Private Lives
Curious Facts about the Famous and Infamous

Also by Mark Bryant

Dictionary of Riddles

Dictionary of British Cartoonists & Caricaturists 1730–1980
(with S. Heneage)

Private Lives

Curious Facts about the Famous and Infamous

MARK BRYANT

CASSELL

This edition first published in the UK 1996 by
Cassell
Wellington House
125 Strand
London
WC2R 0BB

First published in paperback 1997

Distributed in the United States by
Sterling Publishing Co. Inc.
387 Park Avenue South
New York, NY 10016

British Library Cataloguing-in-Publication Data
A catalogue record for this book
is available from the British Library

ISBN 0-304-34923-2

Edited by David Pickering
Designed by Peter Holroyd

Typeset by York House Typographic Ltd, London
Printed and bound in Great Britain

For my father
Robert John Stanley Bryant

PREFACE

Gladstone, in discussing J.W. Cross's *Life of George Eliot*, said 'It is not a Life at all. It is a Reticence, in three volumes.' And, it should be remembered, he was describing a personal memoir written by Eliot's own husband. How much more 'reticent', then, is the average biographical dictionary which, usually in a single volume, barely even informs us that Mary Ann Evans (for such was her real name) even had a husband, let alone two? Or that her first publications were religious works (she did not start writing fiction until she was 'a storm-tried matron of 37') and that her looks were such that Henry James once described her as 'deliciously hideous' and a 'great horse-faced bluestocking'?

Private Lives, it is hoped, will help fill the gap that most biographical dictionaries seem to leap over. Often too, by concentrating purely on achievements, other dictionaries frequently give an unreal slant to what the lives of individuals were actually like. Time-travellers in previous centuries would probably not recognize some of the celebrities of history, for the simple reason that their teachers and school textbooks had not prepared them for something as simple as their appearance. Peter the Great, for example was very tall (six feet seven inches) while Samuel Pepys was tiny (barely five feet high), and – unlike their portrayal by Hollywood actors – some eminent men were extremely unpleasant, had high-pitched voices and quirky mannerisms and were as far from the blonde, blue-eyed athletic figures of wholesome goodness we are led to believe by the drama-documentaries of the silver screen as can be imagined. Other details that are often glossed over are who a celebrity's siblings, parents (especially mother) and other relatives were – information about which may shed considerable light on that person's subsequent career and personality.

This book then re-examines some 200-odd well-known personalities from all periods of history and all walks of life, from Roman Emperors to Victorian composers, from painters to poets, and it is hoped, adds some flesh to the bare bones usually presented in biographical dictionaries. The constraints of time and space have necessarily limited the extent of the book somewhat and the ultimate choice of who should be included has obviously been a personal one. However, nothing presented here is controversial – indeed most of the information can be corroborated from standard reference books and full-length biographies of the subjects covered. It is the emphasis of the book and the presentation of the material which is different. Like many others I have always been fascinated by what the famous and infamous have really been like. Photographs help but they only ever give a static and two-dimensional image of a person. This book tries to round out that picture a little more and, to borrow a phrase from Oliver Cromwell, to portray the subjects covered 'warts and all'.

However, that said, no claim is made to completeness – indeed it is to be doubted whether any such collection could, by definition, be comprehensive – and it is hoped that future editions will both extend the number of celebrities and add further personal information to those subjects already included. Suggestions from readers are welcome.

The one person above all to whom due acknowledgement and credit must go for inspiring this dictionary of biographical curiosities is my late father, who had an uncanny ability to pick up other people's unconsidered trifles and would constantly amaze family, friends and fellow contestants on TV and radio quiz shows with his formidable and detailed knowledge on a wide variety of topics. It is to him, with heartfelt thanks, that this book is dedicated.

Thanks too must also go to the following individuals and institutions for the invaluable help they have given in the preparation of this dictionary: University of London Library, Senate House; the British Library; my editor David Pickering for many helpful suggestions; and to the designer Peter Holroyd, cover artist Peter Ware, the typesetters and printers, and all at Cassell plc for their efforts in turning the end product into such an attractive volume.

Mark Bryant

Alexander III, better known as Alexander the Great, was the son of Philip II of Macedon and Olympias, daughter of King Neoptolemus of Epirus. He was born in Pella on the sixth day of Hecatombaeon (July) – the day the temple of Diana at Ephesus was burnt. His parents split up when Alexander was aged 16, Philip remarrying. He had an elder half-brother (Philip III) and a foster brother Clitus, who once saved his life and whom he later killed with a spear when drunk. His tutor, from the age of 13 to 16, was Aristotle. When his father was assassinated he became king, aged 20, and ruled for 14 years, during which time he inflicted crushing defeats on the Persians at Issus (333 BC) and Gaugamela (331), marched on Palestine, liberated Egypt and founded the city of Alexandria (331 BC) before entering the Persian capital Persepolis in triumph. Subsequent campaigns brought brilliant victories against the Scythians and other enemies. In 327 BC he launched an invasion of India and got as far east as the River Jhelum before ultimately turning back for home (325 BC). His conquests did much to spread the language and culture of the ancient Greeks through the ancient world.

Family/Sex Life: In 328 BC Alexander married Roxana, a Bactrian princess who fell captive to him on the defeat of her father, Oxyartes. His second wife was Statira, daughter of Alexander's defeated enemy Darius, King of Persia; she was killed by Roxana after Alexander's death. Legend also has it that, while drunk, he destroyed the Persian capital Persepolis to please the Athenian courtesan Thaïs (who later married Ptolemy Largus, King of Egypt).

Appearance: According to Plutarch, Alexander was 'Fair and of a light colour, passing into ruddiness in his face and upon his breast.' He was red-haired and had a 'melting eye'. In battle he dressed in a cuirass like his troops but also wore a distinctive buckler and a plume of large white feathers on each side of his iron helmet, which was polished like silver. His soldiers were not permitted to wear beards because, Alexander declared, they were too easy to get a hold of in a fight.

Habits/Mannerisms: Alexander used to incline his head towards his left shoulder (his troops copied this). He kept a copy of Homer's *Iliad*, annotated by Aristotle, under his pillow, together with a sword, calling it 'a perfect portable treasure of all military virtue and knowledge'. It was later kept in a golden casket studded with gems that was found in the tent of Darius after the Battle of Gaugamela. He ate simple food but was a heavy drinker of wine. He washed using olive oil (there was no soap in ancient times).

Sport/Hobbies: Alexander loved hunting and most sports, but could not swim. His great strength was legendary, but so was his decisiveness and his cunning – when he was set the challenge of untying the fantastically complicated Gordian knot, by which Gordius, King of Phrygia, had tied a chariot to a beam using a rope of twisted bark (saying whoever untied it would reign over the entire East), Alexander casually slashed through it with his sword.

Religion/Politics: Alexander was very superstitious, taking the diviner Aristander everywhere. He also greatly admired the Athenian Cynic philosopher Diogenes, who lived in a tub. Such was the cult that grew up around his name that he was considered divine by many admirers. Alexander himself did not contradict the belief that his real father was not Philip but Jupiter (when questioned, his mother remained silent on the grounds that she did not want to get into trouble with the goddess Juno).

Health: His health was generally excellent and he was himself skilled in herbal medicine. During his campaigns he was at various times wounded in the thigh, hit by arrows in the leg and ribs and badly clubbed on the back of his neck.

Temperament: Boastful and violent, Alexander ruthlessly disposed of his rivals, as well as colleagues and friends, often by having them murdered (he may even had had a hand in the murder of his father). As well as destroying Persepolis apparently on a whim, he also razed Thebes to the ground, though he spared the house in which the poet Pindar had lived.

Pets: Alexander conducted his campaigns mounted on Bucephalus ('ox-head'), a wild black stallion he tamed as a boy. The horse wore golden horns in battle (allegedly giving rise to the myth of the unicorn) and had a city named after it. Alexander also named a town after his favourite dog, Peritas.

Work/Daily Routine: He slept till noon, then sacrificed to the gods and ate breakfast. If not campaigning, he spent the rest of the day hunting, writing his memoirs, making military decisions or reading. In the evening he would bathe/be anointed, eat dinner at dusk, then sleep. In battle he led his men from the front (usually fighting with the cavalry).

Manner of Death: Alexander was taken ill after a banquet in Babylon and died of a fever 11 days later on the 30th of Daesius (February) 323 BC, aged 32. His body was mummified, put in a golden coffin and buried in Alexandria.

ANDERSEN, Hans Christian (1805–75) Danish children's writer

Hans Christian Andersen was born in Odense, Denmark, on 2 April 1805, two months after the wedding of his parents, Hans Andersen (a shoemaker) and his illiterate wife Anne Marie Andersdatter (herself one of three illegitimate daughters, each by a different father). He had an older illegitimate half-sister from a relationship his mother had earlier. Educated in a charity school in Odense, after the death of his father (when he was 11) he worked in a cloth mill and a tobacco factory while his mother took in washing. When he was 13 his mother married another shoemaker and at 14½ he went to Copenhagen and, with the intention of becoming an actor and singer, took singing lessons from the opera singer Giuseppe Siboni, then director of the Copenhagen Theatre's song school. He subsequently attended a grammar school at Slagelse aged 17 (in a class of 12- to 13-year-olds) and began to write poems, novels, travel books and libretti to operas. He wrote most of his famous fairytales between 1835 and 1872 – among them such classics as 'The Tin Soldier', 'The Tinderbox', 'The Little Mermaid', 'The Snow Queen', 'The Emperor's New Clothes' and 'The Ugly Duckling'. He was made an Honorary Citizen of Odense and was awarded the order of the Red Eagle (by William IV of Prussia). One of his patrons was H. C. Orsted, the discoverer of electromagnetism.

Family/Sex Life: Andersen never married. A letter from his first sweetheart, Riborg Voigt, was found in a pouch around his neck when he died. He also nursed unrequited loves for Louise Collin, Sophie Orsted and the singer Jenny Lind. It was for Lind, 'The Swedish Nightingale', that he wrote 'The Nightingale'. Somewhat effeminate in character, he resigned himself to perpetual bachelorhood when he reached the age of 40.

Appearance: Tall, gaunt and ungainly, Andersen had a high forehead and a prominent nose. He wore a small moustache as a young man and parted his hair on the right.

Habits/Mannerisms: He was dyslexic and a bad speller and was also over-punctual, habitually arriving at railway stations hours early (he enjoyed travelling by rail, however). He always took a coil of rope with him when staying in hotels in case there was a fire and always turned back twice after leaving a room to make sure the candles were out. He never ate pork for fear of trichinosis and was very fastidious and disliked dirt.

Sport/Hobbies: Andersen was good at sketching and was also very skilled at creating intricate paper-cut designs of dancers, trees, fairies etc. He sang well as a child (he sang and recited for Christian VIII when Crown Prince) but early hopes of a career as an actor and singer came to nothing. The first novel he ever read (at the advanced age of 17) was Scott's *Heart of Midlothian* in translation.

Religion/Politics: Andersen believed in God but was not a churchgoer. He had little interest in politics.

Health: A hypochondriac, Andersen suffered frequent nightmares and 'black moods'.

Temperament: He was very determined but also gauche, extremely timid and hypersensitive to criticism. He was also frightened of animals. Kierkegaard called him a 'sniveller', while a daughter of Charles Dickens, with whom Andersen stayed at Gad's Hill in 1857, found him 'a bony bore'. Apart from Dickens (who also admitted that a little of Andersen's company went a long way), his friends and admirers included Christian VII, with whom he once spent 10 days in the Frisian Islands. Andersen got his own back on his critic Kierkegaard by lampooning him in 'The Snail and the Rose Bush' (Kierkegaard being the snail and Andersen the rose bush).

Work/Daily Routine: Andersen's first published work was the poem 'The Dying Child' (1828). His first book, *Youthful Attempts*, was published under the pseudonym 'William Christian Walter' (he admired both Scott and Shakespeare). His first novel, *The Improvisatore*, published when he was 30, was a great success and was the first to be translated into English. His fairy stories (technically *eventyr* or wonder stories), when first published, were deemed too adult for the nursery. Surprisingly, none of his stories started 'Once upon a time . . .' or ended '. . . and they all lived happily ever after'. He revised his work a great deal.

Manner of Death: Andersen died of cancer of the liver on 4 August 1875, aged 70, in rooms given to him by his banker friend Moritz Melchior in his villa 'Relighed' ('Quietude') near Copenhagen. Not long before his death Andersen consulted a composer about the music for his funeral march, warning him, 'Most of the people who will walk after me will be children, so make the beat keep time with little steps.'

ANNE (1665–1714) Queen of Great Britain and Ireland

The second daughter of James II (when Duke of York) and his first wife Anne Hyde, daughter of Edward Hyde, Earl of Clarendon, Queen Anne was born in St James's Palace, London, on 6 February 1665. Her mother died when she was aged six (1671) and she came to detest her father's second wife, Mary of Modena. She had an elder sister, Mary II, who married William of Orange (William III) and when they both died Anne became Queen of England. She also had a half-sister Isabella and a half-brother James, the 'Old Pretender'. In the nursery rhyme it was Queen Anne whom the cat went up to London to see. She reigned for 12 years (1702–14) and, tragically unable to see any of her many children survive her, was the last of the Stuart monarchy in England. Her time on the throne witnessed the implementation of the Act of Settlement, which designated the Hanoverian descendants of James II as her heirs, the Union of Scotland and England (1707) and the War of the Spanish Succession (1701–13).

Family/Sex Life: In 1683 Anne entered into a very happy marriage with Prince George of Denmark. They had 17 children, but all died young or stillborn. The longest lived was William, Duke of Gloucester, who died in 1700 at the age of 11.

Appearance: According to Smollett, Anne was 'Of the middle size, well proportioned. Her hair was of dark brown colour, her complexion ruddy; her features were regular, her countenance was round rather than oval, and her aspect was comely rather than majestic.' It was generally agreed that she was plain, and later in life she also became very fat.

Habits/Mannerisms: Anne had a soft voice. She enjoyed her food and was very fond of brandy (she was nicknamed 'Brandy Nan'). The simplicity of her tastes, in contrast to the cultivated interests of earlier Stuarts, did much to endear her to the nation.

Sport/Hobbies: Anne enjoyed hunting and had a specially made one-horse open chaise, which she drove furiously in stag-hunts in Windsor Forest. She also had a weakness for gambling.

Religion/Politics: Though James II became a Catholic, Anne had a Protestant upbringing. She was very religious, but also very superstitious, reintroducing the practice of the 'royal touch', which was supposed to cure sufferers of scrofula ('the King's Evil'). One of those thus honoured with her touch was the young Dr Johnson, who regretted that the procedure seemed not to lead to any obvious improvement in his condition. She also prevented Swift becoming a bishop.

Health: Anne was a sickly child and never enjoyed good health. She contracted smallpox and later, exhausted by 17 pregnancies in 16 years, became lame with gout and suffered from convulsive fits. She was already a virtual invalid, in constant pain, by the time she ascended the throne at the age of 37.

Temperament: She was described as very kind but shy, petty, obstinate, ill-educated and dull-witted. She had no interest in art or drama and was considered (even by her closest friends) a dull conversationalist.

Work/Daily Routine: For many years Anne's most valued confidante, whose advice she took in virtually all matters, was the much more intelligent Sarah Jennings, Duchess of Marlborough. She and the Duchess corresponded regularly, addressing each other as Mrs Morley (Anne's name) and Mrs Freeman (Jennings). Blenheim Palace was built at Anne's expense for Sarah's husband, the Duke of Marlborough, after the Battle of Blenheim. They eventually parted company – to Sarah's extreme annoyance – in 1709, when Anne adopted as her new favourite Sarah's cousin, Mrs Abigail Masham, and the Whigs gave place to a new Tory government. In 1704 she established Queen Anne's Bounty for the relief of poor clergy. The question of the succession was a difficult problem that further complicated her last years (she detested her Hanoverian cousins, but was eventually persuaded in the interests of avoiding civil war to allow arrangements to be made for a peaceful handover of power to them after her death).

Manner of Death: According to the *Dictionary of National Biography*, Anne died of 'suppressed gout, ending in erysipelas, which produced an abscess and fever' at 7 am on 1 August 1714, aged 49. Her body was so swollen it had to be buried in Westminster Abbey in a vast square coffin.

ARNOLD, Matthew (1822–88) English poet, critic and school inspector

Matthew Arnold was born in Laleham, Surrey, on Christmas Eve, 24 December 1822, the eldest son of Dr Thomas Arnold, the famous headmaster of Rugby School, friend of Wordsworth and Southey, and later Regius Professor of Modern History at Oxford University who wrote poetry, a history of Rome and translated Thucydides. His mother, who also wrote poetry, was Mary Penrose, the daughter of a Nottinghamshire clergyman. He had an older sister, Jane Martha, and seven younger siblings: Tom, Mary, Edward Penrose (founder of Edward Arnold Publishers), William Delafield (author of the novel *Oakfield*), Susanna Elizabeth, Frances Bunsen Trevenen Whately and Walter Thomas. Named after his paternal uncle, the Reverend Matthew Arnold, army chaplain and Professor of Classics at the Royal Military College, Marlow, his godfather was John Keble. His niece was the novelist Mrs Humphrey Ward – daughter of his brother Tom, later Professor of English at University College, Dublin, and friend of Gerard Manley Hopkins – and he was the great-uncle of Julian and Aldous Huxley (children of Tom's daughter Julia). Educated at Laleham School (1831–2) he was then tutored privately by Southey's cousin and son-in-law Herbert Hill before attending Winchester (1836) and Rugby (1837) schools. In 1841 he entered Balliol College, Oxford (a fellow student was the poet Arthur Hugh Clough), where despite winning the Newdigate Prize for poetry with a poem on Cromwell he only graduated with Second Class Honours. After a period as a schoolmaster at Rugby and a Fellow at Oriel College, Oxford, he became – with his mother's help – Private Secretary to Lord Lansdowne, Lord President of the Privy Council and Head of the Committee of the Council on Education. Then through Lansdowne's influence he worked as a School Inspector for 35 years (from 1851) before becoming Professor of Poetry at Oxford. His most famous poems included 'The Scholar Gypsy', 'Dover Beach' and 'Thyrsis'. He also wrote many acclaimed critical works, including *Essays in Criticism* (1865, 1888) and *Culture and Anarchy* (1869).

Family/Sex Life: In 1851 Arnold married Frances (Fanny) Lucy Wightman, daughter of Sir William Wightman QC – a close friend of John Wilson, whose review of Keats's *Endymion* in the *Quarterly* reputedly hastened the poet's death. Their children were Richard Penrose (a friend of Elgar), Thomas, Trevenen William, Eleanor Mary Caroline (who married the Hon. Armine Wodehouse, a relation of P. G. Wodehouse) and Lucy Charlotte.

Appearance: Six feet tall, Arnold had short black hair with a centre parting and was clean-shaven but for mutton-chop whiskers. He wore a monocle.

Habits/Mannerisms: Arnold liked cold weather and always kept his rooms cold.

Sport/Hobbies: A strong swimmer, Arnold once deliberately swam in the Bay of Spezia, where Shelley had drowned. He was a good high jumper and jumped the five-feet-three-inch-high spiked railings at Wadham College, Oxford, for a bet. He also enjoyed ice-skating, whist and billiards and was fond of gambling (roulette). He was tone-deaf and thought Turner's paintings insane.

Health: Arnold had a bent leg and had to wear cast-iron leg braces as a child. In 1836 he burnt his hand on phosphorus. He also suffered from angina pectoris.

Temperament: Known as 'Matt' or 'Crabby' to his friends, Arnold was cold, stern and reserved in character. His highly critical views often caused offence; when on a US tour, for instance, he and his wife were offered by their hostess some pancakes, which they had never tasted before – Arnold tried one then passed the plate to his wife with the words, 'Do try one, my dear. They're not nearly as nasty as they look.' On his death R. L. Stevenson wrote: 'Poor Matt. He's gone to heaven, no doubt – but he won't like God.' Other friends included Browning, Thomas Huxley and Edmund Gosse.

Pets: Arnold kept a Persian cat called Atossa, the canary Matthias, the dachshunds Geist (brown and black) and Max, and a mongrel collie/dachshund called Kaiser. All feature in his poetry.

Manner of Death: Arnold died, aged 65, at 3 pm on Sunday 15 April 1888, of heart failure after a heart attack while walking in Liverpool awaiting the arrival of his daughter Lucy and her husband from the USA. The day before, weighing 268 lb, he had jumped a two-feet-nine-inch iron railing. He was buried in All Saints' Church, Laleham. His tombstone reads: 'There is sprung up a light for the righteous and joyful gladness for such as are true-hearted' (Psalms xcvii, 11). His express wish was that his biography should never be written.

AUGUSTUS (63 BC–AD 14) Roman Emperor

Gaius Octavius Thurinus was born 'just before sunrise' (Suetonius) in Latium, central Italy, on 23 September 63 BC, the son of Gaius Octavius, Governor of Macedonia, and Atia, niece of Julius Caesar (her father married Caesar's sister Julia) and a relative of Pompey the Great. He had a sister Octavia and a half-sister Octavia by his father's earlier marriage.

His father died when he was four (his mother later married the consul Marcius Philippus). As a child he was known as Thurinus but when he was adopted by Caesar and nominated as his successor he took the name Gaius Julius Caesar, though on Caesar's death he was known as Octavian. The name Augustus ('venerable') was conferred on him by the Senate when he became Emperor (an alternative had been Romulus). He studied under Apollodorus at Polonia in Illyria and fought with Caesar in Spain but only personally commanded two foreign campaigns (Dalmatia and Cantabria). Later he became a triumvir with Mark Antony and Lepidus following Caesar's death (the 'Second Triumvirate'). He ruled with Antony for 12 years, then – after defeating Antony at the Battle of Actium (31 BC) – alone, as Emperor, for another 44 years. His reign saw peace and prosperity as well as steady expansion of Roman territories. Though born in September (the seventh month in the Roman calendar), the month of Sextile (sixth) was renamed August to commemorate the month of his first consulship (he took a day from February so that August would have the same number of days as July – itself named after Caesar).

Family/Sex Life: Augustus's first wife was Mark Antony's stepdaughter (the daughter of Fulvia by her first husband Publius Clodius), Clodia, but he divorced her before the marriage was even consummated. His second wife, Scribonia, had already been married twice and had a child, but ultimately he divorced her too, for nagging. Their daughter Julia proved so licentious in her ways that Augustus had to banish her to a barren island. He took as his third wife Livia Drusilla, though she was still married to Tiberius Nero and pregnant (they had no children, but he took into his household his stepsons Tiberius and Drusus by Tiberius Nero). Having no sons, he adopted Agrippa's sons by Augustus's daughter Julia; when they died he adopted his stepson Tiberius.

Appearance: Around five feet seven inches tall, Augustus wore shoes with thick soles to make him appear taller. Suetonius described him as handsome with a 'very graceful gait'. He wore a serene expression and had clear bright eyes. According to Suetonius, 'His teeth were small, few and decayed; his hair yellowish and rather curly; his eyebrows met above the nose; he had ears of normal size, a Roman nose, and a complexion between dark and fair.' He had seven birthmarks on his chest and stomach in the form of the Great Bear constellation. He dressed untidily, favouring Ancient Roman gowns as opposed to cloaks and wearing a broad-brimmed hat against glare.

Habits/Mannerisms: Augustus ate simple food – 'the coarsest sort of bread, whitebait, fresh hand-pressed cheese, and green figs' (Suetonius). He drank little (a pint of wine-and-water daily and only with meals) and preferred Raetian wine. He ate when hungry rather than at set mealtimes. Augustus not only dated letters but added the exact hour of day and instead of breaking words at line-ends would add missing letters below the word and connect them by a loop. He slept on a low bed and, when travelling, was carried by litter, at night. Once a year he would sit as a beggar in a public place. He softened the hairs on his legs by singeing them with red-hot walnut shells. His favourite expressions were 'quicker than boiled asparagus' and 'don't be a beetroot'.

Sport/Hobbies: He enjoyed fishing, gambling (dice) and watching boxing. He collected antiquities and kept a large collection of prehistoric animal remains ('Giants' Bones') in Capri. He also wrote books, including an autobiography and poetry.

Religion/Politics: Augustus was superstitious. He carried a seal-skin amulet as protection against lightning (of which he was very frightened – his litter was struck once and a slave was killed). He was much encouraged when, before Actium, he met a peasant driving a donkey – the peasant's name was Eutyches (Good Fortune) and the donkey's was Nikon (Victor). After his death he was made a god by grateful Romans.

Health: One leg and both arms were badly crushed when a bridge collapsed during his Dalmatian campaign. He had only partial vision in his left eye and, when old, limped in the left leg. Other problems included ringworm, numbness in the forefinger of his right hand and bladder pains.

Temperament: Augustus was a good ruler but was also brutal – after Caesar's murder he sent Brutus's head to Rome and executed 300 nobles the following Ides of March. He also murdered Caesarion, Caesar's son by Cleopatra. He burnt some 2000 books of Greek and Roman prophesy, but, on the death of Virgil, countermanded Virgil's desire that the *Aeneid* should be burnt because it was unfinished – instead he got others to finish it and had it published.

Work/Daily Routine: Augustus slept seven hours a night and dozed after lunch. Virgil and Horace flourished during his reign and Augustus himself suggested the subject of the *Aeneid* to Virgil.

Motto/Emblem: The personal seal of Augustus was a sphinx, then the head of Alexander the Great, then an image of his own head. He liked to quote the Greek proverb 'More haste, less speed' (*festina lente* in Latin).

Manner of Death: Augustus died of natural causes in the arms of his wife Livia in the family villa in Nola, near Naples (in the room where his father had died), on 19 August AD 14 around 3 pm, aged 50. His body was taken to Rome and burnt on a pyre in the Campus Martius; his ashes were put in the family mausoleum.

AUSTEN, Jane (1775–1817) English novelist

Jane Austen was born on 16 December 1775, the daughter of the Reverend George Austen, Rector of Steventon, Hampshire (a former Fellow of St John's, Oxford) and Cassandra Leigh, a relative of Sir Thomas Leigh (Lord Mayor of London in Elizabeth I's time). Her father also took pupils (including the young Viscount Lymington) and the nearby rectory of Ashe was occupied by Dr Russell, grandfather of the writer Mary Russell Mitford. Her older siblings were James (founder of Austen, Mauden & Tilson's Bank), George, Edward, Henry (Receiver-General for Oxfordshire), Cassandra, Elizabeth, Admiral Sir Francis and William, and she had a younger brother, Rear-Admiral Charles John. She was educated at Mrs Cawley's School, Oxford, then at the Abbey School, Reading (with her sister Cassandra). When her father moved to Bath she and Cassandra followed, then after his death she moved to Clifton (Bristol), Southampton, then to a cottage on the estate of her wealthy brother George at Chawton, Hampshire, and finally to lodgings in Winchester for the last few weeks of her life. She lived a relatively uneventful life but is remembered as the author of six classic novels, four of which were published in her lifetime – *Sense and Sensibility* (1811), *Pride and Prejudice* (1813), *Mansfield Park* (1814), *Emma* (1815), *Persuasion* (1818) and *Northanger Abbey* (1818). *Sanditon* (1817) is incomplete.

Family/Sex Life: Jane Austen never married, though at the age of 27 she accepted a proposal from 21-year-old Harris Bigg-Wither – she accepted him in the evening but by the morning had changed her mind and withdrew her acceptance. She also had a number of other suitors, but there are no records of any other proposals.

Appearance: Tall and slight, Jane Austen had a round face and was fair and pretty. Her niece spoke of her 'clear brown complexion and very good hazle [sic] eyes ... Her hair a darkish brown, curled naturally ... She always wore a cap.'

Habits/Mannerisms: Very neat.

Sport/Hobbies: Jane Austen was very skilled at bilbocatch (cup-and-ball). She also played the piano and sang and danced well, was good at embroidery and could read French and Italian. She had some skill at drawing and wrote verse and charades. Her favourite reading included Fielding, Sterne, Richardson, Fanny Burney, Walter Scott, Cowper and, above all others, George Crabbe.

Temperament: Jane Austen was evidently lively and affectionate, living in a close family and sharing her thoughts in her letters to her sister Cassandra (unfortunately Cassandra expunged references in the letters to private matters after her sister's death). She was very sharp-witted, and on occasion, in her letters, her humour was distinctly coarse.

Work/Daily Routine: Writing about the process of novel-writing, Jane Austen commented that, 'three or four families in a country village is the very thing to work on'. Her last three novels were all written in the family parlour in Chawton, amid all the clamour and noise of Austen family life. She also worked at a mahogany writing-desk and at first wrote on very small pieces of paper so they could be hidden under a blotter if anyone came in.

She rewrote extensively, substantially revising *Pride and Prejudice* and *Sense and Sensibility*, for instance, after they were initially rejected for publication. The original title of *Sense and Sensibility* was *Elinor and Marianne*, while *Pride and Prejudice* was *First Impressions* and *Northanger Abbey* was *Susan* (her brother Henry suggested the final title). *Northanger Abbey* was her first book to find a publisher – Crosby & Sons paid £10 for it in 1803 but she later bought the rights back (1816) as they had hitherto failed to publish it. All her books were published anonymously (until her brother Henry later let the secret out only the immediate family knew she was an author). *Emma* (which was admired by Scott) was dedicated to George IV – then Prince Regent – at his request (though she was no fan of his) and it was said that he kept a set of all her novels at each of the royal residences so that they would always be to hand. Precise though she was, she did occasionally make mistakes – in *Emma*, for instance, she incorrectly had apple trees blossoming in July. Her admirers have been many, but she also has had her detractors. Cardinal Newman lamented, 'Miss Austen has no romance ... what vile creatures her parsons are!', while Jane Carlyle dismissed her novels as 'Too washy; water-gruel for mind and body at the same time were too bad.' Reservations about her work were also expressed by Elizabeth Barrett Browning and Charlotte Brontë.

Manner of Death: Jane Austen died, aged 42, of Addison's Disease in her sister's arms at 4.30 am on 18 July 1817, in lodgings in College Street, Winchester, where she had gone to consult her doctor. She was buried in Winchester Cathedral.

BACH, Johann Sebastian (1685–1750) German composer

J. S. Bach was born in Eisenach near Wartburg Castle, Thuringia, Germany on Saturday 21 March 1685, the son of Johann Ambrosius Bach, a professional violinist at the court of the Duke of Eisenach, and Elisabeth Lammerhirt, daughter of a furrier and Erfurt municipal councillor. He had three older brothers, Johann Christoph (an organist), Johann Balthasar (a trumpeter) and Johann Jakob (an oboist). Bach was educated at the Gymnasium in Eisenach and in Ohrdruf, where he showed a talent in Greek. He was taught the violin by his father and then the organ, the harpsichord and the clavichord by his eldest brother Johann Christoph. After their parents' death (both died before he was 10) the children were brought up by Johann Christoph (organist at St Michael's, Ohrdruf). A good singer, Bach then attended the exclusive choir school of St Michael's, Lüneburg (1700). His first job (aged 18) was as organist at the New Church, Arnstadt, Thuringia, then at St Blaise, Mühlhausen (1707), and then as Court Musician to the Royal Chapel, Weimar, under the patronage of the Duke of Sachsen-Weimar (1708). Rising to Konzertmeister (deputy Kapellmeister) in 1714, he resigned when passed over for promotion and was imprisoned for a month when he tried to leave. Released in 1717 he became Kapellmeister to the Calvinist Prince Leopold of Anhalt-Cöthen, who forbade organ-playing. He then became Curator and Director of Music at St Thomas's Church and Choir School, Leipzig (after Telemann had refused the job) in 1723, adding the part-time role of Court Composer to King Augustus III from 1736. He earnt nothing from his compositions – this was deemed to be covered by his salary. He also took pupils and taught the Duke of Weimar's nephews, Prince Ernst August and Prince Johann Ernst. The

King of Sweden gave him a ring. The true genius of his compositions was only widely realized in the 19th century. Among his most celebrated works are the *St John Passion* (1723), the *St Matthew Passion* (1729), the Mass in B Minor (1733–8) and the Christmas and Easter oratorios, as well as nearly 300 cantatas and much music for the harpsichord, clavichord, violin, cello and lute.

Family/Sex Life: In 1707 Bach married his cousin Maria Barbara Bach. She died in 1720, having borne him four surviving children (out of six) – Catharina Dorothea, Wilhelm Friedemann, Carl Philip Emmanuel (accompanist to Frederick the Great's flute-playing) and Johann Gottfried Bernhard. In 1721 he took as his second wife Anna Magdalena Wilcken, a professional soprano and daughter of the Court Trumpeter at Weissenfels. Their six surviving children (of 13) included Gottfried Heinrich, Johann Christoph Friedrich and Johann Christian.

Appearance: Portly, with a fleshy clean-shaven face and high forehead. While in Weimar he had to dress in full Hungarian Hussar uniform, with a tall cloth cap, a braid-trimmed jacket, tight breeches, high boots and a short cloak hanging from his left shoulder.

Habits/Mannerisms: Bach enjoyed muscat wine.

Religion/Politics: Lutheran.

Health: In 1750 Bach underwent an eye operation, but this did not prevent him from later going blind (though his eyesight returned 10 days before his death).

Work/Daily Routine: A fine violinist and singer, Bach played on the keyboards with curved fingers (against the conventional practice of using straight fingers). He always began new manuscripts with the words 'Jesu Help' and ended with 'S. D. G.' (*Soli Deo Gloria*). He composed a lot in the key of C. At Weimar he had to write a new cantata each month (he wrote 'Jesu, Joy of Man's Desiring' there) – while at Leipzig he wrote 59 in a single year. Also written at Leipzig were the *Magnificat*, the *St Matthew Passion*, the B Minor Mass and other examples of his best work. 'The Well-tempered Clavier' was written at Cöthen as an exercise for his two oldest sons – it contains a piece in every major and minor key (Bach's own title was '48 Preludes and Fugues'); it was scored for the clavier (keyboard), to be played on the harpsichord or clavichord (the fortepiano and pianoforte had not yet been invented). The *St John Passion* was criticized at first for being too operatic. In the unfinished 'Art of the Fugue', Bach had completed the letters of his name, B (German B flat), A, C, H (German B) – it uses a variant of a theme composed by Frederick the Great. Other works included the humorous operetta, the 'Coffee Cantata'. Very few of Bach's compositions were published in his lifetime and his work was largely forgotten for 50 years after his death until it was rediscovered by Beethoven and Mozart. The first performance of the *St Matthew Passion* after Bach's death was conducted by Mendelssohn in 1829. Schumann suggested the publication of Bach's complete works. Bach has also had his detractors. In 1884 the following verse was printed in the *Musical Herald*:

'Though full of great musical lore
Old Bach is a terrible bore
A fugue without a tune
He thought was a boon
So he wrote seventeen thousand or more.'

Manner of Death: Bach died of a stroke, aged 65, in his home town of Leipzig on 28 July 1750. He had no tombstone or monument in the Johanneskirche in Leipzig where he was buried, and the exact location of his grave was uncertain until it was discovered during rebuilding of the church in 1894.

BACON, Francis (1561–1626) English philosopher and statesman

Francis Bacon was born in York House, the Strand, London, on 22 January 1561, the son of Sir Nicholas Bacon, Lord Keeper of the Great Seal, by his second wife Ann Cooke (daughter of Sir Anthony Cooke, and sister-in-law of Sir William Cecil, Lord Treasurer). A cousin of Robert Cecil, Earl of Salisbury, he had an elder brother Anthony (a diplomat, with whom he lived till 1594) and a sister Elizabeth. He was educated at Trinity College, Cambridge, aged 12 (1573–5) then at Gray's Inn, London, where he qualified as a barrister. He later became (with help from his uncle, Lord Burghley) MP for Melcombe Regis, Dorset (and later for Taunton, Liverpool, Middlesex and Ipswich), was confidential adviser to the Earl of Essex then successively Solicitor-General (under James I), Attorney-General (1613), Lord Keeper (1617) and finally Lord Chancellor (1618). He was knighted in 1603, made Baron Verulam (1618) and Viscount St Albans (1621). However, three days later he was accused and subsequently found guilty on 23 counts of corruption, fined £40,000, banished from court and briefly imprisoned in the Tower of London. He spent the rest of his life on scientific projects. His philosophical writings included *The Proficience and Advancement of Learning* (1605) and *Novum Organum* (1620).

Family/Sex Life: In 1606 Bacon married Alice Barnham, daughter of the Sheriff of London. He was also reputedly a pederast.

Appearance: According to Aubrey, 'He had a delicate, lively, hazel Eie; Dr Harvey tolde me it was like the Eie of a viper.'

Habits/Mannerisms: At mealtimes Bacon had the table strewn with herbs and flowers to 'refresh his Spirits and memorie' (Aubrey). Aubrey also reported that he would drink 'a good draught of strong Beer (March-beer) to-bedwards, to lay his working Fancy asleep'. By all accounts he became used to living lavishly and had run up considerable debts by the time of his death.

Sport/Hobbies: Bacon was responsible for laying out the walks and gardens of Gray's Inn, London.

Religion/Politics: Bacon's *The Arrangement and General Survey of Knowledge* was banned by the Vatican and put on the Index of prohibited books (1668).

Temperament: Pope called Bacon 'The wisest, brightest, meanest of mankind.' His friends included Ben Jonson and Thomas Hobbes. He was also admired by Cardinal Richelieu.

Work/Daily Routine: Bacon was a fine poet and wrote a life of Henry VII. It has long been speculated that he may also have been the true author of Shakespeare's plays. 'Proof' of this contention has been offered in the form of the word 'honorificabilitudinitatibus' in *Love's Labours Lost* – an anagram of '*Hi ludi F. Baconis nati tuiti orbi*' ('These plays born of F. Bacon are preserved for the world').

This 'Baconian Theory' was first advanced by the Reverend James Wilmot in 1785 and has won many notable converts, including Henry James and Mark Twain. It has even been suggested that there was no such real person as 'William Shakespeare' and that he was a composite invention through which Bacon, Ralegh and Sydney published their work. Bacon has also been 'identified' as the real author of Montaigne's *Essays*, Burton's *Anatomy of Melancholy* and the plays of Christopher Marlowe. W. S. Gilbert, who lamented Herbert Beerbohm Tree's performances as Hamlet, suggested settling the argument by digging up the corpses of both Shakespeare and Bacon and getting Tree to recite the part over them – whichever corpse turned first was the real author.

Motto/Emblem: Bacon's crest was a boar. His most famous saying (addressed to his closest servant) was, 'The World was made for man, Hunt, and not man for the World.'

Manner of Death: While travelling in his carriage one snowy day, Bacon was struck with the idea that food might be preserved if it was stuffed with snow. Accordingly, he got out of his carriage, procured a chicken and stuffed the carcass with snow to test this theory of 'refrigeration'. Unfortunately he also caught a chill, which turned into bronchitis and, unable to travel any further, he had to be put to bed in Lord Arundel's house in Highgate, London. The bed was damp and Bacon's condition worsened. According to Aubrey, a few days later 'He dyed of suffocation' at Lord Arundel's house, on 9 April 1626, aged 65. He was buried in St Michael's Church, St Albans.

BADEN-POWELL, Robert Stephenson Smyth (1857–1941)
English general and founder of the Boy Scouts

Robert Baden-Powell was born at 6 Stanhope Street, Paddington, London, on 22 February 1857, the sixth son of the Reverend Baden Powell, Savilian Professor of Geometry at Oxford University (who died when he was aged three) and a friend of T. H. Huxley, Alfred Russell Wallace, Dr Jowett and others. His mother was Powell's third wife, Henrietta Grace Smyth (daughter of Admiral Smyth and a great niece of Nelson) – who was 28 years her husband's junior and whose friends included Robert Browning, Thackeray, Ruskin and Harriet Martineau. The engineer Robert Stephenson, son of the locomotive pioneer George Stephenson, was his godfather, and his surviving siblings were Sir George Smyth (an MP and author), Augustus Smyth, Henry Warington Smyth, Francis Smyth, Baden Fletcher Smyth and Agnes (who later helped to found the Girl Guides). He also had two half-siblings – Charlotte Elizabeth and Baden Henry – and two adopted half-sisters from his father's second marriage. Educated at Charterhouse School, he failed to pass the entrance exams for Oxford, despite the academic success there of his father and two brothers (Lewis Carroll failed him for Christ Church, and Dr Jowett said he was 'not quite up to Balliol form'). Instead he became a sub-lieutenant in the 13th Hussars in India, achieving the status of national hero as the defender of Mafeking during the 217-day siege in the Boer War. He retired from the army a lieutenant-general, aged 53, to devote himself to the Boy Scout movement, which he had founded in 1908 (he was made World Chief Scout in 1920). Knighted by Edward VII (1909) and awarded the Légion d'honneur (1922), he was successively GCVO (1922), baronet (1922), 1st Baron Baden-Powell of Gilwell (1929) and was awarded the OM in 1937.

He became Master of the Mercers' Company in 1913 and was nominated for the Nobel Peace Prize in 1939, but none were awarded that year because of World War II. He also worked as an illustrator for the *Graphic* magazine, designed posters during World War I and was author of the famous *Scouting for Boys* (1908).

Family/Sex Life: In 1912, aged 54, he married 22-year-old Olave St Clair Soames, daughter of the heir to a large brewing business (he called her 'Dindo' and she called him 'Bin'). Their children were Arthur Robert Peter, Betty St Clair and Heather. Baden-Powell was 56 when his eldest (Peter) was born.

Appearance: Of medium height and slender build, Baden-Powell had freckles, short sandy hair (prematurely balding) and a moustache. The cowboy hat he wore in Africa earned him the nickname 'Kantankye' ('He of the big hat'). He wore peculiar riding breeches – dark velveteen with skin-tight stockings from thigh to ankle, covered in pearl buttons.

Habits/Mannerisms: Baden-Powell was ambidextrous and had a limp handshake. His practice of scouting at night in Africa earnt him the nickname 'Impeesa' ('The wolf that never sleeps'). He was also known as 'M'hlalapanzi' ('The man who lies down to shoot') because he once shot a hippo by lying on his back and firing between his own legs. He smoked (until he gave up in 1895) and had an obsession with washing his entire body daily, regardless of the circumstances. In India he slept with his feet covered in handkerchiefs, to keep off mosquitoes.

Sport/Hobbies: He enjoyed fishing, polo, football, hockey, pig-sticking and shooting (he was a good rifle shot). He also wrote and illustrated 30 books, including a standard work on pig-sticking. While at Charterhouse and in the Army, he participated in amateur theatricals; he also sang and played the piano and the ocarina and was a good mimic. He blew a koodoo horn at Scout camps. A pioneer motorist, he bought an 18 hp Thorneycroft (1906) and later owned a Rolls-Royce paid for entirely by the Scouts, Cubs, Guides and Brownies – each of whom contributed one penny.

Religion/Politics: Baden-Powell was an anti-clerical Christian; he was also anti-Semitic and showed an interest in Fascist philosophy (he called *Mein Kampf* 'a wonderful book'). He once said 'I would not trust an ordinary politician with my grandmother's toothbrush', but he became an admirer of Mussolini and allowed the Italian Scouts to be absorbed into the Fascist 'Balilla' youth movement. From around 1912 he incorporated the swastika in the Scouts' 'Thanks Badge' design because the word means 'good luck' in Sanskrit and refused to stop using it until obliged to in 1935 when its wearers were attacked by anti-Fascists in Europe.

Health: As a young man, Baden-Powell accidentally shot himself in the leg with a revolver when in Afghanistan.
In old age he suffered variously from lumbago, bronchitis, heart problems and bladder trouble and nearly died after a prostate operation (1934). He also suffered from facial skin cancer.

Temperament: Known as 'Stephe' or 'Ste' by his family, he was commonly referred to as 'B-P' in the Scouting movement. The family surname was legally changed from Powell to Baden-Powell by his mother (1869).

Pets: Apart from his two Labrador dogs, Baden-Powell also kept ponies for his children to ride and a pet hyrax (a nocturnal mammal) called Hyrie.

Work/Daily Routine: Baden-Powell rose at 5 am, had a cup of tea and worked till 7 am, then bathed and dressed, walked his dogs, had breakfast and then worked till lunch. He wrote articles for the *Daily Mail, Daily Chronicle, Graphic* etc. and produced many books, including *Birds and Beasts of Africa* and *More Sketches of Kenya.* The first Boy Scout camp was held on Brownsea Island, Poole Harbour, in August 1907. He was accused of plagiarizing the Scout idea from the American Ernest Thompson Seton's earlier 'Woodcraft Indians'. His first Scout uniform was a South African Constabulary shirt, with trilby hat, shorts and golf stockings.

Manner of Death: Baden-Powell died of natural causes, aged 83, at his home, 'Paxtu', The Outspan, Nyeri, Kenya, at 5.45 pm on 8 January 1941.

BALZAC, Honoré de (1799–1850) French novelist

Honoré de Balzac was born in the Rue de la Grande Armée, Tours, France, on 20 May 1799, the son of Bernard-François Balzac, a hospital administrator and deputy mayor of Tours (originally named Balssa – his father added the aristocratic 'de' later, though they had no title). His mother was the wealthy Anne Laure, who was 32 years younger than her husband. He had two sisters, Laure and Laurence, and an illegitimate step-brother, Henri (from his mother's affair with Jean de Marganne). Wet-nursed by the wife of a gendarme in Saint-Cyr, he did not see his mother, who had been forced into the marriage, until aged four. He was educated in Paris at the Collège de Vendôme, the Lycée Charlemagne and at the Sorbonne, where he studied law. He worked at first for a notary but gave up the law aged 20 when his parents offered to support him (for two years) while he tried to become a writer/journalist. When this failed he became tutor (aged 23) to the children of Madame de Berny (a friend of his mother and goddaughter of Louis XVI and Marie-Antoinette) in Villeparisis. An annual parental allowance plus a substantial loan (45,000 francs) from Madame de Berny (by now also his mistress) enabled him to set up as a publisher of cheap classics and to buy up a printing works and typefoundry. When this failed, he later speculated in mines, shipping and railways, still without success. He also wrote for *Charivari* and was editor of *La Chronique de Paris*. Hopeless with money, he lived far beyond his means and incurred massive debts (he had secret entrances to his lodgings to avoid creditors). He was also once imprisoned for a week for failing to perform guard duty (National Service). A prolific writer, his most important work was the vast novel cycle *La Comédie humaine* (The Human Comedy), which incorporated such classic works as *Le Père Goriot*, *Les Illusions perdues*, *Les Paysans*, *La Femme de trente ans* and *Eugénie Grandet*.

Family/Sex Life: Balzac had affairs with – among others – the already married Madame de Berny, 22 years his senior (he called her 'La Dilecta', she called him 'Didi'), with Laure Permon, Duchesse d'Abrantès (widow of the famous general Junot), with the already married Madame Marie de Fresnaye (to whom he dedicated *Eugénie Grandet*), with Fanny, the English wife of the Italian Conte Guidaboni-Visconti (she called him 'Bally' and reputedly had a son by him and he dedicated *Beatrix* to her as 'Sarah') and with Hélène de la Vallette. Five months before his death, Balzac married (1850),

after a 17-year relationship, the Countess Evelina Hanska (sister of Pushkin's mistress, and to whom he dedicated *Séraphita*). He owned a huge circular divan bed, 50-feet round.

Appearance: Five feet three inches tall, Balzac had a long corpulent body and short legs, with a big head. He had brown eyes flecked with gold, a short black moustache and a tuft on his chin, long sideburns and curly black (often greasy) hair. Some of his upper teeth were missing. He wore dazzling waistcoats but also an old hat too small for his head. He was much caricatured for the fancy canes he carried.

Habits/Mannerisms: Balzac drank vast quantities of strong black coffee to help him work. He wrote while wearing moroccan slippers and a white cashmere robe, like a monk's, with a belt of Venetian gold from which hung a paperknife, scissors and a golden penknife. He had a mania for cleanliness, especially about his hands (he constantly bought gloves). He was a lavish spender, owning Aubusson carpets, an English tilbury carriage with two horses etc. In his youth, when he was struggling to become a writer, he cheered himself up by scrawling on the bare walls, 'Rosewood panelling with commode', 'Gobelin tapestry with Venetian mirror' and 'Picture by Raphael'. He was a copious consumer of good food and champagne, but hated tobacco. He was also very pro-British.

Sport/Hobbies: Balzac was very interested in hypnotism, magnetism and in the supernatural (like his father, he admired Swedenborg). He was also a great collector (pictures, vases, chairs, antiques etc.). He particularly admired Delacroix's paintings. Another pastime was playing cards. His favourite reading included Sir Walter Scott.

Religion/Politics: Roman Catholic, but also superstitious – he kept a rusty key as his talisman and also had a lucky ring featuring Arab characters, which he called 'Bedouck'. All his love stories were banned by the Vatican.

Health: Balzac suffered from neuralgia, breathlessness and headaches and also had two heart attacks.

Temperament: A resolute character, he once declared 'What Napoleon achieved by the sword, I shall achieve by the pen.' His friends included George Sand and Chopin (though Balzac confessed that the latter's music bored him), and he was greatly admired by Hugo.

Work/Daily Routine: Balzac worked 15 to 18 hours a day, going to bed at 8 pm, being woken by a servant at midnight, working till dawn, bathing for one hour (in imitation of Napoleon), then seeing to letters and reading proofs, taking a light lunch (sandwich, egg), writing letters and reading proofs till 5 pm, having dinner and seeing friends before retiring to bed at 8 pm once more. He worked at a table covered in green baize in front of a statuette of Napoleon, the table illuminated by four candles. Writing on blue-tinted paper, he produced 85 novels in 20 years. He rewrote substantially at proof-stage. *Les Chouans* (the first book he signed as 'Honoré de Balzac') took just eight weeks. *Le Père Goriot* took 40 days. *La Comédie humaine* – at first called *Études des Moeurs* but later renamed to reflect Dante's *Divine Comedy* – contained 2000 characters in 97 books (137 books were planned). To help him remember the characters, he fashioned dolls as aide-memoires.

Motto/Emblem: Balzac adopted a fake coat of arms featuring a naked woman and a cockerel, with the motto *'Jour et Nuit'*.

Manner of Death: Suffering from peritonitis and kidney trouble, Balzac's body filled with water and then gangrene set in. His face was almost black when he finally died at home at 14 Rue Fortunée, Paris, on 18 August 1850, aged 51. On his deathbed he called for Dr Bianchon (a character in *La Comédie humaine*). Victor Hugo read the oration at the Père Lachaise cemetery.

BARRIE, Sir James Matthew (1860–1937) Scottish novelist and playwright

J. M. Barrie was born in Kirriemuir, Forfarshire, on 9 May 1860, the ninth child and third son of David Barrie, a hand-loom weaver, and Margaret Ogilvy. His surviving siblings (all older) were Alexander Ogilvy, Mary Edward, Jane Ann Adamson, David Ogilvy (who died in a skating accident aged 13), Sara Mitchell and Isabella Ogilvy. Educated at Glasgow Academy, Dumfries Academy and Edinburgh University (MA 1882), he worked at first as drama critic of the *Edinburgh Courant*, then was leader-writer and sub-editor on the *Nottingham Journal* (1883–4) and a freelance journalist before becoming a professional writer after the huge success of *Peter Pan* (1904). He also wrote as 'Gavin Ogilvy' for the *British Weekly*. Among his most popular works for the stage were the plays *Quality Street* (1901), *The Admirable Crichton* (1902), *What Every Woman Knows* (1906) and *Dear Brutus* (1917). In addition he wrote a biography of his mother and collaborated with Arthur Conan Doyle on a libretto for the D'Oyly Carte company. For many years his secretary was Lady Cynthia Asquith, daughter-in-law of the Prime Minister and herself daughter of the 11th Earl of

Wemyss. Having turned down a knighthood (1909), he accepted a baronetcy (1913) and received the OM in 1922. Elected Rector of St Andrew's University (1919), he succeeded Thomas Hardy as President of the Society of Authors (1928).

Family/Sex Life: In 1894 Barrie married the actress Mary Ansell; they had no children (Barrie was impotent) and he divorced her for adultery in 1910.

Appearance: Barrie stopped growing at the age of 15 and remained only five feet two inches tall. He had a large head and wore a moustache (though he did not start shaving until he was in his twenties).

Habits/Mannerisms: Barrie was naturally left-handed but was compelled to write with his right hand at school, with the result that he later became ambidextrous. Very fond of expensive restaurants (including the Ritz and Claridges), he was a constant smoker (pipes and cigars) and wrote a book on the subject, *My Lady Nicotine.* He could also wiggle his ears.

Sport/Hobbies: Cricket.

Health: Because of his smoking, Barrie had a persistent cough. In 1921 his doctor prescribed heroin to cure the insomnia that came with the coughing.

Temperament: Barrie was most at home in the company of children and cherished his friendships with the children of various acquaintances. The boys in *Peter Pan* were based on the youthful members of the Llewelyn Davies family, while Wendy was Margaret Henley, daughter of his friend the poet W. E. Henley. (Before *Peter Pan* the name Wendy did not exist – Barrie adopted it for his character after the young Margaret Henley took to calling him her 'Friendy-Wendy'). Peter Pan himself was named after Barrie's nephew Peter and the god Pan and was a composite of the Llewelyn Davies boys ('I made Peter Pan by rubbing the five of you violently together, as savages with two sticks produce a flame'). The models for Peter Pan generally had tragic lives: George Llewelyn Davies was killed in World War I, Michael Llewelyn Davies drowned while at Oxford, possibly in a homosexual suicide pact, while Peter Llewelyn Davies, a publisher, threw himself under an Underground train in 1960. Barrie's adult friends included Captain Scott (Barrie was godfather to his son naturalist Sir Peter Scott), Meredith, R. L. Stevenson, General Freyberg, Jerome K. Jerome, Conan Doyle and Quiller-Couch. He was a member of both the Garrick and Reform Clubs. For a long time he refused to pay income tax.

Pets: He kept a brown and white male St Bernard dog Porthos and also a shaggy male black-and-white Newfoundland dog Luath – the model for Nana in *Peter Pan.*

Work/Daily Routine: Barrie's first success came with the (unsigned) 'Auld Licht Idylls' series, retelling his mother's Scottish tales in the *St James's Gazette* (1885). These later became a book. His first novel, *Better Dead* (1886), was published at his own expense (he lost £25 on it). After he contributed the Preface to *The Young Visiters*, many people were misled into believing he was the author, not nine-year-old Daisy Ashford. The huge success of *Peter Pan* was gratifying, but Barrie hurriedly made a minor alteration when he heard that some children were taking Peter Pan's instructions that they could fly if only they believed they could too literally and were risking serious injury. To avoid any further accidents, he stipulated that children could fly only if they were first sprinkled with 'fairy dust'.

Manner of Death: He died in his London flat at 3 Adelphi Terrace House, Robert Street, the Strand, on 19 June 1937, aged 77. The only people in the room were Cynthia Asquith, Nicholas Davies and

Peter Scott. He was buried at Kirriemuir, though there was a memorial service in St Paul's. The statue of Peter Pan in Kensington Gardens (modelled on Michael Llewelyn Davies) was commissioned at Barrie's own expense. Lady Cynthia Asquith was left £30,000 in his will (the highest single beneficiary) and all the rights in his plays and books – except *Peter Pan*, the proceeds from which were left to the Great Ormond Street Hospital for Sick Children, London.

BAUDELAIRE, Charles Pierre (1821– 67) French poet and critic

Charles Pierre Baudelaire was born at 13 Rue Hautefeuille in the Latin Quarter of Paris on 9 April 1821, the son of Joseph François Baudelaire, a high-ranking civil servant, and his second wife (born in England) Caroline Defayis. His father was a former priest and painter who personally briefly helped Condorcet escape the scaffold and whose first wife was a relative of Condorcet. He was 60 when he married Baudelaire's mother (then 26) whom he had known since she was a girl. He died when Baudelaire was six and his mother married Colonel Jacques Aupick, later a general, French Ambassador to Turkey and Spain, and a Senator during the Second Empire – he also co-produced the *New Atlas of the Kingdom of France*. There was a half-brother Alphonse (a judge at Fontainebleau) from his father's first marriage. Charles was educated at the Collège Royal de Charlemagne, Paris (1831), at the Collège Royal, Lyons (1832–6) – where he was often top of his class and won many prizes – and at the Collège Louis-le-Grand in Paris (1836). He studied law in Paris, travelled to India (1841–2) and squandered so much of his father's fortune that he was legally restrained from wasting the remaining money even though of majority age. He then worked as an art critic and translator (especially of De Quincey and Poe) whilst writing poetry. His most celebrated work was the collection of 101 poems *Les Fleurs du mal* (1857), which influenced Symbolist poetry and led to his prosecution for obscenity. Other books included *Les Paradis artificiels* (1860) and *Petits Poèmes en prose* (1869).

Family/Sex Life: In 1842 Baudelaire met Jeanne Duval ('the Black Venus'), a mulatto from San Domingo who became his mistress and who inspired much of his best work.

Appearance: Of medium height, but thin, Baudelaire had a clean-shaven face, the eyes 'small, sharp and anxious, more reddish than brown' (Nadar). He had a thin mouth, which rarely broke into a smile, and prominent ears and his nose was, according to Nadar, 'sensual, and bulbous at the tip'. He was a dandy and wore his hair cut very short.

Habits/Mannerisms: Baudelaire's favourite food was onion soup and bacon omelette. He smoked a pipe and cigars and also regularly took opium and hashish.

Sport/Hobbies: He liked dancing.

Religion/Politics: Suspected of satanist views, he nonetheless took the Roman Catholic sacrament at his death. He was one of those who took part in the Revolution of 1848.

Health: Addicted to alcohol and to opium (the effects of which he described in *Les Paradis artificiels*), he also contracted gonorrhea (1839) and syphilis. In 1845 he attempted suicide in a café by stabbing himself with a knife.

Temperament: Reserved and humourless. His friends included the poet Théophile Gautier (he dedicated *Les Fleurs* to him), Nadar and the art dealer Arthur Stevens (brother of the artist Alfred Stevens).

Pets: Baudelaire loved cats and also kept a pet bat in a cage on his desk.

Work/Daily Routine: His first published work was a song written jointly with Gustave le Vavasseur in the satirical paper *Le Corsaire* (1841). As a result of the famous obscenity trial of 1857, six of the poems in *Les Fleurs du Mal* were banned and Baudelaire was fined, despite his work being praised by Victor Hugo (the offending poems were omitted from new editions). The title of *Les Fleurs du mal* was suggested by the critic Hippolyte

Babou (it was originally called *Les Limbes*). Other less well-known works included a novel, *La Fanfario*. Admirers of his work in later years included T. S. Eliot, who called him 'the greatest exemplar in modern poetry in any language'. In his turn, he admired the poetry of Sainte-Beuve and Poe.

Manner of Death: Baudelaire was paralysed after a Belgian lecture tour in 1866 and spent the last year of his life in the clinic of Dr Émile Duval near the Arc de Triomphe, Paris. He died there, of syphilis, in his mother's arms at 11 am on 31 August 1867, aged 46. He was buried in Montparnasse Cemetery, Paris, in the family vault with General Aupick. Mourners at the funeral included Champfleury, Manet, Verlaine and Nadar.

BEARDSLEY, Aubrey Vincent (1872–98) English artist and writer

Aubrey Beardsley was born at 12 Buckingham Road, Brighton, Sussex, on Wednesday 21 August 1872, the son of Vincent Paul Beardsley, the wealthy heir of a jeweller who squandered his inheritance and later had to work for a London brewery. His mother, Ellen Agnes Pitt, claimed descent from William Pitt and was known as 'the bottomless Pitt' since she was so slender. He had a sister Mabel, who was a professional actress and is mentioned in Pound's *Pisan Cantos* and to whom Yeats dedicated 'To a Lady Dying' (she died of cancer in 1916). Taught piano by his mother from an early age he first appeared professionally as an 'infant musical phenomenon'. Educated at Hamilton Lodge boarding-school, Brighton (1878), he had to leave in 1881 because of tuberculosis. He later went to Brighton Grammar School (1884), where the theatrical impresario C. B. Cochran was a fellow pupil. At the age of 15 (1888), he became a clerk in the office of

the District Surveyor for Clerkenwell and Islington and then a clerk at the Guardian Fire and Life Assurance Company, London (1889). Encouraged in his art by G. F. Watts, he briefly took night classes at the Westminster School of Art on the recommendation of Burne-Jones under Frederick Brown, later Professor at the Slade School. Left £500 by his great-aunt, he eventually gave up his job as a clerk (1892) when a bookseller friend introduced him to the publisher J. M. Dent, who commissioned him to illustrate *Morte D'Arthur*. He also began contributing to the *Pall Mall Budget* (1893) and other journals. Appointed Art Editor of *The Yellow Book* (1894), he was dismissed (1895) – at the insistence of Mrs Humphrey Ward and other Bodley Head authors – for involvement in the Oscar Wilde homosexuality scandal, but later became Art Editor of *The Savoy* magazine (in which Conrad's 'The Idiots' first appeared). Among other works, he also illustrated Wilde's *Salomé* (1894) and Pope's *The Rape of the Lock* (1896).

Family/Sex Life: Beardsley may have been homosexual but was more likely a virgin throughout his life. Wilde said he was neither flesh nor blood but 'a monstrous orchid'.

Appearance: Very thin, with a slight stoop, Beardsley had dark eyes and, according to Wilde, a 'face like a silver hatchet'. Max Beerbohm recorded 'the thin face, white as the gardenia in his coat, and the prominent harshly-cut features; the hair, that always covered his whole forehead in a fringe and was of so curious a colour – a kind of tortoiseshell; the narrow angular figure, and the long hands that were so full of power'. He had reddish-brown hair cut in a fringe and parted in the middle. He dressed elegantly.

Habits/Mannerisms: A quick talker, he used his hands to gesticulate a great deal. He was always a bad speller. His rooms were decorated with orange walls and black skirting boards. He enjoyed a good claret (for instance, Château-Latour 1865).

Sport/Hobbies: Beardsley was too frail for sport, but was a very talented musician and also wrote poetry (he admired Pope) and wrote an unfinished novel, the parody *Under the Hill*. He was fond of the theatre and was very widely read – he particularly liked Balzac and Voltaire (he read French well). He liked Wagner but disliked Turner. He also collected Chippendale furniture and rare books and drew caricatures.

Religion/Politics: Beardsley converted to Roman Catholicism in 1897, but there were rumours that he was also closely linked to satanic sects of the era (Roger Fry called him 'The Fra Angelico of Satanism').

Health: Beardsley suffered from tuberculosis. In 1889 he had a severe lung haemorrhage. Among the medicines he took was one made of ammonia, potassium, belladonna and choloroform.

Temperament: Nicknamed 'Weasel' while at school, his friends as an adult included Oscar Wilde (whom he met through Burne-Jones).

Work/Daily Routine: Beardsley's first paid work (at the age of 10) was a dozen drawings in the style of Kate Greenaway for wedding menus etc. – commissioned by his mother's friend Lady Henrietta Pelham (he received £30). His first published work (at the age of 17) was the short story 'The Story of a Confession Album' in *Tit-Bits* (1890). His first drawings to be published appeared (1891) in *The Bee* (edited by his former Brighton School teacher, Arthur King). He was influenced by Burne-Jones, Whistler and Utamaro and also admired Huysmans's *A Rebours*. He never worked in daylight, always indoors in complete darkness but for the light of two candles in Empire Ormolu holders (he took these everywhere he went). After making preliminary sketches in pencil, he then drew in Chinese ink with a gold pen. The overt eroticism of his illustrations to Wilde's *Salomé* (1894) caused a scandal – they also included caricatures of Whistler (as a faun) and Beerbohm (as a foetus). He also produced a poster for Shaw's *Arms and the Man* (called thereby 'Shoulders and the Woman' by *Punch*). His style was caricatured by Linley Sambourne in *Punch* as 'Daubaway Weirdsley' (1895). In his *New York Times* obituary his work was dismissed as 'a passing fad, a little sign of decadence and nothing more'. His admirers, though, included Kandinsky, Picasso, Eric Gill and Arthur Rackham.

Manner of Death: Beardsley died of tuberculosis at the Hôtel Cosmopolitan, Menton, France, on 16 March 1898, aged 25. His mother and sister were by his side as he died and he was frequently given morphine at the end. He was buried in Menton.

BEETHOVEN, Ludwig van (1770–1827) German composer

Ludwig van Beethoven was born in Bonn, Germany, on 16 December 1770, the oldest of four surviving children of Flemish parents (hence 'van' rather than the German 'von'). His grandfather, also Ludwig, had sung bass in the court chapel (Bonn was the capital of the Electorate of Cologne) and had later been Kapellmeister. His father, Johann, taught piano, violin and singing and was a tenor at court. He was the second husband of Ludwig's mother Maria Magdalena Keverich, daughter of the chief cook at the Elector's summer palace at Ehrenbreitstein and widow of Johann Leym. His surviving younger brothers were (Caspar Anton) Karl – later a musician – and (Nikolaus) Johann, who became an apothecary. His mother died in 1787 and his father was sacked for drunkenness in 1789. The young Ludwig's general education ceased after primary school. Seen as a second Mozart, he first appeared in public playing the clavier on 26 March 1778 (aged seven). He was taught violin and piano at first by his father and later studied with the court organist Van den Feden. He was then a student of and deputy to Feden's successor Christian Gottlob Neefe (1782). After the death of Mozart, he studied for a year with Haydn (who called him 'the Great Mogul') in Vienna (1792) – paid for by the Elector of Cologne, Maximilian Franz (brother of Habsburg Emperor Joseph II). Awarded 4000 florins a year to stay in Vienna as composer he also took pupils, including Czerny, the Countesses Thérèse and Josephine von Brunsvik and Archduke Rudolph (the Emperor's younger brother). He was given a gold snuff-box filled with *louis d'ors* by King Frederick William II of Prussia (1796). Despite the handicap of increasing deafness, Beethoven fulfilled his early promise and won huge acclaim for his two masses, his two ballets, his opera *Fidelio*, his nine symphonies, his five piano concertos, his violin concerto, his 32 piano sonatas, his 10 sonatas for violin and his 16 string quartets.

Family/Sex Life: Beethoven never married but proposed to many women (including Magdalena Willman and Thérèse Malfatti). He refused to flirt with married women. When his brother Karl died of tuberculosis he adopted his nine-year-old son (also Karl), whose attempted suicide while in his care (he fired two pistols at his forehead and missed) led to a court case over the boy's custody. He also fell in love with the Countess Giuletta Guicciardi (aged 17) and dedicated the *Moonlight Sonata* to her.

Appearance: Only five feet five inches tall, Beethoven was of stocky, muscular build, with broad shoulders and a short neck. His face was badly pitted by smallpox; he had a swarthy complexion (later rather florid), with a wide nose, bushy eyebrows and deep-set eyes (sometimes concealed behind black-ribboned lorgnette glasses). His hands were broad and hairy. He had long black hair (grey later) and wore sideburns to the bottom of his ears. He was generally untidy-looking – he was once mistakenly arrested as a tramp.

Habits/Mannerisms: Beethoven was very clumsy – he could not cut quill pens properly, for instance, so these were supplied by friends, and he was also a hopeless dancer. His rooms were always untidy and he had a tendency to overloud laughter. When deaf he bit on a stick placed on the piano in order to 'hear' the music. To communicate with others he wrote in pencil in 'conversation books' (140 of these survive). He had messy handwriting and was very bad at spelling and punctuation as well as being unable to perform even simple multiplication. For many years he believed he had been born in 1772. He liked to call himself a *Tondichter* ('sound poet').

Religion/Politics: Brought up as a Roman Catholic, he was never a regular churchgoer.

Health: Beethoven suffered from oto-sclerosis and started going deaf around 1796. By 1818 he was completely deaf and could not even hear the applause at concerts. His ears would 'whistle and buzz continually night and day'. He also suffered from a form of dysentery. He took the waters at Teplitz and Karlsbad.

Temperament: A deeply unhappy personality, he often flew into rages and started fights. Acquaintances found him difficult, impatient and distrustful. Deafness prevented him going to social functions so he appeared to be misanthropic. Goethe described him as 'an utterly untamed personality, who is not altogether in the wrong in holding the world to be detestable but surely does not make it any more enjoyable for himself or for others by his attitude.'

Work/Daily Routine: Beethoven played the piano, organ, harpsichord, viola and violin. His first published work was *Nine Variations on a March by Dressler* (aged 12, 1782). He was extremely good at improvisation. He dedicated the Battle Symphony to George IV of England, when Prince Regent, and the *Eroica* (Third) Symphony to Napoleon, but removed Napoleon's name in a rage when the latter declared himself Emperor. By the time he wrote his famous Ninth Symphony he was completely deaf. He used books of music paper after 1798 (loose sheets before) and played on a Walter fortepiano, then (from 1803) on an Erard. He rose early, made coffee with an exact number of beans, then worked at his desk until 2 or 3 pm then ate. When composing, he often poured iced water on his head; he was also in the habit of making notes when out walking. He earnt no royalties from his works.

Manner of Death: Swollen feet led to jaundice and dropsy, then to a swollen abdomen from cirrhosis of the liver. He died in Vienna during a thunderstorm around 5.45 pm on 26 March 1827, aged 56. On his deathbed 12 bottles of Rhine wine arrived from his publisher, Schott – his last words in response were 'Pity, pity, too late!' His funeral oration by Grillparzer was spoken to a crowd of around 10,000. He was buried in the Währing cemetery, Vienna, with a simple headstone reading 'Beethoven'. His body was later transferred to the Zentralfriedhof (1888). He left his entire estate to his nephew Karl.

BELLOC, Joseph Hilaire Pierre René (1870–1953) Anglo-French writer

Joseph Hilaire Pierre René Belloc was born during a thunderstorm in La Celle St Cloud, near Paris, France, on 27 July 1870, the son of Louis Belloc, a French barrister (son of Hilaire Belloc, a portrait painter in the school of Delacroix). His mother, the wealthy Bessie Rayner Parkes, an early British suffragette (great-granddaughter of Joseph Priestley and daughter of Joseph Parkes, a founder of the Reform Club) was over 40 at his birth. He had an older sister, later the crime novelist Mrs Marie Belloc Lowndes. His father died when he was two and the family moved to London. Educated at Cardinal Newman's Oratory School, Birmingham, he then entered the naval class of the Collège Stanislas, Paris, and spent his year's National Service in the artillery in the French Army in Toul. He studied Modern History at Balliol College, Oxford (receiving a First and becoming President of the Oxford Union), where fellow students were Maurice Baring, John Buchan and Raymond Asquith (son of the future Prime Minister). Founder of the *Paternoster Review* (1890), his first successful book was *The Bad Child's Book of Beasts* (1896). Among the most popular of his subsequent publications were the *Cautionary Tales* (1907). He was Literary Editor of the *Morning Post* (1905–10), and Editor successively of the political weekly *The Eye Witness* (with Cecil Chesterton), the 'Catholic secular newspaper' *The Illustrated Review* and *G. K.'s Weekly* (which became the *Weekly Review*). Liberal MP for South Salford (1906–9, 1910) he was also Lecturer in Military History at Trinity College, Cambridge (1915–16). He declined the CH (1948).

Family/Sex Life: Belloc was married to the Californian Elodie Agnes Hogan, whose mother was a friend of W. T. Stead, Editor of the *Pall Mall Gazette*. She died in 1914; their children were Louis John, Hilary, Peter, Elizabeth and Eleanor.

Appearance: After the sudden death of his wife he always wore black. In old age he grew a beard. When going out he often wore a huge cloak.

Habits/Mannerisms: He wrote almost exclusively on mourning paper after the death of his wife.

Sport/Hobbies: Belloc was a keen walker – he once walked from Oxford to London in 11½ hours. He also loved sailing and bought a nine-ton cutter, the *Nona*, with his university friend Arthur 5th Baron Stanley.

Religion/Politics: A strong Roman Catholic, when Wells's *The Outline of History* was serialized he wrote a

fortnightly attack on it in the Catholic *The Universe*, claiming it was a religious tract. A Liberal MP, he greatly admired Mussolini and met him (1924) and also supported Franco when Editor of *Weekly Review*. He was also anti-Semitic. When he stood for Parliament in 1906 he was conscious that his Catholicism might be a factor against him. Making a campaign speech at Salford, he told the audience gathered to hear him: 'I am a Catholic. As far as possible I go to Mass every day. As far as possible I kneel down and tell these beads every day. If you reject me on account of my religion, I shall thank God that he has spared me the indignity of being your representative.' He was elected.

Health: Belloc suffered from insomnia in middle age and a stroke in 1942 badly affected his memory.

Temperament: He was a close friend of G. K. Chesterton (who illustrated his novels) – together they were known as 'Chesterbelloc', an appellation invented by G. B. Shaw. Other friends were Lord Basil Blackwood (a Balliol friend), who illustrated his verse (as 'BTB'), and J. B. Morton ('Beachcomber'). Someone who did not take to him was writer Anthony Powell, who commented 'I can't imagine anyone more odiously bad mannered and charmless.'

Pets: Belloc never kept any pets and particularly hated cats – he once wrote a hostile essay 'On Them'.

Work/Daily Routine: He was the author of over 150 prose works of history, political and economic theory and religious apologetics. His first published book was *Verses and Sonnets* (1896). *The Bad Child's Book of Beasts* (1896) sold 4000 copies in the first three months. He often worked quickly, having to produce a constant stream of books (sometimes of indifferent quality) in order to support himself: he wrote a biography of James II in eight days in a hotel at El Kantara on the edge of the Sahara desert. Some of his books were a positive embarrassment to him, because he felt they had so many shortcomings. Once, when he shared a railway carriage with a man reading his *History of England*, he asked the man how much he had paid for it, then presented him with the same sum in cash and tossed the book out of the carriage window. He was always a careless writer and later dictated his work.

Manner of Death: Belloc fell into the fire in the study of his home 'Kingsland', Shipley, near Horsham, Sussex – the consequent shock and burns led to his death on 17 July 1953, aged 82, in Guildford Hospital, Surrey. He was buried in West Grinstead.

BENNETT, Enoch Arnold (1867–1931) English novelist, playwright and journalist

Arnold Bennett was born in his father's pawnbroker's/draper's shop on the corner of Hope Street, Hanley, Staffordshire (now part of Stoke-on-Trent) on 27 May 1867. He was the eldest son of Enoch Bennett, a master potter, pawnbroker, draper and later solicitor and shareholder in the *Staffordshire Knot* newspaper (1882–92), and Sarah Ann Longson, and a distant relation of Margaret Drabble. His siblings included Frank, Fanny Gertrude (Sissie), Emily, Tertia (who wrote children's stories) and Septimus (three others died in infancy). Educated at the Infants' Wesleyan School, Burslem, he also attended the Endowed School in the Wedgwood Institute, Burslem (1877), whose headmaster Horace Byatt later left to become headmaster of Midhurst Grammar and thereby also taught H. G. Wells, later a close friend of Bennett. He also went to Newcastle Middle School (where he was Head Boy) but left aged 16 (1883) to work in his father's solicitor's practice in Hanley but failed to take a law degree. Having studied shorthand he then moved to London to work as a shorthand clerk for solicitors Le Brasseur & Oakley, in Lincoln's Inn Fields (1889). Then, with help from his father who bought shares in the company, he became Assistant Editor of *Woman* weekly (1893) and the magazine's Editor in 1896. He resigned this post in 1900 and wrote pulp serials for money while also working on more serious fiction and producing journalism for *Queen, Sphere, T. P.'s Weekly, Windsor, Academy* etc. After the death of his father (1902) he moved to Paris and did not return to the UK for good until 1912. Chairman of the Board of Directors of the Lyric Theatre, Hammersmith, he sat on the Imperial War Committee and was Director of Propaganda in France in World War I, but refused a knighthood in 1919. His most admired novels included *Anna of the Five Towns* (1902), *The Old Wives' Tale* (1908) and the *Clayhanger* series (1910–18).

Family/Sex Life: Engaged initially to the American Eleanor Green (she broke it off suddenly in 1906), Bennett married his Paris secretary Marguerite Soulié in 1907. They were legally separated in 1921 but his wife refused a divorce. His mistress thereafter was actress Dorothy Cheston (they had a daughter, Virginia).

Appearance: Somerset Maugham described Bennett as a 'thin man with dark hair very smoothly done'. He wore a . moustache and his front teeth stuck out.

Habits/Mannerisms: Bennett had a stammer from childhood (he tried hypnotism to cure it) and retained a strong Burslem accent all his life. The stammer worried him when he was presented at court and he was approached by the Duke of York, later George VI, who had a similar speech impediment – 'Great Scott,' he whispered to a neighbour, 'If he s-s-speaks to me I'll p-p-probably spend my last days in the Tower of London.' He walked stiffly, hated the telephone and had an obsession about punctual mealtimes. His favourite foods included rice pudding and he smoked a pipe and cigarettes (in a cigarette-holder). He dropped the name 'Enoch' after his father's death. His two manservants rejoiced in the names Fish and Pond.

Sport/Hobbies: He played in the First XI football team at Middle School and also enjoyed swimming, tennis, croquet and cycling (then a new sport). Another passion was yachting (he owned the 103-ton yacht *Velsa* and later a larger one, the *Marie Marguerite*). He played the piano, was an amateur watercolourist and later took up calligraphy (the whole of *The Old Wives' Tale* was written thus). He was one of the first to own pictures by Vuillard and also owned a Rolls-Royce. Other interests included canals, quiz games and rare books and bindings.

Religion/Politics: Bennett had a Wesleyan Methodist upbringing. He was a socialist but was not keen on the Fabians. He supported the Suffragettes and Sinn Fein.

Health: In 1897 Bennett dislocated an elbow in a cycling accident. He was a hypochondriac and also an insomniac. Other problems included gastric illness (blood in diarrhoea, 1907), lumbago and pleurisy.

Temperament: Though a shy, nervous and irascible man, his friends included H. G. Wells, Lord Beaverbrook, Frank Swinnerton, Eden Philpotts (author and Assistant Editor of *Black and White*) and Gide. Clive Bell called him 'an insignificant little man and ridiculous to boot', while Somerset Maugham found him 'a very tidy man ... but I didn't very much like him. He was cocksure and bumptious and he was rather common.' To Virginia Woolf, though, he was 'a lovable genuine man'.

Pets: As a child the family dog was Spot.

Work/Daily Routine: *Anna of the Five Towns* was first called *Anna Tellwright*. The 'Five Towns' about which Bennett wrote are actually six (Tunstall, Burslem, Hanley, Stoke, Longton and Fenton). His first masterpiece, *The Old Wives' Tale*, was written in France. The death of Darius Clayhanger in the *Clayhanger* series was much admired – Bennett explained proudly that he had based it on personal experience: 'I took infinite pains over it. All the time my father was dying I was at the bedside making copious notes.' He also wrote poetry and collaborated on plays, farces etc. with Arthur Hooley, Eden Philpotts and H. G. Wells among others. Bennett is Samuel Shodbutt in Wyndham Lewis's *The Roaring Queen*. He admired Chekhov and Swinburne and proclaimed Turgenev's *On the Eve* 'the most perfect example of the novel yet produced in any country'. He thought Robert Browning 'speciously recondite' and disliked Henry James.

Manner of Death: Bennett deliberately drank tap water in the Hôtel Matignon, Paris (December 1930), to prove that the water was safe. As a result, he was taken ill three weeks later and died of typhoid at home in Chiltern Court, Baker Street, London, on the evening of 26 March 1931, aged 64. He was cremated at Golders Green Crematorium; his ashes were interred in Burslem Cemetery. His grey granite obelisk has the wrong day of death engraved on it.

BENTHAM, Jeremy (1748–1832) English philosopher, jurist and social reformer

Jeremy Bentham was born in Red Lion Street, Houndsditch, London, on 15 February 1748, the son of Jeremiah Bentham, a wealthy attorney, and Alicia Grove (who died in 1757 when Jeremy was nine). He had a younger brother, later Brigadier-General Sir Samuel Bentham, a naval architect. A student of Latin at the age of three, he was educated at Westminster School, Queen's College, Oxford (BA aged 16), and at Lincoln's Inn. He worked at first as a barrister and inherited a large fortune when his father died (1792). Among his most celebrated writings were *A Fragment on Government* (1776) and *Introduction to the Principles of Morals and Legislation* (1789), in which he introduced the theory of 'Utilitarianism'. He also wrote on penal and social reform, economics and politics. A founder of University College, London, he was made an honorary citizen of the French Republic in 1792. In 1824, with James Mill, he co-founded the *Westminster Review*, which became a flagship for the expression of philosophical radicalism.

Appearance: According to the *Dictionary of National Biography*, Bentham was 'of dwarfish stature' in his youth. In old age he wore a grey coat, light breeches and white woollen stockings. The *Annual Biography and Obituary* of 1833 recalled how 'his venerable locks, which floated over his collar and down his back, were surmounted by a straw hat of most grotesque and indescribable shape'.

Habits/Mannerisms: He had very difficult handwriting.

Sport/Hobbies: Bentham had no aptitude or liking for games at school. He was, though, keen on chemistry. He often expressed his disliking for 'imaginative' literature, arguing that 'quantity of

pleasure being equal, push-pin is as good as poetry' and further that 'all poetry is misrepresentation'.

Health: Though sensitive and delicate in his youth, Bentham was robust in manhood.

Temperament: Dubbed 'The Queen Square Hermit', after the place where he lived, he 'possessed an unfailing flow of high spirits', according to the *Dictionary of National Biography*. J. S. Mill observed that he was 'a boy to the last'. He always had a spirit of scientific inquiry: as a child he once threw a cat out of the window to test the superstition that it had nine lives. Later, he suggested that every man could be his own statue if he had himself embalmed – these 'auto-icons' could then, he mused, be placed for the enjoyment of all in ornamental gardens.

Pets: Bentham kept a cat called the Reverend Sir John Langbourne. The animal was fed on macaroni and was ultimately buried in his garden, in what was Milton's old house.

Work/Daily Routine: Experience of the practice of English law inspired a dis-illusioned Bentham to set about defining the philosophical foundations of the English legal system. (He once wryly observed that 'Lawyers are the only persons in whom ignorance of the law is not punished.') In penal reform, he developed the concept of the 'Panopticon', a circular prison with a warders' 'well' at the centre, from which all the convicts might be inspected. The idea was tried for the Royal Panopticon of Science and Art, opened in 1854, but the institution did not prosper and the building became the Alhambra Theatre in 1871 (it was destroyed by fire in 1882 and was finally demolished in 1936). Many of his writings on a wide range of topics, from ethics to political economy, remained unpublished by Bentham and were never fully completed. It was left to his loyal disciple Étienne Dumont, of Geneva, to organize the wider publication of his views (1802–25).

Mottoes: In his *Introduction to the Principles of Morals and Legislation* Bentham introduced the famous maxim – the foundation of the theory of 'Utilitarianism' – that 'It is the greatest happiness of the greatest number that is the measure of right and wrong.'

Manner of Death: Bentham died on 6 June 1832, aged 83. True to his principles, he left his body to science, insisting that his friends watch its dissection. His skeleton was later reconstructed, dressed in his clothes and placed (with a wax head, the real one having been mummified) seated in a glass cabinet at University College, London, where for many years it was recorded as present, but not voting, at meetings of University committees.

BOLEYN, Anne (c.1507–36) English queen

Anne Boleyn (also spelt Bullen) was born at Blickling Hall, Aylsham, Norfolk, the second daughter of Sir Thomas Boleyn, Earl of Wiltshire and Ormond, and Elizabeth Howard (daughter of Thomas Howard, Earl of Surrey). She was a niece of the Duke of Norfolk (as was Catherine Howard). Her elder sister Mary had been mistress of Henry VIII and she also had a brother, George, later Viscount Rochford. She was lady-in-waiting to the Queen of France and then to Katherine of Aragon and became the first woman to be created a marquess (as opposed to marchioness, wife of a marquis) in her own right (Marquess of Pembroke, 1532). It is said that when approached by the amorous Henry she refused to become his mistress and only bestowed her favours upon him after they were actually married.

Family/Sex Life: Prior to her marriage to Henry VIII, Anne Boleyn had affairs with the poet Sir Thomas Wyatt and with Lord Henry Percy (the son of the Earl of Northumberland). The relationship with Henry began as early as 1525 and became more serious in 1532. She was secretly married to him in January 1533 before the Pope had formally declared his 18-year marriage to Katherine of Aragon invalid. The marriage was officially announced in May and she was five months pregnant at her coronation in June. The resulting dispute between Henry and the Vatican led directly to the English Reformation. Their daughter became Elizabeth I. The loss of a second child (a son) during pregnancy was enough for the impatient Henry, already tired of her after only three months, to set in course the procedure for ridding himself of her and freeing himself to find another wife.

Appearance: Anne Boleyn, according to one contemporary description, was 'Not one of the handsomest women in the world ... of middling stature, swarthy complexion, long neck, wide mouth, bosom not much raised ... her eyes ... are black and beautiful.' She had long flowing hair thickset with jewels (it was so long she sat on it at her coronation). She had three breasts, and six fingers on her right hand, as well as a defect in one of her fingernails. She also had a large wart under her chin, which, with her other physical flaws, was suggested by enemies to be proof that she was really a witch, who had ensnared the king's affections through the use of black magic. Her jewellery included a pearl necklace with a pendant B.

Sport/Hobbies: When being courted by Henry, Anne Boleyn often accompanied him out riding and hunting.

Religion/Politics: Church of England.

Temperament: Anne Boleyn was arrogant, calculating and a scolder and was easily provoked to anger. She was reviled by the public and very few people cheered or took off their caps at her coronation (many actually booed). She was commonly called a 'goggle-eyed whore' and the public laughed when they saw her initials entwined with Henry's (HA).

Pets: She had a dog that she called 'little Purkoy' and a greyhound named Urian.

Motto: 'The Moost Happi'. Another of her mottoes was *'Ainsi sera groigne qui groigne'* ('Let them grumble; that is how it is going to be').

Manner of Death: After Henry tired of her, Anne Boleyn was formally accused (by Thomas Cromwell) of adultery with Sir Francis Weston, Sir Henry Norris and William Brereton (Gentlemen of the Privy Chamber) and also with Court musician Mark Smeaton. All of these alleged lovers, plus her brother (accused of incest), were

beheaded – all were almost certainly innocent of the charges brought against them. Anne herself was beheaded in the inner courtyard (Tower Green) of the Tower of London at 8 am on Friday 19 May 1536, aged 29. She thus became the first person in the UK to be beheaded in the French manner, with a sword (the executioner came from St Omer). Before she died, Anne refused to allow herself to be bitter against her husband: 'The king has been very good to me. He promoted me from a simple maid to be a marchioness. Then he raised me to be a queen. Now he will raise me to be a martyr.' It is said that the executioner was so put out by Anne's charming manner that he asked someone else present to distract her so that he could regain his composure sufficiently to deliver the fatal blow. After the execution Anne was buried at the Tower, though her heart was stolen and hidden in a church near Thetford, Suffolk. Her ghost reputedly still haunts Blickling Hall every 19 May, sitting with her head cradled on her knees in a coach drawn by four headless horses and driven by a headless coachman. Her brother's ghost has also been reported at Blickling Hall, clutching his severed head while being dragged by spectral horses. One day after the execution Henry announced his betrothal to Jane Seymour (they were married 11 days later).

BORGIA, Lucrezia (1480–1519) Italian duchess

Lucrezia Borgia was born in Subiaio in the Vatican State on 18 April 1480, the daughter of the Spanish Cardinal Rodrigo Borgia (later Pope Alexander VI) and his Roman mistress, Vannozza dei Cattanei. She had two elder brothers, Cesare and Giovanni (later Juan I, Duke of Gandia), a younger brother Geoffredo and, by separate mistresses of her father, three

elder half-siblings: Girolama, Pedro Luis and Isabella. Her mother married Giorgio San Croce when she was two (1482) and Cardinal Borgia broke off their relationship. Her great-nephew (Giovanni's grandson) was St Francesco Borgia, the third General of the Jesuit Order. She was married three times on her father's instructions, apparently to further his political ambitions, but eventually established a prosperous and brilliant court at Ferrara, to which many noted intellectuals and artists were attracted.

Family/Sex Life: At her father's wish Lucrezia Borgia was betrothed (aged 11) to the Spaniard Don Cherubino Juan de Centelles of Valencia, then (aged 12) to Don Gasparo de Procida (son of the Count of Aversa), but in the event was first married (1493) to the widower Giovanni Sforza, Lord of Pesaro and Count of Contignola. They were divorced at her father's wish in 1497. Her second husband (1498) – also chosen by her father – was Alfonso Duke of Bisceglie, nephew of King Frederick of Naples and illegitimate son of King Alfonso III. By him she bore a son, Rodrigo. Shortly after her husband was murdered by her brother Cesare (1500) she was married, aged 22, to Alfonso d'Este, son of the Duke of Ferrara. Their children were Alessandro (who died young), Ercole II Duke of Ferrara, Cardinal Ippolito, Alessandro, Abbess Eleonora, Francesco Marquis of Massalombardi and Isabella Maria. She was also rumoured to have committed incest with her father (giving birth to a son) and with two of her brothers.

Appearance: Lucrezia Borgia was slender and attractive, with blonde hair, grey-blue eyes, an aquiline nose and a receding chin. She wore a gold bracelet in the shape of a serpent (Bembo and Strozzi wrote poems about it) and supposedly also had a ring that contained poison for use as required.

Habits/Mannerisms: Like all the Borgias, Lucrezia had very good manners. She also took daily baths (then unusual).

Sport/Hobbies: Lucrezia Borgia was praised by her contemporaries Ariosto and Bembo as virtuous and as a patroness of the arts and education, attracting to her court in Ferrara many notable artists and men of letters. She spoke Spanish as fluently as Italian and also spoke Greek, French and some Latin, writing poems in all these languages. Other pastimes included Spanish dancing and playing the lute, harp and zither. She was also good at drawing and skilled at embroidery in silver and gold.

Religion/Politics: Devout Roman Catholic.

Temperament: History cherishes the image of Lucrezia Borgia as a murderous and licentious poisoner, and it was this version of her that inspired Donizetti's opera, based in turn on Victor Hugo's book *Lucrèce Borgia*. Gibbon, meanwhile, called her the 'Messalina of Modern Rome'. It was said that Lucrezia and Cesare Borgia often secured the death of their enemies by inviting them to drink pledges of poisoned wine – thus the phrase 'A glass of wine with the Borgias' sometimes used when discussing an honour (typically a political appointment) that is seen to carry with it grave risks. In reality, there was little or no basis for this myth in fact and the real Lucrezia, once settled in Ferrara, lived a relatively peaceful life. Her friends included Cardinal Pietro Bembo (Byron saw her love-letters to him and a lock of her hair in the Ambrosian Library, Milan).

Manner of Death: Lucrezia Borgia died in Ferrara at 11 pm on 24 June 1519, giving birth to Isabella Maria. The doctors cut off her hair before she died. She was buried in the Corpus Domini church in the same vault as Alfonso d'Este's mother.

BOSWELL, James (1740-95) Scottish writer and lawyer

James Boswel (he later added an extra L), the biographer of Dr Johnson, was born in Edinburgh on 29 October 1740, the son of Alexander Boswel, an advocate who became Lord of the Court of Session with the courtesy title Lord Auchinleck, and Euphemia Erskine, daughter of the Deputy Governor of Stirling Castle (who was the grandson of the Earl of Mar). He had an elder sister Euphemia and younger brothers John and Thomas David. Educated at Mundell's School, Edinburgh (1746–8), then tutored at home (1748–52), he studied law from the age of 13 for six years at Edinburgh University (1753), Utrecht and Glasgow University (1759–60). He came to London in 1760 and continued to practise as a qualified lawyer in London and in Edinburgh for the rest of his life. One of the proprietors of the *London Magazine*, he first met Dr Johnson – 30 years his senior – in Tom Davies's bookshop at 8 Russell Street, Covent Garden, London, on 16 May 1763. He succeeded to his father's title in 1782. His most famous writings included his *Journal of a Tour to the Hebrides* (1785) and the celebrated *Life of Samuel Johnson* (1791), which was many years in preparation.

Family/Sex Life: In 1769 Boswell married his first cousin, Margaret Montgomerie. Their children were Veronica, Euphemia, Alexander, James and Elizabeth. He had numerous affairs and had an illegitimate son Charles by Peggy Doig (1762) and an illegitimate daughter Sally and further admitted to having sex with prostitutes in St James's Park. He also had an affair with Rousseau's mistress Thérèse le Vasseur. Mrs Boswell never took to her husband's friend, the lumbering Johnson – she once complained, 'I have seen many a bear led by a man, but I never before saw a man led by a bear.'

Appearance: Five feet six inches tall, Boswell was plump, with a swarthy skin, black eyes, black hair and an alert expression.

Habits/Mannerisms: Boswell drank a lot, especially in his latter years after Johnson's death.

Sport/Hobbies: He enjoyed walking (his most famous trip being the walking tour of the Hebrides that he undertook with Johnson. He also sang comic songs and was a good caricaturist and mimic.

Religion/Politics: Boswell became a Roman Catholic aged 18 (then unusual in Scotland). He also joined the Freemasons (1759, also aged 18), but declined nomination for the post of Grand Master of Scotland. His meeting with Rousseau inspired in him a strong sympathy for those pressing for Corsican independence (he visited Corsica in 1765 and four years later caused a considerable stir when he turned up at the Shakespeare Jubilee in full Corsican dress). His own hopes of a political career were disappointed, though he served as the Recorder for Carlisle (1788–90).

Health: A hypochondriac, he suffered from gonorrhoea (of 19 episodes of urethral disease, 12 were from gonorrhoea). Other problems included an inflamed foot as the result of an ingrowing toenail (1779) and a bad cut on the back of his head and contusions on both his arms when he was mugged (1793).

Temperament: A member of Johnson's Club from 1773, Boswell was generally good-humoured but suffered from fits of depression ('I was born with a melancholy temperament'). His father considered him foolish and extravagant. He was very vain and boastful. Some of the other members of the Club initially resented his presence – when one of them called him a 'Scotch cur' Oliver Goldsmith corrected him, 'He is not a cur, he is a burr. Tom Davies flung him at Johnson in sport, and he has the faculty of sticking.' Johnson and Boswell became very close and Boswell never really recovered from Johnson's death. Apart from Johnson, Boswell also successfully sought meetings with the great thinkers Rousseau and Voltaire. Other friends and acquaintances included Burke and Sir Joshua Reynolds (to whom he dedicated his *Life of Johnson*) – but he was satirized by Rowlandson and the poet Peter Pindar. Macaulay called him 'Senile and impertinent, shallow and pedantic, a bigot

and a sot, bloated with family pride ... weak and diseased mind.' To Irving he was 'an incarnation of toadyism'.

Work/Daily Routine: As well as his famous biographical work, Boswell also wrote verse – first published in the *Scots Magazine* (1758). His first book was *An Account of Corsica* (1768). His journal, which included details of his scandalous private life, was finally published in the 20th century.

Manner of Death: After fever, shivering, headache and vomiting in April, Boswell died of uraemia at home at 122 Great Portland Street, London, at 2 am on 19 May 1795.

BRAHMS, Johannes (1833–97) German composer

Johannes Brahms was born at 24 Specksgang (later 60 Speckstrasse), Gangeviertel, Hamburg, on 7 May 1833, the eldest son of Johann Jakob Brahms (or Brahmst), an orchestral double-bass player (he also played the flute, bugle and most stringed instruments) and Johanna Henrike Christiana Nissen, a seamstress. At his birth his mother was 44 and his father 27. Called Johannes to signify 'son of Johann', he had an elder sister Elizabeth and a younger brother Friedrich. He was taught violin and cello by his father (aged six) and attended H. F. Voss's Privatschule in Hamburg. He also had a private piano tutor and became such a prodigy that at his first public appearance aged 10 an impresario wished to tour with him in the USA. Though his parents were keen, his music teacher thought it a waste of his talent and so was taught (free) by local composer Eduard Marxsen, but was so poor that he had to practise in a piano showroom. To make extra money while studying he also played piano in dockyard inns in Hamburg (from the age of 13).

Praised by Schumann in *Neue Zeitschrift für Musik* (1853), he later toured Europe with violinist Eduard Reményi, and with pianist Clara Schumann and virtuoso violinist Joseph Joachim before becoming a professional composer. Appointed conductor of the Vienna Singakademie (1863–4) and Director of the Gesellschaft der Musikfreunde, succeeding Rubinstein (1872), he resigned in 1875 and refused further professional positions. An admirer of the young Dvořák – whom he helped to get government grants – he never visited the UK and refused an honorary doctorate from Cambridge University (1877), but accepted one from Breslau University (1878). He was elected Honorary President of the Wiener Tonkünstlerverein (1886) and was awarded the Freedom of the City of Hamburg (1889) and the Order of Leopold, conferred by Emperor Franz Josef (1889). His most celebrated compositions included songs and choral works, among them his masterpiece *Ein Deutsches Requiem* (A German Requiem, 1857–68), *Variations on a Theme by*

Haydn (1873), four symphonies and 214 solo songs.

Family/Sex Life: A 'confirmed bachelor', Brahms was very briefly engaged to Agathe von Siebold, daughter of a university professor (1859). He also had a very close and enduring relationship with Clara Schumann (about which there has been much speculation) and when Schumann died he supported his widow and family.

Appearance: Short with fair hair and blue eyes, Brahms was clean-shaven as a young man but later grew a full, snowy white beard.

Habits/Mannerisms: Brahms smoked cigars and loved good food. When he fell ill and his doctor prescribed a strict diet, Brahms protested, explaining, 'But this evening I am dining with Strauss and we shall have chicken paprika!' When the doctor refused to relent, Brahms told him firmly, 'Very well then, please consider that I did not come to consult you until tomorrow.'

Sport/Hobbies: Brahms was very fond of the writings of E. T. A. Hoffmann, especially *Kater Murr*, and when composing lighter works used the pseudonym 'Johannes Kreisler Junior' (Kreisler being the fictional musician who owned the cat Murr).

Religion/Politics: Protestant.

Temperament: Though he could be pleasant and interesting company, Brahms could also be notoriously rude and ill-mannered. He once fell asleep in Liszt's house when his host was playing and on another occasion delivered a tirade of insults at some of his closest friends – as he left the room he paused briefly to say 'If there is anyone here whom I have not insulted, I beg his pardon.' He was, though, very fond of children. His friends included Joseph Joachim, Hans von Bülow and Clara and Robert Schumann.

Work/Daily Routine: Brahms admired Wagner (though Wagner attacked him) but could not take Liszt seriously. Highly self-critical, he rewrote extensively and worked on some pieces for years before he was satisfied ('Whether it is beautiful also is an entirely different matter, but perfect it must be'). He never wrote opera and used pseudonyms (including 'G. W. Marks') for his light music. His First Piano Concerto was hissed on its first performance in Leipzig and some orchestras baulked at his work, finding it too progressive (when the Boston Symphony Orchestra tried one of his compositions an exit sign was altered to read 'Exit in case of Brahms'). Brahms himself admitted, 'My things are written with an appalling lack of practicability!' Paul Dukas memorably dismissed his music as 'Too much beer and beard', while Tchaikovsky exclaimed, 'I have played over the music of that scoundrel Brahms. What a giftless bastard!' Many found his music depressing – Joseph Hellmesberger said, 'When Brahms is in extra good spirits, he sings "The grave is my joy".'

Manner of Death: Brahms died of cancer of the liver (as his father had done) at his home, 4 Karlgasse, Vienna, on the morning of 3 April 1897, aged 63. He was buried, with full honours, in the Zentralfriedhof, Vienna.

BRONTË, Charlotte (1816–55) English novelist

Charlotte Brontë was born in Thornton, Yorkshire, on 21 April 1816, the oldest surviving daughter of Patrick Brontë, Rector of Haworth, near Bradford, Yorkshire, and Maria Branwell (who died when Charlotte was aged five, 1821). Her father, an Irishman (who had also published some poetry), changed his name from Brunty when he moved to England in imitation of Nelson's title, Duke of Brontë. Two sisters, Maria and Elizabeth, died young, leaving Charlotte, Anne, Emily and a brother (Patrick) Branwell. Brought up by her aunt, who moved in after their mother's death, Charlotte was educated at the Clergy Daughters' School at Cowan Bridge (1824) – later portrayed as the appalling Lowood in *Jane Eyre* – then at Roe Head School, Huddersfield, and was later a teacher there (1835–8). Subsequently she endured considerable unhappiness working as a governess before accompanying Emily to Brussels as a student-teacher at the Pensionnat Héger (1842). Recalled to England on the death of their aunt, Charlotte returned to Brussels as an English teacher (1843–4), but eventually rejoined the rest of the family at Haworth. She is remembered as the author of the novels *Jane Eyre* (1847), *Shirley* (1849) and *Villette* (1853).

Family/Sex Life: In 1839 Charlotte rejected a proposal of marriage from the Reverend Henry Nussey. While in Brussels she fell in love with M. Héger, a passion she expressed in her novel *Villette*. In 1854 she married Arthur Bell Nicholls, her father's curate since 1845, thus becoming the only one of the Brontë sisters to marry (the sisters adopted his middle name 'Bell' when choosing pseudonyms for themselves as writers). She died while pregnant a year later.

Appearance: Just four feet nine inches tall, Charlotte was bespectacled, with bad teeth and a poor complexion.

Habits/Mannerisms: As a child, she was fed on potatoes without meat to make her hardy.

Sport/Hobbies: When young, Charlotte and her sisters wrote stories for their own amusement in tiny matchbox-sized books. With Branwell, she invented the miniature world of Angria, full of handsome heroes and passionate women (while Emily and Anne invented the harsher world of Gondal, more similar in nature to the Yorkshire landscape in which they lived). Another pastime was the copying of engravings. Favourite reading of Charlotte and her sisters included Byron, Scott and the *Arabian Nights*.

Health: Very frail, Charlotte blamed her poor health largely on the harsh life she and her sisters were obliged to live while at school at Cowan Bridge.

Temperament: She was shy, with little sense of humour. Her friends included Mrs Gaskell, who later wrote her biography.

Pets: Charlotte had a cat called Tiger and, after her sisters died, looked after Emily's mastiff Keeper (the model for Tartar in *Shirley*) and Anne's black-and-white spaniel Flossy.

Work/Daily Routine: The Brontë sisters had their first poems published at their own expense but only succeeded in selling two copies of these. Charlotte wrote her books under the pseudonym 'Currer Bell' (her sisters called themselves Ellis and Acton Bell) in an attempt to disguise the fact that she was a woman (and thus increasing her chances of being taken seriously as a writer). She continued to use the pseudonym even after her real identity was widely known. When the first books by the sisters appeared, to acclaim, the publishers encouraged speculation about the real identities of the authors and even suggested one person had written them all (Charlotte and Anne were obliged to visit the publishers in person in 1848 in order to reveal their identities and to quash such rumours). Prior to this both Southey and Wordsworth had discouraged Charlotte from taking up writing. Southey wrote: 'Literature cannot be the business of a woman's life, and it ought not to be. The more she is engaged in her proper duties, the less leisure will she have for it, even as an accomplishment and recreation. To those duties you have not yet been called, and when you are you will be less eager for celebrity.' Later, though, he softened somewhat in his attitude and invited her to visit him. She also admired and was admired by Thackeray (who called her a 'poor little woman of genius') – and it was to him that she dedicated her masterpiece *Jane Eyre* (which was an instant success). Not everyone approved of her work, though – Matthew Arnold declared that her mind contained 'nothing but hunger, rebellion and rage'. Besides her three celebrated novels, Charlotte also wrote another full-length novel, *The Professor* (her first, but published posthumously) and the beginning of another, *Emma*, as well as the short stories 'The Secret' and 'Lily Hart'.

Manner of Death: Charlotte Brontë died of a fever while pregnant at Haworth Parsonage on 31 March 1855, aged 38, her father thus surviving the death of all his children.

BROWNING, Elizabeth Barrett (1806–61) English poet

Elizabeth Barrett was born at Coxhoe Hall, near Durham, on 6 March 1806, the eldest daughter of Edward Moulton and Mary Graham. Her father later adopted the surname Barrett on the death of his maternal grandmother, who left him large estates in Jamaica. She had eight brothers, of whom the eldest, Edward, drowned in a yachting accident. Privately educated, she could read Homer in Greek aged eight and her father published her first book of poetry, *The Battle of Marathon*, in an edition of 50 copies in 1819 when she was 13. Among the most celebrated works of poetry that followed were *Sonnets from the Portuguese* (1850), *Aurora Leigh* (1857), *Poems Before Congress* (1860) and *Last Poems* (1862). As well as writing poetry she also translated Greek. In middle age, through marriage she overcame her ill health and escaped the stern life of the Barrett family home to spend the rest of her days with her husband, poet Robert Browning, in Florence, Italy.

Family/Sex Life: In 1846, aged 40, Elizabeth Barrett was married in secret to the poet Robert Browning, six years her junior, against the wishes of her tyrannical father, who had forbidden all his children to marry. Previously, in 1845, Browning had written pledging his love of both her and her poetry after first reading her work, though he had not even laid eyes on her at that point. The months before the elopement were very anxious for both parties (as later dramatized in a popular play). On one occasion, seeking reassurance, Robert Browning opened a book – it happened to be a volume of Italian grammar – at a random passage, hoping that he might thereby glean by magical means what lay in store for them. To his surprise and delight his eye came to rest upon a sentence suggested as an exercise in translation: 'If we love in the other world as we do in this, I shall love thee to eternity.' Their only child was Robert Wiedemann Barrett Browning ('Penini'), who became a sculptor.

Appearance: Elizabeth Browning was, according to Hawthorne, 'A pale, small person scarcely embodied at all.' He added that she had 'a shrill yet sweet tenuity of voice'. She had a diminutive figure, with slender fingers, and wore her hair in black ringlets. She often wore a black silk dress.

Habits/Mannerisms: Elizabeth Browning had fine handwriting and as a child developed great skill at growing white roses.

Sport/Hobbies: Until the accident she suffered at the age of 15 she much enjoyed riding.

Religion/Politics: Elizabeth Browning was very interested in spiritualism and participated in séances. While in Italy, she took an active interest in political life, supporting the cause of Italian unification, and also admired Napoleon III.

Health: A fall while trying to saddle her pony on her own at the age of 15 resulted in an injury to her spine and rendered her a permanent semi-invalid thereafter. In 1838 a burst blood-vessel complicated her medical condition and for a time threatened her demise. The arrival of Robert Browning in her life proved the making of her in more ways than one, however. In terms of her physical well-being, she was inspired by her lover to fight against the bad habits she had fallen into and was soon, for instance, able to walk downstairs unaided for the first time in years (her brother was so startled when she entered the room that he thought she was a complete stranger).

Temperament: Admired by Ruskin and George Eliot, her friends included Hans Christian Andersen, Thackeray and Walter Savage Landor. She was greatly disliked by the poet Edward Fitzgerald, however, who said her death was a great relief.

Pets: As a child she kept a black pony called Moses. Her most famous pet, though, was her red male cocker spaniel Flush, a gift from Mary Russell Mitford, which was later the subject of a spoof autobiography by Virginia Woolf; it also featured in two poems by Elizabeth Barrett Browning herself. Flush bit Robert Browning twice when he was courting his mistress and was kidnapped three times.

Work/Daily Routine: Robert Browning liked to call Elizabeth 'my little Portuguese' and so it was to him that she addressed her 'Sonnets from the Portuguese' – sometimes incorrectly assumed to be translations. She dedicated all her books to Robert Browning and in 1871 he confessed, 'The simple truth is that *she* was the poet, and I the clever person by comparison.'

Manner of Death: Elizabeth Barrett Browning died in her husband's arms at home at the Casa Guidi, Florence, on 29 June 1861 after catching a chill, aged 55. She was buried in Florence.

BRUMMELL, George Bryan 'Beau' (1778–1840) English dandy

George Bryan 'Beau' Brummell was born in London on 7 June 1778, the son of William Brummell, amanuensis to the 1st Earl of Liverpool (and later Private Secretary to Prime Minister Lord North (1770–82) and High Sheriff of Berkshire) and a friend of Fox and Sheridan. His mother (who died in 1793) was a Miss Richardson, daughter of the Keeper of the Lottery Office, sister of Mrs Samuel Brawne – mother of Keats's fiancée Fanny Brawne (thus making Beau Brummell Fanny's cousin) – and a descendant of Sir Thomas Richardson, Chief Justice in the reign of James I. He had an elder brother William and a sister, Maria (later mother of the Countess Linowska and the Baroness de Maltzahn). He was educated at Eton, where he was known as 'Buck' Brummell, and briefly at Oriel College, Oxford, leaving without a degree when his father died (1794). Commissioned into the Prince of Wales's Regiment, the 10th Hussars (1794), he escorted Caroline of Brunswick to her wedding with the Prince Regent and left with the rank of captain (1798). He succeeded to a private fortune of £30,000 in 1799 and never worked again. A close friend of the future George IV when regent to his mad father, he later fell out with the Prince and fled England for good in 1816 to avoid debts of around £50,000. He settled in Calais and was later British Consul in Caen, France (1830–2) but when that post was abolished sank into debt and was briefly imprisoned in Caen (May–July 1835).

Family/Sex Life: Unmarried.

Appearance: Small in stature, Brummell had a long face with a high forehead, grey eyes and a fair complexion. He was clean-shaven and plucked stray hairs from his face with tweezers. He had light-brown hair, sandy side-whiskers and often wore an eyeglass. Each morning he spent two hours washing and dressing (he never used perfume but observed an immaculate standard of personal hygiene). He did not powder his hair after Pitt taxed powder in 1795. Dubbed by Thackeray 'the model of dandyhood for all times' – though he had a rival in Beau Nash – it is arguable that he was a dandy at all. According to the *Dictionary of National Biography*, 'by no means a fop, Brummell was never

extravagant in his dress, which was characterized rather by studied moderation'. His dress was simple but elegant. He usually wore a blue tailcoat, buff waistcoats and buckskins, very white linen (he began the fashion for starching linen neckcloths) and highly polished black Hessian boots (he even polished the soles and claimed he used champagne froth to get the right results). He disliked bright colours, trinkets and gew-gaws in dress – the only ornaments on his outfits were brass buttons on his coat, a plain ring and a heavy gold watchchain, from which hung a lucky sixpence (found in the street). Once, when complimented by a friend on his turn-out, he protested, 'I cannot be elegant, since you have noticed me.' He later became very slovenly. In exile in Caen he carried an umbrella with the handle carved unflatteringly as George IV.

Habits/Mannerisms: Brummell was careful with his money until he took up gambling. In 1813 he won £26,000 (20 times his income), but lost £10,000 in 1814. His luck later took a turn for the worse when he lost his famous lucky sixpence. He reputedly never ate vegetables ('I once ate a pea') but liked biscuits flavoured with maraschino or curaçao. He took snuff and had a silver spittoon because he 'could not spit into clay'. His voice was described as very pleasant. In Caen he never took his hat off to anyone (even to ladies) because this would spoil its exact position on his head. Later in life he had a shambling gait and was shabby and forgetful.

Sport/Hobbies: Though not a keen sportsman, he played in cricket teams at Eton and took part in hunting and shooting. He was a member of White's and Brooks's clubs. He wrote verse, spoke French, drew well and read a lot, as well as collecting prints, pictures, snuff-boxes and buhl furniture.

Religion/Politics: Whig.

Health: Brummell sustained a broken nose

in a fall from a horse. In 1832 he suffered a slight stroke, and another in 1834 left him with facial paralysis (his mouth drawn up to his ear). He eventually went mad and was put in an asylum (in his delirium he held phantom receptions for beauties and magnates of former times).

Temperament: Though seldom ill-tempered, Brummell was arrogant and superior and had a dry humour as well as affected manners. According to the *Dictionary of National Biography* he possessed a 'cool, impudent self-possession rather than wit'. Thackeray called him 'heartless and a swindler, a fool, a glutton, and a liar'. His friends included Byron, the Duchess of Devonshire, the Duchess of York, Lady Hester Stanhope, George IV, Fox and Sheridan.

Pets: His dogs included Atous (in Calais he had a fat female terrier called Vick). He was also devoted to cats – in France he kept the females Ourika and Angolina – and owned a large green macaw, Jacko.

Work/Daily Routine: The quarrel with the Prince Regent was a turning-point. When the Prince ignored him while out walking with a mutual acquaintance, Brummell, on parting, asked the third party, in a deliberately loud undertone 'Who's your fat friend?' In France, he rose at 9 am, took breakfast in his dressing-gown, read the English papers, dressed at noon, took a walk at 4 pm and dressed for dinner at 6 pm. Byron declared him the greatest man of the 19th century (with Napoleon second, then Byron himself). Such was his fame that shopkeepers clamoured for his custom, knowing that many well-heeled clients would follow.

Manner of Death: Sent to the sanatorium/charity asylum of Bon Sauveur in Caen, France, he suffered a last stroke and died soon after on 29 March 1840, aged 61.

BUNYAN, John (1628–88) English preacher and writer

The author of *The Pilgrim's Progress* was born in Elstow near Bedford and baptized on 30 November 1628, the oldest son of Thomas Bunyan, a self-styled 'brazier' (a whitesmith or tinker, a maker and mender of pots and kettles), by his second wife, Margaret Bentley. He had a younger sister Margaret. Without formal schooling, he worked at first as a tinker, then when his mother died (1644) and his father remarried he joined the army, aged 16. During the Civil War he served in the Parliamentary Army on garrison duty in Newport Pagnell, but saw no action. He later joined the Nonconformist Church and, arrested for preaching without a licence (1660), spent 12 years in Bedford gaol where he wrote nine books, including *Grace Abounding* (1666), the first part of *The Pilgrim's Progress*, and made tagged laces to sell to hawkers to support his family. Pardoned in 1672, he was granted a licence to preach but refused to leave Bedford in search of better jobs (he was briefly imprisoned once more in 1676). The second part of *The Pilgrim's Progress* followed in 1684. He was Chaplain to the Lord Mayor of London in the year of his death.

Family/Sex Life: Around 1648 Bunyan married an unidentified woman, who became the mother of his children Mary (who was blind), Elizabeth, John and Thomas. After his first wife died in 1658, he married (1659) Elizabeth (surname unknown), by whom he fathered Sarah and Joseph.

Appearance: Bunyan was tall and strong,

with a ruddy face, sparkling eyes, a grave and sedate countenance, a moustache and red hair that later became grey. He dressed plainly.

Habits/Mannerisms: In his youth Bunyan delighted in blasphemous swearing but he suppressed this weakness after his marriage.

Sport/Hobbies: Prior to his conversion, he was very fond of dancing and music (especially bell-ringing).

Religion/Politics: Bunyan experienced a religious conversion having heard preachers in the Parliamentarian army and committed himself to the Christian church after hearing voices, which warned him that he was bound for hell. A non-conformist and anti-Quaker who was baptized in the River Ouse in 1653, when he was 25, he was commonly dubbed 'Bishop Bunyan' (though some Puritan extremists condemned *The Pilgrim's Progress* as 'a vain story'). The barn where he preached is now preserved as a museum in his honour and Bedford Church contains bronze reliefs from *The Pilgrim's Progress*. Such was his skill as a preacher, it was claimed that he could summon a thousand or more to hear him give a sermon as early as seven in the morning.

Health: Bunyan enjoyed robust health and survived tuberculosis.

Temperament: According to the *Dictionary of National Biography*, the youthful Bunyan was 'a gay, daring young fellow, whose chief delight was in dancing, bell-ringing, and in all kinds of rural sports and pastimes'. He was very mild and affable despite his stern countenance. After his religious conversion, he showed a steadfast determination to follow his calling as a preacher, despite the laws that forbade all but licensed preachers to undertake such work: 'I was made to see that if I would suffer rightly, I must pass

sentence of death upon everything that can properly be called a thing of this life, even to reckon myself, my wife, my children, my health, my enjoyments all as dead to me, and myself as dead to them ... I had this for consideration, that if I should now venture all for God, I engaged God to care for my concernments.'

Work/Daily Routine: Much of Bunyan's finest work was done while confined in Bedford gaol for preaching without a licence and subsequently during his 16 years as pastor at Bedford. When a Quaker visitor claimed he had searched half the gaols in England in search of him, in order to deliver a message from God, Bunyan retorted: 'If the Lord sent thee, you would not have needed to take so much trouble to find me out, for He knows that I have been in Bedford gaol for these past seven years.' While in gaol he kept with him a copy of the Bible and Foxe's *Book of Martyrs* for inspiration. Material for his masterpiece, *The Pilgrim's Progress*, was often drawn from personal experience of life in the army and in rural middle-England. Many of the locales in the epic were based directly on real places. Christian begins his journey, for instance, at the 'City of Destruction' (identified as Bunyan's birthplace, Elstow) and the 'Castle of Beelzebub' is Elstow Church (where Bunyan rang the bells), while the cross on Elstow Green is reputed to be the place where Christian loses his burden. The 'Slough of Despond' is thought to have been modelled on an area between Hockcliffe and Dunstable, while 'Hill Difficult' is Ampthill and his goal, 'House Beautiful', is confidently identified as Houghton Conquest House, a long-since ruined mansion attributed to Inigo Jones. From Houghton Conquest House it is possible to see the Chiltern Hills, renamed the 'Delectable Mountains' in Bunyan's story.

Manner of Death: 10 days after catching cold when riding from Reading to London in the rain, the 59-year-old Bunyan died of a fever in the house of his grocer friend John Strudwick, on Snow Hill near Newgate, London, on 31 August 1688.

He was buried in the Dissenters's cemetery at Bunhill Fields, Finsbury.

BURNS, Robert (1759–96) Scottish poet

Robert Burns was born near Alloway, Ayrshire, on 25 January 1759, the eldest of the seven children of William Burnes (Robert changed the spelling when his first poems were published), a cotter, and Agnes Brown. His brothers and sisters included Gilbert, William, Isobel and Annabella. Educated in Alloway and Ayr, he worked at first as a ploughman on his father's farm and when he died in 1784 moved to Mossgiel and set up another farm with his brother Gilbert. In 1786 the publication of his *Poems, Chiefly in the Scottish Dialiect* brought him immediate acclaim, which persuaded him against moving to Jamaica, where he had been offered the job of overseer of an estate. Attracted to Edinburgh, he was lionized by fashionable society. He gave up farming in 1789, studied surveying in Kirkoswald, worked in a flax-dressing business in Irvine and became an excise officer in Dumfries (where he lived in some style, with a servant etc.). Later he joined the Dumfries Volunteers (1795). His best-loved verse includes satires, animal poems, verse-letters, the narrative poem 'Tam o' Shanter' and the songs 'Auld Lang Syne', 'O my luve's like a red, red rose', 'Ye banks and braes' and 'Scots wha hae'.

Family/Sex Life: Burns had numerous affairs, which provided inspiration for much of his best-loved poetry. These included his engagement to dairymaid Mary – 'Highland Mary' – Campbell (she died in 1786) and a liaison in Edinburgh with Mrs Agnes M'Lehose (addressed as Clarinda in his letters). He also fathered (1785) a child, Elizabeth Paton, by a servant, Anne Park (the child was brought up in his house). In 1785 he fell in love with Jean Armour, but was prevented from marrying her by the objections of her disapproving father. She subsequently gave birth to twins by Burns and they were eventually married in 1788. Their children were Robert, Francis Wallace, William Nicol, Elizabeth, James Glencairn and Maxwell (who was born during his father's funeral service). It was Mary who inspired the famous lines:

'O my luve's like a red, red rose
That's newly sprung in June:
O my luve's like the melodie
That's sweetly play'd in tune.'

Appearance: Five feet 10 inches tall, Burns was very strong, though he walked with a 'ploughman's stoop'. He was good-looking, though he had somewhat coarse features, with a straight nose and eyes that 'literally glowed' (Scott). He was generally untidily dressed.

Habits/Mannerisms: Heavy drinker.

Sport/Hobbies: Burns loved animals and detested fishing and field sports of all kinds.

Religion/Politics: A Freemason and a Jacobite, then for a time a Republican, he supported the French Revolution (he was nearly dismissed from his excise job for selling four ships' cannon to the French) before ultimately turning against the French and resuming a patriotic stance.

Health: Burns suffered from nervous depression and also damaged a knee in a coach accident. His dissipated life-style, with his heavy drinking and womanizing, contributed significantly to his premature death.

Temperament: Contemporaries found the poet witty, gregarious and intolerant of stupidity and arrogance (he could also seem melancholy and stern). He was commonly known as the 'heaven-taught ploughman'.

Pets: Burns kept a pet ewe called Poor Mailie (he wrote two poems about her) and a dog named Luath.

Work/Daily Routine: Like Byron, Burns wrote in a 'white heat' of creative fervour. Many of the folktales and songs that inspired his work came from Betty Davidson, an old woman who lived with the Burns family and who passed the tales on to the poet as a young man. The story for his celebrated narrative poem 'Tam o' Shanter' (1790) came from Davidson, though the name 'Tam o' Shanter' was borrowed from that of a boat which a neighbour, Douglas Graham of Shanter

Farm, used for smuggling purposes. He composed the poem (like many others) while walking in the open air on his farm (he later scratched lines from it on a window-pane at the Globe Inn, Dumfries, now preserved at his cottage). The famous sailing clipper *Cutty Sark* was named after one of the witches in Burns's poem and scenes from it were carved on the vessel's bows.

Manner of Death: Burns contracted rheumatic fever after falling asleep in the open air after a drinking bout and died of rheumatic heart disease on 21 July 1796 aged 36. Three volleys were fired over the grave at his funeral. A mausoleum was built for him in Dumfries by public subscription (1815). Adopted as the national poet of Scotland, the first Burns Club was founded in Greenock in 1802 and his memory is now revered annually throughout the world on Burns Night (marking his birthday, 25 January). Features of the celebrations include a toast to Burns and another 'to the lassies', recognizing his love of women.

BURTON, Richard Francis (1821–90) English explorer and writer

---

Richard Burton was born in Torquay, Devon, on 19 March 1821, the oldest son of Colonel Joseph Netterville Burton, 36th Regiment, who was a descendant of Sir Edward Burton, knighted by Edward IV in the Wars of the Roses. Family tradition had it that he was also reputedly descended from a bastard son of Louis XIV and the Countess of Montmorency. His mother was the wealthy heiress Martha Baker. He had a younger brother Edward Joseph Netterville and a younger sister Maria Catherine Eliza. In the year of Burton's birth, his father was ordered to give evidence in the House of Lords of Princess Caroline's infidelities in Italy but

he refused to lie and was retired on half-pay. This led to financial difficulties and the family moved to Tours, France (where it was cheaper to live), and Burton was educated at the English Colony school there, becoming bilingual in French and English by the age of eight. On the outbreak of cholera he returned to the UK (1830) and attended the Reverend Charles Delafosse's school in Richmond for a year before following his father to Blois, Pisa and Naples, being privately tutored. To curb his increasingly unruly behaviour his father decided he should study for the Church, and sent him to Trinity College, Oxford (1840) but he deliberately got himself rusticated after one year. His father then bought him a commission in the Indian Army, the military wing of the East India Company (1842). Through his language skills and friendship with the Surveyor, he was appointed Assistant Surveyor on the rebuilding of the Indus irrigation system for the East India Company (1844). During the Crimean War he was secretary to General Beatson. He was later British Consul on Fernando Po, off the coast of West Africa (1861–4), in Santos, Brazil (1865–9), Damascus (1871) and Trieste (1872–90). The first non-Muslim Englishman to enter the forbidden city of Mecca of his own free will (disguised as a Pathan doctor, Al-Haj Abdullah), he could reputedly speak 30 languages. He is usually remembered as the translator of *The Arabian Nights* (1885) and *The Kama Sutra* (1883), although he was also the first Western discoverer of the source of the Nile. Awarded the KCMG in 1886, he was never actually physically knighted. He was the founder of the Anthropological Society (1862).

Family/Sex Life: Burton kept an Indian mistress when in Baroda, Gujerat. In 1861 he married Isabel Arundell, without her parents' consent. They had no children, but Isabel was devoted to him, even learning how to fence 'so that I can defend Richard when he is attacked'.

Appearance: Nearly six feet tall, with a broad chest and shoulders though small hands and feet, Burton had a sunburnt face with a spear gash on it. According to the *Dictionary of National Biography*, 'his mouth was hard but not sensual, his nose and chin strongly outlined. His eyes, when in repose, had a faraway look; but they could flash with passion or soften with sympathy.' He had black eyes and short dark hair (he later dyed it black) and wore a very long Chinese-style drooping black moustache. When in India he shaved his head (to keep off headlice) and wore a wig when necessary.

Habits/Mannerisms: Contemporaries described Burton's gestures as dignified and noted that his manners were marked by old-world courtesy. He smoked and drank port and whisky-and-water (to excess). His favourite food was sucking-pig. He was allergic to honey and had a fear of snakes.

Sport/Hobbies: Burton enjoyed falconry and fencing (he wrote books on both and another on bayonet exercises) as well as rowing, boxing, swimming, wrestling and chess. He disliked big-game hunting. Other interests included gambling (whist, piquet, écarté, etc.) and hypnotism (which he practised on his wife). He had a huge collection of pornography, which his wife burnt after his death, including his translation of *The Perfumed Garden* and his diaries.

Religion/Politics: Atheistic but nominally Roman Catholic. He hated egalitarianism and socialism and attacked the hypocrisy of humanitarians and missionaries.

Health: Burton was scarred as a result of a spear piercing both cheeks. He also suffered from gout (from 1883), from fever attacks and from ophthalmia.

Temperament: Spoilt and ill-disciplined as a child, he was always brawling. As an adult, his friends included Swinburne, Tom Hughes (author of *Tom Brown's Schooldays*) and Frank Harris, who noted that 'Burton's laughter had something in it of sadness.'

Pets: Burton took an Oxford bull-terrier with him to India and was also very fond of cats, though his favourite animal of all was a monkey. When in Trieste he liked to buy caged birds and set them free.

Work/Daily Routine: Burton wrote over 50 books. He had minuscule illegible handwriting and often split words (for instance, 'con tradict'). He used the pseudonym 'F. B.' (Frank Baker) for his poetry and also invented a false name for his publishing company – the Kama Shastra Society of London and Benares (actually Stoke Newington) – to publish his notorious unexpurgated version of the *Kama Sutra* (1883).

Motto/Saying: 'To the pure all things are pure' (introduction to *The Arabian Nights*).

Manner of Death: Burton died in Trieste around 5 am on 20 October 1890, aged 68. About 100,000 mourners attended the funeral. His body was returned to the UK but the Dean of Westminster refused burial in Westminster Abbey. He was buried instead in the Catholic cemetery of St Mary Magdalene in Mortlake, Surrey, in a white marble mausoleum in the shape of a tent, 18 feet high and 12 feet square.

BYRON, George Gordon, 6th Baron Byron of Rochdale, Lord
(1788–1824) English poet

Byron was born in rented rooms at 16 Holles Street (now a John Lewis department store), London, on 22 January 1788, the son of Captain John 'Mad Jack' Byron by his second wife Catherine Gordon, 13th (and last) Laird of Gight (a relative of Annabella Stuart, daughter of James I of Scotland). He was the great-nephew of the 5th Baron Byron and grandson of Vice-Admiral Sir John Byron. Brought up by his mother (his father lived in France), on the death of his father (in 1791) his guardian became Frederick Howard, 5th Earl of Carlisle (his first cousin once removed – to whom he dedicated *Hours of Idleness*, described by the *Edinburgh Review* as 'so much stagnant water'). He had a half-sister, Augusta, from his father's earlier seduction of Lord Carmarthen's wife (whom his father later married). Known at first as Geordie Bayron Gordon, he was educated at Aberdeen Grammar School, Dr Glennie's School (Dulwich), Harrow (with Sir Robert Peel) and Trinity College, Cambridge (MA 1808). He inherited his great-uncle's title and Newstead Abbey, Nottinghamshire, in 1798 and travelled extensively from 1809. For his Greek War escapade (1823) he formed the Byron Brigade, hiring 40 Suliots (Christian Albanians) as his bodyguard. He established his reputation as a leading

Romantic poet with such works as *Childe Harold's Pilrimage* (1812) and the verse satire *Don Juan* (1819–24).

Family/Sex Life: As a child, Byron was sexually molested by his nurse, May Gray, and also by Lord Grey de Ruthyn (who rented Newstead Abbey). In 1814 he formed a liaison with Claire Clairmont, stepdaughter of William Godwin and a friend of the Shelleys, who bore him an illegitimate daughter, Clara Allegra. Particularly scandalous were his affairs with Lady Caroline Lamb (née Ponsonby), the niece of the Duchess of Devonshire and wife of future Prime Minister Lord Melbourne (William Lamb) and, allegedly, with his own half-sister Augusta Leigh (her daughter Elizabeth Medora Leigh was thought to be his). Other mistresses included Calypso Polichroni – Pushkin's lover. He also had homosexual affairs (for instance, with Eustathius Georgiou). In 1815 he married Annabella Milbanke, first cousin of Lord Melbourne – she called him 'Duck' and he called her 'Pippin'. They separated in 1816 after she had given birth to Augusta Ada, later Countess of Lovelace and a brilliant mathematician who worked with Charles Babbage on the first computer. Byron's granddaughter Lady Anne Noel married the poet Wilfrid Blunt.

Appearance: Five feet eight and a half inches tall, Byron countered obesity with dieting ('*much* physic and *hot* bathing'), reducing his weight from 14 to 10½ stone. He had a small head, with a pale face, blue-grey eyes, a cleft chin, pouting lips, beautiful teeth, curly dark chestnut hair and delicate hands. He dressed flamboyantly, sometimes in Turkish costume.

Habits/Mannerisms: Byron walked with a limp and spoke with a Scottish accent. He could speak fluent Italian, had a remarkable memory, but was not well read. He never threw anything away. He claimed to have no palate and ate only biscuits and soda water for days, then 'a horrid mess of cold potatoes, rice, fish, or greens, deluged in vinegar' (Trelawney). He was, though, fond of woodcock, lobsters and brandy. He once drank burgundy out of a human skull, occasionally took laudanum and smoked a pipe, and also chewed mastic and tobacco to stave off hunger.

Sport/Hobbies: Byron was a very good swimmer – with Lieutenant Eckenhead he swam the Hellespont breaststroke (four miles in 70 minutes) in imitation of Leander. When returning from visiting mistresses in Venice he reputedly swam down the canals, holding aloft a lit torch so that he would not be hit by the oars of the gondolieri. He also liked boxing, fencing, riding and target pistol shooting. He played cricket at Harrow (using a runner) and owned a schooner, the *Bolivar*.

Religion/Politics: Religious sceptic. He sat in the House of Lords as a Whig (1809), but only made three speeches. He was a Jacobin and a member of the Carbonari secret society dedicated to overthrowing despotic foreign governments and admired Napoleon (at first) and Rousseau.

Health: Byron was born lame and his right foot later became bent inwards (club foot) and he could only hobble a few paces with the foot supported by a brace and an inner shoe. He also suffered variously from malaria, venereal disease, piles, fevers, kidney stones and convulsions. His doctor was Dr John William Polidori ('Pollydolly'), uncle of D. G. Rossetti.

Temperament: Fat and bashful as a boy, he later became 'Mad, bad, and dangerous to know' (Lady Caroline Lamb). He was courageous but vain (he wore curlers at night). His friends included Shelley and John Cam Hobhouse. On his travels he had a valet called Fletcher and a servant Tita (later Disraeli's servant).

Pets: Byron's famous black-and-white Newfoundland dog Boatswain was buried in a tomb in Newstead Abbey intended for himself. He kept a bear at Cambridge as dogs were not allowed. He also had a Newfoundland called Lyon and a bulldog called Moretto (both went to Greece), a mongrel sheepdog named Mutz, 10 horses, five other dogs, three monkeys, five cats, an eagle, a parrot, a crow, a falcon, five peacocks, two guinea-hens, an Egyptian crane, a goat, a badger and three geese.

Work/Daily Routine: A late riser, Byron wrote rapidly, often while his mistresses 'prattled' beside him. He admired Pope, Goethe, Canning, Scott, Coleridge, Samuel Rogers and Thomas Moore but disliked Keats ('piss-a-bed poetry') and called him 'A tadpole of the Lakes'. *Childe Harold* (500 copies) sold out in three days ('I awoke one morning and found myself famous'). *Don Juan* appeared anonymously and was variously called 'filthy and impious' (*Blackwoods*), 'an insult and outrage' (*London Magazine*) and 'a work of art' (Goethe). Byron's memoirs, deemed unfit for publication, were burnt on 17 May 1824 in the London offices of his publisher, John Murray.

Motto/Emblem: '*Crede Byron*' ('Trust Byron').

Manner of Death: Byron caught rheumatic fever after a rainy day in an open boat (his doctors treated him with leeches and brandy) while serving at Missolonghi in the Greek War of Independence. He died in his sleep at 6 pm on Easter Monday, 19 April 1824, aged 36. His lungs were placed in an urn in the church of St Spiridou, Greece. The rest of his body, after burial in Westminster Abbey and St Paul's was refused, was interred at Hucknall Torikard Church, near Newstead. Lady Caroline Lamb accidentally met the cortège, fainted and later went mad. When Byron's coffin was opened (1938) his lame right foot was missing.

CAESAR, Julius (100–44 BC) Roman dictator and soldier

Gaius Julius Caesar (originally pronounced Kaesar) was born on 12 July 100 BC, the son of Gaius Julius Caesar, a praetor and proconsul of Asia (who died when he was 15), and his wife Aurelia. He was delivered by caesarian operation but it is incorrect that the operation is named after him (the word was probably derived from *caesus*, the past participle of the Latin verb meaning 'to cut'). He also had a sister, Julia (grandmother of Emperor Augustus). Having acquired experience as a soldier in the East, Caesar decided to enter politics around 78 BC. Intending to study rhetoric in Rhodes, he was captured by pirates (75 BC): he joked with his captors that he would see them crucified and after he was ransomed led a campaign against his erstwhile gaolers and had them crucified to a man. He was elected consul in 59 BC and formed the First Triumvirate with Pompey the Great and Crassus, becoming governor of Cisalpine Gaul. Caesar's leadership in the Gallic Wars, together with his invasions of Britain in 55 BC and 54 BC, made him a popular hero and in 49 BC he crossed the border (the River Rubicon) into Italy and proclaimed himself sole dictator with the words '*Jacta alea est*' ('The die is cast'). He routed Pompey's forces and subsequently pursued campaigns in Egypt, Africa (defeating Scipio and Marcus Porcius Cato) and Spain. He was elected dictator for life in 45 BC. Among the projects he planned were the drainage of the Pontine marshes, the reformation of the Roman calendar and the codification of Roman law.

Family/Sex Life: Caesar's first wife was Cornelia, daughter of the radical Lucius Cornelius Cinna. The marriage angered Lucius Cornelius Sulla, who was involved in a feud with Cornelia's brother-in-law. Sulla ordered Caesar to divorce Cornelia, but Caesar refused and wisely left for military service in the East. Cornelia died around 66 BC and Caesar married Pompeia, a daughter of Pompey and granddaughter of Sulla. He divorced her, however, in 61 BC after a notorious adulterer, Publius Clodius, allegedly infiltrated the all-female Feast of the Great Goddess and seduced her. Despite a lack of evidence Caesar insisted on the divorce, explaining that 'Caesar's wife must be above suspicion'. In 59 BC he married Calpurnia, daughter of consul Lucius Piso. Caesar's enemies claimed he was both promiscuous and a practising homosexual. One critic observed that 'he was every woman's husband and every man's wife'. He kept several mistresses, including Servilia (mother of his friend Marcus Junius Brutus) and, allegedly, her daughter Tertia. His liaison with Cleopatra led to the birth of Ptolemy XV Caesar, known as Caesarion. His daughter Julia was married off to Pompey in 59 BC (she died in 54 BC).

Appearance: Described by Suetonius as

'tall, fair and well-built, with a rather broad face and keen, dark-brown eyes', he lost much of his red hair and disguised his baldness by combing the remaining hair forward over his pate and by wearing a laurel wreath at all times. He was clean-shaven and something of a dandy, adding wrist-length sleeves with fringes to his purple-striped senatorial tunic, which he wore with a loose belt.

Habits/Mannerisms: Caesar was sober in his ways and drank little.

Sport/Hobbies: A skilful swordsman and horseman, he collected gems, carvings and statues and reputedly invaded Britain in search of freshwater pearls from mussels. He wrote many books and for secret despatches devised the 'Caesar cypher' using third letters (D for A etc.).

Religion/Politics: Became Pontifex Maximus (high priest) through family influence; was later declared a god and his statue was placed in temples.

Health: Good, but suffered from comas and epilepsy.

Temperament: A courageous soldier, he won an oak-leaf crown for saving a fellow-soldier at the Battle of Mytilene. He was, though, a pragmatist and used bribery to advance his career. He was also vain, accepting unconstitutional honours and becoming the first living ruler to feature on Roman coins. He had the month known as Quintilis renamed July in his honour.

Personal friends were invited to address him by the name Gaius.

Pets: His horse, which had hoofs cloven into five 'toes', was immortalized as a statue before the Temple of Venus in Rome.

Motto: Caesar's battle cry was '*Venus victrix*', but he is better known for his remark '*Veni, vidi, vici*' ('I came, I saw, I conquered'), uttered on victory over Mithridates's son Pharnaces (a supporter of Pompey) at Zela, Asia Minor (47 BC).

Manner of Death: Assassinated in the Pompeian Assembly Room at the Senate House in Rome on 15 March 44 BC (the Ides of March), aged 55. Some 60 conspirators – led by Brutus and Cassius – stabbed Caesar 23 times, the first blow being struck by Casca. Legend has it that Caesar attempted to ward off the attack until he recognized Brutus, upon which he uttered '*Et tu, Brute?*' ('You too, Brutus?') and ceased to resist. He fell at the foot of Pompey's statue; his body, laid on an ivory couch, was burnt in the Forum, Rome. Caesar had been warned of danger on the Ides of March by the augur Spurinna – when Caesar encountered Spurinna on his way to the Senate he observed cheerfully that the Ides of March had come, upon which the augur replied darkly: 'True, they have come, but not yet gone.' The night before the assassination Caesar dined with friends: one of them wondered what the best kind of death was, to which Caesar promptly answered, 'A sudden one.'

CALIGULA (AD 12–41) Roman Emperor

Gaius Julius Caesar Germanicus (later known as Caligula) was born in Antium, Italy, on 31 August AD 12, the son of Germanicus Caesar, popular commander of the Roman Rhine Army, and nephew (and adopted heir) of Tiberius, and Agrippina, daughter of Marcus Agrippa. One of nine children, his surviving brothers and sisters were Agrippina the younger, Drusilla, Livilla, Nero and

Drusus (both older and later executed by Tiberius). After the murder of his father (when Caligula was seven) and the exile of his mother he was brought up by his paternal grandmother, Antonia, daughter of Mark Antony and widow of Tiberius's brother Drusus. As a young man he was by all accounts both well educated and intelligent. Proclaimed Emperor, as Gaius, in AD 37 on the death of Tiberius, he was initially welcomed after the previous dissipated reign, but he quickly squandered a vast inheritance and earned the nation's hatred. He reigned for only three years but is still remembered as one of the most dissolute of all the Emperors of Rome.

Family/Sex Life: Caligula's first wife was Julia Claudilla, daughter of senator Marcus Silanus. After Julia died in childbirth, he married Livia Crestilla, only to divorce her a few days later. His third wife, Lollia Paulina, was also quickly divorced and then replaced by Caesonia, who already had three daughters by a previous marriage and an illegitimate daughter (Julia Drusilla) by Caligula himself. Caligula also had numerous affairs as well as committing incest with his sisters and living openly with Drusilla as man and wife. He also had homosexual affairs with the dancer/comedian Mnester and the boy Valerius Catullus, and was fond of the prostitute Pyrallis.

Appearance: Tall, with a pallid complexion, hairy body, thin neck, spindly legs, sunken eyes, hollow temples, broad forehead and near-hairless scalp. He sometimes wore silk (forbidden to men), women's clothes and shoes and a breast-plate stolen from the tomb of Alexander the Great.

Habits/Mannerisms: Nicknamed 'Caligula', meaning 'Little Boots' or 'Bootikins', after the *caligae* military sandals worn by the common soldiers at the camps in which he spent much of his childhood: apparently the youthful

Caligula was given his own miniature uniform, including tiny sandals, in which to play at soldiers. In adulthood, Caligula's vices knew no bounds – as Philo recorded: 'heavy drinking and a taste for delicacies, an insatiable appetite even on a swollen stomach, hot baths at the wrong time, emetics followed immediately by further drinking and the gluttony that goes with it, indecent behaviour with boys and women, and all the vices which destroy body and soul and the bonds which unite them, attacked him simultaneously'. To raise money to support his extravagances, he went so far as to turn part of his palace into a brothel. In later centuries Horace Walpole coined the word 'Caligulism' in referring to the rather tamer debaucheries of his contemporary Frederick, Prince of Wales.

Sport/Hobbies: Very keen on horse-racing, he posted soldiers around the stables of his horses to ensure complete silence, so that the animals enjoyed a good night's rest before the races. He was also a good singer and dancer but could not swim. He admired the comedian Mnester and was fluent in Greek, though he disliked Homer, Virgil and Seneca.

Religion/Politics: Declared himself a god and had a shrine built with a life-size gold image of himself dressed in his clothes for each day. He claimed that on nights when there was a full moon the Moon Goddess herself shared his bed with him: on one occasion he demanded of Aulus Vitellius that he confirm that he had seen Caligula coupling with the goddess – but Vitellius denied this, adroitly excusing himself on the grounds that: 'Only you gods can see one another.'

Health: Epileptic as a boy, he became very ill in AD 37 and was thereafter insanely brutal. Later in his life he suffered from insomnia.

Temperament: Very vain: he insisted his head faced left on coins (not right), renamed September 'Germanicus' in his own honour, and built a bridge of boats across the Gulf of Baiae to better Xerxes's bridge over the Hellespont. He also decapitated many of the most revered and artistically famous statues of Greek deities and put his own head in their place. His taste for cruelty was easily provoked: on one occasion, when the crowd at the gladiatorial games cheered on the 'wrong' team, the emperor leapt up from his seat, shouting: 'Would that the Roman people had but one neck!' During an official banquet he suddenly burst out laughing and, on being asked the cause by two consuls beside him, told them: 'You'll never guess! It suddenly occurred to me that I had only to give a single nod, and both your throats would be cut on the spot.'

Pets: His favourite horse Incitatus had a marble stable, ivory stall, jewelled collar and a house, complete with furniture and slaves. It was Caligula's plan to have him made a consul.

Manner of Death: Caligula was murdered (stabbed in the throat and in the genitals) by Cassius Chaerea, a tribune of the Guard, at noon on 24 January AD 41, aged 29. Caesonia and their daughter Julia Drusilla were also murdered soon after. His body was buried initially in a shallow grave in the Lamian gardens.

CARLYLE, Thomas (1795–1881) Scottish essayist and historian

Thomas Carlyle, 'the Sage of Chelsea', was born in Ecclefechan, Dumfriesshire, on 4 December 1795, the eldest child of James Carlyle, a stonemason, and his second wife Janet Aitken. His brothers and sisters were John Aitken, Alexander, James, Janet, Margaret, Mary and Jane and he had a half-brother John by his father's first marriage. Intended for the Presbyterian ministry he studied at Annan Academy and at the University of Edinburgh but did not take Holy Orders. His first job was as a mathematics teacher in Annan, following which he worked as a private tutor in Edinburgh before becoming a journalist for the *London Magazine*, the *Edinburgh Review*, *Fraser's Magazine* and other publications and translating the works of Goethe. His celebrated *Sartor Resartus* (1833–4) was originally published in *Fraser's Magazine*; he also contributed to the *Edinburgh Encyclopedia* and translated Goethe's *Wilhelm Meister*. After the success of *Sartor Resartus* he moved to London with his wife, in 1834. Later best known for his *History of the French Revolution* (three vols, 1837) and for his huge *History of Frederick the Great* (1858–65) he was one of the founders of the London Library. He was awarded the Prussian Pour le Mérite (1874) for his work on Frederick the Great but declined the Grand Cross of the Order of the Bath from Disraeli. He retired from public life after the death of his wife in 1866.

Family/Sex Life: In 1826 Carlyle married Jane Baillie Welsh – the Jenny of Leigh Hunt's poem 'Jenny Kissed Me' and a relative of John Knox. The couple had no children, apparently because Carlyle himself was infertile. Though the marriage was stormy, Carlyle was distraught at his wife's death and left extensive literary records of her. When a mutual acquaintance regretted that Jane Welsh and Thomas Carlyle had ever married, because of the unhappiness they had caused each other, Alfred, Lord Tennyson demurred, commenting: 'By any other arrangement four people would have been unhappy instead of two.'

Appearance: Full beard.

Habits/Mannerisms: Smoked a pipe; became left-handed after losing the use of his right hand, and always had very bad handwriting.

Sport/Hobbies: A good walker, he once walked all the way from Ecclefechan to Edinburgh University (100 miles). *Tristram Shandy* was a favourite book.

Religion/Politics: Calvinist. He is reputed to have remarked: 'If Jesus Christ were to come today, people would not even crucify him. They would ask him to dinner, and hear what he had to say, and make fun of it.'

Health: Carlyle suffered chronic ill health throughout his life, troubled by stomach pains and by bouts of depression; in old age his right hand shook so much he gave up writing altogether.

Temperament: Violent temper as a child. His friends as an adult included Emerson, Tennyson, Dickens, Thackeray, Fitzgerald, Ruskin and Leigh Hunt (a neighbour in Chelsea). His generosity to the impecunious Leigh Hunt was famous: though often short of money himself, he liked to leave gold sovereigns on his mantlepiece so that Hunt would find them and be able to pocket them without suffering the humiliation of having to ask for help. He disliked Algernon Swinburne greatly, however, and also Shelley whom he described as 'an extremely weak creature; a poor, thin, spasmodic, hectic, shrill and pallid being'. He also took a dim view of the masses in general, sourly describing the population of England as 'Thirty millions, mostly fools' and the public as 'an old woman – let her maunder and mumble'.

Pets: Animals kept in the Carlyle household included a black cat called Columbine and a white terrier named Nero. Carlyle's horse was called Larry.

Work/Daily Routine: Thomas Carlyle hated the noise of London (though Jane loved the city) and he built a soundproof room, lit only from above, at the top of their Chelsea house. He used to paste engravings of the subjects he was writing about over his desk. Explaining his interest in biographical writing he told enquirers: 'A well-written Life is as rare as a well-spent one.' His dogged perseverance as a writer is illustrated by the story of the ill-fated manuscript of *The History of the French Revolution*, the first volume of which the author loaned to philosopher J. S. Mill. A maid in Mill's household, ignorant of the manuscript's importance, used the paper to light a fire, and it was completely destroyed but for a few scraps. Carlyle related the story in his journal, reporting how Mill had 'entered pale, unable to speak' to confess the awful deed. Carlyle confided that the work had taken 'five months of steadfast, occasionally excessive, and always sickly and painful toil', but nonetheless set himself to the task of rewriting the lost volume, which was completed some six months later (though considerably different to the first draft). Jane Carlyle's death in 1866, however, proved a greater blow and he wrote little after that date, rejecting his own conclusion that: 'Work is the grand cure of all the maladies and miseries that ever beset mankind.'

Manner of Death: Thomas Carlyle died at home, 5 (now 24) Cheyne Row, Chelsea, on 5 February 1881. Having declined to accept the honour of burial in Westminster Abbey, he was buried in Ecclefechan beside his parents.

CARROLL, Lewis Lutwidge (1832–98) English writer and mathematician

Charles Lutwidge Dodgson (better known as Lewis Carroll) was born at Daresbury Parsonage, near Warrington, Cheshire, on 27 January 1832, the eldest son of Rev. Charles Dodgson and his first cousin Frances Jane Lutwidge. Known as 'Charlie' at home, he had three younger brothers and seven sisters and was educated in Richmond, Yorkshire, at Rugby School (1846–9) and at Christ Church College, Oxford. A Fellow of Christ Church and Lecturer in Mathematics (1855–81) before becoming a full-time writer, he also became a deacon (1861). He prided himself on his scholarly works on logic and mathematics, but is usually remembered as the author of the classic children's stories *Alice in Wonderland* (1865) and *Through the Looking-Glass* (1872). One probably apocryphal story describes how Queen Victoria, delighted by Carroll's *Alice in Wonderland*, requested that the author send her another of his books – upon which the bemused monarch took delivery of Dodgson's *Syllabus of Plane Algebraical Geometry* (1860).

Family/Sex Life: Though Carroll remained unmarried (a precondition to remaining a Fellow of Christ Church), he exhibited a great fondness for little girls. Among these was Alice Liddell (daughter of Henry George Liddell, Dean of Christ Church), who inspired *Alice in Wonderland*. Carroll first met her when he was 23 and she was just three (Alice Liddell's mother, suspicious of the friendship, later tore up his letters to her). The poem at the end of *Through the Looking-Glass* is an acrostic spelling 'Alice Pleasance Liddell', though Alice Theodora Raikes, daughter of Henry Cecil Parker MP (Postmaster General), was the model for Alice in this sequel (not Alice Liddell). The double acrostic dedication of *The Hunting of the Snark*, meanwhile, is addressed to eight-year-old Gertrude Chataway (who inspired the story). Carroll tired, however, of his young friends when they reached the age of nine or 10 and found new ones to take their place. Alice Liddell went on to be courted by Prince Leopold, son of Queen Victoria, and eventually married one of the author's pupils, Reginald Gervis Hargreaves: she lost two of her three sons in World War I and sold her manuscript copy of 'Alice's Adventures Under Ground' in 1928 for a record £15,400.

Appearance: Nearly six feet tall, he was always neatly dressed (though he never wore an overcoat).

Habits/Mannerisms: Like some of his siblings, Carroll suffered from a stammer, which prevented him becoming a priest. He lost it, however, when talking to children. He only left England once, travelling to Moscow for two months, and from 1877 until his death always took his holidays at 7 Lushington Road, Eastbourne (he never went in the sea, however). He was fond of sherry but ate and drank little, though he kept records of meals that were served to guests to avoid repetition.

Sport/Hobbies: Carroll was an accomplished photographer, exhibiting at the Photography Society in London. His sitters included Tennyson, the Rossettis, Frederick Crown Prince of Denmark, Millais and Bishop Wilberforce. He disliked games but enjoyed walking.

Religion/Politics: Church of England.

Health: Deafness in his right ear as a result of fever in youth meant he preferred people to walk on his left; he also owned a Whiteley Exerciser.

Temperament: Self-centred but kind and modest. Mark Twain described him as 'the stillest and shyest full-grown man I have ever met except Uncle Remus'. Adult friends included Ruskin, Tennyson, Ellen Terry, Lord Salisbury and the painter Arthur Hughes. He liked anonymity, refusing to sit for a *Vanity Fair* caricature by 'Spy' because 'nothing would be more unpleasant for me than to have my face known to strangers'. He never laughed but often smiled (though not when teaching). Endlessly inventive, he introduced many new words in his stories, including 'chortle' and 'galumph'.

Pets: None.

Work/Daily Routine: Carroll wrote some 255 books between 1845 and 1898, including works on tennis, billiards, letter-writing and medicine. His working methods were frequently unusual. The writing of *The Hunting of the Snark*, for instance, began with the last line. The story of the genesis of *Alice's Adventures in Wonderland* is very well known, the original story being told to amuse Alice, Lorina and Edith Liddell on an Oxford to Godstow river trip on 4 July 1862, while Carroll and his friend Canon Robinson Duckworth rowed. The original handwritten 'Alice' story ('Alice's Adventures Under Ground') was only 18,000 words long and took eight months to write. An expanded version was published by Clarendon Press, with plates by Sir John Tenniel, at Carroll's own expense (2000 copies, 1865). Tenniel's illustrations of Alice were based on Mary Badcock. Tenniel had a marked impact upon the author's works: when Tenniel said he did not want to illustrate a chapter about a wasp in a wig for *Through the Looking-Glass* Carroll omitted the chapter altogether. The pseudonym 'Lewis Carroll' was derived from Charles (Carolus) Lutwidge (Ludovicus) and was first used in *The Train* (1 March 1856) at the editor's request (and choice) – other names that the author suggested were Edgar Cuthwellis and Edgar U. C. Westhill. Carroll also kept a diary (13 volumes covering 1854–98, though those for 1858–62 are missing) and he reputedly wrote 98,721 letters. Letters to his young girlfriends were written in violet ink. Otherwise, he wrote in black ink with a fountain pen (a novelty in the 1880s), though he sometimes used a typewriter (also a novelty).

Manner of Death: Carroll died at his unmarried sisters' home, 'The Chestnuts' in Guildford, Surrey, at 2.30 pm on 14 January 1898, aged 66.

CASANOVA, Giacomo Girolamo (1725–98) Italian adventurer, libertine and writer

Giacomo Casanova was born in Venice on 2 April 1725, the supposed son of Gaetano Giuseppe Casanova, an actor, though his real father was Michele Grimani, a distant relative of the Doge of Venice and owner of the theatre that employed Gaetano Casanova and his mother, actress Zanetta Farussi, who had been mistress of George II of England when Prince of Wales. He had a sister, Maria Maddalena Antonia Stella, and two younger half-brothers (both painters). Casanova's father died when he was a teenager and he was brought up by his maternal grandmother and the Grimani family. Entering Padua University aged 12, he worked for a Venetian lawyer before being ordained *abate* (minor clergy) and graduating as a Doctor of Law in 1742. Later he was Private Secretary to Cardinal Acquaviva (Spanish Ambassador) but was dismissed after a minor scandal. He then bought a commission in the Army of Venice, resigned and became a Second Violinist at the S. Samuele Theatre, Venice (1745). After saving the life of Senator Brigadin he was adopted as his son and joined his household (1746). Denounced as a magician and imprisoned in Venice (1755), he escaped after 15 months by cutting through the ceiling of his cell with an 18-inch iron bar and went to Paris where he became a director of a state lottery and owner of a silk-printing business. Imprisoned for debt he was later released and travelled Europe trying to set up lotteries. He was presented at court to Frederick the Great, Catherine the Great and George III of England. In England he was sentenced by Sir John Fielding (half-brother of novelist Henry Fielding) to life imprisonment for attacking a woman, but was immediately released. He then served as Secretary to the Marquis of Roccaforte, as a spy for the Inquisition (1776) and as a writer/publisher of two Venetian magazines. Expelled from Venice in 1783, he became assistant to Sebastian Foscarini (Venetian Ambassador to Vienna) in 1784 and spent his last 13 years as librarian to Count Waldstein in Château Dux (Duchcov), Bohemia. The honorific 'Chevalier de Seingalt' he conferred on himself, but he was genuinely awarded the Order of the Golden Spur by Pope Clement XIII and was elected to L'Accademia degli Arcadi. His patron was Jeanne Camus de Pontcarré, Marquise d'Urfé, ex-mistress of the Regent of France, who paid him a fortune over many years to be reincarnated as a boy through his cabbalistic skills. His numerous sexual adventures were detailed in his *Mémoires* (12 vols, 1826–38), which ensured his reputation as a notorious libertine.

Family/Sex Life: Reputedly the seducer of 10,000 women, Casanova had his first experience of sex in Padua at the age of 11, when he was molested by Bettina Gozzi, sister of the schoolteacher with whom he boarded. He customarily used a pig's bladder as a condom, but nonetheless fathered at least two daughters, Leonilda and Jacomine. He also had an affair with Emma Hamilton in Naples before Horatio Nelson interested himself in her, and engaged in homosexual liaisons.

Appearance: Six feet one and a half inches tall, agile, muscular, with a beaky nose and brown eyes, he was described by the Prince de Ligne as 'tall and built like Hercules, but of an African tint; eyes full of life and fire, but touchy, wary, rancorous ... he laughs little but makes others laugh ...'. As an *abate*, he habitually wore a tonsure.

Habits/Mannerisms: His greatest pleasures included eating oysters off women's breasts. He disliked fish, however, and secured a special dispensation from Pope Benedict XIV so he could eat meat on Fridays. He spoke French and Italian fluently and quoted Homer and Horace *ad nauseam*.

Sport/Hobbies: An accomplished card sharp, he specialized in faro and piquet (he once played for 42 hours without breaking for food). A lover of dancing, music and theatre, he was a good violinist.

Religion/Politics: He was a devout Roman Catholic, but also believed in astrology and in cabbalism; also a Freemason (used name 'Paralis').

Health: A sickly child, suffering from nosebleeds and smallpox (which left three pockmarks on his face). He contracted gonorrhoea and syphilis many times and suffered from piles, epistaxis, pleurisy, pneumonia, gout and prostatitis.

Temperament: Ruthless: he was once imprisoned for selling his family's furniture, but escaped and badly beat up the prosecuting lawyer. He was also brave, fighting several duels. James Boswell, though, called him 'a blockhead'. He kept two faithful Spanish servants, Leduc and Costa, for many years.

Pets: Female fox-terrier dog Melampyge (he wrote verses on her when she died) and another called Finette. He bought a parrot while in London and taught it to shout French obscenities against his former mistress, then sold it back to a street market to embarrass her.

Work/Daily Routine: Casanova wrote over 20 books, including *Venetian Anecdotes of the 14th Century*, the novel *Icosameron* and *History of the Troubles of Poland*. He also wrote verse (for instance, a sonnet on macaroni) and plays and translated the *Iliad* into modern Italian. The original text of his *Mémoires*, written in French and first published in edited form in German, was not published until 1960 (the book was banned by the Vatican and put on the Index of prohibited books in 1834). He used false names when recalling his conquests, unless the women were prostitutes.

Manner of Death: Died of natural causes in Château Dux, Bohemia, on 4 June 1798, aged 72. His last words were: 'I have lived as a philosopher and die as a Christian.' He was buried in St Barbara's churchyard near Dux.

CATHERINE II 'The Great' (1729–96) Empress of Russia

Sophia Augusta Frederica von Anhalt-Zerbst (better known as Catherine the Great) was born on 2 May 1729 in Stettin, then the capital of the Prussian province of Pomerania, the oldest child of German parents, Prince Christian August von Anhalt-Zerbst and Johanna Elisabeth von Holstein-Gottorp. Her mother's brother had been engaged to the Empress Elizabeth of Russia but died of smallpox just before the wedding. She had a French Huguenot governess, Babette Cardel, and took the name Ekaterina (Catherine) Alekseevna when she entered the Russian Orthodox Church in 1744. She became empress in 1762, aged 33, after a *coup d'état*, deposing her husband Tsar Peter III (who was later murdered), and ruled for 33 years. She expanded Russian territory through wars against Turkey and in Poland and attracted many prominent European intellectuals and artists to her court.

Family/Sex Life: Catherine married her mother's cousin Karl Ulrich (the son of Empress Elizabeth's elder sister Anne by the Duke of Holstein-Gottorp – Johanna's brother) at the age of 15. Her husband, heir to the Russian throne, was mentally and physically retarded and the marriage was not a success. The Grand Duke (later Tsar Peter III) deserted her on their wedding night and ordered her to live in a separate household. It was not long before Catherine acquired considerable notoriety for her extra-marital love affairs. Her 21 official lovers – there were probably many more – included her chamberlain Serge Saltykov (by whom she became pregnant twice, but miscarried), Polish Count Stanislaus Poniatowski (whom she made King of Poland), guards officer Gregory Orlov (with whom she lived for 12 years and had a son, Bobrinsky) and one-eyed cavalry officer Gregory Potemkin (to whom she was reputedly secretly married in 1774). By the Grand Duke she had one son, Paul. Catherine's reputation for promiscuity long outlived her: in 1944 Mae West, herself renowned as a sex symbol, wrote and starred on Broadway in a biographical play about Catherine called *Catherine Was Great*. It was in this ill-received production that a fellow-actor playing one of the empress's lovers accidentally prodded West with his sword scabbard in mid-embrace, prompting the actress to quip: 'Lieutenant, is that your sword, or are you just glad to see me?' As the curtain descended at the close of the play each night, West appeared to make a final speech: 'Catherine had 300 lovers. I did the best I could in a couple of hours.'

Appearance: Dark chestnut hair; blue eyes; sweet smile. Her coronation robes were made of 4000 ermine skins.

Habits/Mannerisms: Very intelligent, she retained a marked German accent but also spoke fluent French.

Sport/Hobbies: Catherine wrote plays (*The Paladin of Misfortune* and others), stories (such as the classic fairytale 'Prince Khlor') and memoirs and also compiled a dictionary of the Russian language, employing secretaries to correct her poor spelling and grammar. She enjoyed horse-riding and supervised the construction of the Hermitage Palace in St Petersburg.

Religion/Politics: Lutheran then Russian Orthodox.

Health: Contracted pleurisy (1744). She was one of the first European monarchs to be inoculated against smallpox (which had killed Louis XVI). Late in life she put on weight and suffered from swollen legs, which made walking difficult.

Temperament: Ambitious for power, she may have been involved in the murder of Peter III, arranged by Orlov, and of the death of Ivan VI (Walpole dubbed her the 'Tzar-slayer'). She was keen to promote Russian culture to a level comparable with that of France: her friends included Voltaire, who called her the 'Semiramis of the North' (she bought Voltaire's library and a sculpture of him after his death). Among her more generous acts was the purchase of Diderot's library to help pay for his daughter's dowry (and his appointment as its librarian for life). Early plans to emancipate the serfs were eventually shelved by Catherine, partly in response to the French Revolution and partly in order to secure the support of the aristocracy, who grew ever more powerful under her rule. She did, however, nurse a dream of a reformed Russia, with great new cities to promote industry and progress. This dream was seen as unrealistic by many contemporaries. When the Austrian Emperor Joseph II was invited to mark the inauguration of one of these cities and accordingly laid a second foundation stone upon one already laid by Catherine, he was driven to conclude: 'I have finished in a single day a most important business with the empress of Russia; she has laid the first stone of a city and I have laid the last.' Sure enough, the city was never built and even the location of the site is now forgotten.

Pets: Kitten given to her by Potemkin.

Work/Daily Routine: Rose at 5 am each day.

Manner of Death: Had apoplectic attack and became unconscious on falling from her commode: she died two days later on 17 November 1796, aged 66. Rumours that she died having sex with a horse are untrue.

CERVANTES SAAVEDRA, Miguel de (1547–1616) Spanish novelist

Cervantes was born in Alcalá de Henares, Spain, on 29 September 1547, the second son and fourth of seven children of Rodrigo de Cervantes, a deaf apothecary-surgeon who never studied medicine, and Leonor de Cortinas. His grandfather, Juan de Cervantes, was a wealthy lawyer. He had two older sisters, Andrea and Luisa, two younger brothers, Rodrigo and Juan, and a younger sister, Magdalena. His parents split up in 1563, Luisa and her mother living in Alcalá and Rodrigo and his five other children going to Seville. Educated at the Latin School in Madrid (1561) and the Jesuit College in Seville, Cervantes worked at first in the Vatican as Chamberlain to Monsignor (later Cardinal) Julio Aquaviva, Secretary to Pope Pius V (1568), but left after a few months to join the Spanish Army. He fought against the Turks at the Battle of Lepanto, in which his left hand was maimed and he was wounded twice in the chest (1571). Later he and his brother Rodrigo were captured by the Turks (c. 1576) and imprisoned for five years in Algiers by Hassan Pasha before being ransomed (1580). He then served in the court of Philip II when the king was in Lisbon and became Commissary responsible for provisioning the 130-ship Armada preparing to attack England (1587). Imprisoned for requisitioning Church wheat (1592) he was then a tax-collector and was again gaoled for overzealousness (1597); while in prison he began his classic book *Don Quixote* (part one, 1605; part two, 1615). His other writings included the pastoral romance *La Galatea* (1585), short novels and many plays, of which 16 survive.

Family/Sex Life: Cervantes had an affair with Ana Franca de Rojas, who was already married; by Cervantes she bore a daughter, named Isabel de Saavedra. Subsequently, in 1584, he married Catalina de Salazar Palacios y Voz-mediano, 18 years his junior.

Appearance: According to his own description in the Prologue to *The Exemplary Novels* Cervantes was 'of aquiline visage, of chestnut hair, of open and untroubled brow, of cheerful eyes and hooked though well-proportioned nose'. He also sported a silver beard (formerly gold) and big moustaches and had a small mouth with only six teeth. As regards stature, he called himself slender and 'somewhat bent of shoulder, and not very light of foot'. His left hand, wounded in battle 'to the greater glory of the right', was useless. In *Don Quixote* he concluded: 'Every man is as Heaven made him, and sometimes a great deal worse.'

Habits/Mannerisms: Very fond of *Amadis de Gaul*.

Religion/Politics: Roman Catholic but briefly excommunicated for requisitioning grain for the Armada from the Church (later imprisoned twice for illegal requisitioning). In *Don Quixote* he questioned the worth of religious faith in dire straits, remarking: 'A leap over the hedge is better than good men's prayers.'

Health: Received two gunshot wounds in the chest and one in the left hand at Lepanto; suffered from arteriosclerosis in old age. It was in *Don Quixote* that he made the celebrated observation: 'There's a remedy for everything except death.'

Work/Daily Routine: His first published work was a poem on the death of Queen Isabel de Valois (wife of Philip II of Spain), which was commissioned by his school and was included in a memorial book (1569). He is reputed to have begun his classic romance *Don Quixote* while languishing in prison in La Mancha. The tale was a universal success and secured the author's place among the greatest European writers. Philip III himself became an admirer: when the king happened to pass by a man doubled up with laughter beside the road he observed: 'That man is either crazy or he is reading *Don Quixote*.' History does not record what the king made of the passage in *Don Quixote* in which the queen is discussed: 'She isn't a bad bit of goods, the Queen! I wish all the fleas in my bed were as good.' Though *Don Quixote* proved hugely and lastingly popular, the author's personal favourites among his own works were the romance *La Galatea* and the play *La Confusa*. He wished fervently to establish a reputation as a playwright, but enjoyed only moderate success in this field, partly because of the competition he faced in his rival Lope de Vega and partly because he had sparse talent in writing verse. He freely admitted himself that 'one could expect a great deal from my prose, but little from my verse'.

Manner of Death: Died in Madrid on 23 April 1616, aged 68 (the very same day that William Shakespeare died in England). He was buried in the Convent of the Trinitarians, Madrid, where he was laid to rest without tombstone or inscription.

CHARLEMAGNE (742–814) King of the Franks and Holy Roman Emperor

Charlemagne was born in Aachen in 742, the eldest surviving child of Pepin the Short, Mayor of the Palace (a leading court official) under the last Merovingian king, Childeric III, and later (754) himself King of the Franks. Supposedly illegitimate, his mother was Bertrada and his paternal grandfather was Charles Martel, the conqueror of the Saracens. He had a younger brother Carloman and a sister Gisela (later Abbess of the Convent of Chelles). He was well educated (he learned rhetoric, dialectic, maths and astrology from the English monk Alcuin) and could speak Latin and read Greek. On the death of his father from dropsy (768) he and his brother became joint heirs and divided the kingdom, which then included most of Germany, Holland, Belgium, Switzerland and France. When Carloman died (771), he annexed the rest of the kingdom and was crowned Emperor Carolus Magnus by Pope Leo III in AD 800, ruling as such for a further 14 years (47 in all) – and increasing his dominions greatly – until his death.

Family/Sex Life: His first wife was Desiderata, daughter of Longobard King Desiderius (770, dismissed 771), after whom he married the Swabian Hildigard (died 783), mother of his children Charles, Louis I the Pious, Pepin, Lothar, Rotrude, Bertha and Gisela. His next wife was the German Fastrada (died 794), mother of Theoderada and Hiltrude, and his fourth was Liutgard (died 800). He also kept as mistresses Madelgard (mother of Ruothilde), Gersvinda (mother of Adaltrude), Regina (mother of Drogo, Archbishop of Metz, and Hugo), Adallinda (mother of Theodoric) and Himiltrude (mother of Pepin). He also had a daughter Rothaide by an unknown concubine.

Appearance: Reputedly eight feet tall, he was described by Einhard the Frank as 'tall in stature but not excessively so, for his height was just seven times the length of his own feet'. His eyes were 'piercing and unusually large. His nose was slightly longer than normal, he had a fine head of white hair and his expression was gay and good-humoured ... His neck was short and rather thick, and his stomach a trifle too heavy.' Round his neck he wore a circular talisman made of pure gold set with gems and with two rough sapphires and a portion of the Holy Cross in the centre. He hated foreign clothes and wore Frankish dress: 'linen shirt and linen drawers; and then long hose and a tunic edged with silk. He wore shoes on his feet and bands of cloth wound round his legs. In winter he protected his chest and shoulders with a jerkin made of otter skins or ermine. He wrapped himself in a blue cloak and always had a sword strapped to his side, with a hilt and belt of gold or silver.'

Habits/Mannerisms: Illiterate (he never learned to write but could read better than contemporary rulers, who left this to the monks). He spoke Frankish and Latin and understood Greek. Einhard reported that he 'spoke distinctly, but his voice was thin for a man of his physique'. He was fond of roast meat but was otherwise moderate in eating and drinking and hated to see drunkenness in men. Nonetheless, he lent his name to the classic French white wine, Corton-Charlemagne – the story being that his wife persuaded him to plant white grapes (from which the wine was made) because red wine stained his beard. He particularly admired the works of St Augustine, especially *The City of God*.

Sport/Hobbies: A keen sportsman, he enjoyed hunting, riding and swimming and liked steam baths and thermal springs.

Religion/Politics: Very religious (Roman Catholic); he went to church morning and evening on a daily basis.

Health: A man of limitless energy, and enormously strong. It was said that he could bend three horseshoes at once in his hands. His health was good but he suffered frequent fever attacks in his last four years and became lame in one foot.

Temperament: A man of great resolution, he was generally kind and good-natured – though he hanged 4500 Saxon rebels in one day in 782.

Pets: Kept elephant called Abu al-Abbas presented to him by Harun-al-Rachid, King of the Persians and Caliph of Baghdad. His favourite charger was Blanchard (though his horse in *The Song of Roland* is named as Tencendur).

Work/Daily Routine: Ruled through 12 lords known as Paladins, amongst whom was Roland (whose exploits are recorded in the romance *The Song of Roland*). He ordered the Frankish sagas to be written down and began a grammar of the Frankish tongue. He also built a huge wooden bridge across the Rhine at Mainz: German legend has Charlemagne's spirit crossing a bridge of gold at Bingen, on the Rhine, in order to bless the vineyards and cornfields. After his midday meal, he undressed and rested for two to three hours. A light sleeper, he got up four to five times a night.

Manner of Death: Died of pleurisy in Aachen (Aix-la-Chapelle) at 9 am on 28 January 814, aged 72. He was buried in the church he built in Aachen. He was later embalmed, dressed (with crown and sceptre) and sat on a royal marble throne for 400 years. The corpse was finally removed by the Holy Roman Emperor Frederick II (1215) and buried in a gold and silver coffin in the cathedral of Aachen. He reputedly still waits, armed and crowned, in Oldenburg, Hesse, for the Antichrist to appear so he can go forth and rescue Christendom.

CHARLES I (1600–49) King of England, Wales, Scotland and Ireland

Charles I was born in Dunfermline Palace, near Edinburgh, Scotland, on 19 November 1600, the second surviving son of James VI of Scotland (later James I of England) and Anne, daughter of King Frederick II of Denmark (and sister of King Christian IV of Denmark). He was the grandson of Mary Queen of Scots. His elder brother Henry Frederick died in 1612 (the first recorded case of typhoid, despite being given Walter Ralegh's famous elixir) and he had an elder sister Elizabeth who married Fredrick V, Elector Palatine of the Rhine and King of

Bohemia. Greatly influenced at first by his father's favourite, George Villiers, Duke of Buckingham, after the Duke's assassination (1628) he ruled with the Privy Council. However, his later abuses of Parliament (including suppressing it altogether for 11 years and ruling with the help of Archbishop Laud and the Earl of Strafford) and his attempt to arrest the MPs Pym, Hampden, Haselrig, Holles and Strode in the Long Parliament of 1642 led ultimately to the English Civil War. His defeat (despite his wife's attempts to pawn the Crown Jewels in Europe to raise money for the Royalist cause), led to his imprisonment (1647–9) and a show trial and execution, followed by 10 years of Republican rule under Oliver Cromwell (1653–8) and Richard Cromwell (1658–9). Charles reigned for 24 years.

Family/Sex Life: After unsuccessful negotiations to marry the Infanta of Spain, Charles married by proxy (with arrangements by Cardinal Richelieu) the 14-year-old Catholic Henrietta Maria, daughter of Henri IV and sister of Louis XIII of France, in 1625. They met for the first time a month after the wedding but the marriage prospered (Charles was never unfaithful to his wife). Their children were Charles II, James II, Henry, Mary Princess of Orange (mother of William III), Elizabeth, Henrietta, Anne (who died young), and Catherine.

Appearance: Charles was only four feet seven inches tall, though this is not obvious from his portraits, which show a dignified but sad-looking long face with heavy-lidded eyes. His chestnut hair reputedly went grey during his trial. (Curiously, the famous portrait by Van Dyck shows him carrying two right-handed gauntlets.) The surviving equestrian statue of Charles in Whitehall, honoured by Royalists and Catholics each year, was modelled by Le Sueur in 1633: it was sold for scrap on Parliament's orders in 1650 and was bought by John Revett, who sold cutlery supposedly made from it

– in reality the statue had been hidden away, to be revealed after the Restoration. A bust by Bernini, shown to Charles in the garden of Whitehall Palace, proved a portent of doom: as the bust was uncovered a drop of blood fell from a dead bird being carried by a hawk overhead – the blood landed on the bust's throat.

Habits/Mannerisms: The infant Charles did not speak until the age of five and he never overcame a pronounced stammer; he did not walk until he was seven. Charles was abstemious when it came to food and drink, though he often ate in public.

Sport/Hobbies: Charles loved horses and hunting and rode well. He was also good at tennis and in the tilting-yard. Charles enjoyed good music, drama and fine art. He commissioned Rubens to paint the ceiling of the Banqueting House, Whitehall, and encouraged Van Dyck. He also collected 16th-century Italian paintings (in all 1400 pictures and 400 sculptures). Though 'not a man of thought' his favourite writers were Shakespeare, Spenser, Herbert, Tasso and Ariosto and he also liked masques, especially those by Ben Jonson with designs by Inigo Jones.

Religion/Politics: Very religious; the first English monarch to be brought up in the Church of England (though the Roman Catholicism of his wife caused some disquiet). His insistence on five over-dressed bishops at his investiture in Scotland (1633) and his issue of the Scottish Prayer Book led to riots.

Health: Never a strong child, he suffered especially from weak ankles.

Temperament: Shy and very moral. He would blush if immodest words were used in his presence. He was nonetheless conceited and had little sense of humour (though he kept a famous court jester, Archibald Armstrong). He was dubbed St Coloquintida by the Levellers because he was as bitter as this type of apple. The

Parliamentarians called him the 'Last Man' (in other words, the last king), while to the Puritans he was the 'Man of Blood'.

Pets: Lucky black cat, which died the day before he was arrested by Parliament.

Manner of Death: After his trial in Westminster Hall, at which he was not permitted to speak, Charles was beheaded outside the Banqueting House, Whitehall, on 30 January 1649, aged 48. He wore two shirts on the day of his execution so that he would not shiver in the freezing cold and be thought to be afraid. After the execution, members of the crowd pressed forward to dip handkerchiefs in the king's blood and the soldiers sold bits of the scaffold as souvenirs. The body was buried in Windsor Castle in the same vault as Henry VIII; in 1813 Royal Surgeon Sir Henry Halford stole the fourth cervical vertebra from the coffin and used it as a salt-holder for 30 years before Queen Victoria ordered its return.

CHARLES II (1630–85) King of Great Britain and Ireland

Charles II was born in St James's Palace, London, on 29 May 1630, the second and oldest surviving son of Charles I and Henrietta Maria of Denmark. He had two brothers, Henry (who died of smallpox) and James II, and three sisters, Elizabeth, Henrietta (wife of Louis XIV's homosexual brother Philip) and Mary Princess of Orange (who died of smallpox). His cousins included Prince Rupert – a Royalist commander in the Civil War – and Louis XIV, and one of his godfathers was Louis XIII. He was well educated and Thomas Hobbes served as his maths tutor. During the Civil War he commanded the Royalists in the West Country aged 15 until he was forced to flee to France (1646) and Holland (1648). He returned to Perth in 1650 and was crowned King of Scotland but was defeated by Cromwell at Worcester and was forced to hide in an oak tree near Boscobel House (1651). As 'Will Jackson', a servant, he fled to France, Germany and Belgium and remained there until he was crowned at the Restoration (1660). Charles's 25-year reign witnessed the Great Plague (1665), the Fire of London (1666) and war with Holland (1665–7).

Family/Sex Life: The first of Charles's mistresses – there were at least 13 – was Lucy Walter (1648), whom he met in Holland and by whom he fathered James Duke of Monmouth (his favourite child). In 1661 Charles married Catherine of Braganza, daughter of John IV of Portugal. They had no children and she was no beauty ('her teeth wronging her mouth by stiking a little too far out', according to John Evelyn). Catherine spoke no English and returned to Portugal on her husband's death. Charles's mistresses included Lady Byron, Lady Castlemaine (Mrs Barbara Palmer, née Villiers, later Duchess of Cleveland), the Duchess of Portsmouth (Louise de Kérouaille – his sister Henrietta's French maid) and Hortensia Mancini (Cardinal Mazarin's niece). He fathered numerous illegitimate children. Nell Gwynne, a Covent Garden orange-seller and actress, was the only mistress not a Catholic. She once escaped an anti-papist mob by shouting: 'Pray, good people, be civil – I am the Protestant whore.' One woman who resisted Charles's advances was Frances Stewart ('La Belle Stewart'): Charles put her on the coinage as Britannia.

Appearance: Andrew Marvell described Charles as 'of a tall stature and of sable hue'. He sported black hair in natural ringlets and a moustache and had a swarthy complexion. Evelyn recorded 'his Countenance fierce, his voice greate, proper of person'. On seeing his portrait by Lely he exclaimed: 'Odd's fish, I am an ugly fellow!'

Habits/Mannerisms: A lover of planting and building, Charles enjoyed mutton (also slang for loose women) and telling stories about himself (courtiers heard the same anecdotes repeatedly). 'Odd's fish!' was a favourite expression.

Sport/Hobbies: Charles liked riding, hunting, hawking and horse-racing (he personally won the 12-Stone Plate at Newmarket in 1675) as well as walking, sailing, tennis and pall mall. He danced and enjoyed art, architecture, music and theatre. He also interested himself in science (he founded the Royal Society and the Greenwich Observatory) and had his own laboratory. He understood Spanish and Italian and spoke and wrote French fluently.

Religion/Politics: A deathbed convert to Catholicism, Charles dismissed Presbyterianism as 'Not a religion for gentlemen'. His Cabinet was known as the Cabal after the initials of his chief ministers – Clifford, Arlington, Buckingham, Ashley and Lauderdale.

Health: Charles broke his arm as a child and contracted measles and smallpox. Later, he caught venereal disease (1677) and suffered fits (1679). It was widely believed that his touch would cure scrofula, as John Aubrey reported: 'Arise Evans had a fungous nose, and said, it was revealed to him, that the king's hand would cure him, and at the first coming of King Charles II into St James's Park, he

kissed the king's hand, and rubbed his nose with it; which disturbed the king, but cured him.'

Temperament: Kindly, good-natured – 'A Prince of many Virtues, and many greate Imperfections, Debonaire, Easy of accesse, not bloudy or Cruel', according to Evelyn. Charles was known as the 'Merry Monarch' after the Earl of Rochester wrote: 'Restless he rolls about from whore to whore/A merry monarch, scandalous and poor.' John Dryden called him 'forgiving, humble, bounteous, just and kind'. He was also quick-witted – when Rochester scrawled on the king's bedchamber door 'Here lies our mutton-loving King/Whose word no man relies on/Who never said a foolish thing,/Nor ever did a wise one', Charles responded: 'This is very true, for my words are my own, and my actions are those of my ministers.'

Pets: Charles kept 'King Charles' spaniels (then liver-and-white coloured, not black-and-tan). These lived in his bedchamber 'which rendred it very offensive, and indeede made the whole Court nasty and stinking' (Evelyn, 1685). He even took the dogs to Council meetings. He also kept Arab racehorses, feeding them on soaked bread and eggs. His favourite horse was named Old Rowley (Charles himself was dubbed Old Rowley by satirists).

Manner of Death: Charles suffered an apoplectic fit on 2 February 1685 and died at Whitehall Palace at 11.45 am on 6 February 1685, aged 54. He was buried in Westminster Abbey at night 'without any manner of pomp' (Evelyn, 1685). On his deathbed he requested of James II: 'let not poor Nelly starve'. To the courtiers who assembled at his bed he apologized: 'I am sorry, gentlemen, for being such a time a-dying.'

CHARLIE, 'Bonnie Prince' (1720–88) Scottish pretender to the British throne

Charles Edward Louis John Casimir Silvester Severino Maria Stuart (usually known as 'Bonnie Prince Charlie', the Young Pretender) was born in Rome on 31 December 1720. He was the eldest son of the Chevalier de St George, the Old Pretender, James Francis Edward Stuart (son of James II) and Princess Clementina (daughter of Prince James Sobieski of Poland), who died when he was 14. He had a younger brother Henry Benedict, Cardinal Duke of York. On 23 July 1745 he landed at Eriskay in the Scottish Hebrides, with just seven friends. Subsequently, on 19 August 1745, he raised his father's banner at Glenfinnan, thus launching the 'Forty-five' Jacobite Rebellion against the English in a bid to seize the English crown from George III. Charles's army of Scottish clansmen got as far south as Derby (4 December 1745) before lack of support obliged them to return to the north. When his army of 5000 men was defeated by the Duke of Cumberland ('Butcher' Cumberland) with great loss on Culloden Moor (16 April 1746), the Prince fled to Benbecula in the Hebrides, then Monkstadt on Skye and escaped via Kingsburgh to Portree dis-guised as 'Betty Bourke, an Irish spinning maid' in the company of 24-year-old Flora Macdonald. (The disguised Charles was nearly discovered when, crossing a river, he unthinkingly hoisted up his dress to avoid it getting wet.) After making good his escape he lived on the Continent, mostly in Florence, as the self-styled 'Count of Albany' – though he also claimed the title of Charles III after his father's death in 1766. Flora Macdonald was imprisoned for a time in the Tower of London for her part in the escape, but was released in 1747 under the Act of Indemnity; she married Allen Macdonald in 1750, emigrated to North Carolina in 1774 but finally returned to Scotland in

1779, where she died in 1790.

Family/Sex Life: In 1772 Charles married Louise of Stolberg, 32 years younger than him, but she left him for the Italian poet Count Vittorio Alfieri and they were divorced in 1784 (they had no children). His mistresses included Clementina Walkenshaw (by whom he had an illegitimate daughter Charlotte – both later retired to a convent), his cousin the Duchesse de Montbazon, and the Princesse de Talmont (cousin of the Queen of France).

Appearance: Charles was 'Above the middle height and very thin ... his face is rather long, the complexion clear, but borders on paleness; the forehead very broad, the eyes fairly large – blue but without sparkle; the mouth large, with the lips slightly curled, and the chin more sharp than rounded.' He had light brown hair and was clean-shaven. He was tall but later stooped. Handsome in his youth (he was first called Bonnie Prince Charlie in Edinburgh in 1745) and with a delicate complexion, his face later became bloated and red from drink. He was also a master of disguise and liked dressing as a priest, wearing false noses and so forth.

Habits/Mannerisms: Spoke mostly French, Italian and a little English but no Scots (he had never visited the country prior to the Rebellion of 1745). He was also an alcoholic, his favourite tipple supposedly being Drambuie – a whisky liqueur with a honey flavour, based on secret ingredients. It is said that when Charles wished to reward his supporter Captain John Mackinnon for his loyalty on making good his escape from Scotland, he gave him his only remaining possession: the secret recipe for making Drambuie. To this day, bottles of Drambuie are labelled 'Prince

Charles Edward's liqueur'.

Sport/Hobbies: A good rider and hunter, he was also skilled in country ways and could imitate the call of a plover very accurately. He was a very good golfer, dancer and cellist and was fond of music, theatre and opera. He also played the card game *tarocchi*.

Religion/Politics: Roman Catholic, then Protestant (though he disliked organized Church). He was also reputedly the head of the entire Freemason movement worldwide.

Health: Charles suffered from sea-sickness throughout his life and also contracted chickenpox in 1739. His addiction to alcohol made his leg swell to half the size of his body.

Temperament: Very charming and witty. Arthur, the 6th Lord Balmerino, who was executed in 1746 as a Jacobite leader, called the Young Pretender 'so sweet a prince, that flesh and blood could not resist following him'. Later in life he was often drunk and mistreated his wife (until she left him).

Manner of Death: A severe stroke left Charles semi-paralysed. He died in his daughter's arms in Rome around 9 am on 30 January 1788, aged 67. A plaster cast was made of his face after death and his body was buried at first in Frascati Cathedral, then in St Peter's, Rome.

CHATTERTON, Thomas (1752–70) English poet

Thomas Chatterton was born around 7 pm in his father's lodgings at Pile Street School, Bristol, on 20 November 1752, three months after the death of his father, Thomas Chatterton, a schoolmaster, skilled numismatist (he was the owner of hundreds of Roman coins) and a member of Bristol Cathedral choir. His mother, Sarah Young, opened a sewing school for children after his father's death and took in sewing and created neeedlework designs for local ladies. He had an older sister, Mary, and a brother, Giles Malpas (who died in infancy). He was educated at Pile Street Charity School (where his father had taught) then at Colston's Hospital School. Apprenticed to a Bristol attorney (1767), he worked from 8 am to 8 pm all year round but was eventually sacked. At this point, aged 16, he excited much interest when he announced that he had found 'from an old manuscript' in a chest at St Mary Redcliffe an ancient description of the opening of Bristol Bridge in 1248. This and subsequent medieval poetic 'discoveries' – supposedly the work of a 15th-century Bristol priest, Thomas Rowley – were admired at first by Horace Walpole, who started a correspondence with the boy and said he wished to publish them (he later called Chatterton 'a complete genius and a complete rogue'). Encouraged by his reception, in 1770 Chatterton moved to London and set about consolidating his reputation as a writer. The death of his patron, Lord Mayor Beckford, however, was a massive blow to his fortunes. Reduced to penury, he chose to end his life. The 'Rowley poems' were published by Thomas Tyrwhitt in 1777 but a few years later doubts were voiced about their authenticity, opening a heated and long-running debate that was not finally settled until well into the 19th century. The crucial evidence of forgery was the line 'Life and its good I scorn' – the possessive 'its' not being used before the 17th century. Nonetheless, Chatterton's pastiche poetry was greatly admired by

Coleridge ('Britannia's boast, the wond'rous boy'), Rossetti ('the absolutely miraculous Chatterton'), Wordsworth ('the sleepless soul, that perished in his pride'), Byron, Shelley, Keats (who dedicated *Endymion* to him), Scott, and others. Dr Johnson, however, called Chatterton a 'vulgar uneducated stripling' and omitted him from his *Lives of the English Poets*, though he privately admitted to Boswell that 'it is wonderful how the whelp has written such things'.

Family/Sex Life: Unmarried.

Appearance: Like other pupils, the young Chatterton had tonsured hair (auburn in colour) while at school. Later, he was described as being 'well grown and manly, having a proud air and stately bearing'. He was said to have brilliant grey eyes – one brighter than the other. A single authentic portrait of him, aged 11, has survived.

Habits/Mannerisms: Abstemious – he ate cakes and water at meals, drank tea but disliked hot meat. He later developed a nervous facial tic. He chose to use the pseudonym 'Decimus' when some of his work was published in the *Middlesex Journal*.

Religion/Politics: Christian. He wrote that 'the Church of Rome (some tricks of Priestcraft excepted) is certainly the true Church'. He admired Wilkes and attacked the government of Lords Sandwich and Grafton in the satirical poem *The Consuliad* (1770).

Work/Daily Routine: Chatterton worked at night. He left over 600 printed pages of verse, songs and libretti plus prose pamphlets and letters. Among the journals he worked for were the *Middlesex Journal*, the *London Magazine*, the *Court and City Magazine* and the *Freeholders' Magazine*.

Manner of Death: On the night of 24 August 1770, Chatterton locked himself up in his garret room at his lodgings in 39 Brooke Street, Holborn, London. There the 17-year-old poet committed suicide by drinking arsenic mixed with water. He suffered great pain, which left his features horribly contorted (a detail omitted in the famous painting of the death scene by Henry Wallis, 1856). The body was buried in the Shoe Lane workhouse burial ground, but was later moved to Gray's Inn Road. Just three days before he killed himself, Chatterton, while walking along reading a book, had fallen into a newly-dug grave – he observed to the friend who helped him get out again: 'My dear friend, I feel the sting of a speeding dissolution. I have been at war with the grave for some time, and I find it not so easy to vanquish it as I imagined. We can find an asylum to hide from every creditor but that.' (In the famous romanticized picture of the dead Chatterton by Wallis the model for the poet was George Meredith, whose wife shortly afterwards eloped with the painter).

CHAUCER, Geoffrey (c.1343–1400) English poet and civil servant

Geoffrey Chaucer was born c.1343 in Thames Street, London, the son of John Chaucer, a well-to-do wine merchant, customs collector and property owner, and his second wife Agnes Copton, niece of Hamo de Copton, a maker of coins. After the death of his father in 1366, his mother married another vintner, Bartholomew Chapel. He had a sister Katherine and a stepbrother by his mother's first marriage. Educated, it is presumed, at the Almonry School in St Paul's Cathedral, he worked at first as a page in the court of Elizabeth de Burgh, Countess of Ulster, the wife of Lionel Duke of Clarence (Edward III's third son), aged 14 (1357). In 1359, aged 16 or 17, he served in Edward III's army in France, was taken prisoner by the French at the siege of Reims (1360) and was ransomed (Edward paid £16 for him). He then studied law at the Inner Temple and around 1360 was attached to the court of Edward III as Yeoman of the Chamber and Esquire at Court. He later became Comptroller of the King's Customs and Subsidy of Wools, Hides and Wool Fells for the Port of London (1374–86), Clerk of the King's Works at the Palace of Westminster under Richard II (1389–91), Knight of the Shire of Kent, JP for Kent (1386) and finally Deputy Forester in the King's Forest, Petherton, Somerset (1390–1 and 1397–8). He also went on secret missions to France, Flanders, Spain, Italy (where he may have met Boccaccio and Plutarch) and elsewhere – including looking for a suitable wife for Richard II. He served under three kings: Edward II, Richard II and Henry IV and though never officially knighted was known as Sir Geoffrey Chaucer from 1391. Chaucer is remembered above all as the 'Father of English Poetry'. Among other works, he translated Boethius and the *Roman de la Rose* into English, but he is usually quoted as the author of *The Canterbury Tales* (c.1387), which vividly depicted an assortment of characters among a group of pilgrims journeying to Canterbury to visit the shrine of Thomas à Becket. Other important works by his hand included *Troilus and Criseyde* (c.1385).

Family/Sex Life: In 1366 Chaucer married (by arrangement with her guardian, the Queen of England) one of the Countess of Ulster's household, Philippa Roet of Harvault, daughter of Sir Gilles (Payne) de Roet – an official in the household of Margaret Empress of Germany (sister of Edward III's queen) – and sister of the wife of John of Gaunt, Edward III's youngest son. She died in 1387. They had two sons,

Thomas (later Speaker of the House of Commons and father of the Duchess of Suffolk) and Lewis (to whom he dedicated *A Treatise on the Astrolabe*, 1391), and a daughter, Agnes. In 1380 the poet was charged with rape and had to pay baker's daughter Cecile Champaigne (stepdaughter of Edward III's mistress, Alice Perrers) to withdraw her claim against him.

Appearance: Plump, with grey hair and a two-pointed beard. Surviving portraits suggest a calm, serious expression.

Habits/Mannerisms: As Poet Laureate, Chaucer was entitled to a pitcher of wine every day under the reign of Edward III (modern Poets Laureate qualify for a tun of wine once a year).

Sport/Hobbies: Chaucer spoke French fluently, also Latin and Italian.

Religion/Politics: Roman Catholic. He was a Royalist during the Peasant's Revolt and later served as MP for Kent (1386).

Health: Chaucer lived through the period of the Black Death (then known simply as The Death), which killed a third of the population of England, but survived. His health was also at risk during the 1380s, when several of his associates were executed during a time of mounting political turmoil.

Temperament: His friends included the poet John Gower (who wrote the *Confessio Amantis*). It was to 'moral Gower' that the poet dedicated *Troilus and Criseyde*.

Work/Daily Routine: Chaucer's first work was 'An ABC' – a prayer to the Virgin Mary in which each stanza begins with successive letters of the alphabet. He wrote *Troilus and Criseyde* while living (rent-free) in the gatehouse at Aldgate and he may have embarked on *The Canterbury Tales* when he had time on his hands following the loss of his official posts in

1386 (followed by the death of his wife and mounting debts). He was much influenced by Dante and Boccaccio (especially by *The Decameron*) and invented the 10-syllable, five-stress line, which then became standard in English poetry, as well as the so-called 'rhyme royal'.

Manner of Death: Chaucer died in his lodgings, a house in the gardens of Westminster Abbey, near the Lady Chapel, on 25 October 1400, aged around 60. He was buried in what was later (from the 17th century) known as Poets' Corner, Westminster Abbey, one of the first commoners and the first poet to be buried in the Abbey. His last months were considerably eased by the granting of a generous pension by Henry IV.

CHEKHOV, Anton Pavlovich (1860–1904) Russian playwright and short-story writer

Anton Chekhov was born in Gnutov House, Police Street, in the port of Taganrog – where Tsar Alexander I had died in 1825 – on the Sea of Azov on 17 January 1860, the third son of Pavel Yegorovich Chekhov, owner of a grocery shop and local choirmaster (who later died of a rupture lifting Anton's books), and Yevgenia Yakovlena Morozova, daughter of a cloth merchant. His grandfather, a serf, was the manager of a sugar-beet refinery who had bought his freedom. He had two elder brothers, Alexander and Nikolai (a painter and caricaturist who died of tuberculosis), an elder sister Mariya and two younger brothers, Mikhail and Ivan. Educated at first at a school for Greek children, then at a Russian grammar school (where he founded a paper, *The Stammerer*), when his father was declared bankrupt the family fled to Moscow, leaving 16-year-old Anton as 'hostage' to their main creditor, to whose son he became tutor. He was later awarded a grant to study at Moscow University Medical School, graduating in 1884. While a student he wrote comic stories for St Petersburg humorous magazines under the pseudonym 'Antosha Chekhonte'. He worked as a doctor in Babkino, near Moscow, then travelled to Hong Kong, Singapore and Europe before becoming Cholera Superintendent Doctor for 25 villages in Melikhovo. Though later a successful writer (known as 'The Russian Maupassant') he continued to practise as a doctor. Such was his influence that Lenin said he was made a revolutionary by reading his story 'Ward 6', while George Bernard Shaw said reading Chekhov made him want to tear up his own plays. He was later (1900) elected a Fellow of the Russian Academy of Sciences (becoming with Tolstoy one of the first writers to be admitted) but he resigned (1902) when another Fellow, Gorki, was dismissed. Considered one of the great writers for the modern stage, he was the author of such ground-breaking plays as *Chaika* (The Seagull, 1895), *Dyadya Vanya* (Uncle Vanya, 1900), *Tri Sestry* (The Three Sisters, 1901) and *Vishnevy Sad* (The Cherry Orchard, 1904).

Family/Sex Life: In 1901 Chekhov was secretly married to the actress Olga Knipper, who acted in *The Seagull*.

Appearance: Tall, with thick wavy brown hair, no sideburns and a short beard that later turned grey, he wore pince-nez over his brown eyes. He also carried a scar on his head, dating from an accident he had as a boy.

Habits/Mannerisms: Chekhov ate little, needed little sleep and had a slight lisp. He smoked cigarettes and cigars, liked expensive neckties and favoured 'Vera Violetta' scent. He also laid expensive carpets throughout his house.

Sport/Hobbies: Chekhov enjoyed swimming, fishing and gardening. He could read French, but could not speak it.

Religion/Politics: Russian Orthodox. He lost his faith as a child when forced into the choir by his zealous father. Later in life he supported Émile Zola in the celebrated Dreyfuss case.

Health: Chekhov contracted peritonitis as a child and suffered from heart disease, headaches, piles and intestinal troubles. He caught tuberculosis aged 23 and spent winters in Yalta for the sake of his health. He also took the *koumiss* cure (requiring the drinking of fermented mares' milk) in Ufa.

Temperament: Modest, with a good sense of humour. He used to shoot birds but later came to hate killing animals and released captured mice in the countryside. He admired Tolstoy and Turgenev, but despised Dostoevski.

Pets: When at Yalta he had two stray dogs and a crane, which followed him about everywhere he went.

Work/Daily Routine: The audience rioted on the first performance of *The Seagull* in St Petersburg, with critics calling it 'intellectual rot'. Chekhov, noting that the audience showed signs of 'a strained state of boredom and confusion', was so upset he vowed never to write again for the stage, but the play was later revived and this time proved a great success. Even then, though, it had its detractors. Noël Coward was one: 'I *hate* plays that have a stuffed bird sitting on the bookcase screaming, "I'm the title, I'm the title, I'm the title!"'. Tolstoy was similarly antagonistic, complaining to Chekhov: 'where is one to go with your heroes? From the sofa where they are lying to the closet and back.' Chekhov wrote his works in a chalet on his Melikhovo estate – raising a flag when he was ready to receive guests. He wrote quickly: his one-act farce *Swan Song* was reputed to have taken him just one hour. He sold most of his copyrights to a publisher called Marx for 75,000 roubles – Marx made a fortune. Joshua Logan adapted *The Cherry Orchard* for US audiences, setting it in the southern states and renaming it *The Wisteria Trees*; the press, however, unkindly dubbed the production 'Southern fried Chekhov'. His works were not translated into English until after his death.

Motto: 'Medicine is my lawful wife and literature is my mistress.'

Manner of Death: Chekhov died on 15 July 1904 in a hotel in Badenweiler, in the Black Forest, Germany, on 2 July 1904, aged 44, after his tuberculosis moved to the intestines and bowels. Gasping for breath and in great pain, he died sipping champagne. His coffin was taken to Moscow in a goods wagon marked 'Fresh Oysters'. At his funeral mourners got muddled with those for General Keller of Manchuria and ended up following the wrong procession.

CHESTERTON, G(ilbert) K(eith) (1874–1936) English novelist

G. K. Chesterton was born in Kensington, London, on 29 May 1874, the elder son of Edward Chesterton, head of Chestertons auctioneers/estate agents, and a Frenchwoman, Marie Louise Grosjean. He had a brother Cecil. Educated at

St Paul's School, London (a friend and contemporary was E. C. Bentley), he proved a slow learner. He also studied art at the Slade School, London. He worked for two publishers before becoming a journalist and writer. Journalism came easily to him and much of his prolific output, which included fiction, criticism and verse, was written for publication in magazines. He had few illusions about his journalistic enterprises, however, and once remarked that 'Journalism largely consists of saying "Lord Jones is dead" to people who never knew Lord Jones was alive.' His most celebrated writings included a series of stories about the modest but perspicacious priest/detective, Father Brown, who first appeared in 'The Innocence of Father Brown' (1911), and such novels as *The Napoleon of Notting Hill* (1904) and *The Man Who Was Thursday: a Nightmare* (1908). After converting to Catholicism in 1922, he wrote chiefly on religious themes, his later works including books on Christianity (*Orthodoxy*, 1906), St Francis of Assisi and Thomas Aquinas.

Family/Sex Life: In 1901 Chesterton married Frances Blogg, daughter of a diamond merchant. They had no children (his wife was unable to have them).

Appearance: Chesterton was tall, untidy and grossly overweight. By his own account 'I am six foot two and my weight has never been calculated.' He sported a moustache and glasses and wore a large floppy hat and a huge cloak. He often carried a sword-stick. His considerable girth was in marked contrast to the willowy figure of his friend George Bernard Shaw. Shaw once told Chesterton that if he was that fat he would hang himself. Chesterton replied that if he did decide to hang himself he would use Shaw as a rope. When World War I broke out a young woman tried to hand him a white feather, asking him why he was not out at the front – Chesterton calmly responded: 'My dear madam, if you will step round

this way a little, you will see that I *am*.' On another occasion, addressing a meeting in Pittsburgh, he reassured his audience that he was not really as fat as he appeared: 'Dear me, no. I'm being amplified by the mike.' There were consolations to being so large, though, as he once pointed out: 'Just the other day in the Underground I enjoyed the pleasure of offering my seat to three ladies.'

Habits/Mannerisms: Clumsy and absent-minded, Chesterton frequently managed to get himself lost. During one lecture tour he was obliged to send the following telegram to his wife, who endeavoured to organize his schedules: 'Am in Birmingham. Where ought I to be?' His wife sent back the reply: 'Home.' When he became engaged to Frances Blogg, he was so excited that he decided to write a long letter to his mother at once to let her know the news – quite forgetting that his mother was actually in the room as he wrote it. Not dissimilar was an incident in which, against all expectation, he turned up at his publisher's office at the appointed hour, only to hand over a detailed letter explaining why he could not keep the appointment. By way of contrast, he had very neat handwriting (Gothic script) and spent much time perfecting his style and signature. A heavy drinker, he smoked cigarettes but preferred small black cheroots. He also liked salmon, veal cutlets, cream meringues, burgundy and *Crème de Menthe*.

Religion/Politics: Converted to Roman Catholicism (1922). In politics, he was a Liberal, then 'Distributist', and was controversially pro-Boer during the Boer War. He was also strongly anti-Semitic (though he denied this) and admired Mussolini (but not Hitler). He once observed: 'Democracy means government by the uneducated, while aristocracy means government by the badly educated.'

Health: Chesterton suffered from bad teeth (he never visited a dentist). He broke his right arm in 1912 and also suffered from catarrh and, from 1914, from heart trouble.

Temperament: His school report stated: 'Not a quick brain, but possessed by a slowly moving tortuous imagination – conduct always admirable.' He was very good-natured and had a close friendship with Hilaire Belloc (whose books he illustrated), leading to George Bernard Shaw's appellation 'Chesterbelloc'. Other friends in literary circles included H. G. Wells.

Work/Daily Routine: Chesterton's first published books were *The Wild Knight* and *Greybeards* (both 1900). The famous Father Brown character was modelled on Monsignor John O'Connor, a real Catholic priest.

Manner of Death: Chesterton died at home in Beaconsfield around 10 am on Sunday 14 June 1936, aged 62. He was buried in the Roman Catholic cemetery in Beaconsfield, the mourners including Belloc.

CHOPIN, Fryderyk Franciszek (1810–49) Polish composer and pianist

Fryderyk Chopin (or Chopyn) was born in Zelazowa Wola near Warsaw, Poland, on 22 February 1810 (on his birth certificate, though his mother celebrated his birthday on 1 March). He was the only son of Frenchman Nicholas Chopin, tutor to the children of Countess Louisa Skarbek of Zelazowa Wola and later French teacher at the Warsaw Lyceum and military schools, a famous pupil being Maria Walewska, favourite mistress of Napoleon. His mother was a Pole, Tekla Justyna Krzyzanowska – a relative of Countess Skarbek. He had three sisters, Louisa (older), Isabel and Emily (who died of tuberculosis aged 14). Chopin was first taught piano, aged six, by Albert Zywny; at 11 he was taught by the composer and Director of the Polish National Opera Elsner. At 13 he attended the Warsaw Lyceum; he also studied at the Warsaw Conservatoire (1826–9). At 21 he moved to Paris, where he became a darling of salon society. He played before Tsar Alexander I, Louis Philippe (who gave him a Sèvres porcelain cup) and Queen Victoria – though he later commented: 'I think the English have wooden ears and will never create anything noteworthy in music.' His piano compositions included 50 mazurkas, 27 études, 25 preludes, 19 nocturnes, 13 waltzes, 12 polonaises, four ballades, three impromptus, three sonatas, two piano concertos and a funeral march.

Family/Sex Life: In 1832 Chopin had an affair with his pupil Countess Delphina Potocka, whom he called Phindela. He dedicated his Piano Concerto in F Minor and the 'Minute Waltz' to her. Subsequently he proposed to Marie, daughter of Countess Wodzinska, but they encountered parental objections. From 1838 to 1847 (when they fell out) he lived openly with novelist George Sand (Aurore, Baroness Dudevant, a relative of the King of Poland). He called her Jutrzenka (Polish for Aurore); she called him Chopinet, Chippette, Chip-Chop and Fritz. She was six years older than him and had a 15-year-old son Maurice and a 10-year-old daughter Solange. They were unable to marry because divorce was unrecognized in Catholic France. Strangely, Chopin never dedicated any works to Sand (though she dedicated *La Mare au Diable* to him). He also had an affair with his pupil Jane Stirling (a rich Scottish spinster).

Appearance: According to his 1837 passport, Chopin was five feet seven inches tall. He was thin (six stone 13 pounds in 1840) and had sloping shoulders. He had long silky auburn hair (which he used to curl) and long sideburns. Admirers noted his beautiful hands and Matthew Arnold talked of his blue-grey 'wonderful eyes'. He also had a large nose. He dressed elegantly.

Habits/Mannerisms: In his youth, Chopin slept with wooden wedges between his fingers to extend their span. He had neat handwriting and signed all his letters 'Ch'. He also kept an ivory hand with a black handle for scratching his head.

Sport/Hobbies: Chopin enjoyed riding, skating and playing billiards. He sketched competently and as a child wrote poetry.

Religion/Politics: Roman Catholic (non-practising).

Health: Frail; he suffered from tuberculosis and took opium drops on sugar-lumps. He was also troubled by rheumatism from 1842. On 28 August 1848, at Manchester, he was so weak he had to be carried on and off the stage. That same year he lamented to a friend: 'we are two old cembalos on which time and circumstances have played out their wretched trills ... The *table d'harmonie* is perfect, only the strings have snapped and some of the pegs are missing.' Berlioz put it simply: 'He was dying all his life.'

Temperament: Chopin's friends included Mendelssohn (who liked to call him 'Chopinetto'), Liszt, Delacroix and – very close – Titus Woyciechowski. He was, however, jealous of George Sand's friends and was anti-Semitic. A fastidious man, he complained if friends soiled his manuscripts and one took to wearing white gloves to turn the pages – Chopin still found fault when he inspected the spotless returned manuscript, protesting: 'My dear fellow, you were smoking when you read it!'

Pets: He adopted a stray dog called Mops (Polish for pug-dog) when living with George Sand.

Work/Daily Routine: Chopin was a child prodigy, giving his first public performance aged eight. His first published work, the Rondo in C Minor (1825), came out while he was still at school and was dedicated to the headmaster's wife. The Waltz No. 3 in F major was inspired by a cat walking over the keys. In the 'Black Key étude' a white key is played only once. He felt his A Minor and C Minor études were his best. Around 1830 his routine was to wake early, drink coffee, play the piano until his German teacher arrived at 9 am, play till noon, take a walk, have lunch followed by black coffee, visit friends, return home, go to parties and retire to bed around 10 or 11 o'clock. When preparing for concerts he played Bach. He had two pianos – a grand and an upright – and preferred the Pleyel make. Defying convention, he allowed his fingers to cross when playing.

Manner of Death: Chopin died of tuberculosis at 12 Place Vendôme, Paris, at 2 am on 17 October 1849, aged 39. Artists and photographers recorded the scene and Countess Potocka sang at his bedside at his request. His last words were: 'Play Mozart in memory of me.' He was buried near Bellini in the Père Lachaise Cemetery, Paris, but his heart was taken to the Church of the Holy Cross, Warsaw. The 3000 mourners at his funeral included Meyerbeer, Pleyel and Delacroix. George Sand was not invited.

CHURCHILL, Winston (Leonard Spencer) (1874–1965) English statesman

Winston Churchill was born prematurely in the ladies' lavatory at Blenheim Palace, Woodstock, Oxfordshire, during a dance on 30 November 1874. He was the eldest son of Lord Randolph Henry Spencer Churchill (third son of the 7th Duke of Marlborough, MP for Woodstock, Secretary for India, Chancellor of the Exchequer and Leader of the House), who went mad and died of syphilis. His mother was Jeannette Jerome (daughter of a New York businessman, one-eighth Iroquois Indian and creator of the Manhattan cocktail), whose lovers included Count Kinsky and, allegedly, Edward VII when Prince of Wales. He had a younger brother Jack. At Harrow, he was deemed slow-witted and entered Sandhurst (after three attempts). He fought in the Sudan and reached Lieutenant-Colonel (IVth Queen's Own Hussars, 1895–9) before resigning. He served as war correspondent during the Boer War and escaped from a POW camp. Conservative MP for Oldham, then Liberal MP for 18 years, he was Home Secretary (1910), First Lord of the Admiralty (1911), Minister of Munitions (1917), Chancellor of the Exchequer (1924–9) and Prime Minister (1940–5, 1951–5). Nicknamed 'Winnie', he was Britain's leader in World War II. He received the CH, the OM (1946) and the Order of the Garter (1953) and won the Nobel Prize for Literature (1950) for his historical writings, notably his *The Second World War* (1948–54). Churchill College, Cambridge, was named in his honour.

Family/Sex Life: In 1908 Churchill married Clementine Hozier, daughter of Colonel Sir Henry Hozier. Their children were Diana, Randolph, Sarah, Marigold and Mary. He called her Kat and she called him Pug; the children were nicknamed Puppy Kitten (Diana), Chum Bolly (Randolph), Bumble Bee (Sarah) and Duckadilly (Marigold).

Appearance: Red-haired, Churchill became virtually bald. As a young man he sported a moustache but had a small chest (31 inches at 26). He wore pale pink silk underwear and had many hats. An 80th birthday painting by Graham Sutherland was controversially destroyed by his wife.

Habits/Mannerisms: Churchill drank whisky and soda with ice and also enjoyed claret and soda (though he preferred white wine to red). His consumption did not concern him – when a hostile female MP accused him of being drunk at a dinner, he delivered the celebrated retort: 'And you, madam, are ugly. But I shall be sober tomorrow.' His big cigars were a trademark – favourites were Romeo y Julieta – though he rationed himself to eight or nine a day and did not inhale. His two-fingered Victory V-sign became internationally famous. As a child he had a lisp. He owned a Daimler and only once went on the Underground and never on a bus. Clementine Churchill observed: 'He knows nothing of the life of ordinary people.' Shown Manchester's slums in 1905 he lamented: 'Fancy living in one of these streets, never seeing anything beautiful, never eating anything savoury – never saying anything clever!'

Sport/Hobbies: Rifle-shooting, fencing, riding, polo, gambling, bricklaying and painting. After his resignation over Gallipoli he built a huge model of the Forth Bridge in Meccano. He also bred horses (his colt Colonist II won 13 races), collected butterflies and grew 50 varieties of roses. He reputedly saw the film *Lady Hamilton* 17 times and liked Kipling, Scott, Stevenson, Forrester, Fielding, Maugham, Maupassant, the Brontës,

Orwell, Noël Coward and Gilbert and Sullivan.

Religion/Politics: Church of England, but not religious. Conservative (1900), Liberal (1910), then Conservative again. He praised Mussolini at first for having 'rendered a service to the whole world'. On being elected premier in 1940 he promised 'blood, toil, tears and sweat'. He often clashed with radicals – Nancy Astor told him: 'Winston, if I were married to you, I'd put poison in your coffee', to which Churchill replied: 'And if you were my wife, I'd drink it.'

Health: Churchill suffered from depression (the 'Black Dog'), but enjoyed a good memory. His appendix was removed in 1922 and he suffered pneumonia and a stroke in 1949; he was paralysed down the left side in 1953.

Pets: Churchill kept a green budgerigar called Toby and cats – Margate was a black stray (arriving at 10 Downing Street on the day of Churchill's 1953 conference speech at Margate); Nelson was also black; and Jock, Tango and Ginger (among others at Chartwell) were ginger. He also kept the poodles Rufus I and Rufus II and no one ate before the dogs had been fed.

Work/Daily Routine: Employing a huge staff, he wrote histories, a novel and even film scripts for Alexander Korda (he received £10,000 for a scenario for *The Reign of George V*). During World War I he introduced the first armoured car (a Rolls-Royce with 3½ tons of armour plate and a machine-gun). His powers of oratory were legendary, though he remained unimpressed by the crowds who heard him speak, saying 'ten times as many would come to see me hanged'. Little reported highlights of Churchill's war years included the moment he urinated on the Siegfried Line in 1945.

Manner of Death: After a stroke on 10 January 1965, Churchill died at his London home (28 Hyde Park Gate, Kensington) at 8 am on Sunday 24 January 1965, aged 90 (the day his father died 70 years earlier). He lay in state in Westminster Hall (320,000 visitors) and was given a state funeral (the first for a commoner since Wellington's in 1852) and a service in St Paul's. He was buried in Bladon churchyard, near Blenheim Palace.

CLAUDIUS I (10 BC–AD 54) Roman Emperor

Tiberius Claudius Drusus Nero Germanicus (better known as Claudius) was born in Lyon, France, on 1 August 10 BC, the younger son of Nero Claudius Drusus (Tiberius' brother) and the younger Antonia (daughter of Mark Antony). His father, a consul and a famous general, died in 9 BC when he was just one year old. He was the grandson of Augustus's wife Livia Drusilla and the nephew of Tiberius. His brother was Germanicus Caesar (the popular general and the father of Caligula) and he had a sister, Livilla. He succeeded Caligula as Emperor following the latter's assassination in AD 41, at the age of 50, and ruled for 14 years. He was the first emperor to invade Britain since Julius Caesar and generally proved an able and forward-thinking ruler, though he was criticized for his extravagance, particularly in relation to his wives, whom he indulged with great lavishness, and certain ambitious public projects. He made important administrative reforms and also extended Roman territories with the addition of Britain, Mauretania and Thrace.

Family/Sex Life: Claudius was singularly

unlucky, or unwise, in his choice of marriage partners. He took as his first wife Plautia Urgulanilla, whom he later divorced for scandalous behaviour. Their children were Drusus and Claudia. His second wife was Aelia Paetina, whom he also divorced (by him she gave birth to Claudia Antonia). His marriage to 15-year-old Valeria Messalina resulted in the birth of a daughter Octavia, who married Nero, and a son Britannicus Caesar, fated to be poisoned by his brother-in-law Nero. Despite her youth, Messalina quickly became notorious for her cruelty, lust and avarice and made many enemies. Having engineered the deaths of numerous senators, Messalina finally lost her grip on power when Claudius's secretary Narcissus managed to persuade the Emperor that she had entered into a bigamous marriage with Gaius Silius and was involved in a plot against him – upon which Claudius had her put to death. His fourth wife was Caligula's sister, Agrippina the younger, his previously married niece. They had no children but he adopted her son Lucius Domitius Ahenobarbus (later Nero) – both his son-in-law and his grandnephew – as his successor instead of his own son Britannicus.

Appearance: Claudius was tall, well built and handsome, with white hair.

Habits/Mannerisms: Claudius had weak knees and stumbled when walking. He had an uncontrollable laugh and slobbered at the mouth and nose when he became angry. He also suffered from a stammer and had a nervous tic, tossing his head from side to side, and drank a lot. His physical disabilities probably ensured his survival in his early years, when potential rivals ignored him as a possible future contender for supreme power. When attempts were made by Alexander Korda to film the story of Claudius's life as *I, Claudius* in the 1930s, with Charles Laughton in the leading role, Laughton saw links between the Emperor's character and that of the current king of England,

George VI, who also had a stammer and came to the throne almost by accident (after the Abdication Crisis). This notion alarmed Korda, who wished to be accepted into English society and hoped for a knighthood: when he and co-star Merle Oberon were subsequently injured in a car crash he is thought to have used this as a pretext to abandon the project. Korda got his knighthood in 1942. (Derek Jacobi later played the part of Claudius in an acclaimed, and very bloody, 13-part television series with a script based on the book by Robert Graves).

Sport/Hobbies: The Emperor was very fond of playing dice – he wrote a book on the subject and had a special board fixed to his carriage so that he could play while travelling. He wrote histories in Greek (he spoke Greek well) and – with the encouragement of Livy – a history of Rome. He also invented three new letters for the Roman alphabet.

Religion/Politics: Claudius worshipped the usual Roman gods and expelled all the Jews from Rome because of constant disturbances. He was the first emperor since Augustus to be posthumously deified by the Senate.

Health: A sickly child, apparently stupid, he was scorned by his mother, grand-mother and sister, and also suffered from stomach ailments.

Temperament: Generally scatterbrained and forgetful, Claudius had few qualms about murdering his critics. During his reign he executed 35 senators, 300 knights, his father-in-law, his niece Julia, his son-in-law Gnaeus Pompey and many more.

Manner of Death: Claudius died on 13 October AD 54, aged 64, after eating poisoned mushrooms. It is generally believed that he was murdered by Agrippina to ensure her son Nero's succession.

CLEOPATRA VII (69–30 BC) Queen of Egypt

Cleopatra VII Thea Philopator ('goddess and lover of her father') was born in 69 BC, the third child of King Ptolemy XII of Egypt (nicknamed Auletes or 'flute-player') and his sister – royal incest then being traditional. Like all the Ptolemies, who ruled Egypt after the death of Alexander the Great, she was not a native Egyptian, being of Greek, Macedonian and Iranian stock. She had two younger brothers, Ptolemy XIII and Ptolemy XIV and two elder sisters, Cleopatra VI Tryphaena (who usurped their father's throne) and Berenice (who was executed by their father) and a younger sister Arsinoe. On the death of her father in 51 BC, 18-year-old Cleopatra and her 10-year-old brother Ptolemy XIII were named as his heirs, but after her affair with Julius Caesar (who in the First Triumvirate had supported her father against the rebels) Ptolemy XIII was discovered drowned and she married her brother Ptolemy XIV. When Caesar was killed (44 BC), Ptolemy XIV was murdered and Cleopatra ruled alone with Caesar's son as her heir. She then lived with Mark Antony for seven years until their deaths by suicide after Antony's defeat in battle. Cleopatra's Needle, the monument moved to the Thames Embankment in London in 1878, has nothing to do with her beyond the fact that it stood originally in her capital, Alexandria (it was erected some 1400 years earlier by Thotmes III, c.1500 BC). She was also known as 'the Serpent of the Old Nile'.

Family/Sex Life: Cleopatra married her brother Ptolemy XIV Dionysius, according to prevailing royal custom. She was over 30 when she became the mistress of Julius Caesar and lived in Rome with him for two years (46–44 BC) before his murder. Their son was Ptolemy XV Caesar, known as Caesarion. Her first meeting with Caesar is now the stuff of legend – the

story being that she caught the dictator's attention after she had herself delivered to him rolled up in a priceless carpet. She lived with Mark Antony for seven years (though he was still married to Octavia) and bore him the twins Alexander Helios and Cleopatra Selene, and Ptolemy Philadelphus.

Appearance: Some authorities suggest Cleopatra was not in fact attractive, with a bony face and a hooked nose, but there are virtually no contemporary depictions of her by which to make a judgement. The popular imagination prefers to believe she was ravishingly beautiful and that she used her beauty to sway Caesar and Antony and thus to protect her own and her country's interests against the Roman threat. Her nose was considered the most beautiful of her many beautiful features, and Blaise Pascal wrote: 'If the nose of Cleopatra had been shorter, the whole face of the earth would have been changed.'

Habits/Mannerisms: In order to preserve her beauty, Cleopatra is reputed to have bathed regularly in asses' milk.

Sport/Hobbies: Cleopatra was highly educated and knew several languages, including Egyptian (an accomplishment never attempted by any of her predecessors).

Religion/Politics: Egyptian zoomorphic gods.

Temperament: Very charming and intelligent, if capricious and scheming. To impress Antony with her wealth, she treated him to a costly banquet and dropped a valuable pearl earring into her drink, so that it dissolved to nothing. She was painted in different hues by literary giants of later eras. Shakespeare's

Cleopatra, in the tragedy *Antony and Cleopatra* (*c*.1606), is middle-aged, vain, impulsive, flirtatious, cruel, sensual, unpredictable, fickle, naive and politically astute. Sir John Dryden's Cleopatra, in his play *All for Love* (1678), is nobler and more dignified than Shakespeare's queen, sacrificing all for her love of Antony and maintaining her serenity before Antony's wife. George Bernard Shaw's Cleopatra, in *Caesar and Cleopatra* (1898), is teenage, childlike, timid and egocentric. Many of the most celebrated actresses have presented their own interpretations of her character in these classic plays, some with more success than others. Sarah Bernhardt turned in a *tour de force*, smashing pots, pulling down curtains and throwing herself on the stage floor in her fury at Antony's inconstancy (one member of the audience was moved to observe: 'How different, how very different, from the home life of our own dear queen'). When the US star Tallulah Bankhead essayed Shakespeare's version of the queen the critics were damning, John Mason Brown reporting that: 'Tallulah Bankhead barged down the aisle as Cleopatra and sank. As the serpent of the Nile she proves to be no more dangerous than a garter snake.'

Manner of Death: On learning of Antony's suicide after his defeat at the Battle of Actium, and faced with the humiliation of being paraded through Rome as Octavian's prisoner, Cleopatra committed suicide (30 August 30 BC) by allowing an asp to bite her on the breast. The asp was deliberately chosen because the snake was understood to be the minister of Amon-Ra, the Sun God, and had long been used as a symbol by the Pharaohs, signifying their power over life and death. Antony, not quite dead, expired in her arms. Cleopatra's tomb was discovered on 10 January 1890.

COLERIDGE, Samuel Taylor (1772–1834) English poet and philosopher

Samuel Taylor Coleridge was born in Ottery St Mary, Devon, on 21 October 1772, the youngest son of the 13 children of the Rev. John Coleridge, vicar of Ottery St Mary, headmaster of King Henry VIII Grammar School, Ottery, and author of a Latin grammar, and the tenth child by his second wife Ann Bowdon, a farmer's daughter. He had three older stepsisters and an older stepbrother John, and other older siblings included William, James, Edward, George, Francis Syndercombe (who committed suicide), Anne and Luke. His father died when he was eight. He was educated with Charles Lamb at Christ's Hospital School, London, and at Jesus College, Cambridge, but got into debt and did not take his degree. He enlisted in the 15th Light Dragoons as 'Silas Tomkyn Comberbache' to avoid college debts but was bought out later by a brother under the 'insanity' clause. At first briefly a Unitarian minister in Shrewsbury (1798), he won backing from Thomas and Josiah Wedgwood (£150 a year), which allowed him to leave the ministry. Writing poetry while working as a journalist on the *Morning Post*, he later became Secretary to the Governor of Malta and then a freelance lecturer. Among his most celebrated literary works were the *Lyrical Ballads* (1798), on which he collaborated with William Wordsworth, the epic poem *The Rime of the Ancient Mariner* and numerous translations, plays and philosophical and critical writings.

Family/Sex Life: Coleridge fell in love with Sara Hutchinson ('Asra' in his poems) but was rejected by her (a calamity that inspired his 'Dejection Ode'). In 1795 he married Sara Fricker, by whom he fathered

David Hartley, Berkeley (who died young), Derwent and Sara. His friend Robert Southey married Sara's sister Edith.

Appearance: Dorothy Wordsworth described Coleridge on their first meeting – 'Pale and thin, has a wide mouth, thick lips and not very good teeth; longish loose-growing half-curling rough black hair ... His eye is large and full, not dark but grey ... He has fine eyebrows and an overhanging forehead.' Later in life he became fat. He was usually shabbily dressed and when walking with a friend once suggested, on meeting company, that the friend pass him off as his servant – his companion replied: 'No, I am proud of you as a friend, but would be ashamed of you as a servant.'

Habits/Mannerisms: A brilliant public speaker and conversationalist, Coleridge was vain and enjoyed looking at himself in mirrors. He was called Sam by his family but was addressed as Coleridge by the Wordsworths and even by his wife. After Malta he regularly drank ale at mid-morning and at meals.

Sport/Hobbies: Coleridge was an excellent classicist and translated various German works (such as Schiller's *Wallenstein*). He was a bad horseman but was interested in horticulture and farming and in chemistry. He was also a prolific letter-writer.

Religion/Politics: Unitarian but later rejected this. He founded the radical Christian and political journal *The Watchman* (1796). He supported the French Revolution and with Southey devised 'Pantisocracy', an unrealized scheme to set up a commune in New England. Coleridge was anti-Pitt but admired Fox and David Hartley (after whom he named his son).

Health: Coleridge was addicted to opium in its liquid form, laudanum – by 1814 he was drinking two quarts of it a week. He also took Indian hemp. He suffered from rheumatism and neuralgic headaches and complained: 'I cannot breathe through my nose; so my mouth ... is almost always open.' Further physical ailments included eye infections, rheumatic fever and atonic gout.

Temperament: Carlyle called Coleridge 'a weak, diffusive, weltering, ineffectual man'. Charles Lamb, however, dedicated his *Essays of Elia* to him and said he was 'an archangel slightly damaged'. He recalled how on one occasion, when he was in a hurry, Coleridge had grasped him by the button and had launched into a brilliant but lengthy exposition. Anxious to escape, Lamb took out a knife and cut off the button so that he could depart – five hours later he passed the same spot to find Coleridge still there, talking as before, the button still clasped in his fingers. He was known as 'the Sage of Highgate' in his old age.

Work/Daily Routine: Coleridge had only had one poem published at 21. He composed 200–300 lines of 'Kublai Khan' during a three-hour sleep in a farmhouse between Porlock and Linton, Devon, after reading about Kublai Khan in *Purchas's Pilgrimage* – he woke up and wrote down 54 lines before a tradesman from Porlock interrupted work for an hour, at the end of which he had forgotten the rest. The *Ancient Mariner* began as a collaboration with Wordsworth while walking near Lynmouth (1797). He thought *Tom Jones*, *Oedipus Rex* and *The Alchemist* had the best three plots in literature.

Manner of Death: Coleridge died of heart failure at the London house of his surgeon friend James Gillman (3 The Grove, Highgate) on 25 July 1834, aged 61. An autopsy revealed an enlarged heart and liver and a cyst on the lungs.

COLLINS, (William) Wilkie (1824–89) English writer

Wilkie Collins, the 'father of the detective story', was born in Tavistock Square, London, on 8 January 1824, the eldest son of the landscape painter William Collins and Harriet Geddes (cousin of the famous Scottish painter Andrew Geddes), who were friends of Charles Lamb and Samuel Taylor Coleridge. He was named after his godfather, the painter Sir David Wilkie. He had a younger brother, Charles Allston (who married Charles Dickens's daughter Kate). He was taught at home until aged 11 and then attended Maida Hill Academy for a year. When his parents moved to Italy he spent three years at the Rev. Henry Cole's School, Highbury, where the school bully forced him to tell stories in the dormitory. His first job was working for the London tea merchants Edward Antrobus & Company, where he wrote a novel, *Antonina*. He then studied at Lincoln's Inn (1846) and was called to the bar (1851) but never practised. His father then died and he wrote his biography (Collins's first published book). He received an adequate legacy from his father and £5000 from his mother and eventually earned up to £5000 a year from his writing. Collins is usually remembered for his novels *The Woman in White* (1860) and *The Moonstone* (1868), which T. S. Eliot described as 'the first, the longest and the best of modern detective novels'. He also toured the USA (1873–4) giving readings in the style of Dickens, joined the staff of *Household Words* and wrote short stories, essays and reviews and so forth for *Bentley's Miscellany* and other publications.

Family/Sex Life: Collins never married (by choice) but lived with Caroline Graves (née Elizabeth Compton), the wife of George Robert Graves and with a daughter Harriet, for 40 years. He also had three illegitimate children by shepherd's daughter Martha Reidd (Marian, Harriet Constance and William Charles). When with Martha he called himself William Dawson, barrister, and she was Mrs Dawson (she and the children lived in a separate house). Another mistress was Caroline Courtenay.

Appearance: Collins had very small feet and hands, a very large brown beard, a high forehead, a small nose, hair parted on the left, spectacles and grey eyes. He sported gold studs, cufflinks, watch and chain and also wore a gold locket containing a photograph of his mother and a lock of her hair.

Habits/Mannerisms: Fluent in French and Italian, he was a glutton and loved paté, lobsters, oysters, asparagus, eggs, garlic and black pepper. He drank dry champagne, brandy and gin and smoked cigars.

Sport/Hobbies: Collins enjoyed sailing, riding, fishing and walking and was an accomplished painter (he exhibited at the Royal Academy in 1849). He also loved Italian opera and participated in amateur dramatics, meeting Dickens in 1851 during a charity performance for Queen Victoria.

Religion/Politics: He believed Jesus was the son of God but protested that 'I am neither a Protestant, a Catholic nor a Dissenter.'

Health: He suffered from gout and pains in the knees and back, as well as inflamed eyes and sciatica in his hands. Collins took laudanum for 20 years, drinking a wine-glass full each day (a servant died drinking a similar dose). He injected morphine into his arm each night from 1869 and inhaled amyl nitrite for his angina.

Temperament: Known and addressed as 'Wilkie', his friends included the Lehmanns, Millais, Holman Hunt, the Rossettis, Dickens, Lillie Langtry and Oscar Wilde.

Pets: Collins despised horses but loved dogs. His favourite was Tommie, a brown-and-white Scotch terrier.

Work/Daily Routine: Though he plotted in great detail before writing, Collins rewrote extensively and his manuscripts were very heavily marked. Caroline Graves's daughter Harriet Bartley was his secretary and Caroline herself was probably the model for *The Woman in White* (Collins and Millais first met her in the street by accident at midnight, just as the central character in the novel first appears). He worked from 10 am to 2 or 3 pm daily on *The Woman in White* (which was serialized in Dickens's *All the Year Round*). He was a great admirer of *Robinson Crusoe*, Byron ('beyond comparison the greatest poet that has sung since Milton'), Scott ('the Prince, King, Emperor, God Almighty of novelists') and of Boswell's *Life of Johnson* ('the greatest biographical work that has ever been written'). He was bedridden with gout while writing *The Moonstone* (during which his mother also died): much of the book was dictated, the last part under the influence of laudanum. The detective in the story, Sergeant Cuff, was modelled upon Jonathan Whicher, one of the first six detective sergeants appointed in 1842. Whicher became famous through his involvement in the 'Roadhill House mystery', in which he concluded, on the evidence of a missing nightdress, that the murderer was Constance Kent, a member of the household (he was ridiculed but was later proved correct when Kent confessed). Collins disliked working at night because he saw ghosts induced by the laudanum. He kept the copyrights in 19 of his 22 novels but sold all these to Chatto & Windus before he died.

Manner of Death: Collins died after a stroke at 82 Wimpole Street, London, at 10.30 am on Monday 23 September 1889, aged 65. The only people present at his death were his doctor and Caroline Graves. He was buried at Kensal Green Cemetery; objections by the Dean of St Paul's and others to Collins's unconventional private life prevented a proposed memorial in Westminster Abbey.

COLUMBUS, Christopher (1451–1506) Genoese-born explorer

Cristobal Colombo (who adopted the Spanish version of his surname, Colon, in 1492) was born in the autumn of 1451 in Genoa of Spanish-Jewish parents. His father was Domenico Colombo, a weaver, and his mother was Susanna Fontarossa. His siblings (all younger) were Giovanni (who died young), Bartolomeo (a nautical map maker/seller), Giacomo and Bianchinetta. By the age of 15 he had been to sea several times and in 1474 became a dealer in mastic on the Genoese island of Chios. He was then a naval mercenary in the service of René d'Anjou, King of Naples, and subsequently sailed for various merchants. In 1476 he visited London, Bristol and Iceland. He was in Lisbon when Bartholomew Dias returned from the first successful rounding of the Cape of Good Hope (1488) but left after John II refused to sponsor Columbus's proposed voyage to the spice islands of the East by sailing west and moved to Spain. Here he got backing from Ferdinand and Isabella (changing his surname in their honour) and made four voyages. The first

(1492) was from Palos: with three ships and 90 men he made the first modern crossing of the Atlantic, landing in the Bahamas and thus opening up the exploration of the Americas. His vessel the *Santa Maria* was wrecked after a drunken Christmas Eve on Hispaniola (Haiti): he left his crew behind and returned to Spain in the *Nina*. On the second (1493–6) he led 20 ships and 1200 men to colonize Dominica and brought back around 550 Indian slaves to Spain (200 died in transit). On the third (1498–1500), with only six ships, he went to Trinidad and Venezuela. On the fourth (1502–4) he took four ships to Jamaica, Honduras and Nicaragua. The crew mutinied and he was wrecked and marooned for a year on Jamaica. Though granted the title 'Admiral of the Ocean Sea' Columbus failed to have the New World named after him as his fame had not yet reached Europe when Waldseemuller made a map of the area. The continent was named instead after the discoverer of Brazil, Amerigo Vespucci.

Family/Sex Life: In 1479 Columbus married Felipa Moniz Perestrello, daughter of the Portuguese Governor of Porto Santo, Madeira, who had served under Henry the Navigator. They had one son, Diego. In 1488, three years after his wife's death, he had an affair in Cordoba with Beatriz Enriquez, by whom he had an illegitimate son, Ferdinand.

Appearance: Columbus stood five feet eight inches tall. Ferdinand Columbus described him as a 'well-built man of more than average stature, the face long, the cheeks somewhat high, his body neither fat nor lean. He had an aquiline nose and light-coloured eyes; his complexion was light and tending to bright red ... in youth his hair was blond, but when he reached the age of thirty, it all turned white.'

Habits/Mannerisms: Columbus wrote in Spanish, never Italian, and took Marco Polo's *Travels* with him to the New World.

Sport/Hobbies: A strong swimmer, Columbus swam six miles to shore after he was shipwrecked in a battle off Cape Vincent in 1476. He also wrote a *Book of Prophecies* (1500). Possessing foreknowledge of future events proved useful in 1504, when the natives of Jamaica refused Columbus provisions. Columbus knew that an eclipse was due and threatened to remove the moon if the natives would not trade: when the moon was eclipsed the natives hurriedly complied.

Religion/Politics: Roman Catholic.

Health: Columbus's crew took smallpox, influenza and measles to Hispaniola and brought back an unknown variety of syphilis from the Americas, causing an epidemic in Barcelona (1493). He also suffered from gout and rheumatism (from around 1496), malaria (from 1502) and arthritis (from 1504).

Temperament: Columbus was imaginative but greedy. One reason King John refused sponsorship was that Columbus wanted a tenth of all revenues from the lands he discovered and to be called Governor of them all. He was, however, brave and used cunning to keep crews content. Making his voyage west in 1492, he concealed how far they had come by writing two logs, the one he showed the crew suggesting that they were much nearer Spain (ironically, the falsified log was more accurate).

Work/Daily Routine: Columbus landed at San Salvador in the Bahamas, the first Westerner to set foot in the New World, on Friday 12 October 1492. Among the discoveries he made was that of tobacco-smoking (in Cuba). He called the natives of the New World Indians because he thought these were the Indies. Some critics scoffed at Columbus's achievement, claiming that anyone could have done it. In reply, at a banquet, the explorer challenged all present to make an egg stand on its end. All tried and failed, upon which Columbus crushed the end of the egg so that it stood up, explaining it was easy to follow when someone else had shown the way (any task that is easy once mastered may now be dubbed 'Columbus's Egg').

Manner of Death: Columbus died on 20 May 1506 in Valladolid, Spain, aged 54.

His two sons and his two brothers were present. He was buried in the Franciscan monastery in Vallodolid but was later moved to the Carthusian monastery of Las Cuevas, Seville (c.1509), to the Cathedral in Santo Domingo, Hispaniola (c.1541), to Havana Cathedral (1795) and finally to Seville Cathedral (1899).

CONRAD, Joseph (1857–1924) Polish-born novelist and short-story writer

Josef Teodor Konrad Nalecz Korzeniowski was born on 3 December 1857 at Derebczynka Manor, near Berdyczow, in the Polish Ukraine (then under Russian rule), the only child of Apollo Nalecz Korzeniowski, a Polish noble, man of letters and political activist who taught French, translated Shakespeare, Dickens and Hugo into Polish and who had been banished from Poland for his involvement in the rebellion of 1862. His mother was Eva Bobrowska (both parents died of tuberculosis before he was 12). He was subsequently brought up his uncle Thaddeus Bobrowski. Educated in Lvov and Cracow, he first went to sea (with an allowance from his uncle) aged 17 with the French Merchant Marine. Treated as a nobleman aboard ship (known as 'the Russian Count') he was successively midshipman on the *Mont Blanc* (1875) and steward on the *Saint-Antoine* (1876) before transferring to the British Merchant Marine (1878) serving on coal-freighters, coasters and the real *Narcissus* (1884) – on which his story was based – as well as wool-clippers sailing between England and Australia. Later (1886) he became a master mariner, was involved in gun-running in Spain and received his only sea command – of the cholera-infected barque *Otago* – when its captain died. Resigning from the *Otago* in 1889 he ran a river steamer in the Belgian Congo, worked as a warehouse manager in London (1891) and was first

mate on the clipper *Torrens* (1891–3) where he met John Galsworthy (a passenger). He left the sea for good in 1894 and his first novel, *Almayer's Folly*, was published in English in 1895, when he was 38. Among the celebrated works that followed were *Lord Jim* (1900), *Heart of Darkness* (1902), *Nostromo* (1904) and *The Secret Agent* (1907). He became a naturalized British citizen in 1886, settling in Ashford, Kent, but declined a knighthood in 1924.

Family/Sex Life: In 1896 Conrad married Jessie George, by whom he had two sons, Borys and John.

Appearance: Galsworthy described Conrad as 'Very dark ... tanned, with a peaked brown beard, almost black hair and dark brown eyes, over which the lids were deeply folded.' Edward Garnett called him 'a dark-faced man, short but extremely graceful in his nervous gestures, with brilliant eyes'. He also had full lips, eyes set wide apart and a hooked nose. He dressed elegantly, wearing gloves and a black or grey bowler hat and carrying a cane with a gold knob; he also wore a monocle over his right eye.

Habits/Mannerisms: Conrad could not read or write English (his third language) before the age of 19, and he retained a strong foreign accent. He smoked roll-up cigarettes and had a habit of making bread pellets and flicking them at guests.

Sport/Hobbies: He played cards, spoke French and was one of the first people in England to own a car (he was a furious driver).

Religion/Politics: Roman Catholic.

Health: Conrad suffered from an anal abscess (1877) and from rheumatic gout after a trip to the Congo. At 21, after losing heavily at gambling in Monte Carlo, he attempted suicide by shooting himself but the bullet missed his heart. His back was injured by a flying spar when he was sailing on the *Highland Forest* (1887). He became very ill with dysentery and fever in Africa and suffered from malaria for the rest of his life. His left hand was often dysfunctional; he also suffered long fits of depression, insomnia and bronchitis and had a nervous breakdown in 1909 after finishing *Under Western Eyes*.

Temperament: Conrad himself said: 'I am earnest, terribly earnest. Carlyle bending over the history of Frederick the Great was a mere trifle, a volatile butterfly, in comparison.' He was highly strung and nervy, sensitive, irascible, unpredictable and quarrelsome, frequently leaving ships

because of arguments with the captain. His friends included Edward Garnett. He loved the sea and when he settled in England he observed that it was a country 'where men and sea interpenetrate, so to speak'.

Pets: Conrad kept a pet monkey on the *Narcissus*, and later a dog called Escamillo for many years.

Work/Daily Routine: Conrad dedicated *The Secret Agent* to H. G. Wells, and Arnold Bennett – who shared the same agent – said it was 'steeped in the finest beauty from end to end' (*Books and Persons*). Almayer was based on a real person, Charles Olmeijer. *The Nigger of the Narcissus* was serialized in the *New Review* before the book was published. Conrad worked odd hours – sometimes all night long. He wrote in long-hand, leaving his wife to type everything up. He collaborated with Ford Madox Ford on *The Inheritors* and *Romance*.

Manner of Death: Conrad died of a heart attack at his home 'Oswalds' in Bishopsbourne, near Canterbury, Kent, at 8.30 am on 3 August 1924, aged 66. His epitaph was: 'Sleepe, after toyle, port after stormie seas,/Ease after warre, death after life, does greatly please' from Spenser's *The Faerie Queene*.

COWPER, William (1731–1800) English poet

William Cowper (pronounced Cooper) was born in Great Berkhamsted Rectory, Hertfordshire, on 15 November 1731, the fourth and eldest surviving child of John Cowper, Rector of Great Berkhamsted (a nephew of Earl Cowper, the first Lord Chancellor of Great Britain) and Anne Donne, a relative of Henry III and John Donne (she died in childbirth when Cowper was aged six). His younger brother John (Jack) – the seventh and only

other surviving child – became a Fellow of Corpus Christi College, Cambridge. William was educated at Markyate and Westminster Schools (his usher at Westminster was the Latin poet Vincent Bourne) and was articled to a solicitor for three years with fellow clerk Thurlow (later Lord Chancellor). Called to the bar in 1754, he at first served as Clerk of the Journals in the House of Lords and later became a Commissioner of Bankrupts before being granted a state pension of £300 a year. He declined the Poet Laureateship in 1790 (it went to Henry James Pye). Among other achievements, he translated Homer and edited the works of Milton (as well as translating Milton's Latin poems). His most significant original contributions to English literature included the *Olney Hymns* (1779), which he wrote in collaboration with the clergyman John Newton while living in Olney, Buckinghamshire, the enormously popular comic ballad *John Gilpin* (1782) and the much admired lengthy poem on rural themes *The Task* (1785).

Family/Sex Life: Cowper's engagement to his cousin Theodora Cowper was broken off because her parents disapproved (causing him great distress). He was later engaged to his landlady Mrs Unwin (the widow of the Rev. Morley Unwin, who took the poet under his protection in 1765 and treated him as his adopted son).

Appearance: Clean-shaven.

Habits/Mannerisms: Cowper was very fond of eating fish (he said he was 'the most ichthyophagous of Protestants').

Sport/Hobbies: Cowper excelled at cricket and football at school. He was also a keen gardener and wrote riddles, a reply to one of which in the *Gentleman's Magazine* confirmed the pronunciation 'Cooper'.

Religion/Politics: Calvinist Evangelical. He became very devout after the onset of his mental illness; he also hated slavery and disliked towns, explaining in *The Task* that: 'God made the country and man made the town.' His mental state left him prone to melancholy and he believed in the depths of his depression that God had cast him out. In the words of his own hymn, however, he conceded that it was impossible to know what God's motives might be in excluding him: 'God moves in a mysterious way/His wonders to perform.'

Health: Cowper contracted smallpox at the age of 14 and also suffered from weak sight. He was mentally unstable, hearing voices and experiencing frequent fits of depression/madness (intensified by the breaking of his engagement to his cousin and later by the death of Mrs Unwin in 1796 – a blow from which he never fully recovered). He complained of head pains resembling violent blows and attempted suicide at least six times, feeling compelled to imitate Abraham's sacrifice of Isaac with himself as the victim (failure to kill himself would result, he feared, in eternal damnation). On one occasion he attempted to hang himself with a garter: the garter broke. He was confined to a mental home in St Albans for 18 months in the early 1760s.

Temperament: Sensitive and a hypochondriac, Cowper was very shy and modest. He once declared: 'I have no more right to the name of a poet than a maker of mousetraps has to that of an engineer.' He did, however, have a witty sense of humour and several of his friends were devoted to him, exhibiting considerable patience and sympathy when he was overwhelmed by fits of melancholia.

Pets: Cowper was a great animal-lover and his spaniel Beau featured in his poems. He also kept three male leverets – Puss, Tiney and Bess (he wrote his poem 'Epitaph on a Hare' for Tiney). He hated hunting, calling it a 'detested sport, that owes its pleasures to another's pain'.

Work/Daily Routine: The ballad *John Gilpin* was inspired by Cowper's friend and neighbour Lady Austen, who told him the story in an attempt to lift him out of one of his depressions: he laughed at the tale all night long and set about writing his own version the following day. Lady Austen also provided the starting-point for *The Task*, suggesting his own sofa might make a suitable subject for a poem – Cowper responded by addressing a mock eulogy to the sofa before going on to address other subjects such as his love for animals. He also wrote poems against slavery and in praise of William Wilberforce. His letters have no crossings-out.

Manner of Death: Cowper died at East Dereham, Norfolk, at 4.55 pm on 25 April 1800, aged 68. He was buried in Dereham Church.

CROMWELL, Oliver (1599–1658) English soldier and statesman

Oliver Cromwell ('Old Noll') was born in Huntingdon around 3 am on 25 April 1599, the second son of former MP Robert Cromwell (formerly Williams, a relative of Thomas Cromwell through the female line) and Elizabeth Steward. He was a cousin of the MP John Hampden and had two sisters, Margaret and Jane, and a brother. He was educated at Huntingdon Free School and at Sidney Sussex College, Cambridge, but left after a year, when his father died. Cromwell looked after the family estate in Huntingdon and came into more land in Ely on the death of his uncle Sir Thomas Steward. Elected MP for Huntingdon in 1628 he nonetheless remained a farmer until 1640, when Charles I recalled Parliament after an 11-year break. As a soldier Cromwell served with the Parliamentary cavalry in the Civil War and eventually became commander-in-chief. His Royalist opponent Prince Rupert dubbed him 'Old Ironsides' and his highly disciplined troops were subsequently called Ironsides. He did not at first seek the execution of Charles I, but signed the death warrant when his trial became politically unavoidable. Though offered the Crown he refused it and ruled (from 1653) as Lord Protector of the Commonwealth, the first commoner ever to rule Britain. He conducted a ruthless campaign in Ireland and defeated forces loyal to Charles II. He was also Chancellor of Oxford University (1651–7).

Family/Sex Life: In 1620 Cromwell married Elizabeth Bourchier, daughter of Sir James Bourchier. Their children were Robert, Oliver, Richard (briefly Lord Protector after his father), Henry, Bridget, Mary, Frances and Elizabeth.

Appearance: Sir Philip Warwick wrote of Cromwell: 'His linen was plain, and not very clean ... His stature was of good size ... his countenance swollen and reddish, his voice sharp and untunable, and his eloquence full of fervour.' Thurloe added that he was 'under six feet, I believe about two inches'. He had a strong compact body, long hair, and facial warts – which gave rise to the 'warts and all' phrase from his instruction to the painter Lely: 'I desire you would ... paint my picture truly like me and not flatter me at all; but remark all these roughnesses, pimples, warts, and everything ... otherwise I never will pay a farthing for it.' He also had a big red nose and was nicknamed 'Copper Nose' (or 'Ruby Nosey') because he suffered from *acne rosacea*. Some said his eyes were grey-blue, but their colour varies from one portrait to another.

Habits/Mannerisms: Cromwell enjoyed smoking and drinking wine. His name was originally pronounced Crum-well – hence the Royalist toast: 'God send this crumb well down!' (Royalists also called chamberpots 'Oliver's Skulls' and this name continued in use until 1820.)

Sport/Hobbies: Cromwell banned duelling, cockfighting and horse-racing but liked hunting, hawking and, though a Puritan, organ music. He even had the organ from Magdalen College, Oxford, installed in his residence at Hampton Court (it was returned on the Restoration).

His favourite book after the Bible was Ralegh's *History of the World*; he also employed John Milton (who wrote a sonnet to him) and Andrew Marvell as Latin Secretaries (Marvell was tutor to one of his wards).

Religion/Politics: Fundamentalist Christian. Cromwell was opposed to church ritual and prohibited Church of England clergy from conducting services (1655). He established Puritanism as the state religion but permitted religious toleration. He maintained that congregations should choose ministers, prohibited the Book of Common Prayer and banned swearing. He had the Mace ('this bauble') removed from the House of Commons, but was unsure what manner of government to promote: 'I can tell you, sirs, what I would not have, though I cannot what I would.'

Health: Cromwell was wounded in the neck at the Battle of Marston Moor and suffered from fevers. There were two plots on his life (he was in constant fear of assassination in his later years).

Temperament: Thurloe referred to Cromwell's 'exceeding fiery' temper, but said he was 'naturally compassionate towards objects in distress, even to an effeminate measure'. He was not without a sense of humour: as a young man he reputedly tricked guests into sitting upon sticky sweets he had placed on their chairs at dinner.

Pets: The Cromwell family kept a monkey and the story goes that when Oliver was a baby this monkey snatched him from his cradle and carried him up on top of the roof, from which he was rescued only with difficulty.

Manner of Death: Cromwell died of malaria in Whitehall, London, at 3 pm on 3 September 1658, aged 59. The fact that this was the anniversary of his victories at Dunbar (1650) and Worcester (1651) inspired the allegation that he had made a pact with some witches on the eve of Dunbar to ensure military success in exchange for his soul. His body was embalmed then dressed in robes of state and exhibited at Somerset House on 20 September. He was buried on 23 November in Westminster Abbey, but on the Restoration he was disinterred and, on the twelfth anniversary of Charles I's execution (30 January 1661), his bones were hung on Tyburn gallows and his severed head stuck on a 25-foot pole on top of Westminster Hall: it blew off 24 years later, in 1685, was stolen and was later discovered in a freak show (it was buried at Sidney Sussex College in 1960, while the rest of his body remains buried beneath the site of Tyburn gallows).

DARWIN, Charles Robert (1809–82) English naturalist

Charles Darwin was born at The Mount House, Shrewsbury, on 12 February 1809, the grandson of Erasmus Darwin and fifth of the six children of Robert Waring Darwin, a doctor, and of Susannah Wedgwood, daughter of Josiah Wedgwood II, the son of the founder of the pottery firm (she died in 1817 when Darwin was eight). Francis Galton was his cousin. He had an elder brother, Erasmus Alvey, and four sisters. Taught at home by his elder sister Caroline until the age of eight, he then attended the Rev. G. Case's School before (aged nine) becoming a boarder at Shrewsbury School under Samuel Butler. He left school at 16 and with his brother Erasmus trained in medicine at Edinburgh University (where he met Audubon), but gave it up after two years and studied to become a clergyman at Christ's College, Cambridge. Assured of a private income from his father, he got the (unsalaried) job of naturalist on the 90-foot, 10-gun Royal Navy survey sloop-brig HMS *Beagle* under Captain Robert Fitzroy through his friendship with J. S. Henslow, Professor of Botany at Cambridge University. The world tour (1831–6) included South America, Africa and Australasia. The studies of geology and zoology that he published on his return established him as a leading scientist and he gave up the idea of entering the Church. *On the Origin of Species* (1859) introduced the Darwinian theory of evolution, based on natural selection, and was followed by various important supplementary writings, notably *The Descent of Man* (1871), which controversially applied the theory to human beings. He was Secretary of the Geological Society (1838–41) and was elected a Fellow of the Royal Society in 1839.

Family/Sex Life: In 1839 Darwin married his cousin Emma Wedgwood, grand-daughter of Josiah Wedgwood II. They had 10 children, including four famous sons – Sir George Howard, Sir Francis, Leonard and Sir Horace. Mrs Darwin, though loyal, failed to share her husband's enthusiasm for his work – when he regretted that she must have found a particular lecture wearisome she calmly responded: 'Not more than all the rest.'

Appearance: Around six feet tall and sturdily built, but stooped, Darwin had a ruddy face, blue-grey eyes, deep overhanging brows, bushy eyebrows and long sideburns. In old age he had a high, wrinkled forehead and wore a full beard.

Habits/Mannerisms: Described as clumsy in his movements, he carried a spiral walking-stick made from a climbing plant.

Sport/Hobbies: Darwin was nicknamed 'Gas' at school because of his interest in chemistry. He was also a keen ornithologist and coleopterist (student of beetles) and collected franks, seals, coins, minerals etc. He loved shooting and liked music, reading novels and playing backgammon. He also taught himself Spanish. His father once told him: 'You care for nothing but shooting, dogs, and rat-catching, and you will be a disgrace to yourself and all your family.'

Religion/Politics: Church of England, then agnostic.

Health: Darwin contracted scarlet fever at the age of nine. Though his health was good at first, after 1837 he suffered from palpitations and dyspepsia. He was also seasick on the *Beagle* and contracted Chagas's Disease while in South America (this reduced him to a semi-invalid and made him prone to lethargy, heart trouble and fainting attacks for the last 40 years of his life).

Temperament: Darwin was charming, modest, honest, courteous, unpretentious and a good listener. He was an ardent opponent of slavery and included among his friends T. H. Huxley and Joseph Hooker.

Pets: His dog Bob featured in *The Expression of the Emotions in Man and Animals* (1872).

Work/Daily Routine: Darwin's first published work was a monograph on barnacles (he kept 10,000 barnacles in his house). When taken on the *Beagle* he had no scientific qualifications whatever, but knew how to stuff animals and had made large collections of fossils, rocks and beetles. For reading on the voyage he took *Paradise Lost* and Humboldt's *Personal Narrative*. While on the *Beagle* he slept in a hammock and worked in a small space in the chart room. The first edition (1250 copies) of *The Origin of Species by Means of Natural Selection* (1859) – originally called *The Transmutation of Species* – sold out on publication day and went through six editions in his lifetime (12,500 copies in all). He had developed his theory in 1837 but only published it 21 years later when Alfred Russell Wallace had the same idea and wrote for advice – both then published together in the *Journal of the Linnean Society* (1858). He only worked for short periods – two hours in the morning, followed by a rest and a mid-day walk, then more work and rest. The 'survival of the fittest' phrase was not in fact his but was coined by Herbert Spencer in *Principles of Biology*. The idea that humans evolved from apes encountered opposition in some quarters. Carlyle wrote: 'I have no patience whatever with these gorilla damnifications of humanity', but notable supporters included Huxley, Hooker, Lyell and Charles Kingsley. Karl Marx admired Darwin and wanted to dedicate the English translation of *Das Kapital* to him (Darwin declined). He also wrote books on coral reefs, volcanic islands, insectivorous plants and earthworms.

Manner of Death: Darwin died of a heart attack at his home, Down House, Downe, Kent, on 19 April 1882, aged 73. He was buried in Westminster Abbey beside Sir Isaac Newton.

DAVY, Humphry (1778–1829) English chemist

Humphry Davy was born at 4 The Terrace, Penzance, Cornwall, on 17 December 1778, the eldest child of Robert Davy, a woodcarver who died in 1794 when Humphry was 16, and Grace Millett. His cousin Edmund was Professor of Chemistry at the University of Dublin and he had a brother John (a military surgeon who was the grandfather of Sir Humphrey Rolleston, President of the Royal College of Physicians) and three sisters. Educated at Penzance Grammar School (1787) and Truro Grammar School (1792), he left at the age of 15 and was apprenticed to a surgeon/apothecary in Penzance (1795) after his father died. In 1798 he became assistant to the famous physician Dr Thomas Beddoes, husband of Anne Edgeworth, younger sister of the novelist Maria Edgeworth and founder and principal of the Pneumatic Institution, Bristol, which specialized in research into the use of newly discovered gases as a cure for tuberculosis and other illnesses. Here he discovered the use of nitrous oxide (otherwise known as 'laughing gas') as an anaesthetic and conducted research that led to the discovery of potassium, sodium, boron and other elements. He took on Michael Faraday as his assistant in 1813 and achieved widespread fame as inventor of the Davy safety lamp for miners (1815), which did much to reduce the risks of working underground. Professor at the Royal Institution (1802), he was seven times elected President of the Royal Society (originally succeeding Joseph Banks in 1820) and also helped to found the Geological Society (1807), the Athenaeum Club and London Zoo. Knighted by George IV when Prince Regent (1812), he was created baronet in 1816. His collected prose and verse was published in 1839–40.

Family/Sex Life: In 1812 Davy married the wealthy Scottish 'bluestocking' friend of Sir Walter Scott, Jane Apreece, widow of Shuckburgh Ashby Apreece and daughter and heiress of Charles Kerr of Kelso, to whom Davy dedicated his *Elements of Chemical Philosophy*. They had no children.

Appearance: Short hair.

Sport/Hobbies: Davy enjoyed shooting (snipe, woodcock and so forth), hunting, billiards and especially fishing, about which he wrote and illustrated a book, *Salmonia, or Days of Fly-fishing, by an Angler* (1828). He was also an accomplished poet, writing verse and ballads, and had five poems published in the *Annual Anthology* (1799) edited by Robert Southey. His favourite book as a child was Bunyan's *Pilgrim's Progress*. His interest in the arts did not, however, apparently extend to paintings – having newly returned from Paris he was asked how he enjoyed the art galleries there but only replied drily: 'The finest collection of frames I ever saw.'

Health: Davy had a remarkable memory. In 1807 he became very ill from overwork. A glass splinter lodged in his eye after a lab explosion in 1812 and he had a stroke in 1826.

Temperament: A well-liked and greatly respected man, Davy's friends included Samuel Taylor Coleridge, Southey – whom he once asked to inhale nitrous oxide for the purposes of one of his experiments –

Wordsworth (Davy helped correct the proofs for *Lyrical Ballads*), Walter Scott and James Watt's son Gregory. He had many admirers on the Continent too – Napoleon himself expressed his support for Davy by sending him an award even though France and England were then at war. Such was Davy's international fame that a letter addressed from Italy to 'siromfredevi/Londra' had little trouble reaching its destination. Humble citizens also acknowledged their debt to the distinguished chemist – on one occasion, when Davy dutifully offered the penny fee to look at the moon through a showman's telescope in the London streets, the man recognized him at once and refused to accept the money, explaining: 'I could not think of taking money from a brother philosopher.'

Manner of Death: Davy suffered a stroke in February 1829 in Rome and died peacefully in his sleep en route back to the UK while in Geneva in the early morning of 29 May 1829, aged 50. He was buried in Plain-Palais Cemetery, Geneva, at his own request; a memorial tablet was subsequently dedicated to him in Westminster Abbey.

DEFOE, Daniel (1660–1731) English novelist and political pamphleteer

Daniel Defoe was born in the parish of St Giles, Cripplegate, London, in late 1660, the son of a butcher, James Foe, and his wife Alice (surname unknown). Daniel, who had two older sisters, Mary and Elizabeth, changed his name to Defoe in 1703. Educated at Morton's Academy for Dissenters, Newington Green, London, he intended to become a minister. However, at first he worked successively as a hosiery merchant, civet cat breeder, marine insurance broker and owner of a brick and tile works, as well as travelling extensively

through Europe. In 1688 he took part in the Monmouth Rebellion but managed to escape after the Battle of Sedgemoor and joined William III's cavalry forces. He was declared bankrupt, with debts of £17,000, in 1692. By now already becoming widely known as a writer, he attracted the patronage of the Tory statesman Robert Harley, 1st Earl of Oxford, who employed him as a spy. Defoe's sharp satires brought him into repeated conflict with the authorities. He was imprisoned in Newgate and twice pilloried (1703 and

1712–13) for his writing: in 1703 the public garlanded the Temple Bar pillory with flowers, drank his health and kept ruffians away. Considered the first great English novelist, his works included the satirical pamphlet *The Shortest Way with the Dissenters* (1702), the cause of his first visit to the pillory, the classic novel *Robinson Crusoe* (1719–20), *A Journal of the Plague Year* (1722), *Moll Flanders* (1722) and *Roxana* (1724).

Family/Sex Life: Around 1683 Defoe was married to Mary Tuffley. He had by her eight children – their son Benjamin became editor of the *London Journal*. He also had an illegitimate son, Benjamin Norton Defoe, by an oyster-seller.

Appearance: A wanted poster for his arrest described Defoe as 'A middle-sized spare man ... of a brown complexion and dark brown-coloured hair, but wears a wig; a hooked nose, a sharp chin, grey eyes and a large mole near his mouth.' He often wore a blue cape and a large diamond ring on his finger.

Religion/Politics: Nonconformist. In *The True-Born Englishman* he wrote: 'And of all plagues with which mankind are curst,/ Ecclesiastic tyranny's the worst.' He was gaoled indefinitely in Newgate Prison for seditious libel (1703) but only served a few months (he wrote *Hymn to the Pillory* while in prison). He was inconstant in his political views, supporting Harley and the Tories, then rejecting them, then renewing his allegiance.

Work/Daily Routine: Defoe was nearly 60 when he wrote *The Life and Strange and Surprising Adventures of Robinson Crusoe of York, Mariner*. He got the idea for the book from the true-life adventures of Alexander Selkirk (1676–1721), an outspoken Scottish sailor who in 1704 was marooned on Juan Fernandez, a desert island off Chile, for five years after he fell out with his shipmates while sailing under the explorer William Dampier. On his eventual return to England in 1709, Selkirk repeated his tale to anyone willing to pay – Defoe reputedly hearing it at Ye Llandoger Trow tavern in King Street, Bristol. Selkirk eventually joined the Royal Navy and, dying of a fever, was buried at sea off Africa. A statue of Crusoe now stands on the shore at Largo, Fife, Selkirk's birthplace, and in 1968 the Chilean government renamed two of its offshore islands the Isla Alexander Selkirk and the Isla Robinson Crusoe. The name Robinson Crusoe is supposed to have come from a gravestone Defoe found himself hiding behind in a cemetery following the Monmouth Rebellion. Two sequels about Crusoe – *Farther Adventures* (1719) and *Serious Reflections* (1720) – were less successful, as for the most part were the numerous 'Robinsonnades' subsequently written by Defoe's imitators. *Robinson Crusoe* was the first novel to be serialized (it was pirated in *The Original London Post* in 1719). Fervent admirers of the novel included Samuel Taylor Coleridge, Jean-Jacques Rousseau, who particularly recommended it as reading for young boys, and Karl Marx, who drew on it to illustrate his economic theories in *Das Kapital*. In all, Defoe reputedly wrote 545 works as well as poetry. Among the 500 pen names he used were Eye Witness, T. Taylor, Andrew Morton and Heliostropolis. His *History of the Devil* was banned by the Vatican and put on the Index of prohibited books in 1743.

Temperament: Well educated, Defoe understood Latin, Spanish and Italian, and could read Greek and spoke French fluently. Jonathan Swift, though, called him a 'stupid, illiterate scribbler'.

Manner of Death: Defoe died 'of a lethargy' (a stroke) in his lodgings in Rope Maker's Alley, Moorfields, London, on 26 April 1731, aged 70. He was buried in the Dissenters' cemetery at Bunhill Fields, where an obelisk to him was erected in 1870.

DE QUINCEY, Thomas (1785–1859) English essayist and journalist

Thomas de Quincey was born in Manchester on 15 August 1785, the second son and fifth of eight children of Thomas de Quincey, a linen merchant, and Elizabeth Penson. His father, often abroad, died when he was seven. He had an elder brother William (who died of typhus aged 16) and other siblings were Mary, Richard, Jane and Henry – two more sisters died before he was six. He was educated at Bath Grammar School, in Winkfield (Wiltshire) and at Manchester Grammar School, from which he ran away after being beaten on the head by a school usher. He then lived in Wales and London, later going to Worcester College, Oxford, and studying Hebrew, German, English literature, Greek and Latin but without taking a degree. Later still he studied law at the Middle Temple but failed to graduate to the bar. In 1809 he moved to Grasmere to be close to the Wordsworths and other like-minded writers. In 1822 he acheived fame as author of *Confessions of an English Opium Eater* about his own experiences of drug-taking and his wanderings as a young man. He also worked as a journalist, contributing to *Blackwood's* and the *Quarterly Review* and was Editor of the *Westmoreland Gazette*.

Family/Sex Life: In 1817 de Quincey married farmer's daughter Margaret Simpson, by whom he fathered eight children (Julius, William, Horace, Francis, Paul Frederick, Margaret, Florence and Emily). He later lived separately from his family because, he explained, they made too much noise.

Appearance: Keats's friend Richard Woodhouse described de Quincey as 'short, sallow-looking . . . very gentle, modest and unassuming'. He was a good-looking, clean-shaven man with blue eyes, light-brown hair and long curling eyelashes, though he dressed untidily. The lower half of his face protruded giving him a pouting mouth.

Habits/Mannerisms: De Quincey was a heavy drinker and was notoriously addicted to opium, which he first took to cure neuralgia when at Oxford (1804). As his addiction grew he took up to 340 grains of opium a day but later cut back to six. He was very meticulous, constantly dusting papers and would wash and polish pennies and shillings until they shone and press crumpled banknotes in books. He never threw papers away – when his rooms became too crowded with them he simply moved lodgings (he had filled up six sets of lodgings by the time he died). He disliked cold so had a fire in his rooms all year round and preferred his bedrooms to be decorated in pink and white. He also had a tendency to drop in on people and stay with them for weeks on end. Non-academic interests included a fascination for murders and murder trials (reflected in his *Murder Considered as One of the Fine Arts*).

Sport/Hobbies: De Quincey liked walking, especially by himself at night (he walked 14 miles a day even when aged 70). He was very fond of music, particularly that of Beethoven (though he hated Mendelssohn and the bagpipes). He was also a fine Latin scholar.

Religion/Politics: Non-practising Christian.

Health: De Quincey was plagued by toothache and eventually lost all his teeth. He also complained of 'rheumatism in the head' and stomach pains and was short-sighted. He contracted pleurisy in 1845. He did, though, have a very good memory.

Temperament: A very generous man, De Quincey gave away a great deal of money. He was charming and courteous, though naturally melancholy and very shy. Under the influence of opium, he was carried away on a wave of euphoria when he first experimented with the drug but later terrorized by the dreadful nightmares it induced. The autobiographical substance of *Confessions of an English Opium Eater* suggests that a crucial event in his childhood was the loss of his sister – a loss that was echoed in the subsequent disappearance of a 15-year-old prostitute called Ann, who cared for him when he was homeless and starving in London. His other friends included William Wordsworth (he took over Dove Cottage when the Wordsworths left), Samuel Taylor Coleridge and Thomas Carlyle.

Work/Daily Routine: De Quincey wrote mostly at night, drinking lots of coffee and tea. He wrote *Confessions of an English Opium Eater* at 4 York Street, Covent Garden: it was published in the *London Magazine*. Less well-known works included a novel, *Klosterheim*, essays on philosophy and entries on Shakespeare, Pope and others for the *Encyclopedia Britannica*. He also produced German translations for *Blackwood's* and his writings on economics were admired by J. S. Mill. He used any and every scrap of paper to write on.

Manner of Death: De Quincey died at 42 Lothian Street, Edinburgh, at 9 am on 8 December 1859, aged 74. He was buried in St Cuthbert's Churchyard, Edinburgh.

DE SADE, Donatien-Alphonse-François, Marquis (1740–1814) French writer

The Marquis de Sade (he became a Comte on the death of his father in 1767 but kept the title Marquis) was born in the Condé Palace, Paris – home of the Duc de Bourbon (son-in-law of Louis XIV and Prime Minister to Louis XV) – on 2 June 1740. He was the second child of Jean-Baptiste Joseph François, Comte de Sade, a soldier, diplomat and former French Ambassador to Russia, and a descendant of Laura de Sade, reputedly Petrarch's 'Laura' (he was also a notorious libertine). De Sade's mother was a lady-in-waiting at the palace, Marie-Eléonore de Maillé de Carman, a relation both of Cardinal Richelieu and of Princess Caroline, wife of the Duc de Bourbon. He had an elder sister, Caroline-Laure, who died young. Brought up with the Duc de Bourbon's son, Prince Louis-Joseph, in the Condé Palace, he then lived (1744–6) with his grandmother and (1746–9) with his uncle, Joseph-François, Abbé de Sade – a friend of Voltaire. Aged 10 he entered the Jesuit

school of Louis-le-Grand in Paris, leaving after four years to study at the military academy at Versailles for a year. Commissioned in the Royal Foot Guards aged 15 he fought in the Seven Years' War. He subsequently became a captain in the Burgundian cavalry. After his marriage his father relinquished four small provinces in his favour, of which he became lieutenant-governor. He also became a member of the High Court of Justice of Dijon (1763). Often imprisoned for *debauche outrée* (for the first time only six months after his wedding), in 1768 he was imprisoned for grievous bodily harm (by flogging) of Rose Keller and in 1772 was condemned to death in Aix for 'unnatural offences' and poisoning. He escaped but was later imprisoned in Vincennes for 16 months with Mirabeau (1777). He escaped again and was locked up in the Bastille (1784) where he wrote *120 Days of Sodom* and in July 1789 incited the Revolutionary crowd from his window to storm the prison, saying the guards were going to kill the inmates. Transferred to Charenton Lunatic Asylum near Paris (1789), the Bastille was stormed 10 days later. De Sade was released in 1790 and became a local government official, a member of the National Guard and a judge in a revolutionary court (1793). Arrested as a counter-revolutionary and sentenced to death, he saw 1800 people guillotined before being released after 10 months (1795). Arrested again in 1801 for his licentious publications, he was allowed to stay in Charenton with his wife until his death. Among his most notorious pornographic writings were the novels *Justine ou les malheurs de la vertu* (1791), *La philosophie dans le boudoir* (1795) and *Nouvelle Justine* (1797). He also wrote plays and short stories. Synonymous with sexual perversion, his name gave the language the word 'sadism'.

Family/Sex Life: In 1763 De Sade married René-Péagie, daughter of the President de Montreuil, by whom he fathered Louis-Marie, Donatien-Claude-Armand and Madeleine-Laure. From 1790 he lived with the actress Marie-Constance Quesnet and her son for 24 years. De Sade was bisexual and had a number of regular mistresses, who included Mademoiselle Colette (an actress) and Mademoiselle de Beauvoisin (a ballerina). He also hired prostitutes, whom he liked to flog, and indulged in every variety of sex, willing or unwilling (sodomy with a woman then carried the death penalty) and cut their bodies. He also had sex with his wife's younger sister Anne-Prospère and regularly with his male servant Latour, who participated in his orgies.

Appearance: De Sade was handsome but small, with blue eyes and auburn hair (white by his mid-forties). He wore a grey coat and carried a gold-topped cane.

Habits/Mannerisms: To encourage

partners De Sade offered them sweets impregnated with the aphrodisiac cantharides ('Spanish Fly').

Sport/Hobbies: De Sade had a mania for codes – in prison he used a number code in his correspondence and wrote in invisible ink.

Religion/Politics: Atheist.

Health: Inevitably, in the course of his seductions, De Sade contracted syphilis. He also lost the sight of one eye in prison.

Temperament: As a child De Sade was difficult to control; as an adult he displayed great ferocity of character.

Work/Daily Routine: De Sade wrote most of his books in prison. He wrote *120 Days of Sodom* on a 40-foot roll of paper made from five-inch pieces stuck together, as a book would have been detected. He wrote daily after dinner from 7 to 10 pm and hid the roll in the wall. He wrote quickly, *The Misfortunes of Virtue* (1787) – reissued as *Justine* (1791) and *Nouvelle Justine* (1797) – taking just two weeks. Much of his work was lost when he was moved to Charenton and the mob ransacked the Bastille: *120 Days of Sodom* was not recovered in his lifetime. His private diaries were not published until 1970 (passages concerning sodomy were marked with a special symbol).

Manner of Death: De Sade died in Charenton near midnight on 2 December 1814, aged 74. His will requested that he be kept in an open casket for 48 hours until it was certain he was dead. He wished to be buried in the De Sade family woods at Malmaison with no ceremony or gravestone and the ground to be sown with acorns – instead he was buried in Charenton with Church rites and a stone cross (his remains were later exhumed and his bones scattered).

DESCARTES, René (1596–1650) French philosopher and mathematician

René Descartes (later also known by his Latin name of Cartesius) was born in La Haye, near Poitiers, Touraine, France on 31 March 1596, the third child of Joachim Descartes, a councillor of the Brittany *parlement*, and his first wife Jeanne Brochard, daughter of the Lieutenant-General of Poitiers (his mother died of a lung infection days later). His elder brother Pierre was also later a councillor in the Brittany *parlement* and he had an elder sister Jeanne. In addition he had a half-brother and half-sister by his father's second marriage. He was educated at the newly established Jesuit College in La Flèche (1604–12) and at the Collège de Clermont and graduated in law from the University of Poitiers (1616). In 1618–19 he was a professional soldier in Prince Maurice of Nassau's army in Holland, then joined the Bavarian Army under Duke Maximilian and probably fought at the Battle of Prague (1620). He also served under Count Boucquoi in Hungary (1621). The years 1621–8 were spent travelling and he studied at Leiden University in 1630 before settling in Holland, living in Amsterdam, Utrecht and then finally Egmon-sinnen (1643). In 1649 he became tutor to 19-year-old Queen Christina of Sweden and at her request founded a Swedish Academy of Arts and Letters. Among his most important writings on philosophy and mathematics were the *Discours de la méthode de bien conduire sa raison, et chercher la vérité dans les sciences* (1637) and the *Meditationes de prima philosophia* (1642). He is perhaps best known for the phrase '*Cogito ergo sum*' ('I think therefore I am') which he felt was indisputable and thus could be used as an axiom on which to base his philosophical system.

Family/Sex Life: Aubrey noted that Descartes was 'too wise a man to encumber himselfe with a wife'. He did, though, briefly have a mistress, Hélène, by whom he fathered an illegitimate daughter, Francine (who died in 1640, aged five).

Appearance: Descartes was pale and small, though he had a large head, with a prominent forehead, a projecting lower lip, a distinctive nose, a wart on his cheek, dark grey eyes and black hair, eyebrows and beard – his hair went grey around the age of 40 and he started to wear wigs. He wore a beaver hat with a feather and always a scarf and sword belt. His stockings were always silk (covered in grey woollen hose outdoors).

Habits/Mannerisms: Descartes was secretive and abstemious in his habits. He drank very little wine, never ate rich food and was largely vegetarian, though he ate eggs.

Sport/Hobbies: Descartes enjoyed riding and fencing and was brilliant at geometry (Hobbes thought he could have been the best in the world if he had persevererd and Aubrey claimed 'his head did not lye for Philosophy'). He is reputed to have invented roulette and is said to have constructed a working robot. The robot, in the form of a girl, met an untimely end while being transported by sea: the ship's captain, curious about the contents of Descartes's trunk, opened the box and was horrified to see what he could only assume was the Devil in disguise – he quickly ordered that the trunk be tossed over the side. Descartes was also very interested in spelling (not then standardized) and in the idea of a universal language.

Religion/Politics: Anti-Calvinist but not atheist. He held controversial heretical views on such issues as the rotation of the earth and the infinity of the universe and all his philosophical works were banned by the Vatican and put on the Index of prohibited books. However, he suppressed his own book *Le Monde* (1634), when Galileo was similarly condemned.

Health: A sickly child, Descartes suffered from a dry cough and had a very pale complexion until the age of 20. Later, he suffered from a weak heart and from tuberculosis. He maintained a lifelong refusal to be bled.

Temperament: Generally cheerful but solitary. He was intensely self-conscious and had very few friends.

Pets: He kept a dog called Monsieur Grat when living in Holland.

Work/Daily Routine: Descartes was an early riser but often meditated in bed till mid-day. It was while lying on his bed during his military service that he worked out, while watching a fly hovering over

him, that the position of the fly could be described at any given moment by its distance from three intersecting lines – the basis for Cartesian coordinates. In 1619 the weather was so cold he used to get *inside* the stove and meditate there. He read very little and most of his library was composed of presents from friends. He also wrote few letters and was not a good talker.

Mottoes: *Bene qui latuit, bene vixit* (Ovid, *Tristia*); *Illi mors gravis incubat,/Qui notus nimis omnibus/Ignotus moritur sibi* (Seneca, *Thyestes*).

Manner of Death: Descartes died in Stockholm, Sweden on 11 February 1650, aged 53, after catching a chill on 2 February when teaching Queen Christina (she insisted on having lessons at 5 am). His body was moved to Paris in 1667 and buried in what is now the Panthéon; in 1819 it was moved to St Germain-des-Près.

DICKENS, Charles John Huffam (1812–70) English novelist

Charles Dickens was born on Friday 7 February 1812 at 387 Mile End Terrace, Landport, Portsea, the second of eight children of John Dickens, a clerk in the Royal Navy Pay Office, and Elizabeth Barrow. His family moved to London in 1822 but soon got into debt, John Dickens being gaoled for three months in the Marshalsea Prison – he was the model for Mr Micawber – and Charles having to start work (aged 12) in Warren's Blacking (boot polish) warehouse, owned by a relative of his mother. He later spent two years at Wellington House Academy School and was then a junior clerk in Lincoln's Inn and Gray's Inn. After studying shorthand he became a parliamentary reporter (as, by then, was his father) and, in 1832, polling clerk to

Charles Tennyson MP (uncle of the poet). He then became the first editor of *Bentley's Miscellany* and later founded and edited the Liberal *Daily News* and weekly *Household Words*. The serialization of *The Pickwick Papers* (1836–7) was a huge success and established Dickens as a leading writer. Among the many classic novels that he subsequently wrote were *Oliver Twist* (1837–8), *Nicholas Nickleby* (1838–9), *David Copperfield* (1849–50), *Bleak House* (1852–3), *Little Dorrit* (1855–7) and *Great Expectations* (1860–1). He toured the USA on acclaimed reading tours in 1842 and 1867–8. At the end of his life he achieved his ambition to live at Gad's Hill Place, Rochester, Kent.

Family/Sex Life: In 1836 Dickens married

Catherine 'Kate' Hogarth (whom he called 'Pig' or 'Mouse'), daughter of *Evening Chronicle* Editor George Hogarth. They separated in 1858, having had 10 children: Charles, Mary, Kate (who married Wilkie Collins's brother Charles), Walter Landor, Francis Jeffrey, Alfred Tennyson, Sydney Smith Haldimand, Dora Annie, Edward Bulwer Lytton and Henry Fielding. He had another son (died in infancy) by actress Ellen Ternan, whom he set up in a house in Slough as 'Mr Tringham'. He also fell in love with his wife's 17-year-old sister Mary and was distraught when she died in his arms (he wore her ring and wished to be buried with her); he lived with another sister, Georgiana, until his death.

Appearance: At five feet nine inches tall, Dickens was slim and wiry with a tanned oval face, hazel eyes, long light-brown hair and a moustache and whiskers. He was somewhat dandified and overdressed.

Habits/Mannerisms: Dickens was neat, methodical, punctual and impatient. When concentrating he pulled his hair and sucked his tongue. He spoke quickly and nervously with a slight lisp. If speaking in public, he never allowed anyone to sit behind him and always had a maroon table, maroon carpet and maroon screen. He ate and drank little (but liked cheese and brandy-and-water, and a cigar after dinner). He constantly combed his hair, even at dinner parties. He was super-stitious and felt Fridays were lucky, always slept with his bed in a north–south position and touched things three times for luck. His favourite flower was the scarlet geranium. He hated bats.

Sport/Hobbies: Dickens was keen on amateur theatricals – Hans Christian Andersen said he performed with 'moving sincerity and great dramatic genius'. He also loved rowing, riding, walking, dancing and singing and was interested in hypnotism, phrenology and the occult and did magic tricks at children's parties. He hated croquet.

Religion/Politics: Church of England. Staunch abolitionist (he was shocked by slavery when he visited the USA but did not think slaves should be given the vote if freed).

Health: Dickens was a small, sickly child. An illness in 1865 left him lame in his left foot and that same year he was nearly killed when his train went off a viaduct at Staplehurst, Kent. He suffered from 'rheumatism in the face' and from headaches and was short-sighted. To counter pains in his left side (possibly a kidney stone) he took henbane and from 1853 wore a flannel belt to protect his inflamed kidney. He also suffered from piles and erysipelas and took laudanum to help him sleep, though he was not addicted.

Temperament: Trollope (who called Dickens 'Mr Popular Sentiment') found him energetic and 'hearty'. He laughed a lot and was good-natured, generous, kind and fond of his children. He disliked being called Grandpa so his grandchildren called him 'Venerables'. He wrote hundreds of letters. His friends included Daniel Maclise, Bulwer-Lytton, Augustus Egg, William Thackeray and Wilkie Collins – who called him Dick. He founded a Home for Fallen Women (Urania Cottage in Shepherd's Bush).

Pets: Dickens had a white cat called Williamina and one of her litter (born deaf) was called The Master's Cat – she would snuff his candle with her paw. He also kept mastiffs and St Bernards and a white spaniel named Snittle Timbery. Other animals included his horse, a raven called Grip (which inspired Poe's 'The Raven') and an eagle.

Work/Daily Routine: Dickens's first extant writing is an acrostic to a girlfriend, Maria Beadnell. Some of his work was published under the pseudonym 'Boz', a nickname for his brother Augustus deriving from Moses in *The Vicar of Wakefield*. He always worked at a desk at the window, with a vase of flowers and the same ornaments – two duelling toads in bronze, a gilt leaf with a rabbit on it, a bronze man with dogs swarming over him – and needed absolute quiet. At Gad's Hill, from 1859, he worked in a Swiss chalet in the garden. His page was divided into the main text (middle), story notes (right-hand margin) and chapter notes (left-hand margin) each in a different-coloured ink. He always decided on a title first. He rose at 7 am, had breakfast at 8 am, worked until 2 pm, had a small lunch, walked or rode until 5 pm, then had supper, wrote again and visited the theatre and so forth before retiring to bed by midnight. Using a goose-quill pen, he wrote 2000 words a day on blue-grey slips of paper and said himself 'I never copy, correct but very little, and that invariably as I write' – though he was a poor speller and used erratic punctuation. He always tried to be out of London on publication day.

Manner of Death: Dickens suffered a stroke during dinner at Gad's Hill and died at 6.10 pm on the following day, 9 June 1870, aged 58. He was buried in Westminster Abbey – his oak coffin was covered in scarlet geraniums and thousands filed past as he lay in state.

DISNEY, Walt (1901– 66) US animator

Walter Elias Disney was born at 1249 Tripp Avenue, Chicago, on 5 December 1901 the fourth son of Elias Disney, a fruit and stock farmer in Marcelline, Missouri, where the family moved in 1906. His mother was Flora Call and he had three older brothers, Roy Oliver, Herbert and Raymond, and a younger sister, Ruth Flora. The family moved to Kansas City when Walt was 10 and he attended McKinley High School, Chicago (1917), when they moved back there. He also studied at night school at the Chicago Academy of Fine Arts, where he was taught by cartoonist Leroy Gossett. After leaving school, he became a nightwatchman on the Chicago Elevated Railroad and a postman. During World War I he lied about his age and served in France as a Red Cross van-driver (October 1918) but did not see action. With help from his brother Roy, he worked as an apprentice illustrator in advertising in Kansas City from 1919 but he and fellow artist Ub Iwerks were later laid off and set up on their own as Iwerks & Disney, Commercial Artists. Disney was then offered a job at the Kansas City Film Ad Company (1920) and he later took Iwerks with him. Subsequently he formed Laugh-O-Gram Films Incorporated and began to make live-action films with cartoons drawn straight onto film, notably 'Alice' films based on the Lewis Carroll character. When the company went bankrupt (1923) he worked briefly as a newsreel stringer in Kansas City and then moved to Los Angeles. There, with financial help from his uncle Robert and brother Roy, he set up the Disney Brothers' Studio (later renamed the Walt Disney Studio), producing more 'Alice' films until their first big success with Oswald the Lucky Rabbit, for Universal. After an argument with Universal over copyrights, Disney set up on his own again, creating Mickey Mouse, his first huge success. Among the many classic full-length cartoons and live-action films subsequently produced under his autocratic leadership were *Snow White and the Seven Dwarfs* (1938), *Pinocchio* (1940), *Fantasia* (1941) and *Bambi* (1942). He opened the first Disneyland at Anaheim, California, in 1955. He was awarded a medal by the League of Nations in 1935.

Family/Sex Life: In 1925 Disney married Lillian Bounds, a Disney Studios inker. They had a daughter, Diane Marie, and an adopted daughter, Sharon Mae.

Appearance: He was fairly heavily built, with dark but thinning hair and a moustache.

Habits/Mannerisms: Disney was a heavy drinker (Scotch whisky with ice) and daily smoked up to 70 specially rolled black cigarettes (he had a persistent smoker's cough). He liked to be called 'Uncle Walt' at work (though he was a prejudiced and unforgiving employer).

Sport/Hobbies: Disney played polo and rode well (he was briefly a cowboy extra for Warner Brothers). He also enjoyed poker and was a train enthusiast (he had a half-sized steam railway in his garden).

Religion/Politics: Disney was right-wing, racist, anti-Semitic and sexist (all his top animators were men, while all the inkers and painters were women and were usually sacked at 30). He considered all strikers Communists and used gangsters to intimidate them. He was given special status by the FBI as 'Special Agent in Charge' and identified to the House UnAmerican Activities Committee as subversives many employees and Hollywood figures. He once met Mussolini (a fan of Donald Duck).

Health: A cleanliness neurosis meant Disney washed his hands 30 times an hour. He also had various phobias and twitches. He suffered a neck injury at polo and had massage every evening thereafter. His left lung was removed in 1966.

Temperament: A practical joker, Disney was presented as an avuncular family man, but could be vindictive. He denied that

celebrity was any comfort, observing that: 'it doesn't seem to keep fleas off our dogs, and if being a celebrity won't give one an advantage over a couple of fleas, then I guess there can't be much in being a celebrity after all'.

Pets: While in France he had a pet collie dog, Carey (named after cartoonist Carey Orr).

Work/Daily Routine: Mickey Mouse, who first appeared on 18 November 1928, was originally called Mortimer after a real mouse Disney kept as a pet when working at Newman Laugh-O-Gram (Disney's wife objected so he changed the name). Disney himself did Mickey's voice but did not draw him (he was later taught how to do so). He never could draw lifelike human faces and often signed other people's drawings, causing much resentment. He won 26 Oscars but gave little credit to his team (who got no credits at all until *Snow White*, 1939). He refused to allow workers to form a union so they went on strike – the longest-running dispute in Hollywood. *Dumbo* was mostly made by strike-breakers. He also made three films in the UK (among them *Treasure Island*). Prokofiev composed *Peter and the Wolf* especially for Disney after seeing *Fantasia*. His first colour film, *Flowers and Trees*, was the first cartoon to win an Oscar (1932).

Manner of Death: Disney died after an operation for lung cancer in Burbank Hospital (opposite the Disney Studios), California, at 9.35 am on 15 December 1966, aged 65. There was no funeral; his body was declared to have been cremated and the ashes interred in Forest Lawn Memorial Park, Glendale, California (but Disney was interested in cryogenics so rumours persist that he was frozen for treatment at some future date).

DISRAELI, Benjamin (1804–81) English statesman and novelist

Benjamin Disraeli was born at what is now 22 Theobalds Road, London, on 21 December 1804, the second child and eldest son of Isaac D'Israeli (author of *Curiosities of Literature* and other books and a friend of the publisher John Murray) and Maria Basevi. He had three brothers and a sister Sarah. Educated in Blackheath and at Higham Hall, Epping, he studied law in Lincoln's Inn and was at first articled to a firm of solicitors in the City. He then speculated in South American shares (and lost), founded *The Representative* (with help from Murray), which failed, and then worked as a writer, developing a reputation as a bestselling novelist. His most successful works of fiction were the novels *Coningsby* (1844) and *Sybil* (1848). Having decided to run for Parliament he was defeated in four elections before he was finally elected MP for Maidstone in 1837. Attracting attention as leader of the 'Young England' political group, he eventually became Chancellor of the Exchequer, Leader of the House and ultimately Prime Minister (1868 and 1874–80). As Chancellor, he pushed through the 1867 Reform Bill; as Prime Minister he pressed for diplomatic and social reform and worked for peace in Europe at the Congress of Berlin (1878). In retirement from 1880, he was created 1st Earl of Beaconsfield, refusing a dukedom but accepting the Order of the Garter.

Family/Sex Life: In 1839 Disraeli married Mrs Wyndham Lewis (née Mary Anne Evans), a rich widow 12 years his senior, and it was to her that he dedicated the novel *Sybil*. They had no children, but the marriage was happy – when Disraeli teased his wife that he only married her for her money, she always replied: 'But if you had to do it again, you'd do it for love.' However late Disraeli attended Parliament, Mary Disraeli always waited up for him,

with a hot meal ready – Disraeli once told her appreciatively she was more like a mistress than a wife. After Mary's death in 1872, Disraeli proposed to Lady Chesterfield (she declined). He may also have fathered an illegitimate child, Kate, by Mrs Mary Donovan, and before his marriage had an affair with Mrs Henrietta Sykes (and possibly others). Mrs Sykes provided the model for the central character in *Henrietta Temple* (1837).

Appearance: A dandy with exotic good looks, Disraeli was thin and wore his hair in pomaded long black ringlets (he dyed his hair black from 1830). He also sported a tufted beard on the chin only and a kiss-curl on his forehead.

Habits/Mannerisms: Disraeli's favourite flower was the primrose – the anniversary of his death was officially named Primrose Day in his honour. He smoked and drank brandy (he once drank two bottles during a 3¼-hour speech, aged 68). He slept in a bed with its feet in bowls of salt.

Sport/Hobbies: Disraeli was not a keen sportsman but rode well and was a lover of nature.

Religion/Politics: Disraeli was baptized a Christian in 1817 after his father quarrelled with the Sephardic synagogue. In 1864, regarding the debate then raging on Darwinian theory, he observed: 'The question is this: Is Man an ape or an angel? Now I am on the side of the angels.'

Health: Disraeli's health was generally good, though he suffered from asthma and nervous complaints. He also contracted venereal disease while in Constantinople (1830).

Temperament: Though witty, compassionate and much respected as a novelist and political leader, Disraeli could be conceited and affected. In relation to his writing, on the publication of George Eliot's *Daniel Deronda* (1876), he made the remark: 'When I want to read a novel, I write one.' On another occasion, however, he declared: 'An author who speaks about his own books is almost as bad as a mother who speaks about her children', and was heard to call books the 'curse of the human race', adding that: 'Nine-tenths of existing books are nonsense.' Such views did not prevent aspiring authors sending their works to him for his comments – usually they received in reply a standard acknowledgement: 'Thank you for the manuscript; I shall lose no time in reading it.' In other circumstances, though, he showed himself to be kindhearted and he had many devoted friends, among them Lord Lytton and Queen Victoria. He was widely referred to by the affectionate nickname 'Dizzy'.

Work/Daily Routine: Disraeli's first short story was published by Leigh Hunt in 1820, but it was with *Vivian Grey* that he made his reputation as a writer, aged 20. As in his political life, he had his critics as a novelist: Trollope described his works as 'spurious', while Wordsworth went so far as to label them 'trashy'.

Mottoes: *'Forti nihil difficile'* ('Nothing is difficult to the strong') and 'Never complain and never explain' (a celebrated catchphrase attributed to him by Gladstone).

Manner of Death: Disraeli died of bronchitis and uraemia at 19 Curzon Street, London, at 4.30 am on 19 April 1881, aged 76. Shortly before his death, Queen Victoria, who had paid Disraeli the compliment of visiting him at his home, indicated that she would like to see him one last time – but Disraeli declined the offer, explaining: 'No, it is better not. She will only ask me to take a message to Albert.' The Queen personally laid a wreath of primroses from Osborne House on Disraeli's coffin. He was buried in the family vault at Hughenden, near High Wycombe, Buckinghamshire.

DONNE, John (1573–1631) English poet and priest

John Donne was born in Bread Street, London, the elder son of John Donne, a prosperous ironmonger/merchant and a member of the Ironmongers' Company, and Elizabeth Heywood (daughter of playwright John Heywood, whose wife was the daughter of Thomas More's sister). His uncle Jasper Heywood was Leader of the Jesuits in England and a translator of Seneca. His father died when he was four and his mother remarried (1576) Dr John Syminges and then when he died (1588) Richard Rainsford. He also had a brother Henry (who died in Newgate Prison after harbouring a Catholic priest) and four sisters, Elizabeth, Mary, Anne and Katherine. Educated at Hart Hall (now Hertford College), Oxford, from the age of 12, he left without a degree (Catholics being forbidden to take one) and studied law at Lincoln's Inn (1592). A sailor with the Earl of Essex when he sacked Cadiz, he was also with Walter Ralegh when he sailed in pursuit of Spanish treasure-ships in the Azores. On returning to England he served as Secretary to Sir Thomas Egerton, Lord Keeper of the Great Seal, and in 1601 was elected MP for Brackley, Northamptonshire, but he was dismissed from Egerton's service and was briefly imprisoned in the Fleet after he secretly married Egerton's niece. Elected

MP for Taunton (1614) and ordained priest and deacon in 1615, after serving as Chaplain to James I (1615) he became rector in Keyston, Huntingdonshire (1616) and in Sevenoaks, Kent, before ultimately becoming Dean of St Paul's (1621–31). He received an Honorary MA from Oxford University in 1610 and was made a Doctor of Divinity by Cambridge University. He was also a Justice of the Peace for Kent and Bedford (1622). He is remembered as one of the great English love poets and a leading representative of the 'metaphysical' school of poetry. His sermons were also much admired.

Family/Sex Life: In 1600 Donne was secretly married, without her guardian's consent, to 16-year-old Ann More, daughter of Sir George More and niece (and ward) of Sir Thomas Egerton. The marriage caused considerable outrage and Donne was dismissed from his post as Egerton's secretary. Taking refuge in a house at Pyrford in Surrey, the unhappy Donne – reduced to relying upon the charity of friends and relatives – scratched on a window pane there the words: 'John Donne/An Donne/Undone'. Ann died in childbirth in 1617. They had 12 children in all, including John, George, Constance (who married the famous actor Edward Alleyn), Bridget, Margaret and Elizabeth – the others died young.

Appearance: In his youth Donne wore a moustache; later he sported a full beard.

Habits/Mannerisms: Donne was of a melancholy and sometimes morbid frame of mind and used to lie in his coffin for hours at a time, contemplating death. In *Biathanatos*, which was not published until after his death, he argued in defence of suicide, confessing a 'sickely inclination' to it himself. His favourite passages in the Bible were the Psalms and St Paul's epistles because they were true scriptures and

written as such (poems and letters), and he often used them as the basis of his sermons. He loathed milk.

Sport/Hobbies: Donne was a cultivated man, collecting paintings and enjoying music, the theatre and gardening.

Religion/Politics: Roman Catholic, then Church of England after renouncing Catholicism around 1593. He later published several essays attacking Catholicism and urging adherents to take the oath of allegiance to James. As an MP he served on four select committees.

Health: Donne caught typhoid in 1623 but recovered. Notes made during the month that he lay stricken with fever were published as *Devotions* (1624).

Temperament: Melancholy and serious but also ambitious (at least in his youth) and witty and emotional.

Coat of Arms: Azure wolf salient with a crest of snakes bound in a sheaf; he wrote his motto *'Per Rachel ho servito, e non per Lea'* (taken from Petrarch) on books in his library (as well as his name).

Manner of Death: Donne died on 31 March 1631 and was buried in St Paul's. Some time before his death he agreed to have his portrait painted so that a monumental sculptor would have a design from which to work on a statue of him. He stipulated that he be depicted wrapped in a funeral shroud and, when the painting was done, he had it placed beside his bed as a stern reminder to himself of his own mortality. His monument was one of the very few to survive the Great Fire of London in 1666. His epitaph reads:

'Reader! I am to let thee know,
Donne's body only lies below:
For, could the grave his soul comprise,
Earth would be richer than the skies.'

DOSTOEVSKI, Fyodor Mikhailovich (1821–81)
Russian novelist and short-story writer

Fyodor Dostoevski was born on 11 November 1821 in the Maryinsky Hospital for the Poor, Moscow, where his father Mikhail Andreyevich Dostoevski was senior resident physician. After the death of his mother, Marya Fyodorovna Nechaeva (1837), from tuberculosis, his father resigned his job because of ill-health, took a serf-girl mistress and lived on his small estate, where he was later murdered by peasants resentful of his cruel treatment (1839). Known to the family as 'Fedya', he had an older brother, Mikhail (a literary magazine editor), two younger brothers, Andrei and Nikolai, and three sisters, Varvara, Vera and Aleksandra. Taught French and Latin at home, he attended Chermak's private preparatory school in Moscow, then the Army's Chief Engineering Academy, St Petersburg (1838), where he was nicknamed 'Photius' after a famous monk. After failing and retaking his exams, he eventually became a Second Lieutenant (1842) and worked as a draughtsman in the War Ministry (1843) but resigned in 1844. His first short story, 'Bednye lyudi' (Poor Folk), was published in 1846. In 1849 he was sentenced to death for making treasonable speeches but was reprieved in front of the firing squad and given six years' hard labour and compulsory service with the 7th Siberian Batallion in Semipalatinsk, being released in 1859 on health grounds and eventually returning to St Petersburg. There he wrote his masterpiece, *Prestuplenie i nakazanie* (Crime and Punishment), in 1866. His other classic works included *Idiot* (The Idiot; 1868–9) and *Bratya Karamazovy* (The Brothers Karamazov, 1879–80). In 1873–4 he edited the weekly *Grazhdauin* (The Citizen).

Family/Sex Life: In 1857 Dostoevski married Marya Dmitrievna Isaeva, a widow with a nine-year-old son, Pavel. After the wedding he howled for two hours, eyes staring and face twisted in pain, then suffered a week of depression; the honeymoon was marred by Dostoevski suffering an epileptic fit. Marya died of tuberculosis in 1864 and none of their children survived infancy. In 1867 he took as his second wife Anna Grigoryevna Snitkina, his shorthand stenographer and 25 years his junior. Their children were Fyodor, Lyubov, Aleksey and Sonya (the last two died young). His mistresses included the writer Apollinaria Suslova (1862–3), the translator Martha Brown (1864–5) and the writer Anna Korvin-Krukovskaya (who rejected his marriage proposal). There were also unsubstantiated rumours that he had sex with a child prostitute.

Appearance: Dostoevski was short and thin. He had a straggly beard and fair hair, with a left parting above a high domed forehead. He had freckles and an unhealthy complexion and small deep-set grey eyes, usually bespectacled.

Habits/Mannerisms: A throat infection (*c.* 1837) left him with a hoarse, chesty voice and he foamed at the mouth when excited. He drank tea and smoked cigars and a long pipe, but never touched alcohol.

Sport/Hobbies: Dostoevski was addicted to gambling (cards, billiards, dominoes, roulette) for 10 years, as a result falling frequently into debt, until he saw his dead father in a nightmare and gave it up. He read all the works of Sir Walter Scott (in translation as he never learned English) by the age of 12 but later identified *Don Quixote* as his favourite book. He liked fishing, swimming and gardening and enjoyed opera and dancing. He loved

Mozart and Beethoven but disliked Wagner – 'that utterly dreary scoundrel'. A keen actor, he appeared in St Petersburg as the postmaster in Gogol's *The Inspector General* (1860).

Religion/Politics: Dostoevski was an atheist and socialist revolutionary in his youth but during his imprisonment became very conservative, a Russian Orthodox Christian and a fanatical nationalist.

Health: As well as epilepsy, Dostoevski suffered from long inert death-like trances and consequently had a great fear of being buried alive. Other ailments included emphysema, piles and scrofula. A hypochondriac, he took the waters at Bad Ems, Germany. He was also interested in phrenology.

Temperament: Dostoevski was anti-Semitic, anti-socialist and racist, nursing an extreme dislike of non-Russians, especially Germans. He was conceited, nervous and easily angered, though he could also be warm-hearted (for example, taking responsibility for the family of his brother Mikhail when he died suddenly). He was much disliked by Turgenev, who called him a 'pimple on the face of literature' (Dostoevski responded by lampooning Turgenev as the 'great writer' Karmazinov in *The Devils*). D. H. Lawrence called him a 'rat, slithering along in hate'. Admirers were many, however. Of *Crime and Punishment* R. L. Stevenson commented: 'The greatest book I have read in 10 years ... it nearly finished me. It was like having an illness.'

Work/Daily Routine: Dostoevski worked late into the night, chain-smoking cigarettes and drinking thick sweet tea. He woke about noon, drank two cups of coffee, and then dictated his night's work to his stenographer. He worked fairly quickly, writing 90 pages of *The Idiot* in Geneva in 23 days and sometimes worked on more than one book at a time – *The Gambler* and *Crime and Punishment* were written simultaneously (one in the mornings, the other in the afternoons). He claimed that he never wrote for money alone but often took advances for books he never delivered.

Manner of Death: On 26 January 1881 Dostoevski suffered a lung haemorrhage after moving a heavy bookcase. He died in St Petersburg around 9 pm on 9 February 1881, aged 59. 30,000 people watched his coffin going to the Aleksandr Nevsky Monastery before burial in the Tikhvinsky Cemetery (the largest funeral procession in Russian history).

DOYLE, Arthur Conan (1859–1930) Scottish-born novelist and short-story writer

---

Arthur Conan Doyle was born in Edinburgh on 22 May 1859, the second child and eldest son of seven surviving children of Charles Altimont Doyle, an Irish Catholic clerk in the Scottish Office of Works and an artist/illustrator, and Mary Foley. He was the nephew of the *Punch* artist Richard Doyle and the Director of the National Gallery of Ireland Henry Doyle, and grandson of the portrait painter-caricaturist John Doyle ('H. B.').

His brother-in-law was E. William Hornung (of 'Raffles' fame). He had a younger brother Brigadier-General Innes Doyle and five sisters. Educated at Hodder preparatory school and the Jesuit Stonyhurst School, Lancashire (1870–5), he spent a year at the Jesuit school in Feldkirch, Austria, before studying medicine at Edinburgh University (MD 1885). While a student he spent seven months as a ship's surgeon on the Arctic whaler *Hope* and after graduating he was ship's doctor on a steamer in Africa then a GP in Plymouth and Southsea (1882–90). He then went to Paris and Vienna to train as an eye specialist, set up practice near Wimpole Street but, lacking sufficient patients, started writing full-time. He first introduced the celebrated detective Sherlock Holmes in *A Study in Scarlet* (1887), illustrated by his father. *The Adventures of Sherlock Holmes* were serialized in the *Strand Magazine* (1891–3) and further Holmes stories followed after 1903. Aged 40 Doyle volunteered to work as a doctor in a field hospital during the Boer War. War correspondent for the *Westminster Gazette* in the Sudan, he was knighted in 1902. His other writings included the historical romance *The White Company* (1890).

Family/Sex Life: In 1885 Doyle married Louise Hawkins, the sister of a patient. Their children were Kingsley and Mary Louise. After Louise died, Doyle married Jean Leckie, 14 years his junior, in 1907. Their children were Denis, Adrian and Lena Jean.

Appearance: Doyle had a strong, heavy build, being over six feet tall and more than 17 stone. He had a bronzed face and sported a moustache.

Habits/Mannerisms: Doyle retained his Scottish accent. Like Holmes, he took cocaine; he also smoked cigars.

Sport/Hobbies: Doyle played soccer and cricket for Portsmouth and cricket for the MCC (he hit a century in his first match at Lord's, took 7 wickets for 51 runs against Cambridgeshire in 1904 and once bowled out W. G. Grace). He was also a good boxer and a patron of boxing and played billiards. He rode a tandem tricycle and owned a car as early as 1903, taking part in the Anglo-German car race 'Prince Henry's Tour' in 1911, driving a 20hp Dietrich-Lorraine (England won). He also enjoyed golf, fishing and bowls and helped to introduce skiing to Switzerland (from Norway). He was also a fine amateur photographer.

Religion/Politics: Roman Catholic, but he lost his faith as a teenager and joined the Psychical Research Society (1893). He became very interested in spiritualism – especially after his son was killed in World War I – and believed in fairies (as 'proved' by the famous Cottingley Fairies photographs). He stood twice as a Unionist MP (Edinburgh 1900, Hawick 1906) but was not elected. He detested the Suffragettes but was President of the Divorce Law Reform Society.

Health: Doyle suffered from heart palpitations and later had several mild heart attacks.

Temperament: Doyle was a man of decided, conservative opinions. He disliked the Pre-Raphaelites, for instance, as well as the French Symbolist poets, the Post-Impressionists and the Futurists and signed a petition to remove an Epstein bas-relief in Hyde Park. His friends included the writer Jerome K. Jerome.

Work/Daily Routine: Doyle's first published work was the story 'The Mystery of the Sassassa Valley', which appeared in *Chambers Journal* when he was 19. Sherlock Holmes, Doyle's greatest creation, was modelled on Dr Joseph Bell, Professor of Medicine at Edinburgh University (and a surgeon at the Edinburgh Infirmary), though he was also influenced by Edgar Allen Poe's detective Dupin. Holmes was originally called Sherrinford, rather than Sherlock, and Watson, who was modelled on Doyle's secretary Major Wood, began as Ormond Sacker. At no point in his 60 cases does Holmes ever say 'Elementary, my dear Watson' (though he does occasionally remark 'Elementary'). The success of the Holmes stories proved a burden to the author, who complained: 'I feel towards him as I do towards pâté de foie gras, of which I once ate too much, so that the name of it gives me a sickly feeling to this day.' Always more enthusiastic about his historical works, Doyle attempted to kill the detective off in 1893 by having him plunge over the Reichenbach Falls with his arch-enemy Moriarty (a statue of Holmes has marked the spot since 1988). Eight years later, however, he was obliged by public pressure to revive him in *The Hound of the Baskervilles*. Doyle also produced stage adaptations of the stories and wrote other plays (Sir Henry Irving played in *Waterloo*). Doyle wrote 3000 words daily, working between breakfast and lunch and from 5 to 8 pm. Letters addressed to Holmes continue to arrive at his lodgings, 221B Baker Street, London (now occupied by a building society): they are usually answered to the effect that the great detective has retired, to take up beekeeping.

Motto/Emblem: *'Fortitudine Vincit'*; stag's head.

Manner of Death: Doyle died at Crowborough, Sussex, in the morning of 7 July 1930 (the birthday in 1852 of the fictional Watson), aged 71.

DRAKE, Francis (c.1542–96) English naval adventurer

Francis Drake was born in his grandparents' cottage on Lord Bedford's estate at Crowndale near Tavistock, Devon, one of 12 sons of Edmund Drake, a former sailor who became Vicar of Upchurch, Kent, and his wife, a member of the Mylwaye family (Christian name unknown). His grandparents were wealthy farmers on the Bedford estate and he was also a nephew of the first English slave-trader Sir John Hawkyns. His godfather was Francis Russell, Earl of Bedford, and his brothers included Thomas, Joseph and John. After working on small ships, he was captain of the *Judith* in a squadron commanded by Hawkyns in the war with Spain. He later became the first Englishman to circumnavigate the world (1577–80) and survive the trip (Magellan had died). He bought Buckland Abbey, Devon, with profits from his voyages and reputedly introduced tobacco and potatoes to England in 1586, after leading 25 ships on a voyage of plunder to the West Indies on commission from Elizabeth I. He also made a daring raid on Spanish ships in Cadiz harbour (an escapade known as the 'singeing of the Spanish King's beard') and thus delayed the sailing of the Armada, which he comprehensively defeated at sea in 1588. Knighted in 1581 by Elizabeth I at Deptford on board his ship, the *Golden Hind* (formerly named *The Pelican*), in which he had circumnavigated the globe, he became Mayor of Plymouth (1582) and MP for the town (1593). He set sail on his last voyage to the West Indies in 1595.

Family/Sex Life: In 1569 Drake married Mary Newman. After she died in 1582, he took as his second wife (1585) Elizabeth Sydenham, daughter and heiress of Sir George Sydenham. He had no children.

Appearance: In Stow's *Annals*, Drake is described as 'Low of stature, of strong limbs, broad-breasted, round-headed, brown hair, full-bearded; his eyes round, large and clear; well-favoured, fair, and of cheerful countenance.' He had a mole on the left side of his nose. Evidently a fashionable dresser, judging by his portraits, he owned a suit of silver armour, a present from Elizabeth I.

Habits/Mannerisms: A well-spoken and cultivated man, Drake liked to eat to the sound of violins.

Sport/Hobbies: Drake enjoyed playing bowls and was reputedly doing so on Plymouth Hoe when news arrived that the attacking Spanish Armada had passed Lizard Point in Cornwall. Legend boasts that Drake refused to abandon the game, calmly insisting: 'There's plenty of time to win this game and to thrash the Spaniards too.' Curiously, though, the story is not mentioned in any accounts of Drake's life prior to 1736.

Religion/Politics: Church of England.

Health: In 1579 Drake narrowly escaped death when he was shot in the face by an arrow.

Temperament: Merry, ruthless, and boastful, Drake disliked being confined to port while in England and chafed when political considerations prevented him pursuing his campaigns against the Spaniards. In 1587, when he was finally given reluctant permission by Elizabeth I to undertake the 'singeing of the Spanish King's beard', he set immediately to sea, before any countermanding order could arrive: such an order was indeed sent, but arrived too late to prevent the action taking place. Drake showed more consideration to his sailors than many other commanders. After the victory over the Armada in 1588 he combined with Hawkyns to set up the 'Chatham Chest', a charitable fund to help distressed sailors, who were being offered little reward by the Crown for their efforts against Spain (the cost of defending England against the Armada had almost bankrupted the Treasury).

Work/Daily Routine: Drake was the most successful English seaman of his generation and enjoyed a popular reputation at home. The Queen was one of his most devoted admirers. He returned the compliment by claiming lands in her name. Not all the names stuck, however: the land he named as 'New Albion', for instance, became better known as California. It was near San Francisco, California, that a brass plate in which Drake had claimed the territory for England in 1579 was allegedly found in 1936 – a replica of the plate was subsequently presented to Elizabeth II and was placed with due reverence in Drake's old home, Buckland Abbey, but detailed analysis of the brass in 1977 exposed the plate as a fake.

Manner of Death: Drake died of dysentery on board his ship the *Defiance* off Portobello in the West Indies on 28 January 1596. He was buried at sea in a leaden coffin the next day. His drum was brought back to England and hung up in Buckland Abbey, where – so the story goes – it will beat out a warning tattoo whenever England is in danger from its enemies (it is supposed to have sounded after World War I, at the time that the German fleet was scuttled at Scapa Flow, and again at the time of the Dunkirk evacuation in 1940).

DRYDEN, John (1631–1700) English poet and playwright

John Dryden was born in the vicarage of All Saints, Aldwincle, Northamptonshire, on 9 August 1631, the son of Erasmus Dryden, a landowner and Justice of the Peace for Northampton, and Mary Pickering, daughter of the rector of Aldwincle. His grandfather was Sir Erasmus Dryden and his uncle was Sir John Dryden, and he was also a cousin of Jonathan Swift. Educated at Westminster School (with John Locke) and at Trinity College, Cambridge, where he graduated in 1654, he was at first Secretary to his cousin Sir Gilbert Pickering (one of the judges who had tried Charles I) under Cromwell and then worked for a publisher. Having moved to London in 1657, he soon established a reputation as a poet and playwright and enjoyed the favour of the court. He was appointed Poet Laureate by Charles II in 1668 and Historiographer Royal in 1670 and was later Collector of Customs in the Port of London. He was stripped of the title Poet Laureate by William and Mary (1688) for converting to Catholicism and supporting James II. His most important works included the plays *Marriage à-la-Mode* (1672), *Aureng-Zebe* (1675) and *All for Love* (1678) and the satire *Absalom and Achitophel* (1681), which lampooned the Whig party.

Family/Sex Life: In 1663 Dryden married Lady Elizabeth Howard, daughter of the 1st Earl of Berkshire. By her he fathered Erasmus Henry, Charles and John. It was for her that he suggested the rather ungracious epitaph: 'Here lies my wife: here let her lie!/Now she's at rest, and so am I.' He also had an affair with the actress Ann Reeve.

Appearance: Short, stout and florid, he was nicknamed 'Poet Squab' by John Wilmot, Earl of Rochester. He had a large mole on his right cheek and a 'sleepy eye'.

Habits/Mannerisms: He took snuff.

Sport/Hobbies: Dryden played bowls and was fond of fishing. He was also a member of the Royal Society.

Religion/Politics: Dryden was changeable in his allegiances, according to the prevailing balance of power. He began as a Puritan and wrote the poem *Religio Laici* (1682) in defence of Anglicanism, but later converted to Catholicism, celebrated in *The Hind and the Panther* (1687). He was pro-Cromwell during the Protectorate, then pro-Restoration and then a Jacobite

on the accession of James II. In 1679 he was badly beaten up outside the Lamb and Flag pub in Rose Alley, London, by disguised thugs acting on the orders of the Earl of Rochester and the Duchess of Portsmouth, who believed him to be the author of the *Essay on Satire* (attacking Charles II, Rochester and the Duchesses of Portsmouth and Cleveland). It was actually written by John Sheffield, Lord Mulgrave.

Health: Dryden suffered from gout from 1700.

Temperament: Very modest and generous, Dryden had many friends (Congreve was his protégé). He enjoyed convivial evenings among his friends at Wills Coffee House at the corner of Russell Street and Bow Street, Covent Garden, London, where he had his own chair. On one occasion, while out with the Duke of Buckingham and the Earl of Dorset, he was asked to judge between impromptu poems submitted to him by each person present – he gave the prize to Dorset for the 'poem': 'I promise to pay John Dryden, or order, on demand the sum of £500. Dorset.' Swift, however, hated Dryden for his hostile reaction to his *Odes*: 'Cousin Swift, you will never be a poet.' Dryden's readiness to change tack in mid-course, both stylistically and philosophically, rendered him vulnerable to satire by others. Buckingham had much fun at Dryden's expense, depicting his foibles in the guise of Bayes in his comedy *The Rehearsal* (1672). Lord Macaulay wrote of Dryden: 'His mind was of a slovenly character – fond of splendour, but indifferent to neatness. Hence most of his writings exhibit the sluttish magnificence of a Russian noble, all vermin diamonds, dirty linen, and inestimable sables.'

Work/Daily Routine: Dryden's first published work was the *Heroic Stanzas* (dedicated to Cromwell). Nell Gwynne acted in three of his plays and reputedly attracted Charles II's attention whilst performing as Valeria in his *Tyrannick Love*. In his final years he tired of writing for the stage, complaining that: 'many of my predecessors have excell'd me in all kinds; and some of my contemporaries ... have out-done me in comedy'. Instead, needing to earn more money after the withdrawal of royal patronage, he turned to translations of Juvenal, Persius, Virgil and Ovid among others. Cowper said of him: 'Never ... were such talents and such drudgery united.' Dryden is reputed to have had himself 'blooded and purged' each time he sat down to write.

Manner of Death: Dryden died of blood poisoning, after refusing to have a mortified gouty toe amputated, at his house at 43 Gerrard Street, London, on 1 May 1700, aged 68. His body was embalmed then buried in Westminster Abbey; there were 100 carriages in the funeral procession.

DUMAS, Alexandre Davy de la Pailleterie (1802–70)
French novelist and playwright

Alexandre Dumas *père* was born in Villiers-Cotterets, Aisne, France, on 24 July 1802, the son of General Alexandre Davy-Dumas, 'The Black Devil' (the giant mulatto bastard son of the Marquis de la Pailleterie and Marie Cessette, a negress from San Domingo) and Marie-Louise Labouret – thus Dumas was a 'quadroon' (one-quarter negro). He had an elder sister, Aimée-Alexandrine, a noted singer. His father died when he was four and Dumas worked at first as a junior clerk for a company of solicitors before becoming clerk to the Duc d'Orléans in Paris. He later became Keeper of Museums in Naples for Garibaldi. Among his most popular works of fiction were the historical romances *The Count of Monte Cristo* (1844–5), *The Three Musketeers* (1844–5) and *The Black Tulip* (1850). His most celebrated plays included *Henri III et sa cour* (1829), *Napoléon Bonaparte* (1831), *Antony* (1831), *La Tour de Nesle* (1832) and *Kean, ou Désordre et génie* (1836), as well as stage adaptations of his novels. Several of his plays were first presented at his own Théâtre Historique, the failure of which left him close to bankruptcy.

Family/Sex Life: In 1840 Dumas married the actress Ida Ferrier, née Marguerite

Ferrand. They separated in 1844 and she died in 1859. His affair with the dressmaker Marie-Catherine Labay resulted in the birth of a son, the equally acclaimed writer Alexandre Dumas *fils*, who was later legitimized. He also had affairs with the adventuress Lola Montez and, in his old age, with the US actress/circus performer Ada Menken (a cause of considerable scandal). The actress Mélanie Serre gave birth to his illegitimate daughter Marie-Alexandrine and by Emilie Cordier he fathered Micaella-Clélie-Josepha-Elizabeth when he was 57 and she 19.

Sport/Hobbies: Among the non-literary projects he undertook was the building of a huge house that he later called 'Monte Cristo', after his famous novel.

Health: Dumas was an insomniac and reputedly used to eat an apple under the Arc de Triomphe to cure it. In 1832 he contracted cholera, but survived. Otherwise he enjoyed fairly robust health; in reply to an admirer who wondered how he managed to age so gracefully, he explained: 'Madame, I give all my time to it.'

Temperament: Dumas was vain and provocative but also courageous. He fought his first duel in 1825, when he was 23 (on which august occasion his trousers fell down). Another time he found himself committed to a duel with a man who, like himself, was an excellent shot: it was decided that the duellists should draw lots and the loser should shoot himself – Dumas lost and retired to an adjoining room with his pistol but, unaccountably and to his fervently expressed regrets, missed when he tried to fulfil his part of the bargain. He had a sharp sense of humour. When a friend asked him to contribute 25 francs to the burial of a bailiff, who had died in penury, he responded: 'Here are 50 francs. Go and bury two bailiffs.' When he was introduced to the acrobat Charles Blondin, famed for his exploits on the high wire, he could not resist ribbing the celebrity, questioning his achievements. Blondin, perhaps unused to such irreverence, challenged Dumas to accompany him on the wire over Niagara Falls – to his surprise, Dumas accepted the challenge, but then added: 'but only on condition that I carry you'.

Pets: His pets included a Scottish pointer dog called Pritchard and the cats Mysouff I and black-and-white Mysouff II (Mysouff I 'knew' when he was coming home and would sit at the end of the road). He also kept three monkeys (named after literary critics) and various birds, including a vulture named Jugurtha.

Work/Daily Routine: Dumas's first book was the self-published *Nouvelles Contemporaines*. As an established and wealthy writer, he reputedly employed some 90 collaborators on his work and was not infrequently attacked for plagiarism (his play *La Tour de Nesle* led to a lawsuit and a duel with the original author, Frédéric Gaillardet, whose play Dumas had freely plundered). On one occasion, when he asked his son if he had read his latest novel yet, the young man cheekily replied: 'No. Have you?' When looting the Tuileries Palace with the Paris mob (1830) he found a copy of his own book *Christine* in the royal apartments. All his love stories were banned by the Vatican and put on the Index of prohibited books (1863). He worked with prodigious speed, writing his novels on blue, poetry on yellow and non-fiction on rose-coloured paper. As well as his novels and his plays he also wrote numerous travel books, children's stories, 22 volumes of *Mémoires* and a *Grand Dictionnaire de cuisine* (1872).

Manner of Death: Dumas died on 5 December 1870, aged 68, at his son's villa in Dieppe.

DUNCAN, Isadora (1878–1927) US dancer

Isadora (christened Angela) Duncan was born in San Francisco, California, on 27 May 1878, the youngest child of Joseph Duncan, a poet, and Dora Gray, a musician. She had two sisters, Elizabeth and Augustine, and a brother Raymond. Her mother divorced her father soon after Isadora's birth. She worked at first for the Augustin Daly dance company in New York then came with her mother to England where she and her sisters were 'discovered' by actress Mrs Patrick Campbell as they danced in a park. She then joined Loie Fuller's dance company, toured Germany (where she was hailed as '*Die göttliche, heilige Isadora*') and set up her own school with her sister Elizabeth in Grünwald, near Berlin, and later others in Moscow, Salzburg and Vienna (none of them prospered for very long). She settled in Paris in 1908 but continued to undertake regular European tours. Her free interpretation of a supposedly 'Classical' style of dance had a profound impact upon succeeding generations of choreographers and dancers; she was also widely known for her flamboyant lifestyle. Her autobiography, *My Life*, was published in 1927.

Family/Sex Life: Duncan had a celebrated affair with Edward Gordon Craig, the son of actress Ellen Terry, and had by him a daughter named Deirdre. She also formed a liaison with a millionaire whom she identified only as 'Lohengrin', giving birth to his son Patrick, and with an Italian sculptor (by whom she had a stillborn child). Both her children were tragically drowned with their governess when their taxicab fell into Seine in 1913. In 1922 she married the Russian poet Sergei Yessenin, who was 17 years her junior: he went mad, however, and after leaving her committed suicide. Duncan herself observed: 'So that ends my first experience with matrimony, which I always thought a highly overrated performance.'

Religion/Politics: Duncan was often outspoken about her liberated if somewhat naive views. When the Russian Revolution broke out in 1917, for instance, she appealed to the rest of the world to support the revolutionaries, arguing in Boston in 1922: 'America has all that Russia has not. Russia has things America has not. Why will America not reach out a hand to Russia, as I have given my hand?'

Health: Though in her youth she was presented as a spritely nymph-like figure in flowing robes, she became very flabby and indolent in later life.

Temperament: Energetic, impetuous and

totally absorbed in herself and her dancing, Duncan inspired both admiration and irritation in those who met her. To her critics, she defended herself on the grounds that: 'People do not live nowadays – they get about ten per cent out of life.' Duncan's friends included her patron Paris E. Singer, heir to the Singer Sewing Machine fortune and the world's very first owner of a Rolls-Royce when the company was formed in 1906.

Pets: Duncan hated cats and treated strays in her garden in Neuilly-sur-Seine, near Paris (which was next door to a cat sanctuary) with cruelty.

Work/Daily Routine: Dancing barefoot in a loose, diaphanous tunic in imitation of figures in Greek vase-paintings, Duncan revolutionized ideas about choreography, illustrating how it might be more spontaneous and free-flowing, drawing on personal intuitive interpretations of great music. In a bid to free dance of conventional steps she controversially incorporated skipping, hopping, running and walking in her routines. To the annoyance of many contemporaries, but with the agreement of many more, she claimed that: 'I have discovered the dance. I have discovered the art which has been lost for two thousand years.'

Manner of Death: Duncan was accidentally strangled on the Promenade des Anglais, Nice, on 14 September 1927 when her long red scarf caught in the wheel of a Bugatti sports car she planned to buy. Her last words, cried out to friends as she roared away from her home, were *'Adieu, mes amis! Je vais à la gloire'* : she died a minute later of a broken neck. Her body was taken to Paris and was buried in the Père Lachaise cemetery.

EDISON, Thomas Alva (1847–1931) US inventor

Thomas Edison was born in Milan, Ohio, on 11 February 1847, the fourth surviving child of Samuel Edison, a timber and grain merchant, and Nancy Elliot. Named after Captain Alva Bradley, a Great Lakes shipowner and family friend, he reputedly only had three months' schooling and was taught at home by his mother. He started work as a newspaper and confectionery salesboy on the Grand Trunk Railroad from Port Huron to Detroit and (aged 12) wrote and published a local-interest news-sheet, the *Grand Trunk Herald* (weekly circulation of 400 copies) – the first newspaper printed on a train. He then became a telegraph operator on the Grand Trunk line (1863), later joining Western Union in various locations. His first two inventions – an automatic vote recorder for Congressional proceedings and a duplex telegraph system capable of sending two messages at once – were not commercial successes but led to a job as assistant to the chief engineer at Laws Gold Reporting Company, New York. He later became Chief Engineer before resigning to form Pope, Edison & Company, Electrical Engineers and General Telegraphic Agency, and set up a factory in Newark, New Jersey in 1873 and then at Menlo Park, near New York. In his lifetime he took out 1033 patents for inventions, including the phonograph (1877), the electric light (1879), the kinetoscope (early cinema) and cement.

Family/Sex Life: Edison's first wife was 16-year-old Mary Stilwell, who worked in his Newark factory (she died of typhoid in 1884). Their children were Marion Estelle, Thomas Alva and William Leslie (they nicknamed Marion and Thomas 'Dot' and 'Dash'). In 1885 he married 19-year-old Mina Miller, by whom he fathered Charles, Theodore and Madeleine. The betrothal was unusual in that he proposed to his second wife in Morse code, which he had previously taught her.

Appearance: Edison was clean-shaven and had grey-blue eyes and chestnut hair parted on the right. He was a careless dresser.

Habits/Mannerisms: Edison retained a thick Mid-West accent throughout his life. He developed an unusual vertical handwriting style which allowed him to write very quickly (of great advantage to a telegraph operator). He smoked cigars but drank little alcohol and supported Prohibition. He never slept longer or ate more than necessary – he usually ate only five oz at each meal (including the water in his food), three times a day. He distrusted uncooked foods because they might carry typhus.

Religion/Politics: Edison was anti-Semitic and an atheist, declaring: 'I cannot see that creeds amount to anything and personally I am amazed because apparently sound minds set such great store by them.' He was a pacifist but served as President of the US Naval Consulting Board in World War I (his grandfather had fought with the British in the American War of Independence).

Health: Edison became deaf as a child and had scarlet fever. He was twice operated on for mastoids and also suffered from Bright's Disease, diabetes and uraemic poisoning.

Temperament: Edison was modest and retiring, and not at all egoistic. His friends included Henry Ford, who had Edison's laboratory moved from Menlo Park to Dearborn and reconstructed there as a tribute in 1929 (Edison admired the rebuilt laboratory, saying it was 99½ per cent accurate – the one difference he could discern being that he had never kept the original so clean).

Work/Daily Routine: Edison breakfasted at 8 am on grapefruit, coffee and a slice of toast. He worked either at day or at night and slept either in the night or in the day accordingly. He carried 200-page yellow-leaved notebooks everywhere (filling 3400 in his lifetime). The first recording made on the Edison cylinder phonograph was 'Mary Had a Little Lamb'. Another early recording on wax cylinders featured the elderly Robert Browning reading 'How They Brought the Good News from Aix to Ghent' – after a few lines he forgot the rest and says so on the recording (April 1889). Edison exhibited dynamos and other inventions at the Crystal Palace, London, in 1882 and presented a talking doll to the Archduchess Elizabeth, daughter of the Crown Prince of Austria in 1889. The first US newspaper office to be lit by electricity was James Gordon Bennett's *New York Herald*; the first private home thus lit was that of New York banker Pierpont Morgan. In 1883 Edison helped light up Moscow with 3500 lamps for the Tsar's coronation. The world's first central electricity generating station was opened at Holborn Viaduct, London, using Edison's great dynamo, in 1882. At first Edison used DC not AC current.

Motto: 'Genius is one per cent inspiration and 99 per cent perspiration.' Edison's own work readily illustrated the truth of his assertion: he conducted 50,000 experiments, for instance, before he successfully invented a new storage battery. When a colleague observed that this was a lot of experiments for just one result, Edison countered: 'Results? Why, I have gotten a lot of results. I know fifty thousand things that won't work.'

Manner of Death: Edison died on 18 October 1931, aged 84. At 9.59 pm (Eastern Standard Time) on 21 October 1931 all but essential lights were switched off across the USA for one minute in his honour: even the torch on the Statue of Liberty was turned off and the Broadway lights were dimmed.

EDWARD II (1284–1327) King of England

Edward II was born in Caernarvon, Wales, on 25 April 1284, the fourth and only surviving son of Edward I and his first wife, Eleanor, daughter of Ferdinand III of Castile (she died in 1290, when he was six). His brothers John, Henry and Alfonso all died young. He also had five sisters – Eleanor, Joanna, Margaret, Mary and Elizabeth – and two stepbrothers – Thomas and Edmund – by his father's second wife (Margaret, daughter of King Philip III of France). He was created Prince of Wales in 1301, thus becoming the first English heir-apparent to hold the title. He was crowned king on the death of Edward I six years later, in 1307 (ignorant of Latin, he took the coronation oath in French). Edward's 20-year reign was a troubled one. The barons became highly resentful of his reckless favouritism of certain nobles and sought to reassert their influence by restricting the royal prerogative and by other measures designed to reduce Edward's power. There were also military reverses, as with the crushing defeat by the Scots at Bannockburn in 1314. Ultimately, Edward was deposed by his wife and her lover Roger Mortimer in favour of his son, Edward III. The story of his reign and eventual downfall were memorably dramatized by Christopher Marlowe in his history play *Edward II* (1592).

Family/Sex Life: In 1308 Edward married Isabella, daughter of King Philip IV ('the Fair') of France. Their children were Edward III, John, Eleanor and Joan (who married David, son of Robert the Bruce). Edward also entered into a homosexual relationship with the Gascon knight Piers de Gaveston, whom he created Earl of Cornwall then Regent of Ireland, causing much resentment among other barons. Secure in Edward's protection, Gaveston preened himself before the court and amused his royal master by making up insulting nicknames for the barons: the Earl of Warwick he dubbed the 'Black Hound of Arden' and the Earl of Lancaster 'Churl', while the Earl of Lincoln became 'Burstbelly' and the Earl of Gloucester 'Horeson'. Gaveston's unpopularity eventually obliged Edward to banish him (1308), but a year later he allowed him back to court and civil war ensued. In the end, Gaveston was captured by the Earl of Warwick and executed at Blacklow Hill, Warwick. Edward failed even then to learn his lesson and instead lavished gifts upon another noble, Hugh le Despenser, who became almost as unpopular with the other barons as Gaveston had been. This friendship with Despenser proved the last straw for Queen Isabella, who joined with her lover Roger Mortimer, Earl of March, in leading an army against her husband in order to replace him with her son. Imprisoned initially in Kenilworth Castle, Edward had no option but to renounce his throne in favour of Edward III.

Appearance: Edward was tall, handsome and very strong. At the age of 23 he was described as 'fair of body and of great strength'.

Habits/Mannerisms: A heavy drinker; Edward liked dancing and music and employed Genoese fiddlers to play at his court (he was an accomplished musician himself). He also liked dressing in fine clothes.

Sport/Hobbies: Edward was a good horseman and athlete, and was fond of racing, swimming and rowing. He also played (and lost heavily) at dice and was proud of his skill at digging trenches and at the craft of thatching.

Temperament: Edward was extravagant and frivolous, though also a witty conversationalist. Despite his own considerable strength, he was not, however, keen on fighting.

Pets: Devoted to his horses and his hounds, Edward always took a lion with him on his travels.

Manner of Death: After being deposed, Edward was moved from Kenilworth to Berkeley Castle, Gloucestershire, where he was much humiliated by his captors, Lord Berkeley and Sir John Maltravers. After being crowned with hay and thrown in ditchwater, he was incarcerated in a room over the charnel house where it was assumed he would soon contract a fatal disease. His health withstood such abuse, however, and on 21 September 1327, when Edward was aged 43, he was murdered by the insertion – through a horn (so no wound would be visible) – of a red-hot poker into his rectum. The king's body was subsequently put on display to show that he had died of natural causes and he was then buried in Gloucester Cathedral. Calls from the pious for the murdered monarch to be canonized went unheeded, but his son – Edward III – exacted revenge for his father's death by having Mortimer executed and his mother sent to a nunnery. The sounds of Edward II's screams as he was put to death are reputedly still occasionally heard echoing round Berkeley Castle.

EDWARD VII (1841–1910) King of the United Kingdom and Emperor of India

Prince Albert Edward, later Edward VII, was born in Buckingham Palace, London, at 10.48 am on 9 November 1841, the second child and oldest son of Queen Victoria and Prince Albert of Schleswig-Holstein. His godfather was King Frederick William IV of Prussia. The uncle of Kaiser Wilhelm II, he had two brothers, Alfred and Arthur, and four sisters – Victoria (who married Emperor Frederick III of Germany), Alice, Helena and Louise. After private education by tutors he attended Christ Church, Oxford, then Trinity College, Cambridge (where his history professor was Charles Kingsley). He served with the Grenadier Guards as an ensign and was later (1880) Colonel-in-Chief of the Household Cavalry. In addition he was given Prince Albert's title Duke of Saxony – despite Palmerston's protestations that it was too German. He was aged 59 when he came to the thone (1901). He established the Order of Merit (modelled on the Prussian Pour le Mérite), founded the Royal College of Music (1883), opened Tower Bridge (1894) and was the first king to visit the Isle of Man since Canute.

Family/Sex Life: In 1863 Edward married Alexandra of Schleswig-Holstein, eldest daughter of Christian IX of Denmark. They had five surviving children: Albert Victor, George V, Louise, Victoria and Maud (who married the King of Norway). Most famous of his mistresses was actress Lillie Langtry (who bore him a daughter in 1881). Others were Frances Countess of Warwick, Miss Chamberlayne and Mrs Keppel. He was involved in two major society scandals and such was the notoriety surrounding him that Victoria excluded him from affairs of state.

Appearance: Edward was bearded and portly, boasting a 48-inch waist and chest at his coronation. A dapper dresser, he popularized the fashion for wearing black Homburg hats (he also wore Tyrolean hats and grey felt hats) and sported tweeds at race meetings as well as Norfolk jackets.

Habits/Mannerisms: Known as 'Bertie' to his family and 'Kingy' to his grandchildren, Edward rejected the name Albert when king. He spoke German from his youth and pronounced the letter R in the German manner. He liked brandy-and-soda and preferred claret to champagne. He smoked one small cigar and two cigarettes before breakfast and 12 large cigars and 20 cigarettes later in the day. He was also a glutton. On one occasion, during a typically indulgent repast, a footman accidentally spilt cream on the king, prompting the bemused complaint: 'My good man, I'm not a strawberry.'

Sport/Hobbies: Edward loved shooting (especially partridge, pheasants, grouse and deer) and big game hunting. In accordance with his express instruction all the clocks at Sandringham ran half an hour fast so that guests would rise early for the best shooting (they were not re-adjusted until the death of George V at Sandringham in 1936). During one shoot he came close to killing a beater, accidentally shooting his knee-cap off. He was also keen on horseracing: his horses won the Derby three times (1896, 1900 and 1909) and the Grand National (1900). In 1899 he rode in the Daimler of Lord Montagu of Beaulieu, after which he bought a Mercedes and a Renault, both claret-coloured (thus becoming the first member of the British Royal Family to own a car). He also enjoyed tennis, golf, croquet, ice-skating, ice-hockey and yachting (his yacht *Hildegarde* won the first ever Queen's Cup at Cowes, 1877). Other pleasures included dancing and the theatre – he once played a corpse in Sardou's play *Fedora*, starring Sarah Bernhardt. He spoke French well but read little, except for newspapers. He nursed a passion for baccarat (then illegal) and bridge and as a result was obliged to give evidence in the 'Baccarat Scandal', which arose from the alleged cheating of Sir William Gordon-Cumming during a game in which Edward played.

Religion/Politics: Edward sat in the House of Lords from 1863 but had no party bias. He disliked the Suffragettes (as did Victoria). In 1875 he became Grand Master of the Freemasons.

Health: Edward nearly died of typhoid in 1871 and broke a kneecap in 1898. In 1900 he narrowly escaped assassination by an anarchist at the Gare du Nord, Brussels, and in 1902 his coronation had to be postponed because of an appendicitis operation. He went annually to Marienbad to take the waters and had a face ulcer removed by radium treatment.

Temperament: Edward's friends included Lord Nathan Rothschild and grocer millionaire Sir Thomas Lipton as well as Lord Cole and Sir Frederick Johnstone – named as co-respondents in the divorce of Sir Charles Mordaunt (1871), a scandal that caused the Prince embarrassment.

Pets: Edward was fond of horses and dogs and was patron of the Kennel Club, himself exhibiting dogs. His wire-haired fox-terrier Caesar (which had a collar inscribed 'I belong to the King') followed his coffin in his funeral procession. He inherited a blue Persian cat called White Heather when Queen Victoria died.

Manner of Death: Bedridden with bronchitis, Edward enjoyed a last mid-day cigar, then suffered heart attacks and died at 11.45 pm on 6 May 1910 at Buckingham Palace, London. On his deathbed he heard that his horse 'Witch of the Air' had won at Kempton Park. He was buried in St George's Chapel, Windsor.

EINSTEIN, Albert (1879–1955) German-born scientist

Albert Einstein was born just before noon on Friday 14 March 1879 at 135 Bahn-hofstrasse (which was destroyed by bombing, 1944), Ulm, Bavaria, Germany, the son of Hermann Einstein, proprietor of an electrical engineering company. His mother was Pauline Koch, daughter of a wealthy grain merchant, and he had a younger sister Maria (Maja). Educated in Munich and Pavia, Italy, he became a Swiss citizen in 1901. He entered Zurich's Federal Institute of Technology on the second attempt and studied to be a physics and maths teacher there (1896–1900). After teaching for a year he submitted a thesis on the kinetic theory of gases to the University of Zurich, but it was rejected so he worked in a patent office in Berne,

Switzerland (1902). While there he published five important scientific papers and began lecturing part-time at the University of Berne (1908). Einstein became successively a Professor at the University of Zurich (1909), at the German University of Prague (1911) and at the FIT, Zurich (1912) and in 1913 was invited by Max Planck to become Professor at the University of Berlin. He was Director of the Kaiser Wilhelm Institute in Berlin (1914–33) and during this period published his General Theory of Relativity (1916), which was publicly verified in 1919. He was awarded the Nobel Prize (1921) for his work on the photo-electric effect though he had been nominated for the prize for his Special

Theory of Relativity in 1912. With the rise of Nazism he came to England and lectured at Oxford and Cambridge before emigrating to the USA. There he became Visiting Professor at the California Institute of Technology, Pasadena (1930), and lectured at Princeton. He became a US citizen in 1940. In 1950 he published his Unified Field Theory, in which he attempted (but failed) to merge quantum theory and his General Theory of Relativity.

Family/Sex Life: Einstein fathered an illegitimate daughter Lieserl (1902) by Mileva Maric, a fellow student whom he called 'Doxerl'. They married in 1903 and divorced in 1919. Their other children were Hans Albert (later Professor of Engineering at Berkeley, California) and Eduard (a schizophrenic). Einstein gave Mileva and her children his Nobel Prize money. His second wife (1919) was his cousin, divorcée Elsa Lowenthal, who already had two daughters, Ilse and Margot. They had no more children. Declaring 'all marriages are dangerous', he also had a late affair with another, younger, woman.

Appearance: Born with a very large head, Einstein had black hair and a moustache in his youth, though these later became snowy white. He was a casual and untidy dresser.

Habits/Mannerisms: As a child he constructed whole sentences before uttering single words. The story goes that his first utterance, one mealtime, was: 'The soup is too hot.' When asked why he had never spoken before this, he replied: 'Because up to now everything was in order.'

Sport/Hobbies: Einstein enjoyed sailing and reading. He thought *The Brothers Karamazov* the greatest of all literature and liked Dickens and Balzac. He was fond of music, especially Mozart, and played the violin and piano.

Religion/Politics: Einstein had a non-practising Jewish upbringing but later became an Orthodox Jew. The order of the universe was to him evidence of God's existence and he refuted the principle of uncertainty or indeterminacy on the grounds that: 'God does not play dice with the universe.' He was a Zionist (co-author with Freud of *About Zionism*) but refused the presidency of Israel when it was offered. He was also a pacifist, publishing the anti-war *Why War?* and writing to President Roosevelt in 1939 warning him of the dangers of atomic warfare. He was seen as an 'extreme radical' by the FBI who by 1940 had a 1500-page dossier on him. He did not believe in freedom of will, agreeing with Schopenhauer that: 'Man can do what he wants, but he cannot will what he wills.'

Health: Having flat feet and varicose veins, Einstein was rejected for military service. In 1899 he injured his right hand in a lab experiment. In 1917 he was diagnosed as having a stomach ulcer; he also suffered from jaundice, from an inflamed wall of the heart (1928) and had an aneurysm in the abdominal aorta (a lump the size of a grapefruit).

Temperament: Arrogant in his youth, Einstein became the archetypal absent-minded professor. His friends included Franz Kafka, Max Brod (Kepler in Brod's novel *The Redemption of Tycho Brahe* was based on Einstein), biochemist Chaim Weizmann (leader of the Zionists) and German Foreign Minister Walter Rathenau.

Work/Daily Routine: Einstein read Kant's *Critique of Pure Reason* at 13 and was as much a philosopher as a scientist. He opened up new ways of conceptualizing scientific theory, though he admitted that his ideas sometimes defied common sense (which he liked to call 'the collection of prejudices acquired by age eighteen'). It was claimed that only three people understood his theories – when astronomer

Sir Arthur Eddington heard this he asked: 'Who's the third?' Einstein's wife was baffled by the Theory of Relativity, but added: 'I know my husband and I know he can be trusted.' Einstein claimed he could work anywhere – when a friend worried about wasting his time by asking him to meet on the Potsdam Bridge, Einstein calmly replied: 'The kind of work I do can be done anywhere. Why should I be less capable of reflecting about my problems on the Potsdam bridge than at home?'

Manner of Death: Einstein collapsed at home on 12 April 1955 and was admitted to hospital in great pain four days later, on 16 April. He died of a ruptured aneurysm (having refused surgery) around 1.15 am on 18 April 1955 in Princeton Hospital, New Jersey, aged 76. His brain is preserved in Wichita, Kansas, in the laboratory of Dr Thomas Harvey, formerly Chief Pathologist of Princeton University.

ELIOT, George (1819–80) English novelist and journalist

Mary Ann (later Marian) Evans was born at 5 am on 22 November 1819 in Chilvers Coton, Warwickshire, the youngest surviving child of Robert Evans, forester and former estate bailiff of Wootton Hall, Ellastone, Warwickshire – where Rousseau had begun his *Confessions* – and subsequently of Arbury Hall, Astley, Warwickshire (home of the Newdigate family, founders of Oxford's Newdigate Prize for poetry). Her mother was her father's second wife, Christiana Pearson, and she had an older sister Christiana, a brother Isaac, an older half-sister Francesca Lucy and a half-brother Robert. After the death of her mother (1836) and the marriage of her sister, she kept house for her father. Educated (with Christiana) at Miss Latham's School, Attleborough; at Mrs Wallington's School, Nuneaton; and at the Misses Franklin's School, Coventry, she worked as a German translator and journalist (writing for the *Coventry Herald*, *Fraser's Magazine* and *The Leader*). Her father left her a £120 annuity on his death (1849) and, after travelling abroad, she became Assistant Editor of J. S. Mill's *Westminster Review* (1851–4) before turning full-time writer. She published *Scenes of Clerical Life*, her first book under the pseudonym George Eliot, in 1858; among the most celebrated novels

that followed were *Adam Bede* (1859), *The Mill on the Floss* (1860), *Silas Marner* (1861) and *Middlemarch* (1871–2).

Family/Sex Life: George Eliot lived as the common-law wife of philosopher, writer and magazine editor George H. Lewes. Lewes separated from his wife Agnes and their four sons when Agnes had two children by his friend Thornton Hunt (son of Leigh Hunt) – divorce was impossible because he had condoned her infidelity. After Lewes's death she married (1880) New York banker John Walter Cross, her financial adviser and 20 years her junior. She practised contraception and decided not to have children.

Appearance: With an over-large head, light-brown hair, grey-blue eyes, a fair complexion and a long nose, she had a 'strong masculine face' according to Emily Tennyson, while Edmund Gosse spoke of 'a large, thick-set sibyl . . . massive features, somewhat grim'. Henry James called her: 'Magnificently ugly – deliciously hideous . . . this great horse-faced blue-stocking.' She had a deep voice and her right hand was longer than her left. She always wore a black lace mantilla indoors.

Habits/Mannerisms: Clumsy. She kept a

20-inch cast of Thorvaldsen's risen Christ in her study.

Sport/Hobbies: Eliot enjoyed tennis and shuttlecock. She was also a good pianist and fluent in German. Another interest was phrenology (she had a phrenological cast made of her head).

Religion/Politics: Very religious.

Health: Eliot suffered from neuralgia and kidney stones.

Temperament: Variously called Polly (by Lewes), Pollian, Minie and Marianne, Eliot referred to herself as Clematis ('Mental Beauty' in the language of flowers) in her childhood correspondence. Many found her pompous and self-important and she courted controversy as an advocate of free love, but her friendship was highly regarded by, among others, Herbert Spencer (through whom she met Lewes), Franz Liszt, George du Maurier, Robert Browning, T. H. Huxley, Henry James, Turgenev, Trollope and Hilaire Belloc's mother, Bessie Parkes.

Pets: Eliot kept a pug dog, called simply 'Pug', a gift from her publisher John Blackwood in 1859 after she remarked: 'I wish some nobleman would admire *Adam Bede* enough to send me a Pug.' Blackwood took the hint, confiding: '*Adam Bede* flourishes, so I grins and bears it!' Pug was cherished by the author, who described him as 'without envy, hatred, or malice', unlike some of her human friends. When the dog died after 18 months Blackwood sent her a china pug as a memento. She also had a bull-terrier, Ben, and a dark brown spaniel called Dash. She was very frightened of horses.

Work/Daily Routine: Eliot's first published work was a religious poem (1840) and she did not start writing fiction until 'a storm-tried matron of 37' (in Edmund Gosse's words). She chose George as her pseudonym because that was Lewes's Christian name and Eliot because it was a 'good mouth-filling, easily-pronounced word'. The only book to feature her real name was a translation of Feuerbach's *Essence of Christianity* (1854). *Adam Bede* was admired by Queen Victoria (who wrote in her *Journal* in 1859: 'It has made a deep impression on me. Albert likes and is much interested'), as was *The Mill on the Floss*. She, in her turn, admired Wordsworth and Scott. Free copies of her first book of fiction, *Scenes from Clerical Life*, were sent to such celebrities as Thackeray, Tennyson, Ruskin, Faraday and Mrs Carlyle but only Dickens guessed it was written by a woman: 'If they originated with no woman, I believe that no man ever before had the art of making himself mentally so like a woman since the world began.' Eliot vehemently denied she was the writer but was driven to admit authorship when a man named Joseph Liggins was identified as 'George Eliot' by a psychic medium: Liggins accepted his new-found fame and set about capitalizing on it with a subscription until the truth emerged. Several of Eliot's closest friends were astounded when they learned she was the author, prompting her to remark in her journal: 'This experience has enlightened me a good deal as to the ignorance in which we live of each other.'

Manner of Death: Eliot caught a cold at a London concert and died of a sore throat and kidney infection at 4 Cheyne Walk, Chelsea, at 10 pm on 22 December 1880, aged 61. The Bible and Thomas à Kempis's *De Imitatione Christi* lay on her bedside table. She was buried with Unitarian rites next to Lewes in Highgate Cemetery, London.

ELIZABETH I (1533–1603) Queen of England, Wales and Ireland

Elizabeth I was born at Greenwich Palace, London, on 7 September 1533, the only child of Henry VIII by his second wife Anne Boleyn (beheaded for adultery when Elizabeth was three). She had an older half-sister Mary I (by Henry's marriage to Katherine of Aragon) and a younger half-brother Edward VI (by her father's marriage to Jane Seymour) and was brought up at Hatfield House, Hertfordshire. Well-educated and with a powerful intellect, she knew Latin and French and was taught Italian by Castiglione. Declared illegitimate on her father's third marriage, she came to the throne in 1558 after the short reigns and deaths successively of Edward VI (aged 16), Lady Jane Grey (aged 17) and Mary I (aged 43), the last of whom had Elizabeth locked up in the Tower of London because of her Anglicanism. Elizabeth was crowned queen in preference to Mary Queen of Scots, the legitimate daughter of James V of Scotland, and lived at Richmond Palace. In 1586 she survived the Babington Plot to assassinate her and to put Mary Queen of Scots on the throne and responded by repressing Catholicism and by executing Mary. A strong ruler, she only called Parliament together 13 times in her 44-year reign. Among the many memorable events that occurred during her reign were the defeat of the Spanish Armada (1588) and the development of trade and exploration in the New World.

Family/Sex Life: As a teenager Elizabeth spurned advances by her uncle Sir Thomas Seymour (her stepmother's brother, executed for treason) and later by Henry of Navarre (she once kissed him on the lips in front of witnesses) and Philip II of Spain. Though known as the 'Virgin Queen' she had her favourites. These included Robert Dudley, Earl of Leicester ('sweet Robin'), whose wife Amy Robsart later died in suspicious circumstances; the smallpox-scarred, double-nosed, dwarfish, frog-like Francis Duc d'Alençon (her *'petite grenouille'*); and the popular young general Robert Devereux, 2nd Earl of Essex, who defeated the Spanish at Cadiz. At an early stage of her romance with Essex, Elizabeth presented him with a ring, saying that if he ever caused her offence he had only to return it to her and all would be forgiven: when she signed his death warrant in 1601, for insurrection, he duly sent the ring to her, but it was intercepted by an enemy and never arrived – Essex was executed. It was said that subsequently Elizabeth wept whenever his name was mentioned. She had no legitimate issue but was said to be mother of Arthur Dudley, Leicester's son.

Appearance: 'A little over middle height' with reddish-gold hair, hazel eyes and a slightly hooked nose, her looks were marred by her black teeth (from eating too much sugar). She used a lot of white face powder, especially as she grew older, and had beautiful small hands with long fingers. The extravagance of her dress was legendary, and she passed a law preventing commoners from wearing ruffs.

Habits/Mannerisms: Elizabeth was very coarse – according to the *Dictionary of National Biography*: 'she swore, she spat upon a courtier's coat when it did not please her taste, she beat her gentlewomen soundly, she kissed whom she pleased, she gave Essex a good stinging blow on the face, she called the members of her privy council by all sorts of nicknames'. She drank beer for breakfast. In matters of hygiene, she had her palace at Richmond fitted out with an early lavatory and took a bath at least once a month.

Sport/Hobbies: Elizabeth liked hunting

and enjoyed court masques. She spoke French and Italian, translated Horace, Plutarch, Boethius and Sallust, wrote poetry and was patron to such poets as Spenser and Ralegh to whom she was known as 'Cynthia' (the Virgin Moon goddess) or 'Gloriana'. She played musical instruments well but had no taste for pictorial art. She was also interested in astrology and consulted the sorcerer Dr John Dee for the most propitious date for her coronation. She never visited Ireland, Scotland or Wales and never crossed the Channel.

Religion/Politics: Elizabeth was baptized a Catholic but was later Church of England and prohibited the saying of Mass (she was excommunicated by Pope Pius V). At her coronation a wicker effigy of the Pope, filled with cats, was burned at the height of the ceremony.

Health: Elizabeth enjoyed good health, though she suffered occasional fevers and contracted near-fatal smallpox in 1562 (she is reputed to have wiped her own urine on her face to cure it – and survived unscarred).

Temperament: Proud and conscious of her own importance, Elizabeth resented the ravages of old age and destroyed all the mirrors at her palace so that she could not see her reflection. When she began to lose her hair she wore a red wig. She had a ready wit but was reluctant to part with money. On one occasion, Valentine Dale, a diplomat in Flanders, ran short of money and wrote two letters, one to the queen asking for funds and another, full of terms of endearment and mentioning his money worries only in passing, to his wife – the letters got mixed up and the queen was vastly amused to find herself addressed as 'sweetheart' and 'dear love' in the letter meant for Dale's wife. Touched by Dale's lines, she ordered money to be sent at once (little suspecting that he had engineered the mix-up to catch her attention). Her motto was: '*Semper eaden*' ('Always the same'), later used by Queen Anne.

Manner of Death: Elizabeth caught a cold in January 1603 and collapsed on 20 March. She lost the power of speech on 23 March and died at Richmond Palace around 1.30 am on Thursday 24 March 1603, aged 69, the last of the Tudors and the oldest (though not the longest) reigning English sovereign. She was buried in Westminster Abbey beside her half-sister Mary.

EVELYN, John (1620–1706) English diarist, horticulturalist and civil servant

John Evelyn was born at 2.20 am on Tuesday 31 October 1620 in Wotton, Surrey, the second son and fourth child of Richard Evelyn, a wealthy landowner and Sheriff for Sussex and Surrey, and Eleanor Stansfield, an heiress who died when he was 14 (1635). His grandfather, George Evelyn, was an armaments magnate who introduced the manufacture of gunpowder to Britain. He had an elder brother, George, who inherited the family estate at Wotton, a younger brother Richard and two elder sisters. Brought up by his maternal grandparents in Lewes, Sussex, from the age of four to avoid the Plague in London, he remained there until the age of 16, attending the school at Southover. In 1637 he went up to Balliol College, Oxford, but left without a degree, and later studied law at the Middle Temple, London. His father died when he was 19 and during the Civil War he served with the Royalists very briefly before touring Europe with the poet Edmund Waller and studying medicine at the famous medical school in the University of Padua (1645).

He returned to England in 1652 and after the Restoration served on a number of Royal Commissions for Charles II (for instance, on those for Hackney Carriages, the Mint, Sick and Wounded Mariners, the Council for Forest Plantations and the Supply of Saltpetre). He was also appointed Latin Secretary to the King and Treasurer of Chelsea Hospital. As a writer he was best known in his lifetime as the author of *Sylva, or a Discourse of Forest Trees* – written at the request of the Royal Society – and for the *Halendarium Hartense*, as his celebrated diaries were not published until 1818. However, it was the success of Evelyn's diaries that led to the translation and publication of Pepys's diaries. His 18-room mansion, Sayes Court, Deptford, was formerly the property of his wife's maternal uncle and at the age of 79 he inherited the 7500-acre family estate at Wotton, Surrey, when his elder brother died. He declined a knighthood.

Family/Sex Life: In 1647 Evelyn married Mary Browne, the 12-year-old daughter of Sir Richard Browne, (Royalist) British Ambassador to France. Their children were Richard (who died young), John, George, Richard, Mary, Elizabeth and Susanna.

Appearance: Clean-shaven.

Habits/Mannerisms: Evelyn rinsed his hair once a year with warm water and sweet herbs (it was then unusual to wash at all). He was also one of the first people to carry an umbrella to shield himself from the sun, buying one in Marseilles in 1644.

Sport/Hobbies: Evelyn was an expert gardener and an authority and writer on landscape gardening. He could read French and Italian well, wrote poetry and was a founder member of the Royal Society. He sometimes attended the theatre, but reflected the tastes of his time when he commented of a Shakespearean production: 'I saw *Hamlet Prince of*

Denmark played, but now the old plays begin to disgust this refined age.'

Religion/Politics: Anglican. In politics he was a Tory/Royalist.

Health: Evelyn contracted smallpox in Geneva and was struck by 'quartan ague' (malaria) while at Balliol (1638). He also suffered from a festered hand (1645) and was treated by the physician of the late King Gustavus Adolphus of Sweden (1646). Other ailments included piles, scurvy, kidney and gravel disorders in old age as well as strangury (painful expulsion of urine).

Temperament: Serious and religious-minded. He was also generous, once letting his fine house at Sayes Court to Admiral Benbow who sublet it to Tsar Peter the Great of Russia (whose retinue wrecked it and the gardens). His friends included fellow-diarist Samuel Pepys.

Pets: Evelyn owned a black horse and while in Rome acquired a spaniel (later stolen).

Work/Daily Routine: Evelyn started his famous *Diary* at the age of 11. In comparison to Pepys's diary, which covers nine years from 1660 to 1669, Evelyn's diary spanned the years 1620–1706. Unlike Pepys, who wrote his diary on a daily basis, Evelyn appears not to have written entries day by day but rather at intervals, often some time after the events described took place, and also made some attempt to edit old entries. The fact that it remained unpublished until 1818 was due to the lack of importance given to it by his own family (many of his letters had already been burned). In all he wrote some 30 books and also translated Lucretius.

Manner of Death: Evelyn died on 27 February 1706 at his winter home in Dover Street, London. He was buried at Wotton Church, Surrey.

FIELDING, Henry (1707–54) English novelist and playwright

Henry Fielding was born in Sharpham Park, near Glastonbury, Somerset, on 22 April 1707, the son of Lieutenant-General Edmund Fielding (grandson of the Earl of Desmond) and Sarah Gould, daughter of Sir Henry Gould, a judge on the King's Bench. He had a brother Edmund and five sisters Catherine, Ursula, Anne, Beatrice and Sarah (who also became a novelist). His mother died when he was 11 years old, and he subsequently acquired six half-brothers by his father's second marriage to Elizabeth Rasa, one of whom was the famous blind magistrate, Sir John Fielding, 'the Blind Beak' who once sentenced Casanova to a term of imprisonment. Lady Mary Wortley Montagu was his second cousin. After education at Eton (with Fox, Pitt and Lord Camden), where he was very happy, he studied law at Leiden University (1728–30) and later at the Middle Temple, London. As manager of the New Theatre in the Haymarket, London, he established a reputation first as a writer of theatrical comedies with a sharp satirical and often controversial edge. After his theatre was closed under the Licensing Act of 1737 he had to give up his stage career and took up the law once more, being called to the Bar in 1740 and in due course becoming Justice of the Peace for Westminster, then for the whole of Middlesex from his court in Bow Street, Covent Garden (though ill health often disrupted his work in the courts). After publishing *Joseph Andrews* (1742), a parody of Samuel Richardson's hugely popular *Pamela* (1740), he confirmed his standing as one of the first masters of the English novel with *The History of Tom Jones, A Foundling* (1749). Other novels included *Amelia* (1752).

Family/Sex Life: Having failed to elope with a beautiful heiress at 19, in 1734 Fielding married Charlotte Cradock (despite Fielding's contention that there is 'one fool at least in every married couple' the marriage was very happy and Charlotte provided the model for Sophia in *Tom Jones* and also for the central character in *Amelia*). To Fielding's distress she died in 1744, leaving a daughter, Eleanor Harriet. In 1747 he took as his second wife his wife's former maid Mary Daniel, a marriage which caused a considerable scandal. Children of this second marriage were William, Mary Amelia, Sophia, Louisa and Allen.

Appearance: Thackeray, in *The English Humorists*, described the six-foot tall Fielding as 'Tall and stalwart; his face handsome, manly and noble-looking.' He was popularly known as 'Handsome Harry Fielding'. His portrait was painted by his friend Hogarth.

Habits/Mannerisms: Other branches of the novelist's family spelt their name 'Feilding' – a difference of opinion that Fielding could only explain by suggesting that it was his own branch that first learned how to spell. He enjoyed smoking and drinking champagne.

Religion/Politics: Fielding was a committed supporter of the Whig Party and attacked a range of political and religious targets, especially electioneering abuses, in his plays. His *Historical Register for 1736* proved the final straw for the government of Sir Robert Walpole and led to censorship under the Lord Chamberlain the following year.

Health: He suffered from gout and asthma and in later years had to walk with the aid of crutches.

Temperament: Energetic, determined, industrious and quick-witted, Fielding is thought to have used himself as a model for Captain Billy Booth in *Amelia* (his own favourite among his writings). He was admired by Swift and Hogarth. Fielding disliked Poet Laureate Colly Cibber and (using the pseudonym Captain Hercules Vinegar) once summoned him to court for the murder of the English language (1740). Among his closest friends was the actor David Garrick.

Work/Daily Routine: Fielding started out as a playwright, but withdrew from the stage after the Lord Chamberlain was brought in to license plays. He was paid £700 for his novel *Tom Jones*, which Gibbons dubbed 'that exquisite of human manners' (though it was disliked by Richardson, Smollett and Dr Johnson). The model for Squire Allworthy in *Tom Jones* was George 1st Baron Lyttleton, Fielding's patron to whom the book was dedicated, combined with Ralph Allen, the so-called 'Man of Bath', who was famed for his charity (typically, he provided for Fielding's widow and children after the author's death). Many other characters were drawn from people brought before him in his capacity as a justice of the peace (he was also one of the founders of the famous Bow Street Runners police force). He seems to have been conscious that he had inaugurated a major new school of novel-writing, commenting in the preface to *Joseph Andrews* on 'this kind of writing, which I do not remember to have seen hitherto attempted in our language'.

Manner of Death: Fielding travelled to Lisbon for the sake of his health, but died there on 8 October 1754, aged 47. He was buried in the English Protestant cemetery in Lisbon. His grave bears the Latin inscription:

Henricus Fielding
Luget Britannia Non Datum
Fovere Natum.

FITZGERALD, Francis Scott Key (1896–1940) US novelist

F. Scott Fitzgerald was born in a rented apartment at 481 Laurel Avenue, St Paul, Minnesota, on 24 September 1896, the son of Edward Fitzgerald, owner of a wicker furniture business and later a soap salesman for Procter & Gamble, and Mollie McQuillan, daughter of a wealthy grocer. He had two elder sisters, Mary and Louise, who died before he was born, and a surviving younger sister, Annabel (who married Admiral Sprague). Named after a distant relative (the brother of his great-great-grandfather), Francis Scott Key, who wrote the 'The Star-Spangled Banner', he was educated at the St Paul Academy, then at the Newman School in Hackensack, New Jersey. A legacy of $125,000 allowed him to go to Princeton University (with Edgar Allan Poe Jr, Edmund Wilson and his future publisher, Charles Scribner) but he did not take a degree. In World War I he served in the US Army (1917–19) but was not posted overseas. He worked at first for the Barron Collier advertising agency in New York, writing advertisements for streetcars (for instance, 'We keep you clean in Muscatine' for a steam laundry in Iowa), before becoming instantly famous with *This Side of Paradise* at the age of 23 and moving to the French Riviera (1924). A prominent spokesman for the 'Jazz Age' of the 1920s, his later novels included *The Beautiful and the Damned* (1922), *The Great Gatsby* (1925) and *Tender is the Night* (1934). He returned to Hollywood in 1937.

Family/Sex Life: In 1920 Fitzgerald married 20-year-old Zelda Sayre, daughter of a judge in the Alabama Supreme Court and from a family that had a history of mental illness (she was declared insane by the age of 29). They had a daughter, Frances Scott. He also had adulterous affairs with Dorothy Parker (1934), Mrs Beatrice Stribling Dance (1935), Joyce Grenfell's mother Mrs Nora Flynn (younger sister of Nancy Astor), English actress Rosalinde Fuller, Hollywood gossip columnist Sheilah Graham, actress Lois Moran and Bijou O'Conor (daughter of Sir Francis Elliot and granddaughter of the 2nd Earl of Minto). He also visited prostitutes when at Princeton (1917). In particular, he had a fetish about women's feet.

Appearance: At five feet eight inches and 140 lb (the same as Edgar Allan Poe), 'Fitzgerald was pretty. He had a mouth that troubled you when you first met him, and troubled you more later', according to Ernest Hemingway. Edmund Wilson remarked on his 'pale skin, hard green eyes and yellow hair'. He was slightly pigeon-toed and was shy about his feet.

Habits/Mannerisms: Fitzgerald was notorious for his alcoholism and became drunk very quickly ('My stories written when sober are stupid'). He once observed: 'First you take a drink, then the drink takes a drink, then the drink takes you.' He drank gin and beer, but later gave up and developed a craving for sweets, consuming fudge and Coca-Cola. He also owned a Rolls-Royce.

Sport/Hobbies: He collected stamps and cigar bands as a child. At Princeton he once carried the port into the dining-room for guest of honour John Galsworthy.

Religion/Politics: Non-practising Roman Catholic.

Health: Fitzgerald was an insomniac and was addicted to barbiturates (he took chloral and Nembutal to sleep and benzedrine to wake up). He suffered from tuberculosis and malaria, fractured his right shoulder in a high dive (1928), had heart attacks (1940) and experienced the effects of hypoglycemia (lack of sugar in the blood). He attempted suicide by morphine overdose but vomited it up.

Temperament: Hedonistic and self-destructive, he and Zelda Sayre epitomized the spirit of the age. Cautioned by concerned friends about their habit of diving 35 feet into the sea from the cliffs of the Riviera, for instance, Zelda declared: 'We don't believe in conservation.' Fitzgerald himself admitted: 'Sometimes I don't know whether Zelda and I are real or whether we are characters in one of my novels.' Friends included Ring Lardner, Dos Passos and Ernest Hemingway.

Work/Daily Routine: Fitzgerald's first novel, *This Side of Paradise* (originally *The Romantic Egoist*) sold 20,000 copies in the first week – though critic Franklin Pierce Adams found over 100 spelling and grammatical errors in it. Later, he was one of 15 scriptwriters on *Gone With the Wind*. He wrote *The Last Tycoon* in bed (it was unfinished at his death). Rosemary Hoyt in *Tender is the Night* was based on Lois Moran, while Kathleen Moore in *The Last Tycoon* was based on Sheilah Graham and Boxley on Aldous Huxley. Jay Gatsby, it is thought, was modelled on a neighbour on Long Island, New York, bootlegger Max Gerlack, and on socialite and fraudster Edward M. Fuller. He greatly admired Galsworthy, Conrad and Anatole France.

Manner of Death: Having moved out of his own flat after an earlier heart attack prevented him climbing stairs, Fitzgerald died of a further attack at 3 pm in the ground-floor apartment of Sheilah Graham at 1443 North Hayworth Avenue, Los Angeles, on 21 December 1940, aged 44. Reputedly no one came to the funeral and no flowers were sent, but actually there were 20 people at the Episcopal service. He was buried in the Rockville Union Cemetery, but was moved (1975) to St

Mary's Church. His gravestone (shared with Zelda) reads: 'So we beat on, boats against the current, borne back ceaselessly into the past' (the last line of *The Great Gatsby*).

FLAUBERT, Gustave (1821–80) French novelist

Gustave Flaubert was born in Rouen on 12 December 1821, the son of Dr Achille Cléophas Flaubert, respected chief surgeon and head of the Hôtel-Dieu (Hospital), Rouen – in which the family lived – and Anne Justine Caroline Fleuriot. He had an older brother Achille and a younger sister Caroline. Educated at the Collège Royal, Rouen, he was expelled aged 18 and studied law in Paris but had the first of many epileptic fits just before his finals and did not qualify. After his father died (1846), he lived with his mother (until she died in 1872) and when his sister died took responsibility for her daughter and her daughter's husband, Ernest. However, he was soon bankrupted by Ernest's debts and had to take a government post to pay off his creditors. In the Franco-Prussian War (1870–1) he served as a lieutenant and was awarded the Légion d'honneur. Flaubert's masterpiece was *Madame Bovary* (1857), on the themes of adultery and suicide, which led to a scandal and to the author and his publisher and printer being prosecuted for immorality (they were acquitted). Other important works included *Salammbô* (1862), in which he recreated ancient Carthage, *L'Éducation sentimentale* (1869), *La Tentation de St Antoine* (1874), which was 25 years in the writing, and *Trois contes* (1877), a collection of three short stories.

Family/Sex Life: Flaubert remained unmarried, but had several mistresses. These included the poet and novelist Mrs Louise Colet (1846–55) and two Englishwomen – Gertrude Collier, daughter of a British Naval attaché in Paris, and Mrs Eliza Schlesinger, who was married to a publisher and was 11 years Flaubert's senior. He did not want children.

Appearance: At five feet, 11¼ inches, Flaubert was good looking, with large sea-green eyes, black eyebrows, white skin, full lips and long and slightly curly hair (though he began to lose his hair prematurely from the age of 29). He sported a drooping moustache until 29 then adopted a blond beard. He had a resounding voice. At home he wore trousers held up by a silk cord around the waist, a dressing-gown (brown in winter, white in summer) and a small silk skull-cap.

Habits/Mannerisms: Flaubert smoked a pipe and cigars and also liked very hot baths.

Sport/Hobbies: Swimming, canoeing, riding.

Religion/Politics: He disliked socialists.

Health: Flaubert suffered from epilepsy for many years. His father spilt boiling water on his right hand as a boy (1844), leading to partial paralysis and a permanent scar. In 1850 he contracted syphilis and he subsequently suffered a bad attack of mercury poisoning while trying to treat it (1854).

Temperament: Flaubert had no illusions about his creations, confiding in a letter to Ernest Feydeau in 1857: 'Books are made not like children but like pyramids ... and they're just as useless! and they stay in the desert! ... Jackals piss at their foot and the bourgeois climb up on them.' Flaubert's friends included Victor Hugo, Maupassant (who was Flaubert's protégé), George Sand and Turgenev (who dedicated *A Song of Triumphant Love* to him).

Work/Daily Routine: Flaubert's first published work was a short story in *Le Colibri* magazine (1836). He worked from mid-day to 4 pm, smoking 15 pipefuls of tobacco. *Madame Bovary* caused an immense scandal on publication – it was banned by the Vatican in 1864 and was put on the Index of prohibited books (as was *Salammbô*). *Madame Bovary* was based partly on the real story of Delphine Delamare (1822–48) – a doctor's wife who committed suicide at the age of 24 – and partly on Flaubert's lover Louise Colet. The author himself, however, was apparently reluctant to confirm these identifications: when asked who the real Madame Bovary was, he confined himself to a wry smile and the reply: '*I am Madame Bovary.*' He greatly admired Voltaire (especially his book *Candide*) and kept a bust of Hippocrates and Callot's *Temptation of St Anthony* in his study (he also had an inkwell in the form of a toad). He disliked the addition of any illustrations to his books.

Manner of Death: After a sudden brain haemorrhage – probably the result of tertiary syphilis – Flaubert's face blackened and he lost consciousness at 10.30 am on 8 May 1880: he died at noon the same day. Maupassant stood vigil beside the body for three days. The novelist was buried in Rouen, with Daudet, Edmond de Goncourt and Zola all attending the funeral.

FORD, Henry (1863–1947) US motor manufacturer

Henry Ford was born in the morning of 30 July 1863 near Dearborn, Michigan, USA, the eldest surviving child of William Ford, a prosperous Irish immigrant farmer, railway carpenter and Justice of the Peace, and Mary Litogot, who died in childbirth when Henry was 12 (1876). He had three brothers, John, William Jr and Robert, and two sisters, Margaret and Jane. Educated in Dearborn from the age of seven, he left school at 16 and worked as an apprentice in the James Flower & Brothers machine shop in nearby Detroit (1879), the Flowers being friends of his father. A fellow apprentice was David Dunbar Buick who after a career in plumbing also built cars. Ford then worked for the Detroit Dry Dock Company before returning to his father's farm in 1882. Later (1891) he was mechanic-engineer at Edison Illuminating Company's substation in Detroit and took classes in mechanical drawing, book-keeping and business practice at Goldsmith, Bryant & Stratton Business University, Detroit. Whilst working for Edison he hand-built his first car, the Quadricycle (1896), which so impressed his father's friend, W. C. Maybury, Mayor of Detroit, that the mayor sponsored a second and encouraged backers (including Senator Palmer of Michigan) to fund the Detroit Automobile Company (1899) with a capital of $150,000. Ford made 12 vehicles before the company was declared bankrupt (1900) but managed to get the same backers to fund the Henry Ford Company (1901) when he made a car which beat the world record-holder Alexander Winton (who broke down) in a two-car 10-mile race at Grosse Pointe, Detroit. Sacked the following year for moonlighting, his backers renamed the company the Cadillac Automobile Company (1902) using Ford's designs but with a different engine – so effectively the first Cadillac was actually a Ford. Ford's later models (notably the Model T – the so-called Tin Lizzie 'available in any colour so long as it's black') were so successful that he even bought the prestigious Lincoln Motor Company in 1922. In 1916 he stood unsuccessfully for the US Senate. Awarded the Grand Cross of the German Order by Hitler – the highest award for foreigners (Lindbergh also received one) – in 1938, he also bought a railway, built aeroplanes, published a newspaper and built a hospital.

Family/Sex Life: In 1888 Ford married Clara Jane Bryant. After the birth of their son Edsel, Mrs Ford had a hysterectomy.

Appearance: Ford wore a moustache in his youth, and later had iron-grey hair.

Habits/Mannerisms: Ford was a food faddist – he said meat protein and starches should not be eaten at the same time and he was very keen on soya beans (he even experimented with suits and car panels made from them). He was teetotal and a non-smoker (he banned smoking in his factories but paid employees above the normal rate).

Sport/Hobbies: As a child, Ford enjoyed repairing watches. He was also a keen birdwatcher and a folk-dance enthusiast (he was a good dancer and had small dainty feet). He also had a daily massage, but was otherwise not much interested in physical activities, once declaring: 'Exercise is bunk. If you are healthy, you don't need it: if you are sick you shouldn't take it.' In 1924 he bought a Rolls-Royce Silver Ghost – on visiting a friend in it he declared: 'My Ford was being serviced, so I came in the next best thing!' (he conceded: 'Royce was the only man to put heart into an automobile').

Religion/Politics: Irish Protestant by upbringing, Ford was a Freemason (as was his father). In politics he supported Wilson and was a fervent pacifist – he had a dispute with F. D. Roosevelt over the use of the Ford Company for war production and dispatched a 'Peace Ship' to Europe in the early stages of World War I. He was also anti-Semitic and kept a photo of Hitler on his desk (he was the only American cited in *Mein Kampf* and Hitler was influenced by his writings on anti-Semitism).

Health: Ford had a hernia operation in 1932 and suffered strokes in 1938 and 1941.

Work/Daily Routine: Ford's Quadricycle (1896) was steered by a tiller and could reach 20 mph (then fast). It was built in a shed that had to be demolished to get it out. The first Cadillac was cheaper than the Model T Ford ($750 and $875 respectively in 1903) and contrary to popular belief the world's first low-price car produced in quantity was an Oldsmobile not a Ford. Marianne Moore was hired to name a new Ford in 1955 – when she came up with 'Utopian Turtletop' Ford chose 'Edsel' instead. Bonnie and Clyde, the notorious gun-toting duo, drove a Ford V-8.

Motto/Sayings: 'History is more or less bunk' (said at a libel case against the *Chicago Tribune*, 25 May 1916).

Manner of Death: Ford died at his home, Fair Lane (originally designed by Frank Lloyd Wright's office), in the woods near Dearborn, on 7 April 1947, aged 83. 100,000 people came to see his body lying in state before his funeral at St Paul's Episcopal Cathedral, Detroit. All traffic in Detroit stopped for a minute in respect to him (though it was noted that his hearse was a Packard, not a Ford).

FORSTER, Edward Morgan (1879–1970)
English novelist, short-story writer and critic

E. M. Forster was born in London on 1 January 1879 the only child of Edward Morgan Llewellyn Forster, an architect (who died of tuberculosis before his son was aged two), and Alice Clara ('Lily') Whichelo. His uncle John Whichelo was Marine Painter to the Prince Regent (and painted the famous last portrait of Nelson) and Forster was also related to Sir Lennox Napier Bart, the Earl of Leven and Melville, the Thornton banking family (patrons of Cowper) and William Wilberforce. In addition his aunt Lara Forster was a friend of Hope Wedgwood (wife of the head of the pottery firm), of the sons of Charles Darwin and of Leslie Stephens's sister Caroline. Accidentally christened Edward at Holy Trinity Church, Clapham Common, his birth was actually registered as Henry Morgan Forster. He was educated at Kent House School, Eastbourne, at Tonbridge School and at King's College, Cambridge (Second Class Honours in Classics) when M. R. James was Dean. At first a freelance journalist for the *Independent Review* and others, he published his first novel, *Where Angels Fear to Tread*, in 1905 and by the time *Howard's End* appeared in 1910 was recognized as a major literary figure. A pacifist, he worked for the Red Cross in Alexandria, Egypt, in World War I, and was briefly (six months in 1921) secretary to the Maharajah of Dewas Senior. He stopped writing novels after *A Passage to India* (1924) but lived for a further 46 years. Made an Honorary Fellow of King's College, Cambridge (1946) and a Companion of Honour (1953), he was awarded the Order of Merit (1969) and became the first President of the National Council for Civil Liberties, campaigning against censorship (he testified, for example, in the 'Lady Chatterley' trial of 1960).

Family/Sex Life: Forster was a homosexual and from 1906 had a 17-year affair with his student the wealthy Muslim patriot Syed Ross Masood, grandson of Sir Syed Ahmed Khan (the most influential Muslim in India). It was to him that *A Passage to India* was dedicated. *Maurice*, his novel directly tackling the controversial theme of homosexuality, was published posthumously in 1971. He lived mostly with his mother, who called him Morgan rather than Edward.

Appearance: Forster was very pale and delicate, though large and plump, and had a long reddish nose. Christopher Isherwood wrote of his 'straggly straw moustache ... light gray blue baby-eyes ... elderly stoop'. He usually wore steel-rimmed glasses and a tweed cap.

Habits/Mannerisms: As a child, the young Forster played with dolls, while his favourite book in his youth was *Swiss Family Robinson*. As an adult, he had a habit of standing on one leg and winding the other around it. He was abstemious in most things, but was very fond of trees.

Sport/Hobbies: A good pianist, Forster wrote in *Howard's End* that: 'Beethoven's Fifth Symphony is the most sublime noise that has ever penetrated into the ear of man.' He also enjoyed otter-hunting. He recorded his life in a detailed diary.

Religion/Politics: Agnostic. As a pacifist, he once claimed: '... if I had to choose between betraying my country and betraying my friends, I hope I should have the guts to betray my country' ('What I Believe', *Nation*, 1938).

Health: Forster had a bladder disorder (he underwent two prostate operations) and also sustained a broken ankle (1951) and suffered two strokes (1964).

Temperament: Forster was very shy. In his 'Notes on the English Character' from *Abinger Harvest* he observed of the English temperament: 'It is not that the Englishman can't feel – it is that he is afraid to feel. He has been taught at his public school that feeling is bad form. He must not express great joy or sorrow, or even open his mouth too wide when he talks – his pipe might fall out if he did.' His friends included such notables as Christopher Isherwood, Bertrand Russell, D. H. Lawrence, Virginia Woolf and T. E. Lawrence.

Work/Daily Routine: Forster often drew on his own experience in his novels – the house in *Howard's End* , for instance, was

based on his own childhood memories of Rooksnest, Stevenage, where he spent the years 1883–93. Forster gave up novel-writing after just six books though he continued to involve himself in a range of literary projects, among them literary biographies and the libretto for Britten's *Billy Budd* (1949–51). He included amongst those who had influenced him the most the philosopher G. E. Moore.

Motto/Saying: 'Only connect!' (epigraph to *Howard's End*).

Manner of Death: Forster suffered a stroke at King's College, Cambridge, on 22 May 1970, and at his request was taken on 2 June to the house of his friends the Buckinghams in Coventry. He died there early in the morning of 7 June 1970, aged 91.

FRANKLIN, Benjamin (1706–90) US statesman and scientist

Benjamin Franklin was born on 17 January 1706 in Milk Street, Boston, Massachusetts, the son of Josiah Franklin, a manufacturer of soaps and candles, and Abiah Folger, his second wife. Benjamin was the youngest son of a youngest son for five generations and was Josiah's 10th son and 15th child (there were 17 children in all, seven by the first marriage; Benjamin was the eighth of Abiah's 10). Educated at Boston Grammar School until the age of 10, he worked at first for his father. Apprenticed at the age of 12 to his half-brother James, a Boston printer and publisher of the *New England Courant* newspaper, he travelled to Philadelphia and London (1724–6) before returning to Boston. He bought the *Pennsylvania Gazette* (1729) and gained wide fame as publisher (and writer) of the immensely popular *Poor Richard's Almanac* (annual, 1732–57). He was not, incidentally, the founder of the *Saturday Evening Post*

(though this statement appeared on its masthead for many years). He later became Postmaster of Philadelphia and set up the first postal service in the USA. One of the signatories of the US Declaration of Independence in 1776 (he liaised between England and America and won British recognition of the new republic in 1783), he was later the first US ambassador to France, a Member of Congress and twice served as President of Pennsylvania. He retired from public life after participating in the Federal Constitutional Convention of 1787. As a scientist, he invented the lightning conductor and bifocal spectacles.

Family/Sex Life: Though unmarried, Franklin fathered a son William and a daughter by an unidentified woman, and also had an illegitimate son Francis Folger and a daughter Sarah by Mrs Deborah Rogers (née Read), daughter of his landlady and abandoned by her husband. In the early 1770s he considered marriage to the widow of the philosopher Helvétius.

Appearance: Franklin did not powder his hair with flour as was the fashion but wore it naturally. He carried a gold-topped bamboo cane and wore a beaver cap when ambassador in Paris (where he was known as 'l'ambassadeur électrique').

Habits/Mannerisms: Franklin did not drink alcohol and was mostly vegetarian. He thought it health-giving to take deep breaths in front of an open window, naked, every morning ('fresh air baths').

Sport/Hobbies: A very strong swimmer, Franklin once swam the Thames from Chelsea to Blackfriars (three miles). He also played chess, taught himself French, Spanish, Italian and Latin and was the first US political cartoonist.

Health: Franklin used opium as a pain-killer against discomfort caused by a stone in his bladder.

Work/Daily Routine: Franklin first published under the pseudonym Mrs Silence Dogood – contributing 14 essays in his half-brother's paper the *New England Courant*. Other pseudonyms included Proteus Echo, Richard Saunders ('Poor Richard'), Philomath, Father Abraham, Anthony Afterwit and The Busybody. *Poor Richard's Almanac* made him a household name – it was translated into 15 languages. Less well-known inventions of his included the rocking-chair, the Franklin stove, the water-powered harmonium and daylight saving. His most celebrated experiment was his flying of a kite during a thunderstorm while studying the nature of lightning (a highly dangerous activity that could easily have cost him his life). He also set up the first circulating library in America, discovered the Gulf Stream and coined the word 'harmonica'. He reputedly did a lot of reading and correspondence in his bathtub. Reading was a special pleasure to him – when he was asked to give his definition of the kind of man most deserving of pity, he suggested: 'A lonesome man on a rainy day who does not know how to read.' He did have his detractors, however: D. H. Lawrence hated 'middle-sized, sturdy, snuff-coloured Doctor Franklin', claiming he threatened to take away 'my dark forest, my freedom'.

Mottoes/Sayings: 'God helps those who help themselves.' Other aphorisms that he invented included his advice to the aspiring tradesman: 'Remember that time is money.' On signing the Declaration of Independence in 1776 he confirmed the need for unity with the memorable reminder: 'We must indeed all hang together, or most assuredly, we shall all hang separately.'

Manner of Death: Franklin died on 17 April 1790 in Philadelphia, aged 84. He was buried at the Christ Church Burial Ground, Philadelphia, around 20,000 people attending the funeral. On his death the French Assembly went into mourning for three days. He wrote his own epitaph (aged 22): 'The Body of B. Franklin, Printer; Like the Cover of an old Book, Its contents torn out, And stript of its Lettering and Gilding, Lies here, food for Worms. But the Work shall not be wholly lost: For it will, as he believed, appear once more, In a new and more perfect Edition, Corrected and amended by the Author.'

FREDERICK II 'The Great' (1712–86) King of Prussia

Frederick the Great was born on 24 January 1712, the oldest son of 10 surviving children of Frederick William I of Prussia and Sophia Dorothea of Hanover (daughter of George I of England). His grandfather (Frederick I) was the first King of Prussia and the family (Hohenzollern) claimed descent from one of Charlemagne's generals. He had an older sister Frederica Wilhelmina and other siblings were Augustus William, Ferdinand, Henry, Ulrika (Queen of Sweden) and Amalia. Educated by private tutors, his father forbade him to study Latin or ancient history. Kicked and caned in public by his father as a child, he later ran away from the Prussian court at Königsberg. When caught he was arrested, deprived of the title Crown Prince, court-martialled and imprisoned, and his friend Royal Guards Lieutenant Hans von Katte was beheaded in front of him in an attempt to make him less frivolous. In the war against Louis XV of France he served with the legendary Prince Eugene in Holy Roman Emperor Charles VI's forces. He became king on his father's death (1740) and held court at first at Charlottenburg Palace, Berlin (capital of Brandenburg and Prussia), and later lived in the specially built Sans Souci Palace, Potsdam, Berlin. He was a superb general and distinguished himself in the War of the Austrian Succession (1740–8) and during the Seven Years' War against France and Austria (1756–63). He doubled the size of Prussia and greatly increased its wealth before his death.

Family/Sex Life: In 1733 Frederick married Princess Elizabeth Christina of Brunswick, who was the niece of the Hapsburg Holy Roman Emperor Leopold I. He was also homosexual but kept the female Italian dancer Barbarina as his mistress.

Appearance: Small and clean-shaven with blue eyes, he wore a shabby uniform with tricorn hat and reddish unpolished boots.

Habits/Mannerisms: Frederick wrote and spoke entirely in French, despising German and refusing to keep German books in the library at Sans Souci. Only once, though, did he ever step foot on French soil (incognito, in Strasbourg in 1740). He disliked alcohol but drank cold coffee made with champagne instead of water. He enjoyed heavily spiced food and also took snuff (he was patron of snuff-box makers and collected snuff-boxes). At Sans Souci ('Free from Care') he maintained an all-male court (his sister Wilhelmina was the only woman allowed).

Sport/Hobbies: Frederick was an accomplished flautist (he composed symphonies and music for the flute) and also wrote (all in French) poetry, essays, 31 books and libretti for the Berlin Opera and for musical versions of Voltaire's plays *Montezuma* and *Mérope*. He thought little of Shakespeare and ignored Kant, Goethe, Lessing, Schiller and other contemporary German authors, but he liked Racine. He was keen on architecture ('buildings are my dolls') and collected paintings by Watteau, Pesne and Lancret. He was also a very good dancer.

Religion/Politics: Frederick was an agnostic and a Freemason, though his armies fought as Lutheran Protestants.

Health: Frederick was of a nervous disposition and was always bled before battles to calm his nerves. He was nearly murdered by his cook, who poisoned his drinking chocolate – he was saved when a spider fell in it (a spider was subsequently painted on the ceiling at Sans Souci). In 1740 he became very ill with fever and ague. On another occasion he was nearly killed when a bullet hit the snuff-box in his pocket (in 1758–9 he had three horses killed under him in battle). He also suffered from rheumatism, arthritis, gout, stomach pains and asthma.

Temperament: Known as Fritz to his family, Frederick had many friends, including Voltaire and D'Alembert. It was Voltaire who called him 'Solomon of the North' and first dubbed him 'Frederick the Great'. To his troops, he could be severe, in keeping with militaristic Prussian ideals. During a campaign in Silesia, he once ordered all lights to be extinguished in the camp but then discovered an officer writing a letter to his wife by candlelight: the officer was instructed to add the postscript 'Tomorrow I shall perish on the scaffold' and he was duly executed the following day. When Frederick's cavalry was forced to retreat at the battle of Kolin in 1757 he roared at them: 'Rogues! Cowards! Would you live for ever?'

Pets: Frederick kept female whippets at Sans Souci and also owned greyhounds and a camel.

Work/Daily Routine: Frederick got up at 5 am in the summer and 6 am in the winter and, before coming to the throne, read daily from first light till noon. An enlightened despot, he once announced: 'My people and I have come to an agreement which satisfies us both. They are to say what they please, and I am to do what I please.' His admirers included Bismarck, Kaiser Wilhelm II, Hitler and the historian Thomas Carlyle (who wrote his biography).

Manner of Death: Frederick caught a fever after inspecting troops in the rain in August 1785 and never threw it off. He died at Sans Souci, near Potsdam, a year later at 2.20 am on Thursday 17 August 1786, aged 74. He was buried in the family vault beneath the pulpit of the Garrison Church, Potsdam, beside his father (Frederick himself wished to be buried on the terrace of Sans Souci beside his dogs and favourite horse). Napoleon paid homage in 1806 as, later, did Hitler (the only picture on the wall of Hitler's underground bunker in Berlin was a portrait of Frederick).

FREUD, Sigmund (1856–1939) Austrian-born psychiatrist

Sigmund Freud was born on 6 May 1856 in Freiberg, Moravia (then part of the Austro-Hungarian empire), the son of Jakob Freud, a wool merchant, by his second wife (20 years younger than his father), Amalia Nathanson. The eldest of eight children by his mother, his brother Julius died in infancy, three of his sisters (Rosa, Mitzi and Paula) were gassed at Auschwitz and another sister, Dolfi, starved to death in Theresienstadt concentration camp. His other siblings were Alexander and Anna and he had two half-brothers, Emmanuel and Philipp. The family moved to Leipzig in 1859 and then in 1860 to Vienna, where Freud was educated at the Sperl Gymnasium from the age of nine. Precocious at school, he taught himself Italian and Spanish and kept a diary in Greek. He studied medicine at the University of Vienna (1873), then joined the Physiological Institute under Ernst Brücke (1876–82), where he studied neurophysiology, and qualified as a doctor aged 25. His studies were briefly interrupted by a year's compulsory service in the Austro-Hungarian Army (1879). After a short period teaching at the Institute he became a doctor in the Vienna General Hospital (1882) and in 1883 began work in the Psychiatry Clinic of Theodor Meynert, the leading brain anatomist of his day. Appointed lecturer in neuropathology at the University of Vienna (1885) as a result of his monograph on cocaine, with Brücke's help he studied under Jean Martin Charcot (the foremost neurologist in Europe) in Paris (1885–6). The inventor of psychoanalysis, he was awarded the Goethe Prize in 1930. He came to England in 1938 after Princess George of Greece (aunt of Elizabeth II) paid the Nazi government £20,000.

Family/Sex Life: Reputedly the victim of sexual abuse as a child, in 1886 Freud married Martha Bernays, granddaughter of the Chief Rabbi of Hamburg (her brother Eli had already married Freud's sister Anna). Their children were Martin (named after Charcot), Oliver, Ernst (named after Ernst Brücke), Sophie and Anna. His wife's sister lived with the family after 1896.

Appearance: Above middle height, with black hair, a thick but neat beard, Freud had, according to Hanns Sachs, 'deep set and piercing eyes and a finely shaped forehead, remarkably high at the temples'. Hilda Doolittle noted that 'his beautiful mouth seemed always slightly smiling'. He favoured well-cut suits of English cloth and always wore a black tie and wide-brimmed black hat.

Habits/Mannerisms: Freud smoked 20 cigars a day, even after developing cancer. He seemed unconcerned that, influenced by his own theories, his disciples might interpret his cigars as phallic symbols, remarking that: 'Sometimes a cigar is just a cigar.' He also took cocaine: 'It is the best stomachic after a debauch either in eating or drinking.' He was otherwise abstemious, rarely drinking wine, beer or spirits. He hated the telephone, rarely listened to the radio and only ever flew once.

Sport/Hobbies: Freud learned English and French as a schoolboy and became an Anglophile. He particularly admired Milton, Walter Scott and Byron. Pastimes included playing the Viennese card game tarock. He was also interested in archaeology and collected antiquities (he acquired a statuette from Tutankhamun's tomb), though not artefacts designed to kill.

Religion/Politics: Jewish but not orthodox (his wife was). He greatly admired Oliver Cromwell (who had welcomed Jews back into England) and named his second son after him.

Health: Freud was neurotic and suffered from mild hysteria. He also suffered from a bad heart, pain in his left shoulder, migraines, indigestion, constipation, agoraphobia and fear of trains and travel. He had 33 operations for cancer from 1923 and his right upper jaw and palate and part of his tongue had to be removed. He became nearly deaf in his right ear when the Eustachian tube was damaged in an operation.

Temperament: A pleasant man who was rarely angry with his children, Freud counted among his friends the ear, nose and throat specialist Wilhelm Fliess and Princess Marie Bonaparte (granddaughter of Napoleon's brother Lucien), whose book on her chow dog Topsy he translated from French into German. He did not always apply his theoretical principles to real life. On visiting the USA he once told Carl Jung that he was troubled with erotic dreams about US prostitutes – when Jung suggested he do something about it Freud, foremost expert on sexual repression, looked shocked and protested: 'But I'm a married man!'

Pets: Freud became fond of dogs in his old age, keeping Wolf (an Alsatian), Lun-Yu (a chow, unfortunately run over) and Jo-fi (a chow, who was present during analysis sessions and always got up and stretched when the patient's hour was up).

Work/Daily Routine: Freud's major work *The Interpretation of Dreams* (1899) took eight years to sell out (600 copies). He also wrote an outstanding paper on the nerve cells of crayfish (1882) before switching to psychiatry. He worked 12 hours daily: from 8 am to 1 pm he saw patients, then he took lunch (his main meal), walked through the city for two hours, saw patients between 3 and 9 pm, took supper, then wrote up his notes (he did not make notes during analysis sessions). Only at 65 did he stop for coffee at 5 pm. He was a fluent writer, rarely revising what he had written. He wrote in longhand, as he disliked typewriters.

Manner of Death: Freud died of cancer of the jaw and palate in Hampstead, London, on 23 September 1939.

GALILEI, Galileo (1564–1642) Italian astronomer and mathematician

Galileo Galilei was born in Pisa on 15 February 1564, the eldest child of Vincenzio Galilei, a lutenist, mathematician and writer on music, and Giulia Ammannati. His father's family were of noble birth and were originally named Bonajuti but changed to Galilei in 1343. He was named after Galileo Galilei, Professor of Medicine at the University of Florence and Chief Magistrate of the Florentine Republic (1445), whose brother was the great-grandfather of Vincenzio Galilei. His siblings (all younger) were Michaelangelo, Benedetto, Virginia (who married the Tuscan ambassador), Anna, Livia and Lena. Educated at the school of Jacopo Borghini in Pisa and at home, he studied humanities (aged 12) at the monastery of Vallombrosa, near Florence, leaving in 1579. He then studied medicine at the University of Pisa (1581–4) but became more interested in mathematics and left without a degree. In 1586 he invented the hydrostatic balance and after working as a private tutor was appointed, with the help of his patron, the Marquis Guidobaldo del Monte, Professor of Mathematics at the University of Pisa in 1589, aged 25. He resigned in 1592 when his gravity experiment – dropping a 1 lb and a 10 lb shot from the 179-feet-high Leaning Tower of Pisa – disproved Aristotle's theory (they hit the ground together) and became Professor of Mathematics at Padua University (where William Harvey was then a student). He was also maths tutor to Cosmo de' Medici (c. 1601) when a boy. After resigning from Padua (1610) he became First Mathematician at the University of Pisa and Philosopher and Mathematician to Grand Duke Cosimo II de' Medici. Imprisoned for six months aged 69 (1633) during his trial for belief in the Copernican (heliocentric) theory of the universe, he was released when he recanted to the Inquisition in Rome and exiled to Siena. He was later allowed to return to Florence (1638) – where Milton and Hobbes met him – and settled in Arcetri (his daughters were in a nearby convent) in 1639. He is remembered above all else for his work on telescopes and his first use of them in astronomy and for his determination of the law of uniformly accelerated motion towards earth, of the parabolic path of projectiles and the law that all bodies have weight.

Family/Sex Life: Galileo remained unmarried but from 1599 lived with Marina Gamba (their children were Virginia, Livia and Vincenzio).

Appearance: Above middle height, Galileo was well proportioned and had a fair complexion, sparkling eyes, short reddish hair and a beard.

Habits/Mannerisms: He preferred the countryside and claimed that the city was a prison for a speculative philosopher.

Sport/Hobbies: Galileo made toy machines as a child (as did Newton). He also played the organ and lute and was good at drawing (he had considered painting as a profession). He also wrote sonnets, riddles, a play (1590) and a prose comedy and enjoyed gardening. A connoisseur of wines (he had his own vineyard), he said wine was a compound of humour and light. He could recite Virgil, Ovid, Horace and Seneca and admired Ariosto.

Religion/Politics: Roman Catholic. The Vatican finally acknowledged the truth of his scientific discoveries in 1993.

Health: He suffered from ophthalmia (1579) and was completely blind by 1637. Other ailments included a hernia, fever, hypochondria, rheumatism, gout and insomnia.

Temperament: Cheerful and modest but short-tempered. His friends included the famous enigma composer (and friend of Milton) Antonio Malatesti.

Work/Daily Routine: Contrary to popular belief, Galileo did not invent the telescope (it was invented by Hans Lippershey in 1608) but he developed it significantly. His telescope was a lead tube 70 cm long and 45 mm in diameter with a concave eye-glass and convex object-glass that made objects three times nearer (nine times larger) – less powerful than modern binoculars. With this weak telescope he discovered the four moons of Jupiter, Saturn's rings, the phases of Venus, sunspots and lunar mountains. He recorded his discoveries in cypher. He wrote treatises on military architecture, mechanics and the sphere, invented the sector (a compass), the air thermometer and a machine for raising water. He worked as an astrologer and was designing the first pendulum clock when he died. He admired Plato, Pythagoras and Aristotle but his master was Archimedes.

Motto/Saying: *'Eppur si muove'* ('But still it moves') – allegedly muttered by Galileo after he was obliged to recant his claim that the Earth moves round the Sun. The legend is supported by the discovery of the quotation on a portrait of Galileo around 1640.

Manner of Death: After fever and pains in his limbs confined him to bed (5 November 1641), Galileo was given the last rites and the benediction of Pope Urban VIII and finally died at his home in the Piano de Giullari, Arcetri, near Florence, on the evening of 8 January 1642, aged 77. With his family at the bedside was fellow-scientist Torricelli. He was buried in the church of Santa Croce, Florence. In 1737 his tomb was opened and the thumb and forefinger of his right hand were cut off (they held his pen) by Canon G. V. Capponi, President of the Sacra Accademia Fiorentina and kept in his family until lost in 1845. The index finger of his left hand was removed by A. F. Gori, Professor of Ancient History at the University of Florence, and is now kept in a crystal urn in the Tribuna di Galileo, Florence. Dr A. Cocchi, Professor of Natural Philosophy and Anatomy, took his fifth lumbar vertebra and this is now kept at the University of Padua.

GEORGE II (1683–1760) King of Great Britain and Ireland

George Augustus (later George II) was born in Herrenhausen, Germany, on 10 November 1683, the only son of George I and Sophia Dorothea, daughter of George William Duke of Lüneburg-Celle. His parents were divorced when he was 11 and he was brought up by his grandparents, the Elector of Hanover and his wife Sophia (granddaughter of James I). His sister Sophia Dorothea was later mother of Frederick the Great. Well-educated, he learned Latin, French and English – though he spoke the latter with a German accent (George I could neither speak nor write English) – and became a naturalized British citizen in 1705. As a prince he served under Marlborough and won honours at the Battle of Oudenarde (1708). He came to the throne on the death of his father in 1727, ruled for 33 years and was succeeded by his grandson (son of his eldest son Frederick Louis), George III. He was the last British monarch to lead troops into battle – at Dettingen, during the War of the Austrian Succession, in 1743 (when his horse bolted he led on foot). Other events during his reign included the suppression of the Jacobite Rebellion of 1745, the establishment of British rule in India (1757) and the capture of Quebec (1759).

Family/Sex Life: In 1705 George married Wilhelmina Caroline, the daughter of John Frederick, Margrave of Brandenburg-Anspach. Caroline died in 1737; as she lay dying she told her husband to remarry, to which he gallantly responded that he never would – but then rather spoiled the effect by adding: 'No, I shall have mistresses.' Their children were Frederick Louis, George William, William Augustus, Anne (Princess of Orange), Amelia Sophia Eleonora, Caroline Elizabeth, Mary and Louisa. George's mistresses included the Countess von Walmoden (who bore his illegitimate son, John Louis) and Lady Deloraine. There were also rumours that he was bisexual and that he had had an affair with John Campbell, 2nd Duke of Argyll.

Appearance: Described as small and dapper, though he carried himself rather stiffly, George had striking looks, with a long nose, high forehead, large blue eyes, large mouth, purple-red complexion and fair hair.

Habits/Mannerisms: Known as 'the Little Captain', George had a good memory and never forgot a date and could remember to the last detail the uniforms of his regiments.

Sport/Hobbies: George enjoyed hunting and opera but did not like pictures or literature. He was the founder of the University of Göttingen and was also a patron of Handel. In 1743, at the premiere of Handel's *The Messiah*, he shared the audience's enthusiasm – though during the 'Hallelujah Chorus' he misunderstood the sentiment behind the line 'And He shall reign for ever and ever' and, thinking this was a personal tribute to himself, leapt up with pleasure: the audience, confused, followed suit (for many years afterwards it remained customary for audiences to rise during this section).

Religion/Politics: Protestant. He also believed in the reality of ghosts, witches and vampires.

Health: George survived assassination when a man with a pistol tried to enter his box at the Theatre Royal, Drury Lane, in 1716 (a guard was killed). Later in life he suffered from gout.

Temperament: Having been bullied by his father as a child, George in his turn was impatient with his son and heir Frederick (nicknamed 'Titi') and relations were rarely good between them. His son responded by criticizing his father in the book *Histoire du Prince Titi* (1735). George also had a reputation for avarice and meanness and was popularly supposed to be without wit, manners or morals. Of his personal valour, there was little doubt, however. On one occasion, walking alone in Kensington Gardens, he was approached by a stranger who demanded his money, watch and shoe-buckles. Calmly, the king handed over the requested items then, equally coolly, asked that the relatively inexpensive seal on the watch be returned as it had sentimental value. The robber, evidently impressed by the king's composure but anxious to be gone, agreed to return the seal at the same hour the next day, provided the king said nothing. The king complied and the seal was returned.

Work/Daily Routine: Though he made some effort to involve himself in the government of Britain, George admitted that he cared for Hanover first, the Empire second and England third. He rose between 5 and 6 am, had an hour's siesta in the afternoon and often spent the evening playing cards, eating supper at 11 pm and retiring to bed at midnight. He was a brave soldier, but an ineffective politician and his bellicosity frequently threatened to plunge England into war with European rivals. In domestic policy matters, he allowed Robert Walpole to decide most issues in the first half of his reign, though he also allowed Queen Caroline to influence him significantly, as recorded in a contemporary rhyme:

'You may strut, dapper George, but 'twill be in vain;
We know 'tis Queen Caroline, not you, that reign.'

Manner of Death: George died suddenly, aged 77, in Kensington around 8 am on 25 October 1760, from a rupture of the right ventricle of the heart when preparing for a walk in the gardens. He was buried in Westminster Abbey. He requested that he be interred next to Queen Caroline, with the adjoining sides of the coffins opened so that their dust might mingle.

GEORGE III (1738–1820) King of the United Kingdom

George William Frederick (later George III) was born prematurely in Norfolk House, St James's Square, London, at 7.30 am on 4 June 1738, the eldest son of George II's eldest son Frederick Louis (who died aged 48 after being hit in the throat by a cricket ball, 1751) and Augusta, daughter of Frederick II, Duke of Saxe-Gotha. The first British monarch since Queen Anne to be born and educated in England, he had younger brothers William Henry, Henry Frederick, Frederick William, and sisters Augusta (mother of his eldest son George IV's queen, Caroline), Caroline Matilda (who married Christian VII of Denmark), Elizabeth Caroline and Louisa Anne. A backward child, he was privately educated and became king on the death of his grandfather George II in 1760. He reigned for 59 years (the second longest reign in English history). Decreed mad at the end of his life he spent his last years in Windsor Castle while his son (later George IV) ruled as Regent. Remembered by later generations chiefly for the madness that blighted his later years, his reign witnessed the Industrial Revolution, Britain's loss of the American Colonies and victory over Napoleon.

Family/Sex Life: In 1754 George, then Prince of Wales, took as his first mistress tradesman's daughter Hannah Lightfoot (he had several children by her). Marriage to Lady Sarah Lennox was blocked by parental opposition and instead in 1761 he married Sophia Charlotte, youngest daughter of Charles William Ferdinand, Duke of Mecklenburg-Strelitz. They had 15 children: George IV, Frederick (the 'Grand Old Duke of York' of the popular rhyme), William IV, Edward (father of Queen Victoria), Ernest (King of Hanover), Augustus, Adolphus, Octavius, Alfred, Charlotte, Augusta, Elizabeth, Mary, Sophia and Amelia.

Appearance: According to Horace Walpole: 'His person is tall and full of dignity, his countenance florid and good-natured, his manner graceful and obliging.' He had prominent eyes and a fine voice. In later life, he wore a hat to shade his eyes, grew a long beard and became bald.

Habits/Mannerisms: George wrote English ungrammatically and spelt badly. He ate little meat to avoid getting as fat as his father but was fond of sauerkraut. He ate only one slice of bread and butter and one cup of black tea between breakfast and dinner. When mad he spoke rapidly and incessantly, often ending sentences with 'what? what?' and repeating words. A phase during which he ended each sentence with 'peacock' caused official embarrassment, relieved only when it was suggested to the king that 'peacock' was a royal word and should be whispered before subjects.

Sport/Hobbies: George loved music and played a harpsichord owned by Handel (his favourite composer). He was also interested in mechanics, agricultural science and model ships/dockyards. He collected more than 67,000 books (later presented to the British Museum as the King's Library), spoke French and German and took exercise to prevent getting fat – though he sometimes ate while walking.

He also enjoyed horse-riding, the theatre, astronomy and backgammon.

Religion/Politics: Protestant and fervently anti-Roman Catholic, George was very pious – his Prayer Book had references to 'our most religious and gracious King' replaced with 'a most miserable sinner'. He supported the Tories, appointing Pitt the Younger Prime Minister at 24.

Health: In 1786 George survived assassination by stabbing when attacked by Margaret Nicholson at the gate of St James's Palace. In 1795 he was hit by stones thrown at his carriage and in 1800 he was twice shot at by James Hadfield at the Theatre Royal, Drury Lane. A plot by Colonel Despard to fire a cannon at his coach in St James's Park was foiled in 1803. He suffered his first attack from 'flying gout' (porphyria) on 5 November 1788 (his symptoms including talking nonsense incessantly, foaming at the mouth and passing red urine); he recovered but intermittent insanity plagued him for the rest of his life. A cataract affected his right eye in 1804 and by 1808 he was completely blind. In 1811, blind and deaf, the king was decreed irretrievably mad and locked away until his death. Sometimes speaking for 24 hours without a pause, he claimed to talk with angels and once greeted an oak tree as the King of Prussia. His doctors administered James's Powder (calomel and tartar emetic) and bled him regularly. They also advised him to bathe in the sea (thus encouraging the fad for seaside holidays).

Temperament: Good-natured, conscientious and well-mannered, the younger George was called 'the finest gentleman I have ever seen' by Dr Johnson. Though courageous, saying he would lead his troops in battle if Napoleon invaded, he was dominated by his mother even when king. His confidantes included Swift's friend, the 'bluestocking' Mrs Delany (he bought her a house in Windsor).

Work/Daily Routine: Popularly known as 'Farmer George' because of his interest in farming, the king contributed to *Annals of Agriculture* under the pseudonym 'Ralph Robinson'. At his coronation banquet one of the largest jewels fell out of his crown (seen as an omen of the loss of America). The Americas were irrevocably lost on 4 July 1776 (American Independence Day) – marked in George's diary by the entry:

'Nothing of importance happened today.'

Manner of Death: Over Christmas 1819 George suffered a further bout of madness and spoke nonsense for 58 hours, then sank into a coma. He died in Windsor Castle at 8.32 pm on 29 January 1820, aged 81. He was buried in St George's Chapel, Windsor Castle.

GEORGE IV (1762–1830) King of the United Kingdom

George Augustus Frederick (later George IV) was born in St James's Palace, London, at 7.24 pm on 12 August 1762, the eldest son of George III and Charlotte Sophia, daughter of Charles Louis Frederick, Duke of Mecklenburg-Strelitz. His siblings were Frederick (the 'Grand old Duke of York'), William IV, Edward, Ernest (King of Hanover), Augustus, Adolphus, Octavius, Alfred, Charlotte, Augusta, Elizabeth, Mary, Sophia and Amelia. Educated privately, he was commissioned colonel in the 10th Light Dragoons when the French Republic declared war but never saw action. He ruled as Prince Regent from 1811 for the last years of his mad father's life, then in his own right after George's death in 1820. When he ascended the throne aged 58, his ex-wife Caroline returned from abroad to claim her title as Queen but after a famous trial for adultery Parliament dissolved the marriage. During his reign the Prime Minister (Spencer Perceval) was assassinated in the House of Commons (1812), the Foreign Secretary (Castlereagh) committed suicide on George's birthday (1822), the Cato Street conspiracy to murder the Cabinet was foiled and public unrest led to the Peterloo Massacre. It was also the period that produced the major works of Keats, Wordsworth, Shelley and Byron.

Family/Sex Life: George's first mistress was actress Mrs Mary Robinson (1779–81); in correspondence she was Perdita to George's Florizel (he later paid £5000 for his letters and a £500 pension). In 1785, George was secretly married without the King's consent to Catholic widow Mrs Mary Anne Fitzherbert, née Maria Smythe, a commoner. He was forced to renounce her and in 1795 to marry his cousin Caroline Amelia Elizabeth, daughter of Charles William Ferdinand, Duke of Brunswick-Wolfenbüttel, and George III's elder sister Augusta. They had one daughter, Charlotte Augusta. George was reputedly drunk at the wedding and the marriage was consummated only once (Caroline was eccentric, promiscuous, swore and stank). Legend has it that George's only words on first meeting Caroline were: 'Harris, I am not well; pray get me a glass of brandy.' George corresponded with Caroline by letter even when in the same house and refused to co-habit with her after 1796, seeking solace with Mrs Fitzherbert. A bill to secure a royal divorce was introduced in 1820 and Caroline was refused admittance to George's coronation. The Whigs took up her cause, which attracted public sympathy, but Caroline died a year later. George had many other affairs, especially with older women (for instance, with Frances Countess of Jersey, the Marchioness of Hertford and the

Marchioness of Conyngham – all grandmothers – and with Lady Horatia Seymour, by whom he had an illegitimate daughter Mary).

Appearance: Tall, golden-haired and good-looking in his youth, George later became very fat (Leigh Hunt was imprisoned for calling him 'This Adonis in loveliness ... a corpulent man of fifty' in *The Examiner*). To disguise his bulk he wore corsets. He had a florid complexion and was extravagant in his dress (he spent £10,000 a year on clothes). He also wore rouge and greasepaint. His niece Queen Victoria found him 'large and gouty but with a wonderful dignity and charm of manner'.

Habits/Mannerisms: George was left-handed (as were James I and Victoria) and could converse in French and Italian. He also knew Latin and German, but was a bad speller. He hoarded clothes and all manner of trinkets, quoted poetry and drank a lot (particularly cherry brandy).

Sport/Hobbies: George sang well (bass) and played the cello. He was a keen gambler (especially at faro, whist and loo) and also played écarté, solitaire and patience. He enjoyed riding, fencing, shooting, sea-bathing, cricket and horse-racing (his horse won the Derby in 1788). He liked Shakespeare, Scott, Byron and Jane Austen and requested that *Emma* be dedicated to him. He was also an enthusiastic patron of the arts and an authority on 17th-century Dutch painting, French furniture and English china.

Religion/Politics: Protestant. A supporter of the Whigs, he voted for Fox's India Bill in the House of Lords (he lost interest in politics when Fox died in 1806). He opposed the French Jacobins and continued to give Louis XVIII asylum in England.

Health: George did not enjoy good health and underwent frequent blood-lettings in his youth. He once stabbed himself to get sympathy from Mrs Fitzherbert and took up to 700 drops of laudanum a day after spraining his ankle in 1812. He also suffered from gout, dropsy, pleurisy (1820), bladder trouble (from 1824) and, from 1828, failing eyesight. He also had delusions; his fantasies included riding a winner at Goodwood and he even boasted to the Duke of Wellington of leading a battalion at Waterloo.

Temperament: Despite a strict upbringing, George was dissipated, weak-minded, callous and indulgent. He conducted much official business without bothering to leave his bed, getting up only for dinner. Known as 'Prinny' (Prince) even when king, his friends included Fox, Sheridan and George 'Beau' Brummell.

Work/Daily Routine: George, depicted as a dissolute fop and gambler, was widely resented and his coach was stoned in the Mall in 1817. According to the *Dictionary of National Biography*: 'there have been more wicked kings in English history, but none so unredeemed by any signal greatness or virtue'.

Manner of Death: After a series of strokes (April 1830) George died at Windsor Castle of cirrhosis of the liver, gout, nephritis and dropsy in the early morning of Saturday 26 June 1830, aged 67. He was buried in St George's Chapel, Windsor Castle, wearing the miniature of Mrs Fitzherbert he always carried around his neck.

GIBBON, Edward (1737–94) English historian

Edward Gibbon was born in Putney, London, on 27 April 1737, the only surviving child of Edward Gibbon, MP for Petersfield and Southampton, and Judith Porten (who died when he was 10). His father remarried (to Dorothea Patton) and he was brought up by his maternal aunt, Catherine Porten, in Putney, where she ran a boarding-house for Westminster School pupils. Educated at Westminster School and briefly (for 14 months – 'the most idle and unprofitable of my whole life' – from April 1752) at Magdalen College, Oxford, he was later Colonel Commandant in the Hampshire militia (1759–63) and MP for Liskeard, Cornwall (1774–80) and for Lymington (1781), settling in London despite the debts he inherited from his improvident father. Professor of Ancient History at the Royal Academy of Art and Commissioner for Trade and Plantations, he moved to Lausanne, Switzerland, in 1783 to finish the last three volumes of his most famous publication, *The Decline and Fall of the Roman Empire* (5 vols; 1776–88). He spent his last years in company with his friend Lord Sheffield, who published his *Memoirs and Miscellaneous Works* (1796).

Family/Sex Life: Gibbon remained unmarried, though while in Switzerland he had an affair with Suzanne Curchod (later to be Madame Necker, mother of Madame de Staël). His hopes of marrying her were disappointed by his father's refusal to allow his son to marry a foreigner. Gibbon resigned himself to his fate, writing: 'After a painful struggle I yielded to my fate: I sighed as a lover, I obeyed as a son.' He once proposed on his knees to Lady Elizabeth Foster (the Duke of Devonshire's mistress) but was so fat he could not get up again. Perhaps unsurprisingly the proposal was declined and she eventually married the Duke.

Appearance: Only four feet tall, Gibbon was always rather fat. According to the *Dictionary of National Biography*: 'his features were so overlaid by fat ... as to be almost grotesque'. James Boswell found him an 'ugly, affected, disgusting fellow'. He dressed finely and had a taste for garish waistcoats.

Habits/Mannerisms: Gibbon spoke French well but was also very clumsy and lazy – it was said that he never even cut his own fingernails (a servant had to do it while he read).

Sport/Hobbies: A brilliant and 'pleasant' conversationalist, Gibbon was a member of Dr Johnson's celebrated Club. Besides talk, he also enjoyed playing whist. He hated exercise of any kind.

Religion/Politics: Gibbon converted to Catholicism at the age of 16 but was later persuaded to return to the Protestant faith by the Calvinist pastor with whom he lodged in Lausanne. In Parliament, as an MP, he voted steadfastly in support of the government of Lord North.

Health: Gibbon was sickly as a child. He often complained of great pain in his legs and also suffered occasionally from gout.

Temperament: Affected, pompous and easily offended, Gibbon was classed by Boswell as belonging among 'infidel wasps and venomous insects'. He believed in the worthiness of his historical studies though he did occasionally admit the limitations of his subject and once declared: 'The romance of *Tom Jones*, that exquisite picture of human manners, will outlive the palace of the Escorial and the imperial eagle of the house of Austria.'

Work/Daily Routine: Gibbon had the idea

for his masterpiece *Decline and Fall* when walking in the ruins of the Capitol in Rome in 1764. The Duke of Gloucester, on accepting the second volume of *Decline and Fall* responded with the comment: 'Another damn'd thick, square book! Always scribble, scribble, scribble! Eh! Mr Gibbon?' Gibbon wrote the last words of his classic in the summerhouse in his garden in Lausanne about midnight on 27 June 1787. By that time *Decline and Fall* had already been banned by the Vatican and been put on the Index of prohibited books (1783). Though an MP for a total of eight sessions, Gibbon never spoke in the House of Commons. Every time he thought about it his courage failed him – on one occasion he confided: 'I am still a Mute; it is more tremendous than I imagined; the great speakers fill me with despair, the bad ones with terror.' Another time he explained his silence thus: 'I have remained silent and notwithstanding all my efforts chained down to my place by some unknown invisible power.'

Manner of Death: Gibbon caught an infection following an operation to drain four quarts of liquid from a huge swelling 'almost as big as a small child' that was caused by a hydrocele on his left testicle. He died in London at 12.45 pm on 16 January 1794, aged 56. He was buried in Fletching, Sussex.

GLADSTONE, William Ewart (1809–98) English statesman

William Gladstone was born at 62 Rodney Street, Liverpool, on 29 December 1809, the fourth son and fifth of six children of Scottish parents Sir John Gladstone, a merchant and MP, and his second wife Anne Robertson. He was named after his father's friend William Ewart. His older brothers were Sir Thomas (MP), Robertson (Mayor of Liverpool), John Neilson (MP and High Sheriff of Wiltshire) and he also had an older sister, Anne, and a younger one, Helen Jane. Educated at Eton (1821–7) and at Christ Church, Oxford, at university he was privately coached in the classics by Charles Wordsworth, nephew of the poet, and was President of the Oxford Union. He also studied at Lincoln's Inn but was not called to the Bar. He offered himself to be a clergyman (1830) but had no calling. Conservative MP for Newark (1832), Oxford University (1847), South Lancashire (1865) and Greenwich (1868), he was also Junior Lord to the Treasury (1834), Under-Secretary for War and the Colonies (1835), President of the Board of Trade (1843), Colonial Secretary (1845), Chancellor of the Exchequer (1852, 1859 and 1873) and four times Liberal Prime Minister (1868–74, 1880–5, 1886 and 1892–4). He resigned as Prime Minister and leader of the Liberal Party in 1894. A shareholder in the Metropolitan Railway (London's first Underground railway), Gladstone was also Lord Rector of Edinburgh University (1859) and lived at Hawarden Castle, Flintshire (now Clwyd), Wales (owned by his brother-in-law, Sir Stephen Glynne).

Family/Sex Life: After rejections by Caroline Farquhar and Lady Frances Douglas, in 1839 Gladstone married Catherine Glynne, sister of his Eton schoolfriend Sir Stephen Glynne, MP and a relative of Pitt the Younger. They had eight children: William Henry MP, the Rt Hon. Herbert John MP, Stephen Edward, Henry Neville, Agnes, Jessie Catherine, Mary and Helen (Vice-Principal of Newnham College, Cambridge). In 1849 rumours of liaisons with prostitutes threatened a scandal, but it transpired that Gladstone sought out the company of 'fallen women' in order to offer them assistance and moral strength (Gladstone himself privately admitted to being unclear as to his real motives). Conscious of his ambivalent feelings about these exchanges, he scourged himself with a whip (indicated with a whip symbol in his diary) after these curious meetings. Gladstone apparently saw himself as a Pre-Raphaelite knight and would often read Tennyson to the women. He was never unfaithful to his wife but had a close relationship with the courtesan Mrs Laura Thistlethwaite.

Appearance: Tall, broad-shouldered and muscular but slight, Gladstone had black hair, a pale complexion and eyes 'large, lustrous and piercing; not quite black but resembling agate in colour'. He wore high wing-collars (much caricatured) and gloves – thus concealing the missing tip of his left forefinger, blown off in a shooting accident in 1842. He also wore 'broughams' (check trousers).

Habits/Mannerisms: Abstemious in the use of wine, Gladstone was often criticized for his laborious long-winded manner, charac-teristically holding his lapels as he addressed his listeners (his 1853 Budget speech lasted five hours). Disraeli called him 'a sophistical rhetorician, enebriated [sic] with the exuber-ance of his own verbosity'.

Sport/Hobbies: Gladstone played cricket and football at Eton and was fond of boating, swimming and walking. He also rode and shot, sang well, spoke Italian and read widely (his favourite authors were Homer and Dante though he also liked Scott and Ossian). He thought chess too serious but played whist, collected porcelain and enjoyed cutting down trees. He spent his holidays in Biarritz.

Religion/Politics: Devout and pious – he was a regular churchgoer even on weekdays – Gladstone was 'a great Christian man' according to Lord Salisbury. He was Prime Minister during the Disestablishment of the Church of Ireland Act, opposed the Divorce Bill and was a committed opponent of birth control. First a Tory then a Liberal, Gladstone was a follower of Canning and arch rival of Disraeli.

Health: Gladstone suffered from vertigo and erysipelas and also had problems with cataracts in old age. He had a bad memory for faces.

Temperament: Gladstone was courteous and very generous, giving much money to charity. His friends included Tennyson, Arthur Hallam (subject of Tennyson's poem *In Memoriam*) and Cardinal Manning. He could also be overbearing and moralizing, and Carlyle condemned him as 'one of the contemptiblest men I ever looked upon'. Disraeli claimed 'He has not a single redeeming defect' and Queen Victoria, who doted on Disraeli, was inclined to agree, sending Gladstone only the briefest note when he retired, despite his long service. The tag 'G. O. M.' (Grand Old Man) was much associated with him in later years (it was first used by Lord Rosebery in 1882); he was also nicknamed 'Merrypebble' by Clarendon.

Pets: He kept a black male Pomeranian dog called Petz (later buried in the dog cemetery in Hawarden Park).

Work/Daily Routine: Gladstone wrote a number of books, for instance *The State in its Relation with the Church* (1838), and translated Homer and Farini's *Lo Statto Romano* (The Roman State) as well as contrib-uting Hymn 322 to the *English Hymnal* and writing comic verses and limericks.

Manner of Death: Gladstone died of cancer of the palate at Hawarden Castle early in the morning of 19 May 1898, aged 88. 250,000 visitors filed past his open coffin in Westminster Hall prior to his burial in Westminster Abbey on 28 May. Pallbearers included the Prince of Wales, Lords Salisbury and Rosebery, and Balfour.

GOEBBELS, Paul Josef (1897–1945) German politician

Josef Goebbels (his grandfather had spelt the name Göbbels) was born at 186 (now 202) Odenkirchener Strasse, Rheydt, near Düsseldorf, Germany, on 29 October 1897, the son of Fritz Goebbels, a book-keeper and later plant manager at United Wick Factories, and Katharina Odenhausen, a dairymaid. His older siblings were Konrad, Hans and Maria (died young) and he had two younger sisters, Elisabeth and Maria. Educated at the Gymnasium in Rheydt (1908) he was top of his class in Latin, Geography, German and Maths. He later studied Classical Philology, German Literature and History at the University of Bonn (1917), did a year's military service in the Fatherland Auxiliary (a desk job), then followed a law-student friend to study law at the University of Freiburg (1918), and then at the Universities of Würzburg (1918–19), Munich (1919–20) and Heidelberg (1920), where he received a PhD (1921) for a thesis on the 19th-century dramatist Wilhelm Schutz. He worked at first as a freelance journalist for *Westdeutsche Landeszeitung* and then – with help from his girlfriend Else Jenke – got a job at the Dresden Bank, Cologne (1923), before becoming Editor of the Nazi journal *Volkische Freiheit* (1924–5) while Hitler was in prison. He was then appointed Business Manager of the Rhineland North section (*gau*) of the Nazi Party (1925), Gauleiter (section chief) for Greater Berlin (1926) and in 1927 founded a new Nazi paper, *Der Angriff* (The Attack), featuring vicious caricatures by 'Mjolnir' (Hans Schweitzer, later President of the Reich Chamber of Fine Arts). One of the first 12 Nazi deputies to the Reichstag (1928), he was appointed Reich Minister for Popular Enlightenment and Propaganda in 1933. In Hitler's will he was nominated Reich Chancellor under President Doenitz.

Family/Sex Life: Goebbels had an affair with a rich law student named Anka Stalherm (he met her at the University of Freiburg and followed her to Würzburg and Munich). In 1931 he married Mrs Magda Quandt (née Johanna Maria Magdalena Friedlander – her stepfather was a Jew) who already had a 10-year-old son Harald and two older stepsons by Günther Quandt. Hitler served as witness at the marriage, while Harald attended in the uniform of the Nazi Youth organization. Their children were Helga, Heide, Hilde, Helmut, Holde and Hedda.

Appearance: Small and clean-shaven, Goebbels walked with a pronounced limp.

Habits/Mannerisms: Goebbels was a smoker and wrote novellas and plays.

Sport/Hobbies: A good actor, Goebbels also played the piano, wrote poetry, learnt Dutch and was very well read (especially in the works of Strindberg, Ibsen and Tolstoy).

Religion/Politics: Goebbels was a strong Roman Catholic until 1918. At first he adopted an anti-Hitler stance (he once drew a cartoon of a child on a potty with the caption: 'If I see a swastika/I feel the urge to make caca').

Health: Goebbels nearly died of pneumonia as a child. Osteomyelitis made him lame in the right leg and his right foot became clubbed. Because of this disability he was excused military service during World War I.

Temperament: Known to his friends as 'Jupp', the deeply cynical Goebbels became a fanatical supporter of Hitler and his radical Nazi doctrines. A powerful speaker, he was able to whip up fierce resentment of the Jews and other scapegoats (he was himself anti-Semitic).

Work/Daily Routine: Goebbels proved a master in the manipulation of mass communication, controlling national sentiment about the progress of the war through the information he released to the media. He also wrote articles himself under the pseudonym 'Ulex'. His diaries, published in 1948, reflect his conviction in the justice of the Nazi cause and at times have a semi-religious fervour – when the death of Roosevelt was communicated to the Nazi high command he recorded their reaction in typically grandiose style: 'This was the Angel of History! We felt its wings flutter through the room. Was that not the fortune we awaited so anxiously?'

Manner of Death: After giving morphine injections and then cyanide to their children he committed suicide with his wife by poison in the bunker of the Reich Chancellery in Berlin on 1 May 1945. His body (which also had a bullet in the head) was later burnt and the remains taken to Moscow with those of Hitler.

GOERING, Hermann Wilhelm (1893 –1946) German politician

Herman Goering was born in Marienbad Sanitarium, Rosenheim, Bavaria, on 12 January 1893, the fourth child of Heinrich Ernst Goering, German Consul-General in Haiti, and his second wife Franziska (Fanny) Tiefenbrunn (his parents had been married in London). He had five elder step-siblings by his father's first wife, an older brother Karl, older sisters Olga and Pauli and a younger brother Albert. Brought up in Fürth, Bavaria, for three years while the rest of his family were in Haiti, he attended boarding school in Ansbach, Franconia (1904). His godfather, Ritter Hermann von Epenstein, a doctor of Jewish extraction, was also his mother's lover and for 15 years the whole family lived in his castle, Burg Veldenstein at Neuhaus, near Nuremberg. After school he studied at the military academy in Karlsruhe, then at officer cadet college in Lichterfelde near Berlin and at Mühlhausen. In World War I he was commissioned lieutenant, but caught rheumatic fever (1914) and refused to return to his regiment. His godfather obtained a medical certificate exempting him from service in the trenches and Goering became a cameraman-observer (1915) with the Air Force. Awarded the Iron Cross, First Class, for photographing Verdun fortress, he trained as a pilot and served in Jagdstaffel 5, Jagdstaffel 26 and commanded Jagdstaffel 27. Awarded the 'Blue Max' (Prussia's highest order) after only 15 victories (normally given after 25), his final tally was 22. Leader of the 'Flying Circus' after the death of Manfred von Richthofen ('The Red Baron'), after the war he worked as an acrobatic pilot. He met Hitler in 1922 and was the first commander of the SA (Sturmabteilung), the Nazis' 11,000-strong private army (1923). With Hitler and Ludendorff he led the Munich 'Beer-Hall Putsch' (1923). He was later a salesman for BMW (Bavarian Motor Works) in Berlin and was elected to the Reichstag there, becoming with Hitler and Goebbels one of the first 12 Nazi deputies in the parliament (1928). Later twice elected President of the Reichstag (1932), after Hitler was elected Chancellor in 1933 he served as Minister without Portfolio, Prussian Minister of the Interior and Minister of Aviation. He was later appointed Reichsmarshal (1940) and Hitler's successor and Deputy Führer (1941), but was disgraced by the Luftwaffe's failure in the Battle of Britain and in 1944 staged an abortive coup. He surrendered voluntarily to the US Seventh Army and was sentenced to death at Nuremberg.

Family/Sex Life: In 1923 Goering married the previously married Carin von Kantzow (née Fock), daughter of Swedish Baron Carl von Fock and his Anglo-Irish wife Huldine Beamish – she already had an eight-year-old son Thomas. She died in 1931 and in 1935 Goering married previously married actress Emmy Sonnemann, by whom he fathered Edda (Julius Streicher claimed artificial insemination). Hitler was his best man.

Appearance: The blue-eyed Marshal became very fat and sometimes exceeded 280 lb. He favoured exotic non-regulation uniforms, with solid gold epaulettes and gold marshals' baton (he also inherited a cane from the Red Baron). He wore a huge diamond ring on his fourth finger.

Habits/Mannerisms: A gourmand with a huge appetite, Goering was fond of lobster and of blinis stuffed with caviar and cream. His favourite drinks were champagne and good vintage claret or Moselle. He sweated a lot but was very intelligent – he came out with an IQ of 138, the third highest of the top 21 captured Nazis tested by the Allies.

Sport/Hobbies: Goering enjoyed saunas, massage, swimming and riding to keep his weight down. He was a good shot and was keen on hunting, planting forests and enforcing poaching laws. He collected art and at one stage had the most valuable art collection in the world (mostly acquired legitimately). He also played the accordion and sang (baritone).

Religion/Politics: Goering was curiously

ambivalent about the Jews – he liked Jewish composers (especially Mendelssohn) and artists (such as Rubens) and his (greatly revered) godfather had a Jewish father. Yet, as a Nazi, he was in favour of 'a total solution' to the 'Jewish question' through mass extermination.

Health: Having suffered rheumatic fever in 1914, Goering was badly wounded in the thigh by a Sopwith attack (1916). In 1923 he was shot in the hip and groin in the Beer Hall Putsch and was given morphine twice daily, causing him to become addicted (he also took cocaine and, from 1937, was taking 100 morphine-derivative paracodeine painkillers daily). He was incarcerated in the Langbro Asylum for the insane in Sweden (1927) but later recovered. He also took sleeping pills for his insomnia and suffered from bad teeth.

Mottoes/Sayings: Reputedly said 'When I hear the word "culture" I reach for my revolver' (though he was actually very cultured). A slogan in his office read: 'He who tortures animals wounds the feelings of the German people.'

Manner of Death: Goering was condemned to death by Hitler after the failed coup but escaped; he was again sentenced to death (by hanging) at the Nuremberg trials on 30 September 1946. His request to be shot by firing squad was denied. Refusing to appeal for clemency, he learned that his execution was set for dawn on 16 October and committed suicide in his cell, using an inch-long cyanide capsule hidden in skin cream, at 10.40 pm on 15 October 1946, aged 53. His body, in black trousers and pale blue pyjama jacket, was cremated in Erlangen Crematorium and the ashes discarded (with those of other executed Nazis) in the countryside.

GOETHE, Johann Wolfgang von (1749–1832)
German poet, playwright and civil servant

Johann Goethe was born a 'blue baby' in Frankfurt-am-Main, Germany, at noon on 28 August 1749, the oldest surviving child of Johann Caspar Goethe, a wealthy 39-year-old lawyer and city councillor, and Katharina Elisabeth Textor (then only 18), granddaughter of the head of the judiciary in Frankfurt. Named after his maternal grandfather, Johann Wolfgang Textor, he had a younger sister Cornelia (three other siblings died in childhood). After studying law at Leipzig (1765–8, he was taken ill so did not graduate) and Strasbourg (1770–1) Universities, he became a Licentiate of Law and worked briefly as a lawyer, calling himself (illegally, as his thesis was rejected) Doctor Goethe. He was at first a poet and worked as a freelance journalist (writing book reviews and so forth) in Frankfurt until the (anonymous) publication of the hugely successful autobiographical novel *The Sorrows of Young Werther* (1774). A visit to Italy (1786–8) proved crucial and persuaded him to adopt a more 'classical' style. Later works included the *Wilhelm Meister* novels (1795–6 and 1829) and the poetic drama *Faust* (1808 and 1832). Invited to Weimar by Duke Karl August, he was appointed a member of his Privy Council (1776) and subsequently became President of the War Commission and Director of Roads and Services (1779). He was ennobled as Geheimrat von Goethe (1782) and became Wirkliche Geheimer Rat (addressed as 'Excellency') in 1804 and travelled on diplomatic missions for the Weimar court. Director of the Weimar Court Theatre (1790), he was awarded the Légion d'honneur by Napoleon (1808) and founded the journals *Kunst und Altertum* (1816) and *Zur Naturwissenschaft* (1817).

Family/Sex Life: As a young man Goethe had an unhappy love affair with Lotte Buff, the fiancée of one of his friends, and this helped to inspire *Werther*. In 1775 he was engaged for a time to Lili Schönemann, daughter of a rich Frankfurt banker and niece of the largest snuffmaker in Germany, and it was to her that he addressed his love lyrics. At Weimar he enjoyed a platonic 12-year relationship with the married Charlotte von Stein, which did much to help him mature as a writer. He later lived openly with Christiane Vulpius, sister of the popular novelist Christian August Vulpius (author of *Rinaldo Rinaldini* and other books) and had a son with her in 1789 – August Goethe (the only survivor of five children). After 18 years together the couple married (1806); he called her his 'Little Erotikon', while she called his penis 'Herr Schönfuss'. August, whose godfather was Duke Karl August of Sachsen-Weimar-Eisenach, was a disappointment to his father, leading a dissipated life and dying in Rome in 1830 – prompting his father to observe: 'I was not unaware that I had begotten a mortal.'

Appearance: Tall and clean-shaven, with short hair, Goethe had a very dark brown, almost black, face.

Habits/Mannerisms: Goethe was a non-smoker, drank in moderation and seldom danced. He carried a sword and had some skill at drawing, being given lessons by the painter Adam Oeser (who illustrated the first edition of *Werther*).

Sport/Hobbies: Besides writing, Goethe did important scientific research in the fields of geology, botany, alchemy and anatomy, including the discovery of the intermaxillary bone in man (1784).

Religion/Politics: Christened Lutheran.

Health: Goethe suffered from syphilis, giddiness, lung trouble, severe constipation, a neck abscess (1768), erysipelas (1801) and from a serious kidney complaint (1805). In 1774 he attempted to commit suicide, stabbing himself repeatedly in the heart.

Temperament: Goethe was emotionally intense, as befitted the founder of the *'Sturm und Drang'* movement. His friends included Schiller (for whom he obtained the post of lecturer at the University of Jena) and Beethoven. When Schiller died, Goethe declared he had lost 'half of my existence'. He was greatly admired by Napoleon (an admiration reciprocated by Goethe) and when they met at the Congress of Erfurt (1808) the Emperor was moved to exclaim: *'Voilà un homme!'* ('There is a man!'). Another admirer was Carlyle, who called Goethe 'the Wisest of Our Time' and who translated *Wilhelm Meister* into English. Shelley translated some of his *Walpurgisnacht*.

Pets: Goethe hated dogs and barking – he resigned as Director of the Weimar Court Theatre when Grand Duke Augustus requested a production of Pixérécourt's *The Dog of Montargis* featuring a live poodle. Mephistopheles first appears in the form of a black poodle in Goethe's *Faust*.

Work/Daily Routine: He spent many years on certain works: he worked on *Faust*, which he finished at the age of 81, for some 20 years, having first been inspired by a marionette-theatre drama based on the story. He particularly admired Byron's *Manfred* (Byron later dedicated *Werner* and *Sardanapalus* to him).

Manner of Death: Goethe died of 'catarrhal fever, pneumonia, failure of the lungs and heart' (his doctor's report) in an armchair by his bed at his home in Weimar at noon on 22 March 1832, aged 82. His last words are normally given as 'More light', though what he actually said was: 'Open the second shutter so that more light may come in.' He was buried near Schiller in the ducal vault in Weimar. A curious tribute paid to him years later was the Goethemobile, a car named after him in 1902.

GOLDSMITH, Oliver (1728–74) Irish-born poet, playwright and novelist

---

Oliver Goldsmith was born on 10 November 1728 in Pallas, County Longford, Ireland, the second son and fifth of eight children of Charles Goldsmith, farmer and rector of Kilkenny West, and Ann Jones. He had an elder brother Henry, an elder sister Catherine and other siblings were Margaret, Jane, Maurice, Charles and John. Flogged as a dunce at school, he studied classics at Trinity College, Dublin (a fellow student was Edmund Burke), and then medicine at Edinburgh University (though he did not qualify). After a brief visit to Leiden University to study anatomy he travelled in Europe and returned to work in a school run by his brother Henry. He later had a number of jobs – actor, chemist's assistant and so forth – and was imprisoned on suspicion of enlisting for the French Army when taking ship to France. He was then a proofreader for Samuel Richardson's press and a freelance journalist for the *Monthly Review*, *Critical Review*, *Lady's Magazine*, *Busy Body*, *Public Ledger* and Smollett's *British Magazine* etc. whilst (illegally) working as a physician (calling himself 'Doctor' though not qualified). He also started his own weekly magazine *The Bee* and (through his friend Reynolds's influence as President) was appointed Professor of Ancient History at the Royal Academy of Art. He made his reputation as a novelist with *The Vicar of Wakefield* (1766) and as a playwright with *She Stoops to Conquer* (1773).

Family/Sex Life: Goldsmith never married but was in love with Mary Horneck (his 'Jessamy Bride') and her sister (who married the caricaturist Bunbury).

Appearance: Small (around five feet six inches tall) and stocky with badly formed limbs and an ugly face disfigured by smallpox, Goldsmith was fond of rich and brightly coloured clothes (he wore purple silk underwear and had a scarlet cloak).

Habits/Mannerisms: Goldsmith loved playing cards for money; he also drank a lot, especially madeira and wine (though he also liked sassafras tea). He spoke French fluently.

Sport/Hobbies: Goldsmith was a hammer-thrower and also played the flute pro-fessionally (he paid his way round Europe with it).

Religion/Politics: Anglican (though Irish by birth) and Tory monarchist.

Health: Goldsmith contracted smallpox at the age of nine; later he suffered from inflammation of the bladder (1772) and from kidney trouble (1774). He regularly took Dr James's Fever Powders.

Temperament: Kind-natured but vain, sensual and frivolous, Goldsmith was one of the original nine members of Dr Johnson's Club that met at the Turk's Head, Gerrard Street, Soho. Johnson – whom Goldsmith knew before Boswell arrived (and to whom he dedicated *She Stoops to Conquer*) – said of Goldsmith that: 'No man was more foolish when he had not a pen in his hand, or more wise when he had.' He often referred to him as 'Goldy' (which Goldsmith disliked). Other

friends included Edmund Burke, David Garrick, Joshua Reynolds (Goldsmith dedicated *The Deserted Village* to him) and Bunbury. Horace Walpole summarized Goldsmith as 'an inspired idiot'.

Pets: Goldsmith kept a cat when a student in Edinburgh. As a young man, he also bought a pony called Fiddleback to ride back from Cork to Ballymallon having missed the boat to America, thinking to emigrate (he had sold his horse after the 120-mile journey).

Work/Daily Routine: Dr Johnson helped get *The Vicar of Wakefield* published (Goldsmith received 60 guineas for it, a good price). It sold less than 2000 copies in his lifetime. *She Stoops to Conquer*, about the comic consequences of two men mistaking a private house for an inn, was inspired by an identical error once made by the playwright himself. Travelling in Ardagh he had asked to be directed to the 'best house' in the locality and had been sent to the home of Sir Ralph Featherstone. Sir Ralph, realizing the mistake, played along and allowed Goldsmith to 'treat' the Featherstones with bottles from their own cellar, only letting on in the morning when his 'guest' asked for the bill. Earlier titles of *She Stoops to Conquer* were *The Old House in New Inn* and *The Mistakes of a Night*. A large part of Goldsmith's income came from compiling histories and so forth (Johnson observed that 'he has the art of compiling'); *An Abridged History of England* was put on the Vatican's Index of prohibited books (1823). Goldsmith, though, saw himself primarily as a poet: of 'The Traveller', Johnson wrote: 'since the death of Pope, it will not be easy to find anything equal'. Goldsmith spent his mornings reading, then walked the fields before taking dinner and settling down to his writing. He once tried dictation but this did not work ('I find that my head and hand must go together').

Manner of Death: Goldsmith died in his lodgings at Brick Court, Temple, after violent convulsions around 4.30 am on 4 April 1774, aged 45. Burke and Reynolds attended the funeral. The coffin was opened to give a lock of his hair to Mary Horneck. He was buried in Temple Church, London. His famous epitaph (in Latin) was provided by Johnson: 'To Oliver Goldsmith, Poet, Naturalist, Historian, who left scarcely any style of writing untouched, and touched nothing that he did not adorn.' A medallion by Nollekens was placed on his monument in Westminster Abbey. Garrick contributed a less reverent mock epitaph: 'Here lies Nolly Goldsmith, for shortness call'd Noll,/Who wrote like an angel, but talk'd like poor Poll.'

GORDON, Major-General Charles George (1833–85) English soldier

Charles Gordon was born at 29 Woolwich Common, Woolwich, London, on 28 January 1833, the fourth son of General Henry William Gordon (Royal Artillery) – then Inspector of the Carriage Department at Woolwich Arsenal – and Elizabeth Enderby, the daughter of a shipowner. He was the ninth of 11 children, his surviving siblings being Frederick (younger), Sir Henry, Enderby, Helen, William and Augusta (12 years his senior and his closest companion). After school in Taunton, Devon, he studied at the Woolwich Military Academy but, failing to get into the Royal Artillery, was commissioned in the Royal Engineers instead. He served with distinction in the Crimean War at Sebastopol (winning the British War Medal and clasp and the Légion d'Honneur) and in China after the Anglo-Chinese War. Recruited as the highly successful leader of the Chinese Army against the Taiping Rebellion he acquired the nickname 'Chinese Gordon' and received the yellow jacket and peacock's feather of a Mandarin First Class and the title 'Ti-Tu', the highest military rank in China. He was then about to go to the Belgian Congo when ordered to the Sudan where he served as Governor (1877–80). In 1884 he led the expedition to relieve besieged Egyptian garrisons in the Sudan and to restore order in the region by suppressing the Sudanese rebels. He met with stiff resistance and won enduring fame defending the Egyptian garrison at Khartoum for nearly a year against the forces of the 'Mad Mahdi', Mohammed Ahmed, before the city finally fell. He received the CB (1865).

Family/Sex Life: Gordon never married, deciding at an early age that matrimony would not suit him. According to Lord Elton, 'women in general did not attract him'.

Appearance: Five feet nine inches tall, with short, curly brown hair, a small moustache and later also long side-whiskers, Gordon had a square jaw, very bright light-blue eyes and a spare but strong wiry build. Lytton Strachey in his *Eminent Victorians* spoke of his 'unassuming figure, short and slight ... sunburnt brick-red complexion ... touch of grey on his hair and whiskers'.

Habits/Mannerisms: Explorer Richard Burton referred to Gordon's 'modest, reserved, and even shy expression', while Lord Elton noted 'the unassuming bearing and the searching and magnetic gaze, as of a lion-tamer turned saint'. Strachey reported that he had a 'low, soft and very distinct voice'. Others spoke of his sweet smile and also of his nervous energy, which drove him to pace up and down when talking. He had a very unmilitary bearing and was a heavy smoker, smoking hand-rolled cigarettes. In battle, he led from the front in China carrying only a small cane, which was known to his men as his 'magic wand'. He drank a lot of brandy-and-soda and also enjoyed gin. When in Africa he was in the habit of putting a hatchet and flag at his tent door when he did not wish to be disturbed.

Sport/Hobbies: Skilled at drawing and mapmaking, Gordon was very fond of the poetry of Tennyson and took his works everywhere with him. He once explained: 'The reading of Tennyson is my great relief.'

Religion/Politics: Gordon was very religious, but mixed his conventional Church of England doctrine with mysticism. He was also a committed opponent of slavery.

Health: Gordon contracted smallpox while in China and was also colour-blind. Poor health obliged him to resign as Governor of the Sudan in 1879, though he returned four years later to quell the rebellion.

Temperament: Gladstone called him 'a hero of heroes' and he was both modest and fearless. He also had a naturally hot temper and was brusque in manner yet could be forgiving and sympathetic. He was contemptuous of money and questioned the worth of reputation, however achieved: 'The fact is that, if one analyses human glory, it is composed of nine-tenths twaddle, perhaps ninety-nine hundredths twaddle.'

Manner of Death: On 26 January 1885 Khartoum fell at the end of a year's siege by the forces of Mohammed Ahmed, the 'Mad Mahdi'. Gordon, clad in a white uniform and carrying a sword and revolver but refusing to defend himself, was speared by the Dervish Taha Shahin, then by others and was finally hacked to death, aged 52. The British relief force arrived just two days later, delayed by the indecision of the British Cabinet (Queen Victoria never forgave Prime Minister Gladstone for this). Gordon's head was later fixed to a tree and passers-by threw stones at it. Tennyson provided the epitaph for his monument in St Paul's Cathedral.

GOYA Y LUCIENTES, Francisco José (1746–1828) Spanish painter and etcher

Goya was born on 30 March 1746 in Fuendetodos, 50 km southwest of Saragossa, the capital of Aragon, Spain. He was the son of José Goya, a master gilder, and Gracia Lucientes, and had a brother Camilo and a sister. Aged 14 he was apprenticed to the former Spanish Court Painter José Luzan Martinéz and studied at (though at first he failed to be accepted for) the Academy San Fernando in Madrid. Very little is known of his life between the ages of 20 and 25 but his first professional commission was for a painting of the *Adoration of the Name of God by Angels* on the ceiling of the choir

in the Chapel of the Virgin in the Basilica Nuestra Señora del Pilar, Madrid (1772). He had evidently already established something of a reputation as a sought-after artist for he was paid the enormous sum of 15,000 reals for this work (then equivalent to the annual salary of a Court Painter). He went on to receive a royal commission from the future Charles IV to produce cartoons for tapestries for the Escorial and Prado Palaces and also gained the patronage of the Duke and Duchess of Osuna (formerly the Marquis and Marquise of Peñafiel). In 1785 he became Deputy Director of Painting at the

Academy of San Fernando, Madrid, then Court Painter to Charles III (1786) and in 1788 to his successor Charles IV (his portrait groups including the famous *The Family of Charles IV*, now in the Prado Museum). He was promoted Director of Painting at the Academy of San Fernando in 1795 but retired on health grounds in 1797. He painted the Royal Chapel of San Antonio de la Florida in Madrid (1798) and became First Court Painter (1799). When the French invaded Spain, Goya was allowed to continue to paint and was even granted a French decoration – after the French left Spain Goya was investigated, but found not guilty of collaboration (he never wore the decoration he had been given) and was reinstated as First Court Painter. From 1824 he lived in France.

Family/Sex Life: Goya married Josefa Bayen, sister of his friend Francisco Bayen, an eminent Court Painter; by her he fathered Vicente Anastasio and Francisco Javier. After her death he lived with Leocadia Weiss (a young relative of his daughter-in-law) and her 10-year-old daughter Rosario.

Appearance: He wore glasses.

Habits/Mannerisms: He loved chocolate.

Sport/Hobbies: Goya enjoyed shooting (he was a very good shot), especially partridges, rabbits, etc. He also enjoyed watching bullfights and taught himself to speak French.

Health: Goya contracted meningitis at the age of 47 (1793) and became deaf. From around the same time he also suffered from poor eyesight. Other ailments included paralysis of the bladder and a large tumour on the perineum (1825).

Work/Daily Routine: Goya was profoundly influenced by the paintings of fellow-Spaniard Domenico Tiepolo but maintained that 'I had three masters: Rembrandt, Velázquez and nature.' He was one of the few painters of his time to excel in engraving and aquatint (engraving which imitates wash drawing) and made his first engravings of Velázquez's work. He sold only 27 copies of his famous *Caprices* (sketches) in 1799 before the Inquisition intervened and banned them after just two days. He also painted portraits: the model for the famous *Nude Maja* was Pepito Tudo, mistress of Prime Minister Manuel Godoy (she is sometimes erroneously believed to be the Duchess of Alba). His celebrated paintings *2 May 1808* and *3 May 1808* (painted six years after the events portrayed) depict the shooting of demonstrators by the French after riots broke out in Madrid when Napoleon invaded (even though Spain was France's ally) in 'liberation' to clear the last Bourbons from the thrones of Europe. Vivid and shocking though the paintings are, Goya was not actually an eye-witness of the atrocities. He also painted the Duke of Wellington (who fought France on the Spanish side). He taught himself the new art of lithography. The 'Black Paintings' series were painted on the walls of two large rooms in his house, which was known as 'The House of the Deaf Man'. Among Goya's admirers was Baudelaire, who championed his work in *Le Présent* (1857).

Manner of Death: Goya died on 16 March 1828 in an apartment in the Fossés de l'Intendance, Bordeaux, France, aged 82.

GWYNNE, Nell (1650–87) English actress

Eleanor ('Nell') Gwynne (or Gwyn) was probably born in Coal Yard, Drury Lane, London on 2 February 1650, the second daughter of Eleanor Gwyn, a brothel-owner (who later drowned in a pond in Chelsea), and an unknown father, possibly a Captain Thomas Gwyn, a Welshman. She had an older sister, Rose. At first an orange-seller at the Theatre Royal, Drury Lane, London, she later became the leading comedienne of the King's Company and the most celebrated of Charles II's mistresses. Her first recorded performance, five years before she was taken up by Charles, was as Paulina in Killigrew's *Thomaso* (1664). Subsequently she was particularly admired in plays by John Dryden. She retired from the stage in 1682.

Family/Sex Life: Nell Gwynne was in succession mistress of the actor Charles Hart, then of Lord Buckhurst (Charles Sackville) and ultimately (1668) of Charles II, who gave her a fine house in Pall Mall. By Charles she had two sons – Charles Beauclerk, Duke of St Albans, and James Beauclerk (who died young). Her son Charles Beauclerk acquired his title when, in the king's hearing, his mother called to him: 'Come here, you little bastard' – the shocked monarch protested at her language, to which she demurely replied: 'But, sire, I have no better name to call him by.' Charles quickly appreciated his mistress's concern and had the child raised to the peerage without delay. Charles would have made Nell herself Countess of Greenwich had he lived and on his deathbed his last words (to his brother James II) were, according to Evelyn: 'Let not poor Nelly starve.' James honoured this last request and saw to it that she was provided for.

Appearance: Small, slender and very pretty, Nell Gwynne had a heart-shaped face, hazel eyes and chestnut hair. According to the *Dictionary of National Biography*, 'Her foot was diminutive and her eyes when she laughed became all but invisible.' At the moment when Charles II decided on making her his mistress she was wearing a large hat 'of the circumference of a large coachwheel' and reciting an epilogue. At that point in her career she was in great demand for reciting epilogues and prologues while wearing fantastic hats or clad in fanciful Amazonian dress. Her cartwheel hat (a caricature of French fashions) consequently became all the mode. She also wore a huge pearl necklace.

Habits/Mannerisms: A habitual swearer and illiterate, Nell Gwynne had to dictate her letters and signed them 'E. G.' Pepys testified to her unfettered profanity, reporting how he visited her after an ill-attended performance: 'But to see how Nell cursed for having so few people in the pit, was pretty.'

Sport/Hobbies: Nell Gwynne was a very good singer and dancer, as demonstrated by her performances on stage; she also played basset. She was very fond of silver plate (she had her own marked with her cypher 'E. G.').

Religion/Politics: Staunch Protestant (she was the only one of Charles II's mistresses not a Catholic – a fact that much endeared her to the public at large). She was reported to have given a copy of the Bible to Oliver Cromwell's porter in Bedlam.

Temperament: Samuel Pepys referred to Gwynne as 'Pretty, witty Nell' and added that she was 'the indiscreetest and wildest creature that ever was in a court'. Lively and quick-witted, she called King Charles her Charles the Third (after Hart and

Sackville). When a fellow-performer made to carry her off after she had died in character in an unidentified play she started up in typical fashion with the extemporized couplet: 'Hold off, you d–d confounded dog!/I am to rise and speak the epilogue!'

Work/Daily Routine: As a star of the London stage, she acted in plays by Aphra Behn, John Dryden and Beaumont and Fletcher among others. Dryden even wrote some parts especially for her and Aphra Behn dedicated *The Feigned Courtesans* (1679) to her. She disliked serious acting parts. Her last stage role was as Almahilde (her lover Charles Hart was Almanzor) in Dryden's *Almanzor and Almahide* (1670–1). As Charles's mistress she apparently made little attempt to intervene with matters of state, a restraint that was widely appreciated. Tradition has it that it

was she who persuaded Charles to build the Chelsea Royal Hospital. An anonymous verse of the period pungently expressed the popular preference for Gwynne above the king's other mistresses:

'Hard by Pall Mall lives a wench call'd
   Nell.
King Charles the Second he kept her.
She hath got a trick to handle his p—,
But never lays hands on his sceptre.
All matters of state from her soul she does
   hate,
And leaves to the politic bitches.
The whore's in the right, for 'tis her delight
To be scratching just where it itches.'

Manner of Death: Gwynne was stricken by apoplexy and paralysis on one side in March 1687 and died on 13 November 1687, aged 37. She was buried at her own request in St Martins-in-the-Fields Church, London.

HAMILTON, Emma (1765–1815) English mistress of Horatio, Lord Nelson

Emma Hamilton was christened Amy Lyon in Great Neston, Cheshire, on 12 May 1765, the daughter of Henry Lyon, a blacksmith (who died c.1765 when she was four) and his wife Mary. After her father's death her mother moved to her parents in Hawarden, Flintshire. Amy came to London in 1778 aged 15 and worked as a nursemaid, shop-girl, lady's maid, barmaid and appeared in the guise of the Goddess of Health in Dr Graham's Temple of Hymen, London (a brothel and strip club/health club). She called herself Emma/Emily Hart prior to her marriage to Sir William Hamilton but signed the register 'Amy Lyon'. However, she is best known as the mistress of Lord Nelson, whom she met in Naples, and as the favourite model of painter George Romney. After the deaths of her husband in 1803 and of Nelson at the Battle of Trafalgar in 1805, she quickly spent all she

had and, ignored by the Establishment, was obliged to declare herself bankrupt, being arrested for debt in 1813. She fled to Calais to escape her creditors a year later and ended her days there.

Family/Sex Life: Emma Hamilton was mistress first to Captain John Willet Payne, by whom she had a daughter, Emma. Subsequently she had a stillborn child by Sir Henry Fetherstonhaugh and then, in 1782, came under the protection of the Hon. Charles Greville MP (who also employed her mother as a cook/housekeeper). In 1786 she was sent to Greville's maternal uncle Sir William Hamilton, British Ambassador in Naples, in lieu of payment of his debts. She became Hamilton's wife in 1791, but later became the mistress of the already married Admiral Horatio Nelson, who fathered her daughters Horatia Nelson Thompson and

Emma (who died young) while Hamilton was still alive. The elderly Hamilton seems not to have resented his wife's scandalous association with the great naval hero – he died in Emma's arms, clutching Nelson's hand. In a codicil to his will Hamilton left to Nelson his favourite portrait of Emma, painted in enamel, declaring: 'God bless him, and shame fall on those who do not say Amen.' The liaison concerned the Admiralty, however, and in 1800 they ordered Nelson to come home from Naples, suggesting that in England (in other words, with his wife Fanny) he was more likely to recover his health and strength. Undaunted, Nelson separated from Fanny in 1801 and after Hamilton's death in 1803 lived openly with Emma. When Nelson lay dying at Trafalgar he pleaded with Captain Hardy: 'Take care of my dear Lady Hamilton, Hardy; take care of poor Lady Hamilton.' In a codicil to Nelson's will drawn up on the morning of the battle, he wrote: 'I leave Emma Lady Hamilton, therefore, a Legacy to my King and Country, that they will give her an ample provision to maintain her Rank of Life. I also leave to the beneficence of my Country my adopted daughter, Horatia Nelson Thompson [sic]; and I desire she will use in future the name of Nelson only. These are the only favours I ask my King and Country at this moment when I am going to fight their Battle.' The government decided, however, to ignore Nelson's request and gave Emma and her daughter nothing (though Nelson and Hamilton left them what would have been enough to keep them, had not Emma Hamilton lost it all through her extravagance and recklessness). By way of contrast, Nelson's wife Fanny prospered on a state annuity of £2000, while Nelson's sisters enjoyed grants of £15,000 each and his brother was awarded £90,000 and an annual pension of £5000.

Horatia was adopted by Nelson's younger sister and married a cleric, dying in 1881.

Appearance: Emma Hamilton had a very beautiful face, with dark grey eyes and auburn hair. After Nelson's death, however, she became grossly fat.

Habits/Mannerisms: She enjoyed gambling and this weakness contributed much to her imprisonment for debt in the King's Bench Prison in 1813.

Sport/Hobbies: She sang and danced extremely well and also spoke Italian, though she was still illiterate when living with Greville. She used to pose in *tableaux vivant* 'attitudes', which became famous in society.

Religion/Politics: Emma Hamilton turned to Roman Catholicism in her later years. She was rumoured to be a spy for Pitt and it was claimed that she had obtained a letter from the King of Spain to his brother, the King of Naples (brother-in-law of Marie Antoinette), stating his intention of declaring war on England, and had passed it on to Sir William Hamilton in Naples.

Health: Oppressed by her debts she declined in her later years and became an alcoholic.

Temperament: Emma Hamilton was lively, reckless and devoted to Nelson, who was drawn to her vivacious beauty. After a relatively modest upbringing, she developed a taste for extravagance in all things, a weakness that ultimately proved her undoing.

Manner of Death: Emma Hamilton died in exile in Calais on 15 January 1815, aged 49. She was buried in an oak coffin.

HARDY, Thomas (1840–1928) English novelist, poet and short-story writer

Thomas Hardy was born in Higher Bockhampton, near Stinsford, Dorset, on 2 June 1840, the eldest of four children of Thomas Hardy, a builder/stonemason, and Jemima Hand. Born five months after his parents' wedding, the doctor initially believed he was dead. His siblings, all younger, were Mary, Henry and Katharine, and he was a relative of Vice-Admiral Sir Thomas Masterman Hardy, to whom the dying Nelson addressed his famous last words 'Kiss me, Hardy'. Educated at the new school in Higher Bockhampton (he was its first pupil) in 1848 and at the British School, Dorchester (1849), he was apprenticed at 16 to the ecclesiastical architect John Hicks in Dorchester, restoring churches (1856–61). He then moved to London to work with Sir Arthur William Blomfeld (1862–7) but returned for health reasons to church restoration with Hicks (1867–70). He also assisted in work on St Pancras Station by supervising the removal of bodies from St Pancras cemetery through which the line went. Success as a novelist came with *Far from the Madding Crowd* (1874); it was followed by such classic stories as *The Return of the Native* (1878), *The Mayor of Casterbridge* (1886) and *Tess of the D'Urbervilles* (1891). After the scandal caused by *Jude the Obscure* (1896) he gave up novels to concentrate on poetry. President of the Society of Authors (succeeding Meredith), he was awarded the Order of Merit in 1910.

Family/Sex Life: Around 1867 Hardy fell in love with 16-year-old Tryphena Sparks, possibly his niece, though it is unclear how the relationship developed (the triangle was completed by Hardy's friend Horace Moule). In 1874 he married Emma Lavinia Gifford, the daughter of a Devonshire lawyer. The marriage was unhappy and Hardy later regretted his behaviour to

Emma, expressing his remorse in his poetry after her death. In 1914, two years after Emma's death, the 73-year-old Hardy married his 35-year-old secretary Florence Emily Dugdale. He had no children.

Appearance: Five feet six inches tall, Hardy had short dark chestnut hair parted on the left and sported a full beard (1867–90) but later wore just a moustache.

Habits/Mannerisms: Hardy ate frugally, drank little and was a non-smoker.

Sport/Hobbies: Hardy enjoyed cycling and took regular exercise. A fine draughtsman, he also played the fiddle at local dances (as had his father) and sang bass. He was a member of the Savile and Athenaeum Clubs and also of the Society for the Protection of Ancient Buildings.

Religion/Politics: A Christian, he considered taking Holy Orders but lost his faith in the 1860s (in his drama *The Dynasts* he referred to 'a local cult called Christianity'). He was a supporter of the Suffragettes.

Health: A weak child, he later enjoyed good health, though he suffered an internal haemorrhage in 1880.

Temperament: Emotional, humorous and fascinated by rural life, Hardy was also highly sensitive, reacting badly to criticism of his 'pessimistic' and 'immoral' novels and of his use of dialect words. His friends included Edmund Gosse, the dialect poet William Barnes, A. E. Housman, Algernon Swinburne, Augustus John and T. E. Lawrence. Another admirer was Edward VIII, who visited Hardy's home when Prince of Wales (1923).

Pets: Hardy kept both cats and dogs. His

dog Moss was killed by a tramp, while his wirehaired terrier Wessex was notorious for attacking visitors, with the exception of T. E. Lawrence (it once tore Galsworthy's trousers). Hardy loved the dog as it deterred callers – it featured in three poems and was very spoilt, walking on the table at meals. One of the cats was eulogized in a poem when it died; his last cat, Cobby, a grey Persian with orange eyes, survived him.

Work/Daily Routine: Hardy started writing fiction aged 40. His first published article, 'How I Built Myself a House', was published in 1865 and his first novel, *Desperate Remedies*, in 1871 (Hardy had to guarantee the publisher against loss to the tune of £325 – half Hardy's savings). His own favourite among his novels was his first success, *Far From the Madding Crowd*, commissioned by Leslie Stephen (Virginia Woolf's father) for the *Cornhill Magazine*. In chapter 50 of this book Hardy first introduced the fictional 'Wessex'. *Tess of the D'Urbervilles* was attacked as 'immoral', while a copy of *Jude* was burnt by the Bishop of Wakefield, and the *New York Bookman* called it 'one of the most objectionable books that we have ever read in any language whatsoever'. George Moore

called Hardy 'an abortion of George Eliot', but Arnold Bennett said: 'Never in English prose literature was such a seer of beauty as Thomas Hardy' and Tennyson named *A Pair of Blue Eyes* (set in Cornwall rather than Wessex) his best novel when they met in 1880. In his turn, Hardy admired Shelley and Keats (he quoted Keats's 'Ode to Sorrow' on the title page of *The Return of the Native*). Hardy burned all his papers before he died and his biography, ostensibly by Florence, was actually written by him (100,000 words were delivered to the publisher only three weeks after his death).

Manner of Death: Hardy died in his self-built mansion 'Max Gate', near Dorchester, where he had lived for some 44 years, around 9 pm on 11 January 1928, aged 87, after Florence had read him one verse from *The Rubaiyat of Omar Khayyam*. Pallbearers at his funeral included J. M. Barrie, Galsworthy, Gosse, Housman, Kipling and George Bernard Shaw. He was cremated in Dorchester and his ashes were buried in Poets' Corner, Westminster Abbey, beside Dickens. His heart was supposedly buried in Stinsford Churchyard with his first wife (though there is a tale that his sister's cat stole it).

HEMINGWAY, Ernest Miller (1899–1961) US novelist and short-story writer

Ernest Hemingway was born in Oak Park, near Chicago, Illinois, on 21 July 1899, the son of Clarence Edmonds Hemingway, a doctor who committed suicide by shooting himself in the right ear, and Grace Hall, a music teacher. He had an older sister Marcelline and younger siblings Madelaine, Ursula, Carol and Leicester. Educated at the Oak Park and River Forest Township High School, he then lived with his uncle in Kansas City, Missouri, and worked as a newspaper reporter. Classified

unfit because of defective eyesight, in World War I he served briefly as a Second Lieutenant in a Red Cross ambulance unit in Italy (April 1918). He later moved to Chicago and wrote for the *Toronto Star*. With letters of introduction from Sherwood Anderson to Gertrude Stein, Sylvia Beach and Ezra Pound, he then moved to Paris with his first wife. Here he started a 'Letter from Europe' series for the *Toronto Star* and worked (unpaid) as editorial assistant on Ford Madox Ford's

Transatlantic Review (1924). He published his first novel, *The Sun Also Rises*, in 1926. Among the books that followed were *A Farewell to Arms* (1929), *Death in the Afternoon* (1932), the short-story collection *Winner Takes Nothing* (1933) and *For Whom the Bell Tolls* (1940). He was a war correspondent during the Spanish Civil War and again during World War II (in London, helped by Roald Dahl). He subsequently spent 20 years in San Francisco de Paula, Cuba, then, when Castro came to power, moved to Ketchum, Idaho. He was awarded the Pulitzer Prize (1953) for the novella *The Old Man and the Sea* (1952) and the Nobel Prize for Literature (1954).

Family/Sex Life: In 1921 Hemingway married Elizabeth Hadley Richardson, by whom he fathered John Hadley Nicaner ('Bumby') – named after the bullfighter Nicaner Villalla. He deserted them in 1926 (in his own words, 'Because I am a bastard') and in 1928 married Pauline Pfeiffer. He had by her two sons, Patrick and Gregory. His third wife (1940) was journalist and novelist Martha Gellhorn, while his fourth (1946) was a journalist working for the London *Daily Express*, Mary Welsh. He also claimed to have slept with Mata Hari in 1918 (though she was shot a year earlier).

Appearance: Six feet tall with a broad chest and large feet, Hemingway was, according to James Joyce, 'a big, powerful peasant, as strong as a buffalo'. He wore a short moustache and parted his hair on the left. A scar on his forehead dated from a car crash in London (1944). He often wore a tennis visor when reading and owned a leather belt inscribed '*Gott Mit Uns*'.

Habits/Mannerisms: Hemingway ate rye crisps and peanut-butter sandwiches when working and disliked sweets. When he was too poor to feed his family in Paris he killed pigeons in the Luxembourg Gardens and took them home to eat, concealed in his son's pram. His favourite drinks

included Valpolicella, daiquiris, Scotch, tequila and bourbon. He could not pronounce the letter L – saying 'wiwwies' instead of 'lilies', for instance.

Sport/Hobbies: Hemingway was passionate about hunting and was a good shot – though he needed glasses. He also enjoyed bull-fighting, deep-sea fishing (he founded a marlin fishing tournament in Cuba – Castro winning it in 1960), skiing and boxing and swam half a mile a day. He kept a 38-foot diesel cruiser, *Pilar*, in Key West. He spoke good French, played the cello and sang in church choirs and also collected art – he owned Miró's *The Farm* and works by Braque, Klee, Juan Gris and André Masson.

Religion/Politics: In later life, he became a Catholic and gave the money from his Nobel Prize award to the Shrine of the Virgin in Cuba.

Health: Hemingway was badly wounded by a trench mortar near Fossalta, Italy (1918). Years later, he buried a 1000-lira note at the same spot so he could claim he had contributed both blood and money to Italian soil. His right arm was broken in a car crash in Wyoming (1930) and he was badly injured in a plane crash in Africa (1960). On another occasion he tried to commit suicide by walking into the propeller of a plane. He also sweated profusely and suffered from a defective left eye, haemorrhoids, kidney trouble, a torn groin muscle, bronchial pneumonia, amoebic dysentery, a prolapse of the lower intestine, liver trouble, high blood-pressure, high cholesterol and an inflamed aorta.

Temperament: Known to his friends as 'Papa', he also liked to be called Porthos, Butch, the Old Brute and Hemingstein (he called himself 'Ernie Hemorrhoid' during World War I). He disliked public speaking, declaring: 'A writer should write what he has to say and not speak it' (from his 13-line Nobel Prize speech).

Pets: Hemingway kept dogs – among them the black springer spaniels Blackie (or 'Black Dog', male) and Negrita (female) – and 30 cats (including Boise, Princesa, Bigotes, Fatso, Friendless, Uncle Willy, Uncle Wolfie, Barbershop, Ecstasy, Spendthrift, F. Puss and Christopher Columbus), explaining that he liked cats for their 'absolute emotional honesty'. He once observed: 'Dogs is trumps but cats is the longest suit we hold.'

Work/Daily Routine: Hemingway began writing at first light, commencing by sharpening the pencils with which he wrote on 'onion-skin paper'. He revised his work while typing it up on a Remington or Corona Portable No. 3, standing up (because of a back injury). He wrote mostly in his bedroom or, while in Cuba, in a special workroom. He wrote 500 words a day (*The Sun Also Rises* took six weeks) and rewrote the ending of *A Farewell to Arms* 39 times. In the 1920s his wife Hadley (en route to meet him in Lausanne) left a suitcase containing virtually all his stories and poems – originals and carbon copies – unattended in the Gare de Lyon, Paris, and it was stolen. Hemingway had no option but to rewrite everything.

Manner of Death: Hemingway shot himself with a double-barrelled shotgun placed against his forehead very early in the morning on Sunday 2 July 1961 at home in Ketchum, Idaho, aged 61. He was buried in Idaho.

HENRY VIII (1491–1547) King of England, Wales and Ireland

Henry VIII, 'bluff King Hal', was born on 28 June 1491 in Greenwich Palace, London, the third child and only surviving son of Henry VII and Elizabeth of York, daughter of Edward IV. He had an elder brother, Arthur, who died before succeeding to the throne, an elder sister Margaret (who married James IV of Scotland) and a younger sister Mary (who married Louis XII of France). Well educated (his tutors included poet John Skelton), he became king in April 1509 (aged 17) on the death of his father and reigned for 37 years. Though he visited France (Calais) for the magnificent mutual friendship display called the 'Field of the Cloth of Gold', he only saw the north of England once. His reign witnessed the establishment of the Church of England, with Henry at its head, the suppression of the monasteries and wars with France and Scotland.

Family/Sex Life: Henry was married six times. At the age of 11 he was betrothed to Katherine of Aragon, daughter of King Ferdinand of Spain and his brother's widow. They were married by special dispensation of the Pope in 1509 and she gave birth to a daughter, Mary I. The marriage was nullified in May 1533, by which time Henry had already secretly married the pregnant Anne Boleyn, daughter of Sir Thomas Boleyn and a lady-in-waiting to Katherine of Aragon and younger sister of Henry's former mistress Mary Boleyn. Anne's daughter became Elizabeth I, but when Anne miscarried a second child Henry accused her of witchcraft and had her executed (1536) for adultery and incest. His third wife (1536) was Jane Seymour, daughter of Sir John Seymour, to whom he became engaged the day after Anne's execution. Seymour died in 1537 giving birth to Edward VI. Henry's fourth wife (1540) was Anne of Cleves, sister of William Duke of Cleves, whom Henry knew only from a flattering portrait by Hans Holbein. Anne turned out to be plain and Henry protested that he had been sent a 'Flanders mare', but married her anyway for political reasons. The marriage remained unconsummated and they were divorced the same year. Next Henry married (1540) 19-year-old Catherine Howard, Anne Boleyn's cousin and a maid-of-honour of Anne of Cleves. Catherine was executed for infidelity in 1542. Henry's last wife (1543) was twice widowed Catherine Parr – she outlived Henry and took a fourth husband after his death. The fate of Henry's wives may be remembered by the mnemonic: 'Divorced, beheaded, died,/Divorced, beheaded, survived.' Henry also had an illegitimate son, Henry Fitzroy, through a liaison with Elizabeth (Bessie) Blount, one of Katherine of Aragon's ladies-in-waiting (he died young).

Appearance: Tall and thickset, with blue-grey eyes, short auburn hair combed forward in the French fashion and a fair complexion, Henry was handsome in his youth, but became bloated and fat (he had a 54-inch waist aged 50). The mature Henry had a ruddy face, fleshy cheeks and a beard. He dressed lavishly, wearing a gold collar with a diamond as big as a walnut and jewelled rings.

Sport/Hobbies: A great athlete in his youth, Henry threw the javelin and enjoyed hunting, hawking, archery, jousting and tennis. He spoke French, Spanish, Latin and some Italian and was a good musician (he played the lute and harpsichord well and could sing from sight); he reputedly composed 'Greensleeves' amongst other tunes. His books included the bestselling anti-Lutheran *Assertio Septem Sacramentorum* (1521). A patron of the arts, he encouraged Holbein and built St James's Palace and Nonesuch Palace, near Hampton Court, to rival Versailles. He also built up the Royal Navy – his flagship *Mary Rose* had cloth-of-gold sails and, top-heavy, immediately sank at Southampton (to be raised some 450 years later).

Religion/Politics: Henry was initially a devout Catholic, Pope Leo X dubbing him *Fidei Defensor* ('Defender of the Faith') for his anti-Luther stance. Subsequently he broke with Rome and, ordering the Dissolution of the monasteries, made himself head of the Church of England. He was excommunicated in 1533. He executed many of his advisers after they dared to oppose him, including Thomas Cromwell, Thomas More and Cardinal John Fisher, Bishop of Rochester (the latter after he appealed to the Holy Roman Emperor Charles V to invade England).

Health: Henry enjoyed robust health in his youth but later contracted smallpox (1514), malaria (1521), syphilis and dropsy. Other ailments included headaches, ulcers on both legs (caused by syphilis, varicose veins or osteomyelitis), a painful fistula on one leg (from 1537), loss of speech for a week as the result of a lung blockage (1538) and tertian fever (1541). By 1545 he could neither walk nor stand and had to be carried in a litter and winched up and down stairs.

Temperament: When young flamboyant and good-humoured (he kept the famous court jester Will Somers), as an older man Henry was irascible and ruthless. He showed little remorse for his ruthlessness – when Katherine of Aragon died (1536) he and Anne Boleyn dressed in yellow and celebrated with a banquet, dancing and jousting. Martin Luther called Henry 'the spawn of an adder ... a frantic madman'. Others nicknamed Henry 'Copper-Nose Henry' because (from 1526) he debased the coinage by adding copper to silver coins (the silver quickly rubbed away on the nose of his portrait to reveal the copper beneath).

Work/Daily Routine: Around 1540 Henry's routine was to rise between 5 and 6 am, to hear mass at 7 am, and to go riding till 10 am before settling down to the day's business. He ruled through a Council of State (all church leaders), until

Cardinal Thomas Wolsey (Chancellor for 15 years) was succeeded by layman Sir Thomas More. He only called four parliaments in his reign (1510, 1512, 1515 and 1523), and then only to raise money.

Motto/Emblem: His motto *'Coure Loyall'* (true heart) was embroidered on his clothes in the form of a heart symbol with the word 'loyall'. His emblem was a Tudor rose and the Beaufort portcullis (Henry

VII's mother was the last of the Beauforts).

Manner of Death: Henry died in St James's Palace, Westminster, around 2 am on Friday 28 January 1547, aged 55. His last words were: 'All is lost! Monks, Monks, Monks!' His funeral procession to Windsor was four miles long (a waxwork figure of him had its own chariot). He was buried at Windsor Castle beside Jane Seymour (at his own request).

HITLER, Adolf (1889–1945) Austrian-born German dictator

Adolf (Adolfus on his birth certificate) Hitler was born on 20 April 1889 in Braunau-am-Inn, Austria, the oldest surviving child of customs inspector Aloys Hitler by his third wife, Klara Pölzl. His father, who was illegitimate, at first took his mother's name, Schicklgrüber, and then Hiedler (after his stepfather's brother); in 1876 it became Hitler. He had a younger sister Paula, a younger brother Edmund (who died aged five) and an older half-brother Alois and half-sister Angela. Educated in Linz, he left school at 16 and, intending to be an architect and painter, twice failed to get into the Vienna Academy of Fine Arts. At first he worked by painting postcards and advertisements and later as a draughtsman in Munich. During World War I he served on the Western Front and was awarded the Iron Cross Second Class (1914) and First Class (1918). Subsequently he led the fledgling Socialist German Workers' Party (later the Nazi Party). In 1923 he was imprisoned for five years (released after nine months) after the unsuccessful Munich Putsch (inspired by Mussolini's March on Rome). While behind bars he wrote *Mein Kampf* ('My Struggle'). He became a German citizen in order to run for President but lost; when the Nazis became the largest party in the Reichstag he stood for Chancellor. Failing again to be elected, he

finally became Chancellor in 1933. After the death of Hindenberg (1934) he became President, Chancellor and leader of Germany's armed forces, calling himself *Führer* (Leader), and charted a course that led subsequently to World War II.

Family/Sex Life: Hitler had affairs with 16-year-old Mitzi Reiter (1927) and with Geli Raubal, daughter of his half-sister Angela (Geli shot herself in 1931). In 1945, the day before their deaths, he married his mistress Eva Braun, a photographer's shop assistant whom he met in 1932. She twice attempted suicide because of his infidelities. Hitler's half-sister Angela called Eva *'die blöde Kuh'* ('stupid cow').

Appearance: Hitler had blue eyes and a toothbrush moustache (longer in World War I); his immaculately combed dark hair was parted on the right. Though he was only a lance-corporal in active service, he became leader of Germany's armed forces and during World War II was photographed almost exclusively in the uniform of a senior army officer.

Habits/Mannerisms: Hitler became a vegetarian after Geli Raubal's suicide and was teetotal and a non-smoker. He drank apple-peel tea, opposed the use of cosmetics and refused to fly in Zeppelins, claiming they were against nature.

Sport/Hobbies: Hitler owned two identical Mercedes-Benz 770K cars with armour-plate and bullet-proof glass. He also tried to buy the only Rolls-Royce Silver Wraith in Germany but Rolls-Royce had it driven 300 miles into Poland on 1 September 1939.

Religion/Politics: Hitler was anti-Semitic and highly superstitious. He used to pour molten lead into water to predict the future and timed major offensives for the seventh of the month as he felt seven was lucky. When blinded by gas in World War I he resolved to enter politics if his sight returned. By 1927 he held membership card number one of the renamed National Socialist German Workers' Party, arguing for rearmament and for additional German *'Lebensraum'* ('living space'). Whipping up hatred of foreigners in general and minority groups like the Jews in particular, he created for the NSDAP a distinctive iconography, with Roman standards, eagles, swastikas etc. Adherents of the party included Prince August Wilhelm (the youngest son of Kaiser Wilhelm II), Prince Philip von Hessen (Queen Victoria's grandson), steel magnate Krupp and industrialists Bosch and I. G. Farben.

Health: Hitler recovered from his war wounds but in later years became a hypochondriac and at one time took 28 types of medication, including injections from bulls' testicles. His shoulder was dislocated in the Munich Putsch – when fired on only Ludendorff kept walking. Hitler was uninjured in an assassination attempt at the Munich Beer Hall in 1939, having left early, but was nearly killed in the 1944 Von Stauffenberg plot – he escaped with a fractured nasal septum, but suffered chronic headaches thereafter. He also nursed a lifelong paranoia about

cancer (his mother died of breast cancer in 1907).

Temperament: Obsessed by his vision of a powerful Aryan Germany, Hitler identified himself with past dictators and frequently relied on intuition. He admired Frederick the Great (Goebbels read Carlyle's biography of Frederick to Hitler in the Berlin bunker). At the end of his life he had few admirers left, but in earlier years he could claim many sympathizers, including George Bernard Shaw and Gertrude Stein (who said he should get the Nobel Peace Prize).

Pets: While at the Front in World War I Hitler kept a small dog called Fuchsl (he trained it to walk up and down ladders, but the dog was stolen in 1917). Later he kept alsatians, including Wolf (1928) and Blondi, a gift from Martin Bormann (in the bunker Hitler tested his cyanide on Blondi first – it worked).

Work/Daily Routine: *Mein Kampf* was originally called *Four and a Half Years of Struggle against Lies, Stupidity and Cowardice; Settling Accounts with the Destroyers of the National Socialist Movement.* Hitler first saw the ancient swastika in a coat of arms in a monastery as a child – it was first used as an emblem, together with the *'Heil'* salute, by the anti-Semitic Thule Society and later adopted by Hitler for the Nazis. At his summer residence, the Berghof in Obersalzberg, he had lunch at 4 pm and dinner at 9 pm.

Manner of Death: The evidence suggests that Hitler shot himself in the right temple in the Berlin bunker on 30 April 1945, aged 56, while Eva Braun took poison. His body was burned in the garden of the Reich Chancellery, Berlin, and the remains were reputedly later buried by Soviet troops.

HOBBES, Thomas (1588–1679) English political philosopher

Thomas Hobbes was born in Malmesbury, Wiltshire, on Good Friday, 5 April 1588, the second son of Thomas Hobbes, Vicar of Charlton and Westport, and his wife, a member of the Middleton family (Christian name unknown). The fright of the Spanish invasion supposedly brought on his mother's labour. He had a brother Edmund (a glover) and a sister. His father had a fight with a parson and fled the district, Thomas being brought up in Malmesbury by his uncle Francis, a wealthy glover. He was educated at Malmesbury School and, from the age of 14, at Magdalen Hall, Oxford (BA 1607). At first he worked as a page to the Earl of Devonshire and kept his privy purse, but later became Charles II's maths tutor when Prince of Wales and exiled in Paris. Subsequently he was tutor to the 2nd Earl of Cavendish and after his death to his son, the 3rd Earl, later becoming his secretary. He also served as amanuensis to Sir Francis Bacon and helped to translate Bacon's *Essays* into Latin. After publication of his *The Elements of Law* (1640) he was forced to flee England and spent 11 years abroad. He returned to England under Cromwell in 1651 and was granted a pension after the Restoration. He was also a member of the Virginia Company and a shareholder of the Somer Islands Company (which invested in settlements in Virginia and the Bermudas). His celebrated writings included books on government and the famous *Leviathan* (1651), in which he expressed his political philosophy.

Family/Sex Life: Unmarried, though he fathered an illegitimate daughter by an unidentified woman.

Appearance: Over six feet tall, Hobbes sported a short bristling auburn moustache, though he had jet black hair in his youth and was thus known as 'Crowe' at school. He became completely bald in old age. Aubrey (Hobbes's neighbour in Wiltshire) left the following description: 'Face not very great; ample forehead; whiskers yellowish-reddish, which naturally turned up ... Belowe he was shaved close, except a little tip under his lip ... He had a good eie, and that of a hazel colour, which was full of Life and Spirit, even to the last.'

Habits/Mannerisms: Aubrey recorded that Hobbes 'Spoke broade Devonshire [sic] to his dyeing day.' He used to sing loudly in bed each night to strengthen his lungs, though he also smoked a pipe. He did not drink much and gave wine up altogether after the age of 60. He ate mostly fish and by the age of 70 was both teetotal and vegetarian.

Sport/Hobbies: Hobbes played tennis (even at the age of 75). He spoke French and Italian and translated Greek and Latin, and discovered an interest in geometry aged 40, after which 'he was wont to draw lines on his thigh and on the sheetes, abed', according to Aubrey. Another pleasure was singing, especially songs by Sir Henry Lawes (the foremost songwriter of the day, whose brother set Herrick's 'Gather Ye Rosebuds' to music).

Religion/Politics: An agnostic, he was attacked by critics as an atheist.

Health: Though unhealthy in his youth – 'of an ill complexion (yellowish); he tooke colds, being wett in his feet' (Aubrey) – by the age of 40 he was stronger with a 'fresh, ruddy complexion', though after 1650 he suffered from 'the shaking Palsey in his hands'.

Temperament: Hobbes did not have a

pronounced sense of humour, and Charles II dubbed him 'the Bear' because the Court wits always baited him. His friends included Ben Jonson, Francis Bacon and William Harvey (who left him £10 in his will). He was also admired by Dryden.

Work/Daily Routine: Hobbes rose around 7 am, had a breakfast of bread and butter, then walked and meditated until 10 am, took lunch at 11 am, had a pipe of tobacco followed by a half hour's nap and wrote up his thoughts in the afternoon. He had a walking-stick with a pen and ink in the top and always carried a notebook – it was in this manner that he composed his masterpiece *Leviathan*. His books were

banned in Britain so were published instead in Holland (they were also banned by the Vatican and put on the Index of prohibited books). Hobbes owned very few books himself, but was an indefatigable worker to the end of his long life – writing his autobiography in Latin verse (aged 84) and aged 86 finishing translations of the *Odyssey* and the *Iliad*. He also translated Thucydides's *History of the Peloponnesian War*.

Manner of Death: Hobbes died of 'strangury', paralysed and speechless, on 4 December 1679, aged 91. He was buried in Ault Hucknall Church.

HOGARTH, William (1697–1764) English painter, engraver and caricaturist

William Hogarth was born in Bartholomew Close, Smithfield, London on 10 November 1697, the son of Richard Hogarth, a schoolmaster and hack writer. He had two younger sisters, Mary and Ann. He was taught art at the school of Sir James Thornhill, Serjeant-Painter to the King, and was apprenticed to a silver plate engraver. After the death of his father he set up on his own as an engraver (*c.* 1720), designing illustration plates for booksellers and printsellers. Unfortunately, later much of his work was plagiarized and sold at reduced prices (a situation eventually remedied by the passing of 'Hogarth's Act' in 1735, which aimed to protect the copyright of engravers). His series of pictures *The Harlot's Progress* (1732) was the first of a succession of very popular satirical 'moral pictures' issued in print form. Among the most well-known of the pictures/series that followed were *The Rake's Progress* (1733–5), *Marriage à la Mode* (1743–5), the *Industry and Idleness* series (1747) and the prints *Beer Street* and *Gin Lane* (1750–1). He was also the author of a treatise on aesthetics, *The*

Analysis of Beauty (1753), and in 1757 succeeded his brother-in-law, John Thornhill, as Serjeant-Painter to the king.

Family/Sex Life: In 1729 Hogarth was secretly married to Jane, daughter of Sir James Thornhill, his art-school teacher, without her father's consent. After Thornhill's death his widow lived with Hogarth and his wife at their country retreat, Hogarth's House in Chiswick (now a museum).

Appearance: Very short in stature, Hogarth had blue eyes and a scar over his right eye.

Habits/Mannerisms: Hogarth liked good living and enjoyed fine clothes. He drank beer and port.

Sport/Hobbies: A favourite game was nine-pins.

Temperament: Hogarth was aggressive, outspoken and pugnacious by nature. He was also loyal and committed to social reform, giving generously to charities, especially orphanages and hospitals. He considered himself a serious artist, and resented the public's conception of him as a painter of populist 'vogue' pictures alone. He hated foreigners, especially the French. He was also forgetful – he owned a fine coach but on one occasion, after visiting the Lord Mayor of London, quite forgot it and walked home in the rain. His friends included Henry Fielding, who collaborated with him in the 1730s and defended him against his critics. Other writers who admitted his influence upon them included Smollett, Dickens and Thackeray. Another admirer was Charles Lamb, who wrote the essay 'On the Genius of Hogarth'.

Pets: He had a dog called Trump and painted himself with it in *Portrait of the Painter and his Pug* (1745).

Work/Daily Routine: Hogarth had a great technical memory for art, having the habit of 'retaining in my mind's eye, without coldly copying it on the spot, whatever I intended to imitate'. He established his reputation in his twenties, chiefly with his 'conversation pieces' depicting poignant melodramatic scenes of contemporary London life and with his portraits, notably *David Garrick as Richard III*. He painted numerous portraits of the nobility, but

insisted on portraying his subjects with merciless realism, refusing to disguise physical imperfections. When commissioned to paint the portrait of a particularly ugly nobleman, the finished picture so offended the sitter that he refused to pay for it – whereupon Hogarth threatened to embellish it with a tail and other appendages and sell it for display in a freakshow: the nobleman promptly paid up, took the picture away and burnt it. Copies of Hogarth's engravings were sold at a shilling each. He rarely left London, the subject of many of his most famous pictures, though he twice visited France (on the second occasion, 1748, he was sent back to England after being arrested for sketching the fortifications at Calais).

Manner of Death: Hogarth died, aged 66, after a vomiting fit on 25 October 1764 in the arms of Mrs Mary Lewis, his landlady and the cousin of his wife, at his town house in Leicester Fields, London. He had just written a draft reply to a letter from Benjamin Franklin. He was buried in Chiswick churchyard. Epitaphs included one by David Garrick and the following by Dr Johnson:

'The hand of him here torpid lies,
That drew th'essential forms of grace;
Here, closed in death, th'attentive eyes,
That saw the manners in the face.'

HOUDINI, Harry (1874–1926) US-born magician and escapologist

Ehrich Weiss (later Harry Houdini) was born in Appleton, Wisconsin, on 6 April 1874, the elder son and fifth child of emigré Hungarian Rabbi Mayer Samuel Weiss and Cecelia Steiner. He ran away from home aged 12 and worked briefly (as a magician and escapologist) with his younger brother Theodore, but later his wife became part of the act. He took his pseudonym from the French

magician Robert Houdin, whom he admired, and became famous for his death-defying escapes from locked boxes, cells and coffins, even under water. He later came to the UK and made a sensational escape from Scotland Yard. President of the Society of American Magicians, he also starred in three films.

Family/Sex Life: Houdini married

Wilhelmina Rahner ('Beatrice'). They had no children, but 'invented' a son in their letters to each other.

Appearance: Five feet six inches tall, Houdini was bow-legged.

Sport/Hobbies: He collected playbills and magic/spiritualist material – his collection being donated to the Library of Congress on his death.

Religion/Politics: After failing to communicate with his mother on her death in 1913, Houdini turned against spiritualism, mind-readers and mediums and wrote two books exposing their methods. He inspired great confidence in others – Sarah Bernhardt believed he could restore her lost leg through his magic powers. Arthur Conan Doyle, meanwhile, believed he could dematerialize himself.

Health: Great physical strength.

Temperament: According to the *Dictionary of American Biography*, Houdini – the so-called 'Handcuff King' – had a 'curious combination of aggressiveness and sentimentality ... capable of indulging in bitter feuds and violent bursts of temper'. Among his friends he had something of a reputation for tightfistedness and was notorious for avoiding paying his share of restaurant bills. On one occasion, at the end of a shared meal, his friends outwitted him by promising to show him a new trick – they persuaded him to place his hands palm down on the table, then placed two full glasses of water on them before making good their escape with the challenge, 'Let's see you get out of *that* without paying the bill!'

Manner of Death: Houdini died in Detroit of peritonitis on 31 October 1926, aged 52. His premature death resulted from being punched in the stomach by a man wishing to test his boast that he could withstand any blow – unfortunately the man hit him before he could tense his stomach muscles. He was buried in the coffin he used for his 'buried alive' act in Machpelah Cemetery, New York. Two of the pallbearers at the funeral were Broadway producers Charles Dillingham and Florenz Ziegfeld – as they carried the coffin to the grave Dillingham reputedly whispered to Ziegfeld, 'Ziggie, I bet you a hundred bucks he ain't in here.' Houdini had promised his wife he would return from the dead to communicate with her and to unlock a pair of handcuffs, but he never did. Since his death his name has become synomous with escapology, in a variety of spheres: US President Franklin D. Roosevelt was dubbed the 'Houdini in the White House' because of his ability to wriggle out of tricky situations, while a successor Richard Nixon was called the 'Houdini of American Politics' for similar reasons, prior to the Watergate scandal.

HUGO, Victor Marie (1802–85) French poet, playwright and novelist

---

Victor Hugo was born on 26 February 1802 in Besançon, France, the third son of General Joseph-Leopold-Sigisbert Hugo (Count of Siguenza, Governor of Madrid and adviser of King Joseph of Spain, Napoleon's brother) and Sophie Françoise Trébuchet. Named after his godparents, General Victor Lahorie and Marie Dessirier (wife of the garrison commander at Besançon), he had two older brothers, Eugène and Abel. He was educated at Cordier and Decotte's School and at the École Polytechnique in Paris. His father fled to Bois with another woman (and his fortune) following the fall of Napoleon and his parents separated (1815). The family was then brought up by his father's sister. At first he worked (1819–21) with his brothers on a literary monthly they founded, *Le Conservateur littéraire*. After the successful publication of his first book of poems (*Odes*, 1822, dedicated to Hugo's wife Adèle), Louis XVIII gave him a pension. Among the most celebrated works that followed were the plays *Hernani* (1830) and *Ruy Blas* (1838), such books of poetry as *Les Feuilles d'automne* (1831) and the novels *Nôtre Dame de Paris* (The Hunchback of Nôtre Dame, 1831) and *Les Misérables* (1862). He also served in the 1st Légion National Guard. A member of the Académie Française (1841), he founded the Renaissance Théâtre. Elected to represent his *arrondissement* in the Assembly (1848), he founded the newspaper *L'Événement* (later banned and renamed *L'Événement du Peuple*) the same year. Created a Vicomte (1845), he was not a good speaker but was elected to the Senate in 1875. The Avenue Victor Hugo was named in his honour in his 80th year.

Family/Sex Life: In 1822 Hugo married Adèle Foucher, by whom he fathered Léopold, Léopoldine, Charles, François-Victor and Adèle (whose godfather was Lamartine). His father remained absent from the wedding, while his brother Eugène, who also loved Adèle, went mad at the ceremony and had to be put in an asylum, where he died. Hugo had many mistresses, including actress Juliette Drouet (*c*.1832) – who nicknamed him 'Toto' and worked as his copyist – and Léonce d'Aunet (from 1844), the wife of the painter August Biard (Hugo was acquitted, relying upon the inviolability of peerage, when prosecuted for adultery, but she was imprisoned). His many mistresses in his old age reputedly included actress Sarah Bernhardt, Théophile Gautier's daughter Judith and a 22-year-old maid in Guernsey.

Appearance: Five feet seven inches tall,

Hugo had a large forehead, small black eyes and brown hair. He regularly grew a beard after a throat illness he thought was tuberculosis of the larynx.

Habits/Mannerisms: He drank beer.

Sport/Hobbies: As well as his writing, Hugo was also a good artist.

Religion/Politics: Royalist, then Republican. He supported Louis-Napoleon Bonaparte as President on the abdication of Louis Philippe, but later turned against him and was forced into voluntary exile after the imprisonment of his sons and the Paris massacres – he escaped to Brussels as 'Jacques-Firmin Lanvin, compositor', but was then expelled and went to St Helier, Jersey. Ejected from Jersey, he bought Hauteville House, Guernsey, with the 20,000 francs in royalties from the sale of the long poem *Les Contemplations*. He returned to Paris after 19 years' exile to a huge reception (1870), but was subsequently, during the Commune, obliged to flee once more to Brussels.

Health: Born a puny child with a huge head, he was not expected to live.

Temperament: Hugo was very egotistical – the word 'I' often cropped up in his speech and he lost a lot of friends through his self-obsession. Those remaining included Dumas, Sainte-Beuve and Lamartine. He could be very generous, however – he entertained 40 poor children to dinner every Monday while in Guernsey and paid off Juliette Drouet's enormous debts. Tennyson said of him, 'Victor Hugo lacks commonsense. He is a compound of grandeur and absurdity.'

Pets: He kept a cat called Chanoine and a dog called Chougna.

Work/Daily Routine: While still at school, Hugo wrote riddles and acrostics. He greatly admired Chateaubriand. His first novel *Han d'Islande* (1823) was published anonymously. *Nôtre Dame de Paris* took him six months to write, while the verse play *Ruy Blas* took him just three months. *Les Misérables* and *Nôtre Dame de Paris* were both banned by the Vatican and put on the Index of prohibited books. *Les Misérables*, incidentally, contains the world's longest sentence – 2½ pages, comprising 823 words, with 93 commas, 52 semi-colons and four dashes. In contrast, the telegram he sent to the publishers enquiring after sales of the book read simply: '?' (the reply that was returned read '!'). When in Guernsey he woke at dawn (at the sound of a cannon fired from the nearby fort), worked till 11 am, then stripped and poured ice-cold water over himself, rubbed himself with a friction glove and took lunch at noon.

Motto: '*Ego Hugo*' (invented by himself).

Manner of Death: Hugo caught pneumonia on 18 May 1885 and died on 22 May, aged 83. His last words were 'I see black light.' At his own request his body was laid in a pauper's pine coffin. He lay in state beneath the Arc de Triomphe in Paris and was then buried in the Panthéon before a huge crowd (two million).

IBSEN, Henrik Johan (1828–1906) Norwegian playwright

Henrik Ibsen was born on 20 March 1828 in 'Stockmannsgaarden', a large house in the main square of Skien, Telemark province, Norway, the oldest surviving child of Knud Plesner Ibsen, a wealthy merchant, general store owner and schnapps distiller. His mother was Marichen Cornelia Martine Altenburg, the daughter of a prosperous shipmaster and merchant. Apart from his father, all his paternal relatives had been sea-captains and Ibsen is actually a Danish name (Ib being an old Danish form of Jacob). He had three brothers, Johan Andreas Altenburg, Nicolai Alexander and Ole Paus (a lighthouse-keeper) and a sister, Hedvig Cathrine. When Henrik was seven his father's business collapsed and there were (unfounded) rumours that Henrik was the son of his mother's former lover Tormod Knudsen. Aged 13 he attended a small private school in Skien for two years and then became an apothecary's apprentice in Grimstad. Later he went to the University of Christiania (Oslo) but failed to matriculate. From 1851 he was an assistant at the Norwegian Theatre, Bergen, working variously as writer, director, designer etc. Through such classic dramas as *Brand* (1866), *Peer Gynt* (1867), *Pillars of Society* (1877), *A Doll's House* (1879), *An Enemy of the People* (1882), *Hedda Gabler* (1890) and *The Master Builder* (1892) he established a lasting reputation as one of the great playwrights of the modern stage. In the years 1864–91 he lived in voluntary exile in Italy and Germany. A co-founder of the Norwegian Society (1859), he was made an Honorary Doctor of Letters of Uppsala University in 1877.

Family/Sex Life: At the age of 18½ Ibsen fathered an illegitimate son, Hans Jacob Henriksen, by the 28-year-old maidservant in Grimstad, Else Sofie Jensdatter (he supported them secretly for the rest of his life). In 1858 he married Suzannah Thoresen, daughter of Hans Conrad Thoresen, Dean of Bergen, and novelist/playwright Magdalene Thoresen (who later had an affair with Georg Brandes). The playwright Bjørnson was godfather to their son Sigurd.

Appearance: According to Bjørnson, he

was 'Thin and intense, with a face pale as gypsum/Behind an immense coal-black beard.' He had small blue-grey eyes, dark brown hair and a gap between his front teeth. Later in life he wore mutton-chop whiskers. He was always well dressed, with gold spectacles, spats, white gloves, a black coat, a white cravat and a tall shiny felt hat with a large brim – or else a 'velvet jacket, a white waistcoat with black buttons, and a cape ... with an elegant cane' (Strindberg's description).

Habits/Mannerisms: Breakfast for Ibsen was a small cup of black coffee and a bread roll. He smoked a pipe and drank tea while writing. Before retiring to bed he drank a glass of toddy around 9 pm. He had an obsession about buttons and liked sewing them on himself. He was also very punctual and arrived at railway stations an hour early.

Sport/Hobbies: Ibsen disliked sports but enjoyed fishing, swimming and dancing. He was indifferent to music but a good caricaturist, taking art lessons from the painter Mikkel Mandt. As a child he played with dolls and started his own puppet theatre. He was also good at conjuring tricks and ventriloquism.

Religion/Politics: Ibsen was not a practising Christian, though his favourite book was the Bible. He disliked the works of J. S. Mill.

Health: Ibsen suffered a stroke in 1900 and an apoplectic fit in 1901, which paralysed his right arm and leg and the right side of his face, after which he wrote left-handed.

Temperament: Quiet and withdrawn. Burdened by debt as a young man, he was subject to depression. The character perhaps most like him in his plays was Solness the Master Builder: both men underwent spiritual torment in middle age and both found belated success brought little comfort. Ibsen disliked watching his plays, once describing his involvement in the theatre as a 'daily abortion'. Actors seeking clarification about what he intended in his plays were likely to be asked the same question themselves by the author.

Pets: While writing *Brand* he kept a pet scorpion in a beer-glass on his desk.

Work/Daily Routine: Ibsen's first published work was the poem 'In Autumn', printed in the *Christiania Post* under the pseudonym 'Brynjolf Bjarme'. He liked to rise at 4 am and walked in the woods before working steadily till sunset. His early plays (for instance, *Brand* and *Peer Gynt*) were written in verse. *Peer Gynt* prompted Hans Christian Andersen to speculate that it was 'written by a mad poet, one goes crazy oneself reading this book. The poetry isn't good either, there is something sick and distraught about the whole thing.' When *Ghosts* (concerning venereal disease) opened in London (1891) it caused a huge scandal. When *A Doll's House* was premiered in Germany, Ibsen was persuaded under pressure to give the play a happy ending – in this, Nora decides to stay. He considered the little-revived *Emperor and Galilean* (1876) his greatest work. Often mentioned in the same breath as Strindberg, Ibsen kept a picture of Strindberg over his desk, explaining: 'He is my mortal enemy and shall hang there and watch while I write.' He planned books in the winter and wrote them in the summer. He was greatly admired by, among others, James Joyce, who learnt Norwegian in order to write to Ibsen.

Manner of Death: Ibsen died after a third stroke at 2.30 pm at home at 2 Arbinsgade, Christiania, on 23 May 1906. Assured by his nurse that he was getting better, he retorted 'On the contrary!' – and died. 12,000 mourners attended his state funeral at the Trinity Church, Christiania. His grave was adorned with a column bearing the symbol of a hammer.

IVAN IV 'The Terrible' (1530–84) Tsar of Russia

Ivan the Terrible was born on 25 August 1530, the son of Basil (Vasili) III, Grand Duke of Muscovy. His father had been married to Salome Sabourov for 20 years without issue so, aged 50, he had sent her to a convent (1526) and had married Ivan's mother, his second wife, Helena Glinska, 30 years his junior and the daughter of a Lithuanian refugee. Basil III died when Ivan was three and his mother died when he was seven, leaving Russia in anarchy. He had a younger brother Yuri. Well educated, he was proclaimed Grand Duke Ivan IV in 1533. He took over the reins of government himself at the age of 14 and was crowned the first Russian Tsar in 1547 (rulers had formerly been known as Grand Prince or Grand Duke). He voluntarily gave up the crown in 1575 but took it back the following year. A vicious authoritarian ruler, thousands were killed during 'The Terror' that he instigated against the feudal aristocracy, whom he regarded with deep suspicion. Other events during his reign included the expansion of Russian territory into Siberia, Kazan and Astrakhan and the signing of an important commercial treaty with Elizabeth I after England discovered the sea route to Archangel.

Family/Sex Life: On Ivan's order around 1500 virgins were sent to him so that he might choose a bride from amongst them. Accordingly, in 1547, he married Anastasia Zakharina-Koshkina (of the family later known as the Romanovs). She died in 1560, having given birth to Ivan's children Anna, Maria, Dmitri, Ivan, Eudokia and Feodor. As his second wife (1561) he took Maria, daughter of the Circassian Prince Temgryuk. She died in 1569 and their only son died after five weeks. His third wife (1571) was Martha Sobakin, but she died just two weeks later. In 1572 Ivan married Anna Koltovsky,

but after three years he sent her to a monastery. In 1580 he was married for a fifth time, to Maria Nagoi, and by her fathered a son, Dmitri. Renowned for his enjoyment of sexual indulgences of every conceivable kind, he also kept as mistresses Anna Vasilchikov (1575) and Vasilissa Melentiev (1578). His lifetime obsession with marrying an Englishwoman was never realized (his proposal to Lady Mary Hastings, daughter of the Earl of Huntingdon, was refused).

Appearance: Tall and well-made, with high shoulders and a broad chest, Ivan later stooped (in his last years his head lolled on his chest). He shaved his head (as was then customary) but sported long auburn moustaches and unkempt thick-pointed beard. His face was hawk-like, with a high forehead, beaked nose and close-set piercing eyes. Contemporaries referred to his sinister, fierce expression and his unfailing sardonic smile.

Habits/Mannerisms: Ivan never laughed for joy and took great pleasure watching his victims being tortured. He had a high-pitched strident voice and ate and drank to excess. He was, however, well read in church history and during his reign did much to promote Russian trade and culture.

Religion/Politics: Russian Orthodox (though he had St Philip, the Metropolitan of Moscow, strangled). He commissioned the building of the famous St Basil's Cathedral in Moscow and was so pleased with the result that he had the architects, Postnik and Barma, blinded so they could not produce anything more beautiful. In his later years he became a hermit and, assuming the guise of a monk, had himself addressed by the name Jonah.

Health: Ivan had immense energy and also enjoyed an extremely good memory.

Temperament: Above all else, Ivan is remembered for his cruelty. As a child he amused himself by dropping dogs from the 200-foot-high towers of the Kremlin and also by riding horses at full gallop through crowds of people. On coming to power at the age of 14 he hanged 30 boyars on the Moscow highway and had Prince Shuisky eaten alive by his own hunting dogs. Other atrocities included nailing a French envoy's hat to his head and having a messenger's foot nailed to the floor. He even (accidentally) killed his beloved son Ivan,

then aged 27, when he hit him with an iron-pointed staff in a fit of anger (1580). The campaign against the feudal lords later dubbed 'The Terror' had its roots in the treachery of one of Ivan's counsellors in 1564 – following the uncovering of this betrayal, Ivan was seized by a paranoid fear that he was surrounded by traitors and henceforward he trusted no one. Unsurprisingly, he had no close friends.

Manner of Death: On his deathbed Ivan played a game of chess with the regent-to-be, Boris Godunov. He died on 28 March 1584, aged 63. After death his hair was cut in the style of a monk's, at his own wish.

JAMES I (1566–1625) King of Great Britain and Ireland

James I (James VI of Scotland) was born on 19 June 1566 in Edinburgh Castle, the son of Mary Queen of Scots (great granddaughter of Henry VII) by her second husband, her cousin Henry Stewart, Lord Darnley (heir to the English throne after Mary). His father was murdered in 1567 before he was one year old. When Mary then married Scots army leader James, Earl of Bothwell (who was suspected of Darnley's murder) she was forced to abdicate the Scottish throne in her son's favour, aged 13 months (1567). His regents until he assumed power at the age of 12 were successively the Earls of Moray (his uncle, murdered), Lennox (his paternal grandfather, murdered), Mar (his guardian, died) and Morton (his second cousin). He was brought up by the Earl of Mar and, a clever child, was well educated. His early reliance on favourites provoked resentment and a rebellion, followed by a temporary term of imprisonment. On the death of Elizabeth I he also became King of England, as James I (1603). He reigned for 22 years.

Family/Sex Life: In 1589 James married

Anne, daughter of King Frederick II of Denmark. Their children were Henry, Charles I, Elizabeth (who married Frederick V) and Sophia. He also had homosexual lovers, including Robert Carr, Earl of Somerset, and then George Villiers (Duke of Buckingham) whom he called 'Steenie' (after St Stephen, whose face was said to be like the face of an angel).

Appearance: James was tall and handsome, with a jovial countenance and ruddy complexion. He had blue eyes, a straight well-formed nose, a square-cut beard and pale red then light-brown hair. Not strong in body, he was somewhat bow-legged and had an awkward gait.

Habits/Mannerisms: James did not speak at all until he was three years old and retained a stammer and a thick Scottish accent throughout his life. Though intelligent and well-educated, he was coarsely and loudly spoken. He was left-handed and a vehement anti-smoker – in his book *A Counterblaste to Tobacco* he condemned 'this filthie noveltie ... a custome loathsome to the eye, hatefull to the nose, harmefull to the braine, dangerous to the Lungs'. He was, however, a heavy drinker and enjoyed Canary wine and Scottish ale. Favourite delicacies included soft fruit and boiled sheep's head. The story that it was James I who gave sirloin beef its name, knighting it 'Sir Loin' because he was so impressed with it, is sadly a myth (the name comes from the French *sur loigne*, above the loin).

Sport/Hobbies: James was fond of hunting, though he disliked dancing. Architectural projects included Whitehall Palace, of which only the Banqueting Hall was completed.

Religion/Politics: A Calvinist Protestant married to a Lutheran, James disliked the Puritans as well as the Catholics. He escaped the Gunpowder Plot assassination attempt by the Catholics when about to pass anti-Catholic laws in Parliament. In 1604 he commanded 54 scholars to begin work on the so-called 'King James Bible', destined to remain the most influential book in the English language for some four centuries or more. He was also superstitious: after visiting Denmark to meet his intended bride he became convinced of the reality of a witchcraft invasion of Christian Europe and on his return sanctioned the brutal suppression of Scottish witches, summarizing his opinions in a notorious book, *Daemonologie*. He took great interest in witchcraft trials of the period and personally supervised the questioning and torture of the 'North Berwick Witches' who were accused of plotting his death (the case led directly to the disgrace of the Earl of Bothwell). He regarded Parliament with a jaundiced eye, commenting, 'I am surprised that my ancestors should have allowed such an institution to come into existence.'

Health: James frequently suffered from diarrhoea (probably because he ate so much fruit). Other ailments included arthritis (he eventually had to stamp his signature as he could not hold a pen).

Temperament: Dubbed 'the English Solomon', James was unusually intelligent and well-educated for a monarch of his era (though he was also conceited and idle). This did not mean that he always appreciated similar accomplishments in others – when a young girl skilled in Latin, Greek and Hebrew was presented to him he only enquired, 'Pray tell me, can she spin?' Some criticized him for indecision and incompetence and Count Gondomar, Spanish ambassador, called him 'the wisest fool in Christendom'.

Work/Daily Routine: James wrote poetry in both Scots and English. As well as *A Counterblaste to Tobacco* and *Daemonologie*, he was also the author of *Basilikon Doron* (a treatise on government addressed to his son Henry). After succeeding to the English throne he revenged himself on those responsible for the death of his mother, razing Fotheringhay Castle (the site of Mary Queen of Scots's execution). He also executed Sir Walter Ralegh (imprisoned by Elizabeth I).

Motto: '*Beati Pacifici.*'

Manner of Death: James caught 'tertian ague' (fever one day in every three) on 5 March 1625. He subsequently had a stroke on 24 March, losing the power of speech, and died aged 59 at noon on 27 March 1625 at his favourite residence, Theobalds, Hertfordshire. He was buried in Westminster Abbey.

JAMES II (1633–1701) King of Great Britain and Ireland

James II (James VII of Scotland) was born in St James's Palace, London, on 14 October 1633, the second son and third of six children of Charles I (executed when he was 16) and Henrietta Maria, daughter of King Henri IV of France. His elder siblings were Charles II and Mary, the mother of William III, and his younger ones were Elizabeth (who died a prisoner of Parliamentary forces), Henry and Henrietta (later the wife of Philip Duc d'Orléans). He was a cousin of Louis XIV, his maternal uncle being Louis XIII, but always boasted that he was English, though in reality he had little English blood. During the Civil War he escaped house arrest aged 14½ (1648) disguised as a woman (Mr Andrews and his sister) and fled to his sister Mary Princess of Orange in the Hague, then to his mother in Paris, then to Scotland. He later joined the allied French Army (1652), campaigned during the Fronde rebellion (he was nearly killed at the Siege of Mousson) and achieved the rank of lieutenant-general. However, when Charles I was deposed in England he was forced to leave the French for the Spanish Army. After the Restoration he was re-appointed Lord High Admiral (he had originally received the rank aged 4½ and was appointed a Colonel in the Royal Army aged 10) in 1660. He came to the throne aged 52 on Charles II's death in 1685 but was deposed in December 1688, partly because of public resentment at religious persecution of Protestants and the cruelty of his Lord Chief Justice, 'Hanging' Judge George Jeffreys, during the Bloody Assizes in which hundreds died following the suppression of the Monmouth Rebellion. He escaped from Whitehall Palace when deposed, reputedly threw the Great Seal in the Thames (whence it was recovered by a fisherman five months later) and fled again to France. After an interregnum of two months, he was replaced by his daughter Mary and her Dutch husband – his nephew – William Prince of Orange, who reigned jointly as William and Mary. In 1689 he staged a comeback from Ireland but was defeated at the Battle of the Boyne. He ruled for three years and his supporters were known as Jacobites (from the Latin version of James).

Family/Sex Life: In 1660, while Duke of York, James married his sister Mary's maid-of-honour Lady Anne Hyde, daughter of the Lord Chancellor, Edward Hyde, Earl of Clarendon. She was already pregnant by him and bore him two surviving children, Mary and Anne, before her death in 1671. In 1673, when he was 40, he married the 15-year-old Frenchwoman Mary Beatrice Eleanor d'Este, daughter of Alphonso, Duke of Modena. Their children were Mary (wife of William III), Queen Anne and five others, including James Francis Edward the 'Old Pretender' and Louisa. A notorious womanizer, he also had affairs with Goditha Price, Countess of Southesk, Lady Denham, Anne Carnegie, Arabella Churchill (who bore him several children) and Catherine Sedley (by whom he fathered Lady Catherine Darnley).

Appearance: James was tall with a fair complexion and a commanding appearance.

Habits/Mannerisms: Abstemious in his habits, he did not drink and disliked drunkenness in others (his favourite drink was tea). He never swore or gambled. He kept a dwarf servant (dismissed by Parliament with his other servants in 1646) and another, Bequers, when living on Jersey.

Sport/Hobbies: James enjoyed horse-racing and hunting (at a time when stags and hares were the usual quarry, he was one of the earliest aristocratic fox-hunters). He was also a good seaman, knew French and liked music – he played the guitar and was a patron of Henry Purcell. He had no interest in literature, arts or science (though he was Vice-President of the Royal Society).

Religion/Politics: A devout Catholic, he regularly went to monastic retreats.

Health: James had eye trouble and in 1667 contracted smallpox, but otherwise enjoyed good health (it was widely believed that his touch would cure 'King's Evil' – scrofula). In 1701 he suffered partial paralysis after a stroke.

Temperament: Arrogant, parsimonious and courageous, James was a man of very little humour and no wit and it was alleged that he enjoyed watching torture. A French ambassador wrote of him, 'He has all the faults of his father Charles I, but he has less sense, and he behaves more haughtily in public.'

Manner of Death: A stroke in March 1701 led to a paralysed right arm and leg then (in August) to stomach pain when hearing Mass and an internal haemorrhage. He died in France at St Germain on the afternoon of 6 September 1701, aged 68. His heart was buried in the Convent of the Visitation, Chaillot. His brain was taken to the Scots College, Paris, and his bowels to the English Jesuit College, St Omer, and the Church of St Germain. The rest of his body was buried in the English Benedictine Church of St Edmund, Faubourg St Jacques, Paris, en route to Westminster Abbey, but never reached England. The coffin was broken up for lead and his remains were scattered during the French Revolution.

JOAN OF ARC, St (1412–31) French patriot and martyr

Jeanne d'Arc (English: Joan of Arc) – commonly dubbed 'La Pucelle' ('The Maid') – was born on 6 January 1412 in English-ruled Domrémy, Meuse, France, the daughter of Jacques d'Arc and Isabelle de Vouthon, both peasants. During the reign of Henry VI of England (crowned in London and Paris in 1422) she heard voices two or three times a week from the age of 13 commanding her to join the French during the Hundred Years' War against the English and to fight to get the Dauphin crowned as Charles VII. At first she was sent home, but at the age of 16 the French allowed her to take part and she helped through her inspirational leadership to raise the Siege of Orléans (1429). Subsequently the Dauphin was crowned king at Reims. However, she failed to take Paris the same year – attacking the city on a holy day (then forbidden) – and was badly wounded. Failing to relieve Compiègne, she was captured on 23 May 1430 by the Burgundians and sold to the English for 10,000 livres (Charles VII made no attempt to rescue her). Commonly alleged to be a witch (though these charges remained unproven) she was subsequently tried by a pro-English court on charges of heresy and found guilty, though she defended herself with eloquence and uncompromising honesty.

Family/Sex Life: At 13, when she first heard voices, Joan took a vow never to marry, and remained a virgin (confirmed by the women ordered to examine her by the court by which she was tried). Her proven virginity was an insurmountable obstacle to those eager to try her for witchcraft, as no virgin could be in the Devil's service.

Appearance: Wearing her dark hair cut short like a soldier, she led her forces in a suit of white armour and carried an altar sword with five crosses.

Habits/Mannerisms: Abstemious and illiterate.

Religion/Politics: A devout Catholic, Joan claimed that the voices she heard were those of the martyrs St Michael (patron saint of France and the first voice she heard), St Margaret of Antioch and St Catherine of Alexandria (who was martyred on the 'Catherine Wheel').

Health: Joan was wounded by an arrow in the shoulder when placing the first assault ladder on the castle in Orléans and was later wounded in the leg by an arrow in Paris. A month before her execution she fell ill in prison and might have died but for treatment by the English doctors (the Duke of Warwick observing, 'the King of England had paid too much for her to be deprived of the pleasure of seeing her burn').

Work/Daily Routine: After being initially rebuffed by the Dauphin and his advisers, Joan finally convinced them that she could be of use to the French cause. Legend has it that the Dauphin was persuaded that there was something in her claims of visions of the saints when she repeated word for word his personal daily prayer, known only to himself. As a further test of Joan's supernatural abilities she was ordered to pick out the disguised Dauphin from among his courtiers – a challenge that she easily met, though she had never

apparently laid eyes on him before. Nonetheless, the Dauphin did nothing to save her when she was captured by French forces who were loyal to the English and instead replaced her with a young shepherd boy claiming similar powers (he was also captured by the English and drowned in the Seine). The hapless Joan was taken to Rouen in an iron cage and there questioned by pro-English ecclesiastical authorities. Joan's conduct during her trial was exemplary – when asked to reconsider her evidence, she insisted, 'Whatever I have said about my deeds and words in this trial, I let it stand and wish to reaffirm it. Even if I should see the fire lit, the faggots blazing, and the hangman ready to begin the burning, and even if I were in the pyre, I could not say anything different.' However, when confronted with the stake on 24 May 1431 she recanted, causing the frustrated English soldiery present to stone the French ecclesiastical officials in attendance. Joan was taken away to begin life imprisonment but her cunning gaolers gave her only men's clothes to wear – as soon as she put these on, needing to relieve herself, she was accused once more of heresy. This time, she did not recant.

Manner of Death: Joan was condemned to death for heresy by the Bishop of Beauvais and was burnt alive at the stake, dressed in women's clothes, in the Old Market Square, Rouen, on 30 May 1431, aged 19. When she was dead and her clothes had been burnt away, the fire was raked back to expose her naked body to the public to prove she was human. She was then burnt to ashes and the remains thrown into the Seine. She was canonized in 1920 (feast day, 30 May).

JOHNSON, Dr Samuel (1709–84) English poet, critic and lexicographer

Dr Johnson was born above his father's shop in the Market Square, Lichfield, Staffordshire, at 4 pm on Wednesday 18 September 1709, the elder son of Michael Johnson, a bookseller and magistrate, and Sarah Ford. At the time of his birth his father was 52 and his mother 40. He had a younger brother Nathaniel. Educated at Lichfield Grammar School, he studied Greek and Metaphysics at Pembroke College, Cambridge (1728) for 14 months, but did not take his degree through lack of funds. He was then a schoolteacher and later set up his own private school (maximum eight pupils, one of whom was the actor David Garrick). Subsequently he was a journalist in Birmingham before coming to London (1737) as a hack writer for the *Gentleman's Magazine* and other publications. In 1747 he commenced work on his celebrated *Dictionary of the English Language* (published 1755). He did not meet his biographer Boswell until 1763, when he was 53 and Boswell 22. Eventually he received a Crown pension of £300 a year (1762). Called by Smollett 'The Great Cham of Literature' ('cham' being an old variant of 'khan') he became the foremost figure in London literary circles. Among his most famous writings were the novel *Rasselas* (1759), which was written to pay for his mother's funeral, *Journey to the Western Islands of Scotland* (1775) and *Lives of the English Poets* (1779–81).

Family/Sex Life: Johnson nursed an unrequited love for Olivia Lloyd, aunt of the founder of Lloyds Bank. In 1735 he married a wealthy 46-year-old widow, Mrs Elizabeth Porter, née Jervis, 20 years his senior and already the mother of three children – Lucy, Jervis Henry and Joseph. He called his wife 'Tetty' (she later took to drink and laudanum and died in 1752). Another close friend was Mrs Hester Thrale (née Salusbury, 25-year-old wife of the wealthy brewer Henry Thrale), with whom he fell out permanently (to his great distress) after she married an Italian following Thrale's death.

Appearance: According to the *Dictionary of National Biography*, Johnson was a 'huge structure of bones . . . hideously striking, his head wigless, his gesticulations grotesque'. He was tall and substantially built, with a scarred face, light blue eyes and wore his own brown hair instead of the customary wig. He was a slovenly dresser and had 'no passion for clean linen', according to Boswell. Another contemporary noted that he 'dressed like a scarecrow and ate like a cormorant'.

Habits/Mannerisms: Johnson was always moving, swaying back and forth, making strange gestures and muttering prayers. He used to touch posts and count his steps, even when on horseback. Rarely using the title 'Dr Johnson' himself, he habitually contracted other people's names (for instance, 'Bozzy' and 'Goldy' for Boswell and Goldsmith). He adopted a rustic manner of speech (for example, 'shuperior, woonce, poonsh, thear' instead of 'superior, once, punch, there') and exhaled loudly after long statements. His table manners were poor and he had a voracious appetite. He gave up wine after an illness (1766), though in his youth he drank a lot of 'Bishop' (a punch of port, orange and sugar). He also drank tea in vast quantities (up to 25 cups at a time). He kept a black servant from Jamaica, Francis Barber, for the last 32 years of his life but himself never left Britain – with the single exception of a visit to France with the Thrales.

Sport/Hobbies: Johnson enjoyed hunting, boxing, rowing, swimming, shooting and other forms of physical exercise (he once startled Boswell by rolling down a hill for fun). He was also a good mimic and liked conducting chemistry experiments (he gave these up when living with Mrs Thrale in Streatham). Though he admitted that 'of all the noises I think music is the least disagreeable' he had no taste for it – asked his opinion of a virtuoso violinist's performance he stormed, 'Difficult, do you call it, sir? I wish it were impossible.'

Religion/Politics: Johnson was interested in the supernatural (he exposed the celebrated Cock Lane Ghost imposture). Of women preachers, he famously remarked, 'a woman's preaching is like a dog's walking on his hind legs. It is not done well, but you are surprised to find it done at all.' In politics, he was a Tory (Whiggism was to him 'a negation of all principle') – and he once asserted that 'Patriotism is the last refuge of a scoundrel.'

Health: At the age of three, Johnson was brought to London to be touched by Queen Anne for the King's Evil (scrofula), the ravages of which disfigured his face and damaged the sight of one eye. As an adult, he suffered from melancholia and was a hypochondriac. Physical ailments included asthma, gout, paralysis following a stroke (1783), dropsy, deafness in his left ear, shortsightedness, rheumatoid arthritis, smallpox and bronchitis (for which he took three grains of opium daily). He suffered a breakdown aged 57 and spent three months with the Thrales in their large Streatham mansion.

Temperament: Gracious, courageous, kind to animals and the poor though also impatient, Johnson loved children and had

a good sense of humour. His friends included Garrick, Boswell, Mrs Hester Thrale and the music historian Dr Charles Burney (he gave his daughter, diarist Fanny Burney, Latin lessons). He was a founder-member of the famous Literary Club, created in 1764 at the Turk's Head, Gerrard Street, Soho); other members included Reynolds, Boswell, Burke, Dr Nugent, Goldsmith, Garrick, Gibbon, Fox, Adam Smith and Sheridan. He disliked Rousseau, Voltaire, Gray and all Americans: 'I am willing to love all mankind, except an American.' Some found him arrogant – Horace Walpole said, 'His manners were sordid, supercilious and brutal.'

Pets: He kept a cat called Hodge (which ate oysters) and a 'white kitling' called Lily.

Work/Daily Routine: Johnson employed six assistants on his famous *Dictionary*. In all he defined 40,000 words (an achievement unrivalled until the *Oxford English Dictionary* was published in 1858). A fast worker, he also wrote plays and poetry, though he insisted that 'No man but a blockhead ever wrote except for money.' Certainly, he wrote less when better off. After 1754 he stayed in bed until noon, then dined in a tavern and read and worked at night.

Manner of Death: Johnson died of emphysema, granular disease of the kidneys and dropsy in Bolt Court, London, around 7 pm on 13 December 1784, aged 75. He was buried in Westminster Abbey. The photographic plate of an emphysematous lung in Baillie's *Morbid Anatomy* depicts one of his lungs.

JONSON, Benjamin (1572–1637) English playwright

Ben Jonson was born on 11 June 1572 in Westminster, London, the son of a clergyman who died a month before the playwright was born. His mother (name unknown) remarried a master-bricklayer. He was educated at Westminster School (where he was taught by William Camden, to whom he said he owed 'All that I am in arts, all that I know'). At first he worked at his stepfather's trade of bricklayer and then studied briefly at St John's College, Cambridge (supposedly finding a sponsor after being overheard reciting Homer in Greek whilst building the garden wall of Lincoln's Inn). He served in the English army fighting the Spanish in Flanders and killed an enemy champion in single combat. Later he was tutor to Sir Walter Ralegh's son, Lecturer in Rhetoric at Gresham College, London, and succeeded the playwright Thomas Middleton as Chronologer of London (1628). The first ever Poet Laureate, he received a pension from James I (1616) and an honorary degree from Oxford University (1619). Ranking alongside William Shakespeare as the foremost playwright of his generation, he was the author of such classic plays as *Every Man in His Humour* (1598), *Volpone* (1605), *The Alchemist* (1610) and *Bartholomew Fair* (1614), as well as creator of a number of acclaimed court masques. He fell from royal favour on the death of James I (1625).

Family/Sex Life: In 1592 Jonson married Anne Lewis – 'a shrew yet honest'. Their children, Mary, Joseph, Elisabeth, Benjamin, Benjamin and Benjamin, all died young. He spent a period of some five years living apart from his wife.

Appearance: Jonson was lean in his youth but by 1619 talked of 'my mountaine belly' and weighed around 250–70 lb. According to Aubrey, he had 'one eie

lower than t'other, and bigger' and was 'of a clear and faire skin; his habit was very plaine'. He had an aquiline nose, a full-lipped mouth, a tanned pock-marked face with warts, a scraggy beard and dark brown hair. He had a felon's brand (the letter M) on his left thumb and wore a coachman's coat with slits under the armpits.

Habits/Mannerisms: Jonson had a poor standard of personal hygiene (even by Elizabethan standards) and was prone to lice and bad breath. He was often drunk. 'Canarie was his beloved liquor', according to Aubrey ('Canarie' being a sweet madeira-like wine from the Canary Islands). He had an ungainly lumbering walk and was often so poor his diet consisted of brown bread, beans and buttermilk.

Sport/Hobbies: Jonson's superb library – one of the best in England – was destroyed by fire around 1622.

Religion/Politics: Anglican then Roman Catholic while in prison, then Anglican again. He gave evidence in court during the Gunpowder Plot trial.

Health: Jonson enjoyed generally good health until 1626, when he fell victim to palsy and dropsy. After a stroke in 1628 he remained bedridden until his death.

Temperament: Jonson was arrogant, quarrelsome and pugnacious. In 1598 he killed a fellow-actor, Gabriel Spencer, and was branded a felon. He escaped the gallows by benefit of clergy having pleaded guilty. Aubrey quoted a description of him as 'a great lover and praiser of himself, a contemner and scorner of others'. He was imprisoned for his slanderous satire *The Isle of Dogs* (1597) and for libelling the

Scots in the play *Eastward Ho* (1605), which he wrote in collaboration with Chapman and Marston (he only narrowly escaped having his nose and ears slit as punishment). His friends included Shakespeare (with whom he had been drinking immediately before Shakespeare died), Donne, Bacon, Beaumont, Fletcher and Herrick. He thought Donne 'the best poet in the world in some things'. The convivial literary meetings over which Jonson presided at the Mermaid Tavern, and subsequently in the Apollo Room of the Devil and St Dunstan Tavern, became famous and attracted numerous disciples, who were commonly dubbed 'the tribe of Ben'.

Work/Daily Routine: Beginning as player/playwright for the Admiral's Men troupe, he subsequently joined their rivals the Lord Chamberlain's Men, then the King's Men. Shakespeare acted in the first performance of his plays *Every Man in His Humour* and *Sejanus* and Queen Anne herself acted in his *The Masque of Blackness*, dressed as

a negress. The scenery for his court masques was designed by Inigo Jones, with whom he eventually fell out in acrimonious circumstances. Other works by his hand included the song 'Drink to me only with thine eyes'. He used to study in a 'straw chair', according to Aubrey.

Manner of Death: Jonson died on 6 August 1637, aged 65. He was buried in Westminster Abbey in an upright position by his own request because he could not afford a six feet by two feet plot. His heel bone was later stolen by William Buckland, Dean of Westminster (1849). The only inscription on his tomb was 'O rare Ben Jonson' (possibly intended to read *'Orare Ben Jonson'* – 'Pray for Ben Jonson'). Herrick provided an epitaph:

'Here lies Jonson with the rest
Of the poets, but the best.
Reader, would'st thou more have known?
Ask his story, not the stone;
That will speak what this can't tell
Of his glory; so farewell.'

JOYCE, James Augustine Aloysius (1882–1941) Irish novelist

James Joyce was born at 41 Brighton Square (actually a triangle), Rathgar, Dublin, on 2 February 1882, the eldest child of John Stanislaus Joyce, who worked for the Collector-General of Rates and Taxes for Dublin, and Mary Jane Murray, a noted pianist and daughter of a wine merchant. He had nine surviving siblings – Stanislaus, Charlie, George, Margaret, Eileen, Mary, Eva, Florence and Mabel – and was educated at Ireland's top Jesuit preparatory school, Clongowes Wood College, then at Belvedere College and University College, Dublin (BA Modern Languages, 1902). After studying medicine at St Cecilia's Medical School, Dublin, and (very briefly) at the Sorbonne he returned to Dublin to found and run the

Volta Cinema – the city's first cinema. With the help of Lady Gregory he wrote book reviews for the *Daily Express* and was briefly a teacher at Clifton School, Dalkey, but left Ireland for good (with Nora Barnacle) in 1904. He then taught English at Berlitz language schools in Austrian-ruled Pola and Trieste, was an agent for Donegal tweeds in Trieste, a foreign correspondence clerk for a bank in Rome and contributed journalism to *Il Piccolo della Sera* etc., whilst writing. His brother Stanislaus later came to live with him in Trieste and also worked at Berlitz, frequently helping Joyce financially. After Berlitz he taught at the Scuola Superiore di Commercio Revoltella (later the University of Trieste). During World War I he moved to neutral Zürich before returning to Trieste and then, for 20 years, Paris. From 1917 onwards he was paid £350 every three months by an anonymous admirer (Harriet Shaw Weaver, editor of *The Egoist*) and in Zürich received 1000 Swiss francs a month from Mrs Harold McCormick (daughter of John D. Rockefeller). Later, with support from Yeats and Pound, he received grants from the Royal Literary Fund, the Society of Authors and a Civil List pension. His secretary was Samuel Beckett. His most influential writings included *A Portrait of the Artist as a Young Man* (1915) and the novels *Ulysses* (1922) and *Finnegans Wake* (1939).

Family/Sex Life: Joyce was allegedly first seduced by a prostitute at the age of 14; later he often visited prostitutes. In 1931, after 27 years together, he married (in London) Nora Joseph Barnacle, a former chambermaid at Finn's Hotel, Dublin. Their children, grown up by the time of the marriage, were Giorgio and Lucia Anna (she later became mentally ill and was treated by Jung).

Appearance: Tall and slim, with strong spectacles and swept-back hair, Joyce sported a military-style moustache. Favourite items from his wardrobe included a dark blue serge suit, a yachting cap, tennis shoes, a black felt hat and bow-ties. He carried a cane and used Nora's curling-irons to curl his hair. After his eye operations he wore a patch over his left eye.

Habits/Mannerisms: Called 'Simple-minded Jim' by his wife (who never read any of his books), he took cocaine and was frequently drunk (he drank Guinness in Ireland and white wine elsewhere – especially Neufchâtel, Riesling, white Chianti and the Swiss wine Fendant de Sion). He often sang and danced when drunk. He had very bad handwriting.

Sport/Hobbies: Joyce enjoyed cricket and long-distance running and was a good swimmer. He also played the piano and was a gifted tenor singer (he won a bronze medal in a Dublin singing contest in 1904 but threw it into the Liffey). He taught himself Gaelic, Italian, German and Norwegian (the latter so he could read Ibsen).

Religion/Politics: At first Roman Catholic, then fiercely anti-Catholic.

Health: Glaucoma obliged Joyce to wear glasses from early childhood and he underwent many eye operations from 1917. Other eye problems included iritis (1908), conjunctivitis and cataracts (he was almost blind by 1932). He also had bad teeth (all extracted in 1923) and suffered from rheumatic fever (1907) and fainting fits.

Temperament: Acquaintances found Joyce shy but calculating. He was afraid of thunderstorms, dogs and firearms. His friends included Hemingway, Yeats, Lady Gregory, the English artist Budgen and Ezra Pound, who first serialized *Portrait of the Artist* and *Ulysses* in his magazine *The Egoist*.

Work/Daily Routine: *The Dubliners* was rejected by 40 publishers and when published in 1914 was destroyed by the publisher for fear of libel. *Ulysses* was published on Joyce's 40th birthday – excerpts in the *Little Review* in the USA led to an obscenity trial and a fine for the publishers (1921). The book provoked violent reactions from many established writers. Virginia Woolf, writing to Lytton Strachey in 1922, said of *Ulysses* 'Never have I read such tosh, the work of a greasy undergraduate scratching his pimples.' Edmund Gosse, meanwhile, dismissed Joyce as 'a literary charlatan of the extremist order'. D. H. Lawrence ranted that 'the last part of it is the dirtiest, most indecent, most obscene thing ever written, it is filthy'. Hemingway, on the other hand, found it 'a most goddamn wonderful book'. When *Ulysses* was pirated in the USA by Samuel Roth, 167 protests were lodged by famous personalities, including Einstein, Eliot, Forster and Gide. *Finnegans Wake* provoked similar reactions – Pound called it 'circumambient peripherization', while Stanislaus Joyce summarized it as 'drivelling rigmarole'. Joyce once remarked, 'The demand I make of my reader is that he should devote his whole life to reading my works.'

Manner of Death: Joyce died two days after a successful operation for a duodenal ulcer at 2.30 am on 13 January 1941 at Schwesterhaus von Roter Kreuz Hospital, Zürich, aged 59. He was buried in the Fluntern Cemetery, Zürich.

KEATS, John (1795–1821) English poet

John Keats was born at 24 The Pavement, Moorgate, London, on 31 October 1795, the oldest son of Thomas Keats, manager of the Swan and Hoop Inn and livery stables, and Frances Jennings, daughter of John Jennings who owned the livery stables. His father was killed by a fall from a horse when he was aged eight and his mother remarried to William Rawlings, a bank clerk. On the death of John Jennings, his will was disputed: Keats's mother lost the lawsuit and disappeared and the children were brought up by their maternal grandmother in Edmonton. His mother later returned but died of tuberculosis a year later (1810) when Keats was 14, and John Nowland Sandell (a merchant) and Richard Abbey (a tea-dealer) were appointed his guardians. He had two surviving younger brothers, George and Thomas, and a sister Frances Mary (Fanny). Educated at the Reverend John Clarke's School, Enfield, he left aged 14½ to become a surgeon-apothecary's apprentice in Edmonton for five years. He then worked as a dresser (surgeon's assistant) at Guy's Hospital, London, and later qualified as a licensed apothecary's (1816) and a member of the Royal College of Surgeons. His first poems were shown to Leigh Hunt by Keats's old schoolteacher Charles Cowden Clarke, thus beginning a life-long association with Hunt and other leading Romantics. Clarke also introduced him to the Homer translations of Elizabethan dramatist/poet George Chapman, thereby inspiring one of his famous poems. He was also drama critic of the *Champion*. His works included the long mythological poem *Endymion* (1818) and *Lamia and Other Poems* (1820), which contained such pieces as 'The Eve of St Agnes' and 'Lamia' and his celebrated odes.

Family/Sex Life: In 1819 Keats was engaged to Fanny Brawne, a distant relative of Beau Brummell. He called her 'Millamant' (after Congreve's character).

Appearance: Only five feet and ¼ of an inch tall, Keats was broad-shouldered and stocky, and carried himself erect. He had a small head, with a hawk-like face. According to Hunt, 'His face was rather long, the upper lip projected a little over the under, the chin was bold, the cheeks sunken, the eyes mellow and glowing, large, dark, and sensitive.' He had a bright complexion, mobile features, a large mouth and reddish golden brown, very thick wavy hair. Coleridge described him as a 'loose, slack, not well-dressed youth'. As a student he dressed in a flamboyant Byronic manner.

Habits/Mannerisms: Keats gave up eating meat after getting engaged (1819) but admitted that 'I enjoy Claret to a degree' (his favourite being Château Margaux).

Often after dinner he and his friends amused themselves imitating the instruments of the orchestra (Keats was the bassoon).

Sport/Hobbies: A lover of cricket, Keats also enjoyed watching prize-fights. He also used to shoot tom-tits on Hampstead Heath.

Religion/Politics: Though Protestant, Keats was sceptical about religious orthodoxy, thinking it a 'pious fraud' and did not believe in the Bible. His politics were radical and pro-Whig.

Health: A hypochondriac, Keats suffered from tuberculosis, having his first bad lung haemorrhage in 1820 (he took laudanum as a painkiller). Other ailments included venereal disease (1817), for which he took mercury, throat trouble (1818), and tonsillitis (1818).

Temperament: As a schoolboy, Keats had a naturally pugnacious nature, hitting a teacher at the age of 13. He was otherwise very generous and sweet-natured. His friends included Charles Armitage Brown, Shelley, Leigh Hunt (who published his first poems and to whom he dedicated *Poems*, 1817) and painter Benjamin Haydon (who made a life-mask of his face and painted him as a character in *Christ's Entry into Jerusalem*). Hunt called him 'Junkets' ('John Keats'). He was disliked by Byron and in his turn Keats thought *Don Juan* a 'flash poem' and 'proud bad verse'.

Work/Daily Routine: Keats wrote in a haphazard fashion, scribbling odd lines on scraps of paper, which his friend Brown then retrieved and helped him assemble as complete poems ('Ode to a Nightingale'

was compiled in this way while Keats listened to a nightingale in Brown's garden). 'Ode on a Grecian Urn' was inspired by an urn in the British Museum that was in fact a fake – a Wedgwood copy of a Roman copy of a Greek vase. 'Lamia' meanwhile, had to be completely reworked as Keats had mispronounced most of the Greek names and had thus got the scansion and rhyming wrong (he was also a bad speller). Many of his works received hostile reviews. *Blackwood's* suggested he return to medicine, calling him 'Pestleman Jack' of the 'Cockney poets'. Keats himself said 'I think I shall be among the English Poets after my death.' He invented the term 'bitcherel' for doggerel about women.

Motto/Emblem: The Keats coat of arms was three wild cats passant in pale sable.

Manner of Death: Keats went to Italy with the painter Joseph Severn for the sake of his health and to visit the Shelleys but died peacefully of tuberculosis in Severn's arms at 11 pm on Friday 23 February 1821 in a house on the Spanish Steps, Rome, aged 25. Towards the end he repeatedly tried to commit suicide by drinking laudanum but was prevented by friends. He said he wished his epitaph to be 'Here lies one whose name was writ in water' (inspired by lines in Beaumont and Fletcher's *Philaster*: 'All your better deeds/Shall be in water writ'). He was buried in the Protestant Cemetery, Rome, with Fanny Brawne's letters and a lock of her hair, and with a purse made by his sister. Casts were made of his face, hand and foot and daisies were planted on the grave. Shelley's *Adonis* was dedicated to Keats's memory (and later Shelley's heart was buried in the same cemetery – he drowned with a copy of Keats's 1820 *Poems* in his pocket).

KIPLING, Rudyard (1865–1936) English poet, novelist and short-story writer

Joseph Rudyard Kipling was born on the Esplanade in Bombay, India, on 30 December 1865, the son and elder child of John Lockwood Kipling – an author, potter, architect, architectural sculptor, illustrator, art-school principal and later Curator of the Lahore Museum, India (1837–1911), who designed the emblazoned banners of the Indian princes for the *durbar* proclaiming Queen Victoria as Empress of India in Delhi, 1877. His mother was Alice McDonald, sister-in-law of the painters Burne-Jones and Sir Edward Poynter and aunt of Prime Minister Stanley Baldwin. He had a younger sister, Alice ('Trix'). Named after Lake Rudyard, near Leek, Staffordshire, where his parents first met, he returned to England in 1871 and was educated at a boarding school in Southsea, Hampshire, and at the United Services College, Westward Ho!, Bideford, Devon (four years), but spent Christmases with the Burne-Joneses in Fulham, London. After school he returned to live with his parents in India and his father got him a job as sub-editor on the *Civil and Military Gazette*, Lahore – the largest newspaper in the Punjab (1882–7) and in which he published all the short stories later collected as *Plain Tales from the Hills* (1888). Later he worked for the *Allahabad Pioneer* and the *San Francisco Examiner*. He was the first Englishman to win the Nobel Prize for Literature (1907) but declined a knighthood, the Order of Merit and other awards and was not offered the Poet Laureateship, though he was the pre-eminent national poet of his day after the death of Alfred, Lord Tennyson in 1892. Among his most famous writings, many reflecting his experiences in India, were *Barrack-Room Ballads* (1892), the two *Jungle Books* (1894–5), *Kim* (1901), the *Just So Stories* (1902) and *Puck of Pook's Hill* (1906).

Family/Sex Life: In 1892 Kipling married the American Caroline ('Carrie') Starr Balestier, sister of his US agent/publisher (Henry James gave away the bride). Their children were Josephine (who died young), Elsie and John (who went missing, believed dead in World War I). They lived in Vermont from 1892 to 1896 and settled permanently at Bateman's, Burwash, Sussex, in 1902.

Appearance: Five feet six inches tall, Kipling was lithe and had a dark complexion. He had bright blue eyes, with heavy black eyebrows that went up and down as he spoke, a strongly cleft chin and dark brown hair and moustache.

Habits/Mannerisms: Called 'Gigger' at school because he wore glasses (slang for spectacles was 'gig-lamps'), he never used the name Joseph (he was often called 'Ruddy'). He spoke fluent Hindustani, smoked a pipe, cigars and cigarettes, and owned a Rolls-Royce Phantom.

Sport/Hobbies: Kipling was a keen golfer – he painted his golf balls red so he could play in the snow when in the USA. Another passion was motoring; he was one of the first motorists in the UK and owned a steam-driven American Locomobile. He also enjoyed amateur theatricals and was a talented artist, illustrating early versions of *The Jungle Book*.

Religion/Politics: Described as an imperialist, paternalist, racist, right-wing Conservative, Kipling was, according to Kingsley Amis, 'an oligarch who believed passionately in freedom'. He supported Sir Edward Carson's Ulster Protestant rebellion (1914) but opposed the Fascists, refraining from using the Hindu good-luck swastika symbol on his books when Hitler came to power. He became a Freemason in Lahore in 1885.

Health: Kipling was very shortsighted and wore thick glasses from the age of 11. He nearly died of pneumonia in the USA (1898/9). After the age of 50 he suffered haemorrhages and sickness from a duodenal ulcer. A lifelong insomniac, he had a superb memory, never forgetting a face or name.

Temperament: As a child, Kipling knew Burne-Jones as Uncle Ned and William Morris as Uncle Topsy. As an adult his friends included Henry James, Wolcott Balestier (he dedicated the *Barrack Room Ballads* to him) and Rider Haggard. He had a sharp sense of humour – when a newspaper to which he suscribed mistakenly announced his death, he wrote to the editor immediately: 'I've just read that I am dead. Please delete me from your list of subscribers.' When a fan seeking Kipling's autograph heard that he was paid one dollar a word he sent Kipling a dollar in the hope of realizing his ambition – back came an unsigned postcard with the single word 'Thanks'.

Work/Daily Routine: Kipling only used pitch-black ink, explaining that '*Blue-black used to be an abomination to my daemon*' (quoted in *Paris Reviews*). The *Barrack-Room Ballads* were a huge success – at their peak they were only surpassed by sales of Shakespeare. *Stalky & Co* was based on his experiences at the United Services College and was dedicated to headmaster Cornell Price (a friend of Morris, Swinburne and Rossetti). The *Jungle Book* stories first appeared in the US children's magazine *St Nicholas* (1893–4). Kingsley Amis called *Kim* 'not only the finest story about India ... but one of the greatest novels in the language'. After his son's death in World War I he devoted much of his energy to the War Graves Commission. He only ever broadcast on radio twice.

Manner of Death: Kipling died following an ulcer operation in the Middlesex Hospital, London, on 18 January 1936, aged 70. He was buried in Poets' Corner in Westminster Abbey.

LAMB, Charles (1775–1834) English essayist

Charles Lamb was born at 2 Crown Office Row, Inner Temple, London, on 10 February 1775, the youngest of three surviving children of John Lamb, clerk to the lawyer Samuel Salt MP (a member of the Inner Temple) and Elizabeth Field. He had a brother John and an older sister Mary Anne (11 years his senior) who, overstrained with professional needlework, murdered their mother in 1796 with a table knife in a fit of madness when she tried to stop Mary attacking an irksome apprentice girl. Mary was in his legal care thereafter until his death (she survived him by 13 years). Educated at Christ's Hospital School, London, with Coleridge, he worked at first in a merchant's office. Subsequently, through the influence of Salt (a deputy-governor of the South Sea Company), he became a clerk in the Examiners Office in South Sea House (with his brother John). In 1792 he became a clerk in the Accountants Office of East India House and remained there for 33 years until pensioned off because of ill-health. Success in the literary world came with *Tales from Shakespear* (1807), on which he collaborated with Mary. He published his collected verse and prose in 1818 and later published a celebrated series of essays under the title *Essays of Elia* (1823–33).

Family/Sex Life: Lamb remained unmarried, though always close to his sister Mary (an affair with Ann Simmonds led to a mental breakdown). He and Mary later adopted an orphan, Emma Isola, who stayed 10 years with them until she married. Once, when asked by a lady how he liked babies, he replied drily, 'Boiled, ma'am.'

Appearance: Below middle height, Lamb had a 'small meagre body surmounted by a sensitive, thoughtful head' (Cecil). He had a long melancholy clean-shaven face, with 'a Jewish cast of nose', brown eyes and long curly black hair. He usually dressed in black, with 'tiny black breeches, buttoned to the kneecap and no further, surmounting spindle legs ... in the eyes a kind of *smoky* brightness' (Carlyle).

Habits/Mannerisms: A stutter prevented Lamb taking Holy Orders. He liked strong drink (especially gin), leading Carlyle to accuse him of being a 'confirmed, shameless drunkard'. He also smoked a pipe and took snuff. He never kept still for long, and had a very sweet smile.

Sport/Hobbies: Lamb enjoyed walking and wrote acrostics. He admitted to an unmusical ear.

Religion/Politics: Though a believer in God, Lamb stopped going to church around 1800 and expressed reservations about conventional religion.

Health: Around 1795–6 Lamb became mentally deranged. Subsequently he was much troubled by the threat of permanent madness.

Temperament: Acquaintances found Lamb excitable and nervous as well as shy and melancholy. His friends included Coleridge, Wordsworth, Leigh Hunt, Hazlitt and Southey, though he was disliked by Carlyle ('A more pitiful, ricketty, gasping, staggering, stammering Tomfool I do not know'). Wordsworth, however, said of him, 'Oh he was good, if ever good man was.' As was the case with others, Lamb sometimes found Coleridge's verbose presence tiresome and on one occasion, when Coleridge enquired if Lamb had ever heard him preach, Lamb replied wearily, 'I've never heard you do anything else.'

Pets: He kept a dog called Dash.

Work/Daily Routine: Lamb published his essays under the pseudonym 'Elia' (pronounced 'Ellia'), which was in fact the name of a real clerk (an Italian) working in South Sea House. Lamb used it as a joke. His brother John appeared in the essays as 'James Elia', while Mary was disguised as 'Bridget Elia' and 'Lovel' was presumed to be their father. *Tales from Shakespeare* was published by the philosopher William Godwin (Shelley's father-in-law), Charles working on the tragedies while Mary concentrated on the comedies. In 1797 he dedicated *Poems* to Mary. Not all his literary efforts were well received – his play *Mr H* was so disliked by the audience when it was first performed that Lamb joined in with the hissing and catcalls because he was 'so damnably afraid of being taken for the author'.

Manner of Death: Lamb fell on his face while walking on 22 December 1834 and died of erysipelas at a friend's house, Walden Cottage, Edmonton, on 27 December 1834, aged 59. He was buried in Edmonton Churchyard.

LAWRENCE, David Herbert (Richard) (1885–1930)
English novelist, poet and essayist

D. H. Lawrence was born in Victoria Street, Eastwood, Nottinghamshire, on 11 September 1885, the third son and fourth of five children of John Arthur Lawrence, a coalminer, and Lydia Beardsall, a schoolteacher. He was educated at Nottingham High School. At first he worked in a surgical goods factory (aged 15) before studying, at the age of 21, for a two-year teaching diploma at University College, Nottingham (the College's President was the 6th Duke of Portland, half-brother of Lawrence's friend Lady Ottoline Morell). He was then a teacher at Davidson Road School, Croydon, but after the success of his first novel, *The White Peacock* (1911), he resigned the post and became a professional writer. He toured Europe in 1912–13 and was prosecuted for obscenity after the publication (1915) of his novel *The Rainbow*. He left England in 1919 and settled in Italy, then in Mexico, and (from 1925) once more in Italy. Among his most celebrated later works were the novels *Sons and Lovers* (1913), *Women in Love* (1920) and *Lady Chatterley's Lover* (1928), which gave rise to a sensational trial for obscenity in 1960.

Family/Sex Life: In 1912, just six weeks after meeting her, Lawrence eloped to Metz with Frieda Weekley, daughter of Baron Friedrich von Richthofen (the military governor of Metz) and cousin of the 'Red Baron' air ace – and wife of Professor Ernest Weekley, Lawrence's university teacher at Nottingham. They married in London in 1914; she was six years Lawrence's senior and already had three children (Monty, Elsa and Barbie). They had no further children, Lawrence being sterile.

Appearance: Five feet nine inches tall, Lawrence had a slight build, with narrow chest and shoulders. He had blue-grey eyes and red hair, which was 'bright mud colour, with a streak of red in it, a thick mat, parted on one side', according to David Garnett. As a young man he sported a toothbrush moustache, then later a full beard.

Habits/Mannerisms: Lawrence had febrile hands and a high-pitched, squeaky voice, with a strong Midlands accent. He ate plain food, drank little and never smoked.

Sport/Hobbies: A talented painter, Lawrence had an exhibition of his works in London in 1928, though the police removed some of the paintings as obscene.

Health: Sterile, and later impotent, Lawrence also suffered from tuberculosis. He nearly died of typhoid and malaria in 1925.

Temperament: Known as 'Lorenzo' in Italy, he included among his friends Lady Ottoline Morell and Aldous Huxley (it was Aldous Huxley's wife who typed up the manuscript of *Lady Chatterley's Lover*).

Work/Daily Routine: In all only four of Lawrence's 10 novels were written in England. When *The White Peacock* appeared he proudly showed it to his father, telling him he had been paid £50 for it. The old man was incredulous, 'Fifty pounds! An' tha's niver done a day's hard work in thy life!' Despite this early success, his next major novel, *Sons and Lovers*, was at first rejected by Heinemann. Lawrence never planned his books in advance and was a spontaneous and rapid writer (though he wrote in longhand). He only wrote when in the mood (he never forced himself) and wrote less in the summer. Besides the great novels, he also wrote plays, poetry and stories. The celebrated *Lady Chatterley* obscenity trial of 1960 resulted from the first unexpurgated publication of the book (by Penguin) in the UK, some 32 years after it was written. Notorious moments in the widely-publicized court case included the prosecution's challenge to the British reader: 'Is it a book you would wish your wife or your servant to read?' Witnesses for the defence included such celebrated names as E. M. Forster (who called Lawrence 'the greatest imaginative novelist of our generation' in a letter to *The Nation* on his death), Helen Gardner and Richard Hoggart. Lawrence himself once wrote: 'About *Lady C.* – you musn't think I advocate perpetual sex. Far from it. Nothing nauseates me more than promiscuous sex in and out of season. But I want, with *Lady C.*, to make an *adjustment in consciousness* to the basic physical realities. I realize that one of the reasons why the common people often keep – or kept – the good *natural glow* of life, just warm life, longer than educated people, was because it was still possible for them to say fuck! or shit without either a shudder or a sensation.' The reviewer of *Field and Stream* was among the brave to venture to praise the book in print, admiring Lawrence's descriptions of the duties of a typical English gamekeeper (though also lamenting that 'one is obliged to wade through many pages of extraneous material in order to discover and savour those sidelights on the management of a Midlands shooting estate, and in this reviewer's opinion the book cannot take the place of J. R. Miller's *Practical Gamekeeping*').

Manner of Death: Lawrence died of tuberculosis in Vence, France, on 2 March 1930 in the arms of Aldous Huxley's wife, aged 44. He was buried in Vence, his grave being marked by a mosaic depicting a risen phoenix (his adopted emblem).

LAWRENCE, Thomas Edward (1888–1935) English writer and military leader

---

T. E. Lawrence, later known as 'Lawrence of Arabia' was born in Tremadoc, North Wales, on 16 August 1888. He was the second of five illegitimate sons of Thomas Robert Chapman (who had assumed the name Lawrence), an Anglo-Irish landowner who inherited a baronetcy in 1914. His mother was Sarah Maden, governess to Lawrence's four step-sisters by his father's legitimate wife. Two of his brothers were killed in World War I, the survivors being Willy (younger) – Professor A. W. Lawrence – and Bob (older). Educated at the City School for Boys, Oxford (from the age of eight), he ran away from home in 1906 and spent eight months in the Royal Artillery before his parents bought him out. He later went to Oxford (First in Modern History) and studied Arabic. At first he worked under his friend D. G. Hogarth in a British Museum team excavating the Hittite city of Carchemish, near Aleppo. When Sir Leonard Woolley took over he followed him to the Sinai (then Turkish), secretly mapping the area for British Intelligence. He was then, helped by Hogarth, appointed Temporary Lieutenant-Interpreter to the General Staff Geographic Section to draw up official maps of the Sinai. When war was declared on Turkey he was posted to the Cairo Intelligence Unit (later known as the Arab Bureau) under Hogarth, became military adviser to Sherif Hussein's son Emir Faisal in the Arab revolt against the Turks, and edited the Bureau's *Arab Bulletin*. He is best known for organizing attacks on the crucial Hejaz railway and for his remarkable capture of Akaba. For the latter exploit he was promoted to major, given the Croix de Guerre and caused embarrassment by refusing the Order of the Bath – adding that he might have to fight for the Arabs against the British. After the war he was granted a Fellowship of All Souls College, Oxford, to write a history of the Arab revolt. He was later Arab adviser to the Colonial Office, but in 1922 he disappeared from public view by enlisting as an RAF mechanic under the name 'John Hume Ross' – 352087 A/C Ross. He then joined the RAF School of Photography but when the *Daily Express* exposed him left and worked as a quartermaster in the Tank Corps as 'T. E. Shaw' (1923). Back in the RAF again (1925 for 10 years) he was posted to Karachi, then worked on flying boats (he was part of the RAF team that won the Schneider trophy in 1931) and helped design motor-launches for the air/sea rescue service. He changed his name by deed poll to T. E. Shaw in 1927 and left the RAF in 1935. His publications included *The Seven Pillars of Wisdom* (1926), *Revolt in the Desert* (1927) and *Crusader Castles* (1936).

Family/Sex Life: Lawrence never married, but had homosexual relationships with, among others, the 14-year-old Arab Salim Ahmed (nicknamed 'Dahoum' or 'Darkness'), whom he met in Carchemish, and Sharif Ali ibn al-Hussein. Captured while disguised as an Arab he was raped, badly beaten and whipped by men of Hacim Bey, Turkish military governor of Deraa.

Appearance: Under five feet six inches tall, he was 'physically small, with a head disproportionately large, very unobtrusive with his quiet voice and tendency to long silences' (Leonard Woolley). He had a high forehead, a straight nose, blue eyes and fair yellow hair. He wore Arab dress in the desert.

Habits/Mannerisms: Known by the Arabs as 'El Aurans', he was abstemious in his

habits, neither smoking nor drinking and only eating sparingly. As a teenager he lived and slept in a bungalow at the bottom of his parents' garden. He hated being touched but was also a masochist (his Army friend John Bruce regularly used to beat him at Lawrence's request). He had a very good visual memory.

Sport/Hobbies: At school Lawrence liked cycling, cross-country running and gymnastics. Other interests were pistol-shooting, brass-rubbing, archaeology (especially the 12th century and the Crusades), photography and collecting hand-press books and records. He also liked riding motorbikes fast, notably a Brough Superior, the only type officially recognized by Rolls-Royce as 'the Rolls-Royce of motorcycles'. In the desert he used a fleet of nine Rolls-Royce armoured cars with such names as Bloodhound and Blast. He spoke fluent French.

Religion/Politics: Church of England by upbringing.

Health: Lawrence broke a leg at school (aged 16) and the limb never grew thereafter. He contracted malaria as a student (while in Syria and Palestine) and dysentery at Carchemish (1911). Other problems included boils and cracked ribs and a broken collar-bone sustained when the London–Cairo plane in which he was travelling crashed outside Rome (1919); both pilots were killed. He was wounded over 60 times.

Temperament: Fiery but shy; also neurotic and ascetic. His friends included E. M. Forster, G. B. Shaw (and his wife Charlotte), Robert Graves, John Buchan, Lady Astor, James Elroy Flecker and Henry Williamson (who dedicated *Salar the Salmon* to him and wrote his biography). He was known as Ned to his family. In his *Who's Who* entry he described himself as 'Prince of Mecca'.

Pets: He kept a female racing camel called

Naama (he accidentally shot it in action near Akaba).

Work/Daily Routine: The dashing 'Lawrence of Arabia' image was in fact developed by the American Lowell Thomas, who was sent to the UK to find a British folk hero to make US participation in World War I more acceptable to the US public. As a writer, Lawrence experienced a setback when he lost the manuscript of *The Seven Pillars of Wisdom* when changing trains at Reading – he had no option but to rewrite the whole book (it was dedicated to 'S.A.', Salim Ahmed, who had died of typhoid in 1918).

Manner of Death: Lawrence crashed swerving to avoid two boy cyclists when driving a Brough Special (GW 2275) motorcycle near his rented cottage 'Clouds Hill' near Bovington, Dorset, when returning home from Bovington Army camp. He died of head injuries in a coma in Bovington camp hospital five days later on 19 May 1935, aged 46.

LEAR, Edward (1812–88) English writer and artist

Edward Lear was born in Bowman's Lodge, Holloway Road, London, on 12 May 1812, the 20th child of Jeremiah Lear, a stockbroker who also had sugar-refining interests, and Ann Clark Skerrett. When his father's business collapsed, he was brought up by his sister, Ann, 21 years his senior, who had been left money by their grandmother. Other siblings included Henry, Frederick, Eleanor, Sarah and Mary. Educated at home by Ann, he started work aged 15 drawing bird illustrations for Prideaux Selby, co-author of *Illustrations of British Ornithology* (1828–30) and in 1831, aged 19, was employed by the Zoological Society of London as a zoological draughtsman. Publication of his widely acclaimed parrot book, *Illustrations of the Family of Psittacidae*, before he was 20, led to employment for four years by Edward Stanley, 13th Earl of Derby, at Knowsley Hall, near Liverpool, illustrating plates for a book on his unique private zoo, *The Knowsley Menagerie*. Extensive travels in Europe resulted in the publication of various travel books, including *Views in Rome* (1841) and *Illustrated Excursions in Italy* (1846). He later gave Queen Victoria drawing lessons at Osborne House and Buckingham Palace (1846), studied at the Royal Academy Schools (1849–53), travelled abroad and finally settled in San Remo, Italy (1871). Admired as an illustrator in his own lifetime, he is usually remembered as the author of children's and nonsense verse, notably his limericks, his publications in this vein including *A Book of Nonsense* (1846) and *More Nonsense Rhymes* (1871).

Family/Sex Life: Lear had an affair with and nearly proposed to Augusta Bethell, daughter of Lord Westbury and aunt of the painter Paul Nash. There has been speculation that he was homosexual though there is no proof of this.

Appearance: Nearly six feet tall, Lear walked with a slight stoop. He had broad shoulders and a large shapeless nose (which he exaggerated in his own doodles of himself to accompany his verse). In his youth he wore a moustache but later (around the age of 40) he adopted a full beard.

Habits/Mannerisms: His favourite drink was marsala.

Sport/Hobbies: Holman Hunt observed that Lear 'would rather be killed than fire a pistol or gun'. He did, however, play the piano and composed songs, setting Tennyson's poems to music.

Religion/Politics: Conventional Christian at first, then agnostic.

Health: Lear was an epileptic (he suffered up to 18 attacks a month as a child). He also had very bad eyesight (he wore strong spectacles) and suffered from bronchitis and asthma as a boy. According to Lear himself, he suffered 'every sort of syphilitic disease' as a young man. In old age he was troubled by rheumatism.

Temperament: Lear had a terror of large dogs and horses. He also disliked Germans. His friends included the novelist Prosper Merimée, Holman Hunt, Alfred Lord Tennyson (after whom he named his house in San Remo – the Villa Tennyson), Liberal MP Lord Carlingford (later Lord Privy Seal) and Evelyn Baring (Earl of Cromer). His servant for 27 years (1856–83) was the Corfu-born Albanian Giorgio Cocali.

Pets: Lear kept a striped tomcat with a stub tail, called Foss (the animal died aged 17 in 1887). In 1881, when the family moved from the Villa Emily, San Remo (named after his niece) because a new hotel blocked the view and spoilt the light for painting, Lear built an identical house (the Villa Tennyson) so the cat would feel at home. Foss was drawn in caricature by Lear.

Work/Daily Routine: As a serious artist, Lear was admired as a landscape painter and watercolourist and exhibited at the Royal Academy and elsewhere. He spent some 35 years (intermittently) working on illustrations to Tennyson's poems; in return, Tennyson, after reading Lear's book *Journal of a Landscape Painter in Albania and Illyria*, wrote him a poem 'To E. L. on his Travels in Greece'. Lear's comic writings were to prove more lastingly popular, however. The writer and critic John Ruskin (in the *Pall Mall Magazine* in 1886) placed *A Book of Nonsense* first in his list of 100 best books of contemporary literature. An enlarged edition (1861) had Lear's name on it and went through 30 editions in his lifetime. For a while the public thought 'Lear' was an anagram of 'Earl' and that the limericks were really by Edward, Earl of Derby. 'The Owl and the Pussy Cat' was written for Janet Symonds, daughter of John Addington Symonds, while *Nonsense Songs, Stories, Botany and Alphabets* (1870) was written for Hubert Congreve. Lear admired Byron and Turner. He was also a great letter-writer, writing up to 35 letters a day, usually before breakfast. He was constantly inventing quirky new spellings of words (for instance, fizzicle, eggsi-stens).

Manner of Death: Lear died in San Remo, Italy, on 30 January 1888, aged 75. He was buried in San Remo cemetery beside his faithful servant Giorgio Cocali.

LENIN, Vladimir Ilyich (1870–1924) Russian revolutionary leader

Vladimir Ilyich Ulyanov (later known as Lenin) was born in Simbirsk, capital of Simbirsk Province, Russia, on 22 April 1870, the second son of Ilya Nikolaevich Ulyanov, a school inspector and later Director of Schools for the province of Simbirsk, and Maria Alexandrovna Blank, daughter of a Christian-convert Jewish doctor who later became a wealthy State Counsellor and estate owner in Kazan. He had an older sister, Anna, an older brother, Alexander – who as a student took part in a Populist plot to assassinate Tsar Alexander III and was executed – two younger brothers, Dmitri and Nikolai, and two younger sisters, Olga and Mariya. Lenin went to Simbirsk High School, where Kerensky's father was a teacher, but was banished to his aunt's estate at Kokushkino, near Kazan, after his brother's death. He then studied law at Kazan University but was expelled for political activities and took an external degree in law at St Petersburg University. He later practised as a lawyer in Samara (1892). Exiled to Siberia for three years, where he wrote *The Development of Capitalism in Russia* (1899), he took the name N. Lenin in a letter to Plekhanov in January 1901 and settled on V. I. Lenin in 1902. In 1903 he forced the split between the Bolshevik ('majority') and Menshevik ('minority') factions and, returning from exile in Germany, led the Bolsheviks in the Dumas (Parliament) that seized power in 1917, deposed the monarchy to give power to the proletariat under a Communist government along Marxist lines and took Russia out of World War I. As head of Communist Russia he introduced the New Economic Policy in an attempt to restructure Russian society and industry.

Family/Sex Life: After his proposal to Apollinaria Yakubora was rejected, in 1898 Lenin married Nadezhda Konstantinova Krupskaya. His wife was unable to have children.

Appearance: Described by Trotsky as 'Below middle height . . . Slavonic type of face . . . piercing eyes', Lenin was short but broad-shouldered and well built, with a bald head and dark-red beard and moustache. He had small dark brown slanting eyes and a swarthy Asiatic face, with high cheekbones. He had large ugly hands and usually wore a cloth cap.

Habits/Mannerisms: Known as 'Illyich' by his followers, Lenin was abstemious in his habits and did not smoke. He had a hoarse voice and when speaking put his thumbs in the armholes of his waistcoat and would open and shut his fists in this position. He was shortsighted and tended to screw up his eyes. Some acquaintances spoke of him having a generally shifty look.

Sport/Hobbies: Lenin enjoyed athletic sports and could row, swim, cycle and skate well. He was also a keen walker and enjoyed shooting and hunting. Every morning he performed gym exercises for 10 minutes. Other pursuits included chess, collecting mushrooms and playing billiards. He owned nine Rolls-Royces, including the world's only half-track Rolls-Royce, adapted with skis at the front for snow-driving. His favourite reading included the work of Turgenev (he learnt German and translated Turgenev from Russian into German and back into Russian). He also read Hegel, Aristotle, Napoleon, Clausewitz and Hugo's poetry.

Health: In 1918 Lenin was shot in the left shoulder and neck during an assassination attempt by 28-year-old Fanya (Dora) Kaplan, who saw him as a traitor to the Revolution. He later suffered from sclerosis of the cerebral arteries and was paralysed after a stroke.

Temperament: Known within his family as Volodya, Lenin had a generally reserved nature and did not make friends easily, keeping associates at arm's length.

Work/Daily Routine: Lenin wrote many pamphlets and used to whisper ideas to himself before committing them to paper. He was not well-read in philosophy and had not read Shakespeare, Byron, Molière or Schiller, and of Goethe had only read *Faust*. He disliked Dostoevsky, protesting 'I haven't got time for this rubbish', but admired Pushkin. He thought Mayakovsky's work 'Cheap mumbo-jumbo to which the label "Revolution" has been attached.'

Manner of Death: Lenin died of a stroke following cerebral sclerosis in Gorki on 21

January 1924, aged 53. The post-mortem revealed that his brain had shrunk to a quarter of its normal size. His body was embalmed and laid in a crystal coffin in Red Square, Moscow. Petrograd was renamed Leningrad in his memory, but reverted to its original name St Petersburg with the collapse of Communism in the USSR in the 1990s. In what was dubbed 'Lenin's Testament' he left final instructions to his party, advising against the acceptance of Stalin as his successor.

LEONARDO da Vinci (1452–1519) Italian artist and inventor

Leonardo da Vinci was born in Vinci, near Florence, Italy, on 15 April 1452, the son of unmarried parents, Piero da Vinci, a successful notary to the Florence magistracy or Signoria (subsequently married four times), and a peasant girl named Caterina (who subsequently married someone else). His stepmother, Albiera di Giovanni Amadori, married his father in the year Leonardo was born and he had a stepbrother Bartolommeo – 45 years his junior – by his father's third wife. He never learnt Latin or Greek and studied art under Verrocchio (helping him to make the golden ball for the top of the Duomo church in Florence) and maths and astronomy under Toscanelli. At first he worked as painter, engineer and musician for Duke Ludovico Sforza in Milan (1482–99), then was chief architect and engineer to Cesare Borgia (son of Pope Alexander VI) in Florence (1502). From 1506 to 1513 he worked for Charles D'Amboise (governor of Milan and vice-regent of Louis XII of France) and then for Giuliano de' Medici (Pope Leo X's brother). From 1517 he lived 500 metres from Francis I of France's royal castle at Cloux, Amboise, where he was employed as a painter and thinker. He was a painter, sculptor, musician, poet, architect, engineer, geologist, anatomist, botanist, physiologist, astronomer and philosopher and, according to Vasari, 'He might have been a scientist if he had not been so versatile.' He is credited with inventing air-conditioning, the alarm clock, the automobile, ball bearings, the camera obscura, the flame-thrower, the helicopter, the machine-gun, the parachute, shrapnel, the submarine, the swing bridge and the telescope among other innovations.

Family/Sex Life: A homosexual, at the age of 24 Leonardo was accused of sodomy, with four others.

Appearance: Tall and strong, Leonardo was described by Vasari as 'striking and handsome'. He had a fine long reddish-fair curling beard and long wavy hair; Raphael depicted him in old age as Plato in his painting School of Athens. In his old age he wore spectacles. He had a taste for garish clothing, wearing, for instance, short doublets and tights of blue and crimson velvet and brocade when normal dress comprised a long robe of sober colour. He was particularly fond of wearing pink.

Habits/Mannerisms: Leonardo was left-handed and could write backwards in mirror-writing (which he used in his notebooks). He often used grammalogues (amalgamated words). A vegetarian, he was fond of animals and used to buy caged birds in order to set them free.

Sport/Hobbies: A muscular athlete, he was particularly good with horses. He had a strong voice and also played the lute and the 'lyra' (a sort of lute of his own invention, made of silver in the shape of a horse's skull with its teeth as frets).

Religion/Politics: Leonardo rejected belief in magic or alchemy. He took the Roman Catholic sacrament on his deathbed but was not otherwise Christian (he despised those who worshipped his religious pictures).

Health: According to Vasari, Leonardo 'was physically so strong that he could withstand any violence; with his right hand he would bend the iron ring of a doorbell or a horseshoe as if they were lead'.

Temperament: 'He was so generous that he sheltered and fed all his friends, rich or poor, provided they were of some talent or worth' (Vasari). A practical joker, he included among his friends Macchiavelli and Sandro Filipepi (better known as Botticelli or 'little bottle'). He disliked Michelangelo (the Florence Signoria once commissioned him and Michelangelo to paint opposite walls in the Palazzo Vecchio, Florence).

Work/Daily Routine: The earliest known drawing signed 'Leonardo' was a landscape near Vinci dated 5 August 1473. He usually shaded drawings from top left to bottom right. His *Adoration of the Magi* (c. 1481) was commissioned by the monks of San Donato a Scopeto, whose notary was Leonardo's father. To complete the celebrated fresco *The Last Supper* (1495–7), painted on the refectory wall of the monastery of Sta Maria delle Grazie, Milan, he worked from sunrise to sundown for two years (though while in Milan he maintained six helpers to assist him). The *Mona Lisa* (painted on wood, 1503–6) was a portrait of Lisa di Noldo Gherardini, third wife of the Florentine tradesman Francisco del Giocondo – 'Mona' is short for Madonna. The fact that she has no eyebrows was a reflection of the Florentine fashion for shaving them off. Leonardo spent four years on the painting but Giocondo refused to pay so it was sold to Francis I of France for 492 ounces of gold and he hung it in the Louvre, Paris. Considered the most valuable of all paintings, it was stolen from the Louvre by two thieves posing as workmen in 1911 but was recovered in 1913 after it was offered to a Florentine art dealer. In the intervening two years six US art collectors were duped into paying huge sums to acquire fakes purporting to be the stolen masterpiece. Many of Leonardo's inventions, of which there were over 1000, derived ultimately from ideas by Valturio, Keyser, di Giorgio, Archimedes and Vitruvius. The less well-known included the bicycle chain and the tip-up lavatory seat. He also wrote riddles, jests, stories and arranged court festivities etc. He never published any books – only his notes survive.

Manner of Death: Leonardo died in the arms of Francis I of France at the royal château of Cloux, Amboise, after suffering a paroxysm on his deathbed on 2 May 1519, aged 75. Not long before his death he reflected in his notebook: 'While I thought that I was learning how to live, I have been learning how to die.'

LINCOLN, Abraham (1809–65) 16th US President

Abraham Lincoln, nicknamed 'Honest Abe', was born on 12 February 1809 in a log cabin in Hodgenville, Hardin County, Kentucky, the son of Thomas Lincoln, a farmer, and his first wife, Nancy Hanks. He had a sister, Sarah (his brother Thomas died young) and all his life he thought he was illegitimate (as was his mother). After the family moved to Indiana, his mother died when he was nine (1818) and his father married Sarah Bush Johnston, a widow with two boys and a girl. Tradition has it that he learnt to write with charcoal on the back of a shovel by the light of the hearth and that in all he received no more than a year's formal education. He worked at first as a flatboatman, storekeeper and village postmaster and served briefly as a volunteer in the Black Hawk War (1832) before winning a place in the Illinois State Assembly. Though both his parents had been illiterate, he managed to qualify as a lawyer in 1836, was elected to the House of Representatives in 1846 and ultimately became President (1861–5). His term in office witnessed the victory of the Union Army over the Confederate states in the US Civil War and the end of slavery in the USA.

Family/Sex Life: After love affairs with Mary Owens and (possibly) Ann Rutledge, Lincoln married Mary Todd in 1843. Their children were Robert Todd, Edward Baker, William Wallace and Thomas ('Tad').

Appearance: Lincoln was very tall (six feet four inches) and had long arms and legs – with the result that his trousers often looked too short. He had grey eyes, a large nose and chin and heavy lips. He did not grow his familiar beard (lacking moustache) until 1860, when he was already 51. He paid little attention to his dress, often wearing a battered stovepipe hat and unpolished boots.

Habits/Mannerisms: Teetotal.

Religion/Politics: Lincoln was very interested in psychic research and as President held séances in the White House. Just a week before his assassination he was apparently much disturbed by a dream in which he saw himself walking through a silent White House towards his own coffin covered in black. As a politician, he began as a Whig, but later became a Republican. He was passionately opposed to slavery and it was his stance on

this issue that first marked him out as a leading light in Republican circles.

Temperament: Sincere, fair-minded and direct, Lincoln inspired cult status after his premature death. Opponents, however, criticized his use of his executive powers to rule by proclamation and protested about the detention without trial of certain political rivals. He was not immune to criticism or disappointment, however. Legend has it that when he was asked how he felt when beaten in his campaign to be elected to the Illinois legislature in 1858 he replied: 'Like the boy who stubbed his toe; I am too big to cry and too badly hurt to laugh.'

Pets: Animals belonging to the Lincolns included a cat called Tabby, a yellow mongrel dog named Fido and the goats Nanko and Nanny.

Work/Daily Routine: Lincoln communicated well and was famous as a speechmaker, though he made very few as President. He wrote the celebrated Gettysburg Address ('government of the people, by the people, for the people') on the back of an envelope. Not everyone agreed about the qualities of even this classic speech: the *Chicago Times* dismissed his words at Gettysburg as 'silly, flat and dishwatery utterances'.

Motto/Saying: 'You can fool some of the people all the time and all the people some of the time; but you can't fool all the people all the time' (attributed).

Manner of Death: Lincoln was shot in the head by the actor John Wilkes Booth on 14 April 1865 in Ford's Theatre, Washington DC, while watching Tom Taylor's play *Our American Cousin*. Shouting *'Sic semper tyrannis!'* ('So die all traitors!') and 'The South is avenged!', Booth broke a leg jumping out of the President's box and onto the stage – hence the theatrical good-luck phrase 'break a leg' – but made good his escape. He was later attended by a Dr Mudd (immortalized in the expression 'his name was mud'), but 12 days later was trapped in a burning barn and shot dead. Lincoln died without regaining consciousness the morning after the shooting, aged 56. He was the first US President to be assassinated and he reputedly still haunts the White House. The pistol with which he was shot, together with Booth's diary and other items, are preserved in a basement museum at Ford's Theatre. Lincoln was buried in Springfield, Kentucky. His wife, distressed by the loss of three of her sons and then her husband, went insane for 10 years and had to be institutionalized until 1876.

LISZT, Franz (1811– 86) Hungarian composer and pianist

Franz Liszt was born on 22 October 1811 in Raiding, Hungary, the son of Adam Liszt, a (Hungarian) land-steward on one of the Esterhazy estates at Raiding, near Vienna, and Anne Lager, an Austrian. He was taught at first by his father, an amateur violinist, guitarist and pianist (who died when he was 17), and then, sponsored by Prince Esterhazy, by Salieri (composition) and Czerny (piano) in Vienna (Czerny was so impressed he refused all payment). He was also much influenced by Paganini. A child prodigy, Liszt gave his first public performance at the age of 11 and later performed for George IV and Queen Victoria in England and for Tsar Nicholas II in Russia. He gave up public concerts in 1833, the year the Liszt family moved to Paris, but returned in 1837 for a piano contest with rival virtuoso Sigismond Thalberg (10 times as many turned up for Liszt's concert). In 1848 he settled in Weimar, working as a director of opera and concerts and concentrating on composition rather than on playing. He later joined the Franciscan order (1861) as the Abbé Liszt. Given a jewelled sabre in Pesth, Hungary, he was nearly shot once by an admirer. With Wagner he laid the foundation stone of the Bayreuth Theatre and he also paid for the erection of a statue of Beethoven in Bonn. His most celebrated compositions included 12 symphonic poems, masses, two symphonies and much piano music.

Family/Sex Life: Liszt never married but in 1834 he eloped with Marie Catherine Sophie de Flavigny, Comtesse d'Agoult (the author 'Daniel Stern'). Their children were Blandine (who died in 1862), Cosima (who later married Hans von Bülow and then Richard Wagner) and Daniel (who died in 1859 aged 20). They separated in 1839, shortly after the birth of Daniel, though Liszt continued to spend the summers with her and the children until 1844. Subsequently, in 1847, he eloped with Princess Carolyne zu Sayn-Wittgenstein – he remained with her until his death, though his hopes of marrying her were dashed in 1861 when the Pope revoked his sanction of her divorce. He also had many other affairs (for instance, with the dancer Lola Montez). Many of his liaisons were with titled aristocrats, moving Ernest Newman to observe that: 'He collected princesses and countesses as other men collect rare butterflies, or Japanese prints, or first editions.'

Appearance: Liszt had long grey centre-parted hair, which in later life turned white (admirers would pluck strands with tweezers, and one even framed the seat cover he had sat on). Other distinguishing features included five large warts on his face. He wore green gloves and kept a different cravat for each day of the year.

Habits/Mannerisms: Liszt drank a bottle

of brandy a day and also smoked cigars (one admirer kept one of his cigar stubs in her corsage for 25 years). He disliked being interrupted while playing. When Tsar Nicholas II talked while he was performing he suddenly ceased to play, explaining somewhat sarcastically: 'Music herself should be silent when Nicholas speaks.' An unidentified contemporary vividly recalled the effect his playing had: 'Terrified pianos flee into ever corner . . . gutted instruments strew the stage, and the audience sits mute with fear and amazement.'

Religion/Politics: Very religious. Late in life he became a Franciscan abbé.

Health: Liszt's health was often uncertain, due in part to the demands of repeated tours as a young man. Disappointments in love were also liable to reduce him to illness and left him prone to periods of self-doubt and pessimism.

Temperament: George Eliot spoke very warmly of Liszt, claiming: 'Genius, benevolence, and tenderness beam from his whole countenance.' Heinrich Heine found him 'a man of unruly but noble character, unself-seeking and without falseness'. Beethoven called him a 'Devil of a fellow – such a young rascal!' Other friends included George Sand and Chopin (he owned a marble impression of Chopin's hands and loved all his work with the single exception of the Scherzo in B flat minor). Liszt's friendship with Wagner, in due course to become his son-in-law (initially very much against Liszt's wishes), was close and extended to professional matters. Wagner – whose music was much more popular than Liszt's – once wrote to his friend and mentor apologizing for unconsciously 'stealing' one of his themes. Liszt only said: 'Now at least it will be heard.' When a friend commiserated with Liszt about the neglect of his compositions he replied: 'I can wait.' Opinions about Liszt's compositions were less unanimous than they were about his playing. The critic Neville Cardus memorably summed up Liszt's Piano Concerto No. 2 as 'sawdust and spangles'.

Manner of Death: Liszt died of pneumonia in Bayreuth, Austria, on 31 July 1886. His last word was 'Tristan'.

LOUIS XIV 'The Sun King' (1638–1715) King of France

Louis XIV was born on Sunday 5 September 1638 in the Palace of St Germain-en-Laye, France, the son of Louis XIII (who died when he was four years old) and the Spanish Infanta, Anne of Austria. He was the son-in-law of Philip IV of Spain, the nephew of Queen Henrietta (wife of Charles I) of Britain and had a younger brother Philippe, Duc d'Orléans, who was a homosexual transvestite. (There is a theory that the unidentified 'Man in the Iron Mask', who died in the Bastille during Louis's reign, was Louis's real father, possibly a young Bourbon persuaded to provide the hitherto childless Anne with an heir). Of above average intelligence, Louis was educated privately and learnt French, Italian, Latin, maths, drawing, music and geography. Crowned king aged five (1643), the Queen and Cardinal Mazarin (Louis's godfather) were regents until Mazarin's death (1661). Louis was consecrated king in his own right at Reims Cathedral in 1654. During Louis's reign (at 72 years the longest in European history) France became the most powerful state in Europe, though it also became embroiled in the War of the Spanish Succession (1701–13) among other conflicts. He built the palace at

Versailles, with its staff of 25,000, gave shelter to the exiled Stuart family after the execution of Charles I, employed Racine and Boileau as historiographers royal, and presided over a golden age in French culture.

Family/Sex Life: Permission for Louis to marry Marie Mancini (Mazarin's niece) was refused and he lost his virginity aged 16 to Madame de Beauvais, Queen's Lady of the Bedchamber and 20 years his senior. In 1660 he married the Infanta Maria Theresa, the eldest daughter of Philip IV of Spain. She died in 1683; of their children only Louis survived infancy. After her death Louis married (1684) his mistress Françoise Scarron, Madame de Maintenon, the daughter of a Huguenot malcontent (she was born in prison) and the wife of poet Paul Scarron. He also had other mistresses, including Louise de la Vallière (by whom he had four children), Athénais de Montespan (who, though already married, bore him seven children), and Mademoiselle de Fontanges.

Appearance: Louis was born with two teeth and went through eight wet-nurses before he was weaned. As an adult he was clean-shaven and had blue-grey eyes, a fine mouth, a cleft chin, a prominent irregularly shaped nose and long wavy hair (he wore a wig from 1673). He became fat in old age and in contrast to the rich costumes of his youth preferred a simple brown coat.

Habits/Mannerisms: Louis's life was always exposed to public view – over 100 courtiers assisted in the *grand levée* ceremony in which he was dressed. He only took three baths in his entire life and liked to keep the windows wide open (he called Madame de Maintenon *'Votre Soliditée'* because she overdressed to compensate for the cold). Only he and the queen were allowed to sit in chairs with arms. He touched members of the public to cure scrofula, doing so for the last time in 1715. He collected art and was also a patron of astronomy and fond of tulips. He had a large appetite (though a poor digestion) and enjoyed herb-flavoured food, game, dishes with pistachio nuts and fruit and vegetables (especially globe artichokes and peas). He also took herbal tea and rhubarb, but did not take wine until aged 20 (preferring fruit juice and water). Between 1672 and 1696 he drank champagne on doctor's orders and burgundy from 1696.

Sport/Hobbies: Louis enjoyed hunting, riding, fencing and target-shooting. He also liked music and dancing (he performed in 13 ballets with music by Lully). Other interests included botany, billiards, card games, playing guitar and collecting jewellery and precious stones (for instance, the Hortensia Diamond, the Hope Diamond, the Miroir du Portugal and the 50-carat Grand Sancy).

Religion/Politics: Roman Catholic. Louis's revocation of the Edict of Nantes (allowing freedom of worship) led to the persecution of Huguenot Protestants. He was excommunicated by the Pope in 1689 for supporting an independent French Church. When the Paris *parlement* objected in the interests of the state to Louis's fiscal demands (1655), Louis arrogantly declared (aged 17) *'L'état, c'est moi.'*

Health: Smallpox in 1647 left marks on Louis's face. Subsequent ailments included gonorrhoea (*c.*1655), measles (1683) and a dislocated elbow (1684). In 1685 he had many of his teeth and part of his upper jawbone extracted because of an abscess, with the result that his mouth appeared sunken. In 1686 he had an anal fistula removed. Despite these problems, he remained fit into his old age and was still hunting and having sex in his seventies.

Temperament: Louis was genuinely fond of his lovers and his children. During one protracted labour, for instance, he held his wife's hand throughout her ordeal.

Pets: Louis kept both dogs and horses.

Work/Daily Routine: Louis was called 'the Sun King' because his father had chosen the image of a sun emerging from behind a cloud to publicize his birth. Besides his involvement in affairs of state, Louis wrote a guidebook to Versailles, restored Nôtre Dame Cathedral, laid out the Champs-Élysées, built Les Invalides and rebuilt the Louvre. The building of Versailles was so costly in money and lives that Louis forbade his courtiers to discuss the death toll among the workers. (The palace proved impossible to heat and had inadequate sanitation.) He also introduced 5000 streetlamps (lit by whale oil) and found time to pen his memoirs. His reign is still recalled as the Golden Age of French culture.

Motto: *Nec Pluribus Impar* ('A match for the whole world').

Manner of Death: Gangrene in the left leg and a high fever starting on 10 August 1715 led to Louis's death on Sunday 1 September 1715, aged 76. Noticing tears on the faces of his attendants he asked: 'Why are you weeping? Did you imagine that I was immortal?' During the French Revolution his embalmed heart was stolen and sold to Lord Harcourt, who later sold it to the gourmand William Buckland, Dean of Westminster – who cooked and ate it.

LUDWIG II of Bavaria (1845–86) King of Bavaria

Otto Friedrich Wilhelm II ('Mad King Ludwig') was born at 12.30 am on Monday 25 August 1845 in Nymphenburg Palace, near Munich, Bavaria – the same day his grandfather Ludwig I was born in 1786. His father was Maximilian II (then Crown Prince) and his mother was Princess Maria of Prussia; he was named after his godfathers, King Friedrich Wilhelm IV of Prussia and King Otto of Greece (Ludwig's uncle). His cousin Crown Prince Friedrich of Prussia married Queen Victoria's eldest daughter. At first called Otto, he was later named Ludwig at the suggestion of his grandfather. He also had a younger brother called Otto. Ludwig became king aged 18 on the death of his father in 1864. Though later decreed mad, he reigned for 22 years, uniting with Prussia against France (1870–1) and allowing Bavaria to join the German Empire. He was also the major patron of Richard Wagner. He was eventually deposed by his uncle.

Family/Sex Life: Though a homosexual, Ludwig was engaged to his cousin Sophia, the younger sister of the Empress of Austria (Sophia also admired Wagner). Ludwig called her Elsa, while she called him Heinrich (but the marriage never took place).

Appearance: Tall, slim, athletic and strong, Ludwig had large eyes, prominent ears and sloping shoulders. He wore a small goatee beard and had curly dark brown hair (he once claimed: 'If I didn't have my hair curled every day I couldn't enjoy my food'). He was once described as a 'royal Shelley' in appearance. Contemporaries remarked on his good voice, though he spoke pompously and without humour.

Habits/Mannerisms: In 1870 Crown Prince Friedrich of Prussia observed that Ludwig had 'a nervous, restless way of talking, never waiting for his question to be answered but while the answer is being given asking another question about something quite different'. He turned night into day with artificial light, moons, rainbows etc. and would gallop round and round in his riding school between the hours of 8 pm and 3 am on pretend trips abroad. He also made real nocturnal trips at great speed in a horse-drawn golden rococo sleigh decorated with cherubs. He liked giving flowers to women and adopted a deliberately affected walk (the '*Königschritt*'), lifting his feet high like a horse and then stamping them down again, thinking this resembled Louis XIV's gait. He ate alone but had dinners prepared for others and believed he dined with Louis XIV, Louis XV, Madame Pompadour and Madame de Maintenon among others. He liked champagne and sweet wines and was fond of perfumes. His weakness for sweets resulted in the loss of his front teeth. He also kept diaries in German, French, Latin and Spanish.

Sport/Hobbies: Ludwig was a good rider and a strong swimmer. He disapproved of hunting and shooting but enjoyed fishing, piano-playing and photography. Other pleasures included the theatre, though he disliked the public and so arranged 208 private performances at his Court Theatre. He was fluent in French and loved reading Scott as a child; later he became a voracious reader of Louis XIV's time and of the life of Marie Antoinette. From 1861 he was greatly influenced by the music of Wagner, calling him 'the god of my life' and lavishing money upon him. Another passion was the building of fairytale castles (the most famous of which was Neuschwanstein Castle, unfinished at his death).

Religion/Politics: Deeply religious.

Health: Ludwig first started hearing voices aged 14 and was declared insane in June 1886. There was a history of insanity in the family – his aunt Princess Alexandra thought she had swallowed a grand piano made of glass and his younger brother Otto was locked up as insane around 1876 (he suffered weeping fits and barked like a dog) prior to Ludwig being affected. He had a very good memory but suffered from toothache and headaches.

Temperament: Very shy, but obsessed with his Romantic ideals. He became increasingly withdrawn after Otto went mad. Early eccentricities included sending a sofa out to a palace guard, because he looked tired.

Pets: Ludwig was fond of animals but disliked dogs. As a child he had a pet tortoise. Later he became fond of swans, like the rest of his family – they lived in swan country and named their castles after them. Other pets included peacocks and a parrot that imitated his loud, nervous laugh. He once invited his favourite grey mare, Cosa Rara, to dine with him on soup, fish and roast meat.

Work/Daily Routine: Significant political acts included the famous letter he wrote to King Wilhelm of Prussia inviting him to assume the title of Emperor (*Kaiser*) over a united Germany. Later he concentrated his energies on his mock-medieval castles, which included those at Herrenchiemsee (in imitation of Versailles) and Linderhof.

Manner of Death: On 13 June 1886, a few days after he was declared insane, Ludwig was found drowned (presumed suicide) in shallow water 20 yards from the shore of Starnberger Lake, close to Schloss Berg, near Munich (his watch had stopped at 6.54 pm, suggesting his time of death). He was 40 years old. Beside him was the drowned body of the eminent psychiatrist Dr Bernhard von Gudden, who had been accompanying the deposed king to his mental asylum in Munich (they had stopped for the night at Schloss Berg).

MARLOWE, Christopher (1564–93) English playwright

Christopher Marlowe was born in Canterbury, Kent, on 6 February 1564, the eldest son and second child of John Marlowe (or Marley as he preferred to sign his name), a local shoemaker, and Katherine Arthur. Of his surviving siblings he had an elder sister Mary and a younger brother Thomas. He won scholarships to both King's School, Canterbury (1578), and Corpus Christi College, Cambridge (1580, BA 1584, MA 1587), where he was a pensioner (higher than a sizar) and read Divinity (registered variously as 'Marlin', 'Merling' and 'Marley'). While a student he translated Ovid's *Amores* (publicly burnt by order of the Bishop of London, 1599) and Lucan's *Pharsalia*, and began *Tamburlaine* (1590), the only one of his works published in his lifetime. His friend and patron was Sir Thomas Walsingham, cousin of Sir Francis Walsingham, Elizabeth I's Secretary of State and father-in-law of poet Sir Philip Sidney, and it is now widely held that while still a student he became a spy employed by Sir Francis to uncover Catholic plots against Elizabeth (one of Marlowe's circle was Robert Pole, whose undercover activities revealed the Babington Plot, which led to the execution of Mary Queen of Scots). He travelled to the Continent, apparently in the Queen's service and was deported from Holland for issuing forged gold coins. He wrote plays for the Lord Admiral's Company (the Earl of Nottingham's troupe) and Lord Strange's Men, among them *The Jew of Malta, The Tragical History of Dr Faustus* and *Edward II*, all *c*.1592. During the Plague he stayed on Thomas Walsingham's estate at Scadbury Manor, Chislehurst, Kent, and was working on *Hero and Leander* there when he was arrested, called before the Star Chamber, released on bail pending a trial and subsequently died in a mysterious brawl in nearby Deptford. His reputation was long in abeyance until restored by Swinburne in the 19th century.

Family/Sex Life: Unmarried (probably homosexual).

Appearance: Described by contemporaries as handsome, he had grey eyes and sported a moustache.

Sport/Hobbies: As a boy, he sang in the school choir. One version of his death suggests that he was enjoying a game of backgammon before the fatal fight broke out.

Religion/Politics: It was popularly held that Marlowe was an atheist (he was first accused in print of atheism by the playwright Robert Greene). He was a member of Sir Walter Ralegh's freethinking group the 'School of Night' (other poet members included Chapman, Spenser and Campion), which in pursuit of science, held views judged heretical. Because of his religious views, he was vilified by the Puritans after his death. Some actors believed that the diabolical theme of *Dr Faustus* made it a dangerous play to perform – the celebrated performer Edward Alleyn is reputed to have retired from the stage after a real demon materialized in the wings in answer to his 'summons' in the character of Faustus.

Temperament: Popularly addressed as 'Kit', Marlowe was apparently hot-tempered and provocative, judging from the many brushes he had with the authorities. His friends included the fashionable poet Thomas Watson (he and Marlowe were imprisoned in Newgate for a fortnight in 1589 when they were attacked and Watson killed a man in self-defence), Sir Walter Ralegh (for whom he once stood bail and to whom he wrote a love poem), playwright Thomas Kyd (whose confession to possessing 'atheistic' documents reputedly by Marlowe led to Marlowe's arrest), poet George Chapman (whom he encouraged to publish 'The Shadow of Night'), astronomer Thomas Hariot and publisher Edward Blount.

Work/Daily Routine: Marlowe virtually invented blank verse and English tragedy – according to Swinburne, 'Before Marlowe there was no genuine blank verse and genuine tragedy in our language.' His plays were controversial and *Tamburlaine* was published anonymously (*The Jew of Malta*, first performed *c.*1590, was not published till 1633). The unfinished *Hero and Leander* was completed after Marlowe's death by his friend George Chapman and published posthumously in 1598. In 1903 George Bernard Shaw called Marlowe: 'A barren amateur with a great air.'

Motto: *Quod me nutrit me destruit* (That which nourishes me destroys me).

Manner of Death: Marlowe died aged 29 around 6 pm on Wednesday 30 May 1593 – 10 days after being released on bail by the Star Chamber – after being stabbed above the right eye by Ingram Frizer, personal manservant of Marlowe's patron, Thomas Walsingham. The incident allegedly arose over a quarrel over a bill for a meal shared by Marlowe, Frizer and two others (Nicholas Skeres and Robert Pole – both known government spies) in an inn owned by Eleanor Bull in Deptford Strand, Deptford. Frizer was allegedly attacked first by Marlowe, from behind using Frizer's own dagger, but sustained only minor cuts to the back of his head before retaliating and killing the writer ('his braines comming out at the daggers point'). Frizer was acquitted on a plea of self-defence. Modern opinion suggests Marlowe may have been murdered to protect the School of Night, or alternatively that the murder was faked and another body was substituted to protect Marlowe himself – this latter scenario is favoured particularly by those who claim Marlowe wrote Shakespeare's plays. He was buried in St Nicholas's Church, Deptford.

MARVELL, Andrew (1621–78) English poet, civil servant and politician

Andrew Marvell was born in Winestead-in-Holderness, Yorkshire, on 31 March 1621, the son of the Rev. Andrew Marvell, schoolteacher and Rector of Winestead, and his first wife, Anne Pease, who died in 1638. He had three elder sisters, Anne, Mary and Elizabeth and a brother John (who died young). His father later married Lucy Alured (1638) but was himself drowned in the River Humber in January 1641. Educated at Hull Grammar School (where his father was a teacher) and at Trinity College, Cambridge, aged 12 (BA 1639), he came to London after his father's death and subsequently avoided military service in the Civil War by travelling around Europe (1643–7). At first he was employed at Nun Appleton House, Yorkshire, as tutor to Lord Fairfax's daughter Mary (1650–2), and then at Eton as tutor to Oliver Cromwell's ward William Dutton (1653–7). He was Milton's assistant as Latin Secretary to Cromwell's Council of State (succeeding him as Secretary in 1657) and became MP for Hull in Richard Cromwell's Parliament and under Charles II (1659). Subsequently he worked on undisclosed business (possibly as a spy) in Holland (1662–3) and as Private Secretary to the Earl of Carlisle (1663–5), with whom he visited Russia, Sweden and Denmark. His poetry, of the so-called 'Metaphysical' school, was largely neglected for two centuries after his death before his work was championed by the likes of Charles Lamb, T. S. Eliot and others and his stature was more widely appreciated. He is remembered chiefly for his pastoral and garden poems, the most famous of which include 'Upon Appleton House', 'The Garden', 'The Nymph Complaining for the Death of Her Faun' and 'To his Coy Mistress'.

Family/Sex Life: Marvell never married and lived alone with his housekeeper Mary Palmer. After Marvell's death, Palmer adopted the name Mary Marvell, claiming to be the poet's widow – apparently to acquire £500 Marvell had been holding on behalf of two bankrupt acquaintances. There were no children.

Appearance: Aubrey described Marvell as being 'of middling stature, pretty strong sett, roundish faced, cherry cheek'd, hazell eie, browne haire'.

Habits/Mannerisms: Marvell was a man of few words and was not remarked upon for his social graces. He drank little in company, though he was very fond of wine and drank a lot alone 'to refresh his spirits, and exalt his muse', as recorded by Aubrey.

Sport/Hobbies: He was a skilled fencer and learned several European languages on his travels to Holland, France, Italy and Spain in the 1640s.

Religion/Politics: Marvell became a convert to Roman Catholicism in 1639, being persuaded in his zeal to accompany a group of Catholics to London (from which he was unceremoniously retrieved by his father according to one story). He later became a staunch Protestant and wrote in defence of religious toleration of the Dissenters. An ardent Republican, though he included among his friends several Royalists, he served three times as MP for

Hull and once for Kingston-upon-Hull. It was through his influence that Milton was released from prison after the Restoration. After being elected an MP he wrote less poetry and concentrated on writing (often anonymous) political pamphlets and satires, his targets including intolerance and abuses of power. Many of these were highly controversial, the *London Gazette* actually offering a reward for information about the identity of the author of *An Account of the Growth of Popery and Arbitrary Government in England* (1677). As Cromwell's unofficial Poet Laureate he produced the celebrated 'An Horatian Ode upon Cromwell's Return from Ireland' and another admired poem on the Lord Protector's death (he was among those who walked in the Lord Protector's funeral procession). Earlier in his career, by way of contrast, he had written verses congratulating Charles I on the birth of a daughter, and later Charles II was among those who read his works over and over again. In 1674 he was identified by English agents as a spy in the service of the Dutch, working under the codename 'Mr Thomas'.

Work/Daily Routine: Capable of writing poetry as proficiently in Latin as he could in English, Marvell was little celebrated as a poet in his own lifetime, though he was widely admired as a patriot and satirist opposed to tyrannical government. His poems were published (as *Miscellaneous Poems*) after his death by his housekeeper, who found them amongst his papers; she signed the Preface herself as 'Mary Marvell'.

Manner of Death: Marvell died suddenly, having been given an opiate and being copiously bled for symptoms of tertian ague, on 16 August 1678, aged 57, in his house in Great Russell Street, London. Aubrey reported that 'Some suspect he was poysoned by the Jesuits . . .' He was buried under the pews on the south side of St Giles-in-the-Fields Church, London.

MARX, Karl Heinrich (1818–83) German economist

Karl Marx was born on 5 May 1818 at Brückengasse 664 (now 10), Trier, Prussia, the third child of Heinrich Marx, a Jewish lawyer who had converted to Protestant Christianity, and a Dutchwoman, Henrietta Pressburg, daughter of the rabbi of Nijmegen, Holland. He had an older brother Moritz David (who died young) and an older sister Sophie, while younger siblings were Emilie, Henriette, Luise, Caroline, Hermann and Edward. After attending the Frederick William High School, Trier (1830–5), he studied law at the Universities of Bonn (1835) and Berlin (1836) – where Hegel had been Professor of Philosophy until his death in 1831 – and received a PhD from the University of Jena (1841) after sending his thesis there because doctorates were easier to come by in Jena than in Berlin. Editor of the *Rheinische Zeitung*, Cologne (1842, suppressed 1843) and of the *Neue Rheinische Zeitung* (1848), he was also a regular contributor to the *New York Tribune* (1851–62), *Das Volk*, *Die Presse* and the *New American Encyclopedia*. He was expelled from Paris in 1845 as a result of his radical political writings and was later supported financially by his close colleague Friedrich Engels, with whom he reorganized (1847) the Communist League in London, where he settled permanently in 1849. In 1848 he published the *Communist Manifesto*, attacking conventional ideas of the state. He subsequently elaborated on his economic and political theories in *Das Kapital* (1867, 1884 and 1894) and was a prominent leader of the First International (1864–77).

Family/Sex Life: In 1843, when still a student, Marx married Jenny von Westphalen, daughter of his father's friend Baron von Westphalen and four years his senior. Their children were Jenny, Laura,

Edgar, Guido, Fransiska and Eleanor. He also had an illegitimate son Frederick (born 1851) by his longstanding maidservant Helene Demuth.

Appearance: Marx was thickset with a broad forehead, dark eyes, a heavy beard and (in his youth) very black hair. Other distinguishing features included hairy hands, a monocle and a wound above the left eye sustained in a duel at the University of Bonn in 1836.

Habits/Mannerisms: Marx drank brandy and identified fish as his favourite food. His favourite flower was the daphne and his favourite colour was red.

Sport/Hobbies: Besides his political writings, Marx also wrote poetry and began a comic novel in the style of Sterne. His favourite writers were Shakespeare, Aeschylus, Goethe and Diderot.

Religion/Politics: Marx was brought up as a Christian and was confirmed in the Protestant faith in 1834. Later he made the famous observation: 'Religion ... is the opium of the people.' Prior to coming to London he was exiled from France and Belgium for his Socialist views. Central to his political philosophy was the axiom: 'From each according to his abilities, to each according to his needs.'
Slogans from his *Communist Manifesto* included the oft-repeated revolutionary exhortation: 'The workers have nothing to lose but their chains. They have a world to gain. Workers of the world, unite.'

Health: Marx contracted tuberculosis in 1836 and as a result was deemed unfit for military service in 1841. Work on *Das Kapital* was not made any easier by piles, and he also suffered from the effects of an ulcer on the lung and from bronchitis. He suffered increasingly from ill health in the last decade of his life.

Temperament: Those who met Marx generally found him coldly arrogant and conceited. He was not entirely without friends, however, and included among these Friedrich Engels and Baron Ludwig von Westphalen (to whom he dedicated his PhD thesis). Michael Foot agreed that there was more than one side to Marx: 'Karl Marx wasn't a Marxist all the time. He got drunk in the Tottenham Court Road.'

Work/Daily Routine: The first draft of *The Communist Manifesto* (1848) was actually written by Engels and it was later Engels, using Marx's notes, who finished volumes two and three of *Das Kapital* after Marx's death. Most of the first volume of *Das Kapital* was written by Marx in the British Museum Reading Room (seat G7); Marx was the first reader to use the Government 'Blue Books' in the British Library. Usually, he worked in the morning, walked after lunch and took dinner at 6 pm before meeting with friends at 9 pm.

Mottoes: *Nihil humani a me alienum puto* (I consider that nothing human is alien to me); *De omnibus dubitandum* (You must have doubts about everything).

Manner of Death: Marx died at home at 41 Maitland Park Road, London, on 14 March 1883, aged 64. Only eight friends followed his coffin to Highgate Cemetery, London, and the grave remained ill-kept until 1956 when a massive marble block and cast-iron head was erected over it.

MARY I 'Bloody Mary' (1516–58) Queen of England, Wales and Ireland

The eldest daughter of Henry VIII by his first wife, the Spanish Katherine of Aragon, Mary was named after Henry's favourite sister, Mary Tudor (the 'Tudor Rose'). She was born just before dawn on Monday 18 February 1516 in Greenwich Palace and had an illegitimate younger brother Henry Fitzroy, Duke of Richmond and Somerset, by her father's liaison with Bessie Blount (one of Katherine's maids of honour). She later also had a younger step-sister, Elizabeth I, by her father's second wife, Anne Boleyn, and a younger step-brother, Edward VI, by her father's third wife, Jane Seymour. Deemed illegitimate after Henry's divorce from Katherine, she was accepted back at court after Anne Boleyn's death. The first royal princess to bear the title Princess of Wales, she was the first Queen of England to be crowned in her own right. She came to the throne after contesting (with troops) the 14-day reign of the uncrowned Lady Jane Grey, granddaughter of Mary Tudor, who had been named by Edward VI as his successor. Mary I was nicknamed 'Bloody Mary' because of her persecution of England's Protestants – some 300 people died and she had her father's Archbishop of Canterbury, Thomas Cranmer, burnt at the stake. The future Elizabeth I, suspected of involvement in Wyatt's rebellion, was imprisoned on Mary's orders. Deserted by her husband Philip II of Spain, she was coerced by him into declaring war on France, as a result of which Calais, the last English possession in Europe, was lost. She reigned for five years.

Family/Sex Life: Betrothed at two and a half to the eldest son of Francis I of France in 1518, Mary was subsequently promised at the age of six to the Holy Roman Emperor Charles V (nephew of Katherine of Aragon) and then, at the age of 11, to Francis's second son. In 1554, however,

Mary was married in Winchester Cathedral to 26-year-old Prince Philip of Spain (later Philip II), son of Charles V and Isabella of Portugal and 11 years her junior – he already had an eight-year-old son (left in Spain), Don Carlos, but no children arose from the marriage to Mary. The marriage created many enemies in Protestant England, not least because the birth of a child would have excluded the Protestant Princess Elizabeth from the throne. A plan to strike new coins showing Mary and Philip facing one another and proclaiming Philip King of England, Naples and Spain caused such alarm that a less provocative design had to be quickly introduced (in fact, Philip only visited England twice).

Appearance: Considered to have her father's features and her mother's neck, Mary was short and slender, with a rosy-cheeked complexion and large hazel eyes. She had golden, bright auburn hair and a low-pitched voice that was resonant like a man's. She wore a gold ring given by her father with portraits of Henry and Jane Seymour; favourite jewels included a single ruby in the shape of a gothic H, with a pendant pearl, and a jewelled M set with three rubies, two diamonds and a huge pearl (her father called her 'the greatest pearl in the kingdom'). She preferred Spanish gloves and liked brightly coloured clothes, especially red, purple and cloth-of-gold (her livery was blue and green).

Habits/Mannerisms: Mary was particularly fond of wild boar meat.

Sport/Hobbies: Mary enjoyed riding and hunting and liked to be painted with her Italian greyhounds at her feet. She walked two to three miles after breakfast each day and also danced, gambled at cards and was a good musician (she played the virginals from the age of three and also the regals and the lute). Well educated, she could read Greek and Latin, understood Italian and spoke Latin, French and Aragonese Spanish (though she could not speak Philip's Castilian and he spoke no English

and little French). She maintained at court the female jester/fool, Jane Bold (another gift from her father).

Religion/Politics: A devout Roman Catholic, Mary reunited the English Church with Rome and in 1555 banned English translations of the Bible and works by Luther, Calvin, Coverdale, Erasmus, Tyndale etc. The Mass was reinstated and prominent Protestants were put to death (the first being the married priest John Rogers, burnt at Smithfield, London, in 1555).

Health: Mary contracted smallpox as a child and from 1531 suffered pains in the head and stomach. She had two false pregnancies, caused by 'strangulation of the womb' (ovarian dropsy), and was near-sighted (myopic) like her father.

Temperament: Politically cautious but determined to reinstate Catholicism – a policy that made her deeply unpopular – Mary did win some admirers through her charity, revealed in her generous gifts to the poor. In private she was said to be kind-hearted and fond of children. She was also prone to deep melancholy. Though she was an effective speaker in public, she lacked political insight. One ambassador referred to her as 'so easy to get round, so simple, so little experienced in worldly matters, such a novice in all things'.

Daily Routine: Mary rose at daybreak, said prayers, heard Mass, then worked at her desk till 1 or 2 pm, had a light meal, then worked until after midnight.

Manner of Death: Mary died of ovarian dropsy (believing it another pregnancy) in the early morning of 17 November 1558 while saying Mass in her bedroom at St James's Palace, London, aged 43. Her last words were reputedly: 'When I am dead and opened, you shall find "Calais" lying in my heart.' She lay in state for three weeks and was then buried in Henry VII's chapel, Westminster Abbey. The chief mourners left the funeral trappings unattended while at lunch and they were torn to pieces and stolen as souvenirs.

Mary's subjects celebrated her death with bonfires in the streets. Unusually, there is no monument to her in England.

MARY, Queen of Scots (1542–87) Queen of Scotland

Mary Stuart, 'Queen of Scots', was born in Linlithgow Palace, Scotland, on 8 December 1542, the only surviving child of James V of Scotland and his second (French) wife, Mary of Lorraine, daughter of the Duc de Guise. Her father died a few days after her birth and she became queen on 15 December 1542. In 1547 she was sent to be educated at the French court, where she learned to speak six languages and was taught poetry by Ronsard. After the death of her husband, Francis II of France, she returned to Scotland as Queen of Scots and a legitimate contender for the English throne, Mary I having died and Elizabeth I (crowned in 1558) having been declared illegitimate by Henry VIII. Henri II of France had Mary Stuart proclaimed Queen of England, Scotland and Ireland as well as Queen of France (Elizabeth never forgave her for this) but she met with opposition from Scottish nobles and was eventually deposed (1568) in favour of her son, James I. She fled to England where she was accused, with others, of plotting against Elizabeth and was confined at Sheffield Castle (1570–84) and at various other stately homes, the last being Fotheringhay Castle. After the failure of the Babington Plot, organized by the Catholic Anthony Babington, to release her, and because of her refusal to renounce her claim (and thereby that of her son) to the English throne, she was tried and executed on Elizabeth's orders after 17 years as a prisoner.

Family/Sex Life: In 1558 the 16-year-old Mary was married to the 14-year-old Francis II of France, then dauphin, thus becoming briefly Queen (consort) of

France. He died in 1560 and in 1565 she married her cousin Henry Stewart, Lord Darnley (grandson of Margaret Tudor). Their son became James VI of Scotland and James I of England. Darnley, however, was widely unpopular for his debauched ways and Mary turned against him, relying instead on her Italian secretary David Rizzio (a Catholic). The outraged Darnley and other Scottish nobles murdered Rizzio (the bloodstains where he fell at Holyrood proved ineradicable). On Darnley's subsequent assassination by strangling after a mysterious explosion at Kirk o'Fields, Edinburgh, in 1567, Mary married the Protestant James Hepburn, Earl of Bothwell. Bothwell was widely suspected of Darnley's death, though he was officially acquitted of this charge. The marriage to Bothwell lost Mary popular support and precipitated her abdication.

Appearance: As a young woman Mary was striking, with hazel eyes, a clear complexion, fine hands and ruddy yellow hair, which later turned auburn then prematurely grey. By the time of her death, though, she was corpulent, with a fat face and a double chin. She was sometimes known as the 'White Queen' after she wore white for her wedding to Francis II (this being the traditional mourning colour in France then). She owned a famous set of black pearls (later sold to Elizabeth I) and a huge pendant ('Great Harry') set with large diamond and ruby.

Habits/Mannerisms: Mary had refined manners and ate off silver plates, even when in England. She kept a piece of 'unicorn's horn' from France to test her food in England for poison. While in prison, she also became skilled at secret handwriting and codes, using alum dissolved in water as invisible ink to write secret messages on household bills (to read the message the recipient dropped the paper in water so that the writing appeared).

Sport/Hobbies: Mary enjoyed hawking, dancing, croquet, golf, hunting, riding and 'shooting at the butts'. She also wrote poetry (including love sonnets to Bothwell and a sonnet in Italian to Elizabeth, 1568) and elegant prose, sang well and played the lute. Other pastimes included needlework/embroidery, in which she used emblems to tell stories (the cat and mouse tapestry reputedly by her and now in Holyrood Palace, Edinburgh, for instance, depicts Elizabeth's treatment of her). When she died she left an embroidered bedcover to James I.

Religion/Politics: Mary was brought up a Roman Catholic, making her a focus for Catholic rebellions against Elizabeth. On first arriving in Scotland she insisted on observing the Roman Catholic Mass, though Protestant demonstrations confined the right to hear Mass to her and her entourage alone.

Health: In later years Mary suffered from rheumatic gout in her hands, side and leg, as well as from dropsy.

Pets: Mary kept dogs (including spaniels and bloodhounds), turtle-doves, Barbary fowls and caged birds.

Work/Daily Routine: When in England Mary never went to bed until 1 am and never slept alone, a lady-in-waiting sleeping in a spare bed in the same room. She spent two hours every day reading (as well as reading Livy every day after dinner). She also made a hand-written Book of Hours for her own use.

Motto/Emblem: Mary's personal emblem was a hand-clasped sickle pruning a vine, with the motto '*Virescit vulnere virtus*' – VVV – ('virtue flourishes by a wound').

Manner of Death: Mary was beheaded with two strokes of an axe in Fotheringhay Castle, Northamptonshire, on the morning of 8 February 1587, aged 44. When the executioner held up her severed head (her lips moved for 15 minutes after execution) it fell to the floor and he found himself clutching only her wig, beneath which her hair was 'polled very short'. A pet dog crept onto the scaffold and lay between her body and her head. There were mass demonstrations in Paris at the news of her death. Mary had been denied the services of a Catholic priest at Elizabeth's orders and was also refused burial in France (she was buried instead in Peterborough Cathedral five months later, then moved by order of James I to Henry VII's Chapel, Westminster Abbey in 1612). James also had Fotheringhay Castle razed to the ground.

MAUGHAM, William Somerset (1874–1965)
English novelist, playwright and short-story writer

Somerset Maugham was born in the British Embassy, Paris – deliberately, so that he would be born on British soil – on 25 January 1874, the fourth surviving son of Robert Ormond Maugham, a solicitor at the British Embassy, and Edith Mary Snell (née Todd), daughter of the novelist and children's writer Mrs Snell. Named after his godfather, Henry Somerset Todd (a relation of General Sir Henry Somerset), his paternal grandfather was secretary and solicitor to the Law Society, and as founder and editor of the *Legal Observer* was known as the 'Father of Legal Journalism'. He had three elder brothers, Charles, Frederick (Lord Chancellor in Chamberlain's Cabinet and 1st Viscount Maugham) and Henry (also a writer, who committed suicide by drinking nitric acid, dying three days later) and three sisters. After his mother died (of tuberculosis) when he was eight and his father two years later, he was sent to Whitstable, Kent, to live with his uncle, Henry MacDonald Maugham, Rector of Whitstable. Aged 10 he spoke little English but attended King's School, Canterbury, until at 16 he caught a lung infection and was sent to Hyères, France, for a cure. He then spent nine months in Heidelberg and wrote an (unpublished) biography of Meyerbeer before returning to the UK. With £150 a year from his father's estate he at first tried chartered accountancy, then (1892) enrolled as a medical student at St Thomas's Hospital, London, became a clerk in the outpatients department (1893) and qualified as a doctor but decided to become a writer and moved to Seville, Spain. In World War I he volunteered as an ambulance-driver and dresser and worked for British Intelligence in Russia during the 1917 Revolution. Among his most successful novels were *Liza of Lambeth* (1897), *Of Human Bondage* (1916), *The Moon and Sixpence* (1919) and *Cakes and Ale* (1930). Popular plays included *Home and Beauty* (1919), *The Circle* (1921) and *The Constant Wife* (1926). He was made a Companion of Honour in 1954.

Family/Sex Life: In 1917 Maugham married Mrs Syrie Wellcome, a daughter of Dr Barnardo and the wife of pharmaceuticals magnate Henry Wellcome (26 years her senior), having already fathered a daughter, Liza, by her in 1915. He also had homosexual relationships, especially with the American Frederick Gerald Haxton, who later became his

secretary, then – after Haxton's death from tuberculosis in 1944 – with Alan Searle (whom Maugham legally adopted aged 88).

Appearance: Five feet seven inches tall, the mature Maugham had craggy time-weathered features with sunken cheeks and thinning brown hair (as recorded in a famous but controversial portrait by Graham Sutherland). He also wore horn-rimmed spectacles.

Habits/Mannerisms: Maugham suffered from a severe stutter from childhood. He spoke fluent French and German, smoked cigarettes and in the war years always carried an attaché case containing $100,000. He was also obsessed with tax-avoidance.

Sport/Hobbies: He enjoyed golf, croquet, tennis, swimming and bridge. He also owned paintings by Gauguin, Pissarro, Renoir, Bonnard, Léger, Monet etc. and was given a Matisse in payment for his screenplay for *The Razor's Edge*. In 1946 he founded the Somerset Maugham Award to allow young novelists to travel.

Health: Maugham suffered from tuberculosis and in old age from writers' cramp.

Temperament: A difficult man, who made many enemies, Maugham was nonetheless respected for his acute observations of human nature. Called William by his friends (Willie as a child), Maugham included among his associates Shaw, Beerbohm, Frank Harris, Churchill, Beverley Nichols, Edward VIII and Mrs Simpson, Duff Cooper, H. G. Wells and Kipling. It was alleged that Noël Coward based the embittered homosexual protagonist of *A Song at Twilight* (1966) upon Maugham and a case for libel was feared, but Maugham died before the play opened. Coward commented of Maugham on his death: 'Poor, miserable old man. Not very sadly mourned, I fear.' Maugham was heartily disliked by D. H. Lawrence and was called 'an unhappy and acid man who got no fun out of living' by Frieda Lawrence.

Work/Daily Routine: Maugham read Voltaire's *Candide* before writing each new novel, because it served as 'a touchstone of lucidity, grace and wit at the back of my mind'. As a playwright, he took one week to write each act and one week for a final polish; he once had four plays running simultaneously in London's West End. He admired Ibsen, Hemingway, Sinclair Lewis, Balzac, Maupassant and Stendhal. The title *Of Human Bondage* came from Spinoza's *Ethics*. In *Cakes and Ale* Driffield is Thomas Hardy and Kear is Hugh Walpole. His detractors included Edmund Wilson, who called Maugham 'a half-trashy novelist, who writes badly, but is patronized by half-serious readers, who do not care much about writing'.

Motto/Emblem: Maugham first used his father's Moorish (Algerian) device against the evil eye as his own logo on *The Hero* (1901), but unfortunately it was printed upside down.

Manner of Death: Maugham died at the Villa Mauresque, his home at Cap Ferrat in southern France, on 16 December 1965, aged 91. He was cremated and his ashes buried at King's School, Canterbury.

MAUPASSANT, Henri-René-Albert-Guy de (1850–93)
French short-story writer and novelist

Guy de Maupassant was born on 5 August 1850 in the (rented) Château de Miromesnil, Tourville-sur-Arques, near Dieppe, Normandy, the oldest son of Gustave de Maupassant, a stockbroker, and Laure le Poittevin, daughter of a wealthy cotton-mill owner and sister of Flaubert's friend Alfred le Poittevin (who himself married Gustave de Maupassant's sister Louise). He had a younger brother Hervé who went insane and died in an asylum aged 33. His parents split up in 1856. Educated from the age of 13 at a seminary in Yvetot near Rouen he was expelled in his penultimate year (1868) for writing an indecent poem and passed his *baccalauréat* at the Lycée in Rouen (1869). His law studies in Paris were interrupted by the Franco-Prussian War (1870), in which he served as a private in the Army. With help from his father, he became a clerk in the Naval Ministry while continuing to study law and later, aided by Flaubert, he served in the Ministry of Education. From 1880 he worked as a freelance journalist for *Gil Blas*, *Gaulois* etc. and was in much demand as a short-story writer. A disciple of Zola, he wrote some 300 short stories and six novels, including *Une Vie* (1883), *Bel-Ami* (1885) and *Pierre et Jean* (1888).

Family/Sex Life: Maupassant remained unmarried but had numerous affairs (for instance, with Marie Bashkirtseft).

Appearance: Maupassant had a strong and stocky build and a military bearing. Ruddy faced, he had, according to Alphonse Daudet, 'impenetrable eyes of streaky agate which absorbed the light but did not send it back again'. He wore a long moustache with a tuft under his lip and was always neatly dressed. He also wore a signet ring with his coat of arms.

Habits/Mannerisms: He was in the habit of inhaling ether – at first as a painkiller but later for its hallucinatory effects; he also took hashish and opium and smoked a pipe (though he later gave this up). He was later teetotal, only drinking St Gaulmier water and camomile tea.

Sport/Hobbies: Very athletic, Maupassant liked rowing and made balloon ascents in France (1887). He was also an extremely good shot with pistols (and was thus rarely challenged to duels). He disliked gambling and hated music; his favourite contemporary painter was Millet.

Religion/Politics: Maupassant was confirmed as a Roman Catholic, but later became an atheist before returning to the Catholic faith once more. He admired Napoleon.

Health: He suffered from eye trouble and had terrible migraines, for which he took drugs. He experienced hair loss on his body and head and herpetic eruptions (1878) and, though his hair later grew back, the underlying problem was identified as syphilis. He eventually went mad and suffered progressive paralysis till death.

Temperament: Maupassant's friends included Flaubert (to whom he showed all his work), Zola (who published 'Boule de Suif' in his anthology Les Soirées de Médan), Dumas fils and Henry James (with whom he stayed in London). Another friend was his trusted valet François.

Pets: He loved cats and was never without at least one (he once wrote an essay entitled 'Sur les Chats').

Work/Daily Routine: Maupassant only worked in the mornings (7 am to noon) but worked very fast, producing around 250 stories in the years 1882–7. He started as a poet, being prosecuted in Étampes for immorality in his poem 'Au bord de l'eau' (1876) but being let off with Flaubert's help. He only published one volume of poetry, Des Vers (1880). Less well-known works included plays (for instance, Musotte, which was dedicated to Dumas fils) and travel pieces. He achieved instant fame with the story 'Boule de Suif' (1880), which Flaubert called 'a masterpiece'. Some works were published under pseudonyms, among them Joseph Prunier, Guy de Valmont (from Les Liaisons dangereuses) and Maufrigneuse (from the Duchess in the Comédie humaine who is mistress of 12 characters). In the USA his Collected Works for some years included 65 stories not written by him. Gide, Mauriac and Maurois said Une Vie was one of the 10 best French novels of all time and in the view of his contemporary Tolstoy it was 'perhaps the best French novel since Les Misérables'.

Manner of Death: Convinced that his brain was seeping out through his nostrils, Maupassant tried to commit suicide by cutting his throat in Cannes on 2 January 1892 – he was rescued by a servant who heard his cry and was taken in a strait-jacket to Dr Blanche's sanitarium in Passy near Paris and died there of syphilis on the morning of 6 July 1893, aged 43. He was buried in Montparnasse cemetery, Paris. Zola made a speech at his grave, calling him 'one of the happiest, and one of the unhappiest, men the world has ever seen'. A monument to his memory was erected in Rouen in 1900.

MELVILLE, Herman (1819–91) US novelist and civil servant

Herman Melville was born at 6 Pearl Street, New York City, on 1 August 1819, the second son and fourth of eight children of Allan Melville and Maria Gansevoort. He was a direct descendant of John Melville, Lord of Raith (who was beheaded during the reign of Mary Queen of Scots). His brothers were Gansevoort, Allan and Thomas and he had four sisters. His father died in great debt in 1832 when he was 12. Educated at Albany Academy, he left home at 17 (his mother hated him) and at first worked as a schoolteacher and then as a clerk in the New York State Bank (1834). He then went to sea on the whaler *Acushnet* (1841) but deserted ship on the Marquesas Islands (1842) and was captured by natives (reputedly cannibals) in the Typee Valley. Later imprisoned in Tahiti, he eventually returned to the USA and lived on a farm in Pittsfield, Massachusetts (a neighbour was Nathaniel Hawthorne), before becoming District Inspector of Customs in New York for 19 years. It was from his adventures in the South Seas that he got the inspiration for many of his celebrated novels, among them *Typee* (1846), *Omoo* (1847), *Mardi* (1849), *White-Jacket* (1850) and the classic *Moby-Dick* (1851).

Family/Sex Life: Melville's first wife was a cannibal named Fayaway, whom he married while in the Marquesas Islands. In 1847 he took as his second wife Elizabeth Shaw, daughter of the Chief Justice of Massachusetts. They had four children – Malcolm (who committed suicide), Stanwix (who died young), Elizabeth and Frances.

Appearance: Nathaniel Hawthorne left a description of his distinguished neighbour, emphasizing that there was little in his appearance to suggest the extraordinary life he had led before settling in the USA

with his wife: 'He is a person of very gentlemanly instincts in every respect, save that he is a little heterodox in the matter of clean linen.'

Temperament: Called a 'howling cheese' by R. L. Stevenson, Melville was much troubled by lack of recognition for his literary efforts, to the point of expressing suicidal thoughts (he had a breakdown in the 1850s). His closest friends included Nathaniel Hawthorne and his wife, whom he often visited and with whom he would share reminiscences of his adventures in the South Seas. These included incidents in which he had deserted ship in order to escape victimization by a senior officer and his participation in a mutiny, which had resulted in his being thrown into prison. On one occasion he related to the dumbstruck Hawthornes the tale of a tremendous fight he had witnessed between a Polynesian warrior and his enemies. The Polynesian had laboured in all directions with a mighty club – Melville enthusiastically recreating every blow struck in the terrible battle. At length Melville finished his story and left his much-impressed hosts. Once he was gone, Mrs Hawthorne realized he had left without his club and began looking around for it, but could not find it anywhere. Her husband joined in the search, but still there was no sign of it. It was only later, when they next saw Melville and mentioned the club, that it transpired that there had been no club at all and that they had only imagined it from his vivid narrative.

Work/Daily Routine: Melville's first book, *Typee*, was published in London by John Murray in 1846. During his lifetime he was known primarily for his 'cannibal' books *Mardi* and *Omoo* and it was only many years after his death that the literary establishment hailed him as one of the great American writers. The long story *Billy Budd, Foretopman* was discovered in a bread box 28 years after Melville's death (it was later turned into an opera by Benjamin Britten). He dedicated *Moby-Dick* to Hawthorne. The original for Moby-Dick was probably 'Mocha Dick', a real white whale that terrorized whaling crews around 1850. Legend credited to this beast the destruction of several ships and more than 30 deaths (reports of its activities were given in the *Knickerbocker Magazine* some 12 years before Melville penned his masterpiece). In fact, Jeremiah N. Reynolds had already published a narrative based on the story under the title *Mocha Dick* in 1839 and Edgar Allen Poe wrote tales on a similar theme. Captain Ahab was based on Owen Chase, the first mate on the whaler *Essex* who in 1820 had spent 91 days adrift in a small boat with four companions after his ship was sunk by a sperm whale: to survive, Chase and one of the others were obliged to eat the body of one of their companions after they perished. Melville's book proved a failure at first and sold only 3797 copies in his lifetime (most in the first year).

Manner of Death: Melville died at his home, 104 East 26th Street, New York, on 28 September 1891, aged 72. He was buried in Woodlawn Cemetery. A belated obituary in the *New York Times* identified him as 'Hiram' Melville.

MENDELSSOHN-BARTHOLDY, Jakob Ludwig Felix (1809–47)
German composer

Felix Mendelssohn was born in Hamburg on 3 February 1809, the son of a wealthy banker, Abraham Mendelssohn, and Lea Salomon. His grandfather was the philosopher Moses Mendelssohn (Lessing's 'Nathan the Wise'). He had two sisters, Fanny and Rebecka, and a brother Paul. The name Bartholdy, taken from the former owner of his maternal uncle's garden, was added when he was baptized (though he was of a Jewish family). He was taught to play the piano in Paris aged seven by a woman called Madame Bigot and made his first public appearance two years later. He studied literature and philosophy at the University of Berlin and was later awarded an honorary PhD from Leipzig University. He turned down the Chair of Music at the University of Berlin, even though the post had been created for him, and later became Kapellmeister to Wilhelm IV of Prussia and was founder, director and Professor of the Leipzig Conservatorium (with Schumann) in 1843.

He made many trips to Britain and twice played before Queen Victoria, who called him 'a wonderful genius ... so pleasing and amiable' (at one of these royal concerts the royal parrot drowned out the music and had to be taken from the room). A prolific composer, he included among his most celebrated works the *Midsummer Night's Dream* overture (1826), the *Hebrides* overture and the *Scottish Symphony*, which were inspired by a visit to Scotland, and the oratorios *St Paul* (1836) and *Elijah* (1846), which was commissioned for performance at the Birmingham Festival of 1846. Another universally heard Mendelssohn tune was one composed as part of the *Festgesang* for the Gutenberg Festival, better known as the carol 'Hark! The herald angels sing'. Robert Schumann called him 'The Mozart of the 19th century', while Franz Liszt dubbed him 'Bach reborn'.

Family/Sex Life: In 1837 Mendelssohn

married Cécile Jeanrenand, the daughter of a clergyman in the French Reformed Church (Mendelssohn's sister Fanny described her as 'fresh, bright and even-tempered'). The marriage was happy and they had five children. His 'Wedding March' from *A Midsummer Night's Dream* has long since become the pre-eminent anthem for the entry of brides at weddings throughout the English-speaking world.

Appearance: According to Thackeray, 'His face is the most beautiful I ever saw, like what I imagine our Saviour's to have been.' Distinctive features included long black wavy hair and long sideburns reaching almost to his chin. He was, though, casual about his appearance, leading Fanny Horsley to record after one meeting in 1843: 'Mendelssohn is a generous high-minded creature, but, to descend from these heights, he was dressed very badly, and looked in sad want of a piece of soap and the nail brush which I have so often threatened to offer him.'

Habits/Mannerisms: Mendelssohn had a remarkable memory. After the first performance of the overture to *A Midsummer Night's Dream* (which he composed at the age of 17) a friend left the only manuscript copy of the piece in a cab – but fortunately Mendelssohn was able to rewrite the entire score from memory. He was also one of the first musicians to play a concerto in public without the use of sheet music.

Sport/Hobbies: He was good at billiards, chess, swimming, gymnastics and dancing. He played the piano and the violin well and was also an accomplished water-colour painter.

Religion/Politics: Though born into a Jewish background, he was baptized as a Lutheran Christian.

Health: Mendelssohn enjoyed generally good health until 1847, when news of his sister Fanny's death caused him to faint and triggered recurring health problems. He was never well thereafter, suffering from shivering fits, head pains and depression until the time of his own death.

Temperament: Mendelssohn's first love was always his music, and he was proud of the purity of his motives as a composer, once claiming in a letter that: 'Ever since I began to compose, I have remained true to my starting principle: not to write a page because no matter what public, or what pretty girl wanted it to be thus or thus; but to write solely as I myself thought best, and as it gave me pleasure.' He did not, though, regard his work as remote from his own life and once observed 'Art and life are not two different things.' Generous and noble of temperament, he made few enemies and included among his closest friends Schumann, Chopin and Goethe. While in Scotland he made the acquaintance of Sir Walter Scott, among other notables.

Work/Daily Routine: Mendelssohn worked long and hard, beginning his working day before 5 am each morning – a routine that may eventually have been responsible for breaking his health. *A Midsummer Night's Dream* was largely composed by Mendelssohn while sitting in his garden, where he often worked as a young man.

Manner of Death: Exhausted by his work and saddened by the death of his sister, Mendelssohn suffered a seizure in September 1847 and died in Leipzig on 4 November 1847, aged 38.

MEREDITH, George (1828–1909) English poet and novelist

George Meredith was born at 73 High Street, Portsmouth, Hampshire, on 12 February 1828, the only child of Augustus Armstrong Meredith, a tailor and naval outfitter, and Jane Eliza Macnamara (who died in 1833). His father later married his cook, Matilda Buckett. Educated at St Paul's, Southsea, then at the Moravian School in Neuwied, near Koblenz, Germany, where he was a star pupil, he was articled at first to a solicitor but later rejected law as a career and became a journalist for *The Fortnightly* and other publications, also working as a reader for the publishers Chapman & Hall. He also spent a period as war correspondent in Italy. His novel *The Ordeal of Richard Feverel* (1859) caused a scandal and failed to sell well, though some hailed it as a masterpiece, but he finally achieved success with such subsequent works as *The Egoist* (1879) and *Diana of the Crossways* (1885) and ranked among the most respected writers of his generation by the time of his death. He was Vice-President of the London Library (1902) and served as the second President of the Society of Authors (succeeding Tennyson). He was awarded an OM in 1905.

Family/Sex Life: In 1849 Meredith married a widow seven years his senior (with a daughter – Edith), Mrs Mary Ellen Nicholls (née Peacock, daughter of Thomas Love Peacock). They had a son, Arthur Gryffydh, but in 1856 she deserted him for the artist Henry Wallis (who had used Meredith as a model for his painting 'The Death of Chatterton'). The anguish of this break-up inspired his most celebrated poetry, published as *Modern Love* in 1862, and was also reflected in the themes of the novel *The Ordeal of Richard Feverel*, in Chapter One of which he rather sourly remarked: 'I expect that Woman will be the last thing civilized by Man.' In

1864 he took as his second wife Marie Vulliamy, by whom he fathered William Maxse and Marie Eveleen.

Appearance: Meredith had greyish eyes and a beard and moustache of lighter colour than his hair, which was curly and chestnut-red.

Habits/Mannerisms: Meredith never walked, but always strode. He was a fanatical vegetarian, a believer in homeopathy and a connoisseur of cigars and wines.

Sport/Hobbies: He devised his own form of keep-fit exercise, throwing and catching heavy iron weights at the end of a wooden staff (he called it his 'beetle exercise'). He played the piano well by ear and was a member of the Garrick Club.

Health: A weak stomach meant that Meredith suffered badly from flatulence. He had three operations for bladder stones and was a paraplegic for the last 16 years of his life.

Temperament: Meredith had a roaring laugh and included among his friends Rossetti and Swinburne (he briefly shared a house with both in Chelsea in the years 1861–2 and Swinburne once wrote a famous letter to the *Spectator* in defence of his friend).

Work/Daily Routine: Arnold Bennett, in *Books and Persons*, called Meredith 'not the last of the Victorian novelists, but the first of the modern school'. His first published work was the poem 'Chillianwallah' (1849), which was followed by *Poems* (1851), which he paid for himself and with which he won praise from Tennyson and Charles Kingsley. His first published novel was *The Shaving of*

Shagpat (1856), which George Eliot called 'a work of genius'. He considered himself a poet first and a novelist second – though he is now remembered chiefly for his prose while his poems are largely forgotten. Many readers, however, baulk at the complexity of his stories, and Trollope observed that his plots were self-consciously twisted into 'curl-papers'. Among the writers he most admired was Guy de Maupassant.

Manner of Death: Meredith caught a chill and died at Box Hill, Surrey, on 18 May 1909, aged 81. Burial in Westminster Abbey was refused by the Dean even though requested by Edward VII and other leading figures of the day. Instead he was cremated and buried in Dorking cemetery. His gravestone reads:

'Life is but a little holding,
Lent to do a mighty labour.'

MICHELANGELO (1475–1564) Italian artist and poet

Michelangelo was born Michelagnolo di Ludovico Buonarroti Simoni, on 6 March 1475 in Caprese, near Arezzo, Italy, the second son of Ludovico Buonarroti, a magistrate and mayor of Caprese, and Francesca dei Neri (who died in 1481, when he was six). He had an older brother, Lionardo (a Dominican friar) and three younger ones, only one of whom ever married. The family, who had been money-changers for generations, moved to Florence in 1475. Michelangelo was apprenticed to the painter Domenico Ghirlandaio (1488) for two years and also used to study and draw the collection of antiquities in the garden of Lorenzo the Magnificent with other students, who included the sculptor Pietro Torrigiano. After making a sculpture of a faun he was taken into Lorenzo de' Medici's household (1490) but returned to his father's house when Lorenzo died (1492) and studied anatomy by dissecting corpses at the Hospital of Santo Spirito. Having only received one commission from Lorenzo's successor Piero de' Medici (for a snowman, 1494), he left Florence and travelled to Venice, Bologna and Rome. He later became Governor-General of Fortifications for Florence (1528–9) and Chief Architect, Sculptor and Painter to the Vatican Palace under Pope Paul III (1535). Best known for his ceiling depicting (in its nine main panels) scenes from Genesis for the Sistine Chapel in the Vatican, commissioned by Pope Sixtus IV, he always saw himself as a sculptor, not a painter.

Family/Sex Life: Michelangelo never married and had no children. When a friend regretted this circumstance, he replied: 'I have too much of a wife in this art of mine, which has afflicted me throughout my life, and my children shall be the works I leave.' He did, though, have a very intense love affair with Tommaso de' Cavalieri (1532), writing him love poems, and also enjoyed a very close friendship with Vittoria Colonna (*c.*1536), the widowed Marchioness of Pecara and a friend of Ariosto and Castiglione (he also wrote poems to her).

Appearance: 'Michaelangelo was of medium height, broad in the shoulders ... His face was round, the brow square and lofty, furrowed by seven straight lines and the temples projected considerably beyond the ears, which were rather large and prominent ... his eyes can best be described as being small, the colour of horn, flecked with bluish and yellowish sparks. His eyebrows were sparse, his lips thin ... the chin well formed ... his hair black, but streaked with many white hairs and worn fairly short, as was his beard

which was forked and not very thick'
(Vasari). As a young man Michelangelo
sustained a broken nose during a fight
with Torrigiano, who had made fun of
him. Strongly built and bearded, he was
the model for the figure of Heraclitus in
Raphael's *School of Athens*. In old age
he wore buskins of dog-skin on his legs
and boots of cordswain.

Habits/Mannerisms: Michelangelo was
left-handed and had beautiful handwriting.
He kept the same servant, named Urbino,
for 26 years.

Sport/Hobbies: He was highly literate and
well read in Dante. He was also an
accomplished poet.

Health: Very healthy, though 'in his old
age he suffered from dysuria and gravel
which eventually developed into the stone'
(Vasari).

Temperament: Michelangelo was famed
for his hot temper and generally difficult
character. He was notoriously jealous of
his reputation and resented any rivals. He
particularly disliked Raphael and claimed
that Raphael learnt all he knew from him.
He never signed his work, but on one
occasion, when he overheard admirers
attributing his famous *Pietà* to another
sculptor, he stole back during the night
and carved his name in Latin on a strap
across the Virgin's breast so that there
would be no future confusion. His
relations with the authorities who commissioned works from him were rarely
smooth. When one papal official tried to
get a glimpse of *The Last Judgment* before
Michelangelo was ready he was rewarded
by being depicted among the damned in
hell, being tormented by devils.

Pets: Michelangelo owned horses,

especially valuing an Arab stallion given
to him by a friend.

Work/Daily Routine: He tried to refuse the
Sistine Chapel ceiling commission,
protesting that he was a sculptor not a
painter – he recommended Raphael for the
job instead. The ceiling took four years to
paint and interrupted work he wished to
do elsewhere, including a huge tomb (23
by 36 feet high with three levels and 40
figures) for Pope Julius II, commissioned
by the Pope in 1505. The *Pietà* (finished
c.1500) was commissioned by the French
Cardinal Bilhères de Lagraulas. After the
Sistine Chapel he stopped painting
altogether (though he collaborated with
Sebastiano del Piombo, Michelangelo
doing preliminary drawings and
Sebastiano painting them up) until he
agreed to paint *Leda and the Swan* for
Duke Alfonso I d'Este and *The Last
Judgment* for the Sistine wall (started
1535, finished 1541). Besides his
sculptures and paintings he was also an
architect (his works in this capacity
including St Peter's in Rome, the Capitol,
the Palazzo Farnese and the Reading
Room in the Medici Library). He also
designed military fortifications for
Florence. The work on St Peter's was the
last major project of his life and was much
delayed by the many mistakes he made (attributed to his advanced age). He painted
very few portraits (the only surviving one
is of 18-year-old Andrea Quaratesi). Many
of his nude figures were considered
indecent in later eras and had loin cloths
painted on.

Manner of Death: Michelangelo died on
18 February 1564, aged 88. He was buried
in the Church of Santi Apostoli, Rome,
and later moved to Santa Croce, Florence,
his tomb being designed by Vasari.

MILTON, John (1608–74) English poet

John Milton was born in Bread Street, Cheapside, London, on Friday 9 December 1608 at 6.30 am, the second of three surviving children of John Milton, a composer and scrivener, and Sarah Jeffrey. He had an older sister Anne and a younger brother, later Sir Christopher Milton, a judge. Educated at St Paul's School and Christ's College, Cambridge, he was expelled from university for a term for fighting with his tutor and was one of the last Cambridge students to be publicly flogged. After travelling abroad with a servant for a year he was tutor to his nephews, Edward and John Phillips. He established his reputation as a writer in the 1630s with such works as the poems 'L'Allegro (1632) and 'Il Penseroso' (1632), the masque *Comus* (1634) and the elegy *Lycidas* (1637). In 1649 he became Latin Secretary to Cromwell's Council of State (his assistant and successor was Andrew Marvell) – the job involving translating Government foreign despatches into Latin. He was also Censor of Publications for the Commonwealth. Imprisoned in 1660, Marvell (an MP) successfully petitioned for his release in the House of Commons. Milton spent his remaining years working on his poetry, producing such epics as *Paradise Lost* (1667), *Paradise Regained* (1671) and *Samson Agonistes* (1671).

Family/Sex Life: In 1643 Milton married Mary Powell, 16 years his junior. She died in childbirth in 1652; their children were Anne, who was deformed and suffered from a speech defect, Mary, John (who died young) and Deborah. Mary Powell was a Royalist – she left him six weeks after the wedding but begged to return when the Civil War ended in 1645. Milton's second wife (1656) was Catharine Woodcock, 20 years his junior. She died in 1658, and their only daughter died young.

In 1665 he married Elizabeth Minshull, 30 years his junior.

Appearance: Aubrey left the following description of Milton: 'Well proportioned body. He was a spare man of middle stature ... he had abroun hayre. His complexion exceeding faire – he was so faire that they called him "the Lady of Christ's College". Ovall face. His eie a darke gray.' He wore a grey or black coarse-cloth coat.

Habits/Mannerisms: According to Aubrey, Milton pronounced the letter R very hard. He smoked a pipe, but rarely drank between meals.

Sport/Hobbies: Milton liked walking and was a good fencer. He also sang well and played the organ.

Religion/Politics: Puritan. Milton was very active as a political pamphleteer over a period of some 20 years. When the monarchy was restored he was arrested, imprisoned and fined most of his fortune.

Health: Aubrey testified that in his youth Milton was very healthy and 'seldome tooke any physique'. Later in life, however, he suffered from 'Gowte, Spring and Fall'; moreover, by 1651 (aged 43), he was completely blind (glaucoma). When James II, in the course of a visit to the elderly Milton, suggested that his blindness was a divine punishment for having written in defence of the execution of Charles I, Milton retorted: 'If Your Highness thinks that misfortunes are indexes of the wrath of heaven, what must you think of your father's tragical end? I have only lost my eyes – he lost his head.'

Temperament: Most acquaintances described Milton as very cheerful. His friends included Marvell and Dryden. He did not like Hobbes but admired him, and on his travels met Galileo and Grotius. He also had a very good memory.

Work/Daily Routine: Milton rose at 4 am, had passages from the Hebrew Bible read to him, then indulged in meditation, reading and dictation till mid-day. After lunch he worked for three to four hours and would often enjoy some music. He took supper at 8 pm, usually dining on 'olives or some light thing'. He went to bed at 9 pm after a pipe and a glass of water. After he went blind his daughter Deborah served as his amanuensis. He dictated 30 to 40 lines at a time; often while in bed in the morning. He was paid £10 by Samuel Simmonds for the copyright in *Paradise Lost* (which he dictated whilst blind), while his widow parted with the remaining rights for just

eight pounds after her husband's death. Because of his attacks on Charles II, his books were publicly burnt in London in 1660. *The State Papers* was banned by the Vatican and was put on the Index of prohibited books (1694). Voltaire called *Paradise Lost* 'This obscene and disgusting poem', while Dr Johnson admitted 'Its perusal is a duty rather than a pleasure.' Byron called Milton 'the prince of poets'.

Manner of Death: Milton died of gout on 8 November 1674, aged 65. He was buried in St Giles Cripplegate, London, but his tomb was later desecrated (an act described in a poem by Cowper) and his teeth and hair were sold as souvenirs by grave-robbers. His house at 19 York Street, London, was later occupied successively by Bentham, James Mill and Hazlitt before being demolished.

MOLIÈRE (1622–73) French playwright and actor-manager

Molière was born Jean-Baptiste Poquelin in his father's shop at 96 Rue St Honoré, Paris, on 15 January 1622, the first child of Jean Poquelin, a wealthy upholsterer and interior furnisher to the royal household (*tapissier ordinaire du roi*) of King Louis XIII, and Marie Cressé, daughter of *marchand-tapissier* Louis Cressé. His mother died when he was 10 and his father remarried (to Catherine Fleurette, who died in 1636). He had three surviving siblings (e.g. Marie-Madeleine) and a half-sibling. Educated at the élite Jesuit Collège de Clermont at Clermont under the philosopher Gassendi (a later pupil was Voltaire), he then studied law, was called to the Bar and was nominated as his father's successor in the family business. He decided, however, to become an actor instead and co-founded the Illustre-Théâtre company (1643), whose other founding members included Denys

Beys, brother of the playwright Charles Beys. He later adopted Molière as a stage name (the significance of the name is not known). Twice imprisoned for debt, he attracted the patronage of Philippe, Duc d'Orléans (younger brother of Louis XIV and married to Henrietta Anne, fifth daughter of Charles I of England). He first acted before Louis XIV at the Louvre Palace in 1658 as a member of the Troupe de Monsieur players (whose patron was 'Monsieur', the Duc d'Orléans) in Corneille's tragedy *Nicomède* and at the end of the show performed his own comedy *Le Docteur amoureux*. Louis liked the play and Molière's company was installed at the Salle du Petit-Bourbon. After the playwright's first popular success with *Les Précieuses ridicules* (1659), the troupe acted at the Palais-Royal from 1661. Among the classic comedies that Molière contributed for the company over the following 12 years were *L'École des maris* (1661), *L'Impromptu de Versailles* (1663), *Tartuffe* (1664), *Dom Juan* (1665), *Le Misanthrope* (1666), *L'Avare* (1668) and *Le Malade imaginaire* (1673).

Family/Sex Life: In 1662 Molière married Armande-Grésinde-Claire-Elizabeth Béjart, daughter of a Forestry Department official and sister of Madeleine Béjart, an actress who was also co-founder of the Illustre-Théâtre Company. Of their three children only one daughter survived. Henrietta Anne, Duchesse d'Orléans, stood as godmother to their first child and Louis himself served as godfather. The rumour that Molière's wife was actually his daughter by his former mistress Madeleine Béjart was almost certainly unfounded and the king demonstrated his support for Molière against his detractors by inviting the playwright to dine with him before assembled courtiers at Versailles (an almost unheard-of compliment).

Appearance: Tall and clean-shaven but for a moustache.

Temperament: Introspective and thoughtful, in keeping with the observation in *Le Misanthrope* that: 'One should examine oneself for a very long time before thinking of condemning others.' He inspired loyalty and affection in his friends, who included the playwright Racine. Keen to escape the lowly status of a common comedian, he made the most of his connections at court. On one occasion he was reportedly much dismayed when a chamberlain declined to allow him to assist him in making the royal bed – until another chamberlain invited him to share the honour with himself instead. Signing dedications 'I. B. P. Molière' (Iean Baptiste Poquelin Molière), he dedicated *L'École des maris* to the Duc d'Orléans, *Les Fâcheux* to Louis XIV and *L'École des femmes* to Henrietta Anne, Duchesse

d'Orléans. Louis himself allegedly collaborated on *Les Fâcheux* and suggested the plot of *Les Amants magnifiques*.

Work/Daily Routine: Molière never published his plays but wrote solely for performance. To test whether a new play was satisfactory he usually read it to an elderly female servant in his household, a woman by the name of Laforêt – any jokes that failed to make her laugh were altered or struck out. Actors in the company were also required to bring their children to rehearsals so that the playwright could observe their reactions to certain scenes.

Manner of Death: The playwright was taken ill whilst appearing in the fourth performance of his play *Le Malade imaginaire*, in which he acted the part of the supposedly sick Argan. Racked by a coughing fit during the performance, he managed to get to the end and was carried home, but there he suffered a burst blood-vessel and choked on his own blood, dying on the 17 February 1673, aged 51. The suddenness of his death meant that the playwright had no chance to make a solemn abjuration of his profession and thus be granted burial in consecrated ground. Appeals to the Archbishop of Paris to make an exception in this case were fruitless and the playwright's widow made a last bid to Louis to intervene. The king solved the crisis by enquiring how far down consecrated ground went: when he was informed that it extended downwards some eight feet, he instructed that the playwright be laid in a grave 12 feet deep, thus neatly sidestepping any further theological objections. Molière was duly interred in St Joseph's Cemetery, Paris, after sunset, apparently with only two priests present (the exact location of the grave is unknown and it is possible that he was buried, against the king's orders, beyond the churchyard boundaries).

MONET, Claude-Oscar (1840–1926) French painter

Claude-Oscar Monet was born in the Rue Lafitte, Paris, on 14 November 1840, the son of a grocer who moved to Sainte-Adresse, near Le Havre, in 1845 and became a supplier of goods to the French Navy. After school he was taught painting by Eugène Boudin and sold his first works (he was particularly good at caricatures) in Boudin's stationery/picture-framing shop in Le Havre. His parents then enrolled him at the Académie Suisse, Paris (a fellow pupil was Pissarro) and he soon moved into café society and met Baudelaire, Daudet, Courbet, Zola, Degas, Cézanne etc. In 1860 he began six years' compulsory military service in the Chasseurs d'Afrique in North Africa but, taken ill after two years, his parents bought him out and sent him to the studio of Gleyre in Paris (1862) where fellow students were Renoir, Sisley and Bazille. When his parents cut off his allowance (1865) he shared a studio with Renoir and Bazille and had two pictures accepted by the Paris Salon. During the Franco-Prussian War (1870) he deserted his family and, with Pissarro, fled to Britain. For a time he lived at Argenteuil on a boat on the Seine (painting lastingly popular boating scenes) before moving to the village of Vétheuil near Paris and then to the home of collector and financier Hoschedé – whose widow he later married – in Poissy (1881), finally settling in Giverny (1883). His most famous paintings included *Women in a Garden*, *Gare St Lazare*, *Haystacks*, *Rouen Cathedral*, *Poplars* and his murals of water-lilies.

Family/Sex Life: In 1870 Monet married Camille Doncieux, by whom he had already fathered a child in 1867. Their other children were Jean and Michel. Camille died in 1878 and subsequently, in 1892, Monet married Alice Hoschedé,

widow of the financier/collector at whose house he had been invited to live. Monet's son Jean later married one of Madame Hoschedé's daughters (1897).

Appearance: Perhaps his most distinctive feature was his large beard.

Habits/Mannerisms: He smoked a pipe.

Health: An accident led to temporary loss of sight in one eye (1900); in 1923 he underwent a double cataract operation.

Temperament: Monet's friends included many of the most celebrated French painters of his generation, among them Manet and Renoir. Friends from other circles included Georges Clemenceau (later Prime Minister).

Work/Daily Routine: Under the influence of Boudin, Monet learnt to prefer working in the open air. He once remarked that 'Three brushstrokes from nature are worth more than two days of work at the easel.' Favourite painting sites were at Chailly-en-Bière in the Fontainebleau Forest and Honfleur. Monet's first wife posed for *Woman in the Green Dress* (praised by Zola). He often painted from a high angle looking down. When working on the huge canvas for *Women in a Garden* he had trenches dug to stand in and pulleys to raise and lower the picture as he worked on it (all four women in the picture were based on his first wife). Monet was much troubled by debt: Bazille bought a picture for 2500 francs to help relieve the financial burdens the painter was under, but in 1866 he burnt 200 of his pictures in a fit of pique to prevent them being seized by his creditors. For his own part, he greatly admired the works of Daumier and Turner. The word 'Impressionism' comes from his painting *Impression, Sunrise*

(1872), which was famously exhibited in 1874. Artists featured in the exhibition were lampooned by the art critic of *Charivari* as 'Impressionists', incapable of rendering in detail what they saw and only of vaguely suggesting atmosphere and reality.The tag stuck, but soon lost its original derogatory implications. Characteristics of Impressionism as developed by Monet and his associates included the use of bright colours and coloured shadows and the exclusion of black. The emphasis was always upon light, rather than upon the objects that the light happened to play on. In 1899 Monet exhibited three canvases at the Paris World's Fair (for which the Eiffel Tower was constructed). His famous water-lily mural panels, his last works, were commissioned by Clemenceau for the Orangerie in the Tuileries gardens.

Manner of Death: Monet died on 5 December 1926 at Giverny.

MORE, Thomas (1478–1535) English statesman

Thomas More was born in Milk Street, London, at about 3 am on 7 February 1478, the elder son of Sir John More, a King's Bench Justice, by the first of his three wives, Agnes Graunger. He had a younger brother John and sisters Jane and Elizabeth. Educated at St Anthony's School, London, he served (1490–2) as a page to John Morton, Archbishop of Canterbury and Lord Chancellor, who sent him to Canterbury Hall (later part of Christ Church), Oxford (1492–4), aged 14, but he was later instructed by his father to study law at New Inn and Lincoln's Inn (he was called to the Bar in 1503). He became a Reader in Law at Furnival's Inn (1501), an MP (1504), Freeman of the Mercers' Company (1509) and Under-Sheriff of London (1510). Also Reader at Lincoln's Inn (1510, 1514) and Doctor's Commons he was later High Steward of Oxford and Cambridge Universities, Speaker of the House of Commons and Private Secretary to Henry VIII. Knighted in 1521, he was the first layman to become Lord Chancellor (1529, succeeding Cardinal Wolsey) but resigned in 1532 over Henry VIII's divorce from Katherine of Aragon and was imprisoned in the Tower (1534). He was canonized in 1935. His writings included the celebrated *Utopia* (1516).

Family/Sex Life: In 1505 More married Jane Colt, daughter of Sir John Colt MP, a neighbour of his father's. He actually preferred her younger sister, but when he learned that there was an older sibling he dutifully addressed his attentions to her, conscious of the slight she would suffer if her younger sister married before her. The marriage produced the children John, Margaret (who married William Roper, later More's biographer), Elizabeth and Cicely. Jane Colt died in 1511 and within a month More took as his second wife a widow seven years his senior, Alice Middleton (who already had a daughter).

Appearance: More was of middle height and was clean-shaven (though he was bearded when confined in the Tower). According to Erasmus, he was 'light complexioned . . . his hair is auburn touching upon the black . . . his eyes are of a blue grey colour'.

Habits/Mannerisms: He became an ascetic for a period of four years (1499–1503). He always wore a hair shirt next to his skin, scourged himself every Friday and slept on the bare ground with a log under his head. He drank little wine and, according to Erasmus, preferred 'beef, salt meat and common fermented bread to the usual delicacies – he has a special liking for milk pudding and takes great relish in a bowl of eggs'. He paid little attention to his dress, wearing his gown carelessly and professing a dislike for ostentation and ceremony. He lived in an extended household in Chelsea (then a village in Middlesex) that included his wife, son, son's wife, his son's three daughters and their husbands, and 11 grandchildren as well as his kinswoman Margaret Giggs and his favourite jester Henry Pates (or Pattenson). He had a tendency to hold his right shoulder higher than the left.

Sport/Hobbies: More disliked tennis, dice and cards but played the viol and the flute and wrote epigrams and verse in both Latin and English (he presented one of his poems to the future Henry VIII, then aged nine, in 1499). He also sang in his local church choir.

Religion/Politics: More was very religious and harboured strong anti-Lutheran passions (he used the pseudonym 'William Ross' to attack Luther in a pamphlet).

Health: According to the *Dictionary of National Biography*, More suffered from 'oppression on the chest, gravel, stone and cramp'.

Temperament: More retained his good-humoured wit to the end. As he placed his head on the block he moved his beard out of the way, explaining that 'it had never committed treason'. His friends included Erasmus and Hans Holbein. The tag 'A man for all seasons', which was later used by Robert Bolt for the title of a play about More, was first introduced by Robert Whittinton (1520).

Pets: While living in Chelsea, More kept an aviary and a pet monkey (which featured in Holbein's portrait of him).

Work/Daily Routine: His *Utopia* (which established him as an eminent humanist of the Renaissance and which was first published in Latin, 1516) was originally entitled *Nusquama* but this was changed into the Greek version when being printed. More wrote the Introduction and Part Two before Part One. Other legacies left by More include the phrase 'neither rhyme nor reason', which he first coined in replying to a hopeful author suggesting he turn his work into verse as it was currently neither rhyme nor reason.

Motto/Emblem: More's family crest was a Moor's head.

Manner of Death: More was indicted for high treason by Henry VIII for refusing to recognize him as head of the Church of England. The sentence was commuted from hanging, drawing and quartering to beheading, and More was duly executed with an axe on Tower Hill before 9 am on 7 July 1535, aged 57. On mounting the scaffold, he requested of the lieutenant: 'I pray thee see me safely up, and for my coming down let me shift for myself.' His head was parboiled then stuck on a spike on London Bridge. His body was buried in the Chapel of St Peter ad Vincula in the Tower, then moved to Chelsea Church. His head was later bought by his daughter Margaret, who kept it pickled in spices till she died – it was then buried in the Roper family vault in St Dunstan's Church, Canterbury. He was canonized by the Catholic Church in 1935.

MORSE, Samuel Finley Breese (1791–1872) US artist and inventor

Samuel Morse was born on 27 April 1791 in Main Street, Charlestown, Massachusetts, the eldest of three surviving sons of Jedidiah Morse, a clergyman and geographer, and Elizabeth Ann Breese. His brothers were Sidney Edwards and Richard Cary (eight other siblings died). He was educated at Philips Academy, Andover, and at Yale College (from which he graduated in 1810). While at Yale, he produced miniatures on ivory and began to establish his reputation as an artist of some talent. In 1811 he came to England and studied for four years under Washington Allston and at the Royal Academy under Benjamin West (where his works were also exhibited). He then returned to the USA (1815) and worked as a professional portrait painter (specializing in miniatures), becoming Professor of Painting and Sculpture at New York University in 1832. Founder and first president of the US National Academy of Design (1826–45), he was also one of the founders of Vassar College and twice ran for Mayor of New York. Having first conceived the electro-magnetic telegraph in 1832, he presented the idea before Congress in 1837 and was eventually awarded a grant of $30,000 to construct the first public telegraph line, which was finally inaugurated in 1844. It is as the developer of telegraphy (in conjunction with the Morse telegraphic code system of dots and dashes) for which he is usually remembered. He also helped to lay the first transatlantic cable.

Family/Sex Life: In 1818 Morse married Lucretia Pickering Walker. She died in 1825, having presented her husband with four children. His second wife (1848) was Sarah Elizabeth Griswold, a cousin 31 years his junior. They had four children.

Religion/Politics: Morse was a Calvinist and a committed anti-Catholic. He twice stood for Mayor of New York on Native American then Democrat tickets.

Temperament: His friends included the novelist James Fenimore Cooper.

Work/Daily Routine: In reality, Morse did not actually invent telegraphy – he took the idea from the physicist Joseph Henry, who sued Morse in court for stealing his invention and won. He did, however, invent Morse Code and in collaboration with industrialist and philanthropist Ezra Cornell set up the first telegraph line in 1844. The first message he broadcast using Morse Code, sent from the Capitol, Washington DC to Baltimore on 24 May 1844, was 'What hath God wrought!' This famous message was in fact chosen by Annie Ellsworth, daughter of the Commissioner of Patents. As an artist he experimented by grinding pigments in milk or beer. His paintings were sometimes executed with detailed realism, as was the case of a picture he completed of a man in his death agony – when he showed it to a friend, who happened to be a doctor, with a request for his opinion the immediate response was: 'Malaria.' He also introduced the daguerrotype photographic process to the USA.

Manner of Death: Morse died at his home, 5 West 22nd Street, New York, on 2 April 1872, aged 80. He was buried in Greenwood Cemetery.

MOZART, Wolfgang Amadeus Chrysotom (1756–91) Austrian composer

Wolfgang Mozart was born at 9 Getreidegasse, Salzburg, Austria, on 27 January 1756, the seventh but only the second surviving child of Georg Leopold Mozart, violinist and Vice-Kapellmeister (under Joseph Lolli) to Prince-Archbishop Firmian of Salzburg and composer of *Violin Method* (1756), a standard work on violin technique. His mother was Anna Maria Pertl, herself the daughter of a musician. He was baptized Joannes Chrysostomus Wolfgangus Theophilus Mozart but used the name Gottlieb (the German version of Theophilus) until he visited Italy (1769) when he signed himself Amadeo (the Italian version of the Latin Amadeus). His older sister Maria Anna was known as 'Nännerl', Mozart himself being called 'Wolferl' by the family. After training as a harpsichord player with his sister (herself a talented player and composer but not promoted by their father) he played before George III and Queen Charlotte of England three times and accompanied Queen Charlotte's singing when aged seven (1764). He later worked as Konzertmeister (with Haydn's brother Michael) under his father and Lolli at Salzburg, resigned (1777), returned as organist (1779) and was then sacked (1781). Made a member of the prestigious Accademia Filharmonica of Bologna when below the necessary age of 20, he was also awarded the Order of the Golden Spur by Pope Clement XIV. On Gluck's death in 1787 he succeeded him as 'composer of the Imperial Chamber' to Emperor Joseph II in Vienna. In addition to composing and performing, he also taught music to high society. He wrote 49 symphonies, over 40 concertos, seven string quintets, 26 string quartets and numerous works for the piano and violin as well as classic choral works and the operas *The Marriage of Figaro* (1786), *Don Giovanni* (1787), *Così fan tutte* (1790) and *Die Zauberflöte*

(*The Magic Flute*; 1791).

Family/Sex Life: Mozart fell in love initially with the soprano Aloysia Weber (for whom he wrote *People of Thessaly*) but, rebuffed, in 1782 he married her sister, 18-year-old Constanze Weber, cousin of the composer Weber and eight years his junior. Of their six children only two survived, Karl Thomas and Franz Xavier Wolfgang (who also became a composer).

Appearance: His sister Maria Anna Mozart recorded that 'my brother had been quite a good-looking child. But he was disfigured by smallpox, and, what is worse, he came back from Italy with a sallow complexion like an Italian's.' The singer Michael Kelly recalled him as 'a remarkably small man, very thin and pale, with a profusion of fine fair hair, of which he was rather vain'. As a child he wore a lilac coat; he also wore a ring that some believed gave him magic powers.

Habits/Mannerisms: Mozart signed some of his letters 'Hauswurst' (Jack-pudding) after a character from the puppet theatre. He hated the flute – his favourite instrument was the clarinet. He was very fond of punch.

Sport/Hobbies: He enjoyed riding and dancing and was good at billiards (he had his own table at home). He was excellent at arithmetic as a child and played the piano, the harpsichord, the violin, the viola and the spinet and also sang.

Religion/Politics: From 1784 Mozart was a Freemason (as were Goethe and Frederick the Great). Haydn was a member of the same lodge as Mozart in Vienna, and significantly *Die Zauberflöte* (The Magic Flute) begins and ends in

E-flat major, the Masonic key.

Health: Mozart contracted smallpox and scarlet fever as a child. He also suffered from typhoid and endured painful gumboils. He had a very good memory and once memorized the entire nine-part *Miserere* by Allegri (copying of which was forbidden by the Vatican) and wrote it out.

Temperament: Good-humoured, generous and childlike, Mozart often lent money but kept back little for himself. His friends included J. C. Bach (the youngest son of J. S. Bach) and a favourite pupil, J. N. Hummel, who lived with Mozart and his family.

Work/Daily Routine: Mozart was a child prodigy, writing his first minuet at the age of six and his first opera at 11. Legend has it that at the age of two he identified the squeal of a pig as G sharp. He wrote over 600 compositions in all and his first symphonies were written in London. His own favourites included the Piano Concerto No. 5. Many of his greatest works were commissioned by crowned heads, but mystery surrounds his last masterpiece, the Requiem Mass (1790).

This may have been commissioned by Count Franz von Walsegg in memory of his dead wife, but others have speculated that it was paid for by Mozart's rival Salieri, who wished to pass it off as his own. He worked very fast (he composed *La Clemenza di Tito* in just 18 days). He played and composed at night and in the early morning (he often worked in bed between the hours of 6 and 9 am then did nothing during the day until around 9 or 12 at night). After the age of seven he rarely practised but preferred to sight-read instead. His piano, built by Anton Walter in Vienna, 1780, had a special sustaining device (he also owned one by Stein). Greatly admired by Chopin and Debussy, Haydn called him 'the greatest composer I know'.

Manner of Death: Legend has it that Mozart was poisoned and he himself believed this (Salieri was suspected). Certainly his hands and feet were swollen and his body was partly paralysed in the month before his death – but he actually died of typhoid around 1 am on 5 December 1791, aged 35. He was buried in an unmarked paupers' communal grave in St Mark's Church, Vienna.

MUSSOLINI, Benito Andrea Amilcare (1883–1945) Italian dictator

Benito Mussolini was born on 29 July 1883 in Predappio, near Forlì in the Romagna, Italy, the son of Alessandro Mussolini, a blacksmith and socialist councillor, and Rosa Maltoni, a schoolteacher. Named after Benito Juarez, the Mexican left-wing revolutionary leader and two other left-wing revolutionaries, Andrea Costa and Amilcare Cipriani, he had a younger brother Arnaldo and a sister Edvige. Educated at a boarding-school run by the Salesian Order in Faenza, he was expelled (aged 10) for wounding another boy with a knife. Later he was suspended

from schools another four times (once for stabbing). He worked as a substitute schoolteacher in Gualtieri (1902) and then went to Switzerland as a chocolate-factory worker, builder's labourer, butcher's boy and wine merchant employee. He was arrested as a Communist agitator (1903) and expelled but when he was later found guilty of desertion from military service in Italy he escaped back to Switzerland by forging the expiry date on his passport to 1905. When an amnesty was declared for deserters he returned to Italy and did his military service (1905–6) and resumed work as a teacher. He was then (1909) secretary to the Chamber of Labour, and became editor or sub-editor of various socialist magazines, including *Avanti!* (1912–14). Conscripted in 1915 he served in the Bersaglieri (light infantry), achieving the rank of corporal, but was wounded when a grenade-thrower exploded and was invalided out in 1917. In 1919 he left the Socialist Party to form the Fascist Party and became *Duce* (Leader) in 1922. The Fascists' March on Rome from Milan (1922) led to Mussolini being made Prime Minister; he became Dictator of Italy in 1925. He subsequently annexed Abyssinia (1935–6) and Albania (1939) and formed the Axis alliance with Nazi Germany (1936). He later declared war on Britain and France, but suffered military reverses and was deposed in 1943. Rescued from prison by the Germans, he was reinstated as a puppet dictator, but was ultimately seized by the Resistance.

Family/Sex Life: Having fathered an illegitimate child by Ida Dalser, Mussolini married Rachele Guidi, the daughter of his father's mistress. Their children were Romano, Edda (who married Count Ciano), Bruno, Vittorio and Anna Maria. He also kept as his mistress Clara Petacci.

Appearance: Mussolini was relatively stocky and small (he was given a higher chair than others when in meetings and stood on a footstool to make public speeches, though the stool was rarely visible in official photographs). As Duce he was clean-shaven, though as a youth he wore a moustache. When it became clear that he was losing his hair he had his head completely shaved. When he first came to power he dressed in a dark suit and bowler hat, but he discarded the hat after his similarity to comedian Oliver Hardy was pointed out.

Habits/Mannerisms: Mussolini only spent around three minutes on meals and suffered from very bad indigestion. He had given up alcohol and tobacco by 1923.

When a prisoner during World War II he ate mostly fruit and drank up to four litres of milk a day.

Sport/Hobbies: Favourite sports included boxing. He could read French and German and claimed to have read all of Shakespeare and most of Molière and Corneille. He boasted that he read 70 books a year, including Dante daily, and also that he knew passages of Goethe by heart. He also had pretensions as a writer himself, writing a novel *The Cardinal's Love*, which was serialized in *Avanti!*, a pulp novel *Claudia Particella* and a polemical book, *John Huss, the Man of Truth*. He was also fond of theatre and claimed to be the co-author of three plays, two of which were filmed. Another passion was music (especially Vivaldi, Wagner and Verdi); he played the trombone in the Forlimpopoli school band and later learned the violin. He was also interested in architecture and liked fine motor cars (he owned two Rolls-Royces).

Religion/Politics: An atheist and anti-Christian, he admired Marx, Darwin and Nietzsche. He was, however, superstitious (he refused to meet King Alfonso of Spain because he was reputed to have the power of the evil eye). At first a Marxist socialist and anti-nationalist, he later reversed his position and became an anti-socialist and nationalist.

Health: Mussolini enjoyed generally good health, though at various times he contracted venereal disease and suffered a gastro-duodenal ulcer. In 1926 he survived an assassination attempt by the 62-year-old Irishwoman Violet Gibson – she managed to shoot him in the nose. He survived four assassination attempts in all.

Temperament: Fiery and rarely known to smile or laugh at jokes, he was twice expelled at school for attacking pupils with a knife and was later wounded in a duel with the pacifist Socialist leader, Claudio Treves.

Work/Daily Routine: Notable admirers of Mussolini – at least in the early years – included Ezra Pound, who gave him a draft of his *Cantos* (1935), Gandhi, who called him a 'superman', Edison, who dubbed him 'the greatest genius of the modern age', Belloc, who said 'meeting him was like drinking good wine after marsh water', Archbishop of Canterbury Randall Davidson, who called him 'the one giant figure in Europe' and Winston Churchill, who confided to Il Duce: 'If I were Italian, I am sure I would have been with you from the beginning to end in your struggle against the bestial appetites of Leninism.' The celebrated 'March on Rome' (which inspired Hitler's abortive Munich Putsch) was a fake – Mussolini himself arrived by train.

Manner of Death: Mussolini was captured at Dongo, Lake Como, by Italian Communists (the 52nd Garibaldi Brigade) when trying to escape to Austria disguised in a Luftwaffe greatcoat and helmet and travelling with a group of German soldiers. Aged 61, he and his mistress Clara Petacci were shot at Dongo by the Communists on 28 April 1945. Their bodies were hung upside down and displayed in Como and then in Milan (the former Fascist headquarters).

NAPOLEON I (1769–1821) French emperor

Napoleon Buona Parte (Bonaparte after 1796) was born at Maison Milelli in Ajaccio, Corsica, on 15 August 1769, the second son and one of 14 children of Carlo-Maria Buona Parte, a lawyer, and Maria Letizia Ramolino. He had seven surviving brothers and sisters: Giuseppe (Joseph, later King of Spain), Lucciano (Lucien, captured by the English), Luigi (Louis, King of Holland), Jerome (King of Westphalia), Eliza, Pauletta (Pauline) and Caroline. Educated in Autun (Burgundy), Brienne (Champagne) and at the École Militaire in Paris, he then served as a captain in the Artillery. Second in command during the Battle of Toulon (1793), victory led to promotion to Brigadier-General. Deputy commander of the Army of the Interior in Paris during the counter-revolution (1795), he became commander-in-chief of the Army of Italy aged 26. Successes followed in Italy, Egypt and Malta. He later overturned the Council of 500 and ruled France with two other consuls (1798) before becoming First Consul and effective dictator. When crowned emperor by Pope Pius VII (1804) in Nôtre Dame, Paris, he put the crown on his own head and personally crowned Josephine empress. Napoleon's Grand Army swept through Europe, defeating the Russians and Austrians at Austerlitz and the Prussians at Jena and securing other victories before his failure to retain Moscow (1812) and defeat at the Battle of the Nations, Leipzig (1813). He abdicated in 1814 and was exiled to Elba. He later escaped (1815) and ruled for 100 days before being finally beaten by Wellington and Blücher at Waterloo. He abdicated again in 1815 in favour of his son, Napoleon II, and after failing to escape to the USA and being refused asylum in Britain was finally exiled to St Helena.

Family/Sex Life: In 1796 Napoleon married Josephine (Marie-Josèphe-Rose), a Creole from Martinique six years his senior. She was the widow of Alexandre, Viscount de Beauharnais, commander of the Army of the Rhine (guillotined by Robespierre in 1794), and already had two children, Hortense (who married Louis Bonaparte, King of Holland) and Eugène. The marriage was dissolved in 1809 after Josephine's infidelities (there were no children). In 1810 Napoleon married the 18-year-old Archduchess Marie-Louise, daughter of the Emperor of Austria and 23 years his junior. Their son Napoleon was crowned King of Rome. Marie-Louise never saw her husband again after 1815 and secretly remarried. Napoleon kept mistresses, his favourite being Marie Walewska (wife of Count Alexander Walewski), by whom he fathered the illegitimate Alexandre.

Appearance: Only five feet six inches tall, Napoleon was grey-eyed, olive-complexioned and had a broad chest and short legs (he later became stout). Apparently born with teeth, in his youth he wore his dark brown hair long, in a pigtail; later it was close-cropped. He wore a simple uniform – as emperor, a grey or dark green coat over white breeches, with silk stockings.

Habits/Mannerisms: Napoleon had frugal tastes. He took snuff, drank diluted burgundy and strong black coffee but disliked garlic. He enjoyed chicken; Poulet Marengo was created by his chef to celebrate his victory at Marengo, Italy. He needed little sleep but liked long hot baths. He used English razors to shave himself, preferred Windsor soap and carried handkerchiefs soaked in eau-de-Cologne. When on St Helena he played solitaire constantly. His possessions included a bullet-proof carriage and Frederick the Great's clock (which went with him into exile on St Helena).

Sport/Hobbies: Napoleon hated to lose at anything and would cheat at cards and chess. Other pastimes included billiards and shooting. His reading included Corneille, Racine, Molière, Beaumarchais, Milton, Hume, Voltaire, Rousseau, Macpherson's 'Ossian' poems, the *Iliad*, Plato's *Republic* and Plutarch's *Lives*. He admired Mozart and the paintings of David and Ingres. In exile in St Helena he took up gardening.

Religion/Politics: He was excommunicated by the Pope in 1809 and was a self-confessed agnostic. He once said: 'Were I obliged to have a religion, I would worship the sun.' He had little time for political theorizing, but admired Tom Paine.

Health: Napoleon suffered from malaria, piles and syphilis. He was bayoneted in the thigh at the Battle of Toulon and survived assassination by the Jacobins at the Paris Opéra (1800), by royalists in the Rue Niçoise (1800) and by the German student Friedrich Staps (1809). In 1812 he suffered from an inflamed bladder. In 1814 he tried to commit suicide by taking opium, hellebore and belladonna, but vomited it up.

Temperament: Napoleon's cadet school report stated that he was 'Taciturn, with a love of solitude; is moody, overbearing and egotistical ...' Though he could be charming, he was ruthless, massacring 3000 Turkish prisoners in Jaffa when he could not feed them and sometimes showing callous disregard for casualties (he dismissed the French dead at Eylau as 'small change' and said 'one Parisian night will soon adjust these losses').

Pets: Napoleon hated cats but loved horses. His favourites were the white Arab stallion Marengo, whose tiny skeleton is preserved in the National Army Museum, London, and the white Arab mare Desirée. On his first wedding night Josephine's pug dog Fortuné bit him in bed thinking he was attacking her.

Work/Daily Routine: He dismissed Wellington as a bad general and the English as a 'nation of shopkeepers' (in return, critics called him 'the Corsican upstart' and the 'Little Corporal'). His use of semaphore telegraph gave him a great advantage over his enemies. At Waterloo only 30,000 of the 250,000 troops ranged against his 122,000 were in fact British. David's painting of Napoleon crossing the

Alps on a white charger (1800) is a romanticization – he actually crossed on a mule. He created the Légion d'honneur (at first purely military) and built the Arc de Triomphe.

Motto/Emblem: His personal emblem was a bee.

Manner of Death: After his doctors gave him a huge dose of calomel (mercurious chloride) – which had a horrible effect –

Napoleon died of duodenal-pyloric cancer at Langwood House, St Helena, on 5 May 1821, aged 51. He was buried in Geranium Valley, St Helena. After death his head was shaved for souvenirs and his heart was put in a silver vase and his stomach in a silver pepper pot. After 20 years (1840) his body was transferred to Les Invalides, Paris. In 1972 his dried-up one-inch-long penis was auctioned at Christie's but failed to reach its reserve price.

NELSON, Horatio (1758–1805) English admiral

Horatio Nelson was born on 29 September 1758 in Burnham Thorpe, Norfolk, the sixth child and third surviving son of Edmund Nelson, Rector of Burnham Thorpe. His mother (who died when he was nine), was Catherine Suckling, a relative of Sir Robert Walpole and sister of Captain Maurice Suckling, later Comptroller of the Royal Navy. Named after his godfather and distant cousin Horatio, 2nd Lord Walpole of Wollerton, he had an elder brother William, elder sisters Susannah, Anne and Kate and a younger brother Maurice. Educated at boarding schools in Norwich, Downham Market and North Walsham, he entered the Navy aged 12 (1770), and was midshipman aboard Suckling's ship *Raisonnable* (1771). He captained the frigate *Hinchinbrooke* aged 20, commanded the *Albermarle* in Hood's fleet in New York and met his future wife when in command of the frigate *Boreas* in the West Indies. From 1787 he spent five years with his wife in Norfolk before receiving command of the 64-gun ship-of-the-line *Agamemnon* under Hood in the Mediterranean (1793). He first encountered Emma Hamilton (wife of the British Ambassador to Naples) on a diplomatic mission to pro-Monarchist Naples to gather reinforcements against

the French revolutionary armies. Promoted Rear-Admiral (1797) after success at Cape Vincent, he was made KB the same year, Baron Nelson of the Nile (1798) in the wake of the Battle of the Nile and Viscount Nelson. After further success at Copenhagen (1801) he fought his last and greatest battle at Trafalgar, off Cadiz (1805).

Family/Sex Life: In 1787 Nelson married Mrs Frances ('Fanny') Nisbet, née Herbert, widow of a doctor and niece of the President of the Council of Nevis, West Indies (she already had a five-year-old son Josiah). They separated in 1801, at the height of Nelson's affair with Emma Hamilton (née Amy Lyons), wife of Sir William Hamilton. By Emma he sired a daughter, Horatia Nelson Thompson, the only survivor of twins.

Appearance: Thin and short (five feet four inches), the one-armed, one-eyed, prematurely grey Nelson was an unlikely hero. When young he had a very long pigtail and dressed oddly. Hood's midshipman Prince William Henry, later William IV, called him 'the merest boy of a captain I ever beheld ... full lace uniform; his lank unpowdered hair was tied in a stiff Hessian tail of an extraordinary length'. In reality he rarely wore the black patch over his right eye but had a green shade tucked under his hat to protect his left eye from the sun.

Habits/Mannerisms: Nelson preferred to be called Horace rather than Horatio. He became left-handed after losing his right arm and when agitated the stump of his amputated arm would move about.

Sport/Hobbies: A brilliant tactician, Nelson was a very poor shot.

Religion/Politics: Church of England. A Tory, he made several speeches in the House of Lords.

Health: While in India in the 1770s, Nelson suffered from malarial fever, which left him prone to partial paralysis for the rest of his life. In 1779 he contracted dysentery while in Nicaragua. In 1794 he was blinded in the right eye (he could only distinguish light and dark) by splinters thrown up by shot during a land battle against the French at Calvi, Corsica. His right elbow was subsequently shattered by grapeshot while fighting on land at Tenerife (1797) and his arm had to be amputated (leaving a stump) – he was only saved from death by his stepson's prompt application of a tourniquet. He was also hit in the forehead by scrap iron at the Battle of the Nile in Aboukir Bay, Alexandria (1798). On two other occasions his life was saved by coxswain John Sykes in hand-to-hand fighting at Cadiz. A more minor but persistent ailment was sea-sickness, which he never overcame. The lost eye proved to have its advantages – famously, at the Battle of Copenhagen: when ordered to disengage, he clapped his telescope to his blind eye and denied he had seen the signal, going on to pursue the action to a successful conclusion.

Temperament: Vain and egotistical, Nelson liked to be flattered. His friends included Prince William (later William IV).

Work/Daily Routine: Remembered first and foremost as the victor at Trafalgar, Nelson began hostilities on that fateful day with an almost legendary signal to the fleet. This was originally intended to read 'England confides that every man will do his duty' but 'confides' was not in the signal book so 'expects' was used to save signal flags.

Motto: *Palmam qui meruit ferat* (Let him bear the palm who has deserved it).

Manner of Death: Wearing no sword and bearing four stars of chivalry on the left breast of his coat, Nelson made an obvious target for enemy snipers at Trafalgar. As he stood on the quarter-deck of HMS *Victory* a musket ball fired from the *Redoutable* (part of the Franco-Spanish fleet under Admiral Villeneuve) passed through his left epaulette, lungs and spine and lodged in his back muscles; he died three hours later, at 4.30 pm on 21 October 1805, aged 47. His last words (to Flag Captain Thomas Masterman Hardy) were 'Kiss me, Hardy'. His body, wearing a nightcap, was brought home in a lead coffin, preserved in brandy. His funeral car in London had a bow and stern in likeness of the *Victory*. He was buried in the crypt of St Paul's in a marble sarcophagus designed for Cardinal Wolsey. The 145-foot Nelson's Column by William Railton was erected in Trafalgar Square (1839–42) and surmounted by a bronze capital cast from old Woolwich Arsenal guns and a 17-foot statue (1843) by E. H. Baily. The bronze bas-reliefs were cast from captured cannon and completed in 1849. Landseer's lions were added in 1867.

NERO (AD 37–68) Roman Emperor

Nero was born Lucius Domitius Ahenobarbus in Antium, Italy, on 15 December AD 37, the son of Gnaeus Domitius Ahenobarbus and Agrippina the Younger, sister of Caligula. His maternal great-grandfather was Agrippa. Nero's father died of dropsy when he was three and his mother (whom he later murdered) was banished when he was two. He was brought up by his aunt Domitia Lepida (whom he also later murdered) until Claudius rescinded Agrippina's banishment, married her and adopted Nero as his heir aged 13 over his own natural son Britannicus. He then took the name Nero Claudius Caesar Augustus Germanicus in his stepfather's honour. As a child his tutor was Seneca (whom he later executed). He was created emperor aged 17 when Claudius died (poisoned by Nero's mother) and his reign began promisingly enough under the influence of his mother, Seneca and the Praetorian Prefect Burrus. Later though, Nero abandoned interest in affairs of state and pursued his own personal pleasures. During his reign Boadicea revolted in England, Pompeii was destroyed, Armenia was evacuated and St Peter and St Paul were executed. There was also the Great Fire of Rome (AD 64), which he is reputed to have started in an attempt to create a new city he had designed called Neropolis – though Nero himself blamed the Christians. He changed the month of April to Neronens during his period of office and his death marked the end of the Caesars. He ruled for 15 years.

Family/Sex Life: In AD 52 Nero married Octavia, Claudius's daughter and thus his half-sister. He later divorced her and had her executed. His second wife, Poppaea Sabina, was already married to a noble and died when Nero kicked her in a rage while she was pregnant after she complained of his late return from the races. She had earlier given birth to his daughter Claudia Augusta. After being refused by Antaria, another of Claudius's daughters, whom he subsequently had killed, he married Statilia Messalina (previously married to a consul whom he had murdered). He was also reputed to have had affairs with freeborn boys and married women, to have raped the Vestal Virgin Rubria and to have 'married' a boy called Sporus, whom he castrated and dressed as a woman.

Appearance: Of average height, with a squat neck, spindly legs, a protuberant belly and dullish blue eyes, Nero was described by Suetonius as 'pretty, rather than handsome'. He had a yellow beard (Ahenobarbus means 'bronze beard') and wore his fair hair in rows of curls. He never wore the same clothes twice and did not dress like an emperor, instead wearing a fringed gown or an unbelted silk dressing-gown with slippers and scarf.

Habits/Mannerisms: Nero drank wine and ate lots of leeks in the belief that this would improve his singing voice. On his right wrist he wore a snake skin set in a golden bracelet (the living snake had frightened off assassins when he was a boy). His many eccentricities included having his mules shod with silver.

Sport/Hobbies: Nero had a passion for wrestling and for chariot-racing (he played with ivory models of chariots and occasionally raced himself). He also had a golden net for fishing and was very fond of acting and music, singing and played the lyre (the legend that he played the violin as Rome burned is apocryphal as the violin had not then been invented). He also wrote poems and built a fantasy palace, the Golden House, in Rome.

Religion/Politics: Nero despised all religion and was the first Emperor to persecute the Christians. His Golden House palace included a 120-foot statue of himself in the hall. To fend off bankruptcy he was not above pilfering gold and silver images from the temples.

Health: Described by contemporaries as very healthy, Nero nonetheless had a body that was, according to Suetonius, 'pustular and malodorous'. He did, however, have a very good memory, seldom forgetting a name or a face.

Temperament: Thoroughly ruthless, Nero included many notable people among his victims, besides his mother and his wife.

Among others he murdered were the poet Lucan and Claudius's son Britannicus. He was much dominated by his mother at the start of his reign and she even had her head put on coins with his.

Manner of Death: The Roman armies revolted and when the Senate sentenced Nero to death by flogging he escaped to his villa outside Rome and there stabbed himself in the throat with the help of his scribe, Epaphroditus, as soldiers arrived to take him away. He died on 9 June AD 68, aged 32. His last words were *'Qualis artifex pereo'* ('What an artist the world is losing in me'). He was buried by two of his mistresses on the Hill of Gardens, Rome, wrapped in a white sheet.

NEWTON, Sir Isaac (1642–1727) English astronomer and mathematician

---

Isaac Newton was born two months after the death (aged 36) of his father, also Isaac Newton, on Christmas Day, 25 December 1642, in Woolsthorpe House, near Grantham, Lincolnshire. His mother, Hannah Ayscough, subsequently married Barnabas Smith, Rector of North Witham, Lincolnshire, in 1645 and left Newton in the care of his grandmother. Stepbrothers and sisters from his mother's second marriage were Benjamin, Marie and Hannah. Educated at King's School, Grantham, he was sent (1661) to Trinity College, Cambridge (BA 1665) as a 'poor scholar'. The college closed in 1665 because of the Plague and he continued his influential studies of light and of lenses at home (leading to the construction of the first reflecting telescope in 1668). He was elected a Fellow of Trinity College in 1667 and became Professor of Mathematics at Cambridge in 1669 (aged 26). He went on to publish important works on optics and, through the publication of the *Philosophiae Naturalis Principia Mathematica* (1687), which discussed

gravitation and the 'three laws of motion', became arguably the greatest of all physical scientists. He was not, however, known as a 'scientist' in his lifetime (the word was not coined until 1840). Appointed Master of the Royal Mint in 1699, he did little scientific work in his last 25 years. President of the Royal Society for 25 years from 1703, he was also a Foreign Associate of the Académie Française and MP for Cambridge University. He was knighted by Queen Anne in 1705 (in Cambridge) and spent his last years in the care of his step-niece.

Family/Sex Life: Unmarried.

Appearance: Middle-sized with 'a very lively and piercing eye, a comely and gracious aspect, with a fine head of hair as white as silver', he never wore spectacles and generally had an untidy and slovenly appearance. His head was used as a model in Haydon's painting *Christ's Entry into Jerusalem*.

Habits/Mannerisms: Vegetarian.

Sport/Hobbies: Newton disliked opera: he only went once and left before the third act.

Religion/Politics: Whig MP for Cambridge University (his only recorded utterance in Parliament was a request to open a window).

Health: A very small, weak baby not expected to live, Newton later suffered from phrenitis and gout. A nervous breakdown in 1693 left him insane for 18 months. He was reported to have lost only one tooth in his entire life.

Temperament: Though sometimes generous and charitable, if absent-minded, Newton had few friends. He quarrelled easily with other scientists, including Robert Hooke, Gottfried Leibniz and John Flamsteed. He often sought revenge for both real and imagined insults (typically, if offended, he would delete references to any help he had received from a colleague in his work). His adverse reaction to criticism, amounting to a persecution mania, is sometimes attributed to his abandonment by his mother as a child. On one occasion, when pestered by a woman who, thinking Newton was an astrologer, begged him persistently to use magic to find a lost purse, the scientist showed more forbearing. He carefully drew a magic circle and then intoned: 'Abracadabra! Go to the façade of Greenwich Hospital, third window on the south side. On the lawn in front of it I see a dwarfish devil bending over your purse' – legend has it that the woman duly left the great man in peace and found the purse exactly where she had been told it would be.

Pets: Newton's dog Diamond once knocked over a candle and thus allegedly burned some important scientific notes representing years of work. According to one version of the incident, on viewing the damage Newton confined himself to the comment: 'O Diamond, Diamond, thou little knowest the damage thou hast done.' Others, however, attributed the nervous breakdown Newton suffered in 1693 to the accident. Newton also kept cats and it was for the cat at Woolsthorpe House that he is reputed to have invented the cat flap. Wags of the period claimed that when the cat had kittens the great scientist cut a smaller cat flap next to the original for them to use.

Work/Daily Routine: The theory of gravitation discussed in Newton's *Philosophiae Naturalis Principia Mathematica* was allegedly inspired by the fall of an apple as the scientist, then a young man, sat in the garden at Woolsthorpe House. This anecdote was repeated by Voltaire, whose mistress Gabrielle du Châtelet rendered the first French translation of the book. Voltaire claimed to have heard the tale from Newton's stepniece, Mrs Conduitt; it was also related at an early date by the anti-quarian William Stukeley. On another occasion Newton inadvertently convinced the neighbours that he was mad by sitting in the garden using a pipe to blow bubbles from a tub of soap-suds (he was, in fact, studying the refraction of light upon the bubbles that he made). When an admirer asked Newton how he came to make so many important discoveries he replied simply: 'By always thinking about them', though in a letter to Hooke in 1675 he conceded: 'If I have seen further it is by standing on the shoulders of giants.' He also wrote nearly two million words on alchemy and felt his best published work was his interpretation of the Book of Daniel.

Manner of Death: Newton died in Kensington, London, on 20 March 1727, aged 84. He was buried in Westminster Abbey. At his funeral Voltaire said: 'If all the geniuses of the universe assembled, he should lead the band.' Alexander Pope contributed the epitaph:

'Nature and Nature's laws lay hid in night: God said, 'Let Newton be!', and all was light.'

Newton's reported last words were:

'I do not know what I may appear to the world. But to myself, I seem to have been only like a boy playing on the seashore, diverting myself in now and then finding a smoother pebble or a prettier shell than ordinary, whilst the great ocean of truth lay all undiscovered before me.'

NIETZSCHE, Friedrich Wilhelm (1844–1900) German philosopher

Friedrich Nietzsche (named after Friedrich Wilhelm IV of Prussia, with whom he shared his birthday) was born on 15 October 1844 in Röcken, near Lützen in Prussian Saxony, Germany, the son of Karl Ludwig Nietzsche, a Lutheran clergyman who had been court tutor to the three daughters of the Duke Joseph of Saxe-Altenburg and who died of a brain disease when Nietzsche was five. His mother was Franziska Oehler and he had a younger brother Joseph (named after the duke) and a younger sister, Elisabeth Therese Alexandra, named after the princesses his father had taught. Educated at first in Röcken, after the death of his father his mother moved with the family to stay with his paternal grandmother Edmuthe Nietzsche and two aunts in Naumburg, where Friedrich (known familiarly as Fritz) attended the Dom Gymnasium until 1858. He was then offered a place at the famous classical boarding school at Pforta (alumni included Schlegel and Novalis) where he was frequently top of his class. As his father, both his grandfathers and many other forebears had been in the Church he studied theology at the University of Bonn (1864–5) and philology at the University of Leipzig (1865–7, winning a prize on Diogenes Laertius) before being conscripted for a year in the artillery, reaching the rank of lance-corporal. He became Professor of Classical Philology at the University of Basel at the age of 24 (1869), took his doctorate later the same year, but had to resign in 1879 because of ill-health. He became a Swiss citizen (1869) and served as a medical orderly with the Prussian Army in the Franco-Prussian War (1870–1). His writings, the most important of which included *Also Sprach Zarathustra* (1883–5), were largely ignored until Georg Brandes began lecturing on them in Copenhagen (1888).

Family/Sex Life: Nietzsche never married and it has been suggested that he died a virgin. (He once commented in his writings that 'Woman was God's second mistake.')

Appearance: Softly spoken, with small ears, beautiful hands and hair that remained dark brown until his death, Nietzsche sported a large moustache. He also had a scar across the bridge of his nose as the result of a sword duel when a student. He was always neatly dressed.

Habits/Mannerisms: Nietzsche took snuff and had very neat handwriting.

Sport/Hobbies: A fine rider, he played the piano and composed both piano music and songs as well as writing much poetry as a child (55 poems in 1854 alone).

Religion/Politics: Nietzsche was very pious as a boy and was confirmed as a Christian in 1861, but he subsequently lost his faith while still at school. In his writings he later rejected Christian morality as a valid basis for society and created the concept of the *Übermensch* (Superman) – an ideal that was fated to have immense appeal to the Nazis several decades later. He wrote: 'I call Christianity the one great curse, the one enormous and innermost perversion, the one great instinct of revenge, for which no means are too venomous, too underhand and too petty – I call it the one immortal blemish of mankind.'

Health: Nietzsche was half blind and suffered from migraines, probably as a consequence of his syphilis. He experienced serious eye trouble from the age of 12 (like his mother he had one pupil larger than the other – a symptom of syphilis). Other ailments included rheumatism, a damaged breastbone during army training, dysentery, diphtheria (1870) and shingles on the neck (1872).

Temperament: Though modest and a lover of solitude even as a child, Nietzsche did have a number of close friends, who included Wagner (until Nietzsche

eventually took exception to both Wagner's Christianity and his nationalism).

Work/Daily Routine: Nietzsche's first published book was *Die Geburt der Tragödie* (1872), which he dedicated to his friend Wagner. He had the inspiration for *Also Sprach Zarathustra* while on a path in Èzes, France. Influenced by Schopenhauer and Wagner, he was an admirer of Voltaire, Hölderlin and Byron, but dismissed Plato as 'a bore'.

Manner of Death: Nietzsche suffered a mental breakdown in 1889 and remained insane until he died (of syphilis) after a stroke at midday on 24 August 1900, aged 55, in Weimar, Germany. He was buried at Röcken next to his father in a Lutheran ceremony with a choir and church bells, regardless of his strongly anti-religious views.

NIGHTINGALE, Florence (1820–1910) English pioneer nurse

Florence Nightingale, known as 'The Lady of the Lamp', was born at Villa La Columbaia in Florence, Italy, on 12 May 1820, the second daughter of a very wealthy landowner and later High Sheriff of Hampshire, William Edward Nightingale (formerly Shore, who changed his name aged 21 in order to inherit the estates of his mother's uncle Peter Nightingale). Her mother was Frances Smith, daughter of the abolitionist William Smith. Named after her birthplace, she had an elder sister Frances Parthenope (who later married Sir Harry Verney, 2nd Baronet of Claydon) and her cousin, Blanche Smith, married the poet Arthur Hugh Clough. She was brought up in Derbyshire (where she spent her summers) and Hampshire (where she spent her winters), where Sidney Lord Herbert was a neighbour. She trained as a nurse in

Kaiserswerth and Paris and, after working for a year as Superintendent of the Hospital for Invalid Gentlewomen – a charitable nursing-home in Harley Street founded by Lady Canning – she was sent to the Crimea with 38 nurses supported by *The Times* Fund on recommendation of her friend Sidney Herbert (then War Minister) to improve British nursing standards (French nursing had always been better). She served as Superintendent of the Hospital at Scutari, near Constantinople, reducing the mortality rate from 42 per cent to two per cent. After the war she returned to England (1856) and founded a training school for nurses at St Thomas's Hospital, London (1860). She later became the first woman to receive the Order of Merit (1907) and the second woman to receive the Freedom of the City of London.

Family/Sex Life: Florence Nightingale never married, though research in the 1990s based on her letters suggested she was actually more active sexually than had hitherto been believed. A regular visitor to the home of her sister in Buckinghamshire, she became particularly close to Sir Harry Verney after her sister's death in 1890 and spent almost all her time at his house, ignoring illness to occupy herself with promoting improvements in rural health care in the surrounding villages.

Appearance: According to Lytton Strachey, the young Florence Nightingale was an 'angular woman, with her haughty eye and her acrid mouth', but she later became 'a fat old lady, smiling all day long'. Portraits from her early years attest to her slender frame, wide face and dark, centre-parted hair.

Health: After two years nursing soldiers, she caught a fever and returned to the UK, where her health collapsed, obliging her to live the life of a semi-invalid for the rest of her days. She relieved her physical ailments with drugs and there have been suggestions that she became addicted to these.

Religion/Politics: She was very interested in mysticism, but was otherwise sceptical about religious faith. She once wrote: 'From committees, charity and schism – from the Church of England and all other deadly sins – from philanthropy and all the deceits of the devil – Good Lord deliver us.' She had some sympathy with those who argued for increased rights for women, writing in *Notes for Nursing*: 'No man, not even a doctor, ever gives any other definition of what a nurse should be than this – "devoted and obedient". This definition would do just as well for a porter. It might even do for a horse. It would not do for a policeman.'

Temperament: Energetic, indefatigable and remorselessly passionate about her mission to improve standards of health care, she had many admirers.

Known to her intimates as 'Flo', her friends included Arthur Hugh Clough, Sidney Herbert and Benjamin Jowett (the philosopher and Master of Balliol). She was admired by the Aga Khan and was personally awarded a brooch by Queen Victoria – specially designed for her by Prince Albert (a George Cross in red enamel with the royal cypher surmounted by diamonds and inscribed 'Blessed are the Merciful'). The Sultan of Turkey gave her a diamond bracelet.

Pets: She reputedly kept 60 cats (including the Persians Bismarck, Disraeli and Gladstone); another pet was a small owl which she took everywhere in her pocket (even in the Crimea).

Work/Daily Routine: The 'Lady of the Lamp' tag was a reference to her popularity with the troops she tended in the Crimea, who expressed themselves uniquely cheered by the sight of her visiting their wards, lighting her way with a lamp. This popularity incidentally caused much jealousy and resentment among other medical staff. She was motivated to lead a medical team to the Crimea after reading of the appalling conditions in the army's hospitals. When the chief medical officer there was awarded the KCB she was damning, suggesting the initials stood for 'Knight of the Crimea Burial-ground'. Thanks to her efforts 2000 wounded men no longer had to share just 20 chamberpots and rats, maggots and lice were driven from the wards. It was said that she would never leave the side of a dying man and such was the adoration she inspired that her charges would kiss her shadow as she passed. The author of the standard textbook *Notes on Nursing*, she also wrote translations of Plato.

Manner of Death: Florence Nightingale died at 10 South Street, off Park Lane, Westminster, London, on 13 August 1910, aged 90. Having refused burial in Westminster Abbey she was interred in East Wellow, Hampshire.

ORWELL, George (1903–50) English novelist and essayist

George Orwell was born Eric Arthur Blair on 25 June 1903, in Motihari, Bengal, the son of Richard Walmesley Blair, Sub-Deputy Opium Agent in the Indian Civil Service, and himself great-great-grandson of the Earl of Westmorland. His mother was Ida Mabel Limouzin, daughter of a French teak merchant and 18 years his father's junior. He had an older sister, Marjorie and a younger one, Avril. Leaving their father in India, the family was brought up by their mother in England. Educated at St Cyprian's School (Eastbourne) – with Cyril Connolly and Cecil Beaton – Wellington (one term) and Eton (where he was taught by Aldous Huxley), Orwell worked as Assistant Superintendent of Police in the Indian Imperial Police in Myaungmya, Upper Burma (1922–7) and then lived in Paris (1928–9), working as a dishwasher in a hotel, before returning to England to write up his experiences. As the projected book was too short he became a tramp (never for more than six weeks at a time) in London using the pseudonym 'Edward Burton' and published his account as *Down and Out in Paris and London* (1933). He then taught at a private school in Hayes (1932), was a bookshop assistant in Hampstead, London (1935), and wrote reviews for *The Adelphi*. In 1936 he ran the village shop in Wallington, near Baldock, Hertfordshire, and in the Spanish Civil War fought with the POUM (Workers' Party for Marxist Unity) Republican forces. He served on the Aragon front and was made a corporal. Unfit for service in World War II, he joined the Home Guard and worked as a producer for the BBC, broadcasting to India talks by E. M. Forster, T. S. Eliot, Dylan Thomas etc. (1941–3). He then became Literary Editor of *Tribune* (1943), was War Correspondent for the *Observer* (1945) and also contributed to *New Statesman, Time & Tide* and *Horizon*. He spent his last years alone on the Scottish island of Jura. Among his most celebrated novels were *Keep the Aspidistra Flying* (1936), *The Road to Wigan Pier* (1937), *Homage to Catalonia* (1938), *Animal Farm* (1945) and *Nineteen Eighty-Four* (1949).

Family/Sex Life: In 1936 Orwell married Eileen O'Shaughnessy, daughter of a customs official. She died in 1945; they had no children. In 1949, in a University College Hospital bedside ceremony he married Sonia Mary Brownell, editorial secretary to Cyril Connolly on *Horizon*; they had no children but adopted a three-week-old son, Richard Horatio Blair.

Appearance: Six feet three inches tall, with a pencil moustache (grown when in the police), he had – according to George Woodcock – 'A hard, almost cruel mouth until he smiled.' He had size 12 feet and always wore dark shirts (khaki or navy blue).

Habits/Mannerisms: Orwell had a squeaky voice as the result of a bullet through the throat in the Spanish Civil War and talked in a monotone. He smoked roll-up cigarettes, liked strong tea and dark beer (he refused to buy lager for anyone, even women).

Sport/Hobbies: He enjoyed fishing, growing vegetables and carpentry. He also collected Donald McGill postcards.

Religion/Politics: In his will Orwell asked to be buried with Church of England rites. A Socialist, he joined the Independent Labour Party in 1938.

Health: Orwell suffered pneumonia while in Paris in 1929 and later was wounded by a bullet in the throat (1936). He was first diagnosed with tuberculosis after an attack in 1938. He was also convinced he was sterile.

Temperament: Though solitary and gloomy, Orwell had a good number of friends, including Julian Symonds, George Woodcock and Arthur Koestler. For his part, he disliked Kipling (a 'gutter poet . . . vulgar flag-waver . . . a good bad poet') and Auden ('a sort of gutless Kipling'). Among those he admired were Henry Miller, Conrad, Gissing, Butler, Reade, Jack London, Dickens ('rotten architecture, wonderful gargoyles'), Somerset Maugham and Jonathan Swift (he considered *Gulliver's Travels* one of the top six books of all time).

Pets: He kept a dog called Marx and (while at Wallington) a goat called Muriel.

Work/Daily Routine: Orwell usually wrote three drafts of each book. He first started writing fiction in Paris (1928–9) but later destroyed his early efforts. He wrote *Down and Out* in the comfort of his parents' house in Southwold, Suffolk; after rejection by T. S. Eliot at Faber, the agent Leonard Moore sold it to Gollancz (Orwell was not proud of the book so suggested as pseudonyms P. S. Burton, Kenneth Miles, H. Lewis Allways and George Orwell – after the Suffolk river). Gollancz chose the pseudonym and the title (earlier titles were *Confessions of a Dishwasher* and *Lady Poverty*). Similarly, Orwell thought *A Clergyman's Daughter* (1935) was 'tripe'. His *Homage to Catalonia* sold badly and failed to cover the £150 advance. *Animal Farm* was rejected by Gollancz, Cape and Faber before Secker & Warburg published it – the first printing of 4500 copies sold out in two weeks. By contrast, the first printing of *Nineteen Eighty-Four* was 25,000 (most sold in six months). The title *Nineteen Eighty-Four* was chosen by juggling the number 1948, the year in which he wrote the book.

Manner of Death: Orwell died after a haemorrhage caused by tuberculosis in University College Hospital, London, on the night of 21 January 1950, aged 46. He was buried in Sutton Courtenay, Oxfordshire – at his request he was laid beneath a plain tombstone with the words 'Here lies Eric Arthur Blair' (not George Orwell). He specifically requested that there be no biography of him.

PAGANINI, Niccolò (1782–1840) Italian violinist and composer

Paganini was born on 27 October 1782 in Genoa, Italy, the third child of Antonio Paganini, a poor ship's chandler, musician and dealer in mandolins, and Teresa Bocciardo. He had one surviving elder brother and three younger sisters. After Paganini's mother had a dream in which an angel told her that her son would become a famous violinist, his father taught him the mandolin (aged five and a half) and the violin (aged seven). He wrote a sonata when he was eight and gave his first public performance in Genoa aged 12.

After violin tuition in Genoa a patron helped him study at Parma University under Ferdinando Paer (composer of Napoleon's wedding march). He later turned freelance and moved to Lucca, teaching the violin and giving concerts. In 1805 he and his brother were appointed to the Court Orchestra of Princess Elise Baciocchi, Duchess of Piombino and Lucca (Napoleon's sister), and when it was dissolved they were kept on in the string quartet until he left her service in 1809. After touring Europe with great success he returned to Parma as director of the Court Orchestra of Archduchess Marie-Louise of Austria (Napoleon's second wife). He was co-founder of the Casino Paganini in Paris (which failed) and eventually settled in Nice. Honours heaped upon him included the rank of Knight Grand Cross of the Golden Spur by the Vatican in 1827 (only three other musicians, Gluck, Mozart and Morlachi, had been awarded this before).

Family/Sex Life: Paganini was educated in the arts of love by an unidentified aristocrat, who took him in charge at the age of 19 and maintained him on her estate for three years. Subsequently he became as famous for his affairs as for his music. A plan to elope with Charlotte Watson, singer daughter of the musical director of the King's Theatre, London, was prevented by her father and the police. He was later convicted of the rape and abduction of the pregnant prostitute Angelina Cavanna (he was imprisoned for a week). An affair with the professional singer Antonia Bianchi resulted in a son, Achilles Cyrus Alexander – a financial settlement later gave him legal custody of the child. He also had an affair with Helene, wife of Baron von Dobeneck.

Appearance: Though of medium height, Paganini was very thin (he was described as 'a bag of bones' by 1828 after taking 'Leroy's Cure' for four years). He had a long neck, a very large head, hollow and pale cheeks, an aquiline nose, large black eyes and long jet-black curly hair and sideburns. He had a sardonic smile and his left shoulder was slightly higher than his right. He wore dark glasses in artificial light and owned a diamond ring given to him by William IV of England.

Habits/Mannerisms: When playing, he thrust his right foot forward and pushed out his left hip to take his weight. He often added humorous farmyard animal sounds – birds, cats, dogs etc. – while improvising in concerts (a device much liked by the public).

Sport/Hobbies: He spoke and wrote in French.

Health: Paganini contracted measles and scarlet fever as a child. He suffered a physical breakdown in 1824 and was diagnosed with tuberculosis in 1834. Other physical problems included an injury to the third finger of his left hand (sustained while cutting cheese), syphilis (for which he took opium and mercury), a persistent cough, poor digestion, high fevers, jaundice (1822), a sensitive skin, stomach ulcers and bad teeth, which led to an infected jawbone and rotting gums (part of his lower jaw and all his lower teeth were later removed). Paganini was also a hypochondriac, visiting spas and taking homeopathic remedies.

Temperament: He was imbued with the demonic 'to a remarkable degree', according to Goethe. As a young man, he found success hard to cope with and for a time abandoned himself to gambling and drinking, so that many feared he would be dead before he was 20. Like his friend Rossini, he had a taste for practical joking and uproarious behaviour.

Work/Daily Routine: Paganini played a Guarnerius violin (and later a Stradivarius). He also owned a Stradivarius viola. Before concerts he would relax all day on his bed, without food. He made his British debut at the King's Theatre, Haymarket, London (now Her Majesty's); in 1831 in London alone he earnt over £10,000. He behaved generously with his money, paying off Berlioz's debts and commissioning from him *Harold en Italie*, designed to show off his skills on the viola (unfortunately, Paganini disliked the finished work because it had too many rests and so wrote his own). He greatly influenced Liszt and admired Beethoven. Schubert attended his first concert in Vienna (Delacroix, Donizetti, Liszt, Rossini and George Sand came to the first night in Paris). He is best known as the composer of the *24 Caprices*

(1820), which was later adapted by Liszt, Schumann, Brahms and Rachmaninov.

Manner of Death: Having refused confession and the sacrament, Paganini – who was rumoured to have acquired his skills through a pact with the Devil – died without absolution in Nice on 27 May 1840, aged 57. Cause of death was a disease of the larynx. He spent his last hours improvising on the violin (legend insists it was the greatest performance of his life). He was denied burial in consecrated ground by the Bishop of Nice, so his body was embalmed and left on the deathbed for two months before being moved to the cellar for a year, then to an abandoned leper-house near Villefranche, then to Cap Ferrat, then (after an appeal to the Pope) to Genoa after nearly four years (April 1844). He was still not admitted to consecrated ground so was buried in the garden of the Villa Gaione before he was finally allowed a place in Parma cemetery (1926).

PEACOCK, Thomas Love (1785–1866) English novelist, poet and playwright

Thomas Love Peacock was born in Melcombe Regis near Weymouth, Dorset, at 2 am on 18 October 1785, the only child of Samuel Peacock, a London glass merchant who died when he was three. His mother – who greatly liked reading Gibbon – was Sarah Love, the daughter of a sea-captain and a relative of Admiral Sir Henry Ommanay Love. After his father's death he moved with his mother to Gogmoor Hall, Chertsey, Surrey, home of his grandfather Captain Thomas Love RN. Educated at Wick's Academy, Englefield Green, Surrey, from the age of eight to 14, he did not go to university but worked at first as a clerk for Ludlow Fraser & Company, London, and in 1800 won a prize for a poem in the *Monthly Preceptor* magazine (as did Leigh Hunt). Then, with family help, he was appointed Secretary to Admiral Sir Home Brooks Popham and spent a year aboard his ship HMS *Venerable* (1808). Imprisoned for debt (1815) he joined the East India Company in 1818 as a clerk under James Mill (another colleague was Edward Strachey, grandfather of Lytton Strachey, and Charles Lamb worked in the accounts department). When Mill died he succeeded him as Chief Examiner (1836), retiring in 1856 and being himself succeeded by Mill's son, the philosopher J. S. Mill. He was also music critic for the *Examiner* and *Globe and Traveller*. His writings included the satirical romances *Headlong Hall* (1816), *Melincourt* (1817) and *Nightmare Abbey* (1818).

Family/Sex Life: Peacock's engagement to Fanny Falkner was broken off because of objections by her parents, so instead he married Jane Gryffydh, daughter of a Welsh parson-schoolmaster and described by Shelley as a 'white Snowdonian antelope'. Peacock met her on a holiday, but did not contact her for eight years before suddenly proposing by letter on East India House notepaper. They married in 1819; their daughter Mary Ellen became George Meredith's first wife, but later eloped and had a son with the painter Henry Wallis, while their other children were Margaret Love, Edward Gryffydh and Rosa Jane. They also adopted village girl Mary Rosewall, who looked like Margaret (who died aged three).

Appearance: A handsome man with dark eyes and flaxen hair in his youth, Peacock was clean-shaven but for long sideburns. He wore a white tie and an old-fashioned tailcoat in old age.

Habits/Mannerisms: Peacock nursed an obsessive horror of fire all his life (a fire actually broke out in his house just before his death). He also hated gas and tobacco.

Sport/Hobbies: Peacock wrote riddles (and gave the solution to the famous unsolved riddle *Aelia Laelia Crispis*). He was also good at French, Italian and the classics, taught himself Spanish, and was very fond of Mozart and Italian opera.

Religion/Politics: Agnostic, though later in life he filled his study with pictures of St Catherine.

Temperament: Kind-hearted and friendly, he was described as 'a very mild agreeable man, and a good scholar' by Shelley. Shelley also observed that 'his fine wit/ Makes such a wound, the knife is lost in it.' Shelley was among his closest friends – Peacock lived with him for a while and became his literary executor; he also corrected the proofs of Shelley's *Prometheus Unbound* while Shelley was in Italy and broke the news of his death to Sir Timothy Shelley. Other friends were Sir Henry Cole (who edited a collected edition of his works), Edward Hookham (son of Shelley's publisher Thomas Hookham, who published all Peacock's books after *Palmyra*), Shelley's friend Sir John Cam Hobhouse (later Lord Broughton) and Thackeray.

Pets: He kept cats and dogs.

Work/Daily Routine: Peacock began as a poet but stopped writing poetry in 1818. His first novel did not appear till he was 30. In *Nightmare Abbey* he satirized Shelley (Scythrop Glowry), Byron (Mr Cypress) and Coleridge (Mr Flosky). He greatly admired Burns but disliked Keats and Lamb. Edmund Wilson observed that his books were 'more like operas than novels' and he did in fact write an operatic version of his play *Maid Marian*, produced at Covent Garden (1822), and it was 'all the rage' (Thackeray), being translated into French and German. He wrote *Gryll Grange* (1860–1) aged 75 but otherwise had not written a novel for over 30 years since *Crotchet Castle* (1831).

Motto/Saying: 'The world is a stage, and life is a farce, and he that laughs most has profited of the performance' (Friar Tuck in *Maid Marian*).

Manner of Death: After the shock of the fire in the roof over his bedroom at his home in Lower Halliford near Chertsey, Surrey, Peacock moved into the library and died not long afterwards, on 23 January 1866, aged 80. He was buried in the New Cemetery, Shepperton.

PEPYS, Samuel (1633–1703) English diarist and Admiralty official

Samuel Pepys was born on 23 February 1633 in Salisbury Court, near St Bride's Church, Fleet Street, London. The son of John Pepys, a tailor, and Margaret Knight, he was one of 11 children of whom only three survived childhood. His paternal great-aunt was married to Sir Sydney Mountagu, brother of the 1st Earl of Manchester, Charles I's Lord Treasurer. He had two brothers, Tom (who was reputedly homosexual and died of smallpox) and John (Clerk to Trinity House) and a sister Paulina. Educated at Oliver Cromwell's old school, Huntingdon Grammar, and at St Paul's School, London, he later studied at Magdalene College, Cambridge (BA 1654, Dryden was a fellow student). He then rose, aided by the influence of his father's cousin Edward Mountagu, Earl of Sandwich, to become Secretary of the Admiralty (1673), MP for Castle Rising and Harwich, Justice of the Peace, President of the Royal Society and Master of Trinity House. A close confidant of Charles II and James I, he was twice sent to the Tower (1679, 1690), for misdemeanours in the Admiralty ('I believe unjustly' – Evelyn, 1679) and for being pro-James II. He also ran a privateer, *The Flying Greyhound*. When James II was forced to leave the country Pepys gave up his job and retired to Clapham. He is remembered now for his famous *Diary* (1660–9), a vivid record of his times and an entertaining account of his own character.

Family/Sex Life: In 1655 Pepys married 15-year-old Elizabeth St Michel, the daughter of the Huguenot expatriate Alexander Le Marchant, Sieur de St Michel. She died in 1669 and they had no children – a circumstance that Pepys blamed on his wife's diseased womb (though in fact Pepys was sterile). He had numerous affairs and after his wife's death lived openly with Mary Skinner, niece of Milton's friend Cyriack Skinner (to whom the poet wrote a sonnet) and sister of Daniel Skinner, Milton's last amanuensis.

Appearance: Five feet one inch tall, Pepys was squat, with large enquiring eyes and a sensual mouth. He was foppish about dress, wearing silk shirts, a velvet cloak, buckled shoes and a wig.

Habits/Mannerisms: Pepys often ate at midnight and preferred strong wines (especially from Greece, Italy, Spain and Portugal). He owned a coach decorated with battle-scenes and ships of the line and also had a personal barge. On his 36th birthday (1669) he kissed the 200-year-old embalmed body of Katherine de Valois (wife of Henry V) on the mouth in Westminster Abbey and declared it was the first time he had kissed a queen.

Sport/Hobbies: Pepys sang and played the bass viol, lute and flageolet, which he practised at dawn at home and in St James's Park. He collected clocks, maps, globes, microscopes and model ships. His extensive library was arranged by size of books not by subject matter. Another pleasure was the theatre and he reported his reaction to the plays he saw in his diary – though he found Shakespeare's *The Tempest* 'no great wit, yet good, above ordinary plays' he considered *Romeo and Juliet* the worst play he had ever seen.

Religion/Politics: A Tory, he supported the Roundheads in the Civil War. In 1679 he was accused of complicity in the Popish Plot.

Health: From his youth Pepys suffered from kidney or bladder stones and underwent three operations to remove them. Other ailments included eczema and high fevers, for which he took green hazelnuts and lapis calaminaris as a general panacea. A deterioration in his eyesight in 1669 prompted him to give up writing his celebrated diary (though this would in the opinion of modern physicians have made little difference). In fact, he did briefly resume diary-writing while posted to Tangier with Lord Dartmouth in 1683.

Temperament: According to John Evelyn in 1703, Pepys was 'a very worthy Industrious and curious person, none in England exceeding him in the Knowledge of the Navy ... was universaly [sic] beloved, Hospitable, Generous, Learned in many things, skill'd in Musick'. Other friends included Robert Hooke and Christopher Wren. The diary reveals other sides to his character, however, depicting him as not only unfaithful but cowardly, beating servants and even once blackening his wife's eye (his wife's birthday is never mentioned). He was also mean with money and accepted bribes.

Pets: The last descendant of Pepys's cat was Brutus, who lived at the National Gallery until his death in 1933. Pepys also loved to hear the singing of caged canaries.

Work/Daily Routine: Pepys worked up to 18 or 20 hours a day by candlelight. He wrote his diary in a coded shorthand system, disguising salacious material in Spanish, French and Latin. The code was only finally cracked in 1825 (by John Smith, after three years' study). Other writings included a history of the Navy, *Navalia*.

Motto: *'Mens cujusque is est quisque'* ('What a man's mind is, that is what he is').

Manner of Death: Pepys died in Clapham in his adopted home, the house of his former colleague Will Hewer, at 3.47 am on 26 May 1703, aged 70. He had requested Evelyn to be a pallbearer, but Evelyn was unable to attend. He was buried in St Olave's Church, Hart Street, London.

PETER I 'The Great' (1672–1725) Tsar of Russia

Peter the Great was born in Moscow at 1 am on 30 May 1672, the first child of Tsar Alexis Mikhailovich (who died when Peter was three and a half) and his second wife Natalya Naryshkina. He had two older half-brothers Ivan and Fedor, an older half-sister Sophia and a younger sister Natalya. Peter was elected to power in preference to Ivan (who was frail and half-blind) but Sophia objected and many of Peter's mother's family were murdered by the Kremlin guard with the result that Peter and Ivan ruled jointly with Sophia as regent – the first time in Europe that two co-equal male monarchs had been crowned (1682). After Ivan's death (1696) Peter ruled alone. When he visited England (1698) and was lent John Evelyn's house at Sayes Court, Deptford, his retinue vandalized it, burnt 50 chairs, flattened 400 feet of holly hedge, tore up sheets and feather beds, used pictures for target practice, etc. Influenced by what he had seen in Europe, Peter spent much of his 43-year reign promoting reform of Russian trade and industry and reorganizing government and administrative, cultural, social, military and financial institutions (often with some harshness). He also expanded Russian territory to the west and south-east. In revenge for the murder of his mother's family in the Kremlin, Moscow,

he built a new capital, St Petersburg, and transferred his court there.

Family/Sex Life: In 1689 Peter married Eudoxia Lopukhina. In 1718 their son Alexis died of apoplexy after receiving 40 lashes on being implicated in a plot against his father. Their second son, Alexander, died young. After the failure of his first marriage, Peter took as his second wife his Lithuanian mistress Martha Skavronskaya – renamed Catherine (later Catherine I) when she adopted the Orthodox faith. Peter had numerous children by her, of whom only two survived – Anne (mother of Peter II) and the Empress Elizabeth (a sex maniac and transvestite who often dressed as a Dutch sailor).

Appearance: Six feet seven inches tall, Peter walked with a slight stoop. Saint-Simon described him as 'a very tall man, well proportioned, rather thin with a roundish face, a broad forehead and handsome, sharply defined eyebrows ... His lips were rather thick, his complexion a ruddy brown, fine black eyes, large, lively, and well apart ... a nervous twitching smile ... which contorted his face and his whole expression and inspired fear.' He had a wart on his right cheek, calloused hands from sailing, auburn hair and sported a small waxed moustache. He preferred old clothes and never wore a wig until the end of his life (he had his head shaved for the summer). He never had a hat in summer but in winter wore the tricorn hat of the Preobrazhensky Regiment.

Habits/Mannerisms: The left side of Peter's face twitched uncontrollably when he was agitated. This twitch sometimes led to convulsions and loss of consciousness. He took snuff and drank kummel (aniseed water) in the mornings and beer and wine in the afternoons. He had a huge appetite and liked hard brown bread, cabbage soup, stew, pork with sour-cream sauce, cold roast meat with pickled cucumbers or salted lemons, lamphreys, ham, vegetables and Limburger cheese. He never ate fish. When in London he liked to travel incognito. His court included dwarfs and also the seven-feet-two-inch-tall giant Nicholas Bourgeois.

Sport/Hobbies: Peter disliked hunting but liked ships and sailing. His favourite game was chess (he had a portable folding leather board). He enjoyed working with his hands, doing manual labour etc. Another interest was medicine and he often assisted physicians in operations. On one occasion a courtier came to him for help with his wife, who refused to allow the dentist to extract an aching tooth. Peter gathered his tools and personally pulled out the woman's tooth (only later did he learn that the husband had engineered the incident to get revenge for a domestic squabble and that her teeth had been perfectly all right).

Health: Peter was very strong and was reputedly able to break silver coins with his fingers. Health problems included syphilis and measles (1684).

Religion/Politics: Russian Orthodox.

Temperament: Peter was bad-tempered and ruthless. He had a mistress's former lover executed and his head preserved in alcohol and kept by the bed as a warning. He often hit or caned subordinates, but was himself terrified of cockroaches.

Work/Daily Routine: Peter rose early, dined at 10 am, had supper at 7 pm, and went to bed before 9 pm. On 1 January 1700 he changed the Russian calendar, which ran from the 'beginning of time' (1698 was formerly 7206) and which placed New Year on 1 September, to the Julian Calendar (then in use in the West). Unfortunately the West changed from the Julian to the Gregorian calendar in 1752, leaving Russia out of step once more until the Gregorian calendar was adopted in 1918. In another attempt to westernize Russia, as it was then fashionable in Europe to be clean-shaven, he introduced a tax on beards (1698).

Manner of Death: Peter suffered from strangury, a stone in his urethra preventing him urinating; when he caught cold after jumping into the sea to help rescue a foundering ship in November 1724 this led to complications and fever. He died at 6 am on 28 January 1725, aged 52. The autopsy revealed gangrene around his bladder.

POE, Edgar Allan (1809–49) US poet and short-story writer

Edgar Allan Poe was born Edgar Poe on 19 January 1809 in Boston, Massachusetts, the second son of David Poe Jr, an actor, and the London-born actress Elizabeth Arnold. Both his parents had died by 1811 and the children were split up: his older brother, William Henry Leonard (died 1831), going to their grandparents, his younger sister Rosalie to a family in Richmond, Virginia. Edgar was brought up by foster parents (he was never legally adopted). These were his wealthy godparents, John Allan, a tobacco exporter, and Frances Keeling Valentine (he signed himself Edgar Allan Poe by 1824). John Allan moved to the UK to set up a branch of Ellis & Allan there and thus Edgar was educated in Irvine, Scotland, and at Manor House School, Stoke Newington, London (1815–20). The family returned to the USA in 1820 and Edgar studied at the University of Virginia (1826) but was expelled after only one term for gambling debts and never graduated. He then enlisted in the US Army as ' Edgar A. Perry', rose to become a regimental sergeant-major (1829) and attended West Point Military Academy (1830) to please Allan. However, when Allan's wife died and he remarried, Poe deliberately flunked and was expelled (1831) for 'gross neglect of duty' – in reality he had appeared on parade totally naked except for a white belt and gloves. He later became Assistant Editor of the *Southern Literary Messenger*, then co-Editor of *Burton's Gentleman's Magazine* (1839–40), and Literary Editor of the USA's then most popular magazine *Graham's Lady's and Gentleman's Magazine* (1841–2). He was later co-Editor then proprietor of the *Broadway Journal* (1845–6). In 1845 he achieved immediate fame with the poem 'The Raven'; among his other most celebrated writings were *Tales of the Grotesque and Arabesque* (1840) – which included 'The Fall of the House of Usher' – the short stories 'The Pit and the Pendulum' (1843) and 'The Cask of Amontillado' (1846), and the world's first detective story 'The Murders in the Rue Morgue' (1841), featuring the detective Dupin.

Family/Sex Life: In 1836 Poe, then aged 26, married his 13-year-old cousin Virginia Clemm, with whom he had lived in the same household (also with her mother, his aunt) since 1831. She died in 1847, after which Poe wrote little more. There has been speculation that Poe also had an affair with 21-year-old Mary Rogers, a pretty brunette and cigar-seller on Broadway who was found sexually assaulted and strangled in the Hudson River in New Jersey in 1841. The supposition that Poe may have been the murderer is based on the similarities between the case of Rogers and the events described in Poe's 'The Mystery of Marie Roget', published 18 months later. Poe evidently knew Rogers and she was seen shortly before her death walking with 'a tall dark man aged about 26'. Poe was never questioned about the murder (which remained unsolved) and in his story also failed to identify the killer. He once wrote, in the essay 'The Philosophy of Composition' (1846): 'The death of a beautiful woman is, unquestionably, the most poetical topic in the world.'

Appearance: Five feet eight inches tall, Poe had grey eyes, brown hair, a short moustache and a fair complexion. He habitually dressed in black with an old Army cape on his shoulders.

Habits/Mannerisms: He liked gambling and had very elegant handwriting.

Sport/Hobbies: A very good swimmer and runner, Poe once notched up a leap of 21 feet in the long-jump event while at West Point.

Religion/Politics: Presbyterian.

Health: Poe was epileptic and an alcoholic. He could not hold his drink – according to the *Dictionary of American Biography* 'Less than a little was with him too much.' He also took drugs (opium). He became mentally unbalanced after the death of his wife in 1847 and in November 1848 he attempted suicide by drinking laudanum.

Temperament: The *Dictionary of*

American Biography observed that Poe was 'Greatly loved by a few, hated by many, and memorable to everybody.'

Pets: Poe's tortoiseshell cat Caterina inspired the famous short story 'The Black Cat'.

Work/Daily Routine: Poe wrote riddles and acrostics (his first cryptogram appeared in 'The Narrative of Arthur Gordon Pym'). He began as a poet, his first efforts being published under the pseudonym 'Henri le Rennet'. His first collection of poems, *Tamerlaine and Other Poems* (1827), was published at his own expense under the pseudonym 'A Bostonian', when he was 18. His work was translated and promoted by Baudelaire and Mallarmé in Europe. His immensely successful poem 'The Raven' (first published in *New York Evening Mirror* in 1845) was inspired by his reading of Dickens's novel *Barnaby Rudge*.

Manner of Death: Poe died aged 40 in Baltimore, Maryland, on the morning of 7 October 1849, five days after being found semi-conscious and delirious, from a mixture of alcohol, heart failure and epilepsy. His last words were 'Lord help my poor soul.' He was buried in Westminster Presbyterian Church, Baltimore, his epitaph reading 'Quoth the Raven nevermore.'

POPE, Alexander (1688–1744) English poet and critic

Alexander Pope was born in Plough Court, 32 Lombard Street, London, on 21 May 1688, the son of Alexander Pope, a linen draper, by his second wife Edith Turner (one of whose sisters – Pope's godmother – married the painter Samuel Cooper). He had a half-sister, Magdalen Rackett, by his father's first marriage. Educated at schools in Twyford, Hyde Park (Mr Deane's Seminary) and Windsor Forest up to the age of 12, he was largely self-taught thereafter (he could not go to university because of his Roman Catholicism). He earned his reputation as a poet at the age of 16 with his *Pastorals* (1709) and, after the brilliant *Essay on Criticism* (1711), was introduced to London literary circles by William Wycherley. Pre-eminent among English literary figures for the next 30 years, he proved himself the master of the English heroic couplet in *The Rape of the Lock* (1712, 1714). Other celebrated writings included *The Dunciad* (1728, 1729, 1743), in which he lampooned many contemporary writers, Homer's *Iliad* (1720) and *Odyssey* (1725–6), *An Essay on Man* (1733–4) and *Moral Essays* (1731–5).

Family/Sex Life: Pope never married but nursed an unrequited love for Martha Blount and also for Lady Mary Wortley Montagu (with whom he remained close until they finally fell out in 1723).

Appearance: Pope was deformed and ceased to grow after the age of 12, remaining only four feet six inches tall. He had a handsome but drawn face with the muscles showing, a fine long nose and blue-grey eyes. He was clean-shaven and wore a greyish-yellow wig. He also wore three pairs of stockings because his legs were so thin and was so weak he could not dress without help and had to wear a 'bodice of stiff canvas'. For meals he was obliged to sit in a high chair at the table.

Habits/Mannerisms: Pope's parents lived with him at his house in Twickenham, but he also frequented Wills' Coffee House. After the publication of his vindictive poem *The Dunciad* he took to taking a dog and two loaded pistols for protection whenever he went for a walk. At night he liked to drink coffee; he also enjoyed highly seasoned dishes and potted lamphreys.

Sport/Hobbies: Pope was very interested in landscape gardening and wrote extensively on the subject. His garden at Twickenham boasted the second weeping willow planted in England, and it is claimed that virtually all weeping willows now growing in Britain are descended from this tree. The same is also true of weeping willows in the USA, the first tree there having been grown from a twig taken from Pope's willow by an English officer shortly before leaving for the American colonies. He sang well in his youth and was nicknamed the 'little nightingale' by those who heard him.

Religion/Politics: A Roman Catholic and Tory, he was obliged to leave London for a time in 1715 during the public backlash against the Jacobites.

Health: Pope enjoyed good health until the age of 12, but then suffered from crippling Pott's Disease (tuberculosis of the spine). He suffered constantly from headaches, asthma, neuralgia and insomnia.

Temperament: Pope, nicknamed the 'Wasp of Twickenham', rarely laughed but had a sweet smile and a musical voice in conversation. He was easily offended – Lytton Strachey observed that 'If you looked at him he would spit poison.' His friends included Gay and Swift (with whom he formed the Scriblerus Club, pillorying literary incompetence). He was particularly admired by Thackeray, who called him 'the highest among the poets, the highest among the English wits and humorists'. He made no apology for the 'waspishness' for which he was renowned, writing in his *Epilogue to the Satires*:

'Yes, I am proud to see
Men, not afraid of God, afraid of me.'

Pets: Pope kept a succession of Great Danes all called Bounce ('my only friend', celebrated in a poem by Gay). One of the puppies was presented to Frederick, Prince of Wales (father of George III) with a couplet by Pope on its collar:

'I am his Highness' dog at Kew;
Pray tell me, sir, whose dog are you?'

Work/Daily Routine: *The Rape of the Lock* was based on a real incident – 20-year-old Sir Robert Petre had surreptitiously cut off a lock of society beauty Lady Arabella Fermor's hair, thus causing a feud between the families (Pope dedicated his poem to Lady Arabella). Pope was a great plagiarist – according to Seward, 'Pope stole immensely, but his thefts were from obscure English poets of earlier times ...' He often wrote on the backs of letters etc. (most of his translation of *The Iliad* was written thus) and was thereby dubbed by Swift 'Paper-sparing Pope'. The translations of Homer did not meet with universal approval, however. The classical scholar Richard Bentley admonished the poet, saying of the *Iliad*: 'It is a pretty poem, Mr Pope, but you must not call it Homer.'

Manner of Death: Pope died on 30 May 1744, aged 56. As he lay dying his doctor attempted to reassure him that he would recover, pointing out a host of encouraging signs. Pope only responded: 'Here am I, dying of a hundred good symptoms.' He was buried in Twickenham Church.

POUND, Ezra Weston Loomis (1885–1972) US poet and critic

Ezra Pound was born in Hailey, Idaho, on 30 October 1885 the son of Homer Loomis Pound, Registrar of the US Land Office in Hailey and later Assistant Assayer at the US Mint in Philadelphia. His grandfather was Thaddeus Coleman Pound, Governor of Wisconsin (three times elected to Congress), who owned the Union Lumbering Company and built three railways. Pound was also the great-nephew of Longfellow on the side of his mother, Isabel (though he never admired Longfellow's poetry). Educated at Chelten Hills School, Wyncote, near Philadelphia, he entered Cheltenham Military Academy aged 12 (1897), then attended Cheltenham Township High School, leaving in 1901 to study Arts and Science at the University of Pennsylvania, aged 15 (a fellow student being William Carlos Williams). In 1903 he transferred to Hamilton College, New York State (graduated 1905), then returned to the University of Pennsylvania to study Romance Languages (MA 1906) and became Harrison Fellow of Romance Languages there (1906–7). He began a PhD on 'The Role of the Gracioso in the Plays of Lope de Vega' but did not finish it. He then lectured at Wabash College, Indiana (1907–8) but was sacked after four months and came to the UK where he was Lecturer in Medieval Romance Literature at the Regent Street Polytechnic, London (1908–10). Thereafter he contributed freelance to such magazines as *New Age* and Ford Madox Ford's *English Review* and became Foreign Editor of *Poetry* (Chicago). Co-editor (with Wyndham Lewis) of *Blast*, he invented the name 'Vorticism' with himself and Lewis as the movement's main proponents and *Blast* its organ. He also translated Anglo-Saxon and Chinese and lived in Paris (1920–4) and Rapallo, Italy (from 1925). During World War II he made pro-Mussolini broadcasts on Italian radio and

was arrested in 1945 by the US forces as a traitor. Judged insane, he was confined to St Elizabeth's mental home in Washington (1946–58), and later returned to Italy. He was a member of the National Institute of Art and Letters in the USA (1938). His most celebrated poems were the long series published as *The Cantos* (1930–59).

Family/Sex Life: In 1905 Pound was unofficially engaged to the poet Hilda Doolittle ('H. D.'), daughter of the Professor of Astronomy at the University of Pennsylvania. In 1914, however, he married Dorothy Shakespear, daughter of an English solicitor and the novelist friend of Yeats, Olivia Shakespear; their children were Mary and Omar Shakespear. He also had an affair with the US violinist Olga Rudge (who bore him the illegitimate child Maria Rudge).

Appearance: Five feet 10 inches tall, Pound had grey-blue eyes and brown hair brushed up vertically above his forehead. He also sported a moustache and a goatee beard in his youth (later a full beard). He modelled his dress on Whistler's.

Habits/Mannerisms: William Carlos Williams described Pound as 'gingerly and temperate'. He smoked in his youth but disliked alcohol and was drunk only three times in his life. He hated the sound of church bells and disliked the telephone (the 'gorbloody tHellerfone').

Sport/Hobbies: Pound was taught to box by Hemingway and also enjoyed tennis, fencing, swimming and skating. He liked carpentry, played chess and owned statues by Henri Gaudier-Brzeska. He also wrote operas and violin music (he owned a Dolmetsch clavichord).

Religion/Politics: Pound had a Presbyterian upbringing (his father taught Sunday School). Later he became anti-Semitic and pro-Fascist and interested in astrology. He wrote articles for Mosley's *Fascist Quarterly* in the UK and steadfastly maintained his support for Mussolini. After his release from St Elizabeth's, undaunted, he returned to Italy and joined the neo-Fascists (1961), as well as continuing to write for the right-wing press.

Health: Pound suffered from appendicitis (1924), a urinary infection (1961), had a prostate operation (1961) and also had an anal fistula. He spent 12 years incarcerated in St Elizabeth's mental asylum.

Temperament: Called Ra (pronounced Ray) by his family, he included among his friends T. S. Eliot (it was Pound who christened him 'Old Possum'), Yeats, D. H. Lawrence, Edmund Dulac and Wyndham Lewis.

Pets: Pound regularly fed some 20 stray cats who gathered daily outside his house in Rapallo, Italy.

Work/Daily Routine: Pound greatly admired Yeats and helped to promote the work of Joyce and Eliot. Eliot dedicated *The Waste Land* to him – 'For Ezra Pound, *il miglior fabbro*' ('the better craftsman'), while Yeats called him 'the solitary volcano in modern poetry'. Pound's first published poem was the unsigned 'Ezra on the Strike' in *Jenkintown Time-Chronicle* (1902). He self-published his first book of poems, *A Lume Spento* (1908) in an addition of 100 copies and reviewed it himself anonymously in the *Evening Standard*. His early poetry was described in *Punch* in 1909 as a 'blend of the imagery of the unfettered West, the vocabulary of Wardour Street, and the sinister abandon of Borgiac Italy'. He also wrote ghost stories for the *Ladies' Home Journal* (1908). Composer Walter Morse Rummell (grandson of Samuel Morse) set one of his poems to music. He once tried writing a novel but failed and burnt it, conceding that 'the feminine power of endurance is beyond me'.

Manner of Death: Pound died of a 'sudden blockage of the intestine' in the Hospital of SS Giovanni e Paolo, Venice, at 8 pm on Wednesday 1 November 1972. He was buried on Venice's municipal cemetery island, San Michele, his body being carried there by gondola.

PROUST, Marcel (1871–1922) French novelist

Marcel Proust was born in Auteuil, Paris, on 10 July 1871, the son of Professor Adrien Proust, an eminent physican, and Jeanne Weil, daughter of a Jewish stockbroker. He had a younger brother Robert. Educated at the Lycée Condorcet and at the Sorbonne under the philosopher Bergson (who was a relative), he graduated in law (1893) and philosophy (1895). He worked at first on the staff of the Mazarine Library (1895–1900) and volunteered for service in the 76th Infantry Regiment in Orléans (remaining in the ranks for one year). Increasingly reclusive after the death of his mother in 1905, he produced the first part of his massive 13-volume masterpiece *À la recherche du temps perdu* (Remembrance of Things Past) in 1912. He was awarded the Prix Goncourt for *À l'ombre des jeunes filles en fleurs* (another part of *À la recherche*) in 1919 and won the Légion d'honneur a year later.

Family/Sex Life: Proust was a homosexual. His lovers/secretaries included Reynaldo Hahn, Lucien Daudet (journalist/writer son of author Alphonse Daudet), Alfred Agostinelli (his chauffeur), Henri Rochat and Robert Ulrich.

Appearance: Five feet six inches tall, Proust had very large, round, intense black eyes and a very white complexion. He had black hair and wore a thick walrus moustache in his 30s (he had a thick black beard when he died). He wore a dark fur coat summer and winter and also favoured a violet velvet cloak.

Habits/Mannerisms: To keep out pollen, dust and noise, Proust always kept the windows closed and the curtains drawn. He slept most of the day, wearing a night-shirt and woollen jackets in bed. His bedroom was decorated with Whistler's portrait of Carlyle. When he went out, he frequented the Café Weber and the Restaurant Larne near La Madeleine. He drank large quantities of strong black coffee and tipped servants extravagantly. In 1917 he lived in the Paris Ritz. He was soft-spoken, was a good mimic and liked pansies (the only flower his asthma allowed him near). During the last five months of his life he reputedly ate only ice cream, beer and *café au lait*.

Religion/Politics: Proust was half-Jewish but was brought up as a Roman Catholic. Like Zola, he was pro-Dreyfus and collected 3000 signatures for the petition for his release in 1897–9.

Health: Proust suffered severely from asthma from the age of nine and was reduced as an adult to the condition of an invalid (he inhaled Legras Powder for it and smoked anti-asthma cigarettes). Related ailments included hay fever and insomnia (he took Veronal to sleep). A hypochondriac, he became very ill in 1902 and in 1922 burnt his stomach when he

accidentally swallowed undiluted adrenalin.

Temperament: Proust lived the life of a 'social butterfly' until his mother died (1905) when he was 35, after which he became reclusive and devoted himself to the writing of *À la recherche*. A courageous man, in 1897 he fought a duel with pistols with the journalist Jean Lorrain.

Work/Daily Routine: Proust lived in a soundproof cork-lined flat in his aunt's house at 102 Boulevard Haussman, Paris (he later moved to the fifth floor of a house in the Rue Hamelin). He worked at night, in his bed, and did considerable rewriting at proof stage. He used dozens of pens in case he dropped one, because his fear of catching germs prevented him picking them up. His first writings were published in *Le Banquet* (1892) and *La Revue blanche* (1893). His first book was *Les Plaisirs et les jours* (with a Preface by Anatole France). His masterpiece, *À la recherche*, 1.25 million words long, was inspired by memories that came flooding back with the taste of some madeleine cakes. The first volume (*Du Côté de chez Swann*, 1903) was rejected by three publishers (including André Gide for *Nouvelle Revue Française*) and was only published by Grasset (unread) because Proust offered to pay for its publication. He dedicated *Du Côté de chez Swann* to Gaston Calmette, editor of *Figaro*. The author Françoise Sagan (real name Françoise Quoirez) took her name from Proust's character the Princesse de Sagan.

Manner of Death: Proust died of bronchitis and pneumonia at 44 Rue Hamelin, Paris (near the Trocadero), on 18 November 1922, aged 51.

PUSHKIN, Alexander Sergeevich (1799–1837)
Russian poet, novelist and playwright

Alexander Pushkin was born in Nemetskaya Street, Moscow, on 6 June 1799, the son of Sergey Pushkin, an army major (whose family had helped elect the Romanovs to the throne), and Nadezdha Hannibal. His maternal great-grandfather was an Abyssinian negro slave, Abram Petrovich Hannibal, who was given as a present to Peter the Great and later became General-in-Chief to Empress Elizabeth. He had an older sister Olga. Taught at first by an English governess, Miss Bailey, and by French tutors, he was a student at the exclusive Lycée founded in a wing of the Tsarkoye Selo Palace in St Petersburg and opened by Tsar Alexander I. The 30 pupils included Prince Vladimir Gorchakov, and Pushkin's French teacher was the brother of Marat. He entered government service in 1817, but his liberal views, expressed in revolutionary epigrams, soon encountered opposition and he was sent into exile in 1820, only returning to Moscow on the accession (1826) of Tsar Nicholas I, who later recognized his genius by making him a Junior Gentleman of the Bedchamber (1833). Having established his reputation as a poet with *Ruslan and Lyudmila* (1820), he consolidated his standing as Russia's foremost writer with such works as the novel *Evgeni Onegin* (1823–31) – which is generally recognized as his most sophisticated creation and his masterpiece – and the blank verse historical tragedy *Boris Godunov* (1831). After 1831 he concentrated primarily on his prose writing. As founder and editor of *The Contemporary* he published Gogol's work.

Family/Sex Life: In 1832 Pushkin married Natalya Goncharova. Their children were Maria, Alexander, Grigory and Natalya.

Appearance: Five feet three inches tall, Pushkin was slender, blue-eyed and white-skinned but had a negroid profile, with thick protruding lips. Turgenev referred to his 'small swarthy face, his African lips ... his droopy sidewhiskers ... high forehead, almost without eyebrows, and his curly hair'. He wore long side-whiskers and had wavy chestnut hair, good teeth and very long claw-like fingernails. His expression was usually very gloomy.

Habits/Mannerisms: He took a cold bath every morning.

Sport/Hobbies: Pushkin was very agile. He spoke English and French and was fond of French literature. He gambled heavily at cards.

Religion/Politics: An atheist, Pushkin was nonetheless very superstitious. In politics he held strongly nationalistic Socialist views, though his liberalism caused his temporary exile in 1820. Only his absence from Moscow prevented him taking an active role in the revolt of the Decembrists.

Health: Pushkin contracted typhoid in 1818 and also suffered from a varicose vein in his right leg.

Temperament: Known as Sashka at home, Pushkin was called 'the most intelligent man in Russia' by no less an admirer than Tsar Nicholas I. He was, though, very vain and often challenged people who offended him to duels. His friends included the writer Gogol. After hearing Gogol reading *Dead Souls*, Pushkin burst into laughter and then grew suddenly serious, exclaiming: 'Oh God, how sad our Russia is!'

Work/Daily Routine: Pushkin published some of his short stories under the name 'Ivan Petrovich Belkin'. He was greatly influenced by Byron, while one of his own unfinished works inspired Tolstoy's *Anna Karenina*.

Manner of Death: At 5 pm on 8 February 1837 Pushkin was shot in the stomach and sustained a shattered thigh bone in a pistol duel with his brother-in-law (who was married to his wife's sister Catherine) Baron Georges Heeckeren D'Anthès (a Frenchman in Russian service). D'Anthès was the nephew and adopted son of the Dutch Ambassador in St Petersburg, Baron van Heeckeren, and was a known crack shot – the duel (which was fought in sub-zero temperatures) arose after D'Anthès took a fancy to Pushkin's wife. The mortally wounded Pushkin subsequently died in his lavish flat on the Moyka Embankment overlooking the Winter Palace, St Petersburg, at 2.45 pm on Friday 10 February 1837, aged 37. Just before his death he managed to eat a few cloudberries. 20,000 mourners paid their respects at the funeral. He was buried at Svytogorsk Monastery (though none of his relatives were present).

RABELAIS, François (c.1494–1553) French writer

François Rabelais was born at La Devinière, near Chinon, Touraine, the youngest son of Antoine Rabelais, a landowning lawyer, and an unnamed member of the Frapin family. He had two brothers, Janet and Antoine, and a sister. At first he was a Franciscan monk in the monastery of Fontenay-le-Comte, Bas-Poitou (1521), then, by special permission of Pope Clement VII, he became a Benedictine at the monastery of Saint-Pierre at Maillezais near Poitiers and secretary to Geoffroy d'Estessac, abbott of the monastery and Bishop of Maillezais. He then studied law at the prestigious University of Poitiers, was tutor to the Bishop of Maillezais' nephew Louis and worked as a secular priest in Paris. After taking a degree in medicine at the University of Montpellier (1530) he was a proof-reader for the German printer Sebastian Gryphius in Lyons. In 1532, he was appointed Chief Physician at the Grand Hôtel-Dieu de Nôtre Dame de Pitié du Pont-du-Rhône (the main hospital) in Lyons. Created Doctor of Medicine (1537) he lectured on Galen, Hippocrates and anatomy at the University of Montpellier and edited medical books. One of the most famous physicians of his day, he was among the first to teach medicine using dissection of corpses and was personal physician to the Bishop of Paris, Cardinal Jean du Bellay (later French Ambassador to Rome), when he visited the Pope to petition for the withdrawal of the sentence of excommunication of Henry VIII of England. With Du Bellay's help Rabelais entered service with the Cardinal's brother Guillaume du Bellay, Lord of Langey, and was appointed Master of the King's Requests under Henri II of France before fleeing France to the free town of Metz (1546). Again with help from the Cardinal he was then appointed Canon of St Maur and later (1550) non-resident curé of Meudon. He later resigned this post (1553). His most famous satirical writings were *Gargantua* (1534) and *Pantagruel* (1533) and the sequels *Tiers Livre* (1546), *Quart Livre* (1548–52) and *Cinquième Livre*, which was published posthumously in 1562–4.

Family/Sex Life: Rabelais is known to have fathered an illegitimate son named Théodule (who died at the age of two).

Appearance: He had short hair, a beard

and a long nose. As a Franciscan monk he wore an ash-coloured serge habit.

Habits/Mannerisms: Rabelais was very fond of larch trees, and also of *cannabis sativa* (hemp).

Religion/Politics: Roman Catholic. His scurrilous satires on ecclesiastical institutions caused some difficulty for him and his books were banned by the University of Paris as obscene (1533).

Temperament: Rabelais was naturally inclined to gaiety, as evidenced by the uproarious and often earthy humour of his most famous comic writing. He was also cunning. When he wanted to travel to Paris but found himself unable to afford the fare, he conspicuously placed three small bags on the table of the inn where he was stranded and labelled them 'Poison for the King', 'Poison for Monsieur' and 'Poison for the Dauphin'. Word quickly reached the authorities and he was promptly hauled off to Paris to be inter-rogated – there he explained the fraud and was set free, thus attaining his destination.

Work/Daily Routine: Rabelais's first published work was a translation of *Medical Letters* by Dr Jean Manardi and the *Aphorisms* of Hippocrates (both 1532). He also wrote on archaeology and medicine and edited *Topography of Rome*. He first published *Pantagruel* under the anagrammatic pseudonym 'Alcofrybas

Nasier' (Françoys Rabelais). The giant Pantagruel, son of the giant Gargantua, was identified by many as Henri II of France; Rabelais himself explained the name was derived from the Greek *panta* (meaning 'all') and Arabic *gruel* (meaning 'thirsty'), a reference to the fact that he was born during a drought. Most of the foodstuffs, flora and fauna described in *Pantagruel* and *Gargantua* are from his home province of Poitou. *Pantagruel* and *Gargantua* became immensely popular, with 98 editions being issued in France alone in the 16th century. Admirers in France included La Fontaine, Molière, Racine, Hugo, Montaigne, Voltaire, Balzac and Gautier. Across the Channel Jonathan Swift and Laurence Sterne were at one time or another identified as 'The English Rabelais'. Rabelais made very little money from his books: his will is supposed to have read: 'I owe much. I possess nothing. I give the rest to the poor.'

Manner of Death: Rabelais died (most probably) on 9 April 1553 in Paris, reputedly aged 70 (though his most likely year of birth was 1494). He retained his sense of humour to the end – shortly before his demise he was discovered sitting on his bed dressed in a domino (a mask and cloak): when asked to explain he punned *'Beati qui in Domino moriuntur'* ('Blessed are they who die in the Lord/a domino'). He was buried in St Paul's, Paris, his epitaph being supplied by Ronsard.

RALEGH, Walter (c.1552–1618) English naval commander, explorer and writer

Walter Ralegh was born in Hayes Barton, Devon, the second son of Walter Ralegh, a landowner, by his third wife, Katharine Gilbert, née Champernowne, daughter of Sir Philip Champernowne and sister of Arthur Champernowne, Vice-Admiral of Devon. He had an elder brother, Sir Carew

Ralegh MP, a sister Margaret, three half-brothers by his mother's first marriage to Otho Gilbert (Adrian Gilbert, Sir John Gilbert and the explorer Sir Humphrey Gilbert), two more by his father's first wife (George and John Ralegh), and a half-sister by his father's second wife (Mary

Ralegh). His cousin was the famous sea-captain Sir Richard Grenville. Educated at Oriel College, Oxford (for one year, aged 14–15), his first command was as captain of the privateer *Falcon* against the Spanish. He also served with the Protestant rebel Huguenot forces in France for five years (from 1569), fought in Ireland and was commander during the massacre of Smerwick in which 600 Spanish mercenaries were killed. He was later Warden of the Stannaries (tin mines), Lord Lieutenant of Cornwall, Captain of the Queen's Guard and MP for Devonshire (later Cornwall and Dorset). An explorer of the New World, he was the founder of Virginia (named after Elizabeth I, the 'Virgin Queen') but fell from favour after the accession of James I, being sentenced to death in 1603 and subsequently spending 12 years in the Tower of London before undertaking a last expedition to the New World in search of gold (1617). His name was pronouced 'raw-ly' and was spelt 'Rauley' or 'Rauleygh' *c.*1578 until he adopted 'Ralegh' on his father's death (1581) – he never spelt it 'Raleigh'.

Family/Sex Life: History is unclear whether Ralegh had an actual affair with Elizabeth I around the time when he was 30 and she was 49 – certainly they were close. He attracted her attention by using a diamond to scratch on a glass pane the lines: 'Fain would I climb, yet fear I to fall', to which the queen responded with the lines: 'If thy heart fail thee, climb not at all.' In 1592 Elizabeth was furious when she learned of his love for her maid of honour Elizabeth Throgmorton and had them both imprisoned in the Tower. Ralegh later married Throgmorton; the marriage produced the children Walter (killed on an expedition to Venezuela), Carew and Damerei (who died young).

Appearance: Six feet tall, well-built and handsome, Ralegh had a long nose, thick brown curly hair, a trim pointed beard and was always well dressed. According to Aubrey, ' He had a most remarkable aspect, an exceedingly high forehead, long-faced and sour eie-lidded, a kind of pigge-eie. His Beard turned up naturally.' Portraits show that he wore a fashionable single jewel in his ear.

Habits/Mannerisms: Ralegh spoke with a broad Devonshire accent throughout his life, though 'his voice was small' (Aubrey). He was the first Englishman of rank to smoke – the story goes that his servant, seeing the smoke rising from his master, doused him with a bowl of water. He supposedly introduced from the New World the potato (Drake brought back the sweet potato), bringing it from Virginia to his lands in Ireland (*c.*1585). He also brought the first specimen of mahogany to England and kept in his household a West Indian called Leonard.

Sport/Hobbies: A member of the Society of Antiquaries, Ralegh was also adept in herbal medicine – a cordial he devised to counter fever was later used by Robert Boyle. It was said that he once employed herbal medicine to make himself appear like a leper in order to avoid arrest.

Religion/Politics: Ralegh believed in God but not in Christ. Though not technically an atheist, he was nonetheless condemned as one alongside Marlowe. In 1603 his political views led to his imprisonment in the Tower on charges of high treason.

Health: Ralegh's health was good, though he tried to stab himself when imprisoned by James I.

Temperament: Bold but 'damnably proud' (Aubrey), Ralegh was twice imprisoned in 1580 for fighting duels. He was the essence of Renaissance man, still remembered for his chivalry (exemplified by his throwing of an expensive cloak over a puddle so that Elizabeth I would not get her feet wet). His friends included Drake, Ben Jonson (tutor to Ralegh's son Walter), Marlowe, Spenser (of whom he was patron, and who called him 'The Shepherd of the Ocean') and the

Earl of Essex (godfather to his son Damerei).

Work/Daily Routine: While in the Tower Ralegh lived in comfortable apartments with his wife, son and servants and passed the time writing poems (sometimes under the pseudonym 'Ignoto') and (with several assistants) *The History of the World.* In Part I he got as far as 130 BC, but he gave the project up in a fit of despondency at Man's folly after witnessing two passers-by pick a quarrel outside his window. The single finished volume was the favourite book of Oliver Cromwell. He led two expeditions in search of the legendary El Dorado and built at his own expense the *Ark Ralegh* – later renamed the *Ark Royal,* flagship of the Royal Navy.

Manner of Death: Ralegh was beheaded by order of James I on Tower Hill on 29 October 1618, aged 66. The fact that it was also the Lord Mayor's Day with its attendant pageantry constituted a deliberate attempt to distract crowds from his death. He caused scandal by smoking a last pipe of tobacco before going to the scaffold and then coolly tested the axe's edge, remarking: 'It is a sharp remedy, but a sure one for all ills.' When advised that on placing his head on the block he should face east he replied: 'What matter how the head lie, so the heart be right?' His severed head was put in a red leather bag and sent to his widow, who carried it for the rest of her life. The rest of his body was buried in St Margaret's Church, Westminster.

REMBRANDT, Harmenszoon van Rijn (1606–69) Dutch painter and etcher

Rembrandt Harmenszoon van Rijn was born in the Weddesteeg, near the White Gate, Leiden, Holland, on 15 July 1606, the eighth of the nine children of Harmen Gerritszoon van Rijn, a miller (who owned a windmill), and Neeltgen Willems van Suydtbrouck, a baker's daughter. His siblings included an elder brother Adriaen and a younger sister Lijsbeth. Educated at the Latin School, Leiden, from the age of seven, he also studied briefly at Leiden University but left after a few months. He was then apprenticed to the architectural painter Jacob van Swanenburch for three years (in Leiden) then spent six months studying religious and mythological subjects in the Amsterdam studio of Pieter Lastman (1624) before setting up on his own (1625), sharing a studio with the artist Jan Lievens. Unlike many contemporaries he did not then undertake a tour of Italy to become better acquainted with the works of the Italian masters. Nonetheless, his historical paintings were soon selling for generous sums and his skill

as a portrait artist attracted wide attention; by 1629 his reputation was such that he felt confident enought to present a self-portrait and a portrait of his mother to Charles I of England. Among his most celebrated paintings were *The Anatomy Lesson of Dr Tulp* (1632), *The Night Watch* (1640–2), which depicted members of the local militia, *Bathsheba* (1654) and several acclaimed self-portraits, both as a young and as an old man. He was declared bankrupt in 1656.

Family/Sex Life: In 1634 Rembrandt married Saskia van Uylenburch, the cousin of a wealthy art dealer with whom the artist was closely associated. The marriage was happy, though only their son Titus survived of their four children; Saskia herself died not long after Titus's birth in 1642. Rembrandt then became involved with Titus's nurse, Geertghe Dircx, but this relationship ended in acrimony when the artist began to live openly with his housekeeper/mistress Hendrickje Stoffels

(1649). The discarded Dircx sued Rembrandt for breach of promise. Rembrandt was prevented from marrying Hendrickje Stoffels under the terms of his first wife's will and the local church council issued a formal warning to Stoffels about the sinfulness of her situation – but they continued to live together until her death in 1667. She bore him a daughter, Cornelia, in 1654.

Appearance: Rembrandt had a large, bulbous nose (with a depression at the tip dividing it in two), long curly dark brown hair and, in his youth, a small beard and moustache.

Habits/Mannerisms: Very frugal in his tastes, Rembrandt usually ate just bread and cheese or pickled herring and rarely went out socializing, preferring to stay at home. It is thought that he probably never left his native Holland. His one weakness, though, was his passion for art-collecting. Such was his extravagance in this regard that he was obliged to declare bankruptcy in 1656 (though this had no appreciable effect upon his output as a painter).

Religion/Politics: A Menmonite Protestant, he read frequently from the Bible.

Work/Daily Routine: Rembrandt worked ceaselessly at his art, producing numerous paintings, drawings and etchings. In all some 650 oil paintings, 1400 drawings and studies and 300 etchings have survived. Many of his portraits were commissions from the sitters; for others he used his wife, his son and himself as his models. His second wife, Hendrickje Stoffels, for instance, was the model for *A Woman Bathing, Girl in the Window* and *Bathsheba*. Rembrandt enjoyed success relatively early on his career and became reasonably wealthy, being able to afford to collect Italian paintings himself. The reduced financial circumstances of his last years meant that he had to give up this hobby and by the time of his death he owned little of value besides his painting equipment. He also had to cease socializing with his middle-class friends and find new companions among the less moneyed lower orders. He had many imitators; his pupil Carel Fabritius was perhaps the most promising (unfortunately Fabritius was killed when the powder magazine in Delft exploded in 1654).

Manner of Death: Rembrandt died in Amsterdam on 4 October 1669, aged 63. He was buried in the Westerkerk.

RICHARD I 'The Lionheart' (1157–99) King of England, Ireland and France

Richard I, 'Richard Coeur de Lion', was born in the royal palace of Beaumont, Oxford, on 8 September 1157, the eldest surviving son of Henry II (Henry Plantagenet, Count of Anjou) – ruler of the Angevin Empire that extended from the Scottish borders to the Pyrenees – and Eleanor Duchess of Aquitaine, the divorced queen of Louis VII of France and 12 years Henry's senior. Neither of his parents or grandparents were English, his nearest English relative being his great-grandmother Edith, wife of Henry I. His

wet-nurse, Hodierna, is probably the only wet-nurse in history to have a place named after her, Knoyle Hodierne parish, Wiltshire. His elder siblings were William, Henry and Matilda and his younger ones King John, Geoffrey, Eleanor and Joan. He also had two half-sisters from his mother's earlier marriage. Educated well, he spoke good Latin. Created Duke of Aquitaine and Count of Poitou aged 14 (1172), he and his brothers – led by their mother – rebelled against their father in 1173 in a protracted battle for territory in France during which his elder brother Henry died (1184). Richard thereby inherited the crown when his father died in 1189. A committed Crusader, he led the Third Crusade (1188–92) with Frederick Barbarossa and Philip II of France against the Saracens under Saladin, Muslim leader of Egypt and Syria. Captured by Count Meinhard of Gorz and imprisoned in the castle of Durnstein (1192), he eventually agreed to be ransomed in 1194. He was only present in England twice, briefly, in his 10-year reign, the country being governed by William Longchamp, then Hubert Walter, in his absence. The last years of his reign were occupied in war with Philip II of France.

Family/Sex Life: In 1169 Richard was betrothed to Alice, daughter of Louis VII by his second wife Constance of Castille. In 1191, however, he married Berengaria, daughter of King Sancho VI of Navarre. They had no children and she never set foot in England. He also had an illegitimate son, Philip, and there were allegations of a homosexual affair with Philip II of France (not proven).

Habits/Mannerisms: Richard was the first English king to use the royal 'we'.

Sport/Hobbies: Richard was fond of riding and also of music, writing songs in French and Provençal. Some of his songs were written in collaboration with the famous court minstrel Blondel, who according to legend travelled Europe in search of his master when Richard was captured in Vienna in 1192 – singing songs they had composed together outside castle windows until he found him.

Health: Richard was reputedly covered with some 100 ulcers. In 1196 he was wounded in the knee by a crossbow bolt.

Temperament: Remembered in folklore for his courage, hence the 'Lionheart' tag, in reality Richard was greedy, violent and ruthless – on 20 August 1191, for instance,

he watched from a balcony as 2700 prisoners were put to the sword after the fall of Acre. His motives in leading the Third Crusade had more to do with the prospect of securing vast amounts of gold and silver than they had to do with the publicly stated aims of restoring the Holy Land to Christian control and retrieving relics of the Holy Cross. He once joked that he would sell London itself, if only he could find a buyer. He was a man of few words and always spoke to the point (another nickname was 'Yea and Nay'). According to the historian William Stubbs, he was 'a bad son, a bad husband, a selfish ruler and a vicious man'.

Work/Daily Routine: Richard had considerable success in the Crusades and at one point advanced to within sight of Jerusalem itself, but had to turn back in the face of disunity among his allies and rumours that his brother John was plotting against him at home. Besides his work as a soldier-king, Richard built the castles of Château-Gaillard on the Seine at Andeli and Clairvaux near Chinon.

Motto: His battle cry at the Battle of Gisors (1198) was *'Dieu et mon Droit'* (though this was not adopted as the royal motto of England until the reign of Henry VI).

Manner of Death: Richard was wounded by a crossbow bolt in the shoulder one evening while inspecting (without a shield) the castle of Châlus-Chabrol, Châlus, near Limoges, France, to which he had laid siege for three days believing it to contain a treasure hoard (and having refused the garrison's surrender). He died 11 days later after gangrene set in, on the evening of Tuesday 6 April 1199, aged 42. On his deathbed he forgave the man who had fired the fatal shot (legend has it that his assailant carried a frying pan for a shield). His body was buried at Fontevraud Abbey, France, while his heart was taken to Rouen.

RICHARD III (1452–85) King of England, Wales and Ireland

Richard III was born at Fotheringhay Castle, Northamptonshire, on 2 October 1452, the eleventh child and youngest son of Richard, Duke of York (grandson of Edmund, fourth son of Edward III) and then the most powerful landowner in England after the king, the Lancastrian Henry VI. His mother was Cicely Neville, a relation of Lionel, second son of Edward III. His father and brother Edmund were killed at the Battle of Wakefield in 1460. His other five surviving siblings were Elizabeth, Anne, Margaret, Edward IV and George, Duke of Clarence (who was condemned for treason by Edward IV and drowned in a butt of Malmsey wine). He was brought up by his cousin Richard Neville, Earl of Warwick, at Middleham Castle, Yorkshire. In 1461 he was created Duke of Gloucester by Edward IV and in 1470 he went with Edward into exile, returning with him on his restoration a year later. Aged 17 he was appointed Constable of England and on Edward IV's death in 1483 was made Regent to the 12-year-old Edward V but had him incarcerated (with his younger brother Richard) in the Tower of London and was later accused of having both of them smothered. As his brother George's children were declared attainted Richard inherited the kingdom and was crowned in 1483 by Cardinal Bourchier. He reigned for two years until killed at the Battle of Bosworth Field. The last of the York dynasty, he was succeeded by his victorious opponent at Bosworth, the Welshman Henry Tudor (later Henry VII), a relative of Henry V's widow and John of Gaunt, who had 2000 French convict soldiers fighting with him. His death marked the end of the Middle Ages.

Family/Sex Life: In 1472 Richard married 16-year-old Anne Neville, widow of Henry VI's son Edward and daughter of

Richard's cousin Richard Neville, Earl of Warwick, and with whom he had been brought up in Yorkshire. She died in 1485 (amid rumours that Richard had killed her) a year after their only son Edward. Richard also had at least two illegitimate children.

Appearance: Born with a withered, shrunken left arm, Richard is traditionally portrayed as a hunchback, with his left shoulder considerably higher than his right. There is no hard evidence that he was in fact deformed, authority for this coming only from Sir Thomas More, a propagandist for the Tudors who, 30 years later, described Richard as 'little of stature, ill featured of limbs, crook backed'. He had long hair, brown eyes, thin lips and was clean-shaven.

Sport/Hobbies: Richard enjoyed hawking, hunting and sword and lance fighting. He also liked music and fine buildings (he paid for the completion of King's College Chapel, Cambridge).

Religion/Politics: Richard did not attend mass on the day of his death. His closest political advisers were Francis Viscount Lovell, Sir Richard Ratcliffe and William Catesby.

Temperament: History, influenced by William Shakespeare's hostile depiction, remembers Richard as deformed, ruthless and fundamentally evil. The real Richard was probably less of a monster than is usually believed. There is considerable doubt over who was actually responsible for the deaths of the 'Princes in the Tower', for instance. It has been argued that Richard had little to gain by the Princes' deaths, as his marriage made him the legitimate king – it may in fact have been the future Henry VII (though he was in exile on the Continent at the time of the alleged murders) who ordered the deaths as the boys stood between him and any claim he had to the throne – perhaps significantly it was not until almost a year after the Princes' disappearance that Henry announced that Richard was the culprit). The bones of two small boys were discovered under a staircase in the Tower in the 17th century.

Pets: When he fought at Bosworth Richard was mounted on a fine white horse.

Work/Daily Routine: He rose at dawn, took dinner at 11 am and supper at 5 pm, and went to bed around 7 pm. He commanded his troops himself and is reputed to have personally killed Henry Tudor's standard-bearer at Bosworth.

Motto/Emblem: Richard's emblem was a white boar – hence the famous couplet by William Colyngbourne (a former servant of Richard's mother):

'The catte, the ratte, and Lovell our dogge Rulyth all Englande under a hogge.'

The cat was Catesby and the rat was Ratcliffe, while Lovell was known as 'the King's spaniel'. For his satirical couplet Colyngbourne was hanged and disembowelled. According to the records, he 'lived till the butcher put his hand into the bulk of his body; insomuch that he said in the same instant, "O Lord Jesus, yet more trouble", and so died to the great compassion of much people'.

Manner of Death: Richard was killed, aged 32, during the Battle of Bosworth, near Market Bosworth, Leicestershire, on 22 August 1485, thus becoming the last English king to die in battle. Lack of support from his barons led inevitably to defeat; Richard was cut down shouting 'Treason! Treason! Treason!' as he bravely attempted to reach Henry. His naked corpse was carried by pack horse to Leicester, exposed for two days then buried without ceremony in Grey Friars, Leicester. His tomb was destroyed during the dissolution of the monasteries and his bones were thrown into the River Soar.

RICHELIEU, Cardinal (1585–1642) French priest and statesman

Cardinal Richelieu was born Armand-Jean du Plessis in Richelieu, near Chinon, France, on 9 September 1585, the third son of François du Plessis, Seigneur de Richelieu, Knight of the Holy Ghost and Grand Provost of France during the reign of King Henri III (he was with the king when he was assassinated and personally arrested the regicide). His father died of typhoid when he was five. His mother was Suzanne de La Porte and he had older siblings Françoise, Henri Marquis de Richelieu (who was killed in a duel), Alphonse (Cardinal Archbishop of Lyons and Primate of Gaul) and a younger sister Nicole. One of his brothers thought he was

God and one of his sisters thought that her back was made of crystal. Educated at the Collège de Navarre, Paris, then at the Academy military cadet school in the city, he studied theology at the Collège de Calvi (1602). When his uncle Jacques, Bishop of Luçon, died and his elder brother Alphonse refused the family bishopric in order to become a monk, his mother obtained a special dispensation from Pope Paul V to allow him to take the post though five years younger than was normally allowed. He was thus ordained priest and consecrated Bishop of Luçon on the same day, aged only 22 (1606). Created a cardinal in 1622, he later became Minister of State (Prime Minister) of Louis XIII in 1624 and a duke. He was also chief adviser to Louis XIII's mother, Marie de' Medici, and Governor of Brittany. He founded the Académie Française in 1635 and, as effective ruler of the country, used France's armies to check Hapsburg power in Europe during the Thirty Years' War.

Family/Sex Life: Richelieu never married, but there have been suggestions that he kept a mistress (though there is no firm evidence for this).

Appearance: Richelieu was sickly and had a pale, drawn face, with a sharp nose and prominent cheekbones, wasted with disease. He had black hair and wore a moustache and a pointed beard, and had long tapering fingers.

Sport/Hobbies: Richelieu had cultivated tastes, building the Palais-Royal (originally the Palais-Cardinal) in Paris and becoming the patron of the playwright Corneille. He also played the guitar.

Religion/Politics: Roman Catholic. He was instrumental in crushing the French Huguenot Protestants and in 1628 much reduced the confidence of the Protestants by successfully besieging and capturing their stronghold La Rochelle.

Health: Richelieu suffered from piles and migraines and also from stomach and kidney troubles.

Temperament: Ruthless and iron-willed. To bring France's rebellious barons to heel, for instance, he ordered a series of executions, which quickly had the desired effect. He once remarked, 'If you give me six lines written by the most honest man, I will find something in them to hang him.' He was a fastidious man and took exception to bad table manners. He was disgusted when courtiers in his presence used the pointed daggers they ate with as toothpicks after meals and ordered that the ends of all the knives be rounded (the origin of the modern table-knife).

Pets: Richelieu had 14 cats, including Lucifer, Gazette, Racan and Perruque (twins born in the Academician Racan's wig), Serpolet, Pyramus, Thisbe, Ludovic the Cruel and, his favourite, Soumise. They were all looked after by two attendants and were provided for in his will.

Work/Daily Routine: Richelieu was assisted by his trusted counsellor and secretary Cardinal François Le Clerc du Tremblay, known as Père Joseph – the *Eminence Grise* (so-called after the grey habit of the Franciscan order to which he belonged). Montaigne's literary executor (and adopted daughter), Marie de Gournoy, dedicated Montaigne's *Essays* (1635) to Richelieu. He also wrote a number of books himself, including *Faith of the Catholic Church* (1618), translated into English and published in six editions in the 17th century, and *Instruction of a Christian* (1621), translated into Arabic and Italian and published in 12 editions in the 17th century. He also collaborated on a satirical play, *Miramé* (1641).

Manner of Death: Richelieu died of pleurisy at his home, the Palais-Cardinal, Paris, in the afternoon of 4 December 1642, aged 57. He lay in state for four days and was then buried in the church of the Sorbonne, Paris, which he had built (though it was still unfinished at his death).

RIMBAUD, Jean Nicolas Arthur (1854–91) French poet

Arthur Rimbaud was born in the Rue Napoléon, Charleville, Ardennes, on 20 October 1854, the second son of an Arabic-speaking French Army captain in the Chasseurs d'Orléans, and Marie Catherine Félicité Vitalie Cuif, the daughter of a farmer. His father later became Chef du Bureau Arabe in Algeria, translated the Koran into French and received the Légion d'honneur. After his parents separated in 1860, Rimbaud, his older brother Jean-Nicolas-Frederick, and two surviving sisters, Vitalie and Isabelle, were brought up by his mother with the Cuif family in Charleville. Educated aged eight at the Pension Rossat, Charleville, he then tranferred at the age of 11 to Charleville College, where he was the school's most brilliant pupil. However, he ran away from home aged 15 (his brother had already run away to fight in the Franco-Prussian War), only to be arrested for fare-dodging, bailed out by his former schoolteacher and sent home to Charleville. He then ran way again and lived precariously in Paris and Belgium, returning either to Charleville or his schoolteacher's relatives in Douai until aged 17 he sent (with a letter of introduction) 'Le Bateau Ivre' to the poet Paul Verlaine. He then lived and travelled with Verlaine until their relationship ended with Verlaine's imprisonment for shooting Rimbaud. He then taught briefly in Reading (1874) before returning to Charleville. Having given up poetry by the age of 19, he next enlisted for six years in the 1st Battalion of Infantry in the Dutch Colonial Army (1876) but deserted in the Sunda Isles two months later and went back to Charleville. After a trip to Scandinavia he left home for good aged 25 and became a foreman overseeing 50 men building the Governor's summer palace in Limasol, Cyprus (1880). He then became a coffee exporter in Aden and Harar (Abyssinia), was a gun-runner for King Menelek of Shoa (1885) – one of the rival chiefs in the Abyssinian conflict – and eventually settled in Abyssinia as a trader in coffee, hides, gum, ivory and musk.

Family/Sex Life: Rimbaud had an intense homosexual relationship with the already married poet Paul Verlaine. Verlaine twice tried to kill Rimbaud when he threatened to leave. On the second occasion (in Brussels in 1873) Rimbaud was wounded in the wrist by a pistol shot at very close range (two more shots were fired but went wide). The relationship with Rimbaud was later cited in Verlaine's divorce case. Rimbaud later lived as man and wife with a local woman in Aden.

Appearance: He had a girlish appearance, with blue eyes and reddish gold wavy hair. By 1879 he had dark skin, greying hair and a frizzy beard and moustache. At the time of his death he had short hair and a moustache.

Habits/Mannerisms: A cigarette and pipe smoker from the age of 16, he drank mostly absinthe.

Sport/Hobbies: Piano-playing.

Religion/Politics: Rimbaud was very interested in magic and alchemy, but on his deathbed converted to Roman Catholicism, with assistance from his sister Isabelle.

Health: Besides the gunshot injuries he sustained during his relationship with Verlaine, Rimbaud also suffered from sunstroke and typhoid (1879). In 1891, his right kneecap became so swollen – he said it looked like a pumpkin – that he returned to France and the leg was amputated in Marseilles.

Temperament: Apart from Verlaine, his friends in France included the caricaturist André Gill (who lent him money in Paris and advised him to go home) and the artist Forain ('Gavroche'). His closest friend in Harar was his servant boy Djami.

Work/Daily Routine: Rimbaud's first published poem was 'Les Etrennes des Orphelins', which appeared in *La Revue pour Tous* (1870), when he was 15. He was much influenced by Baudelaire. 'Le Bateau Ivre' – his longest poem and his most popular work – was written at a time when he had never actually seen the sea. While in London with Verlaine (1872) he worked in the British Museum Reading Room. The publication of *Une Saison en Enfer* (1873) was paid for by his mother, but failed to make much impression,

persuading Rimbaud to burn all his manuscripts three months later (November 1873).

Manner of Death: After the amputation of his right leg (July 1891), Rimbaud returned to Charleville, where he lost the use of his right arm. He found Charleville so cold that he decided to return to Abyssinia (August) but only reached Marseilles before he was hospitalized again and succumbed to gradual paralysis. He died, aged 37, on 10 November 1891 in the Hospital of the Immaculate Conception, Marseilles, his only attendant being his sister Isabelle. The cause of death was diagnosed as tertiary syphilis or carcinoma. He was buried in Charleville and a monument to him was erected in the Square de la Gare (1910).

ROBERT I 'The Bruce' (1274–1329) King of Scotland

Robert de Bruce (known as 'Robert the Bruce') was born on 11 July 1274 in Turnberry, Ayrshire, the son of Robert de Bruce, 7th Earl of Carrick, and Marjory, daughter of Nigel, 2nd Earl of Carrick and widow of Adam de Kilconquhar. He had four brothers, Edward (later King of Ireland), Thomas, Alexander (Dean of Glasgow) and Nigel – the last three were all later executed by Edward I – and two sisters, Christina and Mary. He spent his youth in the court of Edward I of England and became Earl of Carrick in 1292. He and his father swore fealty to Edward I in 1296 but when Sir William Wallace raised the Scots against the English he joined him. After Wallace's defeat he again supported the English and was appointed co-regent of Scotland. He later quarrelled with his co-regent John Comyn and stabbed him to death before marching to Scone to be crowned King of Scotland (1306), once again taking up the cause of Scottish independence. However, defeated by the

English, he went into hiding from his enemies on the island of Rathlin, off the Antrim coast, retreating to a cave where he reputedly learnt perseverance by watching a spider spinning its web (a legend later popularized by Sir Walter Scott). After the death of Edward I (1307), Robert and his brother Edward fought back against his weak successor, Edward II, and at the Battle of Bannockburn (1314) won a famous victory for Scottish independence though outnumbered three to one. Incursions into England by The Bruce's armies got as far as York. The independence of Scotland was formally recognized in 1327 by the Treaty of York. No English kings after Edward I ever conquered Scotland.

Family/Sex Life: Robert's first wife was Isabella, daughter of Donald, 6th Earl of Mar. By her he had a daughter, Marjory (mother, by Walter the Steward of Scotland, of Robert II, the first of the

Stuart line). In 1304 he married Elizabeth de Burgh, sister of the Earl of Ulster. Their children were Matilda, Margaret, David II (who married Edward II's daughter Joanna) and John. He also had several illegitimate children, including Sir Robert, Walter, Nigel, Margaret, Elizabeth and Christian.

Appearance: Portraits by artists from later eras suggest Robert the Bruce was strongly built, with a bushy beard and long hair.

Sport/Hobbies: He enjoyed hawking. He also kept a fool and had an interest in shipbuilding. After Bannockburn, when he captured a monk named Robert Baston, who had been sent with the English army to record in verse their expected victory, he ordered the hapless Baston to turn his talents to telling the story of how the Scottish army had prevailed.

Religion/Politics: Though he was excommunicated by the Pope, he won papal recognition as King of Scotland in 1323.

Temperament: Robert was renowned for his courage and prowess in battle. On the eve of Bannockburn, when he happened by chance upon a small party led by the

English knight Henry de Bohun, who charged him with a lance, he felled Bohun with a single blow of his battle-axe. The story of the spider that he encountered on Rathlin was quoted in after years as an example of his innate wisdom. He watched the spider attempt to spin a web six times without success and then, because he too had failed to liberate Scotland six times, paid particular attention to what happened the seventh time. The spider succeeded and, legend has it, the heartened Bruce gathered together 300 followers, landed at Carrick, and launched a successful surprise attack on the English garrison at Turnberry Castle.

Pets: Legend has it that his favourite pet was a lion.

Manner of Death: A scant year after winning recognition of Scotland's independence from England, Robert the Bruce died of leprosy at his home, Cardross Castle, on 7 June 1329, aged 54. His body was buried beside his wife's in Dunfermline. His heart was given to Sir James Douglas with the request that he take it on crusade to the Holy Sepulchre, but Douglas was killed fighting the Moors in Spain so it was buried with Douglas in Melrose Abbey (it was disinterred in 1996).

ROBESPIERRE, Maximilien François Marie Isidore de (1758–94)
French revolutionary leader

Maximilien Derobespierre was born – just four months after his parents' wedding – in Arras, Artois, in French Flanders at 2 pm on 6 May 1788, the eldest child of a lawyer, François Derobespierre, and Jacqueline Marguerite Carrault, the daughter of a brewer, who died when he was aged six. After his mother's death, his father abandoned Maximilien and his younger siblings, Charlotte, Henriette and Augustin, and they were brought up by the

Carrault family. Educated in Arras and at Louis-le-Grand College at the University of Paris – to which he won a scholarship aged 11 – he worked while still a student as a junior clerk in the office of the Procurator of Parliament. He was then a criminal judge in Arras (1782) and was elected a deputy (MP) to the States-General (later the National Assembly) for Artois, aged 30. In 1783 he won a prize from the Academy of Metz for a treatise on whether relatives of a criminal should share his or her legal disgrace. When his maternal grandparents died he gained an inheritance and lived in Arras, with his sister Charlotte as housekeeper. After the Revolution in 1789 he became Public Prosecutor and argued that Louis XVI had to die in order for France to live. Following the king's execution he became President of the Convention and served on the Committee of Public Safety, becoming thereby responsible for the deaths of thousands of citizens by the guillotine and for a brief period the most powerful and feared man in France. At the height of the Terror, between 12 June and 28 July 1794 alone, no less than 1285 people were executed. He dropped the honorific 'de' in his name in 1790 when the Constitutional Assembly abolished titles.

Family/Sex Life: Robespierre never married though he was reputedly engaged three times. He kept a paid mistress and for an English girlfriend, Ophelia Mondlen, he wrote the poem 'Madrigal'.

Appearance: He was short (under five feet three inches) and had a pale complexion, grey-green eyes, a large thin-lipped mouth, high cheekbones and forehead and a pointed chin. His clean-shaven face was slightly pock-marked. His chestnut brown hair was always carefully powdered and he was an elegant and immaculate dresser. He wore glasses (green-tinted in later life) and had a permanent ironic/benevolent smile.

Habits/Mannerisms: Robespierre held his head high and carried himself very erect. He had a tendency to make brusque movements and later developed a number of nervous tics, jerking his shoulders, doubling-up his fists, blinking a lot and turning his head rapidly from side to side. He was a superb orator, though he possessed a high-pitched voice. He was very fond of fruit, especially oranges, but never drank to excess, preferring wine with water. He always carried hair powder and a powder-puff with him.

Sport/Hobbies: Besides writing poetry, Robespierre was skilled at making lace (a craft he was taught by his mother from the age of five).

Religion/Politics: Born a Roman Catholic, he rejected his faith while at college after reading Rousseau. He later introduced a new state religion based on Rousseau's Civic Religion (*Emile*) but did not banish atheists: 'The people of France recognize the existence of the Supreme Being and the immortality of the Soul.' A radical, he emerged as leader of the Mountain group in the National Convention after the Revolution and pursued the Girondins faction with ruthless determination. As he grew more powerful, however, opposition to his ideas intensified, leading ultimately to his condemnation by the Revolutionary Tribunal and his downfall. In 1793 he declared: 'Any institution which does not suppose the people good, and the magistrate corruptible, is evil.'

Health: The day before his execution his lower jaw was broken by a shot fired by a gendarme.

Temperament: Known as 'the sea-green Incorruptible', Robespierre was very virtuous, but also cold, reserved and solitary. His friends included Danton, David and Saint-Just.

Pets: Robespierre kept pigeons all his life and also had a number of canaries.

Work/Daily Routine: Rising around 6 or 7 am, Robespierre breakfasted on a glass of milk, then wrote until 10 am before taking a light lunch. Writing with a fine, crowded, feminine hand, he never used capital letters (except in his signature).

Manner of Death: Robespierre was guillotined by order of the Revolutionary Tribunal in the Place de la Revolution, Paris, on 28 July 1794 (10th Thermidor), aged 36. His death mask was modelled in wax by Madame Tussaud (some years earlier, when Tussaud was led down into the dungeons of the Bastille to begin her work she slipped on the steps and was saved from falling by Robespierre, unaware that one day his severed head would lie in her lap).

ROLLS, Charles Stewart (1877–1910)
English motor manufacturer, engineer and aviator

The Honourable C. S. Rolls was born at 35 Hill Street, Berkeley Square, London, on 27 August 1877, the third son of John Allan Rolls, 1st Baron Llangattock and a Justice of the Peace, and Georgiana Marcia Maclean, daughter of Sir Charles FitzRoy Maclean, 9th Baronet of Morvaren. He had two brothers. He was brought up in Monmouth and educated at Eton and Trinity College, Cambridge (studying mechanical and applied science). While he was at Cambridge he designed and built a four-seater bicycle or 'quadruplet' and became the fourth person in England and the first undergraduate to own a car (a Peugeot). At first he worked as an engineer at the LNW railway works in Crewe, Cheshire, before becoming an engineer on his father's yacht, *Ave Maria*. He then founded C. S. Rolls & Company – selling and repairing Panhard and other foreign makes of motor car – in Fulham, London. In 1904 he joined up with Henry Royce to form the Rolls-Royce company, initially based in Manchester, but from 1906 in Derby. Royce's real name was Runnicles and for the first three months the company was called Rolls-Runnicles until Rolls insisted that he change it. Rolls was managing director of the company, while Royce was chief engineer and works director. Becoming one of the most celebrated figures in the developing British motor industry, Rolls once drove George V (when Prince of Wales) and the future Queen Mary. As a pioneer aviator he was the first Englishman to own a private aircraft, the second to fly (after Griffith Brewster) and the first to fly the English Channel both ways non-stop (1910). A Fellow of the Royal Geographical Society and the Royal Metallurgical Society and an Associate Member of the Institute of Mechanical Engineering and a committee member of the RAC, he also helped found the Aero Club.

Family/Sex Life: Rolls never married.

Sport/Hobbies: He was a keen amateur racing cyclist in his youth, winning a half-Blue for cycling at Cambridge and becoming captain of the University racing team. He was also a balloonist, making 170 ascents between 1901 and his death. He received a Gold Medal for his balloon crossing of the Channel in 1906. He was also a good musician, actor and football player. Motor-racing was another passion: in 1900 he won an RAC Gold Medal racing a Panhard in a 1000-mile trial. In 1903 he established a new world land speed record (84.73 mph) but the French record-holders refused to ratify it. In 1906 he won the Isle of Man TT Race in a Rolls-Royce. His interest in motoring began early. As a child he made his first experiments at motoring using an old bathchair. Positioning the chair at the top of his parents' steep drive in Monmouth, he would launch himself downhill: 'One happy day I bagged a curate, a butcher's boy and a dog cart.'

Temperament: According to his school reports at Eton, 'His thoughts are often far away in dreamland or vacancy, instead of being with his work.' Later in life he earned a reputation for his reluctance to part with money. Tommy Sopwith called him 'the meanest man I know' and it was said that he would sleep under his car to avoid running up hotel bills.

Work/Daily Routine: Between 1908 and 1925 the only car built by Rolls-Royce was the classic Silver Ghost, which epitomized the ideals of refinement and quality ever since associated with the company's cars. It had a top speed of just 65 mph. Many Rolls-Royces were sold under the slogan 'The best car in the world' and it was proudly claimed (quoting an article in *The Motor*) that 'at 60 miles an hour the loudest noise in this new Rolls-Royce comes from the electric clock'. The only

response the company made to this laudatory observation was: 'We really ought to do something about that damned clock.'

Manner of Death: Rolls was killed at the age of 32 when the tailplane collapsed while he was flying his Wright aeroplane in Bournemouth, Dorset, on 12 July 1910. The wreckage of the crashed aeroplane was towed away by a Rolls-Royce Silver Ghost. Thus becoming the first Englishman to be killed flying an aeroplane, Rolls was buried at Llangattock-Vibon-Avel Church, near Monmouth, Wales.

ROOSEVELT, Theodore (1858–1919) 26th US President

Theodore 'Teddy' Roosevelt was born at 28 East 20th Street, New York, on 27 October 1858, the son and second child of Theodore Roosevelt and Martha Bulloch. He had an older sister Anna and other siblings were Elliott and Corinne (Franklin Delano Roosevelt, 32nd US President, was a distant cousin). Educated at Harvard University (graduated 1880) and at Columbia Law School, he trained as a lawyer with his uncle Robert B. Roosevelt and was for a time a freelance historian, writing his first book, *The Naval War of 1812*, in 1882. He then worked in local government in New York before becoming a rancher in Dakota. In the American war with Spain he joined the cavalry and was second-in-command of the 1st Volunteer Cavalry, an untrained group later called the 'Rough Riders'. Fighting in Cuba, his unit led a famous charge on foot, perjoratively referred to as 'the schoolboy charge', an incident that was much reported to bolster morale. A member of the US Civil Service Commission in Washington, President of the Police Board of New York, Assistant Secretary to the Navy and Mayor of New York, he was

elected Vice-President to William McKinley and when McKinley was assassinated (1901) became the 26th – youngest ever – President, aged 42. As President (re-elected in 1904) he introduced the celebrated Square Deal programme for social reform and had a major impact on US foreign policy. He retired in 1909 and was contributing editor of *Outlook* and a contributor to *Metropolitan Magazine* and *Kansas City Star* before travelling to Africa with the Smithsonian Institute. He then lectured at the Sorbonne and Oxford Universities, counted the birds in the New Forest with Sir Edward Grey, represented the USA at the funeral of Edward VII and was awarded the Nobel Prize for Peace (1906). On his return to America (1910), he stood for election but was not elected. He was President of the American Historical Association (1912).

Family/Sex Life: In 1880 Roosevelt married Alice Hathaway Lee. She died in 1884 after the birth of their daughter Alice. His second wife (1886) was Edith Kermit Carow, whom he married at St

George's Church, Hanover Square, London. Their children were Kermit (who died in World War II), Archibald, Quentin (who was killed in the Air Force in World War I), Theodore (who died in World War II) and Ethel.

Appearance: In his youth Roosevelt had 'light-brown, slightly curly hair, blue eyes and an eye-glass . . . clear sharp, boyish voice' (according to *Frank Leslie's Illustrated Paper*, 1884). Later he became quite portly.

Sport/Hobbies: Roosevelt rode, shot and enjoyed boxing. He was also a dedicated hunter of big game and liked shooting bears. The story goes that on one occasion, when the organizers of a hunt were eager that their distinguished guest should successfully shoot a bear, they brought him a bear cub on a rope. Roosevelt, however, took pity on the animal and had it set free. The incident inspired a Clifford Berryman cartoon 'Drawing the Line in Mississippi' (*Washington Star*, 18 November 1902) and subsequently a Brooklyn toy store owned by Mavis Mitcham started making toy versions of 'Teddy's Bear' (the original is now in the Smithsonian Institute, Washington). 'Teddy bears' were later mass-produced by the Ideal Toy Corporation and they became one of the best-loved of all children's toys. Besides bequeathing to the world the teddy bear, Roosevelt also wrote many books, including a biography of Oliver Cromwell. He was also the first US President to ride in a car and fly in an aeroplane.

Religion/Politics: Republican.

Health: A sickly child who suffered badly from asthma, the adult Roosevelt deliberately worked to prove his prowess at manly pursuits. A boxing match in 1904 left him with defective eyesight and he was blind in the left eye after 1908. In 1912 he was shot in the chest before addressing a meeting in Milwaukee: undaunted by his wound he told the stunned crowd, 'I will deliver this speech or die, one or the other' and then gave his speech as planned, only allowing himself to be taken to hospital 90 minutes later.

Temperament: Roosevelt was resolute, moralistic and unswervably honest. As a rancher, he once discovered one of his cowboys putting the Roosevelt brand on an unbranded steer, even though it was on another rancher's property and was thus his by right – Roosevelt instantly dismissed the man, explaining, 'A man who will steal for me will steal from me.' He did not, incidentally, like the nickname Teddy.

Pets: Roosevelt's animals included a large six-toed grey cat called Slippers, another cat called Tom Quartz, a pony Algonquin and a black mongrel dog named Skip.

Mottoes: Roosevelt adopted as his motto the West African proverb 'Speak softly and carry a big stick, you will go far.' This motto led to his foreign policy being called 'big-stick diplomacy'. Another motto was 'Don't hit at all if it is honorably possible to avoid hitting; but *never* hit soft.'

Manner of Death: Roosevelt died peacefully in his sleep on 6 January 1919, aged 60.

ROSSETTI, Dante Gabriel (1828–82) English poet and painter

Dante Gabriel Rossetti was born Gabriel Charles Dante Rossetti (he later dropped the Charles and changed the order of the names) at 38 Charlotte Street, London, on 12 May 1828, the second child of Gabriele Rossetti, a refugee Neapolitan poet, Dante scholar and later Professor of Italian at King's College, London. The brother of his mother, Frances Mary Lavinia Polidori, was Byron's doctor, John Polidori, and her sister went to the Crimea with Florence Nightingale. His father had been librettist to the Naples Opera House and Curator of Antiquities in Naples Museum but fled during the insurrection of 1820–1. He had an older sister, Maria Francesca, and his younger siblings were the poet Christina Georgina and the critic William Michael. His godfather was Charles Lyell (father of the celebrated geologist Sir Charles Lyell) who was a great fan of Dante and subsidized many of Gabriele Rossetti's books. Educated at King's College School, London (aged nine to 13, his art teacher being John Sell Cotman), Cary's Art Academy (four years) and the Royal Academy Antique School (1846), he was later a pupil of Ford Madox Brown. A professional writer and painter, he formed the Pre-Raphaelite Brotherhood with Holman Hunt and Millais around 1848. His paintings included *Beata Beatrix* (1865). Many of his best poems were published in *Ballads and Sonnets* (1881).

Family/Sex Life: In 1860 Rossetti married Elizabeth Eleanor Siddall (a milliner's assistant), known to her intimates as Lizzie or Guggums. She suffered from tuberculosis and, to Rossetti's great distress, killed herself with a laudanum overdose (prescribed for neuralgia) after giving birth to a stillborn child in 1862. Rossetti became increasingly withdrawn and reclusive after Lizzie's death. He later lived in a *ménage à trois* with William Morris and his wife Jane at Kelmscott Manor, near Lechlade, Oxfordshire.

Appearance: He had a high forehead, large dark eyes, a beard worn without sideburns and long hair. He also wore spectacles.

Sport/Hobbies: After his wife's death, he collected old furniture, blue china and Japanese bric-à-brac – especially Nankin blue and white porcelain.

Religion/Politics: Very interested in spiritualism.

Health: Rossetti took chloral and whisky for neuralgia and insomnia in his later years. He had a very good memory but suffered from bad eyesight, sometimes wearing two pairs of strong spectacles at once. In 1872 he suffered a breakdown and took an overdose of laudanum; in 1877 he underwent an operation for hydrocele.

Temperament: As well as the Morrises, Millais and Holman Hunt, Rossetti included among his friends Meredith, Swinburne, and Theodore Watts-Dunton, who shared a house with the Rossetti brothers at 16 Cheyne Walk, Chelsea. Among friends and champions of the Pre-Raphaelite Brotherhood was John Ruskin, who became a patron.

Pets: Rossetti kept a vast menagerie of animals, including an opossum, a racoon, an armadillo, a peacock, a wombat, woodchucks, owls, a raven, a zebra and a monkey – some of which lived in the house. He once announced he wanted to buy an elephant so that he could teach it to wash the windows of the house. He also had a black-and-white cat called Zoe and while at Kelmscott kept three dogs, including Dizzy, a black-and-tan terrier.

Work/Daily Routine: Rossetti admired the poetry of Browning and Poe and shared a studio with Holman Hunt. His sister Christina was the model for the celebrated picture *Ecce Ancilla Domini*. William Morris's wife Jane also modelled for him, as did Lizzie Siddal. Lizzie also modelled for Millais and became seriously ill after posing in a bath of tepid water as Millais's Ophelia. When Lizzie died Rossetti placed the only manuscript copy of some of his poems – inspired by and addressed to her – in her coffin (1862) but later regretted this and had the coffin disinterred so that he could retrieve them (1869). He explained that Lizzie had visited him in the form of a chaffinch and had told him that this would be all right. The exhumation was carried out at night by the light of a fire and the story is that when the coffin was opened it was discovered that Lizzie Siddal's body was perfectly preserved and that her hair had grown till it filled the whole coffin.

Manner of Death: In December 1881 Rossetti became paralysed on his left side.

By then his liver and kidneys had been destroyed by chloral, and he died after a stroke caused by nephritis and uraemia at the bungalow of his architect friend Thomas Seddon in Birchington-on-Sea, near Margate, Kent, at 9.31 pm on 9 April 1882, aged 53. He died in the arms of Theodore Watts-Dunton, his mother and sister also being present. He was buried in Birchington, his tomb being designed by Ford Madox Brown and his epitaph being supplied by his brother William.

ROSSINI, Gioacchino Antonio (1792–1868) Italian composer

Gioacchino Rossini was born in the Via del Duomo, Pesaro, Italy, on 29 February in the leap year 1792, the son of Giuseppe 'Vivazza' Rossini, a town crier, horn and trumpet-player and later Inspector of Public Slaughterhouses, who was a relative of a former ambassador to the Court of the Duke of Ferrara. His mother Anna was a baker's daughter and herself a talented singer. As his parents were constantly on tour in theatres, he was brought up by his aunt and grandmother. Taught the violoncello, piano and the art of counterpoint at the Liceo Musicale, Bologna (1806–10), he was a good singer and was elected a Fellow of the prestigious Accademia Filharmonica in Bologna at the age of 14. With help from his parents he then became composer to the San Mosè Theatre, Venice (1810), when one of their regular composers failed to complete a one-act opera on time. His first really big success, at the age of 21, came with *Tancredi* (1813), which was based on Voltaire's tragedy, but he is perhaps best known for his operas *Otello* (1816), *Il barbiere di Siviglia* (The Barber of Seville, 1816) and *Guillaume Tell* (William Tell, 1829). He came to London in 1823 and Cambridge in 1824 and was received by George IV in Brighton. Appointed Director

of the Théâtre Italien in Paris (1824–5), he subsequently became Composer to His Majesty and Inspector General of Singing (a post created for him). In 1829, at the age of 37, he gave up his professional musical career altogether. Awarded the Légion d'honneur for *Guillaume Tell*, he was also presented with the Order of the Corona d'Italia by King Victor Immanuel of Italy (1868).

Family/Sex Life: In 1822 Rossini married the Spaniard Isabella Colbran, seven years his senior, who was his prima donna and the former mistress of the impresario of La Scala, Domenico Barbaia. They separated in 1837 and had no children (she died in 1845). He then had a long affair with the Parisian courtesan Olympe Pélissier, whom he married in 1846 after Isabella died (they had no children).

Appearance: Handsome, with brown eyes, delicate hands and a roguish smile, Rossini often wore a tie-pin with a medallion of Handel on it and also wore wigs to hide his baldness.

Habits/Mannerisms: Rossini was an epicure and was particularly fond of pâté de foie gras (a weakness that inspired the creation of the dish Tournedos Rossini). On congratulating Adelina Patti on her singing he told her: 'I have cried only twice in my life – once when I dropped a wing of truffled chicken into Lake Como, and once when for the first time I heard you sing.' On another occasion, after enjoying a fine meal at a friend's house, the wish was expressed that he would visit again – 'Right away' came the reply. He kept a fine wine cellar (especially claret) and also smoked cigars and took snuff. He refused to allow any house he lived in to be lit by gas.

Sport/Hobbies: Rossini was an excellent pianist, rarely using the pedals. He also played the viola, the horn, the cembalo and the violoncello and sang (in England he sang tenor to George IV's bass). When not indulging his love of music, he enjoyed a game of dominoes.

Health: Rossini was a hypochondriac and an insomniac. Physical ailments included a throat complaint (with which he became very ill in 1818), urinary disease (for which he had an operation in 1843), neurathesnia (1854), chronic bronchial catarrh, heart trouble and a fistula in the rectum.

Temperament: Cheerful and amusing, Rossini enjoyed his fame. Robert Browning recalled that when writing to his mother he addressed his letters to the 'mother of the famous composer'. His closest friends included Bellini.

Work/Daily Routine: Rossini's first

successes came with *Demetrio e Polibio* (1812) and *La Pietra del Paragone* (1812). *Il barbiere di Siviglia*, which Rossini claimed to have composed in just a fortnight, was actually jeered on its first perfomance by the audience, who were reluctant to see the new work replace *Il barbiere di Siviglia* by the popular composer Paisiello. Donizetti was among his many notable admirers; of *Guillaume Tell* he observed, 'Rossini wrote the first and last acts of *Guillaume Tell*. God wrote the second act.' Rossini prided himself on his ability to write on almost any subject – he once boasted: 'Give me a laundry list and I will set it to music.' He usually rose at 8 am, walked for an hour (10.30 am to 11.30 am) before taking lunch, had dinner at 6 pm, followed by a cigar, received visitors at 8.30 pm and retired to bed at 10 pm. Strangely, he produced virtually no new music after the age of 37, though he lived to be 76.

Motto/Emblem: Rossini's coat of arms was a nightingale perched on a rose.

Manner of Death: Rossini underwent an operation for a fistula in his rectum on 3 November 1868, but septic poisoning led to his death at 11 pm on Friday 13 November 1868 (he had always been superstitious). He was buried in the Père Lachaise Cemetery, Paris, near Cherubini, Chopin and Bellini. A huge crowd attended the funeral. In 1887 his body was moved to Santa Croce, Florence, to lie with Galileo, Michelangelo and Machiavelli.

ROUSSEAU, Jean-Jacques (1712–78)
Swiss political philosopher, educationalist and essayist

Jean-Jacques Rousseau, 'the Father of Romanticism' and inspirer of the French Revolution, was born at 40 Grand Rue,

Geneva, on 28 June 1712, the second son of Isaac Rousseau, a watchmaker and dancing-teacher, and a descendant of a

French Huguenot family that had emigrated to Calvinist Geneva in the 16th century. His mother, Suzanne Bernard, died of puerperal fever a few days after Jean-Jacques' birth so Isaac's younger sister, Suzanne, moved in with the family. However, having been caught trespassing and wounding a local landowner, his father fled Geneva and never returned. Jean-Jacques (then aged 10) and his elder brother François were subsequently brought up by a maternal uncle, Gabriel Bernard (husband of Isaac's elder sister). Rousseau was largely self-taught and after boarding with a pastor in Bossey worked as an apprentice clerk to a notary and then as an apprentice engraver in Geneva for five years. Taken up by the Baronne de Warens (Françoise-Louise de la Tour) in Annecy, Savoy, he was sent to Turin to be baptized as a Catholic. Here he worked as an engraver and a footman before returning to Annecy to train as a priest and also attend the cathedral music school. As 'Vaussure de Villeneuve', he taught music in Lausanne, Vevey and Neuchâtel, was then employed by the Ordnance Survey in Savoy and became tutor to the sons of the Prévôt-Général of Lyons (brother of the philosopher Condillac). Later he was secretary to the Parisian hostess Madame Dupin (grandmother of George Sand), secretary to the French ambassador to Venice (1743–4) and a music copyist. He came to England at the invitation of David Hume (1766–7), received a £100 pension from George III and wrote part of his *Confessions* (published 1782) while staying at Wootton Hall, Staffordshire. His most important writings included *Discours sur l'origine et les fondements de l'inégalité parmi les hommes* (1755), *La nouvelle Héloïse* (1761), *Du contrat social* (1762) and *Émile, ou Traité de l'éducation* (1762), a controversial discussion of education in novel form.

Family/Sex Life: In 1768, after many years together, he married his mistress, Thérèse Levasseur, an illiterate Parisian hotel servant and washerwoman 13 years his junior. Their five children were sent to a foundling hospital, Rousseau having been influenced by Plato's *Republic*. He had many other lovers, especially older women (including the Baronne de Warens – he called her Maman, she called him Petit – and Madame Suzanne-Françoise de Larnage).

Appearance: Around 1762 Rousseau favoured Armenian dress, wearing a long coat and furry hat. He disliked the famous Allan Ramsay portrait of him commissioned by Hume, saying it made him look like a cyclops.

Habits/Mannerisms: A masochist, Rousseau enjoyed being beaten at school and later took to exposing himself to girls at a well in Turin. He was fond of coffee, owned his own personal gondola when in Venice and had neat handwriting. In later life he refused to accept letters with unfamiliar handwriting. The general habit of calling him Jean-Jacques (omitting his surname) annoyed him.

Sport/Hobbies: Rousseau enjoyed playing the spinet and also collected plants. He also wrote operas (his *Le Devin du Village* was performed at Fontainebleau before Louis XV in 1752) and ballets. He invented a new system of musical notation with numbers instead of notes and published a book on it. He also rewrote Rameau's music for a comedy ballet by Voltaire for the Dauphin's wedding (1745). A favourite book was *Robinson Crusoe*.

Religion/Politics: Protestant at first, then Roman Catholic, then Calvinist again (1754). He was exiled from France for criticizing Christianity. Unable to publish his *Dialogues, Rousseau juge de Jean-Jacques*, he tried to place the text on the altar of Nôtre-Dame in Paris.

Health: Rousseau suffered from uraemia and had to press his abdomen to empty his bladder. A doctor's probe once broke in his urethra and was only passed out months later. Other ailments were a hernia and an enlarged prostate. He mistakenly thought he had polypus of the heart. He also had a persecution mania and went mad before his death.

Temperament: Rousseau had no sense of humour and was sensitive, vain and egotistical ('Of all the men I have known in my life, I am firmly persuaded that none was better than I'). Voltaire personally attacked him as a hypocrite, an ungrateful friend and a heartless father. His friends included Diderot, Condillac, Hume (later a great enemy) and Boswell (who had sex with Thérèse Levasseur 13 times) – but not Dr Johnson, who called him 'a rascal ... a very bad man ... I should like to have him work in the plantations' (1766).

Pets: He kept several dogs, including Duke (later renamed Turk) and Sultan (a small brown dog with short ears and a short curled tail).

Work/Daily Routine: *Émile* and *Du contrat social* were written in a summerhouse in the garden of Mont-Louis House, Montmorency, Switzerland. Both were put on the Vatican's Index of prohibited books (Rousseau only evaded arrest in France by fleeing to Switzerland). He was the first person to use the word *'romantique'* to describe scenery (in *Rêveries du promeneur solitaire*).

Motto/Emblem: Rousseau had a seal with the inscription: *Vitam Imendere Vero* (to submit one's life to the truth). Slogans from Rousseau's writings included 'Man is born free, yet everywhere he is in chains' (*Du contrat social*) and 'Liberty, Equality, Fraternity'. He once wrote 'I hate books: they only teach you to speak about what you don't know.'

Manner of Death: After a walk near his home on the estate of the Marquis de Girardin, Ermenonville, near Paris, Rousseau felt pins and needles in his feet, a cold chill up his spine and pains in his chest and head. He died of thrombosis at 11 am on 2 July 1778, aged 66, and was buried on the Île des Peupliers (an island in a lake on the estate). His body was later moved to the Panthéon, Paris (1794), but on the Bourbon restoration (1814) his bones were scattered.

RUSKIN, John (1819–1900) English writer and art critic

John Ruskin was born at 54 Hunter Street, Brunswick Square, London, on 8 February 1819, the only child of John James Ruskin, founder of Ruskin, Telford & Domecq, sherry merchants ('Domecque contributing the sherry, Telford the capital and Ruskin the brains,' according to the *Dictionary of National Biography*). His mother was his father's first cousin, Margaret Cox. Educated at Christ Church, Oxford, he suffered from ill health, prompting his mother to move there to look after him. He later became the first Slade Professor of Art at the university and founded Sheffield Museum. He inherited a vast fortune (£157,000 plus land and houses) when his father died but used it all up (giving a lot to charity) and thereafter lived by his writings. He also founded Mr Ruskin's Tea Shop in Paddington (failed) and the Guild of St George (a utopian scheme). Among those who benefited greatly from his support were Turner and the Pre-Raphaelite Brotherhood. His most influential publications included *Modern Painters* (1843–60), *The Seven Lamps of Architecture* (1849) and *The Stones of Venice* (1851–3).

Family/Sex Life: In 1848 Ruskin married Euphemia 'Effie' Chalmers Gray. Ruskin was reputedly appalled at the sight of his wife's pubic hair and could not consummate the marriage. The marriage was annulled and she left him in 1854 to marry his friend Millais (1855). Equally traumatic was his attachment to Rose La Touche, an 11-year-old girl he met in 1858 and to whom he proposed in 1866 – but he could not accept her Evangelical views and they remained apart (she died mad in 1875 and he was tormented by her memory for the rest of his days).

Appearance: Five feet 10 inches tall, Ruskin was of a slight build (he walked with shoulders bent in later years). He had piercing blue eyes and a radiant smile, though he carried a scar on his upper lip where he was bitten by a dog as a child. He had delicate hands with tapering fingers. His hair remained thick and brown even in old age (he never went completely grey); he added side whiskers in middle age and, from 1879, a beard. The *Dictionary of National Biography* states that his clothes comprised 'light-brown tweed, a double-breasted waistcoat, an ill-fitting blue frock-coat with velvet collar, unstarched wristbands and amplitude of blue necktie worn as a stock'.

Habits/Mannerisms: Ruskin rolled his Rs when speaking and had exquisitely neat handwriting. He lived alone with his parents in Denmark Hill until their deaths (except for the brief period – 1848 – when his wife lived there too); he wrote letters to them daily whenever they were separated. He later lived at 'Brantwood' by Coniston Water in Cumbria and, as his sanity became increasingly precarious in his last years, became a virtual recluse there.

Sport/Hobbies: He liked walking and rowing and also collected minerals. Pet projects of his while at Oxford included the celebrated North Hinksey to Oxford road, which he conceived as an ideal way for his students to try their hand at manual labour while providing some material benefit for local people. He recruited a number of undergraduates, including the youthful Oscar Wilde, and set them to work on the road, directed by his gardener. The undertaking, under the pressure of the toil necessary, collapsed and the road remained unfinished. He also promoted the revival of cottage industries and crafts, such as linen-weaving.

Religion/Politics: Ruskin had a strict Calvinist upbringing. As a child he was not allowed any toys (except a box of bricks) and he never learnt to dance or ride. He had to read the Bible aloud every day in his youth and was forced to memorize whole sections of it. His mother even turned pictures to the wall on Sundays.

Health: Ruskin suffered from pleurisy and tuberculosis as a child. Later he suffered mental breakdowns and saw demons.

Temperament: Some found Ruskin vain, conceited and arrogant, but others appreciated his support and generosity. He had no friends as a child but as an adult was a close friend of, among others, G. F. Watts, the Brownings and Carlyle. Jowett called him 'the gentlest and most innocent of mankind'.

Work/Daily Routine: Ruskin's parents paid him a shilling a page for his juvenile literary writings. He also wrote poetry and contributed to the *Architectural Magazine* under the pseudonym 'Kata Phusin'. He worked very hard, rising with the sun each day. He objected strongly to the painter Whistler charging 200 guineas for one of his paintings, which had taken only two days to complete – the quarrel went to court and Ruskin lost after Whistler argued that he was being paid not for two days' work but for 'the knowledge of a lifetime' (however, Whistler was only awarded one farthing damages). Ruskin greatly disliked the work of Raphael, hence his sympathy with the Pre-Raphaelites.

Manner of Death: Ruskin died of influenza at his home, Brantwood, in Coniston, Cumbria, at 2 pm on 20 January 1900, aged 80. He died in the arms of his cousin Joan Ruskin Severn, wife of the artist Arthur Severn (son of Joseph Severn, in whose arms Keats had died). He had refused to be buried in Westminster Abbey so was buried in Coniston churchyard instead.

SCHOPENHAUER, Arthur (1788–1860) German philosopher

Arthur Schopenhauer was born in the free city of Danzig (his parents wanted him to be born in England) on 22 February 1788, the son of Heinrich Floris Schopenhauer, a wealthy patrician merchant and Polish Court Councillor, and Johanna Trosiener, who later became a novelist. His parents were friends of the poet Klopstock, Madame de Staël's husband, the painter Tischbein (a friend of Goethe) and Dr Reimarus (the son of Lessing's friend). His mother later became a close friend of Goethe and was the first in Weimar society to receive Christiane Vulpius in Goethe's company. He had a younger sister Adele. When Danzig was annexed by Prussia the family moved to the independent (and pro-British) city of Hamburg. Schopenhauer was educated at first in Le Havre for two years (1797) in the care of the family of his father's business partner and then spent four years at the élite Dr Runge's Institute, Hamburg (1799). In 1803–4 he went on a grand tour with his parents and spent some time in a Wimbledon school learning English before beginning his training as a merchant in the country house of Senator Jenisch in Hamburg. After his father was found drowned in a canal in 1805, Schopenhauer followed his mother to Weimar (1807) where he attended the nearby Gymnasium Illustre at Gotha (where a fellow pupil was Carl John, later Goethe's secretary), but was forced to leave after lampooning a schoolmaster in a poem and attended the Altenburg Gymnasium (1807). When he came of age in 1809 he inherited 20,000 Reichstaler. In 1809–11 he studied medicine, natural sciences, Plato and Kant at the University of Göttingen (founded by George II of England) then philosophy under Fichte at the University of Berlin (1811) but fled to Rudolstadt when Napoleon invaded in 1813. Here he submitted a dissertation, 'On the Fourfold Root of the Principle of Sufficient Reason', to the University of Jena (then known for its readiness to confer doctorates), receiving a PhD, a copy of which he sent to Goethe. He then studied the Upanishads and Indian literature in Dresden (1814–18) and when the family's bankers nearly collapsed took a job as lecturer at the University of Berlin (1820). With the outbreak of a cholera epidemic in the city he left Berlin and lived in Frankfurt from 1831 until his death. He was 64 years old before his philosophical work, concerning such subjects as the role of human will, was recognized.

Family/Sex Life: Schopenhauer had a 10-year affair with a chorus girl and actress named Caroline Richter ('Medon'). In 1819 he fathered an illegitimate daughter by a Dresden lady's maid, but the child died that same year. In 1831 he proposed to 17-year-old Flora Weiss, but was rejected. His philosophy of the Will suggested that the only defence Man had against evil in the world was to adhere to ideals of asceticism and chastity.

Appearance: Of medium height, Schopenhauer had a rosy complexion and blue-flecked eyes and usually wore an ironic smiling expression. He had short silvery hair and was always well dressed.

Habits/Mannerisms: Schopenhauer had a large appetite and smoked cigars.

Sport/Hobbies: He enjoyed riding and had a particular passion for music, especially that of Mozart (though he disliked Wagner). He played his ivory flute daily for an hour before lunch (usually arrangements of Rossini). He also learned to speak English and was fluent in French.

Temperament: Schopenhauer was generally pessimistic and misanthropic. He was sued by a neighbour, a 47-year-old seamstress, for injuries she sustained after he forcibly ejected her from his room and had to pay her compensation for 20 years until she died. His friends included Goethe, who gave him a letter of introduction to Byron (then in Venice), though Schopenhauer did not use it. He was also very sensitive to noise. He thought Hegel a charlatan.

Pets: He kept a poodle called Atma ('world-soul').

Work/Daily Routine: Schopenhauer entered an essay for a Royal Danish Society for Learning competition, but failed to win – even though his was the only submission. He is best known for *Die Welt als Wille und Vorstellung* (The World as Will and Representation, 1819), which was published by his mother's publishers, Brockhaus. Other books included *Parerga und Paralipomena* (1851), a collection of essays and other pieces. His concentration on the apparently distorting and corrupting influence of human will left him profoundly depressed and pessimistic, as well as uncertain of his own identity. On one occasion, while examining plants in a Dresden greenhouse, his eccentric behaviour attracted the suspicious attention of an attendant who asked who he was – Schopenhauer only replied: 'If you could only answer that question for me, I'd be eternally grateful.'

Manner of Death: Schopenhauer died, apparently without pain, after getting up and sitting on a sofa on the morning of Friday 21 September 1860, in Frankfurt.

SCHUBERT, Franz Peter (1797–1828) Austrian composer

Franz Schubert was born at what is now 54 Nüssdorferstrasse, Himmelpfortgrund, Vienna, on 31 January 1797, one of 12 children of Franz Theodor Florian Schubert, a schoolmaster, and Maria Elizabet Katherina Vietz, a domestic servant (who died in 1812). His surviving older brothers were Ferdinand, Karl (a painter) and Ignaz and he had a younger sister Maria Theresa. He also had two half-sisters and two half-brothers by his father's second marriage to Anna Kleyenbock (1813). The family was so poor that Franz had to practise piano in a piano factory. Taught at first by his father (violin), his eldest brother Ignaz (piano) and the organist at Liechtental Church, he was accepted as a choirboy in the Imperial Court Chapel, Vienna (1808) and became a boarder at the Imperial and Royal City College under Court Musical Director Salieri (to whom he dedicated *Der Tod and das Mädchen*). In 1814 he became a schoolteacher in his father's school (thereby, but also because of defective eyesight, avoiding seven years' compulsory military service) before becoming music teacher to Count Johann Esterhazy's children, the Princesses Marie and Caroline, in Zseliz, Hungary (1818). He applied for the job of Vice-Director of the Austrian Imperial Court Chapel (1826) but was turned down. His most popular compositions included the 'Trout' Quintet

(1819), his C Major Symphony (1825) and his 'Unfinished' B Minor Symphony (1822). Other works included some 600 *Lieder* (songs) and choral and chamber music.

Family/Sex Life: Schubert never married but reputedly had an affair with his pupil Princess Caroline Esterhazy, youngest daughter of Count Esterhazy (he dedicated his F Minor Fantasy for piano duet to her).

Appearance: Thin and less than five feet tall, he had a high forehead, curly hair, long sideburns and wore glasses.

Habits/Mannerisms: He was nicknamed 'Schwammerl' ('little mushroom' in Viennese dialect) because he was so small.

Sport/Hobbies: When not working on his music, he liked to play charades.

Religion/Politics: Not very religious (his brother Ignaz was a notorious freethinker).

Health: Schubert was diagnosed with syphilis in 1822 and was admitted to Vienna Hospital in 1823. As a result of the illness, he suffered attacks of giddiness and acute headaches; later his hair fell out and he had to wear a wig.

Temperament: According to Johann Mayrhofer, 'His character was a mixture of tenderness and coarseness, sensuality and candour, sociability and melancholy.' Schubert had many friends, including Carl Maria von Weber. He was one of the 36 torchbearers at Beethoven's funeral and the dedication of his Variations Op. 10 to Beethoven read 'by his admirer and worshipper, Franz Schubert'. Beethoven in his turn reputedly said of him, 'Truly in Schubert there is a divine spark.' Liszt enthused: 'Such is the spell of your emotional world that it very nearly blinds us to the greatness of your craftsmanship.'

Work/Daily Routine: Schubert is best known as the composer of more than 600

songs (setting to music poems by Goethe, Ossian, Pope, Petrarch, Scott, Shakespeare, Schiller etc.), though he was also a very good violinist and viola player and wrote dances, sonatas, theatre music and chamber music. 'Erlkönig' was considered his greatest song in his lifetime. He worked usually in the mornings and wrote quickly, composing *Die Zauberharfe* (including the famous Rosamunde overture) in just two weeks. The famous 'Unfinished' Symphony (No. 8) was not his last – he *did* finish the Ninth (Great C Major) Symphony. He reputedly wrote the music for Shakespeare's 'Hark, hark the lark' on the back of a menu. His famous 'Ave Maria' song comes from his setting of Scott's *Lady of the Lake*. Particularly renowned in his day were the 'Schubertiads' (soirées) featuring him and the operatic baritone Johann Michael Vogl singing at the houses of various friends and elsewhere. These evenings were lampooned in 'Parody of the Schubert Circle' by the poet Bauernfeld.

Manner of Death: Schubert died after eating fish in a tavern in Vienna (31 October 1828). After the meal he felt sick and was unable to stomach food for days to follow. He was clearly unaware of the seriousness of his condition, writing to a friend in what was to prove his last letter (12 November): 'I am ill. I have had nothing to eat or drink for eleven days now, and can only stagger feebly and uncertainly between armchair and bed. So please be good enough to help me out in this desperate state with something to read. I have read Cooper's *Last of the Mohicans*, *The Spy*, *The Pilot* and *The Pioneers*. If by any chance you have anything else of him, do please leave it for me at the coffeehouse . . .' He finally died of typhoid (it is presumed) at 3 pm on 19 November 1828, aged 31. He was buried in Währing Cemetery, Vienna, next to Beethoven. A monument to him was erected in 1830 with an inscription by the poet Grillparzer: 'The art of music here entombed a rich possession, but even fairer hopes.'

SCHUMANN, Robert Alexander (1810–56) German composer

Robert Schumann was born at Am Markt No. 5, Zwickau in Saxony, Germany, on 8 June 1810, the fifth child of August Schumann, a writer, bookseller and publisher who translated Scott, Byron and Bulwer-Lytton into German, founded two periodicals and wrote an encyclopedia on Saxony (he died in 1826). His mother was Johanna Christiane Schnabel, daughter of the chief surgeon of Zeitz (she died in 1836) and his siblings (all older) were Julius, Edward, Karl and Emilie (none reached the age of 50). Taught piano at first by his mother and then by the choirmaster and organist of the Marienkirche, Zwickau, he then became a student of Friedrich Wieck. Educated at the Lyceum in Zwickau (1820–8), he also studied law at Leipzig University and later received an honorary doctorate from Jena University (1840). In 1834 he was a founder and editor (with Wieck) of the music journal *Neue Zeitschrift für Musik* and in 1843 he became a professor at Mendelssohn's Leipzig Conservatorium, though he later moved to Dresden and Düsseldorf. His deteriorating mental condition obliged him to vacate his posts and he retired to a mental asylum in 1854. His compositions included the A Minor Piano Concerto (1841–5), four symphonies, chamber music, numerous *Lieder* (songs) and piano music.

Family/Sex Life: In 1837 Schumann married Clara Josephine Wieck, the daughter of his piano teacher (herself a child prodigy and a brilliant concert pianist and later promoter of Schumann's works). The marriage went ahead despite Schumann's brief engagement (1834–5) to another pupil of Wieck's, Ernestine von Fricken, and despite Wieck vehemently refusing permission (he steamed open their letters and did all he could to prevent the union). Their children were Emil, Elise, Eugenie, Felix, Julie, Ludwig, Marie and Ferdinand.

Appearance: Handsome and powerfully built, with blue eyes, a ruddy complexion and a dimple in his cheeks when laughing, Schumann had long, thick dark-brown hair parted on the left. He wore a lorgnette, sported a top hat and in his later years always wore black.

Habits/Mannerisms: Schumann held himself erect when walking but had a loose-limbed gait. When talking he had a habit of nodding his head and when he smiled he tended to purse his lips. He had a weak speaking voice, not sonorous, and spoke quietly. His shortsightedness meant that he often had screwed-up eyes. He was a heavy drinker (usually beer but sometimes Rhine wine or champagne) and constantly smoked cigars.

Sport/Hobbies: Schumann enjoyed fencing, playing chess and collecting quotations (he was working on an anthology of music in poems, *Dichtergarten*, in the mental asylum when he died). He also spoke French.

Religion/Politics: Interested in spiritualism, Schumann was not very political, describing himself as a liberal republican.

Health: Schumann was very short-sighted and suffered from vertigo. In 1832 he broke the third finger on his right hand in a finger-strengthening machine and partly paralysed the index finger, thereby ruining his prospects as a performer. A manic depressive, who also suffered from syphilis, he became mentally ill, perpetually hearing the note A in his ears as well as hearing voices, having shivering fits, becoming terrified of drugs and metal instruments (even keys), hearing sublime or hellish music and tipping over tables. In 1854 he took off his wedding ring and threw himself from a bridge into the Rhine, but was rescued by a boatman. He was then committed, at his own request, to a private asylum in Endenich near Bonn. The threat of madness was something that had troubled Schumann as early as 1833, as he confided to Clara: 'This fear drove me from place to place – my breath stopped at the thought: "What if you were no longer able to think?" Clara, anyone who has once been crushed like that knows no worse suffering, or illness, or despair, that could possibly happen to him.'

Temperament: Schumann was absent-minded, shy and quiet. His friends included Mendelssohn and Brahms (who was his protégé), though Liszt and Wagner were among those who found him dull company.

Work/Daily Routine: The accident to his right hand in 1832 obliged Schumann to give up hopes of earning a living as a performer and subsequently he concentrated on writing and composing (it was largely thanks to Clara's encouragement that he began writing symphonies). He owned a Stein grand piano and smoked cigars while composing. Above his desk he kept a portrait of Napoleon.

Manner of Death: Schumann died alone, quietly, at 4 pm in Dr Franz Richarz's mental asylum in Endenich, near Bonn, on Tuesday 29 July 1856, aged 46. The autopsy revealed brain damage (his brain weighed 7 oz less than it should have done and there were signs of ossification at the base of the skull and atrophy of the brain). Brahms laid the headstone on his grave, as Clara Schumann recorded in her diary (7 June 1857): 'Today Johannes set the stone over my dear one's grave – my whole soul went with him.'

SCOTT, Walter (1771–1832) Scottish novelist and poet

Walter Scott was born in College Wynd, Edinburgh, on 15 August 1771, the fourth surviving child of Walter Scott, a solicitor, and Anne Rutherford, daughter of Dr John Rutherford, Professor of Medicine at Edinburgh University. He had two older brothers, Robert and John, and younger siblings Anne, Thomas and Daniel. Educated in Kelso and at Edinburgh High School (1778), he first went to Edinburgh University aged 12 (he left in 1785 after a bowel haemorrhage) and returned in 1789–92. Apprenticed in his father's practice, he was called to the Bar in 1792. He was also a captain in the Edinburgh Volunteer Light Dragoons (1797) and Sheriff-depute of Selkirkshire (1799) – a judge in a small rural court. He was later a partner in James Ballantyne Printers (1808) and John Ballantyne Booksellers

(1809). When Ballantynes went bankrupt (1826) Scott was personally liable for £114,000 but he refused offers of help from friends, declaring 'This right hand shall work it all off.' Writing furiously and also working as (from 1812) a Clerk to the Court of Session (earning £10,000 a year by 1818), the effort eventually killed him. Created baronet (1818), he was President of the Royal Society of Scotland, but refused the post of Poet Laureate (1813). In his novel writing he claimed inspiration from Maria Edgeworth and hoped to do for Scotland what she had for Ireland. His classic novels included *Waverley* (1814), *Rob Roy* (1817), *The Heart of Midlothian* (1818), *The Bride of Lammermoor* (1819) and *Ivanhoe* (1819). He also founded the *Quarterly Review* and discovered the rural poet James Hogg, the 'Ettrick Shepherd'.

Family/Sex Life: Rejected by Williamina Belsches, daughter of Sir John Stuart Belsches, in 1797 he married Charlotte Margaret Charpentier, daughter of Jean-François Charpentier, Ecuyer du Roi de L'Académie de Lyon. Their children were Walter, Charlotte Sophia, Anne and Charles.

Appearance: Tall and muscular, clean-shaven.

Habits/Mannerisms: Scott liked to answer letters on the day of receipt. He could be impulsive and absentminded; on one occasion, on being presented with a glass goblet by George IV he put it in his coat pocket and broke it the same day. He had a good memory for poetry etc. but was hopeless at remembering names, dates and so on. He would not let his children read his poetry, saying it was too trivial.

Sport/Hobbies: Scott enjoyed long walks, riding, greyhound-coursing, fishing, duck-shooting, gardening and playing chess. He refused to learn Greek and gave up Latin early but knew Italian, Spanish and French and worked as a German translator. He was well read and collected armour, coins and Scottish curios – he owned the Sword of Montrose, Bonnie Prince Charlie's 'quarch' (drinking cup), Rob Roy's dirk, purse and gun and Napoleon's gold bee-clasps. Another passion was his rebuilding of his home, Abbotsford, near Melrose Abbey, as a Gothic mansion (the cost contributed much to his financial problems).

Religion/Politics: He hated zealous religious types but believed in a benevolent Creator and in immortality. He was not, however, superstitious (he once slept in a room with a corpse in the other bed). A Jacobite/High Tory, he defended the Peterloo Massacre and supported the Union of Scotland and England.

Health: Lame in his right leg after poliomyelitis in his youth, Scott subsequently suffered a burst blood-vessel in the lower bowels (1785), stomach cramps (gallstones) – for which he took calomel (1817–20) – and a paralytic stroke (1830). He took laudanum while dictating *The Bride of Lammermoor* because of the pain from his gallstones; *Rob Roy* was also written in great pain. Other ailments included chilblains and rheumatism.

Temperament: Humane, generous and kindhearted, Scott was much liked. His friends included Professor David Hume (nephew of philosopher David Hume), George Canning, Wordsworth, James Hogg, 'Monk' Lewis and Mungo Park. Admirers included Byron ('Wonderful man! I long to get drunk with him'). Scott in his turn greatly admired Burns (he met him once when he was 15 and Burns 28).

Pets: Scott kept dogs and always wrote with one at his side. Among his favourites were the enormous Maida (a cross between a 'deer greyhound and the mastiff, with a shaggy mane like a lion'), Camp (a black-and-tan English terrier crossed with an English brindled bulldog bitch), the bloodhound Nimrod and the greyhounds Bran and Hamlet. His tomcat Hinse of Hinsfield was killed by Nimrod. He also had a pony called Earwig (1796) and a horse named Lenore.

Work/Daily Routine: Scott was the top-selling poet in Britain and made a fortune from *The Lay of the Last Minstrel, The Lady of the Lake* etc. but largely gave up poetry after Byron began writing. He rose at 5 am and was at his desk by 6 am. He finished writing by noon. His huge desk had two desktops so he could work on two projects at once. He worked fast, writing 14 novels in six years (three in 1820 alone). *Guy Mannering* was written in six weeks. *Waverley* was repeatedly put aside because of discouragement from his publisher (he later found the manuscript amongst his fishing tackle and finished it) – it sold out in five weeks. His own favourite was *The Antiquary*. Four of his novels were published anonymously and he denied authorship of *Waverley* to George IV when Prince Regent (1815). Speculation about the identity of the 'Great Unknown' was intense, but Mrs Murray Keith, an old Scottish lady who furnished Scott with tales for his novels was not deceived: 'D'ye think I dinna ken my ain groats among other folks' kail [broth]?' His pseudonyms included Jebediah Cleisbotham, Crystal Croftangry, Malachi Malagrowther, Lawrence Templeton and Captain Clutterbuck. His 'Hail to the Chief' (from *The Lady of the Lake*) is played to honour US Presidents (with music by James Sanderson).

Motto/Emblem: Scott's motto (set below a portcullis) was '*Clausus tutus ero*' ('I shall be safe when closed up') – a rough anagram of his name in Latin. Favourite sayings were 'If it isna weel bobbit/We'll bob it again', 'Time and I against any two' and 'But patience, cousin, and shuffle the cards.'

Manner of Death: Scott suffered a cerebral haemorrhage (1830) that left him temporarily speechless and paralysed. He died at Abbotsford on 21 September 1832, aged 61, of apoplexy. He was buried in Dryburgh Abbey.

SHAKESPEARE, William (1564–1616) English playwright and poet

William Shakespeare was christened on 26 April 1564 in Stratford-upon-Avon, Warwickshire, as 'Gulielmus filius Johannes Shakspere'. He was the eldest surviving child of John Shakespeare – a glover who later became a town councillor, alderman, bailiff and Justice of the Peace – and Mary Arden, eighth and youngest daughter of a wealthy land-owner. Three brothers, Gilbert, Richard and Edmund (also an actor) survived childhood as did one sister, Joan. All predeceased him except Joan. He was educated in Stratford but according to Ben Jonson 'had little Latine and lesse Greek.' He may have worked as a schoolmaster and actor but reputedly had to leave Stratford when caught poaching deer from Charlecote Park. By 1587, having left his wife and three children in Stratford, he was in London – acting with the Queen's Company (*c.*1587) and then with the Lord Chamberlain's Men at The Theatre, Bishopsgate (the troupe included the great actor Richard Burbage, whose father owned The Theatre). He first performed before Elizabeth I at Greenwich Palace (1594) and repeatedly thereafter. The

troupe later moved to the new and larger Swan Theatre before dismantling The Theatre and using the wood to build The Globe in Bankside beside The Rose, home of the Admiral's Men (whose writers included Jonson and Chapman). His main income was as an actor as he only got a maximum of £8 for each play. Nonetheless, by 1602 he owned the finest house in Stratford and a 127-acre estate. On the death of Queen Elizabeth, James I took over the troupe as the King's Men and the actors became Grooms of the Chamber and wore scarlet royal livery. At his death *Twelfth Night* (1601), *Macbeth* (1606), *Antony and Cleopatra* (1606–7) and *The Tempest* (1611) were unpublished but were edited for publication with his other works (in all 36 plays and 150 sonnets, though *Troilus and Cressida* was accidentally left off the contents list for the first edition). His other highly celebrated stage works included the comedies *A Midsummer Night's Dream* (*c.*1595) and *As You Like It* (1599), the tragedies *Romeo and Juliet* (*c.*1595), *Hamlet* (1601) and *King Lear* (*c.*1605) and the history plays *Richard III* (1591) and *Henry V*

(1599). Shakespeare's successor as playwright to the King's Men was the now little known Nathan Field.

Family/Sex Life: In 1582, when he was 18, Shakespeare married the pregnant Anne (also spelt Agnes), daughter of Richard Hathaway, eight years his senior – a special licence was granted by the Bishop of Worcester to call the banns only once. Their daughter Susanna was born six months later and was followed by the twins Hamnet and Judith. He is thought to have had an affair with Mary Fitton, daughter of Sir Edward Fitton and maid of honour to Elizabeth I – and a contender as the mysterious 'dark lady' of the sonnets. There has also been speculation about homosexual relationships.

Appearance: Described by Aubrey as 'A handsome, well shap't man', he had hazel eyes and thick auburn hair, though this later receded. He wore a thin moustache, with a tuft of hair under his lower lip.

Religion/Politics: Some claim that, at the age of 46, he was author of the King James Version of the Bible (1610), offering as 'proof' the 46th word of the 46th Psalm – 'Shake' – and the 46th word from the end of the psalm – 'Spear'.

Temperament: Aubrey related that Shakespeare was 'Very good company, and of a very readie and pleasant smoothe Witt.' Others called him modest, civil and generous. His friends included Jonson (who dubbed him the 'Sweet Swan of Avon ... thou Starre of Poets'). He was not universally admired though – Dryden thought him 'affected', while Addison omitted him from his *Account of the Greatest English Poets* and Hume called him 'a disproportionate and misshapen giant'. Bernard Shaw wrote: 'With the single exception of Homer, there is no eminent writer, not even Sir Walter Scott, whom I can despise so entirely as I despise Shakespeare when I measure my mind against his' (*Saturday Review*, 1896).

Work/Daily Routine: Legend has it that Shakespeare never blotted out a line in his life (Ben Jonson said 'I wish he had blotted-out a thousand'). New coinages ascribed to him include 'aerial', 'assassination', 'barefaced', 'bump', 'clangour', 'critic', 'countless', 'laughable', 'hurry', 'eventful' and 'road'. Influenced as a writer by Sir Philip Sydney and Marlowe, he drew on many sources for his plays, including (for the histories) Ralph Holinshed's *The Chronicles of England, Scotland and Ireland* and (for the Roman plays) North's translation of Plutarch's *Lives*. Some characters were based on real people – Jaques in *As You Like It*, for instance, was based on Jonson. *The Comedy of Errors* (1594) was his only play without a song in it. There is much debate over the parts Shakespeare might have taken in his own works – he almost certainly played the Chorus in *Henry V* and the Ghost in *Hamlet*. Some critics still insist that Shakespeare was not the true author of the plays, and that they were really by Francis Bacon (among others).

Motto/Emblem: Shakespeare's motto was '*Non sans droit*'. His father obtained an official coat of arms in 1596 – 'gould, on a bend sable, a speare of the first steeled argent. And for his creast or cognizaunce a faulcon, his wings displayed argent standing on a wrethe of his coullers, supporting a speare gould steeled as aforesaid.'

Manner of Death: Shakespeare died, supposedly after drinking with Jonson and the poet Michael Drayton, on 23 April 1616, aged 52. He was buried in Holy Trinity Church, Stratford. He left his money to his sister Joan and daughter Judith, his property to his daughter Susanna and his 'second best bed [the one he died on] with the furniture' to his wife. His gravestone reads:
Good friend for Iesus' sake forbeare,
To digg the dust enclosed heare.
Blese be ye man that spares thes stones
And curst be he that moves my bones.

His birthplace in Stratford was a butcher's shop until 1850, when it was preserved as a British monument after US showman P. T. Barnum tried to buy it. Features of the building include the names of distinguished early visitors scratched on the window panes.

SHAW, George Bernard (1856–1950) Irish playwright and critic

George Bernard Shaw was born at 3 (later 33) Upper Synge Street, Dublin, on 26 July 1856, the youngest child of George Carr Shaw – a civil servant – and Lucinda Elizabeth Gurly, 17 years his junior and later a music teacher. He was also related to Sir Robert Shaw, founder of the Royal Bank of Ireland. He had two elder sisters, Lucinda Frances (who caught tuberculosis and later died of starvation) and Elinor Agnes, a professional singer. Educated at the Central Model Boys' School, Dublin, and at the Dublin English Scientific and Commercial Day School, at 15 he worked for Townshend's estate agents in Dublin for four years, later becoming chief cashier. His father being a drunk, the family moved in with their neighbour George Vandaleur Lee, a music teacher and conductor who taught his mother singing. When Lee moved to London, his mother and sisters went too (1872) and Shaw later followed (1876, not returning to Ireland for 29 years). Here he wrote five novels, and, apart from a brief job at the Edison Telephone Company, was kept by his mother for nine years ('I did not throw myself into the struggle for life: I threw my mother into it'). He later worked as art, book and music critic for various papers and was drama critic for the *Saturday Review* (1895–8). He wrote his first play in 1892 and subsequently created some 40 stage works, including *Arms and the Man* (1894), *Candida* (1897), *The Devil's Disciple* (1897), *Man and Superman* (1903), *Major Barbara* (1905), *Androcles and the Lion* (1912), *Pygmalion* (1913), *Heartbreak House* (1919), *Back to Methuselah* (1921) and *Saint Joan* (1923).

He also gave lectures, was a borough councillor for St Pancras (1897) and received the Nobel Prize for Literature (1925) – though he refused a knighthood, a peerage and the Order of Merit. He was also on the council of RADA, and committees for the Stage Society, Authors' Society, Dramatists' Club and Society of Authors. The Malvern Festival was founded in 1927 to present his plays.

Family/Sex Life: Shaw was first seduced, at 29, by Mrs Jenny Patterson, 12 years older. He was reputedly engaged to the Fabian Annie Besant, but found her atheistic marriage contract unacceptable. He continued to live with his mother, until, aged 42 (1898), he married Charlotte Frances Payne-Townshend, daughter of a millionaire Irish barrister. His wife was not interested in either children or sex.

Appearance: Over six feet tall, lithe and broad-chested, though never more than nine stone, Shaw had red hair and beard (which later became snowy white). Beatrice Webb remarked on his 'laughing blue eyes' (though he sometimes wore spectacles). He was a fastidious dresser but disliked vests and wore an all-wool suit designed by Dr Jaeger ('I want my body to breathe'); he also wore grey collars and unlined jackets on principle.

Habits/Mannerisms: Shaw was a vegetarian from the age of 25 (1881) and ate wholemeal bread and never drank spirits, tea or coffee. He was a militant non-smoker and sang every night for his health. He slept with the windows open and ate grapefruit for breakfast. He was famous for his idiosyncratic spelling, which included 'Shakespear', 'program' and no apostrophes in 'didnt', and used spaced letters (not italic) for emphasis. He also owned a chauffeur-driven Rolls-Royce (which once crashed with Danny Kaye inside).

Sport/Hobbies: Shaw enjoyed boxing (Gene Tunney was a friend), swimming, walking and dancing and listed his hobbies in *Who's Who* as 'cycling and showing off'. He also played the piano well and sang (baritone). His favourite music included Wagner. Another passion was letter-writing (he wrote some 250,000 in all).

Religion/Politics: Reared as a Protestant, he was described by G. K. Chesterton as 'A heathen mystic.' He was a founder member (1884) of the Fabian Society, supported women's rights and the Boer War, opposed vivisection, supported Roger Casement and admired Mussolini and Hitler. He was defeated as the Progressive Party candidate for the LCC (1904) and was a member of the Parliamentary Committee on Stage Censorship (1909).

Health: Early health problems included smallpox, a foot injury and a general physical collapse (1884). He was also anaemic and had to have liver injections, despite being a vegetarian.

Temperament: The young Shaw was sensitive, shy and nervous – he later adopted a hectoring manner to counteract this and became egoistic. His friends included the actresses Ellen Terry and Mrs Patrick Campbell (for whom he wrote *Pygmalion*), T. E. Lawrence (who became a sort of honorary son and changed his

name to Shaw), William Morris, the Webbs, H. G. Wells and Thomas Hardy (he was a pallbearer at Hardy's funeral). Oscar Wilde, though, joked, 'He hasn't an enemy in the world, and none of his friends like him!', while Saki disliked him for his egotism and Joyce remarked 'Shaw's work makes me admire the magnificent tolerance and broadmindedness of the English.' Shaw in his turn despised Shelley, Homer, Scott and Shakespeare. When attacked by Belloc and Chesterton, he retaliated by calling them 'the Chesterbelloc ... a very amusing pantomime elephant'. He also disliked Americans, claiming that 'the 100 per cent American is 99 per cent an idiot.'

Work/Daily Routine: Shaw wrote in the mornings in the summer-house in the garden at his home, 'Shaw's Corner' in Ayot St Lawrence, Hertfordshire. A mechanism meant he could revolve the summer-house to catch the sun. He used lots of little notebooks to jot ideas down in. His pseudonyms included Redbarn Wash, G. B. Larking, Corno di Bassetto, Horatio Ribbonson and P. Shaw. He campaigned for simplified spelling and a new 44-letter alphabet, leaving money in his will for his work to be continued. He chose the casts for his plays and used publishers only as distributors, dealing direct with printers, binders, typographers, paper merchants etc. He also wrote five novels.

Manner of Death: Shaw died aged 94 after fracturing a thigh in a fall whilst pruning a tree at Ayot St Lawrence on 2 November 1950. His body was cremated and his ashes were later mixed with those of his wife and scattered in the garden at 'Shaw's Corner'. On his death the lights of Broadway were dimmed and the Indian Cabinet adjourned in respect.

SHELLEY, Percy Bysshe (1792–1822) English poet and political pamphleteer

Percy Shelley was born on 4 August 1792 at Field Place, Warnham, near Horsham, Sussex, the eldest son of Sir Timothy Shelley, Whig MP for New Shoreham, a wealthy landowner and Justice of the Peace – himself the son of Sir Bysshe Shelley Bart (born in New Jersey, USA), of Castle Goring. This made the poet himself heir to a baronetcy and £200,000 when Sir Bysshe died (1815). His mother was Elizabeth Pilfold and he had four sisters – Elizabeth, Mary, Hellen and Margaret – and a younger brother, John. Educated at Syon House Academy (Brentford), Eton (1804–10) and University College, Oxford, he was sent down after one year with his friend Thomas Jefferson Hogg for refusing to disavow atheism in the pamphlet 'The Necessity of Atheism' Shelley had written under the pseudonym 'Jeremiah Stukeley'. Thereafter he worked full-time as a writer, living in Scotland, Ireland, Devon, Wales and (from 1818) Italy but was supported by a legacy of £1000 a year after the death of his grandfather. His most celebrated writings included the poem *Queen Mab* (1813) and the verse drama *Prometheus Unbound* (1818–19).

Family/Sex Life: Shelley eloped with his sister's 16-year-old schoolfriend Harriet Westbrook (daughter of a coffee-house proprietor) when he was 19, marrying her in Edinburgh (1811) then in London (1814). Pregnant by another man, she committed suicide in 1816 (she drowned in the Serpentine, London). Their children were Eliza Ianthe and Charles Bysshe (who died of tuberculosis aged 11). It was to Harriet that Shelley dedicated *Queen Mab*. He then married Mary Godwin, daughter of the philosopher William Godwin and later the author of *Frankenstein*, in 1816, just 15 days after hearing of Harriet's death. Their children were William and Clara, who both died young, and Sir Percy

Florence. He was probably also the father of Elena Adelaide Shelley (registered thus by him in Naples) by Claire Clairmont (the child was fostered). Clairmont was Mary Godwin's half-sister and also the mother of Byron's illegitimate child Allegra; it was to her that Shelley dedicated 'To Constantia, Singing'.

Appearance: Shelley was five feet 11 inches tall and was slim, agile and strong but round-shouldered; he walked with a slight stoop. He had a very small head, with deep blue eyes and a girlish complexion, fair and freckled. He also had long dark brown wavy hair and a soft high-pitched voice. He dressed flamboyantly, wearing open-necked shirts etc.

Habits/Mannerisms: A non-smoker and a vegetarian (he wrote *A Vindication of Natural Diet*, 1813), he did not drink wine but ate a lot of bread, raisins, prunes, honey, fruit and tea.

Sport/Hobbies: Shelley enjoyed horse-riding, target pistol-shooting and sailing his boat *Ariel* (though he could not swim). He spoke Spanish, played the flute and was interested in chemistry, performing experiments while at Oxford. An insatiable reader, he often read at night (consequently falling asleep in the daytime) and collected books. He once took a wooden splinter from the door of Tasso's prison cell in Ferrara and sent it home to Peacock.

Religion/Politics: He was an atheist, though Byron called him 'Shiloh' (the name of the Messiah due to be born in 1814). Influenced by Rousseau and William Godwin, he was a left-wing Radical and wrote numerous political pamphlets. He once entered his occupation in a Mont Blanc hotel register as 'Democrat, Philanthropist, Atheist' (1816).

Health: A hypochondriac, he took laudanum for 'nervous attacks' and also suffered from tuberculosis of both lungs (1815), shortsightedness and (possibly) from kidney stones. He did, though, have a very good memory. In 1811 he escaped death when three shots were fired at him after he killed some diseased sheep in Tan-yr-allt, Wales.

Temperament: Rebellious, with an unbreakable will, he was called 'Mad Shelley' at school. His friends included Byron, Keats (to whom he dedicated *Adonais*), Peacock (who depicted him as Scythrop in *Nightmare Abbey*), Trelawny and Leigh Hunt (to whom he dedicated the play *The Cenci*). Another friend was Southey, but they later fell out, Southey calling Shelley 'a liar and a cheat; he paid no regard to truth, nor to any kind of moral obligation'. Charles Kingsley dismissed him as 'a lewd vegetarian'.

Pets: Shelley disliked cats – he once tied one to a kite and flew it into a stormcloud.

Work/Daily Routine: Shelley's reputation as a poet was almost entirely posthumous. Lesser known works included novels, for instance *Zastrozzi* and *Irvyne, or the Rosicrucian*, a translation of Plato's *Symposium* and a satire on George IV – *Swellfoot the Tyrant*. His pseudonyms included 'John Fitzvictor', 'The Hermit of Marlow', 'Pleyel', 'Victor', 'Jeremiah Stukeley' and 'Mr Jones'. *Queen Mab* was published at his own expense (250 copies). His first published verse was *Original Poetry by Victor and Cazire* (1810), which included poems by his sister Elizabeth and one stolen from 'Monk' Lewis.

Manner of Death: On 8 July 1822, when he was 29, Shelley was drowned in the Bay of Spezia after encountering a storm while sailing in *Ariel* 10 miles out from Viareggio, Italy. He was returning from a meeting with Byron and Leigh Hunt about starting a new journal, *The Liberal*; drowned with him were his friend Edward Ellerker Williams and a sailor friend of Trelawny's, Charles Vivian. Shelley's remains were washed up near Viareggio on the 18 July, his body and face so badly eaten by fish that he was only identified by the volume of Sophocles in one pocket and Hunt's copy of Keats's poems (*Lamia*) in the other. He was buried in the sand by the health authorities but the bodies were later burned on the shore in separate funeral pyres in the style of the ancient Greeks by Trelawny (15/16 August 1822). Byron and Leigh Hunt were present and Byron requested Shelley's skull, but Trelawny, recalling how he had seen Byron use a skull as a drinking cup, refused. His ashes were buried in the Protestant Cemetery, Rome, with his son William and Keats. His heart was given to Hunt, then passed to Mary, who carried it in a silk bag. After her death it was buried in Bournemouth beside their son Percy.

SHERIDAN, Richard Brinsley Butler (1751–1816)
Anglo-Irish playwright, theatre manager and politician

R. B. Sheridan was born at 12 Dorset Street, Dublin, on 30 October 1751, the third son of Thomas Sheridan, actor-manager and author of a two-volume dictionary that rivalled Dr Johnson's, and Frances Chamberlaine, a novelist (who died when he was 15). His elder brother was the Irish MP and author Charles Francis and he had two younger sisters, Elizabeth and Alicia. Educated at Harrow

School (where he was regarded as a dunce), he was left behind there when the entire family emigrated to Blois, France, in 1764. He later studied law at the Middle Temple and then became (1778) manager and eventually sole proprietor of the Drury Lane Theatre (until it burnt down in 1809). He served as MP for Stafford (1780) and later for Ilchester, becoming Under-Secretary for Foreign Affairs (1782) and Secretary to the Treasury (1783). Highly acclaimed for his witty comedies of manners, he is remembered above all for *The Rivals* (1775) and *The School for Scandal* (1777).

Family/Sex Life: Sheridan eloped to France with Eliza Anne Linley, a singer and the daughter of the composer Thomas Linley; they were legally married in 1773. Eliza was very beautiful and her admirers included the (married) Major Matthews, with whom Sheridan was obliged to fight two duels with swords. She died in 1792; their son was Thomas Sheridan MP. In 1795 Sheridan took as his second wife Esther Ogle, daughter of the Dean of Westminster. They had a son, Charles, and it was to her that he dedicated *Pizarro* (1799). Esther, however, was extravagant in her tastes, and her expenditure, compounded by the disastrous burning of the Drury Lane Theatre in 1809, did much to reduce Sheridan to a state of financial ruin in his final years.

Appearance: Fanny Burney, describing Sheridan, spoke of his 'fine figure, and a good, though I don't think handsome, face. He is tall and very upright, and his appearance and address are at once manly and fashionable without the smallest tincture of foppery or modish graces.' He had very fine dark hazel eyes and was clean-shaven; later in life he acquired a very red and blotchy face from heavy drinking.

Habits/Mannerisms: Sheridan frequently drank to excess (Byron often had to take him home). His favourite tipple at first was

claret, though he later preferred brandy. He was arrested for drunkenness on the opening night of *The School for Scandal*. Attempts by friends to point out the danger that he would destroy the coat of his stomach by his drinking were floored with the reply: 'Well then, my stomach must just digest in its waistcoat.' Later, however, he became teetotal and drank only water. Friends found him generally taciturn but brilliant when he did speak and testified that he had a mellifluous voice. He did not much enjoy going to the theatre and reputedly never watched a whole play (except rehearsals of his own) in his entire life. He never himself used his name Butler.

Sport/Hobbies: Sheridan enjoyed fencing, riding and gambling (notably at Brooks' Club). He was also a member of Dr Johnson's Club.

Religion/Politics: A Whig MP and ally of Charles James Fox, he earned a considerable reputation as a witty parliamentary speaker. When he was rebuked by the Speaker for calling another MP a liar, he delivered an apology that became part of parliamentary legend: 'Mr Speaker, I said the honourable member was a liar it is true and I am sorry for it. The honourable member may place the punctuation where he pleases.'

Health: Sheridan was an insomniac and also suffered from varicose veins, which made walking difficult. He was badly wounded in his second duel with Major Matthews.

Temperament: Sheridan was witty, sometimes taciturn, improvident and provocative. His friends in public life included Fox and the Prince Regent himself. In 1809 he behaved with admirable self-composure when the news arrived that his theatre – and thus his fortune – was being lost in a disastrous fire. He chose a seat at the nearby Great Piazza Coffee House (now the Floral Hall) and calmly watched the building burn to the ground. When friends questioned his calm demeanour, he protested: 'A man may surely be allowed to take a glass of wine by his own fireside.'

Work/Daily Routine: Sheridan only spent five years of his life as a playwright (1775–9), but 32 years as a politician. He was greatly admired by Byron, who thought *The School for Scandal* the best comedy, *The Duenna* the best opera and *The Critic* the best farce ever written. He once said, 'Whatever Sheridan has done or chosen to do has been par excellence the best of its kind.' As an MP he could not be arrested for debt but after the fire at the Drury Lane Theatre he lost his seat and the creditors moved in (he was arrested in 1813). His debts were a constant source of anxiety, but Sheridan was often unworldly about his problems. On one occasion,

handing a creditor an IOU, he sighed 'Thank God that's settled.' Asked at least to pay the interest on a large amount he owed his tailor he flatly refused to pay either the principal sum or the interest accruing on it, explaining, 'It is not my interest to pay the principal, nor my principle to pay the interest.'

Manner of Death: Sheridan died in great poverty on Sunday 7 July 1816, aged 64. After he died he suffered a last indignity by being arrested for debt (friends paid the fine to allow him to be buried). He was buried in Westminster Abbey and was honoured with a grander funeral than was arranged for either Pitt or Fox. He had hoped to be buried near Fox and remembered as a politician, but he was laid to rest near Garrick and is remembered above all for his plays.

SMOLLETT, Tobias George (1721–71) Scottish novelist and doctor

Tobias Smollett was baptized on 19 March 1721 in Dalquharn, near Dunbarton, Scotland, the younger son of Archibald Smollett, a landowner who died when he was two (*c.* 1723), and Barbara Cunningham. His grandfather was the judge and MP Sir James Smollett, laird of Bonhill, who was one of the commissioners involved with the Union of Scotland and England. He had an elder brother James and an elder sister Jean. Educated at Dunbarton Grammar School, he studied medicine at Glasgow University and later received his MD from Aberdeen University. He was at first apprenticed to the surgeon Dr John Gordon (1736), then came to London and served in the Royal Navy (1740–4) as surgeon on HMSS *Chichester* and *Cumberland*. In 1741 he sailed with the Navy to the West Indies for the unsuccessful assault on Spanish-held Cartagena. He then became a surgeon in

Downing Street, London, settling in Chelsea in 1750, and was later co-founder of the *Critical Review* and the *British Magazine*. He spent much of his last years travelling Europe with his wife. As a novelist, he is usually remembered for such picaresque works as *The Adventures of Roderick Random* (1748), *The Adventures of Peregrine Pickle* (1751) and *Humphry Clinker* (1771). Less well-known works included his *Complete History of England* (1757–8) and the naval farce *The Reprisal* (1757).

Family/Sex Life: Around 1746 Smollett married the wealthy heiress Nancy Lassells, the Creole daughter of an English plantation owner whom he met while in Jamaica. They had one daughter, Elizabeth.

Appearance: Described by Scott as

'eminently handsome, his features prepossessing', he was said by others to have a roguish smile.

Habits/Mannerisms: Smollett frequented taverns a great deal. On the night of 10 December 1754 he was robbed of his purse and watch in a stage coach between Chelsea (then Middlesex) and London.

Sport/Hobbies: He spoke Italian and Spanish.

Religion/Politics: Though not a Jacobite, his early poem 'The Tears of Scotland' lamented the brutality of the English Duke of Cumberland after Culloden. He once wrote: 'Patriotism is of no party.'

Health: Smollett suffered from chronic rheumatism, ulcers, asthma, colic and skin diseases. While touring Scotland in the 1750s he exhibited symptoms of tuberculosis. He was also much distressed by the death of his 15-year-old daughter (1763).

Temperament: Smollett was surly, proud, independent, argumentative and hated ceremony. According to the *Dictionary of National Biography* he was 'essentially a difficult man', though Scott decided he was 'kind, generous and humane to others . . . a doating father, and an affectionate husband'. Sterne lampooned him as 'Smelfungus' in *Sentimental Journey* and thought him a 'choleric philistine'. Horace Walpole, meanwhile, called him 'a profligate hireling'. His friends included David Hume, David Garrick (whom he satirized as Marmozet in *Roderick Random*) and the poet James Thomson.

It was Smollett who, in a letter to John Wilkes, dubbed Dr Johnson 'the Great Cham [Khan] of Literature' (1759).

Work/Daily Routine: Smollett's first novel, *Roderick Random*, was published anonymously and when translated into French had Fielding's name on it (Lady Mary Wortley Montagu and others attributed it to Fielding). Relations between Smollett and Fielding were not good. He accused Fielding of plagiarism in the (anonymous) pamphlet *Habakkukk Hilding* (1752) and satirized Fielding as Mr Spondy in *Peregrine Pickle*. In his *Continuation of the Complete History* (1760), however, he generously conceded his rival's genius. He wrote *Sir Launcelot Greaves* in the King's Bench Prison after receiving a fine of £100 and a three months' sentence for libelling Admiral Charles Knowles (1760). Debts were a constant problem, exacerbated by the expenses he incurred moving in high society in London and trying to maintain a lavish home in Chelsea. In the attempt to stave off financial pressures he agreed to undertake all manner of literary work, including editing and translation work (he translated *Don Quixote* and *Gil Blas* among other pieces).

Manner of Death: Smollett died after chronic diarrhoea, convulsions and fever led to an acute intestinal infection near Leghorn, Italy, on the night of 17 September 1771, aged 50. He was buried in the English cemetery there. His last words (to his wife) were: 'All is well, my dear.' His tomb had four different inscriptions, in Italian, Latin, Greek and English.

SOUTHEY, Robert (1774–1843) English poet and historian

Robert Southey was born in Bristol on 12 August 1774, the oldest surviving child of Robert Southey, a linen draper, and

Margaret Hill, his siblings being Thomas, Henry Herbert and Edward. He was brought up at first by his mother's half-sister, Elizabeth Tyler, in Bath, but moved to his father's house in Bristol aged six and was educated there and in nearby Corston. His uncle Herbert Hill, chaplain at the British Factory in Lisbon, paid for his education. Expelled from Westminster School for writing an essay against flogging in the school magazine, he then attended Balliol College, Oxford, having been rejected by Christ Church because of the Westminster incident. After studying law at Gray's Inn he became Secretary to Isaac Corry, Chancellor of the Exchequer (based in Ireland). Acclaimed both for his prose writings and for his works as one of the celebrated 'Lake Poets', he declined the editorship of *The Times* and a Baronetcy from Peel but received a government pension in 1807, was elected Poet Laureate in 1813 (recommended by Scott who had refused it) and was granted a further annual government pension of £300 by Peel. His most celebrated writings included the poems 'Inchcape Rock' and 'After Blenheim', his letters and his *Life of Nelson* (1813).

Family/Sex Life: In 1795 Southey married Edith Fricker, thus becoming Coleridge's brother-in-law. Unfortunately, she went mad and had to be incarcerated in a mental home from 1834 (she died in 1837). Their children were Herbert, Isabel, Margaret, Charles Cuthbert, Edith Mary, Bertha and Kate. In 1839 he took as his second wife the poet Caroline Anne Bowles, who had once sent her narrative poem 'Ellen Fitzarthur' to him anonymously.

Appearance: Very handsome.

Sport/Hobbies: Southey's great passion was collecting books – he assembled a library of 14,000 volumes at Greta Hall, Keswick, Cumbria (he was a very rapid reader).

Religion/Politics: As a young man Southey was a Republican radical and in 1794 with Coleridge planned the utopian

'pantisocracy' community that they hoped to establish in the USA. This community, comprising six families, was to be run on the ideals of brotherly love and shared property. Southey was very excited about the plan, saying: 'This Pantosocratic scheme has given me new life, new hope, new energy; all of the faculties of my mind are dilated.' The scheme, though, was never realized thanks to lack of funds (in any case, Southey and Coleridge fell out with one another a year later over a missed lecture engagement, and it was some time before they made up). His views later became more conservative and he sided with the Tories (from 1809 he was a contributor to the Tory *Quarterly Review*). This change in political sympathies was seen as a cowardly desertion by some contemporaries. Thomas Love Peacock, for instance, was incensed enough to lampoon Southey in his *Melincourt* (1817) as Mr Feathernest, a poet who abandons his principles for social advantage. Byron, criticized by Southey in *A Vision of Judgment* (1821), delivered his own attack on Southey in his parody *The Vision of Judgment* (1822):

'He had written for republics far and wide,
And then against them bitterer than ever;
For pantisocracy he once had cried
Aloud, a scheme less moral than 'twas clever;
Then grew a hearty anti-Jacobin –
Had turned his coat – and would have turned his skin.'

Southey was proposed and elected as MP for Downton, Wiltshire (1826) but turned the post down (1827).

Health: Southey's mental health, including his memory, began to deteriorate around 1840, in which year he ceased to recognize even his old friend Wordsworth.

Temperament: By his own account, Southey had 'a heart full of poetry and feeling' and he was naturally at home in the company of other poets. While living in Keswick in the Lake District, he was a close associate of Wordsworth and the Coleridges. He was honest and generous and often helped friends in trouble (he supported Coleridge's family after he deserted them and arranged an edition of Chatterton's works for the benefit of the dead poet's sister and child). Not all aspiring writers benefited from his support, however – when Charlotte Brontë, an admirer, wrote asking his advice about becoming a novelist he replied rather sternly: 'Literature cannot be the business of a woman's life.'

Pets: Southey kept more than 12 cats, including Bona Marietta, The Zombi, Lord Nelson, Pulcherin, Sir Thomas Dido, Hurlyburlypuss and Rumpelstilzchen (a tabby and white with green eyes). He declared: 'A kitten is in the animal world what a rosebud is in a garden.'

Work/Daily Routine: Southey once described his working routine to a Quaker lady, seeking to impress her. According to his own version, he rose at 5 am, read Spanish from 6 to 8 am, read French from 8 to 9 am, read Portuguese from 9 to 9.30 am, then wrote poetry for two hours, then prose for two hours – and so on until bedtime. The Quaker lady's only response was: 'And pray, Friend, when dost thou think?' He produced a huge amount of work, not least of which was the classic children's story 'The Three Bears' (though in his version it is an old woman, not the little girl Goldilocks, who eats the porridge).

Manner of Death: Southey died of fever on 21 March 1843, aged 68. He was buried in Crosthwaite Churchyard, Keswick.

SPENSER, Edmund (c.1552–99) English poet and civil servant

Edmund Spenser was born c.1552 in East Smithfield, London, the son of John Spenser, a free journeyman in the Merchant Taylors' Guild, and his wife Elizabeth. Educated at the Merchant Taylors' School, he was a sizar at Pembroke Hall, Cambridge (1569, MA 1576). He worked at first as secretary to John Young, Bishop of Rochester (and formerly Master of Pembroke Hall in Spenser's time) and then (1579) in the household of the Earl of Leicester, Queen Elizabeth's favourite and the most powerful minister in England. In 1580 he moved to Ireland as secretary to Arthur, Lord Grey of Wilton, (Protestant) Deputy of Ireland, and remained there until the end of his life. He became successively, Clerk for Faculties in the Irish Court of Chancery (1581), Commissioner for Musters in County Kildare (1583), Deputy Clerk to the Council of Munster (1587) and finally High Sheriff of Cork (1598).

Spenser lived in Kilcolman Castle near Doneraille, County Cork (where Sir Walter Ralegh visited him) until it was destroyed in October 1598 during an attack by the Earl of Desmond, after which he fled to Cork with his family before returning to England, dying there in almost destitute circumstances a few weeks later. His most celebrated works included the pastoral poems of *The Shepheardes Calender* (1579) and the epic romance *The Faerie Queene* (1590–6). Among his other writings were *Colin Clouts Come Home Againe* (1595) and the *Prothalamion* (1596), which was inspired by the double marriage of the Lady Elizabeth and the Lady Katherine Somerset, daughters of the Earl of Worcester, and the propagandist prose work *View of the Present State of Ireland* (1596).

Family/Sex Life: Spenser's early work was inspired by 'Rosalind', a 'widow's daughter of the Glenne'. In 1594, having wooed her in the 88 love sonnets of the *Amoretti*, he married Elizabeth Boyle (an event celebrated in the famous marriage poem *Epithalamion*, also published in 1595). Their children were Sylvanus, Peregrine and Catherine. After his death his wife remarried twice.

Appearance: According to Aubrey, Spenser was 'A little man, wore short haire, little band and little cuffs.'

Temperament: Among Spenser's friends were Sir Philip Sidney (in 1579 Spenser dedicated *The Shepheardes Calender* to him) and Walter Ralegh (who greatly admired his work). It was with Sidney that Spenser formed the celebrated 'Areopagus' circle of Elizabethan literary wits.

Work/Daily Routine: Spenser wrote some of *The Faerie Queene* in Kilcolman Castle, Ireland – a place he was inclined to view with a jaundiced eye, considering it a place of exile. The first three books of the unfinished work were dedicated to Elizabeth I (whom he dubbed 'Gloriana'), with a prefatory letter addressed to Ralegh. On one occasion the queen was much pleased when Spenser presented her with some of his poems and instructed her Lord Treasurer, Lord Burghley, to pay Spenser 'what is reason'. Burghley, however, conveniently 'forgot' the instruction. After waiting in vain for his money, Spenser penned to the queen the rhyme:

'I was promised on a time
To have reason for my rhyme;
From that time unto this season,
I received nor rhyme nor reason.'

Suitably embarrassed, the queen scolded her treasurer and ordered immediate payment. The Earl of Southampton, one of Spenser's patrons, was among the first to read *The Faerie Queene*. After a few lines he ordered an attendant to take £20 to the poet. After a further passage he ordered another £20 to be sent. After enjoying yet further delightful verses he exclaimed: 'Go turn that fellow out of my house, for I shall be ruined if I read further.' It is thought possible that several important works may have been lost in the destruction of Kilcolman Castle in 1598 – certainly there are contemporary references to works by Spenser no longer apparently in existence.

Manner of Death: Shortly after the disastrous attack on his Irish home, Spenser, ailing in mind and body, died in lodgings in Westminster on Saturday 16 January 1599, aged 46. He was buried in Westminster Abbey near Chaucer, the funeral being paid for by his friend the Earl of Essex. A monument to Spenser was erected in 1620 by Anne Clifford, Countess of Dorset, and inscribed: 'Edmond Spencer, the Prince of Poets in his tyme, whose Divine Spirrit needs noe other witnesse then the works which he left behinde him.'

STALIN, Joseph (1879–1953) Georgian-born Soviet dictator

Joseph Stalin was born Iosif Vissarionovich Dzhugashvili on 21 December 1879 at 10 Sobornaya Street in Gori, Georgia, the third surviving son of Vissarion Dzhugashvili, a cobbler who died when Stalin was 11 years old, and Ekaterina Geladze, a domestic servant. As

a Georgian, he did not speak Russian until he was taught it at Gori Church School (1888–94). He studied theology at the Tiflis Theological Seminary (the highest seat of learning in Georgia – there was no university) in 1894 but was expelled (1899) for failing to sit his exams. He was then employed as an accountant at Tiflis Observatory (1899) and wrote articles for radical papers. Arrested in 1902, he was imprisoned for 18 months, then deported to Novaya Uda, Siberia, for three years' exile (1903) but escaped in 1904. Arrested again in 1908 he was exiled for two years to Solvychegodsk; he escaped in 1909 but was re-arrested in 1910, released in 1911, then arrested once more, escaped in 1912, was re-arrested and was finally released in 1916. The first editor of *Pravda*, he was elected to the Bolshevik Central Committee (1917) and was People's Commissar for Nationalities in the first Soviet Government (1917). A member of the Politburo (1919), he became General Secretary of the Central Committee on Lenin's recommendation (1922). Subsequently he embarked on a ruthless campaign of extermination of political opponents (including Leon Trotsky) and established himself as dictator. As head of Communist Russia, he instituted five-year plans for the reorganization of industry and agriculture, policies that led ultimately to the deaths of millions of people (some 10 million peasants were murdered by the Communists in 1932–3 alone). He retained control of the country during World War II, signing a Non-Aggression Pact with Hitler in 1939 but siding with the Allies two years later, and kept his stranglehold on power well into the 'Cold War' era of the 1950s, isolating the Soviet Union from the rest of the Western world.

Family/Sex Life: In 1905 he married Ekaterina Svanidze. She died two years later, in 1907, having given birth to their son Yakov. His second wife (1919) was his 16-year-old secretary Nadezhda Alliyeva. In 1932 she committed suicide, shooting herself after an argument with her husband. Their children were Vasily (an alcoholic) and Svetlana (who defected to the West). He also fathered an illegitimate daughter while in exile.

Appearance: Stalin was very small, only five feet four inches tall. To compensate

for this he wore platform shoes and stood on a slab at parades. Trotsky spoke of his 'yellow eyes', while others called them 'tiger's eyes'. In 1911 he had a beard, but thereafter he wore a distinctive heavy black moustache. His face was badly pitted from smallpox. As the result of an accident in his youth, his crippled stiff left arm was shorter than his right arm. The second and third toes on his left foot were joined together.

Habits/Mannerisms: True to his humble origins, Stalin was renowned for his coarse manners, which often caused comment at international gatherings. He spat a lot, drank only wine (usually Georgian) and smoked a pipe in public, though he preferred cigarettes. Nicknamed 'Soso ' (the Georgian abbreviation of Joseph) in his youth, he was later dubbed 'Koba' (after the outlaw hero in Kazbegi's *The Patricide*) before adopting the name Stalin (meaning 'man of steel') in 1912.

Sport/Hobbies: Stalin was a strong swimmer. He had a good voice – he sang in choirs – and wrote poetry when in Tiflis (six of his poems were published in *Iveriya* when he was aged 15/16). He also enjoyed watching films. His favourite painting was Repin's *The Reply of the Zaporozhe Cossacks to the Sultan*, of which he kept a copy in his bedroom.

Health: Having recovered from smallpox, he was otherwise very strong and fit for much of his life. In 1945 he suffered a minor stroke and in his old age he was prone to rheumatism, giddiness, an acid stomach and high blood pressure. He had a very good memory.

Temperament: Stalin was cruel, determined, egotistical, paranoid, coarse and often rude. Many of his traits were inherited from his father, a drunkard who regularly beat his son with considerable brutality. Typical of Stalin's coldheartedness was his refusal of a German offer of prisoner exchange when his son Yakov was captured in World War II – his son consequently died in a prison camp in 1943, killed while trying to escape. When he was introduced to the British politician Lady Astor in 1931 she asked him point blank how long he would go on killing people. He replied coolly, 'As long as it's necessary.'

Manner of Death: On 1 March 1953 Stalin was found speechless but conscious on the floor. Subsequently his face blackened and he choked to death as the result of a cerebral haemorrhage on 5 March 1953, aged 73. Rumours that he had been murdered, having just announced his intention to arrest Jewish doctors working in the Kremlin, have never been fully discounted. In 1961 Stalin was denounced by Khrushchev and his body was removed from the Lenin Mausoleum and buried at a less prestigious site near the Kremlin.

STERNE, Laurence (1713–68) Irish novelist and priest

Laurence Sterne was born in Clonmel, Tipperary, Ireland, on 24 November 1713, the son of Roger Sterne, an infantry ensign and later lieutenant (and great-grandson of Richard Sterne, Archbishop of York under James II and former Master of Jesus College, Cambridge) and Mrs Agnes Hebert (née Nuttle), widow of an army captain. He had an older sister, Mary, a younger one, Catherine, and a younger brother Devijeher (who died aged three). Spending much of his childhood living in barracks, after the death of his father (1731) he was taken in by his cousin, Richard Sterne. Educated at school in Halifax and at Jesus College, Cambridge (BA 1736), he was ordained in 1738 and was then parson of Sutton-in-the-Forest, York, for 20 years. He was also a Justice of the Peace and ran a dairy farm with seven cows. For the sake of his health he lived in France and Italy (1762–4 and 1765). He is usually remembered for the nine-volume comic novel *The Life and Opinions of Tristram Shandy* (1759–67). Other publications included *A Sentimental Journey through France and Italy* (1768) and *Letters from Yorick to Eliza* (1775–9).

Family/Sex Life: In 1741 Sterne was married to Elizabeth Lumley, cousin of the 'Blue Stocking' Mrs Montagu. Their only surviving child was their daughter Lydia. His wife later had a mental breakdown, recovered but remained in France with their daughter when Sterne returned to England in 1764. Sterne adored women and formed liaisons with, among others, the singer Cathérine Fourmantelle (1759), who may have inspired 'dear Jenny' in *Tristram Shandy*, and Mrs Elizabeth Draper (1767), the young wife of an East India Company official who later moved to India (their letters provided the basis for *Letters from Yorick to Eliza*).

Appearance: Five feet 10 inches tall, Sterne had a very small head, with high cheekbones and prominent front teeth. Scott described him as being 'tall and thin, with a hectic and consumptive appearance'.

Habits/Mannerisms: In 1760 Sterne moved to Coxwold near Easingwold, Cheshire, christening his house 'Shandy Hall'. His wife called him 'Laurey'. He disliked smoking and never drank to excess.

Sport/Hobbies: A good shot, Sterne enjoyed game-shooting; he also skated well. He played the bass-viol and the violin and was a painter and collector of books. He also spoke and wrote fluent French.

Religion/Politics: An Anglican and a Whig, he was much influenced by the writings of the philosopher John Locke, which he first encountered while at Cambridge.

Health: Sterne suffered from tuberculosis, which he contracted before going up to Cambridge, and from the ague. He took Bishop Berkeley's tar-water remedies for his ailments, but from 1760 his health steadily declined, prompting the move to France.

Temperament: Sterne's friends included the great actor David Garrick and John Hall-Stevenson, who allegedly provided the model for Eugenius, a minor character in *Tristram Shandy* and *A Sentimental Journey*.

Pets: He kept a pointer dog.

Work/Daily Routine: *Tristram Shandy* was dedicated to William Pitt the Elder (then Prime Minister), but, with its highly inventive form and outlandish even scandalous humour, it did not meet with approval in all quarters. Richardson thought *Tristram Shandy* 'execrable', while Horace Walpole called it 'a very insipid and tedious performance'. It was also disliked by Dr Johnson and Oliver Goldsmith. Some people refused to read the book at all because of its salacious reputation. When Sterne was told by a wealthy Yorkshire aristocrat that she had been informed the book was not suitable for ladies to read, he pointed to her young son, rolling around on the carpet and told her: 'My dear good lady, do not be gulled by such stories; the book is like your young heir there – he shows at times a good deal that is usually concealed, but it is all in perfect innocence.' *A Sentimental Journey*, the only novel to end with a dash, was banned by the Vatican and put on the Index of prohibited books (1819) – then the only English novel on the Index apart from Richardson's *Pamela*. He published his *Sermons* under the pseudonym 'Mr Yorick'.

Manner of Death: Sterne died of pleurisy in his rented lodgings at 41 Old Bond Street, London, at 4 pm on 18 March 1768, aged 54. He died alone but for the company of his nurse. His attendants robbed him of his gold sleeve-buttons as he died. He was buried in St George's Burial Ground, Bayswater Road, London, but his body was subsequently stolen by grave-robbers and was recognized in an anatomy lecture at Cambridge University, upon which it was returned to the grave in secret.

STEVENSON, Robert Louis (Balfour) (1850–94) Scottish novelist

R. L. Stevenson was born Robert Lewis Balfour Stevenson at 8 Howard Place, Edinburgh, on 13 November 1850, the only child of Thomas Stevenson, a lighthouse engineer working for the Board of Northern Lighthouses, and Margaret Isabella Balfour, the daughter of Reverend Lewis Balfour. He changed his name to Louis and dropped 'Balfour' around 1868. Educated at the Edinburgh Academy, he studied engineering at Edinburgh University but later changed to law (he was called to the Bar in 1875). He then moved to Hyères (France), Barmouth (New York) and (in 1890) to Apia in Samoa, where he was known as Tusitala ('teller of stories'). His celebrated writings included travel sketches, short stories and verse, but he is usually remembered for such classic adventure novels as *Treasure Island* (1883), *Kidnapped* (1886), *The Strange Case of Dr Jekyll and Mr Hyde*

(1886), *The Master of Ballantrae* (1889) and the unfinished *Weir of Hermiston* (1896).

Family/Sex Life: In 1880 Stevenson married Mrs Fanny Osbourne (née Van de Grift), to whom he dedicated *Weir of Hermiston*. She was an American divorcee 10 years his senior with a son, Samuel Lloyd, and a daughter (they had no further children by choice). His love for her was all-consuming – after they first met he pursued her to the USA in an emigrant ship, finally winning her hand shortly after her divorce came through.

Appearance: Around five feet 10 inches tall, Stevenson was very thin, with a narrow chest, long limbs and a slight stoop. He had a small head and a long oval face, wide-set dark hazel eyes, an aquiline nose and wore a moustache and had long shoulder-length dark brown hair. He disliked formal dress and favoured a generally 'bohemian' appearance.

Sport/Hobbies: Stevenson liked riding and boating.

Health: Stevenson never enjoyed robust health, suffering from chest trouble and nearly dying of gastric fever in 1858. He also suffered from 'scriveners' cramp'. In the last three years of his life his stepdaughter Mrs Strong acted as his amanuensis, while his wife devoted herself to his care. The move to Samoa was a last attempt to improve his health, but there were those back in London who doubted it was helpful to his writing. Oscar Wilde observed: 'I see that romantic surroundings are the worst surroundings for a romantic writer. In Gower Street, Stevenson could have written a new *Trois Mousquetaires*. In Samoa he wrote letters to *The Times* about the Germans.'

Temperament: As a young child he was known as 'Smout' to other members of his family, then (from the age of nine) was usually called 'Lew'. Friends outside the

family included Henry James, Edmund Gosse, Leslie Stephen, Andrew Lang and Meredith. Another friend was the one-legged poet W. E. Henley, who provided the model for the rascally Long John Silver of *Treasure Island* (it was to Henley that Stevenson dedicated *Virginibus Pueresque* in 1881).

Pets: His donkey Modestine featured in his *Travels with a Donkey* (1879).

Work/Daily Routine: In later years he began his day at 6 am, working solidly until the mid-day meal, then resuming his writing until 4 or 5 pm. Plots came to him in dreams (as was the case with *Dr Jekyll and Mr Hyde*, which was influenced by the real-life story of Deacon Brodie, the respected Edinburgh businessman by day who turned robber gang leader at night). *Treasure Island* began as a game devised with his stepson Samuel Lloyd Osbourne, and was dedicated to him. It first appeared in print as a serial in *Young Folks* under the title 'The Sea-Cook' by 'Captain George North' (1881). He dedicated *A Child's Garden of Verses* to his childhood nurse Alison Cunningham ('Cummie'). *The Master of Ballantrae* was dedicated to Mary Shelley and Shelley's surviving son Sir Percy Florence Shelley. *The Dynamiter* was written with his wife.

Manner of Death: Stevenson died in Samoa of a cerebral haemorrhage at 8.10 pm on 3 December 1894, aged 44. He was working on *Weir of Hermiston* when he died. His death was quite sudden: after an afternoon swim he was talking to his wife when a blood-vessel burst, causing him to collapse into a coma and die within two hours. He was buried on the peak of Mount Vaea, being given a full ceremonial burial by the natives of Samoa. The local chiefs prohibited the use of firearms in the vicinity of the grave in perpetuity, so that Stevenson might be able to enjoy the birdsong in peace. In a will drawn up not long before his demise, he left 'his birthday' to a young child of his acquaintance who had once complained that because her own birthday fell on Christmas Day she only got one lot of presents. The will instructed: 'If, however, she fails to use this bequest properly, all rights shall pass to the President of the United States.'

STRINDBERG, Johan August (1849–1912)
Swedish playwright, novelist and short-story writer

August Strindberg was born at Riddarsholmshamnen 14 on the island of Riddarsholm in Stockholm on 22 January 1849, the third surviving child (and the first born in wedlock) of Carl Oscar Strindberg, a prosperous shipping agent, and Eleonora (Nora) Ulrika Norling, a former maid and his father's housekeeper (whom he eventually married after giving birth to three sons), who died in 1862. He had two older brothers, Carl Axel and Oscar, and younger siblings Olle, Anna, Elisabeth and Nora and a half-brother Emil by his father's second wife, Emilia Charlotte Petersson (the children's governess). Educated in Stockholm at the Klara School, the Jakob School and the Stockholm Lyceum (with his future publisher Isidor Bonnier), he studied at the University of Uppsala but did not take his degree, and also attended chemistry classes at the Technological Institute. He volunteered for the militia (1866), was tutor to the children of a palace secretary, taught at an elementary school and joined the Royal Theatre as a non-speaking extra (1869). In addition he worked as a freelance journalist, proofreader, translator of English children's books, editor of an insurance periodical (1873), staff journalist for *Dagens Nyheter* (1873–4) and at the Royal Library in Stockholm (1874–82). He then went into voluntary exile in France and Switzerland (1883–9, 1892–8), formed his own travelling theatre group, the Scandinavian Experimental Theatre (1888), and enrolled in the Faculty of Natural Sciences at the Sorbonne (1895). He founded the Intimate Theatre group in 1907. After his death, André Gide, Sartre and Camus founded the Société Strindberg. His most celebrated plays, classics of naturalistic theatre, included *Fadren* (The Father, 1887), *Fröken Julie* (Miss Julie, 1888) and *Fordringsägare* (Creditors, 1889).

Family/Sex Life: None of Strindberg's three wives was Swedish. In 1877 he married the Royal Theatre actress and Finnish ex-wife of the Swedish Life Guards officer Baron Carl Gustaf Wrangel, Mrs Siri von Essen – who was six months pregnant with Strindberg's baby (she already had a daughter, Sigrid). They divorced in 1891; their children were Karin, Greta and Hans. In 1893 he married the Austrian journalist and critic Maria Friedrike Cornelia 'Frida' Uhl, daughter of Friedrich Uhl, wealthy editor of the *Wiener Abendpost*. They had one daughter, Kerstin, and divorced in 1895. His third wife (1901) was Harriet Bosse, a 22-year-old Norwegian actress 30 years his junior. They had one daughter, Anne-Marie, and divorced in 1904. He was also engaged briefly to actress Fanny Falkner at the end of his life.

Appearance: Five feet eight inches tall, Strindberg was slim but well built, with small hands and feet. He had melancholy light-blue eyes, a full mouth (though with discoloured and badly shaped front teeth) and curly chestnut hair, as well as upturned moustaches and a tuft on his chin. Bernard Shaw found him 'Quite a pleasant-looking person, with the most beautiful sapphire-blue eyes I have ever seen. He was beyond expression shy . . .' (1908). He commonly wore a severe expression but had a warm smile and a soft and gentle voice. He wore spectacles, large cravats and suede gloves and carried a cane. He often wore his hat indoors so his 'thoughts should not fly away'. Munch's famous portrait of him has his name misspelt 'Stindberg'.

Habits/Mannerisms: Strindberg knew eight languages – German, French, Italian and English among others (including Chinese). He always ate lunch at 3 pm and liked ptarmigan and 'beer and fish dishes'; he disliked desserts. He drank wine (especially burgundy), absinthe, beer, whisky, schnapps and cognac and smoked cigars, cigarettes and a pipe. He blushed a lot and had a nervous habit of patting his moustache. He loved flowers – his favourite was the cyclamen – and his favourite colours were zinc yellow and amethyst violet. He liked to have electric lights everywhere, even in cupboards.

Sport/Hobbies: Strindberg enjoyed fencing and was interested in chemistry and alchemy. He saw himself primarily as a scientist and only secondly as a dramatist/writer (he tried to disprove sulphur was an element, to make gold from copper and iron sulphate and studied nerves in plants and the structure of iodine). He was also a good sculptor, photographer and painter (though he never painted from life). He played the B cornet, sang to the guitar and played the piano. Other pastimes included backgammon.

Religion/Politics: Brought up as a Pietist (like his mother), he was later influenced by Swedenborg's mysticism. The occult fascinated him and he recorded his supernatural experiences in a diary 1896–1908. Though anti-Semitic and left-wing, he did not ally himself with any particular party.

Health: Strindberg was mentally unstable, suffering from a persecution mania (which prompted him to carry a Bowie knife) and experiencing hallucinations. Physical ailments included psoriasis on his hands (he often wore a black glove on his right hand to cover this). He took sulphonal, and also morphine to sleep.

Temperament: Though neurotic, racist and anti-feminist (though not mysogynist), he included among his friends Nietzsche, Mucha, Gauguin, Munch and Delius.

Pets: His favourite creature was the butterfly. He was very frightened of dogs.

Work/Daily Routine: O'Neill called Strindberg 'that greatest genius of all modern dramatists', while Chekhov called him 'a remarkable writer . . . quite unusual power'. He worked very fast – *The Father*, *Miss Julie* and *Creditors* each took less than three weeks. He did not usually bother to read proofs and disliked working in daylight so usually drew the blinds. He admired Dickens (especially *Little Dorrit*), Poe, Balzac, Turner, Hugo, Kipling (though he thought *The Jungle Book* 'dreadful'), Longfellow, Marie Corelli and Kierkegaard. He thought Shakespeare's comedies 'plain rubbish'. In 1884 he was recalled to Sweden to be prosecuted on charges of blasphemy arising from the short stories published as *Giftas I* and *II* (1884–6) – he was acquitted.

Motto: *Speravit infestis* (He was hopeful in adversity).

Manner of Death: Strindberg died of cancer of the stomach in Stockholm at 4.30 am on 14 May 1912, aged 63. He requested an 8 am funeral to avoid attracting a crowd, but still 10,000 mourners followed his coffin (including Prince Eugene).

SWIFT, Jonathan (1667–1745) Irish satirist and clergyman

Jonathan Swift was born at 7 Hoey's Court, Dublin, on 30 November 1667, of English parents, seven months after the death of his father, Jonathan Swift, a steward of the King's Inns. His mother was Abigail Erick and he had an older sister, Jane. Supported as a child by his uncle Godwin Swift, John Dryden was his cousin (his grandfather, Reverend Thomas Swift, having married Elizabeth Dryden). He was educated at Kilkenny Grammar School with Congreve, then at Trinity College, Dublin, but because of indiscipline only received his degree by 'special grace' (he later took a DD at Dublin University, 1701). At first Secretary to Sir William Temple (British envoy to Brussels and architect of the Triple Alliance), he was then ordained in the Anglican Church (1695) and became prebend at St Patrick's, Dublin, and later its dean (1713). His most famous satirical writings included *A Tale of a Tub* (1704), *The Drapier's Letters* (1724), *Gulliver's Travels* (1726) and *A Modest Proposal* (1729).

Family/Sex Life: Swift never married, though at the age of 19 he is reputed to have proposed to Jane Waryng 'Varina' and later had a close platonic friendship with Esther Johnson, the natural daughter of Sir William Temple, whom he first met when he was 22 and she was eight (they always met with a third person present). Esther was immortalized in his writing as 'Stella' (she died in 1728). Another close friend was Mrs Esther Vanhomrigh (pronounced Vanummery), a widow with four children, who was called 'Vanessa' by Swift ('Van' coming from Vanhomrigh and 'Essa' from Esther). She proposed marriage, but Swift rejected her in his poem 'Cadenus and Vanessa' (Cadenus is an anagram of *decanus*, dean). She died in 1723, allegedly from shock after Swift finally rejected her.

Appearance: According to Lord Orrery, Swift had a 'natural severity of face, which even his smiles could never soften'. Pope wrote: 'His eyes are as azure as the heavens and have a charming archness in them.'

Habits/Mannerisms: Swift read aloud from the Book of Job on his birthday each year.

Sport/Hobbies: He enjoyed walking.

Religion/Politics: An Anglican, he was formerly a Whig but later became a Tory after he became increasingly disillusioned with Whig policies, particularly in relation to their treatment of Ireland.

Health: Swift suffered from attacks of giddiness ('labyrinthine vertigo') and from Ménières Disease. The deaths of his two female friends were reputed to have driven him mad and his last years were certainly dominated by his fast deteriorating mental state, suffering from aphasia and then paralysis and his eyes swelling to the size of eggs. Earlier in life he had sadly predicted his own end, telling friends he feared that, like a tree, he would 'die from the top'.

Temperament: Swift was perspicacious and also generous – he spent a third of his income on charities and a third on St Patrick's Hospital for Imbeciles. His friends included Sheridan and Pope (with whom he founded the Scriblerus Club). Voltaire considered Swift 'far above Rabelais' and Thackeray called him 'the greatest wit of all times ... an immense genius', but his relation Dryden, at the outset of his career, advised him, 'Cousin Swift, you will never be a poet.'

Work/Daily Routine: Nearly all Swift's

works were published anonymously. Among pseudonyms he used were Isaac Bickerstaff, A Dissenter, A Person of Quality, A Person of Honour, M. B. Drapier and TRDJSDOPII (The Reverend Doctor J. Swift, Dean of Patrick's in Ireland). He signed himself 'Presto' (Italian for 'swift') in his letters to Stella. He only received payment for one book – *Gulliver's Travels* – for which he got £200. In 1708 he perpetrated a famous hoax on the almanac-maker John Partridge, predicting and then announcing Partridge's death in a rival publication on astrology – all Partridge's attempts to prove that he was still alive were rebuffed and many other contemporary writers joined in the fun.

Motto/Emblem: His maxim was '*Vive la bagatelle*'; he also coined the phrase 'going into the Land of Nod' (meaning to fall asleep).

Manner of Death: Swift died in Dublin on 19 October 1745, aged 77. He was buried in St Patrick's, Dublin, next to Stella.

SWINBURNE, Algernon Charles (1837–1909) English poet and critic

Algernon Swinburne was born in Chester Street, Belgravia, London, on 5 April 1837, the oldest child of Admiral Charles Henry Swinburne and Lady Jane Henrietta Ashburnham, daughter of George, 3rd Earl of Ashburnham. His grandfather was Sir John Edward Swinburne, 6th Baronet of Capheaton, and he had a younger sister, Isabel. His early childhood was spent on the Isle of Wight with his parents and grandparents and he was educated at Eton (where he was bullied) and at Balliol, Oxford, but left without a degree (only achieving a Second in Moderations though he won the Taylorian Scholarship for French and Italian). He wanted to join the Army but was deemed too small and frail. Subsequently he developed links with the Pre-Raphaelite Brotherhood and travelled in Europe (though he was particularly fond of Northumberland, which he called the 'crowning county' of England). He established his reputation as a writer with the play *Atalanta in Calydon* (1865) and with the first of the *Poems and Ballads* (1866) series. Later works included *Songs Before Sunrise* (1871) and *Essays and Studies* (1875) and studies of Shakespeare, Jonson and other major literary figures.

Family/Sex Life: A homosexual, he lived with the novelist Theodore Watts-Dunton in Putney for the last 30 years of his life and dedicated *Tristram of Lyonesse* (1882) to him.

Appearance: Swinburne was thin, with very narrow sloping shoulders. He had a very large head, with a high forehead and a tiny chin with 'a meagre tuft of beard, a faint bit of moustache hovering over fine lips ... light coloured, inquisitive, staring eyes' (Maupassant). He had a shock of red-gold hair.

Habits/Mannerisms: Swinburne's body was always agitated – according to the *Dictionary of National Biography*, 'Alternatively he danced as if on wires or sat in absolute immobility.' He had sado-masochistic tendencies, becoming interested in flagellation while at Eton. He was also a heavy drinker and became an alcoholic until he was rescued after a breakdown by Watts-Dunton. He loved babies and would stop to talk to mothers in the street.

Sport/Hobbies: Swinburne liked climbing and riding and made a daily walk over

Putney Heath. He also enjoyed swimming, though he nearly drowned bathing at Etretat, France, in 1868 (where local inhabitant Maupassant first saw him). He also collected rare books from the age of 14.

Religion/Politics: Brought up a 'quasi-Catholic', he later became strongly anti-Christian (a stance that influenced Thomas Hardy among others). He was seen as 'dangerous' while at Oxford – he admired Orsini (who had tried to assassinate Napoleon III) and supported Mazzini in the Italian independence struggle.

Health: Swinburne was born nearly dead and was not expected to live an hour. He was an epileptic (he had a fit in the British Museum Reading Room on 10 July 1868) and from 1875 suffered increasing deafness. In July 1876 he was poisoned by lilies in his room and taken very ill. In 1903 he contracted double pneumonia. He did, though, have a superb memory.

Temperament: Besides Watts-Dunton, his friends included Jowett, Richard Burton, Burne-Jones, William Morris, Rossetti (a very close friend in the years 1861–71) and Meredith, with whom he lived at 16

Cheyne Walk, Chelsea, for a period. He disliked Byron ('The most affected of sensualists and the most pretentious of profligates') and also Emerson ('A gap-toothed and hoary-headed ape') – Emerson in his turn called Swinburne 'a perfect leper, and a mere sodomite'.

Pets: He was very fond of cats.

Work/Daily Routine: Swinburne once accidentally left the manuscript of his tragedy *Bothwell* in a hansom cab – fortunately it was recovered after he offered a reward. Carlyle commented of him, 'I have no wish to know anyone sitting on a sewer and adding to it', but Bennett was moved to call him 'the greatest lyric versifier that England ever had and one of the great poets of the whole world and of all ages.' He was caricatured in Gilbert and Sullivan's *Patience* as the 'fleshly poet' and was called 'Swine-born' by *Punch*.

Manner of Death: Swinburne died of pneumonia at his home at 11 Putney Hill, Putney, on the morning of 10 April 1909, aged 71. He was buried on the Isle of Wight.

TCHAIKOVSKY, Piotr Ilyich (1840–93) Russian composer

Piotr Ilyich Tchaikovsky was born in Kamsko-Votkinsk, Russia, on 7 May 1840, the second son of Major-General Ilia Petrovitch Tchaikovsky, a mining engineer and later Director of the Technological Institute in St Petersburg, and Alexandra Andreievna Assier (who died of cholera when he was 14). He had an elder brother Nicholas and two younger ones, Modeste and Anatol (twins) as well as two sisters, Hippolyte and Alexandra. He studied jurisprudence and at first worked as a clerk in the St Petersburg Ministry of Justice for

four years from the age of 19. In 1862, however, he gave up his law studies to study music at the St Petersburg Conservatoire. In 1866 he began a 13-year term as Professor of Harmony at the Moscow Conservatoire, as well as working as a music critic for four years. Acclaimed both as a composer and as a conductor he became very rich. His compositions included six symphonies, such classic ballets as *Swan Lake* (1876–7), *The Sleeping Beauty* (1890) and *The Nutcracker* (1892), two piano concertos and a number of tone poems, notably *Romeo and Juliet* and *Capriccio Italien*.

Family/Sex Life: Tchaikovsky was a homosexual, but nonetheless as a young man he had a brief affair with the singer and courtesan Désirée Artôt (she inspired his *Romeo and Juliet*), and in July 1877 he married his Conservatoire pupil Antonina Ivanovna Milyukova. She threatened suicide if he did not go through with it. Tchaikovsky gave in but later confided to his brother that 'Physically she is totally repulsive to me' and fled, subsequently trying to drown himself in the River Neva. They had separated by October that same year (she died insane in 1917). Tchaikovsky then came under the influence of Nadezhda von Meck, the widow of a railway engineer who agreed to act as his patron to the tune of 6000 roubles a year – on condition that they would never meet (the relationship, continued by letter, lasted until 1890). He also had an affair with Count Anton Chelovski.

Appearance: Tchaikovsky sported a neat beard and moustache, without side whiskers (which, like his hair, went white in his later years).

Habits/Mannerisms: When conducting he used to hold his chin with his left hand and conduct with his right hand because he feared his head would roll off his shoulders. If obliged to stay in foreign hotels, he was insistent that everything should be laid out exactly as it had been on the previous occasion. Though not an alcoholic, he was prone to the occasional excessive bout of drinking.

Health: Tchaikovsky was mentally unstable and suffered several nervous breakdowns.

Temperament: Very shy, neurotic, depressive, sensitive and sincere (in his youth his governess referred to him as a 'child of glass'). In 1868 he was introduced to the celebrated group of Russian composers called 'The Five' but, typically, he avoided being associated too closely with them, having a natural disinclination to join cliques.

Work/Daily Routine: In his early years Tchaikovsky showed few signs of any musical ability. He rose at 7 am, took tea and read the Bible, then started work at 9.30. In the afternoon he would continue to compose while taking his daily walk. The evening was devoted to further composition or to proofreading. The premiere of *Swan Lake* was a fiasco, poorly played and conducted by an inadequately trained conductor; Tchaikovsky himself was persuaded to dismiss the work at first, admitting, 'My own *Lake of Swans* is simply trash.' While composing his Sixth Symphony (his own favourite work), he confessed to being so moved he often wept while planning it; it was his brother Modeste who suggested for it the title *Symphony Pathétique*. He hated the music of Mussorgsky and Brahms (Brahms in his turn disliked his).

Manner of Death: Tchaikovsky died, after drinking water infected with cholera at dinner four days earlier, on 5 November 1893, aged 53. Suicide is a strong possibility – as he poured himself the fatal drink his brother Modeste protested, pointing out the dangers, but the composer only replied, 'One can't go tiptoeing about in fear of death for ever.' His body was taken to Kazan Cathedral and thence to the Alexander Nevsky cemetery in St Petersburg (legend insists that every single mourner gladly risked the danger of catching cholera themselves in order to touch the corpse in respect – and that not one of them caught it).

TENNYSON, Alfred (1809–92) English poet

Alfred Lord Tennyson was born in Somersby, Lincolnshire, on 6 August 1809, the fourth of 12 children of the Reverend Dr George Clayton Tennyson, Rector of Somersby, and Elizabeth Fytche. He had two elder brothers, Frederick and Charles (later known as Charles Tennyson-Turner) – also poets – and two sisters, Emily (later engaged to Tennyson's friend Arthur Hallam, son of the historian) and Cecilia. Educated at Louth Grammar School, he left after five years and was taught by his father. He studied at Trinity College, Cambridge (1828–31), with his brother Charles (Frederick had also been there earlier), won the Chancellor's Medal for his poem 'Timbuctoo' (1829) but left without taking his degree. He volunteered (with Hallam) for the army of the Spanish insurgent Torrijos against King Ferdinand VII (1830) – quickly disillusioned, they soon returned. Bankrupted by a speculator who had convinced him to sell his estate, he was given a £200 pension by Peel (1845) and succeeded Wordsworth as Poet Laureate in 1850 (after Prince Albert had admired 'In Memoriam') – borrowing court dress used by Wordsworth for the ceremony. At first he turned down then accepted a baronetcy from Gladstone to become the first English peer whose title was awarded for poetry. As well as the elegy *In Memoriam* (1850), his most famous works included the poems 'The Lady of Shallott' and 'The Lotos-Eaters' and the Arthurian poetry cycle *Idylls of the King* (1859).

Family/Sex Life: In 1850, aged 41, he married 37-year-old Emily Sarah Sellwood, the older sister of his brother Charles's wife; their two surviving sons were Hallam and Lionel. He claimed never to have kissed any woman in love except his wife.

Appearance: Tall and broad-shouldered,

Tennyson, at the age of 80, weighed 9½ stone. According to Carlyle he was 'fine-featured, dim-eyed, bronze-coloured, shaggy-headed'. He was somewhat wild-looking with, in Thackeray's words, a 'big yellow face and growling voice'. He had a large brown-black beard, long black hair and a deep furrow on both cheeks from brow to chin. Hawthorne noted that he had 'a very queer gait, as if he were walking in slippers too loose for him ... he seemed to turn his feet slightly inward'. Queen Victoria described him as 'very peculiar-looking ... oddly dressed, but there is no affectation about him'. He commonly wore a black wideawake hat, spectacles, a famous long black Inverness cape and, in old age, a black velvet skullcap indoors. He described himself in a celebrated photograph by Julia Margaret Cameron as 'The Dirty Monk'. He was the only living poet to have his effigy in Madame Tussaud's.

Habits/Mannerisms: Tennyson (nicknamed 'Ally' by his wife) was very absent-minded. He lost the manuscript of *Poems, Wholly Lyrical* and had to rewrite them all. On another occasion he left the manuscript of 'In Memoriam' in a lodging-house but luckily recovered it. His favourite dinner was beefsteak and a pint of port. He was also a heavy smoker (pipe and cigars). He took three baths a day.

Sport/Hobbies: Tennyson enjoyed yachting, fishing, fencing, dancing and battledore. He learnt Hebrew in order to read the Old Testament in the original.

Religion/Politics: Christian, but with racist sympathies – he once said, 'We are too tender to savages ... Niggers are tigers.'

Health: The sudden death (1834) of

Arthur Hallam was a severe shock to his nervous system. In later years he suffered heart palpitations (1861), eczema (1870), gout in the throat, jaw and knees and rheumatic fever (1888). He was also short-sighted and had a bad memory.

Temperament: Shy, modest and retiring but also vain he shunned publicity. His friends included Hallam (whose death at 22 inspired *In Memoriam*), Dickens, Ruskin, Thackeray, Robert Browning (to whom Tennyson dedicated *Tiresias* without telling him), Carlyle, Elizabeth Browning, Edward Fitzgerald, Gladstone (though he hated his politics), Millais and Lear (who illustrated his complete works and named his house Villa Tennyson).

Pets: His pony Fanny, kept on the Isle of Wight, pulled Tennyson's wife about in a wheelchair. He also had a dog, Old Don.

Work/Daily Routine: Tennyson composed while walking up and down. He worked relatively quickly – 'Crossing the Bar' was written on the back of an envelope in just half an hour while crossing from Yarmouth to Lymington by boat, aged 80 (he insisted it should end every volume of his complete works). He dedicated *Idylls of the King* to Prince Albert (after Albert died) and sold 10,000 copies in the first week. The most popular book in his lifetime, though, was *Enoch Arden*, which earnt £6000 in the first year. 5000 copies of *Maud* were sold on publication day – some critics disliked it, however, with its concentration on suicide, hysteria and madness (one said it had one too many vowels in the title and it mattered little which of them was removed). *In Memoriam*, published anonymously, was dismissed by *The Times* as 'much too long, obscure and difficult'. *De Profundis* meanwhile was parodied by Swinburne: 'God whom we see not is: and God who is not we see:/Fiddle we know is diddle: and diddle we know is dee . . .'). Wordsworth called Tennyson 'the first of our living poets', while Auden later observed of Tennyson that 'He had the finest ear, perhaps, of any English poet; he was also undoubtedly the stupidest; there was little about melancholia he didn't know; there was little else that he did.' Tennyson recorded himself reading 'The Charge of the Light Brigade' and 'Bugle Song' on the phonograph. Poems by his hand were set to music by around 250 composers.

Manner of Death: Tennyson died at 1.35 am on 7 October 1892, aged 83. He was buried with a copy of Shakespeare in Westminster Abbey next to Browning. Alfred Austin wrote *The Passing of Merlin* about him. The Poet Laureateship was left vacant until 1896 as a tribute.

THACKERAY, William Makepeace (1811–63) English novelist

W. M. Thackeray was born in Calcutta, India, on 18 July 1811, the only child of Richmond Makepeace Thackeray, a very prosperous Collector in the East India Company, and Anne Becher. His father died when he was aged five and he was sent to England (his mother married Major Henry Carmichael-Smyth in 1818). William was educated in Southampton, at Charterhouse School (with John Leech) and at Trinity College, Cambridge (with Tennyson and Edward Fitzgerald – his tutor was William Whewell), but left without a degree after two years. Very wealthy from his father's legacy he squandered a fortune (one evening as a student losing £1500 when gambling). He then lived in Germany (1830–1), meeting Goethe, and with his mother and stepfather in Paris. Later he trained as a barrister at the Middle Temple (though he never practised), studied art in London (where he was taught by George Cruikshank) and in Paris and was a cornet in the Devonshire Yeomanry. Forced to work when what was left of his father's money was lost in the Indian banking crisis he became a freelance journalist (he wrote for *Punch*, *The Times*, *Morning Chronicle* among other publications), writer and lecturer. He was the first editor of the *Cornhill Magazine* (1860–2). He is remembered primarily as the author of such classic novels as *Vanity Fair* (1847–8), *Pendennis* (1848–50), *Henry Esmond* (1852) and *The Newcomes* (1853–5).

Family/Sex Life: While in Paris he kept as his mistress Mlle Pauline and then (1836) married Isabella Gethin Creagh Shawe, the daughter of an Irish army colonel. His pet names for her were 'Puss' and 'Trot'. Their children were Anne Isabella (later Lady Ritchie), Jane (who died young) and Harriet Marian (the first wife of Leslie Stephen). His wife went mad (1840) and tried to commit suicide (she died in a mental home in 1894), following which he sent their children to live with their grandparents in Paris and took up the life of a bachelor (the children returned to him in 1846). In the early 1840s he nursed a passion for Jane Brookfield, the wife of a Cambridge friend, but his desire was never realized.

Appearance: Six feet three inches tall and 15 to 18 stone in weight, Thackeray had a massive head (his brain weighed 58½ oz). He was short-sighted and had a broken nose (from his schooldays).

Habits/Mannerisms: Thackeray had tiny, very neat handwriting. He was a considerable gourmet, particularly enjoying lobsters and jam tarts. He also smoked cigars and kept a large cellar of fine clarets.

Sport/Hobbies: Thackeray enjoyed fencing

(he owned a sword that had belonged to Schiller) and was an incorrigible gambler, playing écarté and dice. He liked the theatre – especially ballet, opera and pantomime – and was an accomplished artist and a fine singer.

Religion/Politics: He once stood for Parliament but failed to be elected.

Health: Physical problems included venereal disease (which he contracted in his youth and which left him with urethral stricture) and frequent 'spasms' (about 12 a year in 1854).

Temperament: Thackeray was by all accounts indolent, improvident, a snob and a racist. His friends included Edward Fitzgerald, Leech, Landseer and Watts, and Charlotte Brontë was one of his most ardent admirers (she dedicated *Jane Eyre* to him). In his turn, he admired Cruikshank but hated Byron.

Pets: He kept a cat called Louisa.

Work/Daily Routine: Much of Thackeray's early work was published under pseudonyms, which included Michael Angelo Titmarsh (because of his broken nose and artistic aspirations), Dorothea Julia Ramsbottom, Theophile Wagstaff, C. J. Yellowplush and George Savage Fitzboodle. Pseudonyms used by Thackeray in writing for *Punch* included Miss Tickletoby, Spec, Paul Pindar, Fitz-Jeames de la Pluche, Frederick Haltamont de Montmorency and Our Fat Contributor. The first book he signed as Thackeray was his *Irish Sketchbook*. Thackeray made no bones about his motivation for writing, readily confessing he wrote plainly and simply for money. Unlike the majority of acclaimed writers over the ages he did not write in private, but preferred to work in pubs and cafés, usually between the hours of 10 am and 6 pm.

Manner of Death: Thackeray died of a

cerebral haemorrhage after being sick following a huge meal at his home, 2 Palace Green, Kensington, on Christmas Eve, 24 December 1863, aged 52. He was buried in Kensal Green Cemetery, London.

TIBERIUS (42 BC–AD 37) Roman emperor

Tiberius Claudius Nero was born on the Palatine Hill, Rome, on 6 November 42 BC, the son of Tiberius Claudius Nero, commander of Julius Caesar's fleet and later Chief Pontiff (who died when he was nine), and Livia Drusilla (who was married to Octavian/Augustus when he was aged three, making him the stepson of Augustus). He had a younger brother Drusus. A good soldier, he was a military tribune in Spain aged 16, became quaestor in 23 BC then a general on the northern frontiers of the Roman empire and later a consul. He became emperor aged 56 but later retired to Capri for seven years (AD 27) and let affairs of state slide under his vicious deputy, the Praetorian Prefect Sejanus. After Sejanus died in AD 31 he instituted a new reign of terror. He reigned for 23 years (AD 14–37), a period that witnessed countless executions throughout the Empire, including that of Jesus of Nazareth.

Family/Sex Life: Tiberius's first wife was Vipsania Agrippina, the daughter of Marcus Agrippa (Augustus's admiral). Their son Drusus was later poisoned, then Augustus forced Tiberius to divorce Vipsania and to marry Julia, Agrippa's widow. She was outrageously promiscuous and they were separated around 7 BC. Tiberius later adopted his nephew Germanicus, who became his heir. He was also bisexual and had oral sex with slave boys who swam in the baths with him (he called them his 'minnows'). He also commanded men and women to perform unnatural sex before him in groups of three. Suetonius claimed he even had oral sex with suckling babies.

Appearance: Tall, strong and heavily built, he had broad shoulders and chest but stooped a little. Suetonius recorded that he had a 'Handsome, fresh-complexioned face, though subject to occasional rashes of pimples.' He had remarkably large eyes and his reddish blond hair grew over the nape of his neck. He wore a seal ring on his left hand.

Habits/Mannerisms: Tiberius was left-handed and walked with a stiff stride. He liked trees but was very frightened of thunder and lightning. He disliked flattery and refused the suggested renaming of the month of September as Tiberius in his honour. He was a heavy drinker and was nicknamed Biberius Caldius Mero ('drinker of wine with no water added'). Tiberius was also fond of fruit (especially pears), asparagus, cucumbers and radishes, which he ate with honey and wine.

Sport/Hobbies: He wrote Greek verse and spoke Greek fluently.

Religion/Politics: Tiberius was a student of astrology (though he later had astrologers persecuted) and believed in the action of Fate. He suppressed all foreign religions, especially those of the Egyptians and the Jews.

Health: He was very strong – it was said that he could punch a finger on his left hand through an apple or through the skull of a boy. He suffered from skin disease in later life.

Temperament: Tiberius was unremittingly savage. There were executions every day, even on holy days. The death penalty was imposed for a wide range of offences, serious and trivial. It was even a capital crime to carry a ring or a coin bearing Augustus' head into a privy or brothel, or to criticize Augustus. Sex or youth was no protection. As tradition said virgins could not be killed, he had virgin girls raped before being put to death. Being a family member was no guarantee of safety either: he envied Priam for outliving his family and nearly had all other members of his own family killed so he might do the same. He also issued an edict banning kissing and prohibited the giving of New Year good-luck gifts. He liked to torture men by making them drink lots of wine and then tying up their genitals. He could also be withdrawn and silent and was prone to brooding; the Elder Pliny called him *'tristissimus homo'* ('the saddest of men'). He was also miserly, never paying his staff when they were sent on foreign missions.

Pets: Tiberius kept a pet snake.

Maxim: 'He who knows not how to dissemble knows not how to reign.'

Manner of Death: Tiberius died on 16 March AD 37 in a country house at Misenum while en route to Capri, aged 77. His body was cremated in Rome.

TOLSTOY, Leo (1828–1910) Russian novelist

Leo Nikolayevich Tolstoy was born in Yasnaya Polyana, Tula District (between Moscow and Kiev), Russia, on 28 August 1828, the fourth child of Count Nikolai Ilyich Tolstoy (who died when he was nine) and Princess Maria Nikolayevna Volkonsky (who died when he was two). His mother's grandfather had been Catherine the Great's Commander-in-Chief and later Governor of Archangel, who had retired to the estate in Yasnaya Polyana. His father's relations included Peter the Great's Russian Ambassador to Turkey. His older brothers were Nikolai (who died of tuberculosis in 1860) and Sergei; he also had a younger brother Dmitri and a sister, Marya Nikolayevna. Educated at home (where he had a French tutor), he was brought up by his Aunt Alexandra and his father's second cousin, Tatiana Andreyevna Ergolskaya. When Alexandra died he moved in with her sister, Aunt Pelageya Yushlov, daughter of the ex-governor of Kazan, and later went to Kazan University where he read law and oriental languages but left without a degree. He was an artillery officer (lieutenant) in the Russian Imperial Army (1851–5) and commanded a battery at Sebastopol when it fell in the Crimean War (1855), being three times recommended for the St George's Cross for bravery. He later (1847) inherited the 4000-acre Yasnaya Polyana estate (with its 330 serfs and 34-room mansion) and the title of Count, but sold part of the estate to fund a new army periodical *The Military Gazette*. When the Tsar refused to allow its publication, he gambled away the money he had raised and became an inspector in a factory making military rockets in St Petersburg (living with Turgenev), travelled in France, Switzerland, Prussia, Italy, Belgium and London and set up a school for serf children in Yasnaya Polyana (which eventually had 70 branches). In 1861 he also became an Arbiter of the Peace for Tula and began publishing an educational review *Yasnaya Polyana* (from 1862). The author of just three novels – *Voyni i mir* (War and Peace, 1864–9), *Anna Karenina* (1873–7) and *Voskreseniye* (Resurrection, 1899) – he remains Russia's most celebrated novelist.

He also wrote short stories and plays.

Family/Sex Life: In 1862 Tolstoy married 18-year-old Sonya (or Safya) Andreyevna Behrs, daughter of a Kremlin doctor and 16 years his junior. They had 13 children. He also fathered a son by Aksinya, the wife of one of his serfs, and in his youth visited prostitutes. He continued to have a tremendous sex drive right into his 80s.

Appearance: Tolstoy had small grey eyes and a penetrating gaze that he used as a weapon (he could outstare anyone). He wore a moustache, long sideburns and had bristly hair as a young man; later he grew a long snowy white beard. He had large feet and hands. By day he wore a linen dressing-gown (made by himself) which converted into a sleeping-bag at night. As a student he had his own carriage and personal servant.

Habits/Mannerisms: Vegetarian.

Sport/Hobbies: Tolstoy enjoyed bear-hunting and riding and played solitaire a lot as well as roulette and cards. He liked music, playing the piano and helped to found the Moscow Conservatoire. He also took lessons in English, Greek and Italian.

Religion/Politics: Tolstoy underwent a moral and spiritual crisis in the 1870s and subsequently developed his own brand of Christian anarchism, denouncing the worship of Jesus as blasphemy and founding a new sect purged of faith and mystery. He renounced material possessions in his old age and gave away most of what he had, surrendering his estate to his family. In 1901 he was excommunicated from the Russian Orthodox Church. After his military service he became a pacifist (he corresponded with and influenced Gandhi). He got Gorki released from prison in 1901. He was not, however, politically minded and never thought of freeing his serfs, though he worked to improve the lot of those who worked on his estate.

Health: Aged nine he fell (or jumped trying to fly) from a third-floor window in Moscow, but escaped without breaking any bones. He contracted gonorrhoea in 1847 and again in 1851 (he treated it with mercury). He had very bad teeth but refused to go to a dentist (he was largely toothless by the age of 34).

Temperament: Tolstoy was always crying as a child and so was nicknamed 'the Howler'. He was self-important and self-satisfied in his youth, and was overbearing, selfish and hectoring. Later he questioned the dissolute life he had been leading and strove to redeem himself through his work on his estate and through his writing. His friends included Turgenev (to whom he dedicated *The Woodfelling*).

Work/Daily Routine: *War and Peace*, which has some 500 characters, was not begun until Tolstoy was 35. The title came from Proudhon's treatise on the nature of war (the first title suggested was *Russia in 1805*). He worked in the mornings and played patience between writing bouts (the outcome of one game decided whether or not Katyvisha should marry Nikhlyndov). His wife copied out *War and Peace* seven times in pen and ink. (Turgenev thought the finished work 'a truly bad, boring failure of a novel'.) Tolstoy admitted to being influenced by Sterne and Stendhal and also liked Molière but hated Racine, Homer and Shakespeare.

Manner of Death: Tolstoy died of pneumonia while fleeing from his wife, who could not accept his asceticism, at Astapovo railway station on 8 November 1910, aged 82. Attempts to persuade him to reconcile himself with the Russian Orthodox Church on his deathbed met with the reply: 'Even in the valley of the shadow of death, two and two do not make six.' He was buried near the family estate at Yasnaya Polyana.

TOULOUSE-LAUTREC, Henri de (1864–1901) French painter

Henri Marie-Raymond de Toulouse-Lautrec-Monfa was born at the Hôtel du Bosc, 14 Rue de l'École Mage in Albi, near Toulouse, on 24 November 1864, the son of Count Alphonse-Charles de Toulouse-Lautrec-Monfa and Adèle-Zoe Tapiéde Céleyran. His ancestors were Counts of Toulouse and his family were much intermarried (both grandmothers were sisters and his father's sister married his mother's brother). Henri was named after Henri, Comte de Chabord, last surviving descendant of Louis XIV, whom the Toulouse-Lautrecs hoped would become King of France. He attended the Lycée Fontanes (later renamed the Condorcet), Paris, from the age of eight (1872–5), was taught painting by René Princeteau (a friend of his father, who also drew well) and Jean-Louis Forain, and was then educated at home (1875–83). In 1882 he enrolled in the Paris studio of Léon Bonnat, Paris (Degas' friend and later Director of l'École des Beaux-Arts) and then that of Felix Cormon (fellow students were Van Gogh and Émile Bernard, 'the father of Symbolism'). His first professional work was as a freelance illustrator for such magazines as *Paris Illustré*, *Le Mirliton* and *Figaro Illustré*, and at first he shared a flat with fellow artist René Grenier and his wife (who had been Degas' model). He later produced posters for the Moulin Rouge music hall etc. and made most of his income from lithographs and posters (368 in all). A member of the staff of *Revue Blanche*, he became addicted to alcohol and was sent to the Château Saint-James asylum in Neuilly (1899) to detoxify but without curing the habit. He influenced Van Gogh, Bonnard, Munch and Picasso.

Family/Sex Life: Unmarried, he was a frequenter of Paris brothels and was dubbed 'The Coffee Pot' in Madame Baron's brothel, 24 Rue des Moulins, Paris (the subject of the lithograph album *Elles*) because of his large penis. His mistress was model Suzanne Valadon (mother of Utrillo); he also often had sex with the prostitute Big Gabrielle.

Appearance: Under five feet tall, he had a normal-sized head and torso but short legs, knock knees and short thick arms. He had large hands with thick fingers, a receding chin, thick protuberant very red lips, an enlarged tongue and large nostrils. Yvette Guilbert noted his 'huge dark head, the red face and black beard, the greasy, oily skin, the nose broad enough for two faces, and with a mouth that gashed the face from cheek to cheek, with huge violet-rose lips that were at once flat and flaccid'. He was also short-sighted and wore pince-nez. He always wore a hat – even indoors.

Habits/Mannerisms: Toulouse-Lautrec's large tongue made him lisp and salivate excessively and he had a persistent sniffle. An Anglophile (as was then the fashion), he spoke English well (he had an Irish governess). He sometimes drank absinthe and cognac mixed, a concoction he named *'un tremblement de terre'* ('earthquake'), and was often brought home drunk by the police. His walking-stick was hollowed out to hold a glass container of brandy or absinthe (he took his walking-stick to bed with him to fend off imagined attacks). He also constantly sprayed his studio floor with paraffin because he imagined it alive with microbes. He had a long, sausage-shaped suitcase because he could not carry an ordinary one.

Sport/Hobbies: Despite his deformity, he was a very good swimmer and enjoyed riding, sailing, shooting and dancing. He loved the theatre and collected antiques and dolls.

Health: Toulouse-Lautrec was crippled and deformed following injuries to his legs in two falls at the age of 15, though he also inherited the rare disease pyknodysostosis, which leads to dwarfism. Later in life he became an alcoholic and also suffered from venereal disease. Other problems included piles and a broken collarbone sustained in a drunken fall (1897). He also suffered hallucinations in which he imagined himself attacked by a cardboard elephant, a huge headless animal or a pack of terriers etc.

Temperament: Good-humoured, witty and charming, he numbered among his friends Lionel Sackville-West (former British Ambassador to Paris).

Pets: As a child he kept a male canary called Lolo.

Work/Daily Routine: Toulouse-Lautrec produced oil paintings, watercolours, prints, posters, drawings, caricatures, sculptures, ceramics and a stained-glass window (for Tiffany's, New York). He disliked landscapes, declaring 'the painter who paints purely landscape is a villain'. He used the pseudonyms 'Tréclau' (an anagram of Lautrec) or 'Monfa' (his

mother's family name) until 1887. Another was 'Tolav-Segroeg, Hungarian from Montmartre'. His first important poster commission was for the Moulin Rouge, featuring the artiste La Goulue (1891, 300 copies). He also did advertisements for British firms, for instance Simpson's cycles, as well as illustrations for sheet music, theatres and shops. He used spray paint and was influenced by Manet, Pissarro, Degas and Monet and also admired Whistler. His *Mademoiselle Dihau au Piano* (1890) was called 'amazing' by Van Gogh.

Motto/Emblem: He signed his work with a logo made from an interlocking TL in a circle, sometimes set inside an elephant.

Manner of Death: Paralysed from August 1901, he became almost deaf and delirious, suffering from syphilis and the effects of alcoholism. He died of a stroke in his mother's home, the Château de Malromé, Malromé, near Bordeaux, at 2.15 am on 9 September 1901, aged 36. He was buried in the cemetery of Saint-André du Bois, near Malromé (his father drove the hearse). His body was later transferred to Verdelais nearby.

TROLLOPE, Anthony (1815–82) English novelist

Anthony Trollope was born at 16 Keppel Street (off Store Street), London, on 24 April 1815, the third son of Thomas Anthony Trollope, a barrister and farmer who had been a Fellow of New College, Oxford, and who was related to Baronet Trollope. His mother was Frances Milton, a writer, and both his grandfathers had been clergymen and Fellows of New College, Oxford. His oldest brother Thomas Adolphus was also a prolific writer and later married Frances Ternan, sister of Dickens's mistress. His brother

Henry died of tuberculosis (aged 23), as did his sisters Emily and later, Cecilia (who also wrote novels). Educated with his brothers at Harrow and Winchester (1825), he was left at school for three years when the rest of the family emigrated to Cincinatti, USA (where his mother ran a general store). His mother then wrote *Domestic Manners of the Americans*, which was a big success, but still went bankrupt. His father then died working on letter D of his *Ecclesiastical Encyclopedia* and the family moved to Belgium, where his mother began to support the children by writing 114 books. Trollope himself began work as a junior clerk in the General Post Office in London (1834) – his mother was a friend of the son of its chief, Sir Francis Freeling. He rose through the ranks (working in Ireland, England and the West Indies) to become head of the Eastern Postal District in Britain but took early retirement when passed over for the second-highest job in the GPO of Assistant Secretary (despite the fact that he was by then brother-in-law of the Secretary, John Tilley, who married his sister Cecilia). He then resigned and became editor of *St Paul's Magazine* (1867) but gave it up after three years. The most famous of his 47 novels included the Barsetshire series – *The Warden* (1855), *Barchester Towers* (1857), *Framley Parsonage* (1861) and *The Last Chronicle of Barset* (1867) – and *Phineas Finn* (1869), *The Eustace Diamonds* (1873), *The Way We Live Now* (1875) and *Mr Scarborough's Family* (1883).

Family/Sex Life: In 1844 he married Rose Heseltine, the daughter of a Rotherham bank manager. Their sons were Henry and Frederick. In his old age he had a platonic love affair with a young American, Kate Field.

Appearance: Around five feet 10 inches tall, Trollope was big, burly, balding and bearded (C. P. Snow called him a 'lumbering young man, strong, powerfully muscled'). He had dark blue eyes and small hands and feet. By 1876 he weighed 16 stone and was half deaf and had bad eyesight.

Habits/Mannerisms: Trollope disliked looking at himself in mirrors or being photographed. According to C. P. Snow, 'He had no vanity, and could have done with more.' He drank gin and brandy but later almost no spirits, preferring claret (he was not a heavy drinker). He was a member of the Garrick Club, though Snow observed he was 'without any histrionic

streak . . . a poorish speaker and a bad public performer'. He was almost invariably known as Anthony (not Tony).

Sport/Hobbies: Trollope was a fanatical hunter, hunting three times a week. He played whist daily.

Religion/Politics: High Anglican, but preferred Catholicism to Presbyterianism. He ran as a Liberal candidate at Beverley in 1868 but failed to be elected.

Health: Troubled with asthma, he suffered from angina in old age, had a stroke and experienced paralysis in one of his hands. He also wore a truss.

Temperament: Trollope was bluff, vociferous, blustering and overbearing. Snow called him 'peremptory, aggressive, interrogatory, hectoring'. At a meeting of surveyors he once repeatedly shouted out at a speaker, 'I disagree with you entirely!' – then added, 'What was it you said?' Nonetheless, he counted among his friends Thackeray, Millais (who drew 87 illustrations for his books) and Sir William Gregory of Coole (later Governor of Ceylon and husband of Yeats's benefactor). He disliked Carlyle (whom he called 'Doctor Pessimist Anti-cant') and Dickens ('Mr Popular Sentiment'). He greatly admired George Eliot.

Work/Daily Routine: Trollope rose at 5.30 am and wrote 1000 words an hour for 2½ hours before going to work at the Post Office (office hours were 10 am to 4.30 pm). He wrote nothing before 1843 and his first novel, *The Macdermots of Ballycloran* (1847), was shown to his publishers by his mother. He always delivered manuscripts to his publisher on schedule. He wrote his early work in Ireland, then at Waltham Cross, then in London. The Barsetshire series was inspired by walks he took around Salisbury Cathedral. *The Warden* took four years to sell 700 copies (the original printing was 1000). He thought *The Last*

Chronicles of Barset was his best novel. Not everyone was won over, though – decades later A. N. Wilson dismissed his novels as 'the Victorian equivalent of *The Archers*'. Henry James called him 'the dullest Briton of them all'. Tolstoy, however, praised him extravagantly: 'Trollope kills me ... with his excellence.' He was never paid as much as Dickens or Wilkie Collins (the highest payment he got for a novel was £2800 per volume for *The Claverings*). Outside literature, another claim to lasting fame was his invention of the pillar-box (1854).

Motto: 'No day without its line' (adopted from the original attributed to the Greek artist Apelles).

Manner of Death: A stroke left Trollope with paralysis and rendered him speechless until his death in London on 6 December 1882, aged 67.

TURNER, Joseph Mallord William (1775–1851) English painter

Joseph Mallord (originally Mallad) William Turner was born at 26 Maiden Lane, London, on 23 April 1775, the eldest child of William Turner, a barber and wig-maker, and Mary Marshall (who died insane in 1804). He had a sister, Mary Ann, who died aged seven and a half. Ill-educated, he was sent to live with his butcher uncle in Brentford aged 10 and attended John White's School there. He then stayed with a friend of his mother's in Margate and attended Mr Coleman's School (1786). At the age of 14 he was apprenticed to architect Thomas Hardwick (1789); after working for topographical draughtsman Thomas Malton that year he enrolled at the Royal Academy and exhibited his first watercolour, *The Archbishop's Palace, Lambeth*, there in 1790. After graduating he joined the 'Academy' of Dr Thomas Munro, consultant physician to George III. His first oil painting was exhibited at the RA in 1796 and led to many commissions. He began taking private pupils in 1794–8, was elected a Royal Academician aged 27 (1802), became RA Professor of Perspective (1807–38), a member of the RA Council (1818) and briefly its Deputy President (1845). He was also a founder member of the Artists' General Benevolent Institution (1814) and was its Chairman and Treasurer in 1818 but later resigned (1830). Later in life his father worked as his studio assistant. On his mother's death he inherited houses in Shadwell near Wapping and turned them into a pub, the Ship and Bladebone (1819). His most famous paintings included *The Fighting Téméraire* (1839) and *Rain, Steam and Speed* (1844).

Family/Sex Life: Turner never married but around 1798 took as his mistress Sarah Danby, widow of organist/composer John Danby and already mother of four children (Turner had two illegitimate daughters by her, Evelina – who later married the British consul in Ashanti – and Georgina). Towards the end of his life he kept a secret establishment in Chelsea for his stout, uneducated former Margate landlady, twice widowed Mrs Sophia Caroline Booth, who had a son Daniel John by her first marriage (Turner was known to locals as, variously, Mister, Admiral or 'Puggy' Booth). He was reputedly the father of at least five illegitimate children.

Appearance: Turner was small, stout and sailor-like, with crooked legs and a ruddy complexion. He had a prominent nose, grey-blue eyes and was, according to the *Dictionary of National Biography*, 'of a somewhat Jewish cast of countenance'. He had false teeth in old age and his mouth generally wore a cynical expression. 'He looked like an English farmer, with black clothes, rather coarse, big shoes and a hard, cold manner', according to Delacroix. Turner had long sideburns and, at his death, wore a beard. He was slovenly in his dress.

Habits/Mannerisms: So badly educated he could scarcely write a sentence, he also mispronounced words when lecturing – for instance, 'Mithematics', 'spearides' (spheroids). He spoke little but always to the point, with a strong London accent, and had a short dry laugh. He had a shuffling gait. Ruskin described him as a 'somewhat eccentric, keen-mannered, matter-of-fact, English-minded gentleman; good-natured evidently, bad-tempered evidently, hating humbug of all sorts, shrewd, perhaps a little selfish, highly intellectual'. In old age his diet comprised largely of 'two quarts of milk a day and rum in proportion, very frequently to excess', according to the records of Dr Bartlett, his physician. He was also very partial to sherry. He smoked cigars and took snuff.

Sport/Hobbies: Turner enjoyed fishing and also played the flute and wrote poetry. He never knew any foreign language. Other pastimes included his collection of model ships.

Health: Turner suffered from a nervous disorder, and around 1812 complained of a weak stomach and neck pain.

Temperament: Known as 'William' to his friends, he was cheerful and sociable but could also prove shy, secretive, proud, sensitive, silent, suspicious, surly, avaricious, gruff and bad-mannered. His friends included Ruskin, David Roberts, the sculptor Chantrey, George Dawe RA, Lord Egremont, David Wilkie (a relative of Wilkie Collins) and the landscape painter William Frederick Wells (with whom he stayed in Kent).

Pets: Turner loved animals and kept five or six dirty-white pink-eyed tailless cats at his home in Queen Anne Street, London.

Work/Daily Routine: Turner had a very steady arm and sometimes worked for 15 hours at a stretch, bolting the door of his studio. *The Snowstorm* was painted after Turner had himself lashed to the mast of a ship in order to experience the effects of a storm – critics called it 'Soapsuds and Whitewash'. Mark Twain described another of his paintings as 'A tortoiseshell cat having a fit in a platter of tomatoes.' Once, when he was handed a plate of salad, he observed to a neighbour: 'Nice cool green, that lettuce, isn't it? And the beetroot pretty red – not quite strong enough; and the mixture, delicate tint of yellow that. Add some mustard, and then you have one of my pictures.' He personally witnessed several of the events depicted in his works – notably the fire that destroyed the Houses of Parliament and the final voyage of the *Fighting Téméraire*, which Turner saw being towed to the breaker's yard. He had a roof terrace built on his Chelsea house so he could observe the changing light on the Thames. He hated selling his paintings, complaining to friends, 'I have lost one of my children this week.' Some grossly obscene drawings of Turner's were destroyed in 1858 by the National Gallery for the sake of his reputation – 'they having been assuredly drawn under a certain condition of insanity'.

Manner of Death: Turner died, according to Dr Bartlett, of 'natural decay' at the house of his mistress (Mrs Booth), 6 Davis Place, Cremorne New Road, Chelsea, at 10 am on 19 December 1851, aged 76. His body was taken to his official home, 47 Queen Anne St West. He was buried in the crypt of St Paul's, at his request, near Reynolds.

TWAIN, Mark (1835–1910) US novelist, journalist and lecturer

Mark Twain was born Samuel Langhorne Clemens in Florida, Missouri, on 30 November 1835, the third son of John Marshall Clemens, a storekeeper, landowner (70,000 acres) and lawyer known as 'Judge Clemens' and a descendant of Gregory Clemens, one of the judges who condemned Charles I to death. His mother was Jane Lampton, a distant relative of the earls of Durham. His father died when he was 12 and he was brought up in Hannibal, Missouri. His brother Orion ran a newspaper and he also had a younger brother Henry (who was killed on a boat aged 20) and a sister Pamela. Apprenticed at first to the printer of the *Missouri Courier*, he then trained and worked as a Mississippi river pilot (1857–61), was a goldminer in Nevada and served as a Confederate soldier (Marion Ranger) in the American Civil War. Himself an inventor, he bought four-fifths of the patent for the Kaolotype engraving process for making printing plates and invested heavily in the Page Typesetter (a precursor of Linotype), but lost a fortune when the business collapsed. He was also a publisher – naming the company Charles Webster & Company after his nephew – and as well as his own books published President General Ulysses Grant's *Memoirs*. The Twains moved to Hartford, Connecticut, in 1871. He visited the UK in 1872, was widely fêted and received an Honorary Doctorate from Oxford University. He was declared bankrupt in 1894 and undertook a world lecture tour to recoup his losses. A prolific writer, his most celebrated works included the novels *Tom Sawyer* (1876) and *Huckleberry Finn* (1884).

Family/Sex Life: In 1870 Twain married Olivia ('Livy') Langdon. He had fallen in love with Livy even before meeting her, being shown her likeness in a miniature belonging to her brother when they met on a voyage to the Holy Land. Much later he dedicated *Personal Recollections of Joan of Arc* (1895) to Livy on their wedding anniversary. She died in 1904; their children were Langdon (who died young), Olivia Susan (Susy) and Clara (to both of whom he dedicated *The Prince and the Pauper*, 1882) and Jean.

Appearance: Distinguishing features included a heavy moustache. He was careless about his dress – Harriet Beecher Stowe once scolded him for visiting her without wearing a necktie and, once he was home again, he lost no time in sending her one, instructing her to look at it for half an hour (the period of his visit) then return it to him, as it was the only one he had.

Habits/Mannerisms: Dubbed 'Youth' by his wife, his principal vices were drinking bourbon whiskey and smoking 40 cigars a day (he said quitting smoking was easy – he'd done it 100 times).

Sport/Hobbies: Twain enjoyed hunting and fishing and was very keen on billiards, calling it 'the best game on earth'. He also played the piano and sang and patented numerous inventions, including a self-pasting scrapbook.

Religion/Politics: Agnostic.

Health: In later life Twain suffered from bronchitis and arthritis (for which sympathetic readers sent him hundreds of recommended cures).

Pets: Twain kept cats, whose names included Blatherskite, Beelzebub, Buffalo Bill, Zoroaster, Satan, Stray Kit, Sin, Apollinaris and Sour Mash (some of the names were deliberately chosen to help his children to pronounce difficult words). His daughter Susy once observed that 'the difference between Papa and Mamma is, that Mamma loves morals and Papa loves cats'.

Work/Daily Routine: The pseudonym 'Mark Twain' comes from a river pilot's depth-sounding cry for two fathoms by plumb-line (the journalist and former Mississippi river pilot Isaiah Sellers had already used the name before Clemens adopted it). Twain often wrote in bed and even received visitors without getting up. Some of his early works were published under the pseudonym 'Thomas Jefferson Snodgrass'. He was the first author to type his manuscripts and to double space them for the convenience of his editor (he used a Remington typewriter). In a literary hoax he reviewed his own book *The Innocents Abroad* (1869), attributing the article to the London *Saturday Review* – the joke backfired and he got into trouble, though the book itself established his reputation as a humorist. He intended *Huckleberry Finn* and *Tom Sawyer* for adults and agreed when the former was banned from the Brooklyn New York Public Library Children's Room. He was admired by Kipling but disliked by Faulkner.

Manner of Death: Twain died in Redding, Connecticut, on 21 April 1910, aged 74. He died in the year that Halley's comet appeared, fulfilling his own prediction that, as he had been born on the day when the comet – an 'unaccountable freak' like himself – had last visited the Earth, he would die when it returned. Some years earlier, while he was in London, the rumour had spread that he had died and telegrams starting arriving from the *New York Journal* seeking confirmation of this (in fact, it was Twain's cousin who was ill) – Twain returned the now-celebrated reply: 'Report of my death greatly exaggerated.'

VAN GOGH, Vincent (1853–90) Dutch painter

Vincent Willem van Gogh was born in Groot-Zundert, Brabant, Holland, on 30 March 1853, the oldest surviving son of Theodorus van Gogh, a Lutheran pastor in the village of Zundert, and Anna Cornelius Carbentus, a keen amateur botanist and watercolourist. Three of his uncles were art dealers, one a tax inspector, and one a vice-admiral. He had two brothers, Théo (an art dealer) and Cornelius, and three sisters, Anna, Elizabeth and Wilhelmina. Educated at Zundert village school, he worked for the Hague office of international art dealers Goupil & Company (an uncle was a partner). Promoted to the London office after four years (aged 20), he was then transferred to the Paris branch (1875) but sacked the following year. He then (in brief succession) taught French, German and Maths at Mrs Stokes's school, Ramsgate, was an assistant to the Reverend Mr Jones (a Methodist minister in Isleworth, Middlesex) and worked as a bookseller in Dordrecht. Failing to qualify for university to train as a priest in Amsterdam and as an evangelist in Brussels, he returned home but was eventually thrown out (Christmas Day 1881) for indolence. Thereafter he was supported (often with little thanks) by his younger brother Théo, who also helped him get commissions and with whom he lived in Paris. He later spent one term at the Antwerp Academy of Art (1886) and aged 33 joined the studio of Felix Cormon in Paris (Toulouse-Lautrec was a fellow student). In 1888 he moved to Arles, Provence, in search of a light that would give his paintings a Japanese feel and Gauguin joined him there after Théo guaranteed him 150 francs a month for 12 pictures a year (Gauguin left after the infamous ear incident). The residents of Arles eventually petitioned the mayor and he was interned in the local hospital and then at the asylum of Saint-Paul-de-Mausole at nearby Saint-Rémy (1889). Public recognition came at the end of his life in an article in *Mercure de France* by Albert Aurier (January 1890) and at controversial exhibitions by the Les Vingts association in Brussels (where he sold *Red Vineyard* for 400 francs) and by Les Indépendants. He spent his last days in an inn at Auvers-sur-Oise, near Paris, under the supervision of Pissarro's friend Dr Gachet. His most celebrated paintings included *The Potato Eaters* (1885), *Sunflowers* (1888) and *Cornfields with Flight of Birds* (1890).

Family/Sex Life: Van Gogh never married but nursed an unrequited love for Eugénie Loyer (his landlady's daughter) and later formed relationships with his cousin Kee Vos and with the pregnant prostitute Clasina ('Sien') Maria Hoornik, with whom he lived in The Hague (also with her sick daughter). Margot Begemann, the daughter of his parents' neighbours, fell for him but was rejected and took strychnine (she survived).

Appearance: According to A. S. Hartick, Van Gogh was 'a rather weedy little man, with pinched features, red hair and beard, and a light blue eye'. He also had freckles. On 23 December 1888 he cut off part of his left earlobe after an argument with Gauguin when Gauguin was staying with him in Arles. He took the piece to the local brothel, hoping to find Gauguin there, but gave it instead to a prostitute called Rachel. He liked to wear a shaggy wool-lined cap.

Habits/Mannerisms: Van Gogh ate little and avoided meat. He smoked cigars and a pipe and was a heavy drinker of low-grade absinthe and cheap wine. He was also a masochist – he would beat himself with a

stick if he did not concentrate on his studies and spent his nights in a shed without bed or blanket.

Sport/Hobbies: Van Gogh played the piano and also liked reading Zola and George Eliot.

Religion/Politics: He was very religious and hoped to enter the priesthood. He translated part of the Bible into Dutch, French, German and English and said lengthy prayers at the meal table.

Health: Van Gogh was mentally unstable (schizophrenia). Several times he almost poisoned himself by drinking kerosene and swallowing oil paints. Physical ailments included venereal disease, which he caught from 'Sien', toothache (which affected his right eye and ear and which ultimately resulted in the loss of 10 teeth), a tear-gland disorder that made his eyelids stick together, palpitations of the heart, pains between the shoulders, dizzy spells, insomnia (which he combated by putting camphor on his pillow and mattress) and epilepsy. While in Antwerp he contracted syphilis.

Temperament: A deeply unhappy personality, he always walked with bent head. Though moody and difficult, his friends included Gauguin, Émile Bernard and (through Théo) Monet and Pissarro.

Work/Daily Routine: Van Gogh's first commission was for 12 drawings of The Hague for his Uncle Cor. He reputedly only sold one painting in his entire life (not true). He signed paintings 'Vincent' because Van Gogh was difficult for foreigners to pronounce (early works, though, were sometimes signed 'V. W. v Gogh'). He greatly admired Delacroix, Gauguin, Millet, Daumier, Rousseau, Rubens, the Impressionists, Japanese art and the illustrators of *The Graphic*. He hated Ingres, Raphael and Degas. He insisted on painting landscapes out of doors (like Millet and the Barbizon school), but painted things not as they were but as he 'felt' them to be. He worked rapidly without correcting (he painted *L'Arlesienne* in 45 minutes). He sometimes used Japanese reed pens. When painting at night he put lighted candles in his straw hat and on his canvas in order to see what he was doing.

Motto/Saying: He often insisted that 'One becomes a painter by painting', thus

denying that innate talent had anything to do with it.

Manner of Death: Van Gogh shot himself in the chest with a borrowed revolver in a field near Auvers on 27 July 1890. He died of his wounds in the arms of his brother Théo in his lodgings (an inn kept by M. Ravoux, at Auvers-sur-Oise, near Paris) at 1 am on 29 July 1890, aged 37. Mourners at his funeral included Pissarro.

VERNE, Jules (1828–1905) French novelist and playwright

Jules-Gabriel Verne was born in Nantes, France, on 8 February 1828, the eldest child of Pierre Verne, a lawyer, scholar and poet, and Sophie Allotte de la Fuye, a descendant of a Scotsman (Allott) who had served in the Scots Guards of Louis XI and earnt a title (*fuye* means dovecote, a privilege then in the royal gift) and built a castle near Loudun. His mother was also a friend of the literary hostess Madame Barrère and through her Verne later met Hugo, Dumas and others. He was also related to Chateaubriand, who was the brother of his maternal uncle's first wife. His siblings were Marie, Paul, Anna and Mathilde. Educated at the St Stanislas School, Nantes, and at St Donatien's Seminary, he then studied law in Paris. He also studied maths with his cousin Henri Garcet, Professor of Maths at the Lycée Henri IV and author of books on cosmography and mechanics. In 1852, with the help of Dumas (who had staged Verne's first play in 1850), he became Secretary to the Théâtre Lyrique, Paris. Later he became a partner in stockbrokers Eggly & Company, Paris, a firm owned by a relative of his wife's (1857). He was also Secretary of the Society for Aerial Locomotion (founded by Nadar) and was awarded the Légion d'honneur in 1870. In the year of his death he endorsed the newly formed Esperanto Society. He is usually

remembered for such fantasy novels as *Voyage au centre de la terre* (Journey to the Centre of the Earth, 1864), *Vingt mille lieues sous les mers* (Twenty Thousand Leagues Under the Sea, 1869) and *Le Tour du monde en quatre-vingts jours* (Around the World in Eighty Days, 1873).

Family/Sex Life: In 1857 Verne married Mrs Honorine Morel, née Fraysse de Viane, a widow with two children. By her he fathered a son, Michel.

Appearance: He had short curly hair and sported a large beard. Later in life he wore a peaked cap to shade his eyes.

Habits/Mannerisms: Verne ate huge amounts of food because of the abnormal hunger pains he suffered. He also smoked pipes and cigars. A brilliant speaker, if unable to sleep he did crossword puzzles.

Sport/Hobbies: Verne loved sailing and owned a number of steam yachts, for instance the 92-foot *Saint-Michel III*. He also played the piano and was a good singer (he won a prize for singing while at school); he was especially fond of Wagner.

Religion/Politics: Roman Catholic. He was elected to Amiens town council (1888, 1892, 1896, 1900) as a Conservative

Republican. He did not object to the notorious Dreyfus verdict, believing a judge's decision to be sacrosanct.

Health: In 1886 he was wounded in the foot when his insane nephew Gaston twice shot a revolver at him (he limped thereafter). He had an excellent memory but was a diabetic and suffered repeated attacks of facial neuralgia (he shaved off his beard during these). In old age he was further troubled by dizziness and eye trouble.

Temperament: Verne was taciturn and peaceable. He never entered into arguments and disliked disputes. His friends included George Sand, the *Charivari* cartoonist 'Stop' (Philippe Gille, later Literary Editor of *Le Figaro*) and political cartoonist and fashionable photographer Nadar (Verne called the astronaut in *From the Earth to the Moon* 'Ardan' – an anagram of Nadar).

Pets: He kept a female spaniel, Follette.

Work/Daily Routine: Verne got up at 5 am and worked until 11 am, then took a short walk and had a frugal lunch followed by a small cigar. He produced two books a year. His first performed work was a one-act comedy put on by Dumas at the Théâtre Historique, Paris (1850). His first full novel to be published was *Cinq Semaines en Ballon* (1863) – it became an instant bestseller and the world's first science-fiction novel (as a publicity stunt, Nadar built a huge balloon called 'The Giant'). His most popular book in his own lifetime (and the one that made him world famous) was *Around the World in 80 Days*. Verne was sued for plagiarism over *Journey to the Centre of the Earth* but won the case. In 1969 the moon-rocket Apollo 9 was launched from the same place (Florida), had the same weight and height and splashed down 2½ miles from the point mentioned in Verne's *From the Earth to the Moon*. He also wrote short stories, comedies, tragedies, libretti and comic operas. His style was admired by Apollinaire, who parodied it thus 'Jules Verne! What a style! Nothing but nouns!' His novels were attacked, though, by Zola.

Manner of Death: Verne died in the Boulevard Longueville, Amiens, at 8 am on 24 March 1905, aged 78. He was buried in the cemetery of La Madeleine, Amiens.

VICTORIA (1819–1901) Queen of the United Kingdom and Empress of India

Alexandrina Victoria was born at Kensington Palace, London, on 24 May 1819, the only child of Edward Duke of Kent, fourth son of George III, and the German Princess Mary Louisa Victoria Saxe-Coburg-Gotha (sister of King Leopold I of Belgium and widow of Prince Ernest Charles of Leiningen). Her father died when she was eight months old. She had a half-sister Féodore and a half-brother Charles from her mother's first marriage. Only 18 when proclaimed queen in St James's Palace, she was Britain's longest reigning monarch (63 years – four days longer than George III) and came to the throne on the death of her uncle William IV (1837) because not one of the seven sons and five daughters of her grandfather George III had had a single legitimate child. Created Empress of India (1876) at her own insistence, she had Indian servants at Windsor, Balmoral and Osborne. She devoted herself to the service of country and Empire and became for many the personification of British 19th-century values.

Family/Sex Life: In 1840 Victoria

proposed to and married her cousin Albert, son of her uncle, Duke Ernest of Saxe-Coburg-Gotha. Their nine children were Victoria ('Pussy', mother of Kaiser Wilhelm I), Edward VII, Alice, Alfred, Helena ('Lenchen'), Louise, Arthur (who was named after the Duke of Wellington and was born on his 81st birthday), Leopold and Beatrice. Southey's sister-in-law was superintendent of the royal nursery. Victoria never reconciled herself to Albert's death in 1861 and for a time neglected her state duties; she wore mourning in his memory for the rest of her life.

Appearance: Only five feet tall, Victoria weighed nearly nine stone and had a heavy, jowled face in old age, though she was slim and pretty in her youth. All her adult life she wore a bracelet containing a miniature of Albert painted by Sir William Ross in the year of their engagement.

Habits/Mannerisms: Victoria was left-handed and as a child spoke only German (she never spoke English perfectly). She slept in her mother's room at Kensington Palace until she became queen; after Albert's death she had a huge photograph of his newly-dead corpse placed over her bed and insisted on having his bowl of water set out for him each morning and his clothes laid on the bed each evening. She did not like beer or champagne but enjoyed sweet ale and negus (mulled wine). Intensely patriotic, she was married in clothes entirely of British manufacture. She did not allow knocking on doors, only scratching, and forbade smoking in Buckingham Palace. Treasured possessions included a black walking-stick made from the oak tree in which Charles II hid. Victoria was known as 'Gangan' to her grandchildren. She disliked cars because they frightened her horses.

Sport/Hobbies: Victoria wrote 100 volumes of diaries (from the age of 13 until her death). She also sang and played the piano well (she liked Mendelssohn, but thought Mozart old-fashioned and said 'I prefer Bellini, Rossini, Donizetti etc. to anything else'). Other pastimes included knitting, dancing, riding (side-saddle), sea-bathing (at Osborne) and painting (watercolours, oils, pastels and etchings), which she was taught by Richard Westall RA (1827–36, his first and only pupil) and by Edward Lear (she also admired Landseer and Winterhalter and gave the latter's *Florinda* to Albert for his birthday, 1832). In contrast to the dour lady she became, as a young woman she also enjoyed theatre and ballet – the Old Vic (Royal Victorian) Theatre (formerly the Royal Coburg Theatre) was renamed in her honour (1833). She learnt French, Italian and German and liked playing charades. Her favourite reading included the novels of Walter Scott (the first novel she ever read was *The Bride of Lammermoor*) and George Eliot. She owned the yacht (paddle-steamer and sail) *Victoria and Albert*. She was the first monarch to live in Buckingham Palace (she had Marble Arch removed from in front of the palace as it was too narrow for the royal coach).

Religion/Politics: Church of England. By having chloroform (which had been introduced in the 1840s) during the birth of her seventh child (1853) she ended the Church controversy over the Bible's stipulation that women should give birth with pain. Her tendency to intervene personally in affairs of state led to clashes with her ministers, especially with her Prime Minister Gladstone (though she adored Disraeli). When the Whigs resigned in 1839, she refused to dismiss the Whig ladies of the bedchamber as was the convention, thus triggering a political crisis that led to the Whigs being reinstated for another two years. At one point in her reign she threatened to abdicate over the possibility of war with the USA.

Health: Victoria was a carrier of haemophilia (which only affects males) and passed it on to her son Leopold. She survived assassination by a gunman on Constitution Hill.

Temperament: Victoria was somewhat frivolous in her youth, but was firm-willed as monarch, though she became very depressed and sentimental after Albert's death. The famous 'We are not amused' quotation is thought to have arisen from her frosty reaction to a risqué joke she was told by some of her grandchildren. Her friends and confidantes included Prime Minister Lord Melbourne (the husband of Lady Caroline Lamb), who became her surrogate father, and Disraeli. There were many scurrilous but apparently groundless rumours about her relationship with her faithful retainer John Brown.

Pets: As a child she kept a dog called Fanny. Later she had a King Charles spaniel called Dash (its epitaph was: 'Reader/If you would lived beloved/And die regretted/Profit by the example of/ DASH'). She also had a terrier called Islay and a female greyhound called Eos (Albert's favourite). Her favourite mount was a white horse called Leopold; she also had a Shetland pony chaise, two Blue Persian cats and owned the first Pekinese dog in the West – a fawn-and-white female called Lootie.

Manner of Death: Victoria died at Osborne House, Isle of Wight, on 22 January 1901, aged 81.

VOLTAIRE (1694–1778) French writer and philosopher

Voltaire was born François-Marie Arouet in Saint-André-des-Arts, Paris, on 21 November 1694, the third and last surviving child of François Arouet, a successful notary and close friend of Corneille and Boileau who later became Receiver of Court Fees, Fines and Taxes. His mother (who died when he was seven) was Marie-Cathérine D'Aumard, daughter of the Record Keeper at the High Court. After the death of his mother he was looked after by his godfather, the Abbé de Châteauneuf. His surviving siblings were Armand (10 years older) and Marguérite-Cathérine (nine years older). He attended the Jesuit college of Saint-Louis-le-Grand by the Sorbonne (with Richelieu's great-nephew, Louis de Plessis) and after studying law became page to his godfather's brother, the Marquis de Châteauneuf but was dismissed (1713) for a love affair. He then worked briefly in a lawyer's office in Paris before joining the household of the Marquis de Saint-Ange at Fontainebleau. Imprisoned in the Bastille, Paris (1717–18) for writing lampoons on

the Regent, Philippe Duc d'Orléans, he there began the epic poem *Henriade* – the first ever in French – which was to make him famous. His father left him a fortune when he died in 1721 and he also received an annuity of 4250 livres from the Prince Regent and half his brother's estate after his death (1745). He later became Royal Historiographer and Gentleman in Waiting to Louis XV under the patronage of Madame de Pompadour (to whom he dedicated *Tancrède*). He was also Chamberlain at Sans Souci to Frederick the Great and became very rich buying up lotteries in Paris and the Duchy of Lorraine and speculating in the corn trade. He was a member of the Académie Française and the Royal Society, London. For his last 20 years he lived at 'Les Délices' in Geneva, then in French Ferney, near Geneva (visitors included Casanova, Gibbon and Boswell). His most celebrated writings included the tragedy *Oedipe* (1718), the novella *Candide* (1759) and the *Dictionnaire philosophique* (1764).

Family/Sex Life: In 1713 Voltaire had an affair with Olympe Dunoyer, daughter of the proprietor of a scandal paper. He also had a 20-year relationship with the married Marquise du Châtelet (Gabrielle Émilie Le Tonnellier de Breteuil), with whom he lived at Cirey (from 1734). Other lovers included his niece and housekeeper widow Madame Denis and the actresses Adrienne Lecouvreur and Suzanne de Livry. In old age he adopted a poor young female relative of Corneille.

Appearance: Five feet three inches tall, Voltaire was thin and had a distinctive long nose. A visitor in 1776 said he wore 'white cloth shoes, white woollen stockings, red breeches, with a nightgown and waistcoat of blue linen flowered and lined with yellow: he had on a grizzle wig with three ties, and over it a silk night-cap embroidered with gold and silver'. He was also given a sable wrap by Catherine the Great and owned a cane with a handle in the shape of a crow's beak as well as 12 rings set with cameos and two with diamonds.

Habits/Mannerisms: Voltaire felt the cold and had a fire in his study every day of the year. He drank 50 cups of coffee a day, even in old age. Known as 'Zozo' as a child, as an adult he had 'the eloquence of Cicero, the elegance of Pliny, and the wisdom of Agrippa', according to Frederick the Great.

Sport/Hobbies: Voltaire took fencing lessons, enjoyed gardening, played chess and collected paintings. He settled the spelling in France of 'Anglais' (previously it had been Anglois).

Religion/Politics: Voltaire held controversial views on religion. He believed in a non-Christian God and claimed 'If God did not exist, it would be necessary to invent Him.' In 1769 he became a Catholic and was the first Catholic to own property in (Calvinist) Switzerland. Always provocative, he was beaten up by the Chevalier de Rohan Chabot's men and exiled to England (1726–9). Other writings of his led to the banning of torture in obtaining confessions in Russia, Germany and Austria. He was also anti-Semitic.

Health: A weak and puny child not expected to live, he contracted smallpox in 1722 (it was on his advice that Catherine the Great introduced smallpox inoculation to Russia). A hypochondriac, he suffered from eye infections, bad digestion, gout (for which he took laudanum) and sciatica in old age. In 1778 a blood-vessel burst and he coughed blood for three weeks.

Temperament: Naturally combative, he was challenged to a duel but was arrested. He was also very vain. In England his friends included Pope, Gay, Swift, Lord Bolingbroke (to whom he dedicated his play *Brutus*), Sir Everard Falkner (to whom he dedicated *Zaïre*) and the Duchess of Marlborough.

Work/Daily Routine: 'Voltaire' was an anagram of 'Arouet le Jeune' (Arovet l.i.) but also derived from his nickname as a child, '*Le petit volontaire*' ('Little Wilful'); he adopted it in 1718. He also used the pseudonym 'Sanson' (hereditary French executioners). He worked fast – *Candide* took three days and *Zaïre* 22 days. He drank coffee around 12 pm; had dinner at 9 pm and went to bed around midnight. *Lettres philosophique* was burnt by the public hangman (1733), while the *Dictionnaire philosophique* was banned by the Vatican.

Manner of Death: Voltaire died around 11.10 pm on 30 May 1778 in the Hôtel de Villette, Quai des Théatins (now the Quai Voltaire), Paris, aged 83. He was refused burial in Paris so his body was embalmed (the heart removed and put in a silver vase in his study in Ferney), dressed in clothes, sat in a carriage (propped up by a servant) and driven secretly to the abbey of Scellières, Champagne, and buried there (the prior was later dismissed). All monuments to him were banned. In 1790 his body was transferred to the Panthéon at the request of Villette. The funeral featured the body on a 30-foot high altar pulled by 12 horses and attended by a crowd of 600,000. Reactionaries desecrated the tomb around 1814 and removed the bones. After his death, most of his papers went to Catherine the Great.

WAGNER, Richard (1813–83) German composer

Wilhelm Richard Wagner was born at the house of the Red and White Lion, Der Bruhl Street, Leipzig, on 22 May 1813, the youngest of eight children of Friedrich Wagner, Registrar at Leipzig Police Headquarters (who died in a typhus epidemic when Wagner was six months old) and Johanna Patz. His mother remarried Ludwig Geyer, a society portrait painter, actor/dramatist and friend of Carl Maria von Weber, Kapellmeister to the court opera. Until he was 15 Wagner was known as Richard Geyer (even though Geyer died when Wagner was eight). He had a favourite sister Rosalie, a brother Albert and a half-sister Cäcilie. Educated at the Dresden Kreuzschule (1822) and the Nikolaischule, Leipzig, he studied music with Christian Gottlieb Müller, then at the Thomas-Schule, then took violin lessons with Robert Sipp and studied under Theodor Weinlig, Cantor of the Thomas Kirche. He next attended the University of Leipzig. Aged 17 he conducted his own Overture in B Flat major at a charity concert at the Leipzig Royal Court Theatre but was greeted with laughter. He was later chorus master at the Würzburg Theatre (where his brother worked) in 1833, musical director of a Magdeburg theatre troupe, musical director of the Königsberg Theatre (1837) and musical director of a theatre in Riga, Latvia (1837–9). After this he worked for a music publisher arranging other composers' work and did music journalism. Imprisoned for debt (1840, 1841) he was later Royal Kapellmeister to Frederick August II of Saxony (1843). He took part in the Dresden Uprising (1849) during the German Revolution and fled with help from Liszt into exile in Paris and Zürich (where he composed the *Ring, Tristan* and *Meistersinger*). Frau Julie Ritter gave him 800 thalers a year (1850–9), Queen Victoria attended one of his eight London concerts in 1855 and his patron from 1864 was 18-year-old Ludwig II of Bavaria (until Wagner was expelled by the Bavarian government in 1865). With funds from Ludwig and various Wagner Societies he founded the opera house at Bayreuth exclusively for the *Ring* cycle, laying the foundation stone with a poem by himself and a telegram from Ludwig, and lived in a villa, Wahnfried (Peace from Illusion), nearby.

Family/Sex Life: In 1836 Wagner married the actress/opera singer Minna Planer, four years his senior with an illegitimate six-year-old daughter Natalie. Minna died in 1866. His second wife (1870) was Cosima Liszt, illegitimate daughter of the composer by Countess Marie d'Agoult and former wife of the conductor Hans von Bülow, by whom she already had two daughters, Daniella and Blandine. By her he fathered Isolde (born 1865), Eva and Siegfried. He also had many mistresses, including Friederike Meyer, Jessie Laussot (wife of a wine merchant), Mathilde Wesendouck (wife of a silk merchant patron who bought the copyright of four *Ring* operas for 6000 francs each) and Judith Gautier (daughter of Théophile Gautier and married to the poet Villiers de L'Isle Adam).

Appearance: Five feet six and a half inches tall, Wagner had a large head and a small body, with blue eyes and a beard (though without moustache or chin hair). He owned 24 silk dressing-gowns.

Habits/Mannerisms: He wrote his music in black, red and green ink.

Sport/Hobbies: He liked walking (he once walked from Dresden to Prague).

Religion/Politics: Protestant, but interested in Buddhism. He was a republican and a member of the revolutionary Vaterslandverein (1848). He was a friend of the anarchist Bakunin and was also anti-Semitic (he wrote an essay 'Jewishness in Music' under the pseudonym 'K. Freigedank' in 1850).

Health: A sickly child, he suffered from erysipelas (St Anthony's Fire), which makes the skin red and sensitive (he had to wear silk underwear and trousers and jackets lined with fur and wadding). Other ailments were gastric troubles (he took the waters at Marienbad, Bohemia) and angina (chest pains, 1881).

Temperament: His friends included Nietzsche (who was a good pianist and helped Wagner to publish his autobiography), Liszt, G. B. Shaw and Schumann (though he did not like Wagner's music).

Pets: Wagner kept a Newfoundland dog called Robber.

Work/Daily Routine: Wagner was greatly influenced by Weber, who was a frequent visitor at his home when Wagner was a boy (he arranged for Weber's remains to be brought from London to Dresden in 1844). He also admired Beethoven (his first work, rejected by the publishers, was a piano transcription of the Choral Symphony). He worked at his desk wearing silk and fur dressing-gowns, surrounded by exotic scents (when writing *Parzifal* he bathed in water scented with Milk of Iris perfume for several hours each day). He wrote all his own libretti (at 14 he had wanted to be a poet), including that for *Die Meistersinger*, which took him 30 days while staying in the Hôtel Voltaire, Paris. Not all his works met with immediate acclaim: the command performance of *Tannhäuser* (before Emperor Napoleon III at the Paris Opéra after 164 rehearsals, 1861) was jeered by the audience. Mark Twain joked, 'Wagner's music is better than it sounds.'

Manner of Death: Wagner died of a heart attack in rented apartments in the Palazzo Vendramin, Venice, at 3.30 pm on 13 February 1883, aged 69. His death mask was modelled by Benvenuti and his body was buried in the garden of his house, Wahnfried, Bayreuth.

WASHINGTON, George (1732–99) 1st President of the USA

George Washington was born in Bridges Creek, Westmoreland County, Virginia, on 22 February 1732, one of 10 children of Augustine Washington (who died when he was 11), an estate manager (slave plantation, tobacco, stockbreeding), and Mary Ball, his second wife (four of the 10 children were by an earlier marriage). He had two half-brothers, Lawrence and Augustine. At first he worked as Assistant Surveyor, then Surveyor, of Culpeper County, Virginia (he helped plan Washington DC). When his half-brother Lawrence died he inherited the family's huge estate, Mount Vernon, aged 20. The story that he chopped down a cherry tree with a hatchet in his youth and then freely admitted the crime to his father rather than tell a lie was invented by Parson Mason Locke Weems in his fictionalized biography of the President (1806). He was, however, a colonel in the French and Indian War and Commander of all Virginia troops (aged 23) and served as a member of Virginia's House of Burgesses (1759–74), opposing British rule in the Americas. During the War of Independence he was commander-in-chief of all American forces. In 1787 he presided over the Constitutional Convention and was elected President. He was re-elected for a second term in 1792, eventually retiring after personal attacks and disillusioned by party politics in 1797. He never lived in the White House (it was not built until after he left office).

Family/Sex Life: Washington twice proposed marriage to Betsy Fauntleroy, but was refused on both occasions and in the end married (1759) Martha Dandridge Custis, a rich widow with two children. He later adopted two of his step-grandchildren (he had no offspring of his own).

Appearance: Six feet three inches tall, Washington weighed 220 lb and was muscular, with long arms and legs. His face was badly scarred from smallpox. He had blue-grey eyes, a large mouth, a prominent nose and reddish hair (usually concealed under a white periwig). He later had wooden (e.g. elm) or hippo-ivory false teeth, which he reputedly soaked in port at night.

Sport/Hobbies: He was a very good horseman.

Health: Having himself suffered from smallpox, in 1777 he had his entire army (4000 men) vaccinated against it, at a time when very few American doctors believed in such inoculations.

Temperament: Thomas Paine (who had served in Washington's army) dedicated

The Rights of Man to him, but said that he was 'treacherous in private friendship . . . and a hypocrite in public life'. He showed considerable courage as a soldier and was reputed to have remarked that he found 'something charming' in the sound of bullets whistling through the air. As President he did not keep a personal guard, the story being that if endangered he could rely upon any patriotic American in the street to save him.

Pets: Washington's favourite horse was a chestnut gelding called Nelson. He kept cats at Mount Vernon and was also the first breeder of American jackasses and American mules (he had a mule named Royal Gift).

Work/Daily Routine: Perhaps the most famous episode in Washington's wartime career was his leadership of the beleaguered American forces wintering at Valley Forge (1777–8), when he did much to bolster ebbing morale. Stories were told of how he drank wine with the common soldiers and helped them build barricades and so forth, thus winning their enduring loyalty. Only five other US presidents were professional soldiers (Jackson, Harrison, Taylor, Grant and Eisenhower); in the War of Independence, his 'Continental Army' never numbered more than 20,000 troops (his opponents included 30,000 German troops hired by George III). Known as 'The American Fabius' after Quintus Fabius Maximus, who held that long counselling is needed before action, he was elected unopposed as President – but not by popular vote (such voting was not introduced until 1824). As President he earnt $25,000 a year (he was actually the 15th President of the American colonies but the first under the new constitution of 1789). Among other achievements, he sent the first airmail letter (carried by French balloonist Jean Pierre Blanchard from Philadelphia, then capital of the USA, to New Jersey).

Manner of Death: After suffering exposure

after riding round his estates in winter weather, Washington died at Mount Vernon, Virginia, on 14 December 1799, aged 67. When news of his death reached England, his old enemies honoured him in the form of a 20-gun salute fired by the Channel fleet.

WELLINGTON, Arthur Wellesley, 1st Duke of (1769–1852)
British general and statesman

Arthur Wellesley, later 1st Duke of Wellington (the 'Iron Duke'), was born in Dublin on 29 April 1769, the fourth son of Garrett Wellesley, 2nd Baron and 1st Earl of Mornington (the family name was changed to Wesley around 1790 – Wellington signed himself Arthur Wesley until May 1798). His mother was Anne Hill, daughter of Viscount Dungannon, and his elder brother Richard was Governor-General of India. Educated at Eton until 1784, when his mother took him to Brussels (his father died in 1781), he later studied at a military college in Angers, France. He was at first ADC to the Lord Lieutenant of Ireland and joined the 33rd Highlanders, becoming a captain (1791) and a lieutenant-colonel (1793). He subsequently fought in India and was appointed Governor of Seringapatem and commander of the forces in Mysore. Wellington returned to England in 1805 and was knighted. He entered Parliament in 1807, then saw action against the French in Denmark (1807) and led the British army with success in the Iberian Peninsula (1808–14). He was created a Duke (1814) and promoted to field marshal. After Napoleon's return from Elba in 1815 he combined with the Prussian Army under Blücher to deliver a final crushing defeat against the French at Waterloo. Following his return to politics, he served as MP for Rye and as British Ambassador in Paris before being invited to become Prime Minister (1828–30), though he proved a cautious and conservative leader. He also served as Foreign Secretary under Peel (1834–5) and was appointed Lord High Constable of England in 1848.

Family/Sex Life: In 1806 Wellington married Catherine ('Kitty') Sarah Dorothea Pakenham, daughter of the 2nd Baron Longford (he had first proposed to her, and been turned down, in 1792). They had two sons, Arthur Richard and Charles, but later lived apart, though they were never formally separated. Wellington held that 'no woman ever loved me; never in my whole life', but he also had an affair with Harriette Wilson (he coined the phrase 'Publish and be damned' when he was threatened by the compromising publication of her memoirs). Rumour had it that he had also slept with the French actress Mlle George, whose other lovers included Napoleon – when asked to compare them she reputedly replied, 'Ah sir, the duke was by far the more vigorous.'

Appearance: Five feet nine inches tall, he had penetrating grey eyes and aquiline features, with a large Roman nose (thus the nickname 'Old Nosey', by which he was known to his troops).

Habits/Mannerisms: Wellington never articulated clearly and was not a good speaker.

Sport/Hobbies: As a young soldier Wellington had a weakness for gambling and had got himself into serious debt through his gaming losses by the time he had attained the age of 24 (he consequently determined to give up gambling and to concentrate on soldiering). He played the violin.

Religion/Politics: Irish Protestant by birth, though he later caused controversy through his support for Catholic Emancipation. He served as godfather to one of Queen Victoria's sons. As Prime Minister he acted conservatively and found it difficult to accept the necessity of compromise and was reluctant to agree to radical Parliamentary reform.

Temperament: Renowned for his iron will, his nickname the 'Iron Duke' allegedly arose from an incident when, as Prime Minister, he ordered iron shutters to be placed over the windows of his home, Apsley House, to protect them from an angry mob demanding Parliamentary reform. As a soldier he was courageous – he once fought a duel with pistols but he and his opponent both missed – though he could also be humourless, arrogant and contemptuous of his foot soldiers, calling them 'the scum of the Earth'. When some raw recruits arrived to support him in the Peninsular War he was moved to remark: 'I don't know what effect they will have upon the enemy, but by God, they frighten me.' He had his softer side, though: on one occasion he met a young boy sobbing because he had to go away to school and there was no one to look after his pet toad – the unrecognized Wellington graciously offered to keep the toad for him and a

week after beginning school the boy received a letter reading, 'Field Marshal the Duke of Wellington presents his compliments to Master — and has the pleasure to inform him that his toad is well.'

Pets: He kept a terrier dog called 'Vic' when in Angers. His favourite horse was his chestnut stallion Copenhagen, his mount at Waterloo.

Work/Daily Routine: At one point early in the ultimately glorious Peninsular War, Wellington was actually court-martialled for failing to press home his attacks against the French (he was following orders from his superiors and was duly acquitted of any blame). He played the proper English gentleman when fighting the French – at Waterloo, when an artillery officer reported he could see Napoleon himself and asked for permission to fire, Wellington declined the request, remarking, 'It is not the business of generals to shoot one another.' His legacies to the nation included Wellington boots, Wellington College and the tree Wellingtonia, all of which were named after him.

Manner of Death: Wellington died in the afternoon of 14 September 1852, aged 83. Queen Victoria granted him the most lavish state funeral ever staged; he was buried in St Paul's.

WELLS, Herbert George (1866–1946) English novelist

H. G. Wells was born at 47 High Street, Bromley, Kent, on 21 September 1866, the third son and fourth child of Joseph Wells, a Kent county cricketer who also owned a china shop, and Sarah Neal (who was 43 at the time of his birth). Known as 'Bertie' to the family, he had two elder brothers,

Frank and Fred. Educated at Morley's Commercial Academy, he was then an apprentice draper in Southsea, an apprentice pharmacist, a student teacher at Midhurst Grammar School, Sussex (1883–4), and later won a scholarship to study under T. H. Huxley at the Normal

School of Science in South Kensington, but failed to graduate. He was then a teacher at Holt Academy, Wrexham, then Henley House School, Kilburn, before receiving a BSc (first class) in Zoology. He was subsequently a tutor at the University Tutorial College before becoming a full-time writer. He later received a DSc (from the University of London) for a thesis, aged 78. His most famous writings included the science-fiction fantasies 'The Time Machine' (1895) and *The War of the Worlds* (1898) and the comic social novels *Kipps* (1905) and *The History of Mr Polly* (1910). Among his works of non-fiction were *The Outline of History* (1920) and *The Work, Wealth and Happiness of Mankind* (1932).

Family/Sex Life: In 1891 Wells married his cousin Isabel Mary Williams. Wells left her in 1893 and in 1895 eloped with and married his student Amy Catherine 'Jane' Robbins. He and Jane had two children, George Philip and Frank Richard. Other affairs included relationships with 19-year-old (Dame) Rebecca West, 26 years his junior, which culminated in the birth of their son Anthony West, with Elizabeth von Arnim (the cousin of Katherine Mansfield) and with the novelist Dorothy M. Richardson (whom Wells found 'most interestingly hairy').

Appearance: According to the *Dictionary of National Biography*, Wells was 'short, compact and inclined to plumpness'. He had small hands and feet and short arms but also 'wonderfully clear blue eyes ... birdlike alertness' (Anthony West). He had a piping, squeaky voice and light brown hair and moustache. Like Shaw he wore pure-wool suits made by Dr Jaeger.

Habits/Mannerisms: He moved and spoke very rapidly. Rebecca West said she was attracted chiefly by his smell – 'like walnut'. He always carried two fountain pens in his waistcoat pocket – 'The big one is for the long words, the little one for the short ones.'

Sport/Hobbies: He invented a ball game, was a keen photographer and was also a member of the Reform and Savile Clubs.

Religion/Politics: Wells was an anti-Marxist socialist and a prominent member of the Fabian Society (though he later resigned). He twice stood unsuccessfully as Labour MP for London University (1922, 1923). A republican, he openly attacked the British monarchy as 'this alien and uninspiring court' (1917) and also supported the Suffragette movement.

Health: He broke a leg at the age of seven and later damaged a kidney playing football. Other problems included tuberculosis and, in later life, diabetes.

Temperament: Wells was impatient, querulous but also modest (he told Henry James 'I had rather be called a journalist than an artist'). He espoused high morals, yet found himself incapable of keeping them. Beatrice Webb observed in 1910: 'The tragedy of H. G.'s life – his aptitude for "fine thinking" ... and yet his total incapacity for decent conduct. He says in so many words that directly you leave your study you inevitably become a cad and are indeed mean and dishonourable and probably cruel.' His friends included George Gissing and Bennett; he was also admired by Conrad, who dedicated *The Secret Agent* to him. Arnold Bennett described 'The Country of the Blind' as 'one of the radiant gems of contemporary literature' (*Books and Persons*).

Work/Daily Routine: Wells sold his first article to the *Pall Mall Gazette* (1893) using a formula for writing foolproof saleable newspaper articles suggested by a character in J. M. Barrie's *When a Man's Single*. He predicted through his writings World War II, aerial dogfights/air races, air conditioning, TV broadcasting, video recording and automatic doors (he also claimed that mankind, which was doomed to destroy itself, had just 1000 years left to it). He wrote many of his books in

Malagnon, near Grasse, in the South of France, and drew extensively on personal experience for his characters (to publicize *Kipps*, for which he recalled his own experiences as an apprentice in the drapery trade, he suggested plastering posters all over Southsea proclaiming 'Kipps worked here'). *Ann Veronica* was banned by some UK libraries as 'pornographic'. When *The War of the Worlds*, depicting a Martian invasion, was acted on US radio in 1938 by the Mercury Theater group led by Orson Welles, the story provoked a national panic, with thousands of listeners being misled into thinking the invasion was really happening. One of the listeners was actor John Barrymore who, on hearing that the Martians had reached Madison Avenue, flung open the door of the pen in which he housed 20 St Bernard dogs and drove them out, yelling 'Fend for yourselves!'

Manner of Death: Wells died alone in his sleep at 13 Hanover Terrace, Regent's Park, London, at 4.15 pm on 13 August 1946, aged 79.

WHISTLER, James Abbott McNeill (1834–1903) US painter

James Whistler was born in Lowell, Massachusetts, on 10 July 1834, the son of George Washington Whistler, a military engineer who built railways for the Tsar of Russia in St Petersburg. Educated at West Point Military Academy, he failed his chemistry exams ('Had silicon been a gas, I would have been a major-general') and was expelled. A fine draughtsman, he worked at first as a map engraver employed by the US Coastal Survey in Washington DC, but left after six months. Living on an allowance from his mother, he then moved to Paris and later settled in London (1859). President of the Royal Society of British Artists, he was bankrupted by a court case with Ruskin – Whistler won but was only paid a farthing in damages and had to sell his house in Chelsea. Sickert was one of his pupils. Among his most celebrated paintings were the evening scene *Nocturne in Black and Gold* and the so-called *Whistler's Mother* (1871–2). He also produced etchings and lithographs, many depicting scenes of the Thames.

Family/Sex Life: Whistler's mistress for 10 years was a woman named Joanna (who called herself Mrs Abbott and who modelled for such paintings as *Wapping*). He also had an affair with Maud Franklin and eventually married Mrs Beatrix Godwin, the widow of the architect of his house (she was the model in *Lamplight* and *The Siesta*).

Appearance: Whistler was a dandy. He wore a monocle and had a white forelock in his hair.

Sport/Hobbies: He collected blue and white china porcelain and Japanese prints. He also spoke fluent French – or at least thought he did (at a restaurant a friend offered to order for him after he inadvertently asked for 'a flight of steps').

Temperament: Whistler was a famous wit, often engaging in verbal fencing with Oscar Wilde (whom he accused of stealing some of his best quips). On one occasion, when Wilde was moved to exclaim 'I wish I had said that!' Whistler murmured, 'You will, Oscar, you will.' He was also self-obsessed, argumentative and pugnacious and picked fights (he once threw his brother-in-law through a plate-glass window). To those who differed from his views he would say, 'I am not arguing with you – I am telling you.' He was also immodest. When his attention was drawn to a particularly resplendent night sky, with a myriad stars on display, he lamented, 'Well, not bad, but there are decidedly too many of them, and they are not very well arranged. I would have done it differently.' His friends included Rossetti, Degas and Proust (who based his character Elstir on Whistler and Monet) and he was praised by Baudelaire. George du Maurier based his popular novel *Trilby* upon his and Whistler's experiences as art students in Paris. Examples of his legendary wit included the reply he gave to a woman who wondered rather preciously why he had been born in such an unfashionable place as Lowell, Massachusetts – 'The explanation is quite simple. I wished to be near my mother.'

Pets: He owned a brown, gold and white cat and also a French poodle.

Work/Daily Routine: Whistler used paint so runny that he had to work flat on the floor in order to control it. He was much influenced by designs on Japanese porcelain. His models had to pose for up to 70 sittings for each portrait and he reputedly destroyed 70 per cent of his portraits when they failed to meet his exacting standards. When one sitter complained that the resulting portrait was not a great work of art, Whistler uttered the unabashed response, 'Perhaps not, but then you can't call yourself a great work of nature.' Ruskin attacked his *Symphony in Red and Green*, calling it 'absolute rubbish', and also his *The Falling Rocket*, which prompted him to remark that he 'never expected to hear a coxcomb ask two hundred guineas for flinging a pot of paint in the public's face'. Whistler consequently sued him for libel, arguing that though a painting like the famous *Nocturne in Black and Gold* only took two days to paint, he charged such high prices for the 'knowledge of a lifetime'. The derisory damages he was awarded ruined him. The difficulties he had with Ruskin and many other critics prompted him to write a book entitled *The Gentle Art of Making Enemies* (1890).

Emblem/Motto: Whistler used a butterfly emblem as his signature ('Butterfly' was the pet name his mother gave him as a child).

Manner of Death: Whistler died in London on 17 July 1903, aged 69.

WILDE, Oscar (1854–1900) Irish playwright, novelist, poet and wit

Oscar Fingal O'Flahertie Wills Wilde was born at 21 Westland Row, Dublin, on 6 October 1854, the son of Sir William Wilde, a celebrated surgeon and antiquary, and Jane Francisca Elgee, better known as the poet and society hostess 'Speranza'. His elder brother was the Fleet Street journalist William Robert Charles Kingsbury Wills Wilde (who died in 1898). He also had a younger sister, Isola Francesca Emily, and an illegitimate older half-brother, Dr Henry Wilson, and two older illegitimate half-sisters, Emily and Mary, from earlier pre-marital liaisons by his father. Educated at Portora Royal School, Enniskillen, he studied classics at Trinity College, Dublin, and at Magdalen College, Oxford (where he took a Double First in Greats and won the Newdigate Prize for the poem 'Ravenna'). He was later Editor of *Woman's World* magazine (1887–9). As author of such classic plays as *Lady Windermere's Fan* (1892) and *The Importance of Being Earnest* (1895), he was celebrated as one of the most flamboyant and brilliant playwrights of the

1890s, but subsequently fell from grace and was declared bankrupt after losing his famous libel case against the Marquess of Queensberry (who had publicly called him a 'Somdomite' [sic]). Wilde failed to clear himself of the libel and was himself tried for homosexual offences (then illegal). He was sentenced to two years' hard labour and was imprisoned (1895–7) in Wandsworth and Reading gaols. His prosecutor was Sir Edward Carson, a childhood friend and fellow-student at Trinity College who later led the Ulster Protestant Rebellion (1914) and became Attorney-General. After his release Wilde lived in exile in France. His other publications included the novel *The Picture of Dorian Gray* (1891) and the poem *The Ballad of Reading Gaol* (1898).

Family/Sex Life: Though a homosexual, in 1884 Wilde married Constance Lloyd, granddaughter of John Horatio Lloyd QC and fathered two sons, Cyril and Vyvyan. The most infamous of his homosexual affairs was with Lord Alfred Douglas ('Bosy'), son of the Marquess of Queensberry – the relationship that was fated to result in Wilde's public exposure as a homosexual and in his inevitable exclusion from fashionable society. After serving his sentence, Wilde attempted to 'prove' his heterosexuality by making a well-publicized visit to a French brothel (though he confided to a friend that 'it was like cold mutton').

Appearance: Six feet three inches tall, Wilde had a large pale face and was slim in his youth, but later became stouter in build, with heavy blue eyes, thick lips and protruding teeth (which later turned black then greenish after mercury treatment for syphilis). He was clean-shaven but wore his dark brown hair long. A dandy, he often wore a green carnation in his buttonhole.

Habits/Mannerisms: Wilde had a swinging walk, though Max Beerbohm remarked on his 'cat-like tread'. He spoke rapidly, in a low voice, with distinct enunciation. While at Oxford he collected blue china and peacocks' feathers and his eccentric ways led to him being ducked in the Cherwell and to his rooms being ransacked. He was a founder of the 'Aesthetic' cult, whose symbols included peacocks' feathers, sunflowers, dados, blue china, long hair and velveteen breeches. He smoked cigarettes and drank absinthe. He was lampooned as 'Archibald Grosvenor' in Gilbert and Sullivan's *Patience*.

Sport/Hobbies: Wilde enjoyed riding, rowing, shooting, fishing and sailing but otherwise hated all sport (though he was a good boxer), especially hunting ('the unspeakable in pursuit of the uneatable'). He spoke fluent French and some German.

Religion/Politics: He received the last rites as a Roman Catholic. In politics he was a nationalist and an anti-Tory.

Health: While at Oxford Wilde caught syphilis from a female prostitute. In 1900 he underwent an operation on his right ear. He took chloral and opium as painkillers.

Temperament: Debonair and self-confident. In reply to a New York customs official's 'anything to declare?' he replied, 'Nothing but my genius' (1882). At school he was nicknamed 'the Grey Crow'. His experience of prison broke his health, but he retained some vestige of his wit, remarking as he waited handcuffed in the rain for the carriage to take him to gaol, 'If this is the way Queen Victoria treats her prisoners, she doesn't deserve to have any.'

Work/Daily Routine: 'The Ballad of Reading Gaol' was published under the pseudonym 'C3.3' – his prison number. After his release (May 1897) he used the pseudonym 'Sebastian Melmoth' (from St Sebastian – a reference to the arrows on his prison clothes – and the character in *Melmoth the Wanderer*, a popular Gothic novel by the Reverend Charles Maturin, his great-uncle). He wrote the play *Salomé* (1893) originally in French.

Manner of Death: Wilde died of cerebral meningitis after an ear infection at the Hôtel D'Alsace, Paris, at 1.50 pm on 30 November 1900, aged 46. At the moment of death, liquids erupted from his ears, nose, mouth and other orifices ('the debris was appalling' – Richard Ellman). Legend has it that on his deathbed Wilde quipped 'Either that wallpaper goes, or I do' and that he accepted a last glass of champagne with the words 'I am dying beyond my means.' He was buried in Bagneux Cemetery on 3 December 1900, but was later moved to the Père Lachaise Cemetery (1909), with a monument by Epstein.

WILHELM II (1859 –1941) German Emperor and King of Prussia

Wilhelm II ('Kaiser Bill') was born to the sound of a 100-round cannon salute at about 3 pm on Thursday 27 January 1859 in Berlin, Germany, the eldest son of Prince (later Crown Prince) Frederick William of Prussia, son of Prince Regent William (who became King William I of Prussia in 1861). His mother was an Englishwoman, Princess Victoria (daughter of Queen Victoria, aged 18 at his birth). Christened Prince Frederick William Albert Victor, he was known as Willy and was Queen Victoria's first grandson (she and Prince Albert were his godparents). A descendant of Frederick the Great, George III and Catherine the Great, he was also a nephew of Edward VII and a cousin of George V. His younger siblings were Charlotte, Henry and Victoria. Educated at first by private tutors, he attended the Gymnasium at Kassell aged 18 (1874) and studied law, history and science at the University of Bonn (1877). The British Government refused Victoria's wish that he be granted the Order of the Bath, but at 18 he did become the youngest foreigner to be made a Knight of the Garter. Nominally commissioned in the Foot Guards Regiment aged 10, he was promoted to captain in 1881 and rose to the rank of general (1888) – in 1889 he was also made an Admiral of the Fleet in the British Royal Navy (he later became colonel-in-chief of the British 1st Royal Dragoons and was promoted to field marshal by Edward VII).

When his father died of throat cancer (1888) and the Emperor Frederick III died the same year, he became King of Prussia and Emperor (Kaiser) of Germany. He later dismissed the much-admired Chancellor, Prince Bismarck – unifier of Germany – giving rise to the famous *Punch* cartoon 'Dropping the Pilot' by Tenniel (1890). In 1914 he sided with Austria-Hungary after the assassination of Archduke Franz Ferdinand at Sarajevo, but then tried unavailingly to prevent war. After World War I he abdicated (9 November 1918) and escaped to Holland, thereby evading trial for war crimes; he was interned in Doorn Castle for nearly 27 years. His uncle, Edward VII, called him 'the most brilliant failure in history'.

Family/Sex Life: In 1881 Wilhelm married 'Dona' – Princess Augusta Victoria of Schleswig-Holstein-Sonderburg-Augustenburg, daughter of Duke Frederick of Augustenburg. She died in 1921, having borne him William, Joachim, Eitel Frederick, Adalbert, Augustus William, Oscar and Victoria Louise. When she died he took as his second wife (1922) Princess Hermine of Reuss, one of his former wife's godchildren, who was aged 35 (he was 63) and who already had five children (they had no more).

Appearance: Wilhelm weighed around 11 stone and had a crippled left arm (not obvious from his many portraits in full military uniform). He wore upturned waxed moustaches and did not allow his hair to appear grey until he was in his fifties. At Doorn he often wore a straw boater and white spats.

Habits/Mannerisms: He was an abstemious eater, but a heavy smoker.

Sport/Hobbies: Wilhelm enjoyed riding, hunting, shooting, croquet and sailing – he won the Queen's Cup at Cowes in his yacht *Meteor* (1893). Other pastimes included music, archaeology and card-playing (he popularized the game 'skat'). He disliked duelling, gambling and excessive drinking. His favourite reading included P. G. Wodehouse, Dorothy L. Sayers and Ellery Queen. Determined to build up the German navy to rival that of England, he actually designed his own battleship, the equal of anything then afloat, with massive armament and spacious quarters for the crew (unfortunately, the experts agreed, it was highly unlikely that it would float).

Religion/Politics: Wilhelm was patriotic but anti-Nazi (his son Augustus William became a Nazi). He especially disliked the racist and pagan element of Nazism.

Health: Wilhelm was born with a dislocated elbow and shoulder and was paralysed thereafter in the left arm. He was also deaf in his left ear. Other health problems included a hernia and pneumonia.

Temperament: Resentful of British imperialism and influence overseas, he could be very ruthless (he had his own – English – mother arrested in 1888). He disliked Disraeli (whom he met) because of his 'cleverness and cold calculation'. He had a good sense of humour, but banned *Punch* from his palace when it attacked him. He once allowed the US sharpshooter Annie Oakley to shoot a cigarette from his mouth.

Manner of Death: Wilhelm died of pneumonia at Doorn Castle, Holland, on the morning of 4 June 1941, aged 82. He requested no swastikas to be displayed at his funeral but Hitler's wreath and the uniforms of Nazi officers present had them. He was buried at Doorn without an oration, music or bells.

WILLIAM I 'The Conqueror' (*c.*1027–87)
King of England and Duke of
Normandy (as William II)

William the Conqueror (or 'The Bastard') was born in Falaise, France, *c.*1027, the illegitimate son of Robert I ('The Devil'), 6th Duke of Normandy, and Herleve Fulbert, who was a tanner's daughter. His mother was married off to Herluin, Vicomte of Conteville, soon after William's birth, and he consequently acquired two famous stepbrothers, Bishop Odo of Bayeux (later Regent of England and Earl of Kent) and Robert of Mortain (later one of the largest landowners in England), and a stepsister Muriel. He also had a sister Adeliza by Robert and Herleve and Edward the Confessor was his cousin (both were descended from Duke Richard the Fearless). His father, who was a direct descendant of Rolf (or Rollo) the Viking, who first conquered Normandy from the French, left the duchy for good in 1034 to go on a pilgrimage to Jerusalem. He died when William was eight (1035) and during the ensuing wars William was hidden and cared for by his maternal uncle Walter Fulbert. He visited Edward the Confessor in England in 1051 and was made his official heir. In 1064 he captured Harold Godwinson (later Harold II) – whose father Earl Godwin had killed Edward the Confessor's brother – when shipwrecked off Ponthieu and made him swear support for William's claim to the English throne before releasing him. After the death of Edward, William arrived with his army in southern England and defeated Harold II at the Battle of Hastings (1066). He was crowned king in Westminster Abbey that same year and made his brother Odo regent when abroad (he later imprisoned Odo for mismanagement). There were many revolts until 1070 (including that of the Lincolnshire thegn Hereward the Wake). He reigned for 21 years, during which period he commissioned the celebrated 'Domesday Book' detailing his English possessions.

Family/Sex Life: Around 1051 William married Matilda, daughter of Baldwin V, Count of Flanders, and Adela, daughter of King Robert II of France, who at four feet two inches was Britain's smallest ever queen. Their children were Robert Duke of Normandy, Richard, William II 'Rufus', Henry I, Adela, Agatha, Adeliza, Constance, Cecily and Matilda.

Appearance: Around five feet 10 inches tall, William had a very powerful physique, though in later years he became very fat. He had a bald forehead, a stern countenance, close-cropped red hair and a short moustache.

Habits/Mannerisms: William was described as having a harsh gutteral voice. He was moderate in eating and drinking and disapproved of drunkenness in his men. He introduced the concept of the curfew – in Caen in 1061 a bell was rung each evening as an invitation to prayer and as a signal to shut all doors for the night. In England he held court in Winchester at Easter.

Sport/Hobbies: William enjoyed hunting and riding (he had three horses killed under him during the Battle of Hastings). He also presided over the building of the Tower of London as his fortress.

Religion/Politics: A Roman Catholic, William was very religious. He built the abbey of St Stephen in Caen, France, and Battle Abbey in Sussex. His invasion of England was offically backed by Pope Alexander II. He also introduced the Jews to England (from Normandy).

Health: A formidable warrior, he was wounded in the hand during a fight with his eldest son Robert, who demanded Normandy and Maine.

Temperament: William had an iron will and was described as morose and ruthless – he decreed that all who illegally slew deer should be blinded. By way of contrast he had only one man condemned to death during his reign (though many others were blinded and mutilated on his orders).

Work/Daily Routine: William invaded England in 1066 sailing across the Channel in his ship *Mora*. He sailed from Saint-Valéry on the mouth of the River Somme and landed on 27 September at Pevensey, though it was not until 9 am on 14 October that battle was finally joined near Hastings (as recorded in the Bayeux Tapestry). As he landed on English soil William stumbled and his men instantly began muttering at what they considered a bad omen for their enterprise – but William got back to his feet, held out his muddy hands, and proclaimed, 'By the splendour of God I have taken possession of my realm; the earth of England is in my two hands' – and morale was restored.

Manner of Death: William was badly injured when he was thrown against the pommel of his horse's saddle in Rouen on 15 August 1087. He lingered in great pain for several weeks before dying, aged 60, early in the morning of Thursday 9 September 1087 in Rouen. On his deathbed he confessed that he had acted with brutality in subjugating England to Norman control and asked God's forgiveness for his sins. He was buried in St Stephen's Church, Caen. A monument raised by William II was destroyed by the Huguenots in 1562 and his remains were scattered, except for a thighbone. His tomb was completely wrecked in 1793 and his last remains scattered.

WODEHOUSE, Pelham Grenville (1881–1975) English novelist

P. G. Wodehouse was born at 1 Vale Place, Epsom Road, Guildford, Surrey, on 15 October 1881, the third son of Henry Ernest Wodehouse, a magistrate in Hong Kong, and Eleanor Deane. He was the great grandson of Sir Armine, 5th Baronet Wodehouse – a descendant of Anne Boleyn's sister Mary – and the great-nephew of Cardinal Newman (his maternal grandmother was a sister of Newman's mother). His two elder brothers were Philip Peveril and Ernest Armine and he had a younger brother Richard Lancelot. Educated at Dulwich College, he received an Honorary Doctorate from Oxford University in 1959. As his father could not afford to pay for another son at Oxford, after school he worked for two years in the Hong Kong & Shanghai Bank in London and while there was a freelance journalist, writing comic verse and articles for numerous publications and public-school stories for *The Captain* (1902–13). He then got a part-time job on *The Globe* through his old Dulwich School teacher, William Beach-Thomas (who was Assistant Editor) and became Assistant Editor of the paper when Beach-Thomas left (1903) and its Editor in 1904. He was then staff lyricist at the Aldwych Theatre, London. In New York he was theatre critic for *Vanity Fair* in 1915 (succeeded by Dorothy Parker) and collaborated with Jerome Kern and Guy Bolton on musicals. During World War II he was captured by the Germans in Le Touquet (1940) and when interned in Berlin broadcast for CBS Radio describing camp life (for this he was later accused of collaboration). He became a US citizen in 1955 and was knighted in 1975 just before his death. He established his reputation as a comic novelist with *Psmith in the City* (1910) and other early stories; among the most popular of his many subsequent books were the Jeeves and Wooster novels – *Right Ho, Jeeves* (1934), *The Mating Season* (1949) etc. – and the 'Blandings' stories.

Family/Sex Life: In 1914 Wodehouse married widow Ethel May Rowley (née Newton), whom he called 'Bunny'. She already had a daughter, Leonora, to whom he dedicated *The Heart of a Goof* (1926). There were no further children.

Sport/Hobbies: Wodehouse enjoyed golf, gambling and crossword puzzles. In 1905 he took up motoring, buying a second-hand Darracq car (unfortunately he drove it into a ditch, left it there and never drove again).

Health: Wodehouse suffered from the skin disorder pemphiguf and also from arthritis. He suffered a stroke in 1951.

Temperament: Known to his friends as 'Plum', Wodehouse was rather like his creation Bertie Wooster – cheerful but naïve (hence the trouble he innocently got into broadcasting from occupied Europe). He could be rather shy, however – when his wife was searching for an apartment for them in New York he begged her to find one on the ground floor ('I never know what to say to the lift boy').

Pets: Wodehouse was reputedly captured at Le Touquet during World War II because he did not want to leave behind his dogs Winks and Boo (both Pekineses), which he would have had to do because of British quarantine laws. Pekineses were a great favourite of his (others that he owned included Wonder and Squeaky). He also kept a foxhound called Bill and a cat called Poona. He gave $35,000 for a shelter for stray dogs and cats near Westhampton, New York.

Work/Daily Routine: Sean O'Casey called Wodehouse 'English literature's performing flea'. He wrote 2000 words a day, seven days a week, thus taking about three months to write a novel and producing over 100 in all. Before starting writing he made around 400 pages of notes. Jeeves and Wooster first appeared in 'Extricating Young Gussie' (*Saturday Evening Post*, 1915). The fictional Jeeves was named after Warwickshire cricketer Percy Jeeves (who died in 1916) and bore some resemblance to Wodehouse's own personal valet, Eugene Robinson. Wooster was a development of his earlier characters Bertie Mannering-Phipps and Reggie Pepper and had certain traits in common with the author's friend George Grossmith and Wodehouse's son-in-law, Anthony Bingham Mildmay, 2nd Baron Mildmay of Flete (who died in 1950). Psmith was based on Rupert D'Oyly Carte, son of the founder of the D'Oyly Carte opera company. The name Emsworth comes from Emsworth House preparatory school in the village of Emsworth on the Hants/Sussex border, where Wodehouse's friend Herbert Westbrook was a teacher. He often collaborated with others, for instance with Westbrook on *Not George Washington*. His own favourite humorous writers were Thurber and Robert Benchley – he was also very fond of Kipling's work and admired (and was admired by) Agatha Christie, who dedicated *Hallowe'en Party* (1969) to him (Evelyn Waugh was another fan and Belloc called him 'the "best" writer of our time: the best living writer in English').

Manner of Death: Wodehouse died in hospital on Long Island, USA, on 14 February 1975, aged 93.

WOOLF, Virginia (1882–1941) English novelist

Adeline Virginia Woolf was born Virginia Stephen at 22 Hyde Park Gate, London, on 25 January 1882, the second daughter of Sir Leslie Stephen, editor of the *Dictionary of National Biography* (whose first wife had been Thackeray's daughter Minny), by his second wife Julia Duckworth (née Jackson) – who died in 1895 when Virginia was 13 – widow of the publisher Herbert Duckworth and a cousin of the Duchess of Bedford. Her godfather was US Ambassador James Russell Lowell and her maternal great-aunt was the photographer Julia Margaret Cameron. Her older siblings were Vanessa (later Vanessa Bell, the painter) and Julian Thoby (who died in 1906) and she had a younger brother Adrian and older half-siblings Gerald and Stella Duckworth. Educated largely at home, she took classes in Greek and History at King's College, London, and was taught Latin by Walter Pater's sister Clara (later Vice-Principal of Somerville College, Oxford). She then worked as a freelance journalist for the *Guardian* and others and taught evening classes in History and English at Morley College for working men, London (1905–7). Later, with her husband Leonard Woolf, she founded and ran the Hogarth Press from 1917 but withdrew her half-share to allow John Lehmann to join the company (1938). A prominent member of the Bloomsbury Group of writers, she was the author of such admired novels as *The Voyage Out* (1915), *Jacob's Room* (1922), *Mrs Dalloway* (1925), *To the Lighthouse* (1927), *Orlando* (1928) and *The Waves* (1931).

Family/Sex Life: Having rejected proposals from the homosexual Lytton Strachey (1909), from Hilton Young – later Lord Kenet and then Assistant Editor of *The Economist* – (also 1909) and from diplomat Sydney Waterlow, she married (1912) her brother Thoby's Cambridge University friend and Fabian Society member Leonard Sidney Woolf, the son of a barrister. They had no children by choice. She also had lesbian affairs with her sister Vanessa and with Vita Sackville-West.

Appearance: Virginia Woolf was very tall and had a rather long, gaunt face. She received the *Evening Standard* award for Tallest Woman Writer of 1927 (beating Elizabeth Bowen).

Habits/Mannerisms: After the death of her parents (her father died in 1904) she lived with Adrian, Thoby and Vanessa at 46 Gordon Square, Bloomsbury, London, then (after Thoby's death and Vanessa's marriage) at 29 Fitzroy Square until her own marriage. She liked to smoke cigarettes in a long holder. She hated shopping and kept a cook and servants to perform all the domestic chores.

Sport/Hobbies: She drove a Singer car.

Religion/Politics: A voluntary worker for the Women's Suffrage office, she testified at the trial of the lesbian novel *The Well of Loneliness* (1928). She was also anti-Semitic.

Health: Woolf was mentally unstable, hearing voices and suffering a nervous breakdown after the death of her father (1904). The Hogarth Press was founded in 1917 partly as therapy for her. Thinking she would go permanently mad, she repeatedly tried to drown herself and eventually succeeded. She was sexually molested at the age of nine by her 18-year-old stepbrother Gerald Duckworth (he did not have sex with her, but just touched her all over).

Temperament: Innovative and serious as a writer, she did have a sense of humour. In 1910 she participated in a celebrated public hoax with Horace de Vere Cole and others to gain access to the top secret battleship HMS *Dreadnought* by posing as the retinue of the 'Emperor of Ethiopia'. The naval authorities were completely taken in and showed the 'dignitaries' (disguised in beards, turbans, etc. and made up by Sarah Bernhardt's make-up artist) all round the vessel without suspecting the fraud, which when subsequently revealed caused the Naval establishment considerable embarrassment. Her friends included Hugh Walpole, Rupert Brooke and members of the Bloomsbury Group – Fry, Keynes, Forster and Clive Bell. Within family circles she was known as 'The Goat'.

Pets: Her pets included a marmoset called Mitz, a blonde cocker spaniel bitch called Pinker (a present from Vita Sackville-West) and Potto (a cat).

Work/Daily Routine: Her first novel, *The Voyage Out* (1913), was published by the family firm of Duckworth. Her more eccentric works included *Flush*, a spoof biography of Elizabeth Barrett Browning's spaniel – reviewed as 'the most tiresome book which Mrs Woolf has yet written' (Geoffrey Grigson). The jackets for her books were designed by her sister Vanessa Bell. *Night and Day* was hostilely reviewed by Katherine Mansfield in *Athenaeum*.

Manner of Death: Virginia Woolf died by drowning (suicide), having filled her pockets with heavy stones, in the River Ouse near her home, Monks House,

Rodmell, Essex, some time before 1 pm on Friday 28 March 1941, aged 59. Her corpse was discovered three weeks later. Her body was cremated and the ashes buried beneath an elm tree at Monks House.

WORDSWORTH, William (1770–1850) English poet

William Wordsworth was born in Cockermouth, Cumberland, on 7 April 1770, the second son of John Wordsworth, a lawyer and agent for Sir James Lowther, Earl of Lonsdale (who died of dropsy when he was 13), and Ann Cookson (who died of pneumonia when he was seven). His grandfather, Richard Wordsworth, had been Receiver-General of Cumberland. After his parents' death he was brought up by two uncles, Richard Wordsworth (Controller of Customs at Whitehaven) and Christopher Crackanthorpe (his mother's brother, who changed his surname to inherit Newbiggen Hall). He had a younger sister, Dorothy, an older brother Richard and two younger ones, John and Christopher (Master of Trinity College, Cambridge). Educated in Cockermouth with Fletcher Christian, he was sent away aged nine to board at Hawkshead Grammar School. He was later a sizar at St John's College, Cambridge – where his uncle Reverend William Cookson was a Fellow – and took the Maths Tripos but opted out and went to France and Switzerland with fellow student Robert Jones (1790) before his finals, so only got an ordinary degree (BA 1791). With his sister Dorothy he worked at first as tutor to Basil Montagu's two children at Racedown Lodge, near Lyme Regis, in Dorset. He then received two legacies and moved to Alfoxden, Somerset, and to Cumbria, living in Dove Cottage (formerly a pub, the Dove and Olive Branch) and later at Rydal Mount (where visitors included Queen Adelaide, widow of William IV). He joined the Volunteers when war was declared on France. With help from Lord Lonsdale (who also gave

him £100 a year) he was appointed Stamp Distributor for Westmorland – effectively a tax collector giving government stamps to legal documents. He resigned in 1842, with a Civil List pension, and became Poet Laureate on the death of Southey in 1843 (and was himself followed by Tennyson). His most famous publications included the *Lyrical Ballads* (1798), which were written with Coleridge, and *The Prelude* (written in 1805 and published posthumously).

Family/Sex Life: While in Orléans, France, Wordsworth met and later had an affair (1791–2) with Frenchwoman Annette Vallon, daughter of a surgeon in Blois. She bore him an illegitimate child, Anne-Caroline, but they did not marry. In 1802 he married primary school friend Mary Hutchinson, daughter of a tobacconist. Their surviving children were John, Dorothy ('Dora') and William (Thomas and Catherine died young).

Appearance: Five feet 10 inches tall, Wordsworth was gaunt, angular, wiry, large-boned, sturdy but clumsily built (De Quincey observed 'Wordsworth's legs were certainly not ornamental'). He was white-skinned, had a heavy mouth, with good teeth, a prominent Roman nose and receding hair. He dressed quaintly – in later life he wore rough plaid trousers, a brown frock coat, a black handkerchief around his neck, a straw hat with a veil against the sun, green glasses and big heavy shoes. Some said he looked more like a curate or shepherd than a poet.

Habits/Mannerisms: Wordsworth slept half-sitting, propped up on a bolster, rather than flat. He lived with his wife and his sister Dorothy (who later went mad and just sat by the fire, though she retained the ability to recite all his poems). He spoke with a North Country accent, with a 'deep guttural intonation, a strong tincture of the Northern burr ...', according to Hazlitt. He was austere and very frugal – he never wasted candles, travelled on the outside of coaches, wore second-hand clothes and papered a room at Dove Cottage with newspaper – but employed a daily cleaner. Wordsworth ate mostly porridge and only occasionally boiled mutton, though he did like Cheshire cheese. He was virtually teetotal and hated tobacco. His possessions included an umbrella (then considered effeminate), 200–300 books (mostly in tatters as he treated them badly) and a portable (candlestick-like) eye-shade. As an old man he gave away locks of his hair.

Sport/Hobbies: Wordsworth was a good skater and also liked walking, fishing, boating, dancing and playing cards.

Religion/Politics: A supporter of the French Revolution, he was nonetheless pleased when Robespierre was executed. Coleridge called him 'a republican, and at least a semi-atheist'. Later, however, he canvassed for the Tories and became staunch Church of England, opposing Catholic Emancipation and the Dissenters. When living at Alfoxden he and his family were watched by the Home Office as possible French spies. In the Lake District he tried to stop the coming of the railways.

Health: Wordsworth was never ill but suffered from piles and from poor eyesight (he could not read for more than 15 minutes by 1830). After moving from Racedown, Dorset, he had no sense of smell.

Temperament: The young Wordsworth was mild-mannered but he later became arrogant, pompous and didactic. His friends included Coleridge (whom Wordsworth greatly respected), the painter Benjamin Haydon (who made a life mask of him and included him with Voltaire and Newton in *Christ's Entry into Jerusalem*), Humphry Davy (who read the proofs of *Lyrical Ballads*), De Quincey, Charles Lamb and Southey. He was disliked by Browning, Hazlitt, Keats, Shelley and Byron – 'Let simple Wordsworth chime his childish verse,/And brother Coleridge lull the babe at nurse.'

Pets: He kept a dog.

Work/Daily Routine: Wordsworth wrote his first poem at the age of 14 (1784). He never wrote at a table but at a chair with a writing board on its arm. He usually composed aloud while out walking, often in wind or rain. The *Lyrical Ballads* were published anonymously, with Coleridge and Wordsworth hoping to make enough money to visit the Continent (it was badly reviewed). It was Wordsworth who suggested the albatross in Coleridge's *Ancient Mariner*. *The Prelude* was intended as the preface to a larger work entitled *The Recluse*, but this was never completed. Wordsworth became the most parodied of all the English poets. Most famous of the parodies was the White Knight's song by Lewis Carroll. J. K. Stephen, in *Granta* (1891) offered: 'There are two voices; one is of the deep,/And one is an old half-witted sheep/And Wordsworth, both are thine ...' By agreement with Prime Minister Sir Robert Peel, he did not write a single line of poetry as Poet Laureate.

Manner of Death: Wordsworth died of pleurisy at noon on 23 April 1850, aged 80. He was buried in Grasmere Churchyard.

WREN, Sir Christopher (1632–1723) English architect

Christopher Wren was born in East Knoyle, Wiltshire, on 20 October 1632, the son of Christopher Wren, later Dean of Windsor, and Mary Cox (who died when he was very young). One uncle was the Bishop of Ely, and the first of his designs that was actually built was the chapel at Pembroke College for another relative, Bishop Matthew Wren. He had an older sister and a younger one, Elizabeth. Educated at Westminster School and Wadham College, Oxford, he became a Fellow of All Souls in 1653. He was later Professor of Astronomy at Gresham College, London (1657) and Savilian Professor of Astronomy at Oxford University (1661–73). Three times elected an MP (for Plympton, Windsor and Weymouth), he was Surveyor-General during the reigns of Charles II, James II, William and Mary and Queen Anne (but was dismissed in 1718 after a Court intrigue). He was a founder of the Royal Society, its President (1681–3), and was knighted by Charles II in 1672.

Family/Sex Life: Wren's first wife was Faith Cargill, daughter of Sir John Cargill; their children were Gilbert and Christopher. His second wife was Jane, daughter of Lord Fitzwilliam, by whom he fathered Jane and William.

Appearance: Short and clean-shaven.

Religion/Politics: Wren was a Freemason.

Temperament: Subtle, determined and a skilled diplomat, Wren used all his wiles to get his plans approved by the authorities. He was fairly resilient to the criticism that constantly came his way, though when his ambitious plans for St Paul's were initially declined it is said that he wept. His friends included the diarist John Evelyn (who was godfather to one of his sons in 1679 and

who, when Wren was just 21, described the as yet unrealized architect as 'that miracle of youth').

Work/Daily Routine: Wren was a highly skilled draughtsman, though he only turned to architecture in his early thirties, following an inspirational visit to Paris. After the Great Fire of London (1666) Wren produced ambitious plans for the wholescale rebuilding of the city on a Continental model, with piazzas and squares, but these were never put into action. Instead, funded by a tax put on coal coming into the capital, he rebuilt 52 London churches and also designed the Chelsea Hospital and the Greenwich Observatory and, elsewhere, the Ashmolean Museum and the Sheldonian Theatre in Oxford and Marlborough House. His feats of design were beyond the understanding of many contemporary architects – when he produced a design for the interior of Windsor Town Hall local building inspectors insisted that he had not included enough pillars to support the ceiling. Obligingly, Wren added an extra four pillars, but unnoticed left them several inches short of the ceiling, thus deceiving the inspectors and satisfying his own contention that his original design was sound (the pillars remain short of the ceiling to this day). His masterpiece was St Paul's Cathedral in London, which remains the only classical cathedral designed and completed within the designer's lifetime. The original designs, with the breathtaking classical dome, horrified the authorities, who demanded the conventional spire. Wren accordingly amended his designs, but gradually, during building, he reinstated his original ideas without attracting attention. When the money for the project threatened to run dry he had himself elected an MP and got the tax on London's coal tripled so that he could continue. He also invented a corn-planting machine, a method for making fresh water at sea and a language for the deaf and dumb. He wrote important works on mathematics and was greatly admired by Newton as one of the 'leading geometers of this age'.

Manner of Death: Wren died on 25 February 1723, aged 90. He was buried in St Paul's; his epitaph reads, *'Si monumentum requires, circumspice'* ('If you seek a monument, look about you'). Hours before his death, as a frail old man, he paid his last visit to his masterpiece, sitting beneath the huge dome and watching the sunlight on the stonework.

YEATS, William Butler (1865 –1939) Irish poet, playwright and statesman

W. B. Yeats was born at 'Georgeville', 5 Sandymount Avenue, Dublin, on 13 June 1865, the eldest son of Pre-Raphaelite portrait painter and art teacher John Butler Yeats (a friend of actor Henry Irving) and Susan Pollexfen, daughter of a prosperous shipowner. His surviving brother was the painter Jack Butler Yeats (another brother, Robert, died as a child) and he had two sisters, Susan ('Lily') and Elizabeth ('Lolly'), who later founded the Cuala Press (fine art printers). The family moved to London when Yeats was three (1868) and did not return to Ireland (to Howth) until he was 15. Educated at Godolphin School, Hammersmith (1874), and at the Erasmus Smith High School, Dublin, he also studied art (1884) at the Metropolitan School of Art, Dublin, where his father was a teacher (and the poet 'AE' – George Russell – was a fellow pupil), but gave it up after three years, aged 21 (1886). 50 years old before his income from books exceeded £200 a year, he was successively a Senator in the Irish Free State (1923–8), Chairman of the Commission on Coinage and first President of the Irish Literary Society. He also founded (with George Moore, Edward Martyn and Lady Gregory) the Irish Literary Theatre (later called the Abbey Theatre) for the production of Irish plays, financed by the Englishwoman Miss A. E. Horniman. Co-founder, with Shaw and 'AE', of the Irish Academy of Letters and a member of the Academic Committee for the Royal Society of Literature, he received a Civil List pension (1910) and was awarded the Nobel Prize for Literature (1923). Among his most admired publications were the plays *The Countess Cathleen* (1892), *The Land of Heart's Desire* (1894) and *Cathleen ni Houlihan* (1903) and the poems of *The Tower* (1928), *The Winding Stair* (1929) and *A Full Moon in March* (1935).

Family/Sex Life: Yeats nursed an unrequited love for the actress and revolutionary Maud Gonne (Madame Gonne MacBride) and proposed to her in 1891. Later he also proposed to her adopted daughter, Iseult, but was again refused. At the age of 50 he was married (1917) in London to the Englishwoman Georgie Hyde-Lees, who became a medium. Their children were Michael and Anne.

Appearance: Over six feet tall and slim, Yeats had an olive complexion and wore pince-nez glasses. He wore his gloves on a string.

Habits/Mannerisms: Known as 'Willie' to his friends, for some 30 years he spent his summers at Lady Gregory's home, Coole Park House, Galway (he also bought the ruined Norman castle Thoor Ballylee in Coole).

Sport/Hobbies: Yeats was tone-deaf and understood 'no music but that of words'.

Religion/Politics: He was influenced by the Theosophists (he was a friend of Madame Blavatsky and joined the Blavatsky Lodge of the Theosophical Society in London) and by Indian theology and astrology. He was also a member of the Hermetic Order of the Golden Dawn (1890), whose other members included the notorious Aleister Crowley. He was a firm believer in the occult, though when questioned he could not claim ever to have seen a spirit – though, with his wife's help, 'he had often *smelt* them'. In politics, he was an ardent Irish nationalist and joined in demonstrations for independence (especially if Maud Gonne was involved).

Health: Yeats suffered from lung congestion and influenza (1927) and was something of a hypochondriac in his later years. In the 1930s he went to the extreme of having new sex glands implanted by a certain Dr Steinach in the confident belief that this rather radical procedure would have the beneficial effect of curing him of one of his most distressing ailments – falling asleep after lunch.

Temperament: Though haughty, snobbish and aloof, he included among his friends the poet 'AE' (to whom Yeats dedicated his first volume of poems), William Morris, Ezra Pound, Lady Gregory (Augusta Persse, second wife of Sir William Gregory), Arthur Symonds (editor of *The Savoy*) and George Moore (with whom he wrote the play *Diarmuid and Grania*).

Work/Daily Routine: Despite his lack of musical ability, Yeats hummed and beat time while writing poems. His first published prose work was *Celtic Twilight* (1893). His first published verse appeared in the *Dublin University Review* (1885). He produced his best work between the ages of 50 and 70. He greatly admired J. M. Synge, but deliberately excluded Wilfred Owen and Lord Alfred Douglas when editing *The Oxford Book of Modern Verse* (1936), considering them unworthy.

Manner of Death: Yeats died of myocarditis (heart failure) in Roquebrune, France (near Monaco), on 28 January 1939, aged 73. He was buried in Roquebrune (1939), but later his body was moved to Drumcliff, near Sligo (1948). He wrote his own epitaph: 'Cast a cold eye/On life, on death./Horseman, Pass by!'

ZOLA, Émile Edouard Charles Antoine (1840–1902) French novelist

---

Émile Zola was born at 10 Rue St Joseph, Paris, at 11 pm on 2 April 1840, the only child of the celebrated Italian/Greek civil engineer Dr Francesco Zola – consultant on Europe's first public railway (Budweis to Linz) – and a Frenchwoman, Émilie Aubert, daughter of a glazier. His father, who was more than 20 years older than his mother, died when he was six. Educated at the Collège d'Aix – where he won physics and drawing prizes (beating his schoolmate Cézanne) – then at the select École Normal Supérieure, Paris (where he failed his *baccalauréat* oral), he worked at first as a copy clerk in the Excise Office, Paris, and then in the postroom of Hachette publishers. He was later Hachette's chief of sales and promotion and as 'Claude' was art critic for *L'Événement*, praising Manet and attacking the Paris Salon Jury. When his second novel, *La Confession de Claude*, caused a scandal he left Hachette and became gossip columnist on *L'Événement* until it closed (1866). He then moved to its sister paper *Le Figaro*, freelanced for *Le Globe*, *La Marseillaise* and others, and became private secretary to the Republican politician Alexandre Glais-Bizain (founder of *La Tribune*) in Bordeaux during the siege of Paris (1870). He was later parliamentary correspondent for *La Cloche* and *Le Semaphore*, and drama critic for *L'Avenir National* (1873) and *Le Bien Public* (1876–8). He was President of the French Society of Authors (1891). His most famous publications included the novel *Thérèse Raquin* (1867) and the 20-volume novel series *Les Rougon-Macquart*, which incorporated such acclaimed books as *Nana* (1880), *Germinal* (1885), *La Terre* (1887), *La Bête humaine* (1890), *La Débâcle* (1892) and *Le Docteur Pascal* (1893).

Family/Sex Life: In Paris Zola lived with a prostitute called Berthe until his mother moved in with him when working at Hachette. He then lived with Alexandrine-Gabrielle Meley, whom he eventually married (1870) and he and his mother moved into her flat. His affair with his wife's 20-year-old servant Jeanne-Sophie-Adèle Rozerot, when he was 48 (1888), resulted in the birth of two children, Denise and Jacques.

Appearance: He was short and later in life became very fat (in 1887 he had a 44-inch waist and weighed 212 lb, but he then dieted, keeping off starchy foods and wine, and lost 30 lb in three months). He had an olive complexion and a high forehead, a disdainful mouth and a long nose with a cleft tip (two deep grooves). His hair was very black and at the age of 20 he wore a dark 'Newgate frill' beard (no hair on the cheeks or chin), but he later grew a full heavy beard. He used a lorgnette before switching to pince-nez glasses.

Habits/Mannerisms: Zola had very mobile, expressive hands and a nervous tremble (which prompted him to give up pipe-smoking in 1885). He was shortsighted and spoke with an attractive tenor voice, with a slight lisp. He was also a glutton.

Sport/Hobbies: A good swimmer, he shot birds as a child and became a keen photographer. He only ever knew French.

Religion/Politics: Zola became the most controversial figure in France in 1898 when he published the open letter 'J'Accuse!', addressed to the French President Félix Faure, on the front page of *L'Aurore* in defence of Captain Dreyfus, a Jewish military officer who had been unjustly court-martialled and sent to Devil's Island for passing secrets to the Germans. Zola alleged anti-Semitism and the forging of evidence etc. and generally questioned the integrity of the authorities involved. The Establishment's reaction was severe – Zola was sentenced to a year's imprisonment and a 3000-franc fine was imposed. While his appeal was being heard he fled to England, where he remained for 11 months in exile. He eventually returned, to a hero's welcome, after getting Dreyfus a retrial (Dreyfus was pardoned and reinstated with the army rank of major and awarded the Légion d'honneur).

Health: Zola, a hypochondriac, suffered a nervous breakdown (1882), while other ailments included neuralgia and kidney trouble.

Temperament: His friends included Cézanne (very close), Pissarro and others of the Café Guerbois circle (Monet, Whistler, Degas etc.) as well as the Goncourt brothers, Flaubert, Turgenev, Daudet, Maupassant and Huysmans.

Pets: He had a Labrador dog called Bertrand.

Work/Daily Routine: Zola wore a loose peasant smock when working at home and planned all his books in great detail. He wrote 1000 to 2500 words daily and worked for nine to 10 hours. The plot of *Thérèse Raquin*, his first major success, was derived from a novel by Adolphe Bélot. The famous 20-novel series *Les Rougon-Macquart* was influenced by Balzac's *Comedie humaine* and was described by Havelock Ellis as a 'study in social mathematics'. The police stopped the serialization of *La Curée* in *La Cloche*, but *Nana* was a huge success (the 55,000 sale of the first edition was then the largest ever known in France). His personal favourite among his own books was *La Terre*, which was attacked for gratuitous pornography (Anatole France called it 'a heap of ordure'). The English publisher Vizetelly was fined for obscene libel (he was later imprisoned and his company closed) for publishing *Nana*, *Pot Bouille* and *La Terre*. Samuel Smith MP, in the House of Commons, claimed of his books that 'Nothing more diabolical had ever

been dreamed up by the pen of man; they were only fit for swine, and those who read them must turn their minds into cesspools.' All Zola's works were banned by the Vatican and put on the Index of prohibited books. Zola's biography (by Paul Alexis) appeared when he was only 42.

Motto/Saying: Zola's motto was 'All or Nothing'.

Manner of Death: Zola was found dead in his Paris rooms, asphyxiated by carbon monoxide fumes from a smokeless-fuel fire in his bedroom (which had a defective chimney) in the morning of 29 September 1902 (his wife survived because she fell on the bed, while Zola fell to the floor).